Time Honored

A Global View of Architectural Conservation

Time Honored

A Global View of Architectural Conservation

PARAMETERS, THEORY, & EVOLUTION
OF AN ETHOS

John H. Stubbs

Foreword by Sir Bernard M. Feilden

*With a contribution of images from the photo archive
of the World Monuments Fund*

WILEY

John Wiley & Sons, Inc.

Library of Congress Cataloging-in-Publication Data:

Stubbs, John H.
  Time honored : a global view of architectural conservation : parameters, theory & evolution of an ethos / John H. Stubbs.
    p. cm.
  Includes bibliographical references.
  ISBN 978-0-470-26049-4 (cloth)
1. Architecture—Conservation and restoration. 2. Historic preservation—Philosophy. I. Title.
  NA105.S79 2009
  363.6'9—dc22
                                                                              2008021419

Printed in the United States of America

10 9 8 7 6 5 4 3 2 1

Contents

Preface

People's awareness of the importance of protecting the world's cultural patrimony—in particular its architectural heritage—is at a record level, and it is growing. *Time Honored: A Global View of Architectural Conservation* explores the reasons for this phenomenon, explains how international architectural heritage practice operates, and considers where this firmly rooted global interest may lead.

Protecting historic buildings and sites as a way of making the best use of the built environment is an important consideration for architects, landscape architects, urban planners, and others in disciplines that depend on heritage protection, such as archaeologists and museologists. Indeed, protecting at least representative examples of human-made heritage and the countless actions exerted each day toward its accomplishment are a worldwide concern that characterizes life and societal values in our time.

Restoring and preserving historic architecture throughout the world is a very broad topic. A balanced portrayal of it seemed possible when research for this book began in 1998 for two main reasons: the cumulative experience and amount of information on the subject that had been amassed and a vastly improved means for accessing it. Equally important was the coincidental development of participating government organizations, nongovernmental organizations, and members of the general public. Their combined successes in the field demonstrated how powerful they could be when working in concert. The resulting cultural heritage protection system, which includes topics beyond matters of historic sites and architecture, is the universe in which we work and live today.

As the first of a multipart series that profiles architectural conservation practices in different regions of the world, the present volume offers a gateway to this large and diverse topic. Its overall aim is to provide a convenient means for learning about contemporary international conservation practice—whether the reader is a student, a professional in the field, or an interested layperson seeking to know more about the subject—and to highlight architectural conservation solutions that have been developed in different parts of the world. This volume seeks to define the physical and conceptual parameters of the field of architectural conservation, its background, and its position today as a major influence on the world's built environment. In the near term, more volumes are planned that focus on architectural conservation practice from the mid-twentieth century onward: in contemporary Europe, the Americas, the Middle East and Africa, and in Asia, Oceania, and the Polar Regions.

In *Time Honored*, the subject is addressed via an introduction to aims, characteristics, context, and language of the profession, an outline of humankind's long experience in protecting its built heritage, and a discussion of the evolution of its principal theories and their applications. These are followed by examples of representative problems, solutions, and promising new directions from around the world.

Time Honored is written from the perspective of both a participant and an observer of a wide range of architectural conservation projects in more than one hundred countries, experience I have gained through my work both as director of field projects at the New York–based World Monuments Fund since 1990 and through teaching for more than two decades at Columbia University's Graduate Program in Historic Preservation. Because the field is synoptic, in this instance demanding the attention of a variety of special interests and talents, I should stress here that I was one participant among many, and the views contained herein are my own. Indeed, the more I traveled to view progress at established field projects, to see prospects, to participate in conferences, to advocate, or simply to observe, the more I became aware that my interests and actions were but a fraction of the countless efforts exerted over the centuries that have resulted in the historic built environment we know and enjoy today. If *Time Honored* helps in any way to achieve the conservation of more of the world's amazing artistic, architectural, and cultural patrimony, it will have served its purpose.

JOHN H. STUBBS

Foreword

The main appeal of architectural conservation for me has been its physicality. One need only look around to see the need for it; it's real, site-specific, and relevant. Today's demands on heritage conservation practitioners are at an all-time high. Examples of its successes — and, it must be said, its shortcomings as well — can be seen practically everywhere on earth.

Time Honored: A Global View of Architectural Conservation is a rich and ambitious offering steeped in the author's experiences in architectural conservation practice at both the local and international levels over a period of nearly forty years. John Stubbs, a native of Louisiana, was trained in both architectural technology and historic preservation. He has taught the subject at the graduate level at three institutions, including Columbia University. He worked for the US National Park Service's Technical Preservation Services Division in Washington, DC, and later practiced for a decade as a restoration specialist at the firm of Beyer Blinder Belle Architects & Planners in New York. And for nearly two decades Stubbs has been in charge of the field projects for the renowned World Monuments Fund (WMF).

I know of no one other individual who could have produced such a book. His postgraduate training at the International Centre for the Study of the Preservation and Restoration of Cultural Property (ICCROM), and later, his close work with the eminent educator and historic preservation practitioner James Marston Fitch in New York, certainly exposed him to the leading thinking in the field. (I first met Stubbs when he attended ICCROM in 1977. I worked with him most recently, at WMF's invitation, at Angkor Wat in 2004.)

In normal architectural and engineering practice, the technical challenges of conserving historic architecture can range from addressing large, vexing engineering solutions to simply showing the way through problem solving and leadership. Architectural conservation, however, is distinct from the modern building industry in one main respect: It inevitably deals with history and changes to buildings over time. When compared to building anew, dealing with extant buildings can be a simple task — though, more often, it is considerably more complex. The problems of documentation, diagnosis, and the prescription of solutions — and dealing with endlessly changing variables — can be specialties in and of themselves. Implementing architectural conservation solutions at important historic buildings that are publicly owned, held in trust, or in possession of owners having differing affections for the task often brings with it added scrutiny that often requires informed answers.

At this stage in the evolution of architectural conservation practice throughout the world, questions of what to do and how to do it are remarkably clear. In addressing these matters in my own work, through nearly a half century of practice, teaching, and writing, I am amazed by the growing sophistication of the specialties comprising building conservation science and practice. Curiously, what has been lacking is a single published resource that offers explanations of how and why architectural conservation practice — now a recognized specialty profession — has come to be and outlines the extent of it. *Time Honored: A Global View of Architectural Conservation* offers the best and certainly the most convenient answers to these questions to date.

There has long been a need to delve into how architectural conservation has become such a pervasive subject, not only in the building professions but also in today's global society. *Time Honored* aims to do just that. The present inaugural volume addresses the fundamentals of the topic by defining the field and its structure, outlining its more remarkable examples and theories over time, and citing the key challenges faced and solutions being applied today. The book offers a plethora of examples and explanations with the help of hundreds of useful illustrations followed by four carefully considered appendices. There are further volumes planned, detailing the role and solutions for architectural conservation around the world. Singly or together, the books should prove to be a valuable resource to those wishing to learn the subject from the beginning or to supplement an existing knowledge of the field. The comprehensive nature of the book should prove useful for reference purposes as well. Stubbs stands beside the topics he presents here in a refreshingly objective way, more in the manner of an anthropologist or some other social scientist than a deeply involved advocate and stakeholder, as he thoughtfully says, "Conservation for the sake of conservation—a phenomenon of our time."

John Stubbs has witnessed and participated in more conservation projects in more places than probably anyone else. In *Time Honored: A Global View of Architectural Conservation*, Stubbs documents and explains what he has observed on his countless trips around the world and offers the first truly comprehensive review and balanced portrayal of today's field from a professional perspective. The results—often amazing—reassure us that concerted efforts at this kind of cultural heritage protection are a vital and essential aspect of life in the twenty-first century.

BERNARD M. FEILDEN
DUniv. DLit, Hon FAIA, FSA, FRIBA, AADipl
Director Emeritus, ICCROM
Norwich, England
March 2008

Acknowledgments

Time Honored: A Global View of Architectural Conservation is in large measure based on the writings, teachings, and ideas of others. While I have endeavored to be thorough in giving credit throughout, not all sources—such as the people who created the buildings, places, and conservation schemes referred to herein—could be included. To those named and not, especially the pioneer researchers, thinkers, and those who *acted* to conserve the world's architectural heritage that we may enjoy today, I extend my sincere respect.

My first thanks for assistance in producing this book go to President Bonnie Burnham, the trustees, and my colleagues at the World Monuments Fund in New York for supporting my participation in numerous architectural conservation projects and programs throughout the world since 1990. Without this subvention, this attempt at portraying architectural conservation practice around the world would not have been possible. Of equal importance has been my teacher, mentor, and friend, James Marston Fitch, who put me to the task of writing this book in 1998. I also thank Martica Sawin Fitch, who offered encouragement and help of all kinds along the way.

The Graham Foundation in Chicago provided generous support during the final phase of writing and while choosing illustrations. The Samuel H. Kress Foundation in New York underwrote a research mission to Rome during the initial stages of research. The Bogliasco Foundation in Genoa, Italy, provided a haven for completing the first draft. I also received helpful financial and moral support from Joan K. Davidson through the Furthermore grants for publications program of the J. M. Kaplan Fund in New York.

Sincere appreciation is extended to colleagues, deans, and former students at Columbia University's Graduate Program in Architecture, Planning and Historic Preservation, in particular: Tenzing Lobsang Chadotsang, Brian Curran, Dorothy Dinsmoor, Tania Garth, Catherine Gavin, Jennifer Ko, Bruno Maldoner, and Professor George Wheeler. Special thanks go to Emily Gunzburger Makas and Rob Thomson, who helped greatly with research, content development, and shaping the text. Special thanks is also extended to Sharon Delezenski Genin, who helped prepare several drafts, including the final manuscript, and who served as general assistant for much of the project.

I am grateful to the numerous friends, hosts, and colleagues I have met in connection with the projects and programs of the World Monuments Fund who provided assistance, especially Amita Baig, Andrea Baldioli, Norma Barbacci, Nancy Berliner, William J. Chapman, Jonathan Foyle, Ian Morello, Gaetano Palumbo, Michelle Santoro, and Mark Weber. The World Monuments Fund also generously allowed the use of its photographic archives, from which over one-third of the images in this volume are derived. Heritage conservation consultant Arlene Fleming helpfully provided the compendium of conservation charters and declarations that forms one of the book's appendices.

I especially thank Sir Bernard Feilden, Professor Cevat Erder, Brian Fagan, and Lisa Ackerman for suggestions that improved the content of the book, and editor and writer Ann ffolliott, who did much to improve the text at various stages.

Time Honored: A Global View of Architectural Conservation is dedicated to my parents, King and Sue Stubbs, and my wife Linda Stubbs, whose support and encouragement above all else made it possible.

PART I

Conserving History in Changing Contexts

Machu Picchu (c. 1460 CE), southeastern Peru.

CHAPTER *1*

Introduction

How would the lives of the world's population be different if there were no great *historic buildings* or sites? What if the Parthenon, Pompeii, or Hagia Sophia no longer existed? Imagine Paris without Notre Dame, Florence without the Duomo, and Jerusalem without the Wailing Wall or the Dome of the Rock. What if St. Petersburg had no palaces, if Jordan had no Petra? What if China had no Great Wall or Forbidden City, if India had no Taj Mahal? What would Chicago be without its early skyscrapers, Peru without Machu Picchu, or Easter Island without its mysterious stone *moai*? Apart from these iconic historic buildings and places, what if the more ordinary historic buildings that we encounter in our daily lives were also gone? Imagine if everything was new and undistinguished by change and invention over time, that there was nothing in the *built environment* to remind us of what came before us. How would today's world be different?

The answer to these questions is that civilization as we know it today would not exist. The cultures that inherited these cultural legacies would lack their distinctiveness and their sense of accomplishment. Individuals would have a diminished sense of history and memory of the places they live in and visit. People would lack the variety and reassurance that preceding historic events and places provide.

The sense of one's physical position and place in time is in large part based on historic places, whether they are individual buildings, or entire cities, or the countries in which they are situated. Just thinking of the *historic monuments*[1] and cultures of Rome, London, Egypt, and China helps each individual who knows of these places understand his or her position in space and time. Local landmarks, both cultural and natural, can provide similar orientation. The river, the steeple, the square, the *maison de ville* all help individuals know where they are. The sequences and patterns these objects occupy in a particular location form an environmental context that has meaning for those who experience them.

Many of the buildings, monuments, and places cited above have influenced history. All offer lessons about our forebears and inspire wonder, pride, and additional works of art and architecture.[2] The historic architecture around us enriches human existence and makes our knowledge of the past more comprehensible. Our identity as human beings, both individually and collectively, would be less sure and less meaningful without their presence. It has been convincingly argued that notions of shared history and identity have fostered improved human relations by highlighting a common sense of belonging. Just beginning a list of reasons to preserve artistic and architectural legacies demonstrates that without such tangible reminders, life today would not be as colorful, interesting, or inspiring.

A Russian architectural historian expressed it well: "Historic buildings are a concrete expression of a people's *cultural heritage*. They are products of human activity that reflect sociological trends, national character and 'the spirit of the time.' They provide the means of studying the development of relations among peoples, the mutual influence of their cultures, and the mutual enrichment that has resulted. As an incarnation of the creative activity of mankind, historical monuments are the *heritage* of the whole of humanity."[3]

At the practical level, a continually used historic site adds tangible economic value to its locale on several different levels. The restoration, rehabilitation, and *preservation*—that is, the *conservation* of an old building—embodies an expenditure of time and materials that has usually been repaid many times over, especially considering the indirect financial benefits that can accrue in locales where historic buildings are conserved.

Each component of the world's architectural patrimony, whether it is a site recognized as having "outstanding *universal value*" and included on the United Nations Educational, Scientific and Cultural Organization's (UNESCO's) World Heritage List or simply an old building that we pass in the course of our daily lives, connects us to the past more effectively than does any other human creation. Without memories in the form of physical evidence of who and what preceded us, life today would be less structured and peaceful than it is.

But any structure made by humans, irrespective of the length of time and care it took to create, can easily be taken away, as the destruction of New York's World Trade Center on September 11, 2001, dramatically demonstrated. A secure future for the world's cultural patrimony—of which historic buildings, sites, and *cultural landscapes* are its most tangible and visible manifestations—is by no means assured no matter how valuable it may be.

Fortunately, there is a growing awareness of the fragility of both the world's natural and its cultural heritage. A parallel interest in the conservation of both types of heritage is developing worldwide. Helping to facilitate the protection of both cultural and natural environments are a host of sophisticated heritage management models and systems situated within both the public and the private spheres. Likewise, many new professional specialties are developing within the fields of cultural and natural heritage protection. Each seeks to maintain irreplaceable natural and cultural resources for use and enjoyment both now and in the future. The cultural heritage conservation movement—most noticeably the component that addresses architectural conservation—speaks to an issue of fundamental importance: integrating the past into the future.

But even with the current technical sophistication of the field of architectural conservation, the likelihood of saving all that could or should be saved is not great. It has been estimated that some 50 percent of the world's historic architecture has disappeared during the twentieth century.[4] Given this statistic, one might ask why are people drawn to the practice of architectural conservation. Is it not, in the end, a hopeless task? Some reassurance lies in the hard-earned successes that have been achieved by those who have helped pass architectural legacies on to the present generation. Another assurance lies in the remarkable "rightness" of the activity. The eminent American economist John Kenneth Galbraith commented in 1980, when there were far fewer examples of architectural conservation to see: "The preservation movement has one great curiosity. There is never any retrospective controversy or regret. Preservationists are the only people in the world who are invariably confirmed in their wisdom after the fact."[5]

This book takes on the task of sharing the knowledge gained through the cumulative experiences of over two centuries of organized efforts to conserve architecture—especially as they relate to professional best practices developed in different locales around the world. At this point there are numerous notable examples of conserving historic buildings and sites in most countries. Together, these form a foundation for qualitative and quantitative improvements in contemporary conservation practices elsewhere for both the present and future.

Today's ethos of conserving historic buildings and sites reflects both a maturation of a relatively new discipline and a profession within the practice of architecture. The related specialties of art, archaeological, urban, historic landscape, and architectural conservation attempt to satisfy the important and unavoidable need to maintain and present humanity's physical creations through a variety of conservation-minded actions. These actions together were labeled by the eminent American preservation educator and pioneer in the field, James Marston Fitch, as "curatorial management of the built world."[6]

Today's cultural heritage conservation field faces a daunting and multifaceted challenge driven by difficult questions: What do we want to conserve from the present for the future? What do we value highly? For whom are we maintaining this heritage? Who owns the past? How exactly should we intervene? Adding to the complexity is that approaches to conserving cultural heritage—as well as views about past approaches—also change. Another noted American historic preservation expert and educator described the problem well: "Our answers will not be the same answers we have grown used to.... Each passing day gives new meaning to old places and new character to the nation."[7]

The challenges in architectural conservation faced by every country are the result of certain patterns of cause and effect. As complicated and seemingly overwhelming as these challenges may be at times, there are a finite number of problems that can be met by a finite number of solutions. The accomplishments of the architectural conservation field over the past two centuries—combined with the present local, national, and global interconnectedness of interested agencies, institutions, and individuals—offer today's practitioners great hope for even bolder and more effective cultural heritage conservation schemes. In fact, heritage conservationists of the twenty-first century have certain advantages: No previous generation has possessed more technical tools and means to address conservation challenges.

INEVITABLE CHANGE

The experiences of the twentieth century alone prove that destruction of the built environment by both humans and nature forever alters the character of a place. The variety of possible natural disasters—storms, fires, earthquakes, and floods—is exceeded only by the number of possible man-made threats, which range from benign neglect and poor planning to willful destruction and war. Recently, these traditional human threats have been joined by a number of more modern ones, such as air pollution, tourist wear, vast redevelopment schemes, and increasingly sophisticated and powerful weapons of war.

The cataclysmic changes brought on by the twentieth century's two world wars and the full extent of destruction of the built environment and its inhabitants are almost inconceivable. In the postwar years, changes to cityscapes in Europe, Asia, and the Americas have been unprecedented, exceeding in many cases even the scale of wartime destruction. In his seminal book *Preserving the World's Great Cities*, American urban planner and preservationist Anthony M. Tung writes, "Half a century after World War II numerous planners throughout Europe, including Germany, have concluded that far more architectural history was destroyed in the urban redevelopment that followed the fighting than by the tens of millions of bombs themselves."[8]

Figure 1-1 Dresden, Germany, after the aerial bombing on February 13 and 14, 1945, exemplifies the most powerful and immediate threat to the world's architectural heritage posed by humans: the calculated destruction of war. *(akg-images Ltd., London)*

The built environment has always been created to accommodate human populations; it is therefore helpful to review a few facts regarding patterns of world population growth and movement to illustrate the subsequent enormous pressures on towns, urban areas, and remaining habitable open land. The first concerns population growth: In 1800 the world population was estimated at 978 million; in 1900 it was 1.65 billion; in 2000 it was 6.07 billion, a figure that is expected to double by the year 2200.[9] The second concerns population distribution: By the early twenty-first century, for the first time in history, more people will live inside cities than outside of them. The United Nations predicts that by 2025 about 61 percent of the global population, or 5.2 billion people, will reside in urban areas.[10]

The last century also saw developments in telecommunications, transportation systems, industrial processes, data management, and everyday conveniences that were unimaginable in previous eras. These developments were largely the creations of the so-called first- and second-world industrialized nations, where change and growth were viewed as synonymous with progress. An undeniable result of this trend has been increasing global affluence, although progress has not eradicated the significant imbalances in wealth and well-being, especially for those who live in the developing world. Previously, growth patterns of affluence have been uneven; in modern times, however, demands on the world's natural and cultural resources have consistently increased.

The power and the ruthlessness of change to the built environment, particularly when that change has had a negative impact on large numbers of people, have been increasingly questioned in recent decades. The cumulative reaction to the wholesale loss of cultural patrimony over the past five hundred years has generated the current global concern, or movement, to *safeguard* both our significant and surviving built and natural environments.

Taking a static snapshot of the world's dynamic historic built environment at any given time is not possible. The countless numbers of historic buildings that exist, plus the exponential growth of new construction that will in time become historic, make any attempt at such a precise quantitative survey pointless.[11] But two similarities among all human-made structures make the task of characterizing the present global phenomenon of the architectural conservation movement conceptually manageable. First, the uses and construction methods and materials of all structures are definable and typologically limited. This means that even when considering all the variables the number of physical, material, and construction problems that can be encountered are finite, as are the number of possible remedies. As a result, lessons, however approximate, can be inferred by quantitative and qualitative analyses of existing building stocks.

Second, most human-made creations serve, or served, a purpose, and each represents an expenditure of time, energy, materials, and economic resources. Thus, most physical creations by humans contain some degree of value, whether it is material, artistic, symbolic, economic, or due simply to age. The simplest way to appreciate the value of any creation, either handmade or natural, is by attempting to reproduce it.

In places where historic buildings exist, there are usually also a finite variety of time-tested building traditions. For example, for residential structures, there are functional similarities between the traditional wooden houses of the Baltic region and the mud-brick domestic architecture of the Middle East. There are often amazing general similarities in certain building types across time, as can be seen by comparing the first-century multistory apartment houses of ancient Ostia near Rome with those of nineteenth-century London or New York. Basic functional similarities can also be observed between the ruined atrium houses of ancient Pompeii; the empty stone and adobe Native American habitations at Chaco Canyon, New Mexico; and the fast-disappearing courtyard houses within Beijing's *hutong* neighborhoods.[12]

In the broadest sense, the conservation of architecture is all about managing change. Change is an inevitable life process with which every living creature contends. Anticipating and managing change, whether personal or collective, has always been a human concern. Failure to do so would mean extinction. But buildings have lives, too; they were created under dynamic conditions and will be in a dynamic state when considered for refurbishment. Remember, too, that the field of architectural conservation is itself constantly changing. Accommodating change is at the heart of cultural resources management, and the tools for handling it begin with innate common sense based on observation and experience.

Recent developments in computer modeling can provide highly realistic simulations of almost any imaginable scenario. Examples range from likely growth predictions for towns, states, and entire countries to analyzing structural failure points in Gothic cathedrals and impact studies for potential ecological disasters. Such tools, however, have their limitations, because it is unlikely that virtually every potential cause-and-effect scenario in the built environment is predictable. This is because certain combinations or sequences of variables may not be anticipated, although they may be individually predictable.

Consequently, the cumulative experience of the relatively young field of architectural conservation offers the best basis on which to predict what may happen when change occurs and, perhaps more importantly, *why* change occurs. A working knowledge of the cause-and-effect aspects of managing change in the built environment is essential

Figure 1-2 Destruction of a traditional *hutong* block, Beijing, China, 2007. Such superblocks, consisting of dozens of courtyard houses, represent a time-tempered architectural form suitable to Beijing's climate; they reflected the capital city's grand plan dating from the early fifteenth century. Despite the fact that en masse they helped make Beijing one of the most beautiful cities in the world, only a few *hutongs* have survived the city's recent modernization.

for those engaged in the field if effective remedies are to be applied. Such knowledge, enhanced by an ability to appraise historical value and significance objectively, is what distinguishes those who are trained and experienced in architectural conservation from those who are not. Such an understanding can be crucial given the importance of "doing the right thing" with a historical resource—and there are rarely second chances.

The sizable losses of the world's significant architectural patrimony in modern times have, in turn, provided a major impetus for today's burgeoning heritage conservation field. Saving historic buildings and sites was once an esoteric interest of a few antiquarians and advocates, but in thousands of communities throughout the world it has evolved into a widespread movement involving millions. The sound logic of the obvious returns that can be derived from conserving cultural heritage is its greatest appeal. After all, everyone cares, at least to some degree, about the place in which he lives.

Most preservation-minded individuals probably developed their interest in the subject by witnessing the loss of cultural heritage sites in their own communities. The cumulative effect of the loss of landmarks, familiar environments, and treasured works of art has fueled a widespread and growing interest around the world in organizing efforts to protect cultural heritage sites. This was especially true in the last three decades of the twentieth century. Those who are thus involved find themselves part of a widespread human activity—a new culture, so to speak. Proof of the existence of this phenomenon lies in the fact that the language, procedures, and purposes of architectural conservation are remarkably similar wherever it occurs. Proof of it also comes to light when valued sites are imminently threatened.

By the beginning of the twenty-first century, the ***architectural heritage*** conservation movement had matured. Today, it is fast coalescing into an increasingly global concern that is well-served by a growing number of international participants who are adding to local and national efforts; their primary aim is conserving and presenting tangible examples from history as useful and vital necessities for both individuals and for the world's population in general.

Although the integration of the world's economy can be said to have begun with European exploratory and colonial missions in the fifteenth and sixteenth centuries, it was standardized and codified much more recently, beginning with the removal of international trade barriers after World War II.[13] Certain coinciding factors in the late twentieth century, including the development of the Internet and the end of the Cold War, have accelerated this process dramatically by allowing both communications and markets to become truly global.

GLOBALIZATION AND CULTURAL HERITAGE CONSERVATION

Globalization is fundamentally an economic process enabled by political and techno-logical change and characterized by increasing international trade and harmonizing world financial systems. British sociologist Roland Robertson, an early proponent of a social theory of globalization, offers a broader definition, suggesting this concept "refers both to the compression of the world and the intensification of consciousness of the world as a whole."[14]

The internationalization of the world economy has meant that developing countries are both positively and negatively affected by the involvement of foreign governments, transnational corporations, and major international financial institutions. These major financial institutions, which both regulate world trade and promote global economic development, include the World Trade Organization, the World Bank, the International Monetary Fund, the Inter-American Development Bank, and the European Bank for Reconstruction and Development. Funds have been channeled into local communities and the living conditions of local populations have been improved, but simultaneously the self-sufficiency of local economies has been challenged and local sociocultural patterns have been changed. Examples in the case of the World Bank include city center infrastructure and revitalization efforts in Fez, Morocco, and Stone Town, Zanzibar, Tanzania, and the restoration of Constantin Brancusi's Endless Column monumental sculpture complex in Tîrgu Jiu, Romania. The European Bank for Reconstruction and Development (EBRD) and the Inter-American Development Bank (IADB) likewise made low-interest, long-term loans in support of several historic centers. Notable EBRD project sites are Zagreb, Croatia, and Moscow, Russia; for the IADB, Cartagena, Colombia, and Quito, Ecuador, deserve mention. Somewhat similar government-to-government grants, often with fewer conditions, can be seen in German government support for the conservation of Durbar Square at Baktapur in the Kathmandu Valley, Nepal, and significant aid from China to restore structures in Ulaanbaatar, Mongolia, and at Angkor in Cambodia. Often, such grants incorporate technical and training assistance and are joined to a parallel goal of improving trade relations.

Significant debate has also surrounded the degree to which globalization is controlled and directed by the policies of governments, corporations, and international organizations. Some argue these institutions simply enable and facilitate that which is an inevitable historical process, calling change a healthy, natural, and unavoidable process that, if well-managed, can result in better global living conditions. Others contend that substantial loans to, gifts for, and investments in developing countries from wealthier nations and institutions simply redistribute global wealth. Supporters of globalization reason that change brought about by a country's increased growth brings progress and should therefore not be impeded but rather guided.[15]

Skeptics, however, counter that it is a self-serving process orchestrated by the parties who benefit disproportionately from it. Pessimistic views of globalization see it as uncon-

Figure 1-3 The infrastructure and several buildings in Plaza de San Francisco, the historic center of Quito, Ecuador, were restored with loan assistance from the Inter-American Development Bank.

Figure 1-4 The medina in Fez, Morocco. Infrastructure improvements and select building restorations in the commercial center of one of Morocco's two most intact historic cities were accomplished with funding from the World Bank.

trolled modernization causing massive, dehumanizing change along with disorientation and disruption. The most dire of these views is exemplified by American political scientist and professor Samuel P. Huntington in "The Clash of Civilizations?" in which he writes that current economic and political processes are leading the world head on into global conflict along cultural fault lines.[16]

A look around us in the first decade of the twenty-first century shows that all of the above-mentioned positions on globalization are both true and ongoing. In retrospect, the accelerating process of globalization in the second half of the twentieth century had a direct and obvious bearing on cultural identity and cultural resource management worldwide. It had a homogenizing effect that has reduced cultural diversity. Many aspects of culture have indeed become global, particularly American contributions like MTV, Coca-Cola, and Microsoft. Traditional draped and loose-fitting garments worn in hot climates, such as the *galabia* worn by men, still give way to Western-style fitted clothes, especially the ubiquitous sneakers, jeans, and T-shirts, even if these are less practical or climate friendly.

Globalization and the encroachment of Western culture and values have created a threat, both real and perceived, to communities that feel their proud artistic and cultural traditions are at risk, even though these changes are more often embraced voluntarily than as the result of forced acculturation.[17] The concern is not just that traditional ways and customs—ranging from agricultural practices and regional cuisines to traditional music and manners of dress—will change, but that the values, ways of life, and histories they represent will be lost or forgotten as well. For example, critics of globalization suggest that in Istanbul, opening a Starbucks café that offers customers takeout coffee could accelerate the closure of nearby local coffee shops, which in turn might also contribute to the demise of a centuries-old cultural habit of leisurely interpersonal exchanges at Turkish coffeehouses. There is certain irony in the same franchise having a presence in the Forbidden City, which until a century ago was famously the most inaccessible place in the world to outside influence.

At the same time that globalization has standardized certain lifestyle elements among many of the world's populations, it has also led to an increased awareness of the multiplicity of cultures worldwide and helped individual cultures recognize their own uniqueness. A better understanding of the culture and heritage of others raises one's consciousness and estimation of one's own culture. As British political scientist Mary Kaldor advises, "Globalization conceals a complex, contradictory process that actually involves both globalization and localization, integration and fragmentation, homogenization and differentiation."[18]

The recent awareness of cultural, national, and regional identities and interest in local ways of life have led to increased local, national, and international efforts at heritage protection worldwide. Particularly vivid examples are found in countries such as Indo-

Figure 1-5 Starbucks café franchise in the Palace Museum, Forbidden City, Beijing, China, 2004.

nesia, Cambodia, and Morocco, which are endowed with significant—though until recently underappreciated—cultural or natural assets. Today, the unique heritages of Bali, Angkor, and Fez are well-known throughout the world. Moreover, their nationally led redevelopment schemes to celebrate, preserve, and present such places have stimulated similar actions at other nearby heritage sites.

Much of the world's poor live in ancient towns that may be in decrepit condition when compared with more recent settlements. Where such environments involve historic buildings, a special opportunity exists to incorporate community revitalization efforts in heritage conservation. Integrated neighborhood and infrastructure improvement schemes that simultaneously address environmental, social, and health conditions have proven effective. Experience gained from world food programs, such as those administered by the United Nations and its Food and Agriculture Organization, has shown that simultaneous environmental improvement and heritage conservation schemes in impoverished areas should be a priority among both rich and poor countries in the future. It therefore makes eminent sense for world governments and organizations such as the European Union and the United Nations to further cooperate to conserve, and sensitively develop more deteriorated historical residential areas as well as historic town centers for the benefit of all.

Though the concept of world heritage implies worldwide understanding and appreciation, actions to promote, conserve and present such heritage rely ultimately on national and local participation. Through global programs like UNESCO's World Heritage List and the World Monuments Fund's Watch™ List of 100 Most Endangered

Figure 1-6 In coordination with local architectural conservation agencies in Ahmadabad, India, an innovative approach was developed by a not-for-profit organization aided by funding from the Ford Foundation. Called the Health and Heritage Program as the health concerns of families were addressed, improvements were made to eighteenth- and nineteenth-century *havelis* (finely detailed courtyard houses) in a representative historic district in which they lived.

Sites, individual governments and communities are encouraged to identify and protect significant sites within their boundaries. Optimally, these schemes stimulate local empowerment and private entrepreneurship, which can result in real contributions to local economies. An excellent example is the church of Jesús Nazareno of Atotonilco, located near the town of San Miguel Allende in the state of Guanajuato, Mexico. The church was constructed between 1740 and 1776, and behind its unpretentious *façade* the church and its side chapels contain an extremely elaborate decorative scheme consisting of wall and ceiling murals, silver inlay work, and a rich array of sculpture. The artistic program reflects well a "syncretism" of Catholic religious iconography mixed with native religious beliefs and as such served as a spiritual center and is the destination of frequent religious pilgrimages. In addition the site served as the terminus of the famous Mexican Independence Route. In the mid-1990s, the church suffered from leaking roofs, rising damp, and general neglect as a result of its nearby village being essentially abandoned. In 1995 the fate of Atotonilco changed when local supporters in San Miguel Allende drew the attention of the World Monuments Fund to the site. After placement of the site on WMF's 1996 World Monuments Watch list of most endangered sites, and with start-up funding of $20,000 from the American Express Company, a slow but sure effort to restore the church, one component at time, gained momentum. A key partner early in the project was Adopte una Obre de Arte, a not-for-profit organization based in Mexico City, which was just beginning to take on whole architectural restoration projects at the time. Toward its participation, WMF applied funding from its Wilson Challenge to Conserve Our Heritage, which in turn attracted other support for the project from foundations and private donors from as far away as Los Angeles and London. As the conservation project neared completion after nearly a decade of effort, the critical mass of interest and support for the site expanded even further in September 2008 when Atotonilco was placed on UNESCO's World Heritage List.[19]

The motives of international heritage conservation advocacy organizations are rarely questioned, especially when their lists of architecturally distinguished sites and priority conservation projects are backed by the promise of financial assistance, both direct and indirect. Some localities view these actions as paternalistic or even hegemonistic, but most realize the associated benefits of increased visibility, technical assistance and exchange, and leveraged funding is worth the introduction of foreign influence and aid. That organizations such as these are working in all countries, not just developing countries, is testament to both their fairness and their usefulness.

Resourceful and thoughtful *managed change*, performed through an open and inclusive process and based on facts, has proven to be the most viable method for accommodating humanity's environmental needs in the era of globalization. As heritage conservation specialists at the World Bank have said, "Cultural heritage is, in a sense, 'knowledge management' based on simple common sense and sustainable use of resources."[20]

Our ever-expanding knowledge of other people and places, both in the present and across time, offers improved abilities to interpret and present heritage sites as well as increased opportunities for international exchange and cooperation. The marvels of humanity's past—and the issues we face in understanding and conserving them—are topics of concern as never before.

CULTURAL SENSIBILITY

There is more to architectural heritage conservation than arresting or impeding the process of physical decay through technical intervention. It also encompasses the challenging task of fully appreciating and accommodating both the past and present cultural

▲ **Figure 1-7** Restored exterior of the church of Jesús Nazareno in Atotonilco in north central Mexico, which in the 1990s suffered extensively from both rising damp and roof water leakage.

▶ **Figure 1-8** Interior ceiling murals of Atotonilco, which are part of the church's highly ornate interior decorative features, seen after restoration.

values the objects being observed represent. Conservation assumes an attitude about a building or site, so therefore its interpretation must reflect these cultural sensibilities. To do this effectively, not only are the essential talents of the historian, architect, engineer, and archaeologist tapped but often those of specialized *conservators*, researchers, restoration artisans, and project implementers as well. Input from educators, museum professionals, tourism experts, sociologists, and anthropologists is often equally important. These and other specialists in the social sciences and the humanities would best understand the audience that is served by the conserved buildings and sites.

In all cultures, heritage conservation practice is nearly always inclusive and reflects the complexity of the host society in decisions and its organizational structure. Why conserve an object or a tradition in the first place unless it serves a purpose and benefits the local population? Where intellectual, philanthropic, and educational activities unite with wider community interest and action, the merits of heritage conservation leave an impression on all aspects of modern life.

To date, the socioeconomic impact of architectural conservation projects on communities remains poorly understood because neither the variables nor the benefits are easily measurable. Pride in local customs and the special characteristics of a particular locale, termed *genius loci* — or sense of place — are difficult to define. Assigning a precise monetary value to these intangible concepts is clearly impossible. Even attempts at formulating the replacement cost of vanished landmarks are limited because such replacements can never carry exactly the same meanings as the originals due to their lack of authenticity. Nonetheless, pride in ownership and *associations* with historic places — as reflected in the measures extended toward their protection, maintenance, and presentation — are usually an obvious feature of any community. Pride and interest in a place's upkeep can be fragile and change quickly for reasons ranging from demographic shifts to external traumas to ill-advised planning decisions.

Typically, changes in *genius loci* occur subtly. For instance, interventions at heavily visited conserved sites can be disruptive and disorienting to a locality's sense of ownership, even if the work has been initiated locally. Work that has been orchestrated by foreign specialists can also produce the unhelpful impression of a site's having outside ownership. Some recent efforts in architectural heritage conservation and related activities by local governments, foreign nongovernmental organizations (NGOs), and quasi-autonomous non-governmental organizations (QUANGOs) have radically changed the meaning and purpose of heritage sites as far as local inhabitants are concerned — and not always for the better. Note, for example, the almost too great popularity among visitors in recent years of sites such as the Athenian Acropolis, the Valley of the Kings in Egypt, Borobodur in Indonesia, Beijing's Forbidden City, and the Italian cities of Venice and Florence.

From the initial stages of planning, cultural heritage interventions should carefully consider their social, cultural, and economic implications as objectively as possible. Sharing experiences and best practices through publications, training programs, cooperative ventures, and exchange programs are among the ways to achieve culturally sensible and sensitive heritage conservation management.

Despite ever-present challenges facing cultural heritage protection, an overriding concern for its protection usually exists. This instinct to preserve represents a certain cultural sensitivity, if only for practical purposes. Stefano Bianca, former Director of the Historic Cities Support Programme for the Geneva-based Aga Khan Trust for Culture once complemented this fact in saying:

"The richness and variety of many pre-industrial historic cities we admire today result from a seemingly incoherent, if not careless, attitude to the past…. When judged in our own terms of preservation, though, we have to admit that the very genesis of this accumulated heritage was fundamentally anti-historic and non-scientific."[21]

Figure 1-9 The temple of Tanah Lot, the oldest Hindu temple in Bali, Indonesia, pictured here during a religious festival, is an example of *living heritage.*

Figure 1-10 Tourists viewing a sunset from atop the ninth-century state temple of Phnom Bakheng, Angkor, Cambodia.

Herein lies a certain paradox: Should heritage conservationists disrupt traditional (organic) cultural growth and death processes? By today's principles in heritage protection the answer is yes, especially where the process of alienation has taken place—where members of a society no longer recognize the deeper values and motivations in its **material culture**. Preservation can thus be a substitute for living tradition, though it lacks the power of procreation and may no longer be able to engage the society as a whole.[22]

Bianca's argument points to a larger concern: While some heritage site protection measures may at times seem culturally insensitive, they can, when following recognized tenets of conservation practice, actually reflect a greater cultural sensibility than those undertaken by the local communities themselves. Reviewing the track record of the heritage conservation movement allows us to evaluate its accomplishments and failures and see how its philosophy and approaches have evolved over time. Modern heritage conservationists recognize the necessity for continued professional evolution bolstered by improved measures involving the careful use of new conservation materials and techniques as well as more effective technological and project-assembly processes.

Through the activities of organizations such as WMF, UNESCO, the International Council on Monuments and Sites (ICOMOS), the International Centre for the Study of the Preservation and Restoration of Cultural Property (ICCROM), the International Council of Museums (ICOM), the Getty Conservation Institute (GCI), and others, professionals in the field of international cultural heritage protection are more closely in touch than ever before. And as more people become aware of the social and economic benefits of cultural heritage protection, more government agencies throughout the world are committing significant time and resources to such tasks.

As the demand for professional services grows, cultural heritage managers, training institutions, and the allied professions are responding to meet that need. New teaching venues—from workshops to college courses to complete academic programs—are being established in more places around the world. These positive developments are expanding the accomplishments of previous generations, which set the stage for contemporary cultural heritage conservation practice. Our debt to those who preceded us, who likely struggled against even greater odds than those that we face today, should be remembered. The legal

Figure 1-11 The countless actions to maintain historic buildings over generations have a direct relation to their survival. As such it is the daily custodians of the world's architectural heritage, including its advocates in government, site managers, curators, historians, repair technicians, and daily maintenance personnel, who are the unsung heroes of cultural heritage protection. This worker is repainting a precinct division wall within the Forbidden City in Beijing, China.

and operational framework for cultural heritage protection today depends on the efforts and resources expended to preserve many of the buildings, sites, and objects that draw our attention generations later. Throughout history and in every corner of the world, there have been countless unsung heroes of the cultural heritage conservation movement, usually anonymous men and women who protected and maintained old buildings, sites, and other forms of the world's cultural heritage. Through their efforts, today's conservators have a wealth of cultural heritage to work with and are better prepared for assuming the challenge of heritage conservation.

Great challenges lie ahead in the field of cultural heritage protection, and in particular for its main subfield, architectural conservation. Understanding these challenges will be as important as having the vision and will to address them.

ENDNOTES

1. *Random House Unabridged Dictionary*, 2nd ed. (New York: Random House, 1993), defines *monument* thus: from the Latin *monere*, "to remind"; "something erected in memory of a person, event, etc., as a building, pillar or statue; any building, megalith, etc., surviving from a past age and regarded as of historical or archaeological importance; an area or site of interest to the public for its historic significance, great natural beauty, etc., preserved and maintained by a government; any enduring evidence or notable example of something."

2. For example, the remains of ancient Rome inspired the art, architecture, and literature of the Renaissance. Historicism in the nineteenth century in Europe and the Americas was concerned with reviving past styles in architecture.

3. Alexander Halturin, "Monuments in Contemporary Life," in International Council on Monuments and Sites (ICOMOS), *Colloque sur les Monuments et la Societé / Symposium on Monuments and Society: Leningrad, URSS / USSR, 2–8 Septembre 1969* (Paris: ICOMOS, 1971), 21–22.

4. Anthony M. Tung, *Preserving the World's Great Cities: The Destruction and Renewal of the Historic Metropolis* (New York: Clarkson Potter, 2001), 414.

5. John Kenneth Galbraith, "The Economic and Social Returns of Preservation," in *Preservation: Toward an Ethic in the 1980s*, ed. National Trust for Historic Preservation (Washington, DC: Preservation Press, National Trust for Historic Preservation, 1980), 57.

6. James Marston Fitch, preface to *Historic Preservation: Curatorial Management of the Built World* (Charlottesville, VA: University of Virginia Press, 1990).

7. Robert E. Stipe and Antoinette J. Lee, eds. *The American Mosaic: Preserving a Nation's Heritage* (Washington, DC: US National Committee of the International Council on Monuments and Sites [US/ICOMOS], Preservation Press, National Trust for Historic Preservation, 1987), quote within by W. Brown Morton III, 41.

8. Tung, *Preserving the World's Great Cities*, 17.

9. United Nations Department of Economic and Social Affairs, Population Division, http://www.unesco.org.

10. During the twentieth century alone, the global urban population increased more than tenfold, and it is still growing.

11. Preservation planner Anthony Tung has derived some meaningful conclusions on estimates of the amount of loss to the built environment in his *Preserving the World's Great Cities*.

12. The same may be said of other building types, such as religious buildings, civic architecture, commercial structures, parks and plazas, city walls, street systems, bridges, and cemeteries. While the existence of such similarities may be convenient for general comparison purposes, each building possesses its own history and distinct characteristics.

13. The globalization of the world economy in recent decades has been evidenced and perpetuated through the formation of political-economic alliances such as the ever-expanding European Union (EU), trilateral trade agreements such as the North American Free Trade Agreement (NAFTA), and membership trade organizations such as the Association of Southeast Asian Nations (ASEAN).

14. Roland Robertson, *Globalization: Social Theory and Global Culture* (London: Sage Publications, 1992), 8.

15. For example, George Soros argues in favor of globalization because it increases wealth and creates open societies. He suggests, however, that institutional reforms are necessary to ensure that the newly generated wealth is fairly distributed, arguing that "all the evidence shows the winners could compensate the losers and still come out ahead" (*George Soros on Globalization* [New York: Public Affairs, 2005], 9). He recommends removing biases from the market, sponsoring parallel social and poverty-reducing actions on a global scale, and ending "corrupt, repressive or incompetent governments" (ibid., 7).

16. Samuel P. Huntington, "The Clash of Civilizations?" *Foreign Affairs* 72, no. 3 (Summer 1993): 22.

17. Resistance to the spread of foreign influences has been heroic in some places. For example, in the 1990s in France, legal measures were taken to protect the French language from unwanted intrusions of foreign words.

18. Mary Kaldor, "Cosmopolitanism Versus Nationalism: The New Divide?" in *Europe's New Nationalism: States and Minorities in Conflict*, ed. Richard Caplan and John Feffer (New York: Oxford University Press, 1996), 42.

19. The effort over a 10-year period to research, document, and carefully restore Atotonilco brought to light the site's extraordinary historical and artistic significance. When complemented with a plan for the protection and operation of the site in the future, the church and its immediate surroundings were technically qualified for nomination to the UNESCO World Heritage List

20. Ismail Serageldin and June Taboroff, eds., *Culture and Development in Africa: Proceedings of an International Conference* held at the World Bank, Washington, DC, April 2 and 3, 1992 (Washington, DC: World Bank, 1994), 65.

21. Stefano Bianca, "Direct Government Involvement in Architectural Heritage Management: Legitimation, Limits, and Opportunities of Ownership and Operation," in *Preserving the Built Heritage: Tools for Implementation*, ed. J. Mark Schuster, with John de Monchaux, and Charles A. Riley II (Hanover, NH: University Press of New England, 1997), 14–15.

22. Ibid. See also information about the Maori concept of permanence in Chapter 15.

Figure 2-1 Each of the dozens of buildings dating from the Gothic, Renaissance, and Baroque periods that forms the town square in Telč, Czech Republic, has its own history, identity, and conservation challenge. In aggregate, the town's buildings, generous square, and surrounding farmland create something that is greater than the sum of its parts, giving it a special sense of place.

CHAPTER **2**

What Is Architectural Conservation?

Aside from the effects of land cultivation as seen from above, the built environment is the most visible expression of man's presence on earth. But conceptualizing this legacy at a discernible scale is at once both simple and difficult. Although evidence of man's creations is easily found in all corners of the globe, making sense of this vast array of constantly changing cultural heritage for conservation and interpretation purposes is a complicated task. The complex tapestry of human history and the broad geographical circumstances through which its many threads occur creates a seemingly infinite number of possibilities for the physical form, condition, and context of the human-made environment. Each artifact, building, town, or cultural landscape has a unique story, character, and significance that reflect the culture that created it, the time of its creation, and its subsequent history. Correspondingly, each architectural heritage site has its particular conservation challenges.

Conservation of **cultural property** has been defined as all actions aimed at safeguarding cultural property for the future in order to study, record, retain, and restore the culturally significant qualities of the object, site, or building with the least possible intervention.[1] It is, first and foremost, a process intended to ensure that cultural property endures and can be used now and in the future.[2] Thus, **architectural conservation** constitutes actions and interests that address the repair, restoration, **maintenance**, and display of historic buildings and sites as well as their associated accoutrements, such as furnishings and fittings.

Architectural conservation is widely regarded as the predominant activity within the larger and more diverse field of *cultural heritage conservation*, which is also referred to as *cultural heritage (or resource) management*. This field is concerned with the **documentation** and preservation of all forms of human culture, including tangible artifacts such as architecture, archaeological sites, cultural landscapes, arts and crafts, and other objects of material culture. In addition, cultural heritage conservation addresses intangible manifestations of human activity, including manners and customs (folkways); spiritual

Conserving History in Changing Contexts

Figure 2-2 The broad label of cultural heritage conservation includes architectural conservation as its principal subcategory. Some of the many types of cultural heritage are on display at the opening ceremony of the restored theater building on the town square in the village of Shaxi in western Yunnan Province, China, where in 2004 several specially dressed ethnic minority groups celebrated with music, song, dance, traditional food, and religious offerings.

practices; and musical, craft, and cuisine traditions of indigenous populations, all of which are considered *living heritage*. The various theories and practices of architectural conservation are best understood in light of the broader activity of cultural heritage management.

Any attempt to define architectural conservation comprehensively is elusive due to the field's constantly evolving concerns. Because of the simultaneous and growing interest in new aspects of cultural heritage, the purview of heritage conservation is ever expanding. Such breadth and eclecticism is useful; an all-inclusive attitude that embraces and juxtaposes disparate facts and incidents can find within them a new significance. This book attempts to survey and explain a phenomenon of our times—what one observer described as "the current almost obsessional desire to preserve the past in a physical form. Preservation for religious reasons is as old as the first rudimentary tomb. Preservation for aesthetic reasons is as old as civilization. But 'preservation for preservation's sake,' because an object is old, regardless of its religious or aesthetic content, is a thing very much of our day."[3]

Today, most countries are involved with heritage conservation actions ranging in scale from modest objects in museums to various isolated buildings to entire urban areas and cultural landscapes. Against this backdrop a multitude of activities related to the field are occurring daily: significant *historic objects* are selling for record prices, as is antique furniture; debate about exported national heritage—especially illicitly traded archaeological objects—continues; sites and objects in areas experiencing civil unrest are of wider concern; and prominent museum exhibitions are promoting universal notions of humanity's shared heritage. The sheer quantity of such activity as reported in

Terminology differences between British English and American English underscore a much larger issue within the field of architectural conservation, which today uses both long-established and newer terms to describe its various types and levels of intervention. Established terms include *restoration, reconstruction, replication, rehabilitation*, and *conservation.* Terms describing specific types of interventions include *stabilization, consolidation, anastylosis, repair, replacement, duplication*, and *extended* or *adaptive use*. Terms borrowed from allied and distant fields such as art conservation and medicine include *facsimile, palimpsest, lacunae, regeneration*, and *building forensics*. Newer terms coined to describe evolving issues in the field include *gentrification, re-restoration, museumification*, and *reversibility*. Less established and more informal American slang describing aspects of the field include *renovation, remodel, overhaul, fix up, revamp*, and *Disneyfication*. Romance language terms that have gained currency in diverse distant cultures include *valorization, façadism, degagement*, and *toute ensemble.*

Due to the relative newness of the profession of architectural conservation—which evolved from restoration traditions primarily in Italy, France, England, and Germany from the late eighteenth through early twentieth centuries—most countries today recognize and use Romance language–based terminology. These terms are easily translated, and their common Latin roots are easily recognizable. The English terms *restoration, conservation, historic monument, restorer*, and *conservator* translate, respectively, to *restauro, conservazione, monumento nazionale*, and *restauratore (-trice)*, and *conservatore* in Italian; *restauration, conservation, monument historique, restaurateur (-trice)*, and *conservateur (-rice)* in French; *Restaurierung, Konservierung, Baudenkmall, Restaurator (-in)*, and *Konservator (-in)* in German; and *restauración, conservación, monumento, restaurador (-a)*, and *conservador (-a)*, in Spanish. The architectural conservation field is known as *restauração* in Portuguese, *restauracja* in Polish, and *реставрация* or *restavratsia* in Russian.

Understandings of what restoration or conservation entails can vary in different parts of the world, as is vividly illustrated by comparing Western (Euro-American) and Eastern (East Asian) approaches. East Asian restoration and conservation tends to involve more radical interventions, which Westerners often consider rebuilding and reconstruction. Certain Eastern approaches are based on long-standing traditions in art and cultural practices, such as the Buddhist practice of rebuilding for merit or the age-old Japanese aesthetic of *wabi-sabi*, the belief that values attributable to age, imperfection, and even breakage are inherent to every object. While an academic knowledge of *wabi-sabi* is useful for Western conservators, its meaning—and applications—rests almost exclusively among Japanese conservators and connoisseurs.

It is a saving grace for those confronted with international nomenclature differences that the meaning behind most of the field's terms and their counterparts are remarkably similar. Professional conservators and laypersons alike have remarkably little difficulty communicating both the intent and procedures of architectural conservation because the issues and possibilities encountered throughout the field are often similar. Borrowed terms, principles, and procedures, as well as the use of foreign legislative models and internationally recognized charters, help to harmonize nomenclature, standards, and practices to a certain degree. As a result, professionals from all over the world are increasingly working together in collaborative ventures with remarkable ease, harmony, and success.

Detailed definitions of four essential terms used in architectural conservation follow:

Conservation: "The processes of caring for a place so as to safeguard its cultural heritage value" and "Conservation may involve, in increasing extent of intervention: non-intervention, maintenance, stabilization, repair, restoration, reconstruction or *adaptation*. Where appropriate, conservation processes may be applied to parts or components of a structure or site."[4] Architectural conservation also refers to the applied science of conserving building materials. *Restoration*: "The return of something to a former, original, normal, or unimpaired condition; a *reconstitution* or reproduction of an ancient building…showing it in its original state or its appearance at some other specific point in time."[5] Restoration requires a maximum amount of research and authenticity because it may include reinstating or replicating missing elements or removing later additions. The goal of any restoration project is to re-create a historic site's aesthetic and historical *integrity* by presenting its appearance at some earlier point. More than any other type of intervention, a successful restoration requires the most careful research and documentation since it often involves removing existing *fabric* or

(continued)

re-creating missing elements. Restoration is only appropriate if there is sufficient evidence of an earlier state of the fabric.[6] Examples include the Windsor Guildhall near London; the Château de Versailles near Paris; Ho Chi Minh's residence in Hanoi; parts of the Qianlong Garden complex in the Forbidden City, Beijing; and Mount Vernon, Virginia.

Rehabilitation: The modification of an historic architectural resource to contemporary functional standards, which may involve adaptation for new use.[7] In rehabilitation, those portions of the property important in illustrating historic, architectural, and cultural values are preserved or restored. Rehabilitation is also defined as actions—including cleaning, strengthening, adding modern elements, and so on—taken to prevent a structure, site, or group of structures from further change or decay. Examples include the Guimet Musée National des Arts Asiatiques in Paris; the Pension Building in Washington, DC; Raffles Hotel in Singapore; and the Gostiny Dvor shopping center in St. Petersburg, Russia.

Adaptive use: The modification of a structure, site, or group of structures to fit a changed environment.[8] Adaptive use accommodates a contemporary function that meets the needs of the community and contributes positively to the urban environment. It should be limited to what is essential and is acceptable only where it has minimal impact on the **cultural significance** of a place.[9] Examples include New York City's South Street Seaport and Ellis Island, London's Covent Garden, Paris's Musée d'Orsay, the Palazzo Altemps in Rome, former commercial buildings adapted to residences in the French Concession district in Shanghai, and the numerous *paradores*, *posadas*, and *pousadas* (hotels within historic castles, monasteries, and towns) of Spain and Portugal.

The three terms defined above betray both distinctions and similarities. Occasionally, they are used interchangeably. *Adaptive use*, for example, usually entails rehabilitation. However, recognizing the sometimes subtle differences in meaning among the field's terminology is especially important when studying and practicing architectural conservation internationally. The glossary of this book (see page 375) contains expanded definitions of the nomenclature of the architectural conservation field.

the news media every day is a testament to both the popularity and the validity of the heritage movement in our time. As such, it has been impossible to avoid questions and issues related to the preservation of the past. While the battle for the minds of some is far from won, there can be no return to the days when governments and developers could ignore the value of built heritage or treat it merely as an inconvenient obstruction to "progress."

Since its origin as an independent discipline in the late eighteenth century, acts of restoring, rehabilitating, and conserving works of architecture have relied on an increasing number of terms drawn from several languages that are specific to the field. The British term *architectural conservation* will be used in this book to refer to the overall enterprise of conserving historic buildings and sites that were created by or affected by humans. This term is being increasingly used throughout Western Europe and elsewhere in the world, both officially and informally.

The equivalent term in the United States is *architectural preservation*, but in truth this is outmoded and not as literally descriptive as architectural conservation. Thus, in the United States as well, the terms **historic preservation** and **architectural conservation** are increasingly used interchangeably as both laypersons and professionals acquire a more complete perspective on the importance of safeguarding both America's and the world's cultural patrimony.[10] In both the United States and Great Britain the term *architectural conservator* is used to describe one who practices *building conservation science*. Architectural conservators research the degradation and destruction of building materials as well as their scientific remedies. The terms *architectural conservationist* and *architectural conservation professional* are recognized and used in most countries in preference to the term *architectural preservationist*.

ORIGINS AND CONCERNS OF ARCHITECTURAL CONSERVATION

It is easy to appreciate the fruits of architectural conservation efforts because conserved historic buildings and sites are widely seen and enjoyed by much of the world's population today. Humans have always been distressed by the loss of valued possessions or aspects of their surroundings. The genesis of "preservation-minded" actions—even if relatively primitive and only at the level of individual actions—theoretically dates from the time the first person attempted to control unwanted changes to his living environment. While no one will ever know for sure, it is probably safe to assume that the "instinct to preserve" dates to not long after early humans began creating objects and structures that could be used continually. Researchers date the earliest creation of durable stone implements to about 3,000,000 BCE; the oldest evidence of durable expressions of artistic and spiritual beliefs date to at least 50,000 BCE, and the earliest evidence of the construction and maintenance of built works and settlements dates to about 8000 BCE. Somewhere within these dates—that is, from time immemorial—humankind became interested in safeguarding its practical and symbolic creations.

The history of architectural conservation can be divided into premodern and modern phases, roughly demarcated by the Industrial Revolution, which began in England in the mid-eighteenth century. Our current widespread interest in history and its physical remains is largely attributable to humanity's awareness of a distant past, which in the Western tradition was first formally recognized during the Renaissance. Tangible evidence of documenting and preserving the artistic creations of the distant past dates in China to the Northern Song dynasty (960 to 1127 CE), when inventories and collections of ancient bronzes were formed.[11] Deep respect for tradition carried preservation consciousness in China into the twentieth century, when it and a number of its neighboring countries developed wider interests in preserving the past—an interest that included architectural conservation. Beginning in the fifteenth century, educated Europeans exhibited a growing understanding of human history as elements of the age of humanism, and later, the Age of Reason developed in concert with important changes in the realm of arts and sciences. The unfettered pursuit of knowledge and its popular dissemination from the Renaissance onward meant that with every passing year, humankind knew more about its past than ever before. (See Part III).

Over the past 250 years, the modern field of architectural heritage conservation has advanced hand in hand with allied developments in history, museology, archaeology, and ecology. It began as an upper-class European concern that focused on saving ancient monuments, important religious buildings, and national symbols, with motivations ranging from an appreciation of an object's spiritual significance and practical value to ethnic or national pride and nostalgia. In time, less monumental, less famous, and less historically and artistically significant examples of built heritage would also be considered important.

From the late eighteenth century, architectural restoration increasingly entailed "restoration for restoration's sake." More and more, heritage-minded individuals aimed to restore historic buildings and sites to the way they were thought to have previously appeared. There are many countries that can boast of examples of restoring and preserving historic buildings from hundreds of years ago. In the United States, one of the world's younger nations, the earliest known example of protecting a historic building dates from 1749, when a Swedish traveler in Philadelphia reported the purposeful retention of an old log house as a relic from the settlement era.[12] The first substantial and influential architectural conservation effort in the United States occurred a century later, when the Mount Vernon Ladies' Association successfully fought to save the house of the first US president, George Washington. Over time, the restoration, preservation, and display of historic buildings and sites in the United States extended to other nationally and locally

significant places and grew to include both historic enclaves and entire towns. A similar evolutionary process of taking on interventions of greater scale and depth has occurred in most other countries as well; the greatest number and range of examples are found in Europe.

During the last quarter of the twentieth century, preserving the architectural legacies of the less privileged has become a concern. Architectural conservationists now value traces of serfs, slaves, farmers, and industrial workers—and their cultural expressions—via primitive, vernacular, and traditional crafts, folklore, and other evidences of farm and village life.[13] The modern cultural heritage conservation field is not only concerned with less elite themes but also has a growing popular base. Somewhat ironically, the countries that have led the way in developing these nontraditional areas in heritage conservation have been young—notably, Australia and the United States.[14]

Architectural conservation is now a well-integrated global concern that regularly engages large segments of the world's population. It has become a vibrant, independent field with many centers of interest, including conservation science, museology, education, urban planning, tourism, and even national economic policy. The best barometer of this modern social phenomenon is the growing public and institutional support dedicated to the conservation of historic buildings and sites.[15] The popular appeal of cultural heritage is readily seen through observations of the modern tourism industry, especially in the component called *heritage tourism*. Advanced training opportunities are now available to specialists in such diverse locations as Ankara, Turkey (whose Middle Eastern Technical University in 1964 became the first to offer degrees in historic preservation), and at Columbia University in New York City, which began to offer graduate study in historic preservation in the same year. As early as 1958, architects and materials conservators could participate in a postdegree training program that offered a certificate of participation in architectural conservation at the UNESCO-supported International Centre for the Study of the Preservation and Restoration of Cultural Property (ICCROM) in Rome. Today there are scores of degree-granting university and postgraduate educational opportunities in architectural conservation throughout the world. (See also Chapter 15.)

Global and local movements to conserve cultural heritage have been paralleled by separate movements to preserve the world's *natural heritage*. Environmental conservation has also developed into an established discipline of professionals with significant popular support and participation in the past century.

The world's ecological heritage is threatened by many of the same human and natural forces that affect cultural heritage, including development, pollution, tourism, and natural disasters. Conservation biologists, like cultural heritage conservators, are motivated to protect sites because of their tangible and intangible values, including their environmental benefits, uniqueness or representativeness, aesthetic qualities, recreational potential, their perceived right to exist, as well as for the perpetuation of biodiversity and endangered species.[16]

Though they face the same challenges and share the goal of maintaining sites for future generations, the fields of natural and cultural heritage protection have seldom collaborated effectively in Europe and North America. In fact, these two fields have often been in competition for funding and other resources as well as in priorities at sites having both natural and cultural significance. While the ecological contexts of historic buildings are often ignored and despoiled, man-made structures at wildlife refuges and parks are often seen as detracting interventions to be removed, and the human cultures assigning value to those environments are often overlooked.[17]

This traditional separation between the conservation of natural and cultural heritage has resulted in large part from the institutional compartmentalization of their prac-titioners and donors as well as the government agencies responsible for each; there has also been a lack of inter-communication because of differing disciplinary concerns, terminology, and approaches.[18]

On a global scale, both natural and cultural sites are protected by the same 1972 World Heritage Convention Concerning the Protection of the World Cultural and Natural Heritage, and those deemed to be of universal significance are included on the same World Heritage List. This shared international structure, developed and maintained by UNESCO, with the International Union for Conservation of Nature (IUCN) and ICOMOS serving as its principal advisors, offers a framework for collaboration between architectural conservators and conservation biologists, as well as for partnership with museum curators, archivists, and other professionals concerned with different forms of heritage protection. Places referred to as *mixed cultural and natural heritage sites*, especially cultural landscapes, offer opportunities for natural and architectural conservators to join forces to achieve their common goals and learn from one another's experiences. Efforts are currently underway to retroactively include more site elements and broader cultural heritage concerns at a number of World Heritage sites that were originally listed only for other, more dominant values.[19]

Integration and cooperation on heritage conservation will only be possible, however, if international organizations, government agencies, local institutions, and professionals all broaden their agendas to include each other's concerns and organize pilot projects and shared forums to open lines of communication between their disciplines, as has been effectively done in Australia at Ayers Rock for instance.

Modern technology, especially television, the Internet, and extensive air travel networks, have nurtured the growth of the international proliferation of interest in cultural heritage preservation. Geographically disparate professions and institutions utilize remarkably consistent operational objectives, standards, and methodologies thanks in part to rapid and efficient information transfer. Every professional, regardless of location, can benefit from an ever-increasing array of innovative new methodologies and best-practice technologies that are easily disseminated throughout the field. International meetings and activities, publications, and improved transportation and communications systems convey information to a large international audience with unprecedented speed.

From this process of discovering history has come the realization that the past not only precedes us but also surrounds and shapes us. Throughout the world, various social traditions are successfully incorporated into modern life and help to shape national identities. And the field, too, has become more broadly inclusive; the narrowly drafted charters of its early years—such as the Athens Charter (1931) and the Venice Charter (1964)—are being augmented by layers of new text that broaden the framework of professional practice to include non-Western concepts of heritage value, places, and living heritage. Examples include the Burra Charter and the China Principles. (See also Chapter 9.)

The field's broadened scale and complexity have been met with an increased understanding of the challenges architectural conservationists face. An optimal first goal—although admittedly not the most practical—is to attempt to save any artifact of even the slightest historic and artistic merit. This archetype assumes that the physical integrity and functionality of every inherited object, building, or site is useful and deserves to be maintained until facts that prove otherwise come to light. This ideal world will certainly never exist. Change is inevitable; practically all materials used in the creation of art and architecture are in the process of decomposition, however slowly it may be occurring. Therefore, compromise and the frequent and often difficult need for prioritization are called for.

The purview of the field of architectural conservation is extensive and continues to expand, involving everything from individual artifacts and buildings to large-scale urban *settings* and cultural landscapes. As time goes by, everything slowly but inexorably passes into history in a manner one heritage conservationist likens to a moving gla-

▼ **Figure 2-6** Ayers Rock, or Uluru, in north central Australia, a site sacred to local aboriginal inhabitants, is an example of a mixed cultural and natural heritage site on UNESCO's World Heritage List.

cier.[20] During the twentieth century, several important events have contributed to making the conservation of historic buildings and sites a participatory concern for millions of people worldwide. National rebuilding in the aftermath of two world wars set the stage for the development of a network of supportive legislation for architectural conservation. Comprehensive coverage was created in France (the Malraux Act of 1962), England (the Historic Buildings and Ancient Monuments Act of 1953), Japan (the Ancient Capitals Preservation Law of 1966, as amended in 1976), and in the United States (the National Historic Preservation Act of 1966). Today, these join with a host of international heritage conservation charters, programs, and projects promulgated by international organizations such as UNESCO and the International Council on Monuments and Sites (ICOMOS) to create a profession that is no longer an ancillary special interest tied mainly to the profession of architecture but is largely autonomous and vital in its own right.

ENDNOTES

1. International Institute of Conservation-Canadian Group (IIC-GC) Code of Ethics and Guidance for Conservation Practice, 1989.

2. Bernard M. Feilden, *Conservation of Historic Buildings* (London: Butterworth Scientific, 1982), 3.

3. E. R. Chamberlin, *Preserving the Past* (London: J. M. Dent, 1979), ix, which in turn echoes the definition of restoration offered by a founder of the field, Eugène-Emmanuel Viollet-le-Duc, in *Dictionnaire raisonné de l'architecture française du XIe au XVIe siècle* (Paris: A. Morel, 1854–68).

4. ICOMOS New Zealand Charter sections 22 and 13, respectively.

5. *Random House Unabridged Dictionary*.

6. Australia International Council on Monuments and Sites (Australia ICOMOS), Burra Charter, article 19, adopted November 1999, http://www.icomos.org/australia/burra.html.

7. D. Bell, *The Historic Scotland Guide to International Conservation Charters* (Edinburgh: Historic Scotland, 1997), ICOMOS Canada, Appleton Charter, section B, 25.

8. *Random House Unabridged Dictionary*.

9. Australia ICOMOS, Burra Charter, articles 1.9, 21.1; New Zealand Charter, articles 22, 23, in Bell, *Historic Scotland Guide*.

10. In the United States, heritage conservation is called historic preservation, and conservationists are known as preservationists. The terms *architectural* and *historic preservation* will likely endure in the United States. The term *preservation* was employed in the formation of the country's laws on the subject and is also immortalized within the name of the US National Trust for Historic Preservation, the nation's largest membership organization concerned with preserving and presenting historic buildings.

11. Referred to as the Bogutulu collection of ancient bronzes, the emperor Sun He, who reigned during the Northern Song dynasty (960–1121 CE), especially prized bronzes from the Shang and Zhou dynasties (collectively ca.1600–256 BCE). Its possible predecessor in the West was the Mouseion ("museum") established in the third century BCE in Alexandria, Egypt. The ruling Ptolemaic dynasty built a special storage facility exclusively to house cultural treasures. There is no evidence, however, that inventories and typological analyses were made of the Mouseion's collection.

12. Charles E. Peterson, "Historic Preservation U.S.A: Some Significant Dates," *The Magazine Antiques*, February 1966, 226–32.

13. Fitch, *Historic Preservation*, 40.

14. Colonization of both Australia and the United States displaced indigenous peoples, legacies that both these countries also tried to preserve early on. In the United States, the first national legislation for historic preservation was the Antiquities Act of 1908, which afforded protection to Native American heritage sites.

15. Chamberlin, *Preserving the Past*, ix.

16. Graeme Aplin, *Heritage: Identification, Conservation, and Management* (South Melbourne, Australia: Oxford University Press; 2002), 85–87.

17. Ibid., 6.

18. Howard Gilman Foundation and the World Monuments Fund, (New York: Howard Gilman Foundation and the World Monuments Fund, 1998), 12–15.

19. S. I. Dailoo and F. Pannekoek, "Nature and Culture: A New World Heritage Context," *International Journal of Cultural Property* 15 (2008): 25–47.

20. Michael Hunter, ed., *Preserving the Past: The Rise of Heritage in Modern Britain* (Stroud, Gloucestershire, UK: Alan Sutton, 1996).

CHAPTER 3

What Do We Conserve?

W hile decisions about what architectural heritage should be conserved are sometimes controversial, most people agree that those that represent the best of their type and those with the greatest historical and artistic significance should be saved. Because of the fame and popularity of sites such as Machu Picchu in Peru, Westminster Abbey in London, Independence Hall in Philadelphia, the pyramids in Giza, and the Taj Mahal in Agra, they have been considered worthy of preservation for most, if not all, of their existence. These examples were, of course, built to last in the first place.. In fact, the degree of *authenticity* (i.e., the intactness of original elements) of heritage sites such as these and all others considered for the World Heritage List is considered by some to be their most essential quality. This is an important topic for debate—one about which lively exchanges have been ongoing for some time.

Monuments conservation in non-Western societies reflects the profound impact of cultural attitudes. In *The Future of the Past*, American journalist Alexander Stille discusses the ongoing Chinese and Japanese tradition of conserving a monument by copying or rebuilding it. A famous example of this practice is Japan's Ise Shrine, a seventh-century wooden Shinto temple that for centuries has been ritually dismantled and rebuilt every twenty years. Despite the complete replacement of the temple's original fabric, it is perceived as being thirteen hundred years old. Japanese cultural belief in the eternal renewal of cyclical time provides the framework for perpetuating the perception of Ise's antiquity and value. Nevertheless, the World Heritage Committee of the United Nations Educational, Scientific and Cultural Organization (UNESCO), operating primarily from a Western perspective, would likely deem Ise to be ineligible for World Heritage site listing because the fabric of the current shrine structure is neither ancient nor **authentic**.

There will always be an ample supply of candidates for inclusion on the World Heritage List. While most historic sites are less globally significant than those mentioned above, their preservation may nonetheless be equally important. Almost every nation in the world has a list of nationally, or locally, significant historic and architectural sites. Because aging is relentless—new sites are therefore becoming worthy of protection with each passing year. And sites can jump in significance unexpectedly due to extrinsic historical events, such as Chernobyl, Ukraine's radiation disaster, or the music festival in Woodstock, New York. Increasingly, sites (and objects) with negative connotations, such as Hiroshima, Japan, and Auschwitz in Poland, are also receiving attention from conservationists and the museum-going public. Today, UNESCO'S dynamic World Heritage List includes sites chosen solely for their historic significance, with little consideration given to aesthetics. In sum, it is an easily accessible reminder of the omnipresence of the world's incontrovertible historical and architectural landmarks.

Determining what should be conserved and what should not is one of the most crucial questions in architectural conservation. It is also one of the most difficult. Criteria for defining significance or value are often not easy to apply due to the ever-changing global context and evolving popular attitudes toward history. Subtle changes in philosophies of history and new realizations about the histories and meanings of objects and places keep heritage conservation practice dynamic. A seemingly exponential number of objects, buildings, and sites are created with every passing decade. When added to vast amounts of neglected and threatened built heritage, cultural heritage managers find themselves in the unavoidable position of performing triage, deciding what can be treated, when it can be treated, and which treatment is best. There is truly a sense of urgency in the field.

Deciding what to conserve is a question of what we value. Concepts of value reflect an ever-changing contemporary society. While professional practice in heritage conservation today carries with it a certain continuity of purpose and approach from generation to generation, this is against the backdrop of another truism: Every generation has its way.

As always, inheritors of the past will be faced with difficult choices. Will it ever be possible to satisfy the wishes of all interested parties? Somehow, we must, because buildings surviving from prior times sooner or later demand our attention—in their favor or not. This may explain the observation once made that "historic preservationists don't merely contemplate the past—they act upon it."[1]

DETERMINING SIGNIFICANCE AND VALUE

In the architectural conservation field, the *significance* of historic objects or sites is synonymous with *historic, cultural* and *artistic value* rather than with their monetary value or replacement cost. Historical and cultural significance encompasses both tangible and intangible realms of the past, including the built environment and myriad forces that have given it shape and meaning over time.[2]

Assessing value has always been problematic for heritage conservationists. It remains so despite an expanded contemporary knowledge base that to some extent facilitates making subjective judgment calls in new situations. For example, despite Europe's long history of cultural heritage protection, the processes and importance of architectural conservation in some places remain ambiguous. In many historic European towns, for instance, one can sense tension between two issues: good housekeeping in a society that sensibly protects and enhances the assets it has acquired from its forebears, and the right to "improve" what has been inherited. While a community might be satisfied with the relative stasis of managed change as afforded by local heritage protection laws and their administration, others fear that any artificial intervention, including heritage conservation, might upset natural patterns and inhibit natural vitality and growth. Then there will always be those who vehemently argue against maintaining the status quo. Such opinions about the value and usefulness of preserving elements of the past advance an ongoing dilemma with no clear-cut solution.

Figure 3-1 A carved stone Buddhist religious figure being consumed by a sacred tree at a temple in Ayutthaya, Thailand, is an assemblage within a national heritage site that has additional special associations, values, and significance.

Although the professional field of architectural conservation largely developed first in the West, Euro-American cultural values are only one among many options available. Each architectural conservation professional holds an individual concept of cultural significance that reflects his or her own personal belief system. Nonetheless, these opinions can usually be batched into schools of thinking due to the range of choices posed by the conservation challenges at hand. These schools of thought can be—and often are—in diametric opposition. The 1931 Athens Charter, the first international agreement on the protection of architectural heritage, focused on Western cultural heritage values associated with Europe's heritage of monumental buildings. Since then, the entire field has been enriched by new charters and declarations of purpose and procedures that have codified more sophisticated approaches that embrace multicultural choices and non-Western values as well.

In order for heritage management standards and guidelines to remain useful, they must be accepted by an audience that is capable of understanding the significance of the resources being conserved. As the field becomes more sophisticated, an unforeseen and

Values in Heritage Conservation

In recent decades, the significance of cultural heritage and the values associated with it have become a subject of increasing interest and inquiry. Definitions of monuments and historic sites have expanded, as have the meanings behind them and the reasons for which those sites are appreciated and protected. As a result, the heritage conservation field has moved toward *value-led planning*, which integrates cultural significance assessments and involves diverse interest groups.

Two institutions that have led the important recent concern for *values* in heritage conservation are the Australia International Council on Monuments and Sites (ICOMOS) and the Los Angeles–based Getty Conservation Institute (GCI). Through its public advocacy and sponsored publications, Australia ICOMOS has encouraged dialogue about the role and importance of values in heritage conservation. Australia's Burra Charter—from its initial discussion in 1979 to its most recently amended and adopted 1999 version—has promoted the inclusion of less tangible values in conservation theory and practice as well as the participation of indigenous peoples in the conservation of their

heritage. These efforts have been studied and imitated in many countries.

The GCI has also made heritage values a priority of its research programs and publications, including the convening of a multidisciplinary workshop on the topic in 1998. The results of this conference of conservation professionals included the report *Values and Heritage Conservation*, which explores how heritage is valued as well as its place in conservation decision making. The GCI researchers have been joined by cultural anthropologists and sociologists, who have offered advice and guidance on culturally sensitive interpretations and the management of conflicting values and priorities at heritage sites.

These pioneering projects and documents are significantly aiding contemporary conservation practice by clarifying and underscoring the centrality of values to the field and by making it a more inclusive process. Professionals and historic property owners alike have been reminded that heritage sites are protected for their significance and that those values for which it is appreciated should therefore guide any conservation management plan.

potentially serious trend is also emerging: the creation of a powerful "architectural elite" that could alienate community-based heritage proponents from their own history. In the words of Canadian heritage conservation professional Frits Pannekoek, "The priesthood of professionals is now to be formally placed between the people and their past. Professionals no longer advise or counsel—they decide."[3]

American historian Roger Kennedy echoes Pannekoek's observation. Kennedy advises that the only way to cope with changing notions of values and significance is to recognize the crucial roles of continuity and community—the line of history and the extension of community—as realities of human activity.[4] Both writers are correct in their assumption that, as Kennedy puts it, "Communicating significance is best done from meaningful local histories in which people are involved and can identify"[5] (see also Chapter 5).

In any case, the expert in charge, be it the historian, the architect, the engineer, the museum professional, the archaeologist, the anthropologist, or the educator, will all tend to determine significance from the standpoint of his or her respective specialty. Historical and cultural significance is determined from the study of the building, place, or object itself as a specific historic entity under the assumption that everything is potentially significant.[6] Because there are many valid ways to look at anything, one must consider as many different viewpoints as possible before a decision is reached: Thought, reconsideration, and reassessment are important.

Stressing the objective view, British conservation consultant David Baker argues that each object, building, and landscape requires distinctive techniques of investigation and care. They equally belong to the same continuum of past human activity, contribute to the sense of a particular place, can be registered on the same record system, and face the vast choice between preservation and destruction.[7]

It has been said that architectural conservation is both a self-referencing and a reflexive activity.[8] This idea is echoed by David Lowenthal, the American historian and chronicler of the cultural aspects heritage conservation movement. In his book, *The Past Is a Foreign Country*, he questions how we can understand the past if we can only exist in the present. Much depends on our imagination, which is inevitably influenced and changed by the process of studying the past. "In attempting to learn about history, we inevitably make it part of our present-day selves. In doing so, we simultaneously make that understanding about our present-day selves part of the past. To put it simply — the past, present, and the future are self-referencing."[9]

The philosopher Friedrich Nietzsche salutes the quest for history and its uses in contemporary society, writing, "That which distinguishes truly original minds is not being the first to see something new, but seeing something old, well-known…by all."[10] This may help explain the increasing tendency toward heritage protection at the present time. Clearly the architectural conservation field is moving in the right direction, with its reputation for being vital, proactive, inclusive, and above all *relevant*. However, to sustain and further build this position will require renewed efforts and fresh thinking. Ultimately, architectural heritage protection should not be considered an exclusive peripheral activity but should be as routine as the recycling of everyday objects — something most of us do every day.

TYPES OF VALUE OR SIGNIFICANCE

Local, national, and international heritage protection organizations choose to preserve ruined buildings that serve no contemporary practical function, such as the former libraries at Pergamon and Ephesus in Turkey, the open ruins of the Acropolis in Athens and the Forum in Rome, the ruins from Egypt's Pharaonic era, the centuries-old Jantar Mantar open-air astronomical observatories in India, and China's Great Wall. Obviously, the aesthetic and historical meaning of such sites to their local protectors outweighs any logical conclusion to replace them with something more functional. Clearly, there are a variety of ways of valuing architectural heritage.

Figure 3-2 The eighteenth-century Jantar Mantar astronomical observatory in Jaipur, India, is the most intact of its type in India and considered a historic scientific site.

Riegl and the Meaning of Monuments[11]

In his 1903 essay "The Modern Cult of Monuments: Its Character and Its Origin," Austrian art historian and aesthetician Alois Riegl (1858–1905) sought to define and categorize architectural heritage and to probe the question of its changing significance and role in contemporary culture. The terminology and distinctions he developed in this essay had little impact on discussions of heritage by his contemporaries beyond German-speaking countries. However, following its translation into English and its republishing in 1982, Riegl became an important influence on later twentieth-century understandings of monuments and architectural heritage worldwide.

Riegl identified three types of monuments, which he suggested "form three consecutive phases of the generalization of what a monument means."[12] These categories are increasingly inclusive and open-ended.

1. The first type are *intentional monuments*, which "recall a specific moment or complex of moments from the past," and whose "commemorative value has been determined by its makers."[13] Riegl argued that intentional monuments could be traced back to the beginnings of human culture; his examples included the Mausoleum of Maussollos at Halicarnassus (now Bodrum, Turkey) and Trajan's Column in Rome, which held the emperor's remains.

2. The second type are *historical monuments*, a category "enlarged to include those which still refer to a particular moment, but the choice of that moment is left to our subjective preference."[14] These sites were not necessarily built as monuments but became such over the course of history (Riegl therefore calls them *unintentional monuments*). For Riegl, the term *historical* referred to "everything that has been and is no lon-

ger."[15] His examples included practically every surviving fragment of ancient Roman and Greek building, such as capitals, lintels, and inscriptions.[16]

3. Finally, the also unintentional *age-value monument* was Riegl's broadest category, including "every artifact without regard to its original significance and purpose, as long as it reveals the passage of a considerable period of time."[17] At the turn of the twentieth century, Riegl speculated that perceptions of age-value could easily predate the nineteenth century. Subsequent research in the history of architectural conservation has proven him right; there are examples of this from as long ago as classical antiquity that come to us through the writings of Vitruvius, Pausanias, and Strabo.

Riegl's three categories of monuments correspond to the three commemorative values he identified, including intentional value, historical value, and age value. In addition, Riegl recognized and defined noncommemorative, present-day values for monuments, including *use value*, *newness value*, and *relative art value*. Use value covers our practical need to maintain historic buildings in use, newness value covers the modern preference for the latest thing, and relative art value covers changing taste as certain aspects and periods of the past appeal more to the present than others.

While modern terminology varies a little from that suggested by Riegl, his overall premise retains its validity. Riegl argued that each of these values competes in our interpretations of monuments and that their relative significance determines our attitudes toward any given site as well as our decisions about whether or not to preserve it.

The value categories by which architectural heritage are most commonly classified include universal, associative, curiosity, artistic, exemplary, intangible, and use. In addition, different types of value or significance are often ranked and weighed against one another before making a final determination about heritage preservation. As the architectural heritage conservation field evolves, it becomes closer to the allied fields of archaeology, cultural anthropology, and cultural geography, and cultural heritage protection decisions have begun to more closely reflect those fields' complex matrices of types of values, which range from the broadest and most easily recognized to the more specialized and esoteric.

Figure 3-3 Trajan's Column in Rome is considered to be an intentional monument, as the aim of its builder was to memorialize himself.

Universal Value

The concept that a historic site is valuable worldwide, and that it constitutes part of the world's heritage, dates to antiquity, when a list of seven wonders of the world was created.[18] Today's rather grand term, *universal value*, is an outgrowth of attempts made since the 1960s to define "divine" models (archetypes) in nineteenth-century philosophy and apply them to developments in international heritage conservation practice.[19]

The concept of universal value needed to be clarified when it began to be used in connection with UNESCO's 1972 Convention Concerning the Protection of the World Cultural and Natural Heritage (or, more simply, the World Heritage Convention).[20] While the convention does not specifically define universal value, it does clearly set out detailed criteria for inclusion on the World Heritage List. To be included, a site must meet some of the following criteria:

1. Represent a masterpiece of human creative genius;

2. Exhibit an important interchange of human values over a time span or within a cultural area of the world, regarding developments in architecture or technology, monumental arts, town planning, or landscape design;

3. Bear a unique—at a minimum, an exceptional—testimony to a cultural tradition or to a civilization that may be either living or extinct;

4. Be an outstanding example of a type of building or architectural or technological ***ensemble*** or landscape that illustrates a significant stage(s) in human history; or

5. Be an outstanding example of a traditional human settlement or land use that is representative of a culture (or cultures), especially when it has become vulnerable under the impact of irreversible change; or

6. Be directly, or tangibly, associated with events or living traditions: ideas, beliefs, or with artistic and literary works of outstanding universal significance.[21]

Of these criteria, Jukka Jokilehto, architect, architectural conservation historian, and UNESCO advisor, places major emphasis on "true [authentic] expressions of specific cultures."[22] He addresses the complex relationship of authenticity and universal value in his book, *A History of Architectural Conservation*:

*"Modern society…has given a new focus for the issue of universal significance…. [It] does not…derive from the notion that all products resemble a particular ideal or model, but from the conception that each is a creative and unique expression…[that] represents the relevant cultural context. For a cultural **heritage resource** to have universal value does not—in itself—imply that it is 'the best'; rather it means it shares a particular creative quality of being 'true,' original, authentic, as a constituent part of the common, universal heritage of humanity."[23]*

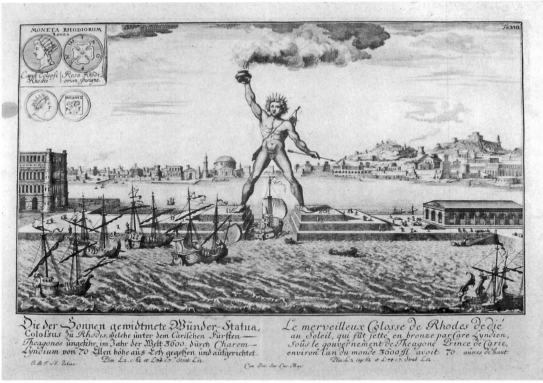

Figure 3-4 Early eighteenth century graphic speculations of four of the Seven Wonders of the Ancient World (the Temple of Zeus at Olympus, the Colossus of Rhodes, the pyramids at Thebes [sic], and the Mausoleum of Maussollos at Halicarnassus), the first list of historic architectural monuments of *universal value* or *significance*. (*Johann Bernhard Fischer von Erlach*, Entwurf einer historischen Architektur, *1721*)

Eine der Prachtigsten Ægyptischen Pyramiden, wovon
man die ruinen noch bey der berühmten Statt Thebæ findet.

Vne des plus magnifiques Pyramides Egyptiennes
dont on trouve les ruines auprés de la fameuse Ville de Thebe.

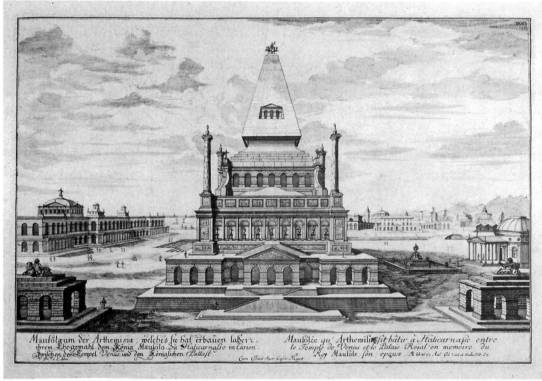

Mausolæum der Arthemisiæ, welches sie hat erbauen laßen,
ihrem Ehegemahl dem König Mausolo zu Halicarnasso in Carien
zwischen dem Tempel Venus und den Königischen Pallast.

Mausolée qu' Arthemilis fit bâtir à Halicarnasse entre
le Temple de Venus et le Palais Roïal en memoire du
Roy Mausole son epoux.

Assigning these significance criteria to sites and prioritizing them accordingly is problematic, because despite all efforts to objectify qualities, the decision is both subjective and relative—and therefore often controversial. One only needs to consider the World Heritage List nomination and selection process to appreciate exactly how difficult the task of assigning universal value has become. (See also Chapter 15.) Past experiences in preventative conservation and site maintenance have resulted in emphasizing effective conservation planning and sustainability when selecting sites for inclusion. This relatively new consideration has added to the complexity of the World Heritage listing process. At the same time, new and broader categories of cultural heritage sites are being considered. In 2003, UNESCO declared that sites possessing outstanding "intangible heritage qualities" might be eligible for World Heritage site listing; one such listed site was the Richtersveld Cultural and Botanical Landscape in northwestern South Africa, the land of the nomadic Nama people.

Given the increased participation of new member states in the convention in recent years, UNESCO has been under increasing pressure to add more sites to its World Heritage List. As of October 2008, it included 878 cultural and *natural heritage sites* located in 145 countries. Cultural sites that have made the cut include the Parthenon in Athens and the Great Wall of China. Examples of natural sites include Kenya's Mount Kilimanjaro and Uluru (Ayers Rock) in Kata Tjuta National Park, Australia. A site proposed for World Heritage listing must first be recognized in its home country as being of the highest national significance. Sites of national, regional, and local significance are therefore first defined by nations themselves, using criteria supported by national laws that are remarkably consistent throughout the world.[24] There is no consensus as to how many sites of universal value could be eligible for listing.

ASSOCIATIVE VALUES: HISTORIC AND COMMEMORATIVE

An accurate appraisal of associative values of a cultural heritage site requires understanding its specific history from the time of its creation until the present. Inevitably, the historic meanings associated with objects, buildings, and sites will vary, with some aspects being of greater importance than others. The events and details of a site deemed significant greatly depend on how and when these aspects are being interpreted, and by whom, and the criteria for judging those values at the time.

The concept of *historical value* or *age value* is rooted in the Italian Renaissance, when various social, political, religious, and economic changes resulted in a new appreciation for ancient art, whose forms came to be seen as the arbiter for artistic truth and beauty. The concept was not new: centuries earlier, in twelfth-century China, Emperor Huizong of the Song dynasty had demonstrated antiquarian appreciation of then-ancient collected bronze objects by collecting and cataloguing them.

For the rulers of the Northern Song dynasty, it was more a matter of reviving a traditional art within the context of unbroken cultural continuity. As detailed further in Section III, such interest in the long-dead past is analogous to the Renaissance curiosity for, and use of, ancient Rome's remains dating from over one thousand years earlier. The Renaissance view was not historical in the modern sense, because it did not yet recognize chronological and stylistic development. However, it was from late-Renaissance experiences in investigating the lost lessons of the ancients that objective and holistic approaches to the study of history developed in the West.

In the late eighteenth and nineteenth centuries in the West, the cherished goal of historians was to gain encyclopedic knowledge of historical facts. Historical value was tied to details of history and transformed itself slowly into "developmental value," for which specific details were less important than patterns of development. In the first decade of the twentieth century, Riegl correctly surmised that "if the nineteenth cen-

Figure 3-5 The primary associative values of the Brandenburg Gate in Berlin have changed several times since its creation in the late eighteenth century. From 1961 to 1989, it was the portal to the principal checkpoint between East and West Berlin. Since its restoration in 2000 (illustrated here), it has served as a symbol of a reunited Germany.

tury was the age of historical value, then the twentieth century appears to be…that of age-value."[25]

Riegl's "intentional commemorative value" is another form of associative value. The creators of intentional monuments sought to preserve a moment in the consciousness of future generations, which would presumably make it vital and significant in perpetuity. As such, an intentional monument makes a claim to immortality. The present-day value of most historical monuments, however, never seems to be based on their original commemorative significance. The meaning of monuments and the memories they are intended to commemorate usually change over time.

The meaning of most architecturally significant and famous sites has varied over time. Istanbul's Hagia Sophia, Berlin's Brandenburg Gate, and Beijing's Tiananmen Square are all sites valued today for associations that were acquired long after their construction. Charged with meaning, such sites that are imbued with social historical significance can be mythologized as national, if not international, symbols.

Other sites that Riegl termed unintentional monuments acquired value during their existence because of their historic associations. Examples include literary and artistic landmarks such as writer Leo Tolstoy's residence in Moscow, painter Pablo Picasso's birthplace in Malaga, Spain, and Robben Island prison in South Africa, where former South African president Nelson Mandela was held for nearly twenty years. In several urban settings, commemorative markers indicate the presence of historic structures, extant or long vanished. One blue plaque on the front of 180 Ebury Street, Westminster, London, reads: "Wolfgang Amadeus Mozart (1756–1791) composed his first symphony here in 1764." In New York City, the site where patriot Nathan Hale was hanged by the British is now a coffeehouse. At both, the aesthetic qualities of the site are secondary to their historical significance, their associative value.

Paradoxically, conservation can complicate the changing value of a site: The aging process lends value to a thing, value which can then be reduced or destroyed by restoration. The prevalent modern expectation that historic buildings and sites retain a pristine condition exacerbates this problem. Riegl's notions of age value did not anticipate that future conservators would have few reservations about artificially creating a timeworn look for a building or an object, while others might go to great lengths to seek out and conserve as is unrestored objects for their authentic and *sublime* qualities. For Riegl, "The more faithfully a monument's original state is preserved, the greater its historical value; disfiguration and decay detract from it."[26] He clearly supported the conservation of monuments in the condition that reflected their appearance at the time of acquiring historical value.[27] In cases where historic value conflicted with preserving a site's age value, Riegl favored age value as the only viable strategy."[28]

Curiosity Value

People are curious about the past and preserved buildings; sites and objects satisfy this desire. While it is rarely referred to in today's criteria for determining historic values, all historic buildings, sites, and objects have some degree of *curiosity value*.

Saving unusual objects and sites for their value as mementos of times past is an ancient practice. An early example was noted by the first century BCE Roman architect Vitruvius, who wrote, "In Athens on the Areopagus there is to this day a relic of antiquity with a mud roof." In his native Rome, Vitruvius noted that the hut of Romulus on the capital was "a significant reminder of the fashions of the old times."[29] Sites preserved for their curiosity value could also be mysterious and spiritual places, such as Stonehenge in Wiltshire, England, or the site of the geoglyphs in Nazca, Peru.

Both the site managers and visiting public are well aware that people flock to see the World Heritage sites of Asia, for instance, simply out of curiosity. They want to see, to learn about, and to touch, if possible, the grandness of the imperial past of the Forbidden City—now that it is accessible to all. Who would not want to see the very private quarters of the emperors of China, or the state temples of the former imperial capitals of Mongolia, Vietnam, and Cambodia? That's why the government ministries of culture and tourism of all these countries have made their restoration—through improved conservation and interpretation—a top priority.

Aesthetic Value

Oftentimes, a particular building or site is protected simply because it is beautiful and viewers derive pleasure from experiencing it. Even if such places were not old and had no historic associations, most people would argue that St. Peter's Basilica in Rome or the Umayyad Mosque in Damascus are worth preserving. Sometimes structures originally intended as temporary are made permanent because of their aesthetic appeal. For example, in California, the city of San Francisco could not bear to remove American architect Bernard R. Maybeck's wood and plaster Palace of Fine Arts after the 1914 Panama-Pacific Exhibition closed. In the 1960s, after the structure had nearly completely disintegrated, it was rebuilt in concrete.

Although the practice of assigning value to the art and architecture of the past on the basis of aesthetic quality is nothing new, it has broad implications for heritage conservation. In the Renaissance, an assessment of the aesthetic characteristics of a historic building or artifact extracted a set of abstract ideals from the visual elements of the object. Thus, during this period in the West, the development of a fresh appreciation for art and architecture produced in classical antiquity rested on the conviction that ancient Roman art forms were the only objectively "true" models. The fascination with the lost principles of ancient architecture as seen in the remains themselves is evidenced by the first official measures for the preservation of ancient Roman buildings: a papal bull issued by Pope Paul III in 1534.

By the middle of the eighteenth century in the West, the appreciation of historic art and architecture had acquired a new dimension—a fascination with the *picturesque*. Originally an English interest, it quickly spread to the European continent. Despite rationality's preeminence during the Age of Enlightenment, a growing spirit of romanticism had begun to emerge in European society. Romantics turned their attention to

Figure 3-6 The Italian Renaissance fascination with the antique took on a new meaning in the eighteenth century, when Rome was the ultimate destination for *grand tourists* in search of lessons from the classical past, inspiration for designs, and objects to adorn their own homes and museums. Here, students draw ancient sculpture in the Capitoline Museums in Rome. *(Engraving by G. D. Campiglia, from Bottari's* Musei Capitolini, *1755)*

Figure 3-7 *Grand tourists* with the aid of their cicerone, or local guide, examining the tomb of Lucius Arruntius. *(G. B. Piranesi, The Antiquities of Rome II, 1757)*

the mysterious and evocative forms of the medieval world, which provided them with an escape from the excessive concerns about the mechanical and ordered nature of the universe that dominated so much of eighteenth-century European thought.

Romantic sensibilities moved away from the rational facts of a building or site's history to focus on the "sublime emotions"[30] evoked by the aesthetic qualities of decaying artifacts. Architectural ruins were valued for the sentiments they evoked—as pleasing ornaments in designed landscapes. Such sensibility was one of several influences imported into England by eighteenth- and nineteenth-century Grand Tour participants, whose trips to Italy and Greece were considered an important and obligatory experience for every European "person of taste."[31]

The traditional concept of the picturesque and the associated notion of what English painter John Piper called "pleasing decay" are integral to the history of architectural conservation. In eloquently defining *pleasing decay* in a 1947 article by the same title in *Architectural Review*, Piper made the novel suggestion (for the late 1940s) that his colleagues consider retaining the tower of the "redundant" church, and any similar distinctive architectural feature, as visual points of interest in any new development scheme to provide relief and contrast in the overall plan.[32] English conservation architect and educator Derek Linstrum credited Piper's vision as being fundamental to the establishment of British conservation philosophy and claimed, "This remarkably prophetic statement about visual qualities in architecture and planning has become the basis of our recent thinking and legislation."[33]

Determination of aesthetic worth has indeed been a significant factor in the treatment of historic buildings since the nineteenth century. Riegl defined *relative art value* as seeing a relationship to something contemporary in the old. Relative art value contributed to both the Gothic revival movement of the early nineteenth century and to the revived interest in classical idioms in art and architecture during the previous three centuries. The fascination of artists and architects with the qualities and techniques of their predecessors is an age-old tradition that certainly continues to the present time. Twentieth-century European artists Pablo Picasso, Henry Moore, and Constantin Brancusi acknowledged their debts to their predecessors. Similarly, architects as varied as Leon Battista Alberti, Claude-Nicolas Ledoux, Le Corbusier, and Louis I. Kahn were among countless of their peers from the Renaissance forward who were inspired by classical traditions in architecture. Training in the arts in East Asia for centuries entailed copying the work of masters until the artist or craftsman was considered proficient to create on his own. This role of historic works serving as exemplars for later works is often underappreciated, even by experts who may be charged with valuing the past.

Exemplary and Instructive Value

Examples of aesthetically significant cultural heritage are often viewed as paradigms with instructional value. Historic architectural exemplars are especially useful for what they can reveal about the past. Included in this category are archetypes—sites representing innovation—such as the urban conception and façade treatments Michelangelo created for the Campidoglio in Rome (1546). The Iron Bridge at Coalbrookdale, Shropshire, England, erected by Abraham Darby in 1778, was the first structure of its kind in the world, as was Alexandre Gustave Eiffel's tower in Paris dating from 1889. The Tel Dan gate in Israel, dating from about 1800 BCE, was formed by the oldest known use of the true arch in architecture. Exemplary architecture, if appreciated mainly at the national and local levels, include Cass Gilbert's Flatiron Building (1902), New York's first steel-frame and stone-clad skyscraper; Erich Mendelsohn's modernist Einstein Tower in Potsdam, Germany (1921); and the ten-story wooden pagoda in Ying County, Shanxi Province, China, dating from 1056.

Sites valued for their exemplary nature include not only firsts but also those that are particularly good or rare surviving examples of a specific style or type of building—such as the Ottoman era in Damascus and Cairo or the early twentieth-century Russian avant-garde in Moscow. Preserving the last examples of original buildings, sites, and artifacts usually entails a special sense of importance and urgency.

Use Value

A building or site that has served the same purpose without interruption for a long period of time can be viewed as having a special quality that supplements age value. *Use value* is of considerable importance, given that most buildings eventually fall victim to functional obsolescence and are usually replaced with more efficient alternatives;[34] buildings with long useful lives tend to be self-preserving.[35] Thanks to their viable uses, they may turn out to be the oldest of their type to survive. Examples are the oldest pharmacy in the Balkans, operating in a Franciscan monastery in Dubrovnik, Croatia, since 1391; an area in Rome in the vicinity of the Porto Ostiense used to bury the dead since antiquity; and Acoma Pueblo in Acoma, New Mexico, which has been continuously inhabited since the twelfth century.

Figure 3-8 Abraham Darby's Iron Bridge in Coalbrookdale, Shropshire, England, built in 1778, was the first monumental single-span iron bridge in the world and thus has an exemplary value in the history of architecture and engineering.

The use value of a structure also refers to the continued usefulness of a building or site in the present, even if its original function is not maintained. An inner-city industrial building that can be reused as loft apartments or a plantation manor house that can become a bed-and-breakfast are more likely to survive and be preserved.

Values associated with cultural heritage can take on yet additional meanings when viewed in combination with one another. Also to be considered is both the intentional and unintentional **valorization** of the past. (See also page 53.) An example of intentional valorization would be the upgrade of an eighteenth-century English country house and its grounds from Grade III to Grade II due to new information that had come to light about it by English Heritage, the British government's advisory agency on the country's *historic environment*. That the same site is accessible to the general public and that its original landscape features have matured and are even more enjoyable might be said to be an example of unintended or incidental valorization.

ENDNOTES

1. William C. Baer, "The Impact of Historical Significance on the Future," in *Preservation of What, for Whom? A Critical Look at Historical Significance*, ed. Michael A. Tomlan (Ithaca, NY: National Council for Preservation Education, 1998), 75.
2. David Aimes, "Introduction," in Tomlan, *Preservation of What, for Whom?* 6.
3. Frits Pannekoek, "The Rise of a Heritage Priesthood," in Tomlan, *Preservation of What, for Whom?* 30.
4. Roger Kennedy, "Crampons, Pitons, and Curators," in Tomlan, *Preservation of What, for Whom?* 20.
5. Ibid.
6. "Historical significance is determined from the study of the object itself as a document with the assumption that everything is potentially significant." Quoted from Richard Striner, "Determining Historic Significance: Mind over Matter?" in Tomlan, *Preservation of What, for Whom?* 10.

7. David Baker, *Living with the Past: The Historic Environment* (Bletsoe, Bedford, UK: D. Baker, 1983), 10.

8. Baer, "The Impact of Historical Significance on the Future," in Tomlan, *Preservation of What, for Whom?* 72.

9. Ibid., 75.

10. *Human, All Too Human: Parts One and Two (Menschliches, allzumenschliches)*, trans. Helen Zimmerman and Paul V. Cohn (Amherst, NY: Prometheus Books, 2008; translated from *The Complete Works of Friedrich Nietzsche*, v. 6-7 [London: T. N. Foulis, 1909–1913]). Nietzsche's work was originally published in 1880.

11. The word *monument* comes from the Latin *monere*, "to remind." See the glossary for other definitions of *monument*, a word with several meanings.

12. Alois Riegl, "The Modern Cult of Monuments: Its Character and Its Origin," trans. Kurt W. Forster and Diane Ghirardo, *Oppositions* 25 (1982): 24.

13. Ibid., 23.

14. Ibid., 24.

15. Ibid., 21.

16. Riegl's specific examples of historical monuments included the Ingelheim Columns at Heidelberg Castle in Germany and the Campanile di San Marco in Venice.

17. Riegl, "Modern Cult of Monuments," 24.

18. The oldest known enumeration of the Seven Wonders of the Ancient World is referenced in the writings of Herodotus in the fifth century BCE. Despite their recognized importance, only one—the Great Pyramid of Giza—has survived to our time.

19. Alois Riegl was the first in the nascent profession of heritage protection to suggest in writing that some heritage monuments, sites, and works of art could be seen as having "universal" significance to humankind. The idea of universal heritage in relation to the legal consequences of warfare had been advanced earlier in 1758 by the Swiss jurist Emmerich de Vattel in his *Droit des gens,* ("The Law of Nations"). J. Jokilehto, "International Standards, Principles, Charters of Conservation" in Stephen Marks, ed., *Concerning Buildings*: Studies in Honor of Sir Bernard Feilden (Oxford and Boston: Butterworth-Heineman, 1996) 74.

20. The convention aimed to identify and protect the best examples of both man-made and natural sites for placement on the World Heritage List.

21. Criteria for listing natural heritage sites can be found on UNESCO's Web site, http://whc.unesco.org/en/criteria/.

22. Jukka Jokilehto, A *History of Architectural Conservation* (Oxford: Butterworth-Heinemann, 1999), 295–296.

23. Ibid.

24. Among the many nationally recognized, highly significant cultural heritage sites that are theoretical candidates for receiving the distinction and protection of a World Heritage listing are Charles Garnier's Palais Garnier, also known as the Opéra de Paris and the Opéra Garnier; A. W. N. Pugin's (with Sir Charles Barry) Houses of Parliament in London; James Oglethorpe's plan for the city of Savannah, Georgia; and Oscar Niemeyer's modern capital of Brazil, Brasília.

25. Riegl, "Modern Cult of Monuments," 29.

26. Ibid., 34.

27. Riegl's "cult of age value" opposes the restoration of monuments, and he warned against interfering with the natural weathering or deterioration of a site. Fifty years prior, British art critic and writer John Ruskin had passionately argued for preserving age value. Unfortunately, these highly evolved and rational arguments for natural weathering usually prove impractical if the continued use of a building is desired. Beyond this, Riegl suggested, "Permanent preservation is not probable because natural forces are ultimately more powerful than all the wit of man, and man himself is destined to inevitable decay."

28. Riegl, "Modern Cult of Monuments," 37. Although historic sites—such as the "living museums" of Hancock Shaker Village in Pittsfield, Massachusetts, or **Skansen** historic museum in Stockholm—are effective in countering obsolescence, copies or replicas tend to counter Riegl's argument as well. The Campanile di San Marco in Venice is a copy of the one that collapsed in 1902.

29. Vitruvius Pollio, *De Architectura* [Vitruvius: *The Ten Books on Architecture*], trans. Morris Hicky Morgan (Cambridge, MA: Harvard University Press, 1914), bk. II, chap. 1.

30. David Lowenthal, *The Past is a Foreign Country* (Cambridge: Cambridge University Press, 1985), 173.

31. Great Britain's associations with times past developed to the point that ruins, whether original or artificial, became objects of great interest, to be used as landscape design conceits wherever possible. In the mid-nineteenth century, honoring and preserving both the actual fabric and the spirit of Gothic designs in church restoration schemes became central to the English scrape versus anti-scrape debate. Broad segments of the population became interested in the question, which encompassed how best to treat genuine relics of the past.

32. John Piper, *Buildings and Prospects* (London: Architectural Press, 1948), 70.

33. Derek Linstrum, "Conservation and the British," *Commonwealth Foundation* (London) Occasional Paper XXXVIII (1976): 35.

34. Rome's Porticus Ottaviae is an example of a building having both age value and use value. Originally built in the first century BCE as part of a pagan temple complex and later converted to be the Christian Church of Sant'Angelo in Pescheria, it has served the same function from its construction until the present day.

35. Although it is often a certain historical event that triggers the takeover of such places by conservation agencies, which then preserve them and feature them for different purposes.

CHAPTER 4

Why Conserve Buildings and Sites?

Why do people think they must act to protect their remarkable architectural heritage and its contribution to history? The question—why preserve?—is intimately connected to the question of *what* to preserve. In fact, the reasons to save architectural heritage are the same as the reasons why it is valued. Nevertheless, these motivations for conservation can be separately assessed. A significant work of architecture is a remarkable thing regardless of its function, representing the creative abilities of its builders and their culture. Historic buildings have educational values in that they are a tangible representation of human accomplishment and past ways of life. They illustrate the cultural history of places. As the eminent British conservation architect Sir Bernard Feilden says, "The qualities that created civilizations are measured in the architecture that is left behind as much as in their literature or their music. Societies may disappear but the cultural artifact remains to provide intellectual access to those who created it."[1]

Historic architectural fabric indicates the techniques and circumstances of its construction period. For architectural conservationists, retaining as much original fabric as possible for presentation purposes and possible further scientific analysis later on should be primary goals.

The towns and cities of the world's earliest organized settlements—from the Fertile Crescent in Mesopotamia to Mohenjo Daro in Pakistan to Banpo in Xi'an, China—are marvels of human ingenuity. Market squares, principal streets and buildings, and water sources have provided important orientation points for a community's individuals since people began living in towns and cities.

A delicate equilibrium exists between physical cultural sites and its social existence. Safeguarding the architectural heritage of a place can also account for distinct urban character and galvanize communities through an increased sense of pride and belonging. Cultural and familial traditions, reminders of one's origins, and familiar surroundings and objects serve as markers of memory and thus provide an important sense of orientation. People who are deprived of their environmental past lack tangible evidence of their own history, and this sense of loss can result in instability and a yearning for security.

Figures 4–1 and 4–2 Rising waters of the Euphrates River contained by the Birecik Dam, built in Turkey in July 2000 just north of its border with Syria, resulted in the inundation of scores of towns, settlements, and archaeological sites, including the old village of Halfeti, seen here. While its inhabitants were resettled in modern, more organized surroundings with more reliable amenities, there were complaints from both young and old about the loss of friendships, a sense of community, and the day-to-day activities that had shaped their lives.

Slowing Time and Valorizing the Past

The idea that under certain environmental conditions and with proper maintenance, material expressions of human creativity and industry can last indefinitely has been a key factor in the development of the world's heritage conservation consciousness: Witness the enduring structural stability and usable condition of the Pantheon in Rome. With consistent attention and protection throughout its lifetime, it has remained essentially intact for nearly two thousand years. Millions of objects conserved in museums' stable environments the world over offer ample evidence of the possibilities for extending the life of physical cultural heritage.

The products of civilizations can be shielded from the destruction of time by acts of nature as well as by those of humans. In the mid-1700s, excavations at Herculaneum and Pompeii revealed two cities that had been preserved almost completely intact for centuries, buried beneath the thick blanket of ash, stone, and mud that was produced by Mount Vesuvius's eruption in 79 CE. Today, these sites provide researchers with much valuable information about daily life on the Italian peninsula during the early years of the first millennium. The same can be said about finds made at many burial sites, such as those in the Valley of the Kings in Luxor, Egypt. Many societies—Egyptian, Chinese, Incan—carefully prepared the deceased with objects thought to be useful in the afterlife, often going to great lengths to ensure that such burials would last "forever."

There are at least three routes to the past—memory, written accounts of past events, and artifacts.[2] Of the three, artifacts may reward investigators with the most compelling picture of the past. Tangible and replete with the evidence of age, they are usually the most eloquent witnesses to the imagination and resourcefulness of our predecessors.

As David Lowenthal notes in *The Past is a Foreign Country*, "Only by selectively shaping available sources can any historian coherently convey knowledge of the past."[3] In "selectively shaping" primary source material, the historian uncovers and presents its essence—the context of attitudes, beliefs, and events in which it was created and its place in the cultural, social, and political life of the age in which it was made or written. Over time, however, the perceived significance of an artifact or a written account of an historical event is constantly revised and adjusted—sometimes subtly and at other times dramatically—to conform to society's ever-changing values and concerns. "The truth lodged in an historic resource, and our current perception of the significance of that same resource, is rarely an exact match. Thus, the significance or importance of a place is constantly undergoing reinterpretation because significance and importance are manifestations of our human curiosity."[4]

The loss or threatened loss of physical landmarks that help orient a population to its locale has often stimulated a reassessment of their value and a determination to preserve them in as intact a condition as possible. One of the earliest instances of clear concern for the protection of historic resources in an organized way occurred during the third century BCE in Alexandria, in northern Egypt. The ruling Ptolemaic dynasty built a special storage facility exclusively to house cultural treasures. It was named Mouseion, from the Greek "of the muses," and is the basis of the English word *museum*.

A contemporary example of a swift and widespread reassessment of a structure's architectural significance is that of the World Trade Center's Twin Towers following their destruction by terrorists on September 11, 2001. Since their construction in the early 1970s, the towers had been dismissed by most architectural critics as intrusive and discordant additions to New York City's architectural mix. But following their loss, they acquired the status of unique examples of engineering ingenuity and vital elements in the aesthetic balance of the city's skyline. This view is now widely held by many critics as well as the general public, at least locally.

One of the most important tasks for architectural conservationists and urban planners is to preserve genius loci or sense of place—a location's unique qualities as defined by its geography and its past and present human, cultural, and industrial activities. This involves preserving the physical integrity of a place's key existing features and maintaining its aesthetic coherence and values, whether the place consists of one building, an enclave of buildings, a growing community with several historic districts, or entire historic towns.

Plans for preserving places and social traditions must also accommodate change, especially those improving human health and basic conveniences. While there have been many attempts to freeze the appearance of historic buildings and sites in order to represent a static moment in time, most heritage conservationists today consider the preservation of the continuity of traditions—layered onto historic sites over time—more important.

TO SAVE THE PROTOTYPE

According to James Marston Fitch, "The main reason to conserve buildings, sites, artifacts from the past is to preserve the prototype so that future generations can see what the past was *really* like. There is no equal for the authentic or the original. Likewise there is no substitute for direct observation of the real thing, which 'represents the shortest distance in time and space that an object [or a place] and a viewer can have.'"[5]

The **prototype**, or original, is considered important because it is **authentic**. Authenticity relates to a work being genuine and true and does not take into consideration its artistic or creative qualities.[6] There can be only one true original of an authentic work of art, although copies can often be made.

In his writings—notably, in the 1930s essay "The Work of Art in the Age of Mechanical Reproduction"—Walter Benjamin questioned the meanings of the original and the copy at a time when new technologies like photography allowed endless reproduction of artworks.[7] For Benjamin, this meant that in many cases, there was no unique original that held special value, and that authenticity was less easy to identify—and perhaps less important than it had been previously. More recently, Fitch also addressed the relationship of mass production, mass media, and industrialization to the idea and significance of the original.[8] But for Fitch, in an era when readily available copies made the prototype's very existence less discernable—and therefore questioned its value—its identification and preservation was even more important.

While **replicas** and approximations of the prototype are not the same, there have been instances where a well-forged surrogate has been practically indistinguishable from the prototype. One such example was the production of an exact **facsimile** of the house in which German philosopher Johann Wolfgang von Goethe was born. In 1999, the 250th anniversary of his birth, a replica was built about 110 yards (100 meters) away from the extant original garden house in Park an der Ilm in Weimar, Germany. In it, his writing desk, chair, and writing implements were precisely duplicated with extreme accuracy—down to a reproduction of worn edges on his desk and ink stains on its surface.[9] That this was done, and especially that the prototype and the facsimile were in view of each other, caused a stir among conservation professionals and the public alike. The project's creators rationalized it by explaining their goals: first, to honor the great writer in a special way; second, to relieve visitor traffic in the original building; third, to intensify the public's appreciation of the prototype; and fourth, to have a spare exhibit that could perhaps travel to other locations.[10]

In America, the restoration and reconstruction of Colonial Williamsburg, Virginia, in the late 1920s, was endowed both financially and with a sense of purpose by American philanthropist John D. Rockefeller, Jr. He called Colonial Williamsburg a "lesson...that teaches of the patriotism, high purpose, and unselfish devotion of our forefathers to the common good." Picturesquely re-created Colonial Williamsburg is not a real eighteenth-century town, though the effort comes remarkably close to one. The effort represented a serious attempt to approximate the capital of the British colonies before its destruction during the American Revolution—as influenced by the twentieth-century imagination. As such, when it opened to the public in 1931 it was without the full extent of the smells, dirt, and realities of life as it would have been in the previous century. Williamsburg has been described as having "no round-the-clock life to sustain it, and little sense of continuity of past, present and future."[11] Nevertheless, it has become a very popular tourist destination for Americans and foreigners alike. The fact that its restored buildings and town are located on their original sites makes it much more truthful than most other historic town representations of this kind.

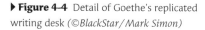
▲ **Figure 4–3** The residence in which the German philosopher Johann Wolfgang von Goethe was born in 1749 in Park an der Ilm, Weimar, Germany, was restored in 1999 on the occasion of the 250th anniversary of his death. To further celebrate the event, a scrupulously accurate full-scale replica of the house and its contents, down to the ink stains on his writing desk, was created only about 110 yards (100 meters) away. (A photographer's "pushed" image here captures the two buildings in one frame.) Organizers of the project offered several explanations as to why the prototype and a copy of it were built within sight of each other, one being their aim to provoke thought about the relevance of authenticity. (©BlackStar/Mark Simon)

▶ **Figure 4–4** Detail of Goethe's replicated writing desk (©BlackStar/Mark Simon)

Heritage conservation practice has become increasingly relaxed in its view of the role of replicas, both because of the number of replicas that exist and because of the powerful didactic role they can play.[12] Replications of palatial and temple forms is so commonplace in the history of East Asian architecture that it characterizes the genre in general. The nearly unbroken Western tradition of reviving Greek and Roman classical architecture has produced some astonishing examples of impressive and literate replication and revivals: Witness the extent of the classical revival in Edinburgh; Stockholm; St. Petersburg, Russia; and Washington, DC.

Some commemorations of events of national importance have entailed the re-creation of related symbols. Examples that exemplify both social history and transportation history are seen in two maritime heritage projects. The replication of a "famine ship" in Wexford, Ireland, in 2001 commemorated the mass Irish immigration to the New World following the potato famine of the 1840s; the replication of an eighteenth-century ship (that remains in Boston Harbor) memorializes the Boston Tea Party, the symbolic start of the American Revolution in 1776.

HISTORICAL, RELIGIOUS, AND NATIONAL RESPECT

Figure 4-5 The monumental remains of Great Zimbabwe (eleventh through fifteenth centuries), a UNESCO World Heritage Site, served as the namesake of the modern country.

All human beings recognize and, to some degree, respect history. Much of the world's literature is rich with descriptions of the past, and there is an almost universal curiosity or respect for things or places that are obviously historic. They are further imbued with special meaning when they are the oldest, or the last of their kind, or have special historical associations. Nearly every settlement older than a few generations has at least one structure or site recognized as being the oldest place. Similar respect is frequently afforded to the oldest part of town, the oldest tree, or even the oldest living person, because he or she may have the oldest memory of a place.

When places or objects are created according to spiritual beliefs, they become both complex and imbued with special meaning.[13] Correspondingly, respect and care for such creations has almost always merited special attention.[14] This applies to both natural and human-made sites with spiritual associations.

In the words of the Indian Hindu holy man Sri Sri Ravi Shankar: "Sacred places keep alive the legends and traditions for all future generations. Respecting sacred natural sites such as mountains, rivers, and even trees such as the *bodhi* tree and the *neem* tree, has an impact on ecology; there is desire to preserve that place."[15]

Every town, settlement, and many households possess sites and objects of veneration; they can range from formal places of worship and cemeteries to cherished possessions passed down through generations. In addition to the powerful historical and spiritual associations that physical objects can have at the individual level, collective efforts are often made to preserve sites and objects deemed to have national significance. This is evidenced in the number of cultural heritage sites and objects that help define the cultural identity of a place and a people saved in the national interest of every country of the world.[16] The existence of and conservation of the remains of the stone city of Great Zimbabwe in southern Africa was so important to the local people that when they finally gained independence from Great Britain in 1980, they renamed their country for the site.

Defiance and national pride were the principal motivations behind Poland's extensive post–World War II rebuilding of Warsaw's Stare Miasto ("Old Town") to its late eighteenth-century appearance. By special order of Adolf Hitler, it had been largely destroyed as punishment for a nationalist uprising in 1944; 85 percent of the buildings were reduced to rubble. From 1947 to 1965, the government restored it to commemorate Communist and Polish nationalist resistance to fascism.

AESTHETIC APPRECIATION

Respect for, or at least a curiosity about, high artistic accomplishments is a basic human trait. One only needs to observe the place that antiques, antiquity, and historic buildings have in today's society, and the values placed on them, to appreciate the role of history in world culture today.

But apart from the more spectacular accomplishments of famous individual artists, there is an ever-widening appreciation of artistry and craftsmanship—such as Roman mosaic inlay, Chinese jade carving, or Shaker furniture design and joinery—which, although less historically significant, are nonetheless interesting. That such intrinsically valuable artistic creations have aesthetic merit (and frequently high monetary value as well) is borne out by the worldwide proliferation of both permanent and temporary museum exhibitions devoted to them—and in the robust contemporary antiques and antiquities trade.

There has been a recent increase of scholarly and popular interest in all manner of historic buildings, their arrangements, and the landscapes in which they may be situated. Most architectural historians and architectural conservationists view the field in terms of types of buildings from specific periods, while planners and cultural anthropologists tend to view uses, arrangements of buildings, and their infrastructure as wholes. Other views are held by building conservation scientists and historians of technology, who may be interested in details of historic construction technology or the subtle evidences of history as seen in the *patina* on an object. (See Chapter 8.)

ROMANTICISM AND NOSTALGIA

The veneration of the past and its traditions is reflected in Western art, architecture, and literature from the Renaissance onward. A major revival of interest in architecture and other art forms from classical antiquity began in Italy in the late fifteenth century.

Nostalgic interests in the historic past took on a new turn from the late eighteenth century against the backdrop of rapid social change and the onset of industrialization. This sentiment is well represented in Europe's nineteenth-century age of historicism, when what were perceived to be national styles were sought out and celebrated in new architecture. Eventually western Europe countered the pervasiveness of the classical revival with several other trends, the first and most notable being the Gothic revival. Accomplishments in archaeology and historical research also served as a stimulus to pursue the past for modern purposes. English *picturesque gardens* became popular throughout Europe during this period. In addition to using real or re-created ruins as focal points, architects and landscape designers often incorporated naturalistic settings with new structures into exotic historic architectural styles, such as classical, medieval, Chinese, and Moorish.

Pride in indigenous styles and artistic creation could also represent potent social forces. William Morris, the late nineteenth-century British designer, writer, and social reformer, led a school of thought that prized traditional craftsmanship over modern modes of production. Among his many accomplishments was the founding of the Society for the Protection of Ancient Buildings in 1877, considered to be the first membership organization to advocate the conservation of historic buildings.

During the nineteenth century, this increasing fascination with the material remains of the past and the techniques used to produce them resulted in greater conservation efforts, which started in Europe and spread elsewhere. Interest in craft traditions and their documentation (followed often by systems of inventory and heritage protection techniques) was carried to many parts of the world through the process of European colonization. Legacies of European-style historic research and cultural heritage protection seen today in South and Southeast Asia, Africa, and parts of the Americas are testament to this.

SHORTCOMINGS IN MODERN ARCHITECTURE AND PLANNING

New construction and urban and rural development schemes radically changed the face of most countries during the twentieth century, often with grave consequences for their historic built environments. Quantitatively, there was likely more new building during the past century than in all previous centuries combined. Despite all the time, energy, and money expended by the modern construction industry, planning for new development has been deficient in certain areas, and considerable numbers of new buildings have had problems, mainly due to the use of unproven materials, designs, and construction methods. As a result, many people throughout the world have become disillusioned with modern architecture and planning, which not long ago was championed as the best solution by far to the world's urban problems and people's desire to live comfortably.

The chief complaints about modern architecture have focused on its scale, its lifeless and monotonous design, and its frequent inability to respond to the needs of its users. In the former Soviet Union, tens of thousands of multistory public housing buildings were erected based on erroneous assumptions of efficiency and people's desire to live in highrise, high-density neighborhoods. Post–World War II planning is filled with examples of overscale, inefficient, and inhospitable spaces, many of which have become national embarrassments.[17] Tens of millions of buildings from this period are found throughout the world; many have neither proven durable nor served their inhabitants well.

Failures in modern architecture have been particularly acute when imported modern styles and building methods represented a complete break from local building traditions and failed to respond to local environmental demands. There are numerous examples of glass-clad skyscraper designs transported from the United States and Western Europe to completely different physical environments—in Asia, for instance—that did not serve as well. In the early years of the world's adoption of the International Style, protection of interior spaces from direct sunlight via overhangs or other screening devices was minimal or nonexistent, even when a building was located near the Saudi Arabian desert or in a tropical locale like Bangkok, Kuala Lumpur, or Singapore. Such insensitivity to local environmental conditions incited criticism simply on the basis of energy inefficiency; many modern architects and engineers had designed mechanically conditioned interior spaces with the erroneous assumption of limitless inexpensive fuel for heat, air conditioning, and lighting.[18] The growing "green architecture" movement is one response. (See Chapter 7.)

As the deficiencies of modern architecture and planning are recognized, corrective efforts are being made. The present architectural conservation movement can take considerable credit for pointing modern architecture in new directions, since it has for many years insisted that old buildings should be recycled whenever possible. As the American architectural historian Vincent Scully has said, "The historic preservation movement— a mass popular movement—has been a matter of people taking architecture back from

Figure 4–6 Time has proven that many new building designs and modern construction techniques are no better, at least aesthetically, than traditional designs, as seen in this modern apartment building clad predominately in glass and stucco, erected adjacent to an Empire-style mansion in Boston.

the hands of planners and architects."[19] In fact, much of American landmark legislation followed popular efforts to save specific sites threatened by the prospect of replacement with what was considered inferior architectural solutions.

Not surprisingly, one of the biggest growth areas in both the building industry and in architectural conservation today is the rehabilitation of twentieth-century buildings. The quantity of relatively new construction, regardless of its quality, that will inevitably require updating and rehabilitation is tremendous. Many modern building materials, such as metal alloys, plastics, specialized sealants and finishes, and new types of glass, require specialized research and restoration techniques.[20]

Architectural conservation started primarily as a historian's concern but has increasingly become of consequence to anyone who is interested in aesthetics and the environment. A healthier and stronger new blend of interests now exists, one that offers a revised and improved *cultural ecology* for utilizing and shaping the human built environment. The search for a viable modern architecture has caused many architects and planners to reassess historic building designs and traditions. At this stage, the preservation of historic buildings and the crafts traditions used to create them is in everyone's interest. The recent demands that new architecture be more respectful of physical context, continuity, and the cultures it serves have raised the stakes in contemporary architectural design and construction. When today's concerns for sustainability and energy efficiency are added in, modern architecture has some exciting new purposes to fulfill and expectations to meet.[21]

PRACTICALITY

People also preserve historic buildings because they are useful resources, whether they continue serving their intended purpose or are capable of adapting to new, contemporary use. It has always been human nature to repair a building for as long as it serves its function and can be maintained at a reasonable cost. Special efforts are often made to prolong the usefulness of some buildings—places of worship, civic architecture, memorials, palaces, institutions of learning, select *vernacular architecture*, and the like. Their owners usually seek to maintain them for uncomplicated, practical reasons. Such structures created with longevity in mind have been termed by British architectural conservationist John Earl "celebratory monuments," which, if they survive public scrutiny and remain in political favor, sooner or later acquire public monument status.[22]

Usually, it is external forces that make a building obsolete—not infeasible repairs. For example, when well-designed, solidly built warehouses and industrial constructions lose their original function, they can often remain in use for a different purpose.

The 1970s sparked a new interest in energy-efficient buildings. More recently, an awareness of the need to reduce carbon emissions associated with the building industry has furthered interest in the sensible reuse and extended use of existing buildings. (See also Chapter 7.)

TOURISM

The desire to visit historic buildings and sites in order to experience different cultures and see evidence of different historical periods firsthand is yet another reason to conserve such places. Today, both nationals and foreign tourists expect to find conserved historic buildings and sites nearly everywhere they go, as these destinations define the character of a place and add to their interest. Cultural tourism increases both educational experiences and revenues.

While the economic importance of tourism cannot be overstated, its potentially negative impact on heritage conservation should not be underappreciated. General tourism is the fourth largest industry in the world; in 2003 it generated more than $733 billion.[23] Heritage tourism is a major component of this growing industry: It constitutes as much as 15 percent of general tourism's total revenue and much higher percentages in certain regions.[24] For example, 60 percent of all visitors to Europe cite culture as a purpose of their trip. Tourism is the largest industry in many of the countries with large inventories of historically significant sites, such as Italy.

Unfortunately the increasing demands of tourism can lead to unrestrained commercial exploitation of historic towns, buildings, and sites, especially in developing countries, where there may be few other opportunities for local economic development. While tourism has focused unprecedented attention on cultural heritage in the developing world, its expansion has also created one of the biggest challenges in the cultural heritage management field. There is an urgent need to decrease the stress that many well-known places, such as Venice, Prague, the Taj Mahal, Borobudur, and Angkor are under today. The future of heritage tourism lies in large part in increasing access to more sites in order to relieve pressure on the most popular sites and on managing mass tourism at existing sites more effectively. (See also Chapter 7.)

Heritage tourism stands alongside ecotourism, health tourism, and leisure tourism as an important and specifically recognized subcategory within the tourism industry. Tour agencies offer alluring trips to Egyptian monuments, ancient sites of the Aegean, and European cathedrals; to archeological sites in Sri Lanka and religious sites in the Holy Land and Europe; even tours that retrace medieval Christian pilgrimage routes,

Figure 4–7 The statistics on the popularity of heritage tourism's share of general tourism do not take into account that when given a choice, "brief stay," transient, and business travelers usually choose well-preserved and presented cultural capitals over others. Paris is one example.

"the way of Saint James," to Santiago de Compostela in Spain. To paraphrase the English writer L. P. Hartley, the past is increasingly becoming another country that we can visit.[25]

British archaeologist Ian Hodder has suggested that a more specific term for travel aimed at learning history would be *time tourism*[25]—and that *sustainable time travel* would be an even better term. But in reality, heritage tourism is almost always as much about the present as about the past. Where people choose to travel and the sites they collectively choose to preserve says a lot about modern societal values. The global appeal of heritage tourism coupled with new notions of ownership of the past underscore Hodder's point that "[n]o one owns the past, though we all pass through it as time travelers… and we have a responsibility to others who pass through it."[26]

ENDNOTES

1. Feilden, *Conservation of Historic Buildings*, xiii.
2. Lowenthal, *Past is a Foreign Country*, 187.
3. Ibid., 237.
4. W. Brown Morton III, "Managing the Impact on Cultural Resources of Changing Concepts of Significance," *Preservation of What, for Whom? A Critical Look at Historical Significance*, ed. Michael A. Tomlan (Ithaca, NY: National Council for Preservation Education, 1998), 145.
5. Fitch, *Historic Preservation*, x, Fitch's clarion rationale for conserving authenticity is rare even among the experts because he projects what the importance of the authentic (thing), or the prototype, will be to the future, not just to the present. The late Ecuadorian architect Hernán Crespo Toral echoed Fitch, stating the issue even more plainly: "We must fight to preserve authenticity during the restoration process, otherwise we will pass on to our descendants a *pastiche*

of history." (World Monuments Fund Regional Conference on Architectural Restoration and Preservation, São Paolo, Brazil, May 2002.)

6. Literary critic and philosopher Walter Benjamin (1892–1940) has noted that in the pre-modern era, what mattered most was "cult value." Art value was only generated with the start of collections and exhibitions (Walter Benjamin, 'The Work of Art in the Age of Mechanical Reproduction," *Illuminations: Essays and Reflections*, ed. Hannah Arendt (London: Fontana-Collins, 1969), 219–254. Also, Jokilehto, *A History of Architectural Conservation*, 296.

7. Walter Benjamin, *Illuminations: Essays and Reflections*.

8. Fitch, *Historic Preservation*, chap. 1, 1–12.

9. Jan Otakar Fischer, "Ask Not Which House Is Real, but Which Is Not," *New York Times*, September 23, 1999.

10. The Goethe garden house facsimile was the idea of Lorenz Engell, dean of media studies at Bauhaus University, a man eager to provoke essential questions about authenticity. The intricacies of determining what is "real" have particular relevance in this postwar landscape, where great tracts of the national heritage were destroyed and had to be rebuilt.

11. Derek Linstrum, "The Conservation of Historic Towns and Monuments," *Commonwealth Foundation* Occasional Paper XXXVIII (1976): 19.

12. Wim Denslagen, "Restoration Theories, East and West," *Transactions/Association for Studies in the Conservation of Historic Buildings* (ASCHB) 18 (1993): 3–7.

13. Examples of places venerated for their religious significance and that are carefully protected include Mount Nebo in Jordan, where Moses is said to have first viewed the Holy Land; Jerusalem's Dome of the Rock, the seat of the Islamic faith; Jagannath Temple, one of India's key Hindu pilgrimage destinations; and the sites in Rome where Roman Catholic St. Peter was said to have been crucified and buried. Every country has its examples of highly venerated national historical symbols, among them Les Invalides, Napoleon Bonaparte's tomb in Paris; Kemal Atatürk's residence and tomb in Ankara, Turkey; and London's Westminster Abbey and St. Paul's Cathedral. In the United States, a memorial has been created at Plymouth Rock in Plymouth, Massachusetts, where the Pilgrims are said to have first landed.

14. As has been proven through archaeology, preserving and venerating objects and places having religious or cultic significance dates to prehistoric times.

15. His Holiness Sri Sri Ravi Shankar, speech at Museum of World Religions conference, Taiwan, November 10, 2001.

16. Occasionally, conserved historic buildings, sites, shrines, and objects represent not only respect for the past but also national glorification, furtherance of political goals, or substantiations of political legitimacy. Preserved sites that memorialize nationally or internationally significant events include battlefields and war sites: Yorktown and Gettysburg, Pennsylvania, in the United States; Waterloo in Belgium; Verdun in France; Stalingrad in Russia; and Hiroshima in Japan.

17. Large numbers of residential buildings—referred to by locals as *panelák* (prefabricated concrete slab housing blocks)—and commercial buildings erected during the interwar and post–World War II years throughout Eastern Europe, as well as countless other low-quality buildings in thousands of towns and cities elsewhere in the world, have frequently proven to be substandard when compared with those constructed using both earlier and later building techniques.

18. Due to such miscalculations, builders, governments, and users alike are frequently disappointed in the final quality of modern architectural projects. Retrofitting or replacing failed parts of relatively new construction is now commonplace.

19. Vincent Scully, lecture, New York Landmarks Conservancy, New York, NY, March 23,1994.

20. This growing trend in the United States in rehabilitating buildings dating from the twentieth century is reflected in statistics published in building industry magazines such as the *Dodge Reports*.

21. The architecture of tomorrow might heed some recent lessons about looking backward in order to go forward. One such lesson is apparent in many postmodernist American and European designs of the 1970s and 1980s, when historic building motifs were used as appliqué to add recognizable character to modern architecture, thus making them more acceptable. In subsequent efforts to be au courant, postmodernist historicism was—and continues to be—emulated throughout the world, especially in developing countries. A more recent trend in architectural practice has been neotraditionalism, which involves the conscientious revivals of traditional styles updated with modern amenities. The present burgeoning green architecture movement

toward more environmentally friendly and energy-efficient buildings, often using variations on traditional materials and construction techniques, offers a more useful and resourceful new direction.

22. John Earl, *Building Conservation Philosophy* (Reading, UK: College of Estate Management, 1996), 14.

23. Only the chemical, automotive products, and fuel industries have generated more revenue than tourism worldwide in recent years. United Nations World Tourism Organization (UNWTO), *Tourism Highlights: 2006 Edition* (Madrid: World Tourism Organization, 2006), 3; UNWTO, "Tourism and the World Economy," http://www.world-tourism.org/facts/tmt.html; and UNWTO, *Cultural Heritage and Tourism Development* (Madrid: World Tourism Organization, 2001): 4–5.

24. Ian Hodder. (Presidential Colloquium: *The Politics of Archaeology in the Global Context*, lecture, Archaeological Institute of America annual meeting, Dallas, Texas, January 4, 2000).

25. Based on the famous phrase, "The past is a foreign country: they do things differently there," which was used as the first sentence in L. P. Hartley's *The Go-Between*, London, 1953.

26. Hodder, Ibid.

CHAPTER 5

Who Owns the Past?

Who owns the past? Potential answers have serious implications both for the stewardship of historic cultural sites and their presentation.

The interpretation of history is a dynamic process. The vast amount of information available to us about all aspects of human history, and the ease with which it can now be accessed, has fundamentally altered humankind's appreciation of history. Modern scholarly historical research, especially archaeological investigations, has done much to reshape modern views of the past. Any of the recent great historical research projects—studying the fate of Black Sea cultures, discovering new tombs in Egypt's Valley of the Kings, or conducting ancient population studies for the greater Angkor region in Cambodia—bears this out. New information comes to light on an almost daily basis and occasionally forces us to revise our understanding of previously considered truths and facts.

Popular interest in history can be gauged by the number of related programs on television and through the popularity of genealogy. Media sources constantly bombard us with new information about the past: the daily lives of the ancient Egyptians and Romans, the rise and fall of cities and civilizations, epic military exploits in history, and almost firsthand tours to exotic historic places. Tracing one's ancestors has never been easier, thanks to the Internet.

During the twentieth century alone, approaches to historiography—the study of how history is recorded—have radically changed; so have the allied fields of anthropology, archaeology, genealogy, and architectural conservation. Each of these fields is derived from intellectual concerns raised during the Age of Enlightenment centuries ago, but each has advanced according to the needs, interests, and methodological developments of its specific field. Today, the cultural heritage conservation movement is synthesizing information gained in many of these diverse disciplines into new and practical cross-disciplinary applications.

An uneven knowledge about the past—and the population's varying levels of interest in it—means professionals who research and interpret history must recognize that the past is something different to everyone. In this sense, the mantra of anyone in the history business, including architectural heritage conservationists, must be: Whose history is it?

A HERITAGE OF UNIVERSAL IMPORTANCE

The concepts of *world heritage* and sites of *outstanding universal value*, which imply that historic cultural sites belong symbolically to all people,[1] were raised and codified by the 1972 World Heritage Convention of the United Nations Educational, Scientific and Cultural Organization (UNESCO).[2] Although they are supported by the International Council on Monuments and Sites (ICOMOS) and recognized by myriad heritage organizations and entities, these core concepts are neither perfect nor without controversy. The idea of universal, globally recognized cultural heritage and the increasing importance that certain international organizations and standards play in conservation has raised some important questions regarding ownership and accountability.

UNESCO's fundamental principle—that the heritage of each culture is the heritage of all humankind—has been used to support the argument that decisions about the treatment and future of historic sites can and should be made by outsiders rather than local communities.[3] This same principle of universality has been used to explain the occasionally troublesome problem of local communities with listed World Heritage sites abdicating responsibility for caring for their own cultural heritage because outsiders had assumed the obligation. In response, the 1996 Inter-American Symposium on Authenticity in the Conservation and Management of the Cultural Heritage of the Americas concluded that "responsibility for cultural heritage and the management of it belongs, in the first place, to the cultural community that has generated it, and subsequently, to that which cares for it."[4]

The World Heritage List expands annually, but it is paltry compared to many thousands of sites worthy of consideration. The convention clearly indicates that its own list is "not intended to provide for the protection of all properties of great interest, value or importance, but only for a select list of the most outstanding of these from an international viewpoint."[5] (See also Chapters 9 and 15.)

The decision to request a listing rests with each of the 185 signatory states that are party to the convention. Even the worthiest site cannot be listed if its sponsoring state cannot or will not undertake various site-supportive responsibilities (an idea ironically at odds with the notion of universal or world heritage).

Usually, obtaining the historical facts about World Heritage sites is the least difficult part of the nomination process for the sponsoring state. The main challenge lies in preserving and presenting the physical site and in determining what kind of visitor experience will be appropriate for the public. The host state must also secure the site by guaranteeing regular monitoring and control. Unfortunately, as of September 2008, thirty World Heritage sites were considered threatened for reasons ranging from human-related causes and war to ecologically inflicted damage and threats.[6]

Transnational cooperation has successfully generated various international conservation programs, but the efforts of different programs have occasionally undermined one another. The enhanced global attention generated by a World Heritage listing broadens a site's interest, which usually translates into increased visitor attendance—and all its attendant advantages and disadvantages.

The interests and capacities of special interest groups within cultural heritage conservation are vital to the overall heritage conservation movement. Expatriated descen-

Figure 5-1 The Aga Khan Trust for Culture, committed to conserving Islamic heritage, has provided significant financial and technical assistance toward planning and conservation work at the UNESCO World Heritage site of the Citadel of Aleppo in Syria.

dants of those who had at one time settled a place and left behind physical legacies sometimes represent a cultural diaspora that can become the most interested party in its preservation. Examples of special interest cultural heritage organizations include the Aga Khan Trust for Culture, with its mission to conserve Islamic heritage, and the grant program of the Calouste Gulbenkian Foundation, with its long-standing interest in conserving both Portuguese heritage abroad and Armenian architectural heritage wherever it may be found. (See also Appendix B.)

The past is most visible when it has been manifested in objects of national pride. Nevertheless, the practical aspects of conserved national treasures—such as their income-generating tourist appeal and their reassuring effects on local society—cannot be underestimated. Famous national symbols such as the Colosseum and the Kremlin are seen by millions daily, whether in person or in the media. The celebrations at the turn of the third millennium showcased these icons to hundreds of millions of television viewers worldwide, who were able to compare the national displays. Each representation of a national symbol, be it the Taj Mahal, the pyramids, the Parthenon, the Eiffel Tower, or the Statue of Liberty, simultaneously embodied both a national and a universal significance. The most prominent of the world's architectural icons may belong to individual nations, but they are rightly perceived as belonging to the world at large. These sites are simultaneously valued and claimed by local, national, and worldwide populations as part of humankind's inherited identity.

The question of "who owns the past" is best answered by examining the site or object in question within its own context. Some ownership problems related to overlapping heritage are legendary: disputed religious sites in Jerusalem, a holy city for three major religions; the claims of Serbian nationalists over Muslim property in the former Yugoslavia; the repatriation of skeletal remains by descendants of American Indians.

The year 2008 witnessed two extraordinary developments pertaining to ownership of internationally recognized architectural heritage. The first was the return to Ethiopia of the 78-foot (24-meter) high Aksum stone obelisk dating from the fourth century CE, which had been taken in pieces to Rome and erected on the Esquiline Hill in 1937 to commemorate the conquest of Ethiopia the year before and the birth of Mussolini's "Third Rome." Based on a much earlier agreement to do so and in a technical effort beginning in 2003, the 166-ton former monolith was flown and hauled in three pieces back to the ceremonial center of Aksum, re-assembled on a strengthened foundation, and re-dedicated in a national celebration on September 4, 2008. (See Figures 17.48 a and b.) The second development was the apparently successful resolution of national political tensions that flared between Thailand and Cambodia in mid-July and August on news that the ancient Khmer temple of Preah Vihear, which is situated in Cambodia's Preah Vihear Province along its border with Thailand, had been placed on UNESCO's World Heritage List. Despite a 1962 International Court of Justice ruling on the matter, groups within Thailand claimed the Preah Vihear Temple was Thai national heritage; military units from both sides were dispatched to the region, and after weeks of international diplomatic efforts, tensions abated. The details of an accord between the two countries on the matter are pending as of the time of this publication.

Even more examples exist relative to movable heritage, since these items can be easily transported; the most famous ownership dispute concerning a movable monument is the Greek government's repeated demands for the return of the Parthenon frieze, which was taken to England in 1804 by Lord Elgin. Numerous other calls for the restitution of cultural property are heard each year, often in countries whose patrimonies were vulnerable to plunder or cheap purchase before the development of national heritage protection policies. These demands have often become catalysts for new protective legislation.

The process of determining historical and/or artistic significance of a site or object is fraught with difficulties because any such process is always, in part, subjective. For example, the more than three hundred Native American cultures and religions that exist in the United States today hold diverse views on heritage topics. Native American sites are lost when smaller communities, which tend to be politically fragmented, are unable to present a powerful, cohesive front that can effectively argue for site preservation. Therefore, non–Native Americans unfamiliar with the perspectives and preferences of these communities make decisions about site significance.[7] The same problem exists throughout the world for hundreds of other indigenous peoples.

So decisions about what history is preserved and how it should be presented are of utmost importance. Given the vastness of human history and the ever-present curiosity to know what happened in the past, there are pressing needs for cultural heritage conservationists to be conversant in history and its research methods. Moreover, heritage conservation professionals must objectively and sensibly judge *which* history is presented in which manner and be able to defend their rationale. Opinions representing differing points of view from local communities as well as from historians, conservationists, museum administrators, archaeologists, anthropologists, sociologists, and technicians such as architects and materials conservators, when combined, can best determine what should be conserved, how it should be done, and for whom.

ENDNOTES

1. Apart from the precedent of the Seven Wonders of the Ancient World, which were presumably considered shared heritage in their day, the first mention in modern times of a historic monument or site being of universal significance—and thus "owned" by humankind in general—is credited to Austrian philosopher Alois Riegel.

2. UNESCO, World Heritage Convention, http://whc.unesco.org/en/conventiontext/.

3. Margaret MacLean et al., *Proceedings of the Inter-American Symposium on Authenticity in the Conservation and Management of the Cultural Heritage of the Americas,* (Washington, DC, and Los Angeles: US/ICOMOS, and the Getty Conservation Institute, 1999), xix.

4. Ibid.

5. UNESCO. *Convention Concerning the Protection of the World Cultural and Natural Heritage,* adopted by the General Conference at its seventeenth session, Paris, 16 November 1972 (Paris: UNESCO, 1972), http://whc.unesco.org/archive/convention-en.pdf.

6. Since 1995, the World Monuments Fund's World Monuments Watch program and its Watch List of 100 Most Endangered Sites have complemented the aims of the World Heritage List by helping to raise worldwide awareness about the importance of historic buildings and their conservation.

7. A concern first articulated in the United States by archaeologist Sherene Baugher, "Who Determines Significance of American Indian Sacred Sites and Burial Grounds?" in *Preservation of What, for Whom? A Critical Look at the Historical Significance,* 9.

CHAPTER 6

History, Historiography, and Architectural Conservation

Since the past is the medium of all cultural heritage, it is in the cultural heritage conservationist's interest to know as much as possible about history, historical methods, and attitudes toward history. A heritage conservation professional is expected to be conversant, if not expert, on the conditions during which a building, site, or object was created as well as how it survived to the present time. He or she is also expected to use that information to substantiate informed and defendable professional opinions about the heritage in question. This knowledge puts the person in a key position for deciding on the historical elements and themes to be highlighted in a conservation project. Experience with the methods and applications of art and architectural history is essential to deciding what should be conserved and how it could be presented.

HISTORY AND THE PASSAGE OF TIME: FACTS, VALUES, AND NOTIONS OF HISTORY

The concept of history has evolved as an expression of humanity's attempts to understand the world and its place in it. The English word *history* is derived from the ancient Greek word for "inquiry" and is related to the Greek verb "to know." Histories are orderly, factual, explanatory accounts about human existence over the course of time.

Webster's Dictionary defines *historiography* as "the writing of history," "the principles, theory, and history of historical writing," and "any body of historical literature, such as classical or medieval history." Varying historiographical approaches can significantly affect a population's appreciation and treatment of historic places.

Historians interpret the physical evidence of human activities. This vast range of material and intellectual output includes products with a purpose, such as tools and machinery; the remains of social environments, such as residential, civic, and religious structures; and the symbolic and expressive products we call art. Historians' interpretive skills extend as well to written records and oral testimonies of human struggle, conflict, and achievement. In the best histories, narratives about the past embody the scholar's awareness of the influence that present-day perspectives and historiography inevitably have on events that occurred long ago.

◀ **Figure 6-1** One of the first printed books on architecture, the *Hypnerotomachia Poliphili* (1485), attributed to Francesco Colonna, is richly illustrated with woodcut engravings of both real and imagined ruins of the distant classical past.

The development of writing and print technology profoundly influenced the world's understanding of the past and thus had an effect on efforts to conserve and interpret it. Though writing emerged more than five thousand years ago and printing presses with movable type were invented in eleventh-century China, it was the invention of a different form of this technology using a simpler alphabet in mid-fifteenth-century Europe that led to a widespread awareness of past cultures and their differences from contemporary culture.

Also, from the Renaissance forward, a modern consciousness of past and present developed in western Europe. History was separated into distinct periods, and the ability to critically evaluate artifacts and cultural characteristics from former periods eventually developed. From the fifteenth century, ancient classical sites were recognized as special, worth studying, and deserving of protection.[1] But in Asia, few cultures placed great importance on original historical artifacts; ancient items were used and copied instead. Therefore, the spread of printing did not have the same effect there as it did in the West, where it raised awareness of the past and promoted conservation movements. From the onset of printing history both in the East and in the West, illustrations including artistic objects and works of architec-

ture were depicted. The proliferation of illustrated books on architecture from the sixteenth century forward in Europe is responsible for the wide and rapid influence of stylistic developments as well as the documentation of specific buildings, the concerns of historians and conservationists.[2]

Mass literacy and mass printed media came even later, in the nineteenth century, and allowed a burgeoning interest in the past to become truly widespread. The ideas and projects of influential thinkers and practitioners, such as Eugène-Emmanuel Viollet-le-Duc, John Ruskin, and William Morris, who were committed to preserving historic architecture and related things, were disseminated; they affected architectural conservation practice throughout Europe. As publishing activity increased, so did documentation of the past, which in turn facilitated the expansion of popular knowledge about the existence of the surviving elements of the past and of opportunities for its comparison and interpretation. In the twentieth century, new media, such as television and the Internet, radically increased humankind's knowledge of history, especially in relation to cultures distant from the reader, and thereby also contributed to conservation actions at popular cultural heritage sites worldwide.

VIEWING TIME THROUGH THE LENS OF HISTORY

The aim of the historian is to portray time.[3] Over the centuries, whatever values historians brought to the description and interpretation of past events and human-made objects, the purpose of their work has remained consistent: to deliver a meaningful pattern of historical information in narrative form that depicts the passage of time. That this pattern was invisible to the historian's subjects when they lived it, and unknown to his or her contemporaries before they detected it, suggests the importance of the historian's role in giving meaning to past events and cultural traditions.

But when does a historical event occur? A generation or perhaps centuries ago? Or can it be almost instantaneous—say, what happened just a second before? Austrian historiographer Ernst Breisach notes that psychologists have found that "the span of time which we actually experience as 'now,' the 'mental' present, is only about one-fiftieth of a second long." Thus "human life is never simply lived in the present alone but rather in three worlds: one that is, one that was, and one that will be."[4] Of course, our sense of the present is relative. When we think of ourselves, the present may mean this moment or year—but when we think of history, the present may mean this decade. In many ways, our modern attitude about the past is more complex than either our experience of the present or our concept of the future.

In every culture, the link between past, present, and future accounts for a sense of continuity. The continual presence of physical objects such as old buildings and artifacts links the present with the past and provides reference points for proceeding into the uncertain future. Every historic object or place exists simultaneously in the past and in the present. What leads us to identify things as antiquated or ancient varies with environment and history, with individual and culture, with historical awareness and inclination.[5]

In the modern context of cultural heritage conservation, it is generally agreed that buildings acquire something of a mantle of age after about two generations, or about fifty to sixty years. To be listed on the US National Register of Historic Places, a building or district must be at least fifty years old, but there is flexibility in the application of this criterion for younger sites of exceptional importance. For example, the facilities from which the first astronauts were launched into space at Cape Canaveral Air Force Station in Florida were added to the National Register in 1984, just twenty-three years after that program ended. Despite this site's relative youth, its historic value was unquestioned.

The National Board of Antiquities of Finland generally ignores the criterion of age in determining the eligibility of heritage places for listing on its state inventory, recognizing that perceptions of time are, in fact, rarely acknowledged as determining factors in heritage conservation decisions. The country, therefore, has the most flexible and viable of all architectural heritage listing procedures, at least with regard to age-limit criteria.

American architect Kevin Lynch, in his thought-provoking work *What Time Is This Place?* dissects the interrelationships of views of the past, present, and future to demonstrate their profound effects on environmental planning and architectural conservation: "The present…is a mental construction, a conscious recital to oneself of immediate events and actions, a renewable answer to the question 'What am I up to?' …[T]he past and the future, although they refer to more distant events, exist only in this same immediate time, as present processes of recall or anticipation."[6]

An awareness of concepts like these can heighten one's sensitivity to issues pertaining to the preservation and presentation of historic buildings and sites. According to British historian Michael Hunter, "Present-day preservation stems from a threefold awareness of the past…that it was unlike the present, that it is crucial to our sense of identity, and that its tangible remnants are rapidly disappearing."[7] He argues that we often forget that awareness of change is relatively new, since the present is so different from even the very recent past as a result of the rapid changes of modern society. Thus, in most of today's world, where change is increasingly evident, it is hard to avoid receiving nonstop reminders from myriad sources about perceptions of the past, present, and future. A growing derivative of this reality is contemporary interest and commitment to cultural heritage protection, the subject of this book.

PERCEPTIONS OF TIME

Historical time is the medium through which all human actions and experiences are organized. In Western societies, time is perceived to be a linear structure for a chain of events that moves forward from a fixed point in the past through the present and on toward a future goal. In contrast, traditional Asian societies view the passage of time as cyclical, a continuous and infinite repetition of natural and human behaviors. During the sixteenth and seventeenth centuries, Western means of measuring time and viewing the past and present spread as distant places and cultures were colonized or otherwise strongly affected by trade relations. One of the greatest results is the present world's recognition of twenty-four separate time zones, which encircle the earth and synchronize the global perception of daily time.

There is, however, no consensus as to an annual "starting point" for time. Time in imperial China began anew with the ascension of each dynasty. The familiar and widely used Western chronological framework, the Gregorian calendar, was created only in 1582 CE by Pope Gregory XIII, who revised the Julian calendar of 46 BCE. The Hebrew calendar marks lunar years beginning with the creation of the world, which its adherents believe occurs 3,760 years before the start of the Gregorian calendar. The Islamic calendar is also lunar and marks the beginning of time from when the prophet Muhammad moved to Medina in the seventh century CE. China's traditional lunar calendar was introduced in 2953 BCE and remains an honored cultural reference in East Asia. It is used in China, Japan, and Korea alongside the adopted modern Western calendar. In India, the Gregorian calendar is widely used, but the official civil calendar is the Saka (or Hindu) calendar, which was introduced on March 22, 1957 to harmonize the preparation of religious calendars for Hindus. There remain many other locally popular variants as well. These examples cover only contemporaneously active calendar systems and do not begin to describe how various other human civilizations, such as the ancient Egyptians and pre-Columbian Maya, understood time.

PERCEPTIONS OF HISTORY

Figure 6-2 A *lukasa,* or memory board, is used by designated elders among the Luba people of Congo to recall history by the means of mnemonics. *(Image courtesy of Susanne K. Bennet and the Museum of African Art. Jerry L. Thompson, photographer)*

How history has been perceived and recorded has been similarly varied, depending on the age and complexities of a culture. Some tribal societies use art objects as a central means of communicating historical events and cultural values derived from past experience. The Maori of New Zealand traditionally ascribe spiritual power to carvings that have been applied to houses, war canoes, and figurative sculptures. Widely understood oral traditions provided the basis for the historical stories illustrated by the carvings. The aesthetic merits of the precious objects were incidental: Their value lay in their ability to convey these important stories about ancestor gods, their descent lines from the time of creation to the present, and the eternal stability of the particular landscape occupied by the community. The supernatural aspect of carving also served a religious function for the Maori community and created a conduit to their various gods and revered ancestors.[8]

In southeastern Congo, the historical consciousness of the Luba people also rests on oral traditions and the use of prized objects to bolster memory. A remarkable range of decorated and carved objects fulfills this role, from beaded necklaces and headdresses to the thrones and staffs of precolonial kings and chiefs. One of the most concrete and illuminating examples of a Luba **mnemonic** object is the *lukasa,* or memory board. This wooden board about the size of a human hand is covered with intricate patterns of beads, shells, and metal pins. These coded signs form a kind of map of past events organized around an element representing a topic or an important place, such as the royal court. Through narrative or song, a reader interprets the memory board to the Luba group. The complexity of the *lukasa's* design allows for a great variety of content in the readings, says Ernst Breisach, "depending upon who the reader is and what points she or he wishes to stress…. The diversity of the interpretations stimulated by a single board does not indicate error, deceit, or misperception. Rather, it proves that *lukasa* readings are rhetorical moments for the persuasive argument and defense of a particular point of view" about history.[9]

Although history did not emerge as a modern scientific discipline until the nineteenth century, historians in every period sought to identify the causes and effects of humanity's considerable impact on the world. The methods—and purpose—of the study of history have, however, changed dramatically since recorded history began. With the invention of writing in about 4000 BCE in Mesopotamia and in around 1500 BCE in China, the measure of time began to take on new meanings. History could be placed on chronological frameworks in a more rational and recognizable way.

HISTORIOGRAPHY UNTIL ITS PROFESSIONALIZATION

The Greek historian Herodotus is generally credited with founding the discipline of historiography. His fifth-century *The Persian Wars* was succeeded by another literary milestone, Thucydides' *History of the Peloponnesian War*. Both writers viewed public instruction and inspiration as history's overriding purpose and were committed to the social usefulness of accurate historical accounts. Such sentiment was echoed by others such as Cicero, whose commentary on contemporary events often included philosophical speculations on the nature of human progress and on the higher moral purpose of history.

Such concerns were expressed through numerous examples of preserving historic buildings and sites in antiquity. In ancient Greece and Rome, damaged monuments were repaired with a variety of techniques that were often designed to preserve the form of the original.[10] Conservation measures were motivated both by religious beliefs (upkeep honored the deity within) and practical concerns (maintenance and repair were less expensive than replacement) rather than by the aesthetic and historical considerations of modern heritage conservation.

The European scholastic approach to history changed during the fifteenth century, when Renaissance writers were freed from the religious constraints of the Middle Ages and began to explore the work of ancient historians. Humanist scholars began investigating the classical past not only through the surviving writings of ancient authors but also through relics, architectural remains, carved inscriptions, tombstones, and coins. The Middle Ages were dismissed as irrelevant to an understanding of historical cause and effect, characterized as barbarous, and derisively labeled "Gothic," after the name of a barbaric tribe.

Perhaps the most far-reaching aspect of early Renaissance scholarship's new historical awareness was a shift in attitude toward the architecture and some of the other arts of earlier civilizations. Whereas medieval writers had demonstrated an interest in ancient Rome's patriotic monuments (such as Trajan's Column), fifteenth-century Italy assigned a new commemorative value to a broader range of buildings and relatively insignificant architectural fragments, such as lintels and capitals. Inscriptions on *spolia* (prized architectural fragments) were mainly recorded not for their inherent informational content but rather because they had survived the passage of centuries. As early as the mid-1440s, antiquarian Flavio Biondo had conducted site visits and combed literary evidence to produce fourteen regional governmental surveys that described a range of ancient structures, including baths, temples, gates, and obelisks.[11]

This fresh interest in historical events and the artistic products of the past was essentially confined to those of ancient Greece and Rome, the two civilizations that were perceived as precursors of contemporary Renaissance society. "For the first time, people began to recognize earlier stages of their own artistic, cultural, and political activities in the works and events that lay a thousand years in the past," observed Alois Riegl.[12] In the East, interests in the documentation of history took a different course. (See Chapter 15.)

Throughout Europe in the late Renaissance, one astounding discovery followed another, altering perceptions of the world beyond recognition. The sixteenth-century experiments of Leonardo da Vinci uncovered new principles in botany, geology, and mechanical engineering. Relying on sensory observation, Copernicus, Galileo, and Isaac Newton tackled the physical universe, while René Descartes and other seventeenth-century philosophers explored the principles that shaped human thought and the ability to know the universe. The struggle among religious philosophies profoundly influenced art, politics, and intellectual debate, and the discovery by courageous mariners of continents previously unknown to Europeans opened new avenues of thinking in every field of intellectual activity.

Amid this background emerged new ways of looking at the world that relied on observation and experimentation. Thus emerged the revolutionary scientific method that characterized the eighteenth-century Age of Enlightenment.[13]

Figure 6-3 Excavators measuring discoveries at Pompeii. During the Age of Reason, methods of documenting history changed and the modern disciplines of archaeology and architectural conservation were born. *(View toward Herculaneum Gate, ca. 1815 by Charles François Mazois, from* Les Ruines de Pompeii, *Firmin Didot, Paris, 1809–1838).*

In the midst of the intellectual ferment of the nineteenth century, Western history writing was "professionalized" and for the first time moved into a discrete discipline at European and American universities. Early in the century, at the German universities of Göttingen and Berlin, scholarly historians developed the formal basis for the modern discipline of history, adopting the empirical methods of the physical sciences in order to objectively determine the "truth" about the past. Written sources and material evidence were approached in a systematic and critical fashion, documentary archives were created, and publication activities were expanded. Information was assembled in a manner that broadened the scope of history and presented historical explanations of events "in terms of a wider, more complex range of causes."[14]

The nineteenth-century German historian Leopold von Ranke is generally credited with the founding of "scientific" history. He claimed his intentions were not to judge the past but to describe it "as it actually occurred"[15] and to reconstruct it from documentary evidence. Believing that one could best understand the past by analyzing primary sources, von Ranke emphasized an approach that involved "a sense of history, an awareness that the past was fundamentally different from the present."[16] Unlike earlier antiquarian and Enlightenment interests, such historicism rejected measuring the historic past.

Historicist views remained highly influential in all areas of European thought throughout the nineteenth century. For heritage conservationists, "the stress placed by historicist thinkers on the uniqueness of historical change—which, in the nineteenth century, took on strong nationalist overtones—gave great significance to the origins and development of nations and localities as key to their distinctive character. When the national past was seen as enriching the present through tradition and continuity, tangible relics of previous epochs acquired urgent importance as guarantors of historical identity."[17]

During World War I and the interwar years, scholars who believed historicism had resolved many of the ambiguities of earlier historiographical thinking were faced with an ideological challenge that continues today. Against a background of unsettling changes in the social, cultural, economic, and political environments of the European nations, historical relativism took center stage, sweeping aside "the very notion of rationality."[18] Followed to its logical, if radical, conclusion, the reasoning of the historical relativists "pronounced history to be no science at all but a creative act that gave meaning to meaningless life."[19] Most European and American scholars maintained their historicist orientation after World War II, but their assertions of the objectivity of their source evaluations were somewhat tempered in response to relativist criticisms.

During the social and political upheavals of the 1960s in Europe and North America, historical objectivity was once again vehemently debated. By the 1970s, poststructuralist theory had expanded the notion of relativism and declared the impossibility of acquiring objective historical knowledge. Some historians announced that the "end of history" was imminent.

HISTORICAL METHOD AND THE ELUSIVE IDEAL OF ACCURACY

A scientific approach to historical sources begins with a critical analysis of its form and content in order to determine authenticity. Such was the path taken in the eighteenth century among the rationalist thinkers of the Age of Reason. In architecture, the polemics over the true sources of the classical style in the 1750s in Rome is one example of this phenomenon. In authenticating a record of the past, today's historians can call upon a wide variety of tools, many of them developed initially for use in other scholarly disciplines (the sophisticated dating techniques invented for archaeology, for example). For historians dealing with ancient written sources, the science of paleography—the study of ancient handwriting—offers techniques to reveal long-faded ink on even fragmentary remains of parchment and paper.[20] Statistical tools have proven to be especially useful for crafting demographic histories of pre-modern and modern Western societies.[21] Linguistics contributes an understanding of the evolution of language in different cultures and brings the historian closer to an accurate assessment of the meaning of documents from the past. Economic history and social anthropology provide insight into the likely motivations and relationships of people in the past.

But even with today's wide assortment of analytical tools, historiography's inherent constraints restrict the degree of historical accuracy any historian can achieve. The most important limitation is the presence of the historian himself, who wears the same "present-day mental lenses" as his audience.[22] Whether or not the author and his audience share the same perspective and values, a twofold process of interpretation introduces unavoidable inaccuracy into the historical narrative.

A second constraint on accuracy is the linear nature of the Western historical narrative, which encourages the mistaken assumption that history unfolds on a one-dimensional plane. As an organizing tactic, chronology is an indispensable means of clarifying the cause-and-effect relationship of events. However, it fails to convey the rich complexity of the past—the interlocking, overlapping layers of human activity through time—and must present an edited flow of events in order to be coherent. In the 1970s, postmodern approaches to the historical narrative attempted to capture that complexity by narrowing the framework to cultures or nations and imposing a thematic form of organization. More recently, the chronological narrative technique has reemerged as a valid means of providing context and of demonstrating causal connections among events. Even given its limitations, the sequential ordering of past events enhances our comprehension and offers a subtle, reassuring parallel to the life experiences that unfold for each individual. (Further discussion of non-Western perceptions and meanings associated with the past can be found in "European Heritage Conservation Principles Abroad" in Chapter 15.)

The third factor that inhibits the attainment of perfect historical accuracy is the influence of cultural trends and political concerns on the historian's presentation of events, an influence the historian may only be partially aware of. Nineteenth-century European historians approached past events selectively and constructed narratives that were clearly fashioned to bolster national identities. Today, especially in education, history is largely a values-driven undertaking. Although many Euro-American educators would deny it, fostering a steadfast appreciation of national achievements becomes part of the national character, and promoting patriotic ideals remains a chief objective of the historical enterprise in Western culture.[23] The same is true for other cultures. This is most vivid in East Asia, where a commodification of history has been on the rise over the past three decades.

Perhaps the most significant constraint on a full portrayal of history is human imperfection: only a fraction of all events have been noted, only a few lives are ever remembered, and only fragments of flawed records survive in decipherable form.[24] As for the dimension of history that can bring narrative to life—the ideas and emotions of historical figures—we are largely in the realm of conjecture. In the end, as George Kubler writes in *The Shape of Time*, "The fullness of history is forever indigestible."[25]

ANTIQUARIANISM: PUTTING THE PAST ON A PEDESTAL

The term *antiquarianism* emerged in the sixteenth century, when the collection of antiquities and study of monuments of the past became sufficiently widespread to merit identification as a cultural pursuit among Renaissance humanists. (The term *ancient scholar* more aptly describes the antiquarian in the East.) The earliest attempt to produce a comprehensive survey of national antiquities was undertaken in England by William Camden in his *Britannia*, which was published in a series of editions from 1586 to 1606. It was not known at that time in Europe that a precedential effort to collect and record all known ancient artistic and literary expressions, especially bronzes and porcelain, had been conducted by Emperor Huizong during the Northern Song dynasty (960–1127). Efforts similar to Camden's followed in other countries.

The appeal of ancient relics, especially prehistoric ones, rested on a complex assortment of cultural attitudes and values. David Lowenthal lists the virtues of antiquity that were most important to antiquarians: "great age, uniqueness, scarcity, ancient skills, non-recoverable techniques, and the assumptions that primitive man lived in harmony with nature, treated technology and art as one, and made everything for both use and beauty."[26] Today it is a widely held belief that, overall, the early antiquarians demonstrated an admirable curiosity and instinctive appreciation for the merits and singularity of historical objects. Ultimately, their attentive regard for the products of the past formed the foundations of both history as a science and the architectural conservation field.

Seventeenth-century European antiquarianism profoundly influenced the arts as well as collectors' activities. Antique Roman ruins functioned as settings for sacred and mythological figural groups in paintings that were rendered with exaggerated grandeur, as Riegl says, "to convey to the beholder the truly baroque contrast between ancient greatness and present degradation."[27] A developing sense of national pride, reinforced by the growing interest in historical study, supported the inclination to venerate the past and its local material remains. Europe's abundant medieval monuments were no longer denigrated but instead received increasing attention from eighteenth-century connoisseurs.

The MOST NOTABLE

ANTIQUITY

OF

GREAT BRITAIN,

Vulgarly called

STONE-HENG,

ON

SALISBURY PLAIN,

RESTORED,

By *INIGO JONES*, Efq; Architect General to the King.

To which are added,

The *CHOREA GIGANTUM,*

OR,

Stone-Heng Reſtored to the *Danes,*

By Doctor *CHARLETON;*

AND

Mr. *Webb's* Vindication of *Stone-Heng* Reſtored,

In Anſwer to Dr. *Charleton's* Reflections;

WITH

OBSERVATIONS upon the Orders and Rules of ARCHITECTURE
in Uſe among the Antient *ROMANS.*

Before the whole are prefixed,

Certain MEMOIRS relating to the LIFE of *INIGO JONES;*
with his Effigies, Engrav'd by *Hollar*; as alſo Dr. *CHARLETON's,*
by *P. Lombart*; and four new Views of STONE-HENG, in its
preſent Situation: With above twenty other Copper-Plates,
and a compleat INDEX to the entire Collection.

LONDON:

Printed for D. BROWNE *Junior,* at the *Black-Swan* without *Temple-Bar,*
and J. WOODMAN and D. LYON, in *Ruffel-Street, Covent-Garden.*

M. DCC. XXV.

◀ **Figure 6-4** The architect Inigo Jones demonstrated the seventeenth-century English antiquarian's view of antiquity in his speculations on the origins and intent of Stonehenge. Title page: *The Most Notable Antiquity of Great Britain, Vulgarly called Stone-Heng, on Salisbury Plain...Restored, by Inigo Jones..."* (1725).

▼ **Figure 6-5** Numerous others wondered as well about Stonehenge, including William Camden, considered Great Britain's first true antiquarian. Camden's own essay on the topic is included in this posthumous edition of Jones's essays on Stonehenge.

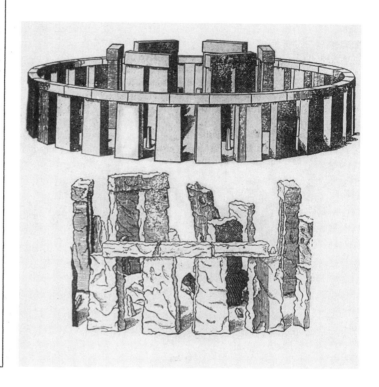

As the European industrial age developed during the eighteenth century, attention focused on "progress" and "the perfectibility of all things." Popular concern for the past receded,[28] and damage and destruction of ancient monuments accelerated as roads and other modern "improvements" were rapidly built to accommodate swelling populations. Factories multiplied, cities grew at a staggering rate, and migration to urban areas introduced new social pressures and economic theories.[29]

Industrialization's continuing advance in nineteenth-century Europe combined with the growing importance of science and created a conflict between the ancient and the modern.[30] Organizations such as William Morris's Society for the Protection of Ancient Buildings provided a forum for traditionalists while advancing the practical concerns of early architectural conservationists. (See also Chapter 9 and Appendix B).

Like the expanding field of historical study, antiquarianism was initially the exclusive province of the well-educated. By the nineteenth century, however, antiquarianism had become a popular diversion in the West, as reflected in the growing market for books on historical topics, an increasing number of museums, and the proliferation of historical societies. One of the earliest, most active, and most influential was the Society of Antiquaries of London. Established in 1580, it eventually acquired a reputation as England's custodian of ancient monuments. For much of its history it was the country's most active pressure group and regularly mobilized its membership to prevent the demolition of medieval remains; the society lists several prominent British conservation architects and architectural historians among its members today.

With the arrival of the twentieth century, the past and its artifacts began to lose much of their luster as antiquarianism's uncritical veneration was replaced by an increasingly rigorous, fact-based historical approach that valued relics only for the information they could provide. Many modern historians share one historian's definition of the distinction between antiquarianism and history writing: "The historian composes a meaning from tradition, while the antiquarian only re-creates, performs, or re-enacts an obscure portion of past time in already familiar shapes."[31] Nonetheless, in the latter part of the twentieth century attention from the mass media boosted popular interest in relics of the past, so much so that world populations are constantly exposed to the "pasts" of practically every place on earth.

ARCHAEOLOGY AS A PATH TO HISTORICAL CERTAINTY

Since its eighteenth-century beginnings, the scientific discipline of archaeology has provided concrete data for historical interpretation. The social context for its development was provided by the pervasive influence of antiquarianism; early archaeologists, in fact, were essentially collectors of relics seeking to fill their cabinets with the romantic remnants of a distant past.

Archaeology's purpose is to study ancient human behavior using the material remains of the past by employing modern techniques and analytical tools designed to yield verifiable results. Its specific objectives are fourfold: to develop cultural histories; to study ancient life ways; to explain why cultures changed in the past; and to conserve the archaeological record

Figure 6-6 Charles Thomas Newton's painstaking efforts to identify and assemble the surviving fragments of the Mausoleum of Maussollos at Halicarnassus (in modern Bodrum, Turkey) and publish his findings in *A History of Discoveries at Halicarnassus, Cnidus and Branchidae* in 1862, represented early scientific archaeological method used in the research of an architectural monument.

for future generations. Archaeology is both aided by, and is a contributor to, history, geography, anthropology, the physical sciences, and other disciplines. It is a profession that benefits from a light touch; both archaeological research work and the conservation of archaeological sites are potentially subject to even more destructive threats than those encountered in the conservation of historic buildings and sites.

Archaeology began to define its own disciplinary territory in Europe, the Americas, and the Middle East during the early nineteenth century. Even then, the field remained essentially underdeveloped despite the groundbreaking work of such pioneers as Austen Henry Layard and his methodical research on Assyria in the 1840s, and Auguste Mariette. François Auguste Ferdinand Mariette's strengths lay more in the office than they did in the field…. While he was not a particularly careful excavator, he was a good first director of the Egyptian Service of Antiquities in the 1870s, where he regularized, systematized, and controlled all excavation and research in Egypt.

Other early shapers of the field include Charles Thomas Newton, who painstakingly tracked down many of the widely dispersed fragments of the Mausoleum of Maussollos at Halicarnassus (in Bodrum, Turkey) and Ernst Curtius and his German colleagues who, at Samothrace and Olympia in Greece, realized the importance of ordinary finds and preserved most all that they excavated. Heinrich Schliemann, inspired by Homeric legends, investigated the origins of Greek civilization at Troy and Mycenae in the 1870s with a sensational find that did much to popularize the notion of archaeology as an exciting and useful scientific pursuit. In the eyes of the public, English archaeologist Howard Carter topped Schliemann's finds at the Mycenaean shaft graves and Troy's early layers with his discovery of the Tomb of Tutankhamen at Luxor's Valley of the Kings in 1929.

Late eighteenth and nineteenth-century archaeology did produce a number of promising demonstrations of innovative scientific methods and field techniques that are impressive even today. Notable is the work of the Swiss engineer Carl Weber at Herculaneum in the 1750s, who kept scrupulous records of his deep excavations. English archaeologist Augustus Henry Pitt-Rivers is considered the father of British archaeology. He was one of the first to perceive the value of precise documentation during excavation of a site. His painstaking, large-scale excavations were conducted on his 29,000-acre estate, Cranborne Chase in Wiltshire, and revealed prehistoric, Roman, and Saxon villages, cemeteries, and burial mounds. A former military man, General Pitt-Rivers was named Great Britain's first inspector of ancient monuments following passage of the Ancient Monuments Protection Act in 1882.

Another great founder of archaeological method from the same period was Flinders Petrie, whose work in Egypt was based on the following principles: "First, care for the monuments being excavated, and respect for future visitors and excavators; Second, meticulous care in excavation and in the collecting and description of everything found; Third, the accurate planning (documentation) of all monuments and excavations; [and] Fourth, the full publication of all excavations as soon as possible."[32]

Archaeology in Eastern Asia originated on the sites of some of the world's most ancient civilizations. From the late nineteenth century, modern archaeological methods began to be utilized in the Yellow River area of China, informed by knowledge of European methodologies being used in French Indochina and British India.

In western Europe, the archaeology of architecture developed as a specialized area of inquiry in the nineteenth century due to a renewed interest in classical and medieval building styles. Partly in reaction to the Renaissance rejection of "brutish" Gothic buildings, parish churches and cathedrals were among the first old buildings in Europe to receive the thorough examinations that archaeology could provide. This was not simply antiquarianism, but the architectural manifestation of the revival of Catholicism—and the Evangelical reaction to it. Restoration was equated with a moral and religious duty.

As the pace of archaeological discoveries picked up in the early twentieth century, new methodologies followed. The development of excavation and research systems included

Figure 6-7 Modern archaeology in Asia was initially informed by methods developed in Europe and North America. The differing nature of some of its finds, such as the famous terra-cotta army of the Emperor Qin Shi Huang at Xi'an, dating from the third century BCE, has produced some specialties in archaeological method and site conservation unique to China.

approaches that are still used today, such as archaeological grids, aerial photography, and the typological analysis of pottery and other finds. After World War II, a range of new technologies was devised to facilitate accurate archaeological research. These evolved into a sophisticated range of advanced techniques: carbon-14 and potassium-argon dating, zooarchaeology, proton magnetometry, and a variety of methods of archaeological prospecting, including magnetometer and electronic resistivity testing and ground penetrating radar.

Among the early twentieth-century archaeologists who reshaped the discipline's theory and methodology, none was more influential than V. Gordon Childe, who focused on large ideas of neolithic and urban revolution. His scholarship focused on how trade contributed to the diffusion of innovation and cultural ways. Other notable archaeologists of our time include Grahame Clark, who was concerned with ecological settings; Mortimer Wheeler, for his contributions to excavation technique; Gordon Willey, for his work in the Americas and culture history; and Lewis Binford and Ian Hodder, for their contributions to theory.

Figure 6-8 Modern technologies applied to archaeology have included the acquisition of ground-penetrating radar images of the historic city of Angkor, Cambodia, taken from the space shuttle *Endeavor* in November 1994. The results revealed new information about the ancient megalopolis and broadened the interests of several archaeologists, historians, planners, and cultural heritage experts. *(Image: JPL/NASA)*

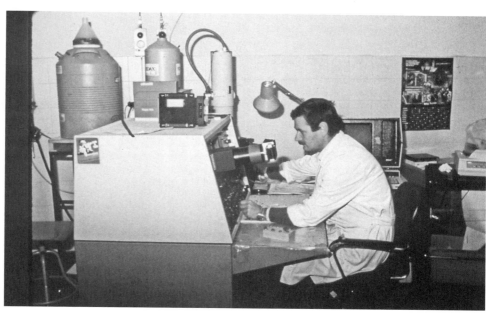

Figure 6-9 The Misericordia Laboratory established on the island of San Giorgio in Venice in 1971 was the first architectural conservation laboratory there. The building conversion and equipment were funded by the New York–based Samuel H. Kress Foundation in partnership with the World Monuments Fund.

Today, archaeology focuses as much on the cultures that produced the sites and artifacts as it does on the surviving material evidence. In the past decade especially, archaeology has widely established its role in cultural heritage conservation practice. American archaeologist Susan Alcock and Australian archaeologist Lynn Meskell point to examples of heritage consciousness in ancient societies. Meskell has also raised questions about the traditional practices of foreign archaeological expeditions and their effects on host countries and cultures. Individual practitioners and museums alike are rethinking archaeology's traditional role in the sourcing of new collections, especially those removed to other countries.[33] Such trends draw archaeology, as well as its related fields of anthropology and sociology, well within the purview of cultural heritage conservation. The multidisciplinary nature of these fields has been there all along, but the trend is now global, and the future promises yet more interdisciplinary analysis and its benefits.

The emergence of architectural conservation as a profession in Europe and the Americas in the 1960s was due in large part to extensive developments in conservation science and technology. This technical side of the profession developed from the work of a few art restorers, scientists, restoration architects, and engineers and became in many ways the core of the field today. The specialized methodologies of architectural conservation science grew to meet the needs of architectural monuments protection. That growth—and its applications—was remarkable: it has both kept up with and served well a burgeoning demand, all while developing simultaneously in several different places.

Modern conservation science and its practical applications in Europe and the Americas derive from four major sources: conservation traditions associated with collecting and museum collections management; building industries over the past century; observations and importations from elsewhere; and firsthand experiences in technical problem solving by restoration architects, chemists, engineers, archaeologists, and craftspeople. It was this latter group, in particular, whose job it was to preserve authentic historic fabric (materials and historic building systems) at architectural conservation projects in which they were involved.

Since the main objective of architectural conservation practice is to slow or arrest the decay process, that is, to extend the lives of objects, the task often entails sophisticated technical intervention. Adding to the challenge is that each building material has its own physical characteristics, each with its own range of possible solutions. (See Chapter 8.)

It is in sources other than this book that the full range of scientific and technical solutions for architectural conservation is covered. Examples include Bernard Feilden's *Conservation of Historic Buildings*, Martin E. Weaver's *Conserving Buildings*, the Butterworth-Heinemann series on architectural conservation edited by John Ashurst, Giorgio Croci's *The Conservation and Structural Restoration of Architectural Heritage*, Harold James Plenderleith's *The Conservation of Antiquities and Works of Art*, and a plethora of journals and occasional publications such as the journal of the Association for Preservation Technology (*APT Bulletin*), *The Architectural Conservation Journal*, the publications of the International Institute for Conservation of Historic and Artistic Works, and the technical brief series of Technical Preservation Services, a department of the National Park Service. It is among these sources and others, including well-indexed bibliographies on the World Wide Web, that constantly evolving developments in architectural conservation science and methodology are best researched. (See Appendices B and D.)

It is likely that the earliest competent restorers involved in the scientific aspects of architectural conservation learned their craft on sculpture and paintings and the occasional need to blend old and new in the repair or adaptation of earlier buildings. Restoring and conserving works of art dates to at least the Italian Renaissance, when European restorers were themselves artists who became experienced in the repair and restoration of damaged works of art.[34] Along the way the attendant issues of theory and technique, and the wider implications of both, evolved. Questions from the beginning must have included how to preserve authenticity, deal with *lacunae* (missing elements), distinguish old from new, and use restoration materials effectively. These issues are of great importance to a project's success in both art and architectural conservation; thus it is not surprising that as expertise in these matters grew, specialties in restoration and conservation science developed.

As the specialty artist-restorer's techniques for treating objects evolved to become a discipline in its own right (often associated with museums and at academic institutions), its early practitioners—restorers, scientists, and technicians—developed abilities for addressing *immovable heritage*—buildings. Some early names in the formative years of modern European art and architectural conservation included the Swiss Italian brothers Gaspare and Giuseppe Fossati, who restored the mosaics and painted finishes of Hagia Sophia in Istanbul in the 1840s. Succeeding generations of pioneers in architectural conservation science and technology included Belgians Albert Philippot and the director of the Institut Royal du Patrimoine Artistique in Brussels Paul Coremans; Italians Roberto Longhi, Piero Sanpaolesi, Cesare Brandi, Giorgio Torraca, and Paolo and Laura Mora; and Harold James Plenderleith of the British Museum, later the first director of the International Centre for the Study of the Preservation and Restoration of Cultural Property (ICCROM), from 1959 to 1971. Some early art and architectural conservation experts in the United States included George Stout and Rutherford Gettens of the Fogg Art Museum[35] and Craig Hugh Smythe, Sheldon Keck, and Lawrence Majewski, who were all associated with prominent museums or universities.[36] As the larger field of architectural conservation developed from the mid-twentieth century forward, the work of these pioneers grew in importance, and their students and others who followed went on to define and populate the robust field of architectural conservation science and technology that exists today.

From the 1980s on, specializations in conservation science were seated at national or regional institutes such as the Laboratoire de Recherche des Monuments Historiques in Paris; the Geological Institute of the Rheinish-Westfälische Technische Hochschule (RWTH) in Aachen, Germany; the Center for Architectural Conservation of the Austrian Federal Office for the Care of Monuments (Bundesdenkmalamt) in Mauerbach, Austria; at English Heritage in the United Kingdom; and the distinguished Opeficio delle Pietre Dure (OPD) in Florence. Other national or university-based initiatives included the German and Austrian nationwide stone conservation surveys that began in the 1970s and lasted over a decade, the Istituto Centrali per il Restauro in Rome, the Riksantikvarieämbetet (National Heritage Board) of Sweden, the conservation facilities of the Middle Eastern Technical University in Ankara, Turkey, and the Tokyo Research Institute. Most of these institutions were and remain state-supported organizations of scientists and scholars responsible for the scientific aspects of the protection of state monuments.

In the Americas, the national agencies devoted to conservation science within the United States began the conservation facilities of the US National Park Service at Independence Park in Philadelphia. Under the aegis of Technical Preservation Services, a department of the US National Park Service, the National Center for Preservation Technology and Training in Natchitoches, Louisiana, presently serves this function. Its counterpart in Canada is the Canadian Conservation Institute of Heritage Canada; in Mexico, the Instituto Nacional de Antropología e Historia in Churubusco; and in Peru, the National Institute of Culture. Beyond the nationally oriented work of these institutions and others like them is a supranational capacity that exists in two key forms: the ICCROM laboratory in Rome, which serves projects and countries with which ICCROM is involved, and the scientific and technical expertise represented worldwide by the network of national and scientific committees of ICOMOS. (See Appendix B.)

The building industry also played a key role in the development of conservation sciences, as its specialists within the research and development branches of product manufacturers responded to markets needs. The industry has made considerable contributions in the areas of masonry, wood, glass, and paint conservation. Various independent chem-

ists, scientists, and technicians became associated with the field through their interests in the building trades. The proliferation of the architectural restoration and preservation industry throughout Europe, the Americas, East Asia, the Indian subcontinent, and Australia is reflected in the increasing number of specialty publications and mentions of conservation projects in more mainstream architectural publications.

The transfer of knowledge in architectural conservation science is one of the field's most impressive characteristics. For instance, American fact-finding missions to Europe in the early 1960s to observe architectural restoration practices brought back news of established government commitment to—and schools training in—architectural conservation practices that served as models. Today, scientists and restorers who relocate or travel in relation to their work continue to share new ideas with their colleagues. But by far the most effective means of transmitting information on conservation science and practice has been through formal educational training. (See Chapters 15 and 16.)

Today's practice of architectural conservation science and technology is served by several professional interest groups, including the scientific committees of the International Council on Monuments and Sites (ICOMOS), the International Institute for Conservation of Historic and Artistic Works (IIC), and the Association for Preservation Technology (APT). Two major institutions on both the American and international scenes are the Getty Conservation Institute (GCI) in Los Angeles and its counterpart in Canada, the Canadian Conservation Institute (CCI).

As important as developments in materials conservation science is its application. As in all good science, most technical conservation applications have been learned through experimentation (developments in masonry cleaning is a good example). Conservation science—an exemplar of applied scientific methodology—serves as the basis of cultural heritage protection today precisely because conservation scientists have cooperated with each other, sharing information with the building trades and at professional conferences and journals. In light of the thousands of often sizable—and expensive—conservation projects undertaken annually, it is clear why conservation science and technology have so distinguished the entire field of cultural heritage protection.

HISTORY AND HERITAGE CONSERVATION

Like history, the cultural legacy known as *heritage* is concerned with past events, physical remains, and human relationships. The two endeavors have different purposes, however, with important implications for the conservation of historic buildings and sites. Despite historiography's limitations, pursuit of the "truth" about the past is history's mandate. Heritage, in contrast, presents the past for public consumption as an enriching and entertaining experience, and in so doing selectively modifies the established facts of the past to convey a clarity that history never had.

An increased awareness of built cultural heritage and its conservation in the nineteenth century coincided with the professionalization of history. In western Europe, the unease created by the Industrial Revolution and the sense that excessive materialism might erode spiritual values motivated much of the aggressive restoration activity that characterized the late nineteenth century. Restoration was understood as correcting mistakes made by preceding generations and regularizing the decay, patina, and stylistic muddle that reflected a building's history.

As continuing industrialization changed Europe's social structure and exploded urban populations, its architects and historians more fully realized the value of the irreplaceable corpus of fine old buildings that had been inherited from the past. The need to develop legal means to protect historic structures from the ever-present threat of destruction emerged and in many places gained a new sense of urgency. Critics of heavy-handed restoration such as John Ruskin and William Morris were sensitive to the historical integrity of old buildings and objected to prevailing restoration practices. Ruskin maintained that attempts to "improve" the definition of detail and the regularity of finish transformed and diminished the aesthetic character of the entire building. Morris pointed out the subjectivity and hypocrisy of treating historic buildings in this way. (See also Chapter 14.)

The possibility to distort historical facts remains in the twenty-first century; it occurs more often where period restoration is practiced, however, and is minimized where events of major historical significance have occurred. Even so, at sites deemed historic as the result of a single event, preservation decisions seem straightforward. For example, Ford's Theatre in Washington, DC, where President Abraham Lincoln was assassinated on April 14, 1865, has been restored to its appearance on that night. At the fifteenth-century Vistulamouth Fortress in Gdansk, Poland, the first shots of World War II were fired on September 1, 1939, by the German ship *Schleswig-Holstein*. The enormity of the event led to the erection of an imposing bronze monument. While both sites may eventually gather other interesting associations, these two primary facts of history will never be erased.

For heritage conservation professionals approaching sites with more layered pasts and with multiple significant historical associations, deciding which event is to be memorialized and why can be a complicated question. Indeed, all historic buildings are far more than a simple historical document. Inflexible attachment to the literal facts of their history limits their potential to be perceived as vital contributions to their environment. Conservation projects that take into account the complexity of a site and that include broad and accessible information about the past utilize the value of history more fully. In the words of Paul Philippot, the prominent Belgian art historian and former director of ICCROM, architectural conservation can lessen the gap between the past and present.[37]

David Lowenthal goes further, saying that a unified view of the past promotes pride in one's membership in a group and adherence to that group's cultural values. He characterizes heritage as a "declaration of faith"[38] in the past that is being presented, whether through historic buildings, battle reenactments, historic villages, films, or the myriad other expressions of contemporary heritage consciousness. "The heritage fashioner," he writes, "...seeks to design a past that will fix the identity and enhance the well-being of some chosen individual or folk."[39]

Kevin Lynch is undoubtedly correct in noting that "preservation is not simply the saving of old things but the maintaining of a response to those things."[40] The popularity of cultural heritage today is due to its capacity to distill the complexity of the past into a coherent message that speaks to present values and implies their reassuring continuation into the future. At its best, the conservation of architectural and other kinds of cultural heritage can—as Lynch continues—craft a valuable "social image of time which enlarges, celebrates, and vivifies the present, while increasing its significant connections with the past and especially with the future."[41]

RELATED READINGS

Breisach, Ernst. *Historiography: Ancient, Medieval & Modern.* 2nd ed. Chicago: University of Chicago Press, 1994.

Choay, Françoise. *The Invention of the Historic Monument.* Translated by Lauren M. O'Connell. Cambridge: Cambridge University Press, 2001.

Conti, Alessandro. *Storia del restauro e della conservazione delle opera d'arte.* Milan: Biblioteca Electra, 1988.

Denslagen, Wim, and Neils Gutschow, eds. *Architectural Imitations: Reproductions and Pastiches in East and West.* Maastricht, Netherlands.: Shaker Publishing, 2005.

Fitch, James Marston. *Historic Preservation: Curatorial Management of the Built World.* Charlottesville, VA: University of Virginia Press, 1990.

Getty Conservation Institute. Research on the Values of Heritage. Los Angeles: Getty Conservation Institute, 2000. http://www.getty.edu/conservation/field_projects/values/.

Huntington, Samuel P. *The Clash of Civilizations and the Remaking of World Order.* New York: Simon & Schuster, 1998.

Jokilehto, Jukka. *A History of Architectural Conservation.* Oxford: Butterworth-Heinemann, 1999.

Kubler, George. *The Shape of Time: Remarks on the History of Things.* New Haven, CT: Yale University Press, 1962.

Laurence Kanter, "The Reception and Non-Reception of Cesare Brandi in America," *Future Anterior: Journal of Historic Preservation; History, Theory and Criticism* 4, no. 1 (Summer 2007): 31–34; Frank G. Matero, "Loss, Compensation, and Authenticity: The Contribution of Cesare Brandi to Architectural Conservation in America," *Future Anterior* 4, no. 1 (Summer 2007): 45–63.

Lowenthal, David. *The Heritage Crusade and the Spoils of History.* Cambridge: Cambridge University Press, 1998.

———. *The Past is a Foreign Country.* Cambridge: Cambridge University Press, 1985.

Lynch, Kevin. *What Time Is This Place?* Cambridge, MA: MIT Press, 1972.

Marks, Stephen, ed. *Concerning Buildings: Studies in Honor of Sir Bernard Feilden.* Oxford: Butterworth Heinmann, 1996.

Meskell, Lynn, ed. *Archaeology Under Fire: Nationalism, Politics and Heritage in the Eastern Mediterranean and Middle East.* London: Routledge, 1998

Riegl, Alois. "The Modern Cult of Monuments: Its Character and Its Origin." Translated by Kurt W. Forster and Diane Ghirardo. *Oppositions* 25 (Fall 1982): 21–51.

Robertson, Roland. *Globalization: Social Theory and Global Culture.* Thousand Oaks, CA: Sage Publications, 1992.

Schama, Simon. *Landscape and Memory.* London: Harper Collins, 1995.

Stanley-Price, Nicholas, M. Kirby Talley, Jr., and Allesandra Melucco Vaccaro, eds. *Historical and Philosophical Issues in the Conservation of Cultural Heritage.* Readings in Conservation. Los Angeles: Getty Conservation Institute, 1996.

Stille, Alexander. *The Future of the Past.* New York: Farrar, Straus and Giroux, 2002.

Tomlan, Michael A., ed. *Preservation of What, for Whom? A Critical Look at Historical Significance.* Ithaca, NY: National Council for Preservation Education, 1998.

Tung, Anthony M. *Preserving the World's Great Cities: The Destruction and Renewal of the Historic Metropolis.* New York: Clarkson Potter, 2001.

UNESCO. Convention Concerning the Protection of the World Cultural and Natural Heritage [World Heritage Convention]. http://whc.unesco.org/pg.cfm?cid=175.

Endnotes

1. Alexander Stille, *The Future of the Past*, 312–39.

2. Even earlier if one takes into account works by Dante and Petrarch based on ancient texts.

3. George Kubler, *The Shape of Time*, 12.

4. Ernst Breisach, *Historiography*, 2.

5. Lowenthal, *Past is a Foreign Country*, 241.

6. Kevin Lynch, *What Time Is This Place?* 121–22.

7. Michael Hunter, "Preconditions of Preservation," in *Our Past Before Us: Why Do We Save It?* ed. David Lowenthal and Marcus Binney (London: Temple Smith, 1981), 17.

8. Bernie Kernot, "Maori Artists of Time Before," in *Te Maori: Maori Art from New Zealand Collections*, ed. Sidney Moko Mead (New York: Harry N. Abrams, 1984), 155.

9. Mary Nooter Roberts and Allen F. Roberts, "Mapping Memory," in *Memory: Luba Art and the Making of History*, ed. Mary Nooter Roberts and Allen F. Roberts (New York: Prestel USA, 1996), 144.

10. Jokilehto, *History of Architectural Conservation*, 3.

11. As Breisach comments, "[Flavio Biondo's] enthusiasm for the skilled use of nonliterary remainders of the past stimulated the rise of the antiquarian movement, which in time would enhance the scope of historiography, strengthen the importance and awareness of primary sources, and evoke in historians a sense of the wholeness of past life" (Breisach, *Historiography*, 156).

12. Riegl, "The Modern Cult of Monuments," 26–29.

13. As science presented developmental interpretations of natural phenomena, philosophers and historians increasingly argued for interpretations of history based on the idea of humankind's progress toward greater perfection. As Breisach said, "Past, present, and future were once more linked in a development with a common direction, this time not towards a spiritual goal"—as in the medieval past—"but towards human betterment in this world" (Breisach, *Historiography*, 205).

    An important competing view of history was proposed by Giambattista Vico (1668–1744) in his *New Science 1725* (trans. Thomas Goddard Bergin, Max Harold Fisch, Cornell University, Ithaca, NY: 1970). Challenging the assumption that reason alone could reveal truth and lead to a permanent state of progress, Vico argued for a dynamic model of history based on the observation of human behavior in groups. Like Voltaire, Vico maintained that cultural practices were both learned and variable. Belief in an unchanging human nature was incorrect; different historical ages were expressed in a diversity of cultures, and monuments were the direct evidence of the human past. Vico's work formed a cornerstone for the development of the historicist view that became prominent in the nineteenth century.

14. Baker, *Living with the Past*, 28.

15. Martha Howell and Walter Prevenier, *From Reliable Sources: An Introduction to Historical Methods* (Ithaca, NY: Cornell University Press, 2001), 12.

16. Georg G. Iggers, "Historicism," in *Dictionary of the History of Ideas: Studies of Selected Pivotal Ideas*, ed. Philip P. Wiener (New York: Scribner, 1973–74), 2:458.

17. Hunter, "Preconditions of Preservation," in Lowenthal and Binney, *Our Past Before Us*, 28.

18. "The principal argument of the historical relativists," as historian Peter Novick describes it, "was that so far as they could see, historical interpretations always had been, and for various technical reasons always would be, 'relative' to the historian's time, place, values, and purposes" (Novick, *That Noble Dream: The "Objectivity" Question and the American Historical Profession* [Cambridge: Cambridge University Press, 1988], 166).

19. Breisach, *Historiography*, 329.

20. Howell and Prevenier, *From Reliable Sources*, 46.

21. Ibid., 53.

22. Lowenthal, *Past is a Foreign Country*, 216.

23. David Lowenthal, *The Heritage Crusade*, 110.

24. Lowenthal, *Heritage Crusade*, 113.

25. Kubler, *The Shape of Time*, 12.

26. Lowenthal, *The Past is a Foreign Country*, 57.

27. Riegl, "The Modern Cult of Monuments," 31.

28. Hunter, "Preconditions of Preservation," in Lowenthal and Binney, *Our Past Before Us*, 26.

29. In its teleological design, Marx's theory of class struggle mirrored the structure of the revolutionary philosophy of history formulated by Georg Wilhelm Friedrich Hegel (1770–1831). Human history began when an abstract, impersonal Idea, or pure thought, first manifested itself in time as Spirit (*geist*). This manifestation, or thesis, took the concrete form of a particular society with its moral, cultural, and political "spirit," Hegel's famous *zeitgeist*.

30. According to Lowenthal, Victorian Britons took refuge against "the evils of rampant change and the dangers posed by the new industrial order" by "extravagantly re-creating architecture, art, and literature…. By the turn of [the twentieth] century the past had lost its exemplary and pedagogical justification but continued to supply intimate connections with pre-industrial ways of life" (Lowenthal, *Past is a Foreign Country*, 102).

31. Kubler, *The Shape of Time*, 13.

32. Glyn Daniel, *150 Years of Archaeology* (London: Duckworth, 1978), 175.

33. The success rate of recent claims by ministries of culture in Turkey, Italy, Egypt, and other countries for the restitution of antiquities in foreign hands that are thought to have been illicitly acquired will likely continue to affect museum acquisition policies and the antiquities trade.

34. The Florentine artist Giorgio Vasari refers to restorations of both buildings and paintings in his *Lives of the Artists* (1568) (New York: Oxford University Press, 1988).

35. George Wheeler (lecture, Historic Preservation Theory and Practice course, Columbia University Graduate School of Architecture, Planning and Preservation [GSAPP], New York, NY, November 10, 2006).

36. Namely the Fogg Art Museum at Harvard University, the Metropolitan Museum of Art in New York, and New York University.

37. Paul Philippot, "Restoration from the Perspective of the Humanities," in *Historical and Philosophical Issues in the Conservation of Cultural Heritage*, 225.

38. Lowenthal, *The Heritage Crusade*, 121.

39. Ibid., xi.

40. Lynch, *What Time Is This Place?* 53.

41. Ibid., 134.

PART II

Problems, Principles, and Process

Author's note: Due to the lengthy nature of this subject, examples of a number of points are further cited and elaborated on in this section's endnotes.

Today's architectural conservation field is faced with several paradoxes. One is that the widespread appreciation of historic buildings and sites engenders the satellite threats of large-scale tourism and physical interventions that such usage may require. When historic buildings and sites are restored or rehabilitated and adapted to economically viable new uses, the necessary interventions are often both radical and complicated. Bonnie Burnham, president of the World Monuments Fund, has described the special concerns faced by architectural conservation professionals, arguing that their task is even more complicated than the conservation of movable heritage. According to Burnham:

> *The main issues [in objects conservation] are authenticity, integrity and appropriate use…whereas architectural conservation must address two special additional concerns: continuity of function—the preservation whenever possible of the uses for which a structure was intended or the visual and architectural evidence of that function; and sustainability—self-sufficient community use within its original context.*[1]

These and many other practical and philosophical concerns inform every decision made in architectural conservation practice. Not only does today's heritage protection field require a clear understanding of the theoretical issues that underlie it, but a cumulative, in-depth knowledge of available scientific methods and technologies is also indispensable to the conservation professional. Remaining up-to-date in state-of-the-art architectural conservation techniques and technologies requires diligence, because knowledge of experiences in the field—including information about applications that did *not* work—develops rapidly.

Figure 7-1 A craftsman restoring exterior stucco work at Gostiny Dvor, the historic central market building in St. Petersburg, Russia.

CHAPTER 7

Perils to Built Heritage

The work of architectural conservation is challenged by a multitude of threats to the built environment. The destructive forces that threaten architectural heritage are both natural and manmade; in recent centuries, however, the effects of humans on the environment have proven more complicated and extensive. These threats can be instantaneous and dramatic, such as earthquakes or terrorist attacks, but are more often gradual and barely perceptible, such as the deterioration of stone building materials by pollutants, the decay of wood in damp climates, or the effects of climate change.

It is essential to understand what causes the physical aspects of cultural property to deteriorate and weaken in order to make an accurate and effective conservation diagnosis. Finding solutions for causal effects calls mainly upon deductive reasoning coupled with careful observation, training and experience, scientific analysis, and common sense. The testing and careful experimentation of various solutions is immeasurably beneficial.

AN EVOLUTION OF AWARENESS

Of all the works of art and architecture that have been produced, those that remain today represent a mere fraction of what could have survived had more care been taken to preserve them. Even today, considerable numbers of the world's historic buildings and sites are destroyed annually. At the same time, however, the odds of survival for the best, the most representative, and the most useful examples of art and architecture are far greater today than ever before because of the increased potency of the heritage conservation movement.

In the past, most civilizations tended to condemn that of their predecessors, and little prevented the continuous destruction and replacement of their objects and sites. In Japan and China, it was customary for each succeeding ruler or dynasty to build a new palace — and often a new capital. Before the current Parthenon was constructed on the Athenian Acropolis, two previous temples on the site had been successively razed. In medieval Eu-

Figure 7-2 Remains of an entablature depicting Christian motifs from the church that preceded the Hagia Sophia in Istanbul; that church dated from 415 CE.

rope, numerous Romanesque churches gave way to Gothic ones, which were in turn extensively renovated or replaced several centuries later by churches built in the classical style. Globally, there are numerous examples of the religious architecture of one faith replacing another.[2] To name just one, the place where the Hagia Sofia stands today in Istanbul was the site of earlier religious structures of the same and other faiths. This is the case for other building types and town architecture in general; numerous earlier settlements—now almost completely lost—flourished beneath the centers of Paris, Naples, Beijing, Mexico City, and New York.

Nevertheless, throughout history there is also an abundance of examples of conservation-minded actions taken to preserve objects, buildings, and sites. It is the sum total of these experiences that has changed popular attitudes toward the architectural and artistic treasures of the past. The enlightened worldview that developed in the Renaissance in the West and in the mid-nineteenth century in the Americas and parts of Asia increasingly recognized the practical benefits of conserving historic buildings. What began as an occasional interest in preserving the more remarkable monuments of the classical past in southern Europe was followed by considerable interest in restoring the more monumental religious buildings from the Gothic period. An interest in conserving examples from all historic periods followed and progressively expanded to encompass an increasing variety of building types, including ordinary buildings that served remarkable historical personages or events and groups of buildings without exceptional aesthetic merits that contributed to the special character of a historic place. Eventually, the built environment became inextricably linked to the surrounding natural site as the interest grew to include restoring and conserving *historic gardens* and human-made landscapes.

Classifying the types of perils facing historic buildings and sites is made difficult by the emergence of new threats and the many variations of known threats (e.g., mechanized pumping of groundwater for modern industrial use can alter the water table below historic buildings and lead to differential settlement of the soil, which in turn leads to the progressive deterioration of other building components, including wall, floor, and roof joints, and ultimately affects the building's interior finishes). Defining risk is further complicated when several problems occur simultaneously (e.g., a combination of weather-related masonry failure, inexpert earlier restoration, and poor maintenance), a frequent occurrence.[3] There can also be sequential cause-and-effect actions: a postearthquake fire, or the loss of potentially reusable building components due to their removal in a postdisaster cleanup process.

Irrespective of the types of threats to historic architectural resources, the creation and enforcement of protective legal and administrative measures is one route to finding answers to many of these perils. The Council of Europe, which has been concerned with heritage conservation since the 1960s,[4] considers an administrative division of powers to be essential. In many cases, the nature of governmental heritage protection involves the ministries of culture, education, tourism, and domestic affairs, and at times also the national ministries of finance and foreign affairs. Some countries have mandated religious

Figure 7-3 Armenia's wealth of early Christian architecture is mostly in ruins. The Cathedral of T'alin (seventh century CE) and scores of similar sites around the country could be featured again as stops along a revived system of cultural heritage trails that was established in the 1960s.

authorities to oversee historic religious sites.[5] These additional layers of oversight are best viewed as added protection.

Despite such layered administrative responsibilities, additional funding for cultural heritage conservation is needed in every country, a situation that is expected to persist for the foreseeable future.[6] The availability of funding for cultural heritage conservation will always depend on national budgetary priorities at every level of government, even in the wealthiest countries. Ironically, the abundance of heritage sites in need in some poorer countries, such as Cambodia and Armenia, offers them their greatest hope for an improved economy through tourism.[7]

THE DESTRUCTIVE ACTIONS OF TIME AND NATURE

No structure can escape natural decay. All building materials are vulnerable to deterioration over time with some materials, such as wood, being more vunerable than others. In Turkey, for example, sixteenth- and seventeenth-century Ottoman-era wooden structures are rare, but there are many surviving contemporaneous mosques and palaces, which were built to impress and to last longer, constructed of stone.

Nature's destructive forces have always greatly affected cultures, historic buildings, and landscapes. The violence of these forces is unchanged over time, although modern forecasting techniques can mitigate the related loss of human life and property.[8] Unfortunately, a few days' or hours' notice can do little to lessen damage to significant works of immovable architecture and landscapes. More radical preventative measures, such as cinctures, structural reinforcing—even the mounting of entire buildings on shock absorbers—to strengthen buildings in earthquake zones have proven helpful, although often of limited effect.

Among the most destructive natural forces are:

- *Avalanches, landslides, and glacial movements.* Hilly areas where natural water-drainage patterns have been altered by modern development are especially susceptible to landslides.

- *Hurricanes, tsunamis, raging winds, and storms.*[9] Islands and coastal settlements are obviously at greatest risk from these threats.

- *Earthquakes.* These occur with relative frequency in countries along tectonic plate fault lines.[10]

- *Volcanic eruptions.*[11] Volcanoes are frequently located along tectonic plate edges, although there are significant exceptions.

- *Floods.* While floods due to torrential rains are a natural phenomenon, they can also be caused or exacerbated by human decisions: the alteration of land areas for agriculture; the damming of a river; the alteration of tributary flows or runoff patterns.[12]

- *Fire.*[13] Fires can result from lightning strikes on a drought-stricken landscape or from human carelessness—preventable fires that are especially tragic.[14]

Nature's impact on cultural patrimony does not need to be violent to be threatening. In addition to the effects of nature's sudden destructive forces, exposure to the elements (including sun, wind, rain, and temperature change) over long periods of time can cause serious damage to the built environment.

Climatic effects are determined by localized topography along with a variety of natural physical actions including solar radiation variances, temperature and thermal expansion, moisture action, and wind erosion.[15] All of these conditions concern architectural conservation professionals, who must not only take them into account but must also be aware of the rare instances when extreme conditions could occur over longer periods of time.

Effective architectural conservation requires a solid knowledge of conservation science and a good understanding of the pathologies of building materials. For example, water is the chief culprit in the deterioration of historic buildings, whether its source is precipitation, rising damp (moisture rising from below via capillary action through building foundations), forced moisture movement laterally or from below (aided by hydrostatic pressures), or condensation and atmospheric moisture. Moisture traveling through building materials can not only degrade plaster and painted finishes but may also carry harmful salts that can cause unsightly and at times damaging spalling and efflorescence.[16]

Annual temperature variations can also be destructive, especially in regions that suffer extreme climatic changes. For example, the building materials and construction techniques used in Hungary's rich architectural heritage are considerably stressed by cyclical temperature extremes, from over 86°F (30°C) in the summer to a winter low of –4°F (–20°C). Finnish log structures are particularly susceptible to freeze-thaw cycles and the associated actions of expansion and contraction that occur during Scandinavia's harsh winters.

Another natural danger for historic structures is organic: lichens, molds, fungi, trees, and plants. Cambodia's famous tree-enshrined temples of Ta Prohm and Preah Khan (See Fig. 7.5) at Angkor impressively demonstrates the relentless power of nature. Over centuries, tropical vines and trees have taken root in crevices between its stonework and, as they grow, are dislocating its large, built components.

Other natural destructive agents include animals and insects such as deathwatch beetles, powder-post beetles, carpenter bees, termites, and marine borers. Natural residues left by animals and birds, and damage caused by their presence, are also deleterious.

Figure 7-4 Four of many natural threats to architectural heritage: a. the total destruction by fire of a commercial building in Monroe, Louisiana, in 1968; b. flood damage in Teunom, Indonesia, after the 2004 tsunami; c. earthquake damage in Mexico City (1985); and d. biodeterioration. *(Tsunami image: AFP Photo/ CHOO Youn-Kong 2005)*

Of all the risks—both human made and natural—that architectural heritage conservationists face globally, the one that poses the most serious threat in the long run is probably climate change. The *greenhouse effect* is caused primarily by the release of fluorocarbon, carbon dioxide, and methane gases into the earth's atmosphere. Global climate change has in recent years been proven to be gradually altering the mean temperature of all places in the world. The rate of change remains a matter of debate, although few would disagree that unless adequate measures are taken to address the issue on a global scale, average temperatures will continue to increase.

This phenomenon is expected to have a major impact on the world's cultural heritage in ways that are still being determined by a growing body of experts. Most at risk will be low-lying coastal cities and towns vulnerable to flooding like Venice and New Orleans, where problems already exist. Poised for serious trouble are coastal regions in Bangladesh and Myanmar and island countries such as the Maldives and scores of others in the Indian Ocean and the South Pacific. In places that have coped well with extreme tidal conditions in the past, such as the Netherlands and London, prospects of expensive additional protection measures are of serious concern. Even a very slight increase in average annual temperature has been proven to affect ice melt in the polar regions and high-altitude countries in the Alps and Himalayas. The silting of shallow water bodies, a reduction of freshwater sources, changing farming patterns, and increased desertification will affect vulnerable human-shaped environments, both new and old, which number in the thousands. The Scientific Council Cultural Heritage and Global Climate Change Working Group of the International Council on Monuments and Sites (ICOMOS), an interdisciplinary body, has been researching the effects of climate change on specific historic building materials, building typologies, and intangible heritage.[17]

Among greatest concerns are changing socioeconomic conditions, as most scenarios do not bode well for the conservation of historic cultural resources. For instance, what happens when populations that sustain historic places are displaced due to a reduction of available freshwater or higher food and energy costs? There is a reduction in the viability of such places—and in the priority for maintaining them—perhaps leading to their demise. In countries where financial resources are already limited or where extraordinary burdens, such as inadequate food supply, disease, and civil unrest already exist, cultural heritage conservation priorities often wither to nothing.

A veritable catalogue raisonné of these kinds of threats and discussions of each are found in the writings of conservation architect and engineer Bernard Feilden, notably in his *Conservation of Historic Buildings*.[18] In it, he poses several questions that are central to the decision of how to conserve threatened or damaged architectural heritage: What are the weaknesses and strengths inherent in the structural design and the component materials of the object? What are the possible natural agents of deterioration that could affect the component materials? How rapid is their action? What are the possible human agents of deterioration that could affect the component materials or structure? How much of their effort can be reduced at source?[19]

DESTRUCTIVE ACTIONS OF HUMANS

The permanent and universal dangers that time and nature represent to the global built patrimony are magnified by the presence of humankind. Perils wrought by humans fall into one of three categories: ancillary effects of modern life (pollution, economic, religious, social, or lifestyle changes); willful calculations (vandalism, war, or terrorism-related destruction); and oversights (ignorance, neglect, profligate use of natural resources, or insensitive or inadequate work).

Figure 7-5 The growth of trees and ground vegetation at many of the temples in the historic city of Angkor affects its monumental remains in a variety of ways. They provide more stable microenvironmental havens from Cambodia's harsh climate, aiding in preservation; however, the root and trunk growth and falling trees also do damage.

Ancillary Effects of Modernity

The radical changes of modern life have subjected the world's cultural patrimony to a number of dangers. It is no mere coincidence that the architectural conservation field has grown in tandem with the developments of the eighteenth- and nineteenth-century industrial and technological revolutions and the plethora of additional developments broadly called "modernization" that followed. The life changes made possible by mechanization, mass production, vastly improved communications and transportation systems, and some government-sponsored development schemes have radically changed the world's historic built environment, both for better and for worse.[20] The main result has been a complete revolution in the spatial distribution of most of the world's populations from rural to urban settings, irrevocably changing land settlement patterns that had existed in some places for thousands of years.

Decay of cultural heritage sites related to modernization is a problem that has no easy solution. The same forces that threaten historic sites and the life ways of those who sustain them are often also sources of financial support and generators of increased interest. This applies not only to tourism and increased economic activity but also to the social and religious changes that have taken place in recent decades.

According to Anthony Tung, who has dubbed the twentieth century "The Century of Destruction," residents of the world's greatest metropolises systematically demolished huge percentages of their own cities during that time. Tung notes that though only eight cities had over one million inhabitants in 1900, by 2000, 323 cities did, and that "early in the twenty-first century, for the first time in history, more people will live inside cities than outside them."[21] The building demands of this population explosion and shift combined with the preferences and ideals of the modern movement in architecture have long been seen as detrimental to most existing urban architectural sites. In addition, the by-products of modernization, urbanization, and industrialization—such as pollution as well as economic and social change)—have had an effect on cultural heritage well beyond the world's cities.

Technological Change

The positive side of the technological changes of the past few centuries is the vast improvement in health, education, and amenities they have facilitated for millions of people. Industrialization's economic and social developments have eased life's burdens for nearly every human being. Inexpensive computers, radically improved methods of communications, and vastly improved transportation systems connect distant regions of the world. New concepts of leisure time for a record number of today's workers permits their travel to historic sites. Unfortunately, there remain imbalances among those who can enjoy these benefits. Further, the increased demands for the fulfillment of these new lifestyles and the development costs of an industrialized world—such as land and resource exploitation and pollution—have been detrimental to the historic built environment.

Transportation

Motorized transport—a fact of modern life—has, probably more than any other single factor, negatively affected the historic built environment. Historic enclaves, towns, and cities simply did not envision the volume of motorized traffic, especially passenger automobiles, that has grown at astonishing rates. Modifications to infrastructure to accommodate modern traffic, from incorporating new arteries to improving existing street patterns, have altered the character of nearly all of the world's historic cities and frequently subject residents and buildings alike to traffic's harmful side effects—vibrations, noise, and the risks of accidents. One of the best-known and ambitious projects in urban planning history was Baron Haussmann's nineteenth-century Parisian road works, which replaced large parts of the medieval city with straight, broad boulevards. Post–World War II highway construction programs in the United States and throughout the world also resulted in the loss of large numbers of significant historic buildings and sites.

Even the islands of Venice are not immune to vehicular vibrations and pollution; the dense volume of watercraft on its canals contributes to the erosion of building foundations at and below their waterlines. This is best exemplified by the rate of deterioration in the palaces along the Grand Canal. They are sinking at an annual rate of almost ⅖ inches (1 centimeter); elsewhere in Venice the rate is barely one-tenth of that.[22]

In the 1950s, Istanbul drove major urban arteries through its city center, destroying numerous riverside wooden palaces (*yales*) in order to make way not only for increased traffic but also for more profitable buildings. Such urban renewal occurs for a variety of reasons: to accommodate new styles of living and greater population densities, to replace areas considered to be blighted, and to correct perceived health concerns, among others. The world's great historic cities offer numerous examples of these kinds of urban changes. In Athens, particularly around Lycabettus and the Acropolis, old houses were demolished to accommodate new buildings in a completely different style. As a result, the character of whole areas like parts of the Plaka has been seriously compromised.[23] Anthony M. Tung describes this situation well in *Preserving the World's Great Cities: The Destruction and Renewal of the Historic Metropolis*.[24]

Over the past half century, the pathologies affecting historic residential and commercial districts and their influences on their inhabitants have been the basis of urban planning theory and numerous physical and sociological studies. Some of the first to question the prevailing theory that blighted urban areas should all be destroyed and replaced anew were in the United States: Jane Jacobs in her seminal *The Death and Life of Great American Cities* and Kevin Lynch in *What Time Is This Place?* European publications on this topic include the Council of Europe's *Dangers and Perils: Analysis of Factors which Constitute a Danger to Groups and Areas of Buildings of Historical or Artistic Interest* by Pierre-Yves Ligen, *The Conservation of European Cities* edited by Donald Appleyard, and *Conservation and Sustainability in Historic Cities* by Dennis Rodwell.

The deterioration of some urban centers eventually provoked protective public measures. French examples include the Marais district in Paris, the Quartier de la Balance in Avignon, and the *centre ville* ("town center") of Sarlat in the Dordogne. Initially, it was thought that all such undertakings were likely to be more costly than building anew, but they proved to be more economical in the long term and continue to provide healthy places for people to live and work—without the need for ongoing capital investment. The growing number of successful urban renewal schemes that incorporate the old and the new has, in fact, inspired more such developments.

A final negative influence of modern life on historic architectural resources comes from air transportation. Initially, airspeed regulation of supersonic aircraft over Europe and the United States merely sought to avoid disturbing ground populations, but in recent years the overflight of planes and helicopters in populous areas of cities and historic sites, such as at Angkor in Cambodia, has also been banned. The prohibition was enacted both to avoid intruding on visitors' experiences and to protect the monuments themselves, because the vibrations can accelerate deterioration. Similar restrictions became more widespread and stringent in the years following September 11, 2001, when the world became cognizant of the destructive potential of ordinary commercial aircraft.

Pollution

Airborne industrial pollution, a major danger to both human health and to natural and historic sites, is found in almost every city in the world. Moist air pollution intensifies surface erosion, and its unsightly ash and soot mottles the exteriors of urban historic buildings. While systematic operations like those now undertaken to clean and maintain the historic buildings of Paris help guard against unkempt appearances and future "stone disease,"[25] dramatic examples of this pollution-related blight are noticeable between cleanings of the delicate sandstone exteriors of Notre Dame and on the nearby Tour St.-Jacques.[26] Airborne pollutants also threaten both new and garden landscape features, as can be seen in the surviving historic trees and plant materials in Beijing's former imperial gardens.

Important attempts to combat this problem have been addressed locally in many countries by various pollution control measures and via international accords like the Kyoto Protocol and at the Earth Summit in Rio de Janeiro and the UN Climate Change Conference in Bali, which seek to restrict global carbon emissions and greenhouse warming levels. Compliance with them and with air-quality standards established by various national environmental protection agencies should directly improve both global health and better protect the human-built environment. Three decades ago, in the 1970s, the United States made a notable contribution to environmental and heritage protection by passing legislation that required prospective federally funded projects to be analyzed by means of a publicly reviewed environmental impact statement (EIS) before any interventions are undertaken. Executive Order 11593, signed by President Richard Nixon in 1971, has proven to be an invaluable first step in addressing these issues in planning safe, new and preserved historic environments.[27] Similar planning actions exist today in many European countries.

As a result of such legislative initiatives, large development schemes are more closely scrutinized today than ever before. An ancillary benefit from the EIS is a considerably improved urban planning and heritage conservation planning practice, which often results from the care taken to comply with it. For example, the "smart growth" techniques that are used increasingly in the United States entail more efficient use of both undeveloped and previously developed land that can include *easements* for both cultural and natural *conservation areas*. Planned efforts in resourceful land use were commonplace in the Netherlands, Germany, Slovenia, and parts of France for centuries, the results of which can be seen today. Some of the last remaining examples on earth of authentically resourceful land use where cultural heritage traditions have also changed little are seen

Figure 7-6 Traffic in Bangkok, Thailand, where vehicular congestion is so bad that some traffic signals are timed to change every ten minutes. Recognition of the scientifically determined negative effects of pollution on the historic built environment is not new. In a 1968 Council of Europe report, the French urbanist Pierre-Yves Ligen reported that atmospheric pollution was at the heart of a vast complex of hazards to historic buildings, noting that chemical and bacterial components, when solubilized by water (precipitation) multiply the effects of attrition and age, especially on exterior stone surfaces.

Figure 7-7 Stone deterioration caused by air pollution in Venice is exacerbated by the island's humid environment. In recent years, however, the problem has been reduced.

among cultures found in Bali, Indonesia; Bhutan; and remote parts of Latin America and Africa.

While today's new ecofriendly technologies—biodegradable products, wireless fidelity (WiFi), solar panels on little-seen roof surfaces, and a host of others that support *sustainable development*—are often less intrusive than others; some installations, such as quarries, oil refineries, and highly visible wind power and telecommunications towers and relay facilities, continue to have a negative impact on the aesthetic character of both the natural and the built environment. Despite the introduction of new fuel-efficient technologies, Mexico City's vehicular traffic releases over 1,307,951 cubic yards (1 million cubic meters) of carbon monoxide into the air each month, greatly degrading both the urban fabric and the quality of city life. But improvements are being made: Since the 1970s, Parisian laws aimed at reducing harmful air pollutants have significantly reduced the deterioration of its historic building exteriors.[28] Bold measures at reducing the number of motorized vehicles in urban centers such as London and Rome in recent years are also having noticeable positive effects.

Social and Economic Change

Industrialization has profoundly redefined societies, engendering potentially damaging social changes that can also influence the historic built environment. Beginning in the nineteenth century, relations between the landed gentry and the servant class that supported their estates rapidly changed. Due to political upheaval and social reforms, job seekers massed to urban centers. In Europe, for instance, affluent owners abandoned ancient rural manor houses in favor of modern amenities or decided that the operation of a large estate was no longer economically feasible because of high operating costs and tax burdens. There, as elsewhere, population movements stressed both the built and natural environments as the rural exodus depleted countryside populations; small settlements and farms were abandoned in favor of high-density urban settlements and their improved employment prospects.[29] Rural society declined in practically every country as demographics shifted in response to economics.

In the twentieth century, this process of urbanization only accelerated. Today it is not uncommon for town and city populations to double in size within a few years, as those of Bangkok, Beijing, New Delhi, Istanbul, Moscow, and Berlin have done. The population of Saõ Paolo, Brazil, grew from approximately seventy thousand in 1900 to ten million in the 1970s to eighteen million in 2005.

In some nations, however, more affluent city dwellers have migrated to rural areas— even if only to second homes—resulting in the rescue of many obsolete or underutilized country houses, farmsteads, and country settings. But while this process can breathe new life into historic areas, *gentrification* can also affect the traditional ways of life of the local inhabitants.

Tourism

Increased leisure time, secondary residences, improved transportation, reduced working hours, more hours spent away from home—all have become facts of life for at least parts of the populations of most of the wealthier nations of the world in recent years. The related phenomenon of mass tourism is the proverbial double-edged sword for many cultural heritage sites. Much needed foreign and local revenue from tourism may support economic development and growth in a host country, but it invariably comes at a cost.

Figure 7-8 The overburdening of Venice with crowds of visitors— fourteen million in 2008—has had its effects on both the city's historic buildings and its dwindling resident population.

The term *tourist pollution* was popularized in the 1970s by the prominent English architectural conservation advocate John Julius Norwich in reference to what happens when too many tourists overwhelm a historic place. Tourist pollution can be deleterious to the fabric of historic sites and also create the kind of negative experience to which visitors and inhabitants of Venice can attest.[30] Recently, proposals have been circulated to sell entrance tickets to nonresidents of "essential" tourist destinations like Venice and the center of Florence in order to curb the numbers of visitors at any one time. While this radical approach has not yet been implemented, its consideration underscores how seriously the wear and tear caused by tourists is taken at some imperiled sites.

At the level of the actual historic resources, tourism-related problems include damaged architectural finishes, such as what happened to Westminster Abbey's bronze floor reliefs and to the Mayan carved stone stelae in Guatemala in the 1970s (after which tourists and local merchants were forbidden to make rubbings); the purloining of stone idols like those on ancient Khmer temples throughout Cambodia; and wanton vandalism, as occurred when a disturbed person took a hammer to Michelangelo's unprotected statue, the *Pietà*, in St. Peter's Basilica in 1972.

Regardless of their location and popularity, historic sites open to the public pose a constant challenge for site managers and conservators, who must effectively both protect and display their sites. But managing visitors at cultural heritage sites is not easy, and trends show steady increases in the numbers of both visitors to heritage sites and the opening of new venues to receive them. Permitting more visitors than sites can accommodate, however, can result in physical wear to the resource, grossly uneven visitation patterns, visitor frustration, negative publicity, and the deterioration, rather than the enhancement, of the local populations' lives.[31] Despite the difficulties that mass tourism may pose, most governments today strive to promote their tourist destinations to an international audience.

Specialist heritage conservation professionals, experts on the tourism industry, government agencies, and a few concerned tour companies have recently made significant progress in determining criteria for sustainable tourism as a certain goal for specific sites.[32]

Judging by recent trends in tourism and the role the tourism economy plays in global financial realms, all popular heritage tourism destinations should have viable cultural resources management plans that take into account the concerns of all interested parties and that correlate the intrinsic qualities of heritage places with both the actual and anticipated demands upon them. In the past, poor decisions have been made in the interest of exploiting the economic potential of historic sites, but not necessarily in conserving them. For example, in Peru, the rural Incan seat of Machu Picchu, located high among Andean peaks, is accessed via the rambling shanty town of Aguas Calientes, where tickets must be purchased, further transportation must be arranged, and visitors are greeted by a gauntlet of stands selling local wares. Atop the summit at Machu Picchu's actual entrance is a guest lodge concession, while the famous site's well-designed interpretive center and museum is so remote that most visitors miss it completely.[33]

Responsible heritage tourism allows for the interpretation of a site's values and historical significance in accurate and engaging ways while integrating its economic value to its region. When located near an economically depressed area, a popular historic resource can sustain and even improve the local quality of life. Heritage tourism employment opportunities keep residents from abandoning their towns in search of jobs elsewhere. Local participation offers the visitor a broader, more interesting experience that is often more memorable. Countless heritage conservation projects have proven that diverse community groups are most effective when acting in a unified manner, regardless of their ethnic or religious backgrounds. Such cohesion is broadly beneficial and can mean the difference between an isolated act of conservation and the revival of a vital and lasting community. To this end, heritage conservation professionals must always strive to understand the interests of local inhabitants and other stakeholders with legitimate ties to the cultural heritage sites in question and the impact those users will have on the sites.[34]

Religious Differences

The secularization that accompanied modernization in the twentieth century has also affected architectural heritage. Changes in religious convictions have often mandated changes in building forms. For example, the number of practicing Jews and Orthodox Christians in the countries of the former Soviet Union dropped precipitously during World War II and in the postwar Communist period. This, in turn, led to the loss of a number of historic synagogues and churches through abandonment and decay or targeted vandalism and destruction. Since the end of the Cold War, these faiths have revived, stimulating the restoration and conservation of many related religious sites in central and eastern Europe.[35]

Liturgical reforms and changing attitudes among practitioners of a faith can also be destructive to religious structures. Between 1960 and 1980, Roman Catholic liturgical changes required a presiding priest to face his congregation rather than the altar on the church's back wall and to no longer be separated from it by a gated communion rail. In order to accommodate new church law, major alterations to the sanctuaries of many historically significant church interiors were made.[36] In addition, the call for more austere decorations saw some statues and other large components removed; artistic works such as mural paintings and altar fittings subsequently disappeared.[37]

Significant architecture, new and old, has always elicited an emotional response from those who encounter it. From apathy and benign neglect, through ignorance or error, to antipathy and avarice, to the calculated destruction of war and terrorism, such reactions affect built heritage. The effects of time on unmaintained building materials can be dramatic, depending on macro- and microclimatic conditions, the nature of the materials involved, and their assembly. When a building, site, or object is neglected by its caretakers, it deteriorates—and once decay begins, it progresses at an increasing rate.[38]

Figure 7-9 The abandoned former Jewish ghetto in the center of Vilnius, Lithuania, which was forcibly vacated in 1941, as it appeared in 1998.

Often, ordinary citizens are unaware of the relevance of architectural patrimony to contemporary culture and as a result take no interest in historic sites or fail to treat them with the respect and care they deserve. For those who do appreciate such places, there can be the added problem of the *perceived* responsibility of their upkeep: Too often people feel that the protection, conservation, and presentation of historic buildings and sites are governmental or institutional responsibilities. Cultural heritage site administrators around the world spend a good percentage of their time trying to counter this belief by showing the myriad ways the public can participate in and support heritage conservation.

Design Defects

Occasionally, a structure is inherently defective due to faulty design or construction. Making repairs to such buildings can be costly and pose complex theoretical issues. The Leaning Tower of Pisa, a renowned example of an inherently flawed building, began to tilt in 1178, even before its construction was completed. In 2001, the structural stabilization of the foundations and base of the tower, then at a 5.6-degree tilt, was carried out, surely just prior to its collapse.

Extending the life of buildings and art works originally constructed of temporary or unproven materials can pose similar problems. In particular, many new building materials and construction systems used in the past century have proven to be remarkably short-lived. The Lever Building, a landmark of 1950s modernism in New York City, required resheathing with more resilient metal spandrels and replica tinted glass only forty years after its construction. The ubiquitous high-rise government buildings clad in glazed terracotta erected beginning in the 1930s throughout Russia and Eastern Europe are also not faring well today because this stone substitute, especially when poorly maintained, is not suitable for use in harsh climates.

Figure 7-10 The Leaning Tower of Pisa, which began to tilt from the time of its construction, is probably the most famous example in history of defective architectural design.

Poorly Planned Adaptive Use

Even the best-intentioned *adaptation* of a historic building makes it vulnerable to damage from extensive alterations that can turn out to be visually and physically unsympathetic. It is important to understand the economic context and marketability of restored and rehabilitated historic buildings. Sometimes success and failure can be seen in the same type of project, but in different locations. At the South Street Seaport in New York City, a 1980s renovation unified one city block of eleven eighteenth- and nineteenth-century four-story buildings into commercial and residential spaces. The scheme reclaimed the rear yards of these properties as a shared amenity for commercial ground-floor tenants and turned narrow loft-type spaces on the upper floors into open-plan offices. Because of the abundance of modern office space in nearby Lower Manhattan, the seaport's commercial office space offerings were unsuccessful. The ground-level, mixed-use commercial spaces, however, were well received.[39]

A more successful example of tying diverse historic buildings together for new functions can be seen in Philadelphia, both at the rehabilitated former Reading Terminal and in the commercial heart of its historic center, where several late nineteenth- and early twentieth-century high-rise buildings were connected with both subterranean passageways and sky bridges to form multiuse conference facilities. This intervention redefined downtown Philadelphia for local inhabitants and visitors alike and has made an important contribution to the city's revitalization.

Incompatible Additions and New Architecture

Modernizing historic buildings for new or extended commercial purposes with insensitively designed new storefronts and façades, oversized window glazing, and unsympathetic modern advertising can have a deleterious effect on both their character and their locale. Preventing such intrusions is one of the objectives of most local historic architectural conservation commissions.[40] However, there are millions of buildings and districts that possess historic and architectural character that are not afforded such protection. Likewise, not all countries have yet created such oversight and protection systems.

New architecture that accommodates new specialty functions can add value to traditional urban settings, as the Pompidou Center in Paris did for its historic Marais district in 1976. More commonplace, however, are less successful attempts. In 1994, the city of Lisbon built a conference and cultural center and museum complex in the center of its triangular sixteenth-century Belém district, the site of some of the most famous historic buildings in Portugal. The oversize and visually intrusive Belém Cultural Center was so controversial that it was proposed that the entire historic enclave consisting of the city's famous Manueline-style Jerónimos Monastery, the Tower of Belém, and the nearby Our Lady of Belém Church be removed from UNESCO's World Heritage List.

The main problems created by most new architecture in historic settings derive from changes in scale, both in plan and elevation, as well as from alterations to visual harmony and perspective. One of the most famous examples of the intrusion of a new high-rise in a neighborhood of traditionally low buildings was the Montparnasse tower project built in Paris in 1973. The construction of this 689-foot (210-meter) structure

Figure 7-11 Obviously built to make a statement, the new headquarters of the Russian Union of Architects on Granatny Lane in Moscow entailed the re-creation of a recently destroyed nineteenth century building with a markedly new storey above it, which is described by locals as its "cap".

proved so controversial it resulted in local building laws that enforce stricter height limitations than those in listed historic districts.

As was the case in Lisbon's Belém neighborhood, historic districts are often impacted by adjacent new construction, which affects the views both from and toward the districts. Avoiding this has proven very difficult in most countries, to such an extent that many architectural conservationists yield to such forces as being a lesser negative consequence.[41]

Insensitive Prior Interventions

Given how heavy-handed many restorations and rehabilitations were in earlier times, the need to re-restore historic structures that were damaged or disfigured by previous interventions is not uncommon. This often involves removing liberal applications of concrete used in masonry repairs and structural stabilizations and installing more efficient and visually discreet heating, ventilating, and air-conditioning systems.

These kinds of problems are often the result of a lack of experience and the use of inappropriate materials. While re-restoration can be disruptive and costly, expediently performed earlier conservation interventions should not always be judged harshly. Previous architects and administrators often simply did the best they could with the materials and information available to them at the time. For example, a temporary roof was placed on the Alexander Palace in Tsarskoe Selo, near St. Petersburg, Russia, soon after World War II, when resources were extremely scarce. It served the purpose of preserving the fabric of the building until a more appropriate replacement could be constructed nearly one-half century later.

Figure 7-12 The use of reinforced concrete in reconstructing the upper stories and roofs of some of the more important buildings at Pompeii in the 1970s has since created serious structural problems. The weights of these new structures exceed the load-bearing capacities of lower historic wall fabric, and their rigidity poses dangers during the regions many seismic events. A failing reinforced concrete roof support is seen here.

CULTURAL BIAS

Cultural bias within heritage conservation practice is a subtle but potent threat that can be focused on types of physical cultural heritage or certain historical eras. It can manifest in a lack of maintenance or protection, or the assignment of insufficient funds, for the upkeep of buildings that have undesirable associations. Regarded as unimportant or distasteful, perfectly viable or reusable architectural forms have been swept away. As frivolous as this may sound, much has been lost to the ever-present, influential, but not infallible notions of fashion. On close examination, these influences can also be discerned in choices made by many countries in which sites are nominated for World Heritage designation or for protective listing, raising the question of whose history will be enshrined and celebrated.

The history of art is replete with examples of negative attitudes toward the styles of earlier periods. As Ligen puts it, "Nothing is more fluctuating and fragile than the appreciation of what is beautiful and what is not."[42] Only in the past half century have the Spanish recognized that the country's national patrimony included Moorish sites earlier than the fifteenth century. Similarly, until the 1970s, Turkish heritage conservation efforts exclusively favored sites associated with the more charismatic of the ancient civilizations represented within the country's borders and practically all sites reflecting Islamic heritage. Omnipresent vestiges of the Byzantine Empire that lasted one thousand years were largely ignored, while the non-Christian periods were portrayed as the authentic history and culture of Turkey. A somewhat analogous policy existed in Greece.[43]

Often, a succeeding culture is ignorant of, or oblivious to, the importance of an inherited past and its relevance to the present, but more often the simple preference for modernity makes older, out-of-date things vulnerable to loss. Throughout the United States, planners, architects, and citizens alike have exhibited impatience with, or distaste for, the past in general. This was especially evident during the progressive era between the 1930s and the mid-1960s, when wholesale modernization seemed to be the only path to the future. Fortunately, intolerance and disdain for the past and its remnants has reversed in past decades with the recognition and acceptance of a broader spectrum of aesthetic values and social acceptability. The reason for this change in attitude is primarily due to what one prominent chronicler of the field termed the "heritage crusade."[44]

Profligate Use of Resources

The potentially profitable nature of many civic and corporate development projects can offer powerful disincentives for real estate developers and their investors toward regulations protecting historic sites. Arguments for aesthetic considerations rarely prevail over technical, financial, or economic necessities.

Modern methods of demolition and a need for deeper foundations to support tall structures have major consequences for archaeology. Construction over ancient sites in cities such as Naples, Marseilles, Athens, Istanbul, and Beirut often leads to clandestine excavation and rebuilding as developers seek to avoid the additional costs and delays associated with documenting and protecting archeological finds.[45] A new structure hastily built atop earlier remains represents a lost opportunity to do historical research and to incorporate interesting amenities into new designs. The presentation of *in situ* ancient remains in entranceways to the underground rail systems in Rome and Athens and the featuring of citadel remains discovered in excavations for a new entrance to the expanded Louvre Museum in Paris are examples of successfully incorporating old and new within contemporary infrastructure development projects.

▼ **Figure 7-13** Despite certain legal protections and its popularity among both local residents and foreign visitors, the characteristic French colonial shop houses of Hanoi's 36 Pho Phuong, or 36 Streets district, have frequently been replaced.

Chart 7-1 Some facts about energy and material consumption relative to new building construction and rehabilitation in the United States

Common Sense, Resource Consumption, and Development

Destroying any physical object wastes the energy expended on its creation. Simply defined, *embodied energy* is the energy required to extract, process, manufacture, transport, and install building materials.[46]

James Marston Fitch best summed up the historical awareness of the economic benefits of conservation when he said:

> *Throughout history the cost of making anything—a city, a house, even a quilt—has been quite high in terms of both labor and materials. Thus every artifact was used and reused until it "wore out" or "fell apart." Final dissolution was postponed as long as possible [until]…the artifact was cannibalized [with] every possible bit and piece being salvaged for reuse in new combinations. This sort of conservation of energy cut across every level of pre-industrial societies. In any case, the material value of a constructed building was always seen as something great.*[47]

Since the 1970s, experts have been able to quantify the expenditure of energy and enterprise on building in terms of British thermal units (Btus).[48] Their results are not just academic. When the sum of the billions of Btus expended in the creation of a specific building is translated into terms such as numbers of trees felled or gallons of gasoline consumed, the value of conserving recyclable existing buildings—as opposed to replacing them—becomes more meaningful.

Many real estate developers have discovered that the rehabilitation of historic buildings is economically justifiable. In conserving old buildings, the savings begins at construction, as there is less need for excavation, site clearance and demolition, and waste removal. The major foundation and structural components are usually reusable, and significant savings can be realized on the cost of materials. In preserving the mature landscape features of a historic site, significant cost and energy savings can be realized as well. Such features can also significantly enhance property values.

Putting a monetary value on the artistic, historic, or aesthetic merits of a building or object runs counter to established notions of material appraisals. What is the price of the remains of the Parthenon in Athens, Petra in Jordan, the Great Wall of China, or Frank Lloyd Wright's home and studio in Oak Park, Illinois? For historic buildings and sites such as these, which are imbued with historic significance and meanings that no copy can replicate, calculations of pure replacement costs are irrelevant. It may be wiser to reason that the economic argument is secondary to the fundamental purposes of historic continuity and cultural retention.

Approaches to this question can be found in feasibility studies done by architects and engineers who analyze the question of repair versus replacement of more ordinary historic buildings. Comprehensive cost-benefit analyses include expert opinions of quantity surveyors, real estate appraisers, marketing experts, and economists, who discuss aspects of economic feasibility and return on investment as well as various direct and indirect economic benefits: land values, tourism revenues, and improving the local tax base. Conserving old buildings can also help unemployment statistics because rehabilitation can be more labor intensive than new construction.[49] Rehabilitation also provides an alternative to the high costs of new housing and office space and often creates more interesting spaces in which to live and work.[50]

In many countries economic development is increasingly tied to the well-being of the cultural heritage, and vice versa. When attention is paid to cultural sensitivities utilizing sound technical expertise, development projects aid not only

Figure 7-14 The rehabilitation of London's Covent Garden produce market in the late 1980s accommodated a mix of new uses, including evening activities, thereby avoiding the need to completely replace it. It now provides a vibrant new amenity to this part of the city. The efficiency of recycling the complex is abundantly clear: At its busiest hours, some local residents would argue that the four-hundred-year-old market area is now too successful.

those seeking the economic benefits but heritage conservation efforts as well. This dual relationship can be cemented by providing working incentives, a regulatory framework, and up-to-date information—and through cultural diplomacy. When such projects are realized, the policy of resourceful intervention in support of conserving historic buildings produces net gains in both real and cultural assets.

Historic buildings tend to be amply built from the standpoint of structural engineering and are thus often useful for a surprising number of new purposes. In addition, buildings constructed before the development of modern air-conditioning would necessarily have been carefully and intuitively designed for human comfort. Practical devices used include high ceilings, cross-ventilation, generously sized window openings for light and air, overhangs, and shutters for shade. Site placement with regard to orientation for prevailing breezes and sun angles was commonplace. It is no surprise, therefore, that many old buildings are more inherently energy efficient than newer structures—and built in more temperate climates as well.[51] The Energy Research and Development Administration in Washington, DC, has determined that rehabilitation consumes around 23 percent less energy than new construction.[52]

Urban rehabilitation projects have the phenomenal capacity to inspire. There are thousands of examples of how a single restored residential or commercial building motivated its neighbors to follow suit. When such initiatives serve as exemplars, the results can be amazing, with whole districts, or even entire cities, following the same path of regeneration, as was the case in St. Petersburg, Russia; Avignon, France; the Marais district in Paris; and more recently, at the Factory 798 industrial district in Beijing.[53] Examples in the United States include Boston's waterfront; College Hill in Providence, Rhode Island; SoHo in New York City; Philadelphia's Society Hill; and the downtowns of Annapolis, Maryland; Charleston, South Carolina; and Savannah, Georgia. The historic character of these neighborhoods, which made them eligible for landmark protection and—for the US examples—tax incentives, were an essential ingredient to their regeneration.

But as with all interventions, extensive urban regeneration is not without a downside. Wholesale improvements to neighborhoods can displace less established or less affluent residents through gentrification. They have also occasionally invited extraordinarily heavy usage and long hours on weekends and holidays—in the Georgetown section of Washington, DC, for example, or the Covent Garden district in London.

This growing global trend toward propagating reuse and recycling techniques marks a significant shift away from the former mentality of Western societies, which considered most resources as cheap and unlimited. Beginning in the last few decades of the twentieth century, populations all over the world are experiencing a cultural shift toward a civilization rooted in balance, order, and permanence—especially when it comes to things previously taken for granted. As one American energy conservation researcher and policy maker argued, "Through the examples set by architectural conservationists, it is obvious that two vital social goals—resource conservation and historic preservation—are self-reinforcing."[54]

Thus, the destruction of any historic structure, regardless of its artistic merit, should be carefully considered in light of the energy waste that destruction represents. Adaptive reuse is especially relevant in a world in which primary resources are constantly being depleted by modern life. While all old buildings cannot be saved, the decision to demolish and replace—especially with a structure of a similar size—must account for the whole costs of energy consumption during both creation and operation. When examining the question at the scale of a nation's entire existing building stock, such considerations cannot be overlooked.

War and Terrorism

War-related destruction to historic cultural resources is usually broad: bomb and shell damage, vandalism, theft, neglect, and further demolition during cleanup and reconstruction operations.[55] From earliest antiquity the fate of conquered cities frequently involved the destruction of their major buildings, especially those of symbolic or military value. The enormous increase in the destructive power of modern armaments has multiplied this danger to an unparalleled degree, as recent wars have demonstrated. Of the many risks to the world's cultural heritage attributed to humanity, both the willful and collateral destruction of buildings, sites, and objects during wartime conflict is by far the most destructive.

Cultural heritage can be a prime target for calculated destruction by those opposed to a specific ideology, nationality, or race. Isolated incidents of targeted damage have also happened outside of the context of battle. According to a Museum of World Religions conference report, "Sacred images, artifacts, and sites have been destroyed throughout the millennia but no act of destruction of sacred sites in history had the same impact, simultaneously and globally, as the annihilation of the Buddhas of Bamiyan in Afghanistan in March 2001."[56] The motives, impacts, and reactions to the destruction of the Old Bridge at Mostar in Bosnia in 1993, and the World Trade Center in New York on September 11, 2001, were not dissimilar.

During the modern era, humanity has made the world a healthier and better place in which to live; it is ironic that during this same period we have also witnessed an unprecedented loss of cultural heritage through warfare. World War II exacted a particularly heavy toll on the built environment.[57] Examples of the extensive destruction it caused can be found in many countries—notable losses on an urban scale were sustained at Italy's famous Abbey of Montecassino and in Dresden, Germany; Coventry, England; and Warsaw and Gdansk in Poland. The destructive effects of the nuclear bombing of the Japanese cities of Hiroshima and Nagasaki set a new standard for wholesale destruction.

Sixty years later, the evidence of destruction and postwar reconstruction efforts are still easily identifiable—especially in Germany, where nearly every historic urban area was seriously damaged. Some, like the old quarters and squares of Karlsruhe, Mainz, and Düsseldorf, were rebuilt according to the original plans. Others— Cologne, Hanau, and Ulm—

▲▲ **Figure 7-15** The medieval seaport Dubrovnik, Croatia, avoided conquest and conflict throughout its long life until October 1, 1991, when it was besieged and shelled over a seven-month period.

▲ **Figure 7-16** The quick replacement of traditional town architecture in Dresden, Germany, after World War II left the historic town with architecture, seen here, that was little admired. The city is currently replacing many such buildings with higher quality new architecture reflecting traditional forms.

Recent Destruction and Reconstruction: From Ground Zero, New York, to Baghdad, Iraq

During the eighteen months following the September 11, 2001, al-Qaeda attacks on the Pentagon and World Trade Center, international forces led by American and British troops were deployed to Afghanistan and Iraq. As a result, the governments of both countries were overthrown in a military action whose related calculated physical destruction and economic loss was immense.

While the US-Afghan conflict mainly entailed the destruction of relatively modern domestic buildings, the most important cultural heritage casualties of this unfortunate period in Afghanistan's long history had occurred earlier, during its long war against the Soviet Union, and later, during a civil war that ended with the victory of the Taliban. In April 2001, the Taliban regime deliberately destroyed Bamiyan's famous, rock-hewn buddhas; between 1996 and 2001, the national museum in Kabul was systematically looted. The most widely attributed motive for both was religious intolerance.

In contrast, Iraq's loss of cultural patrimony to collateral war damage was sustained by its museums and archaeological sites, which were looted for the value of the antiquities they contained. Such losses occurred both during the Gulf War in 1991, and during the 2003 invasion that ousted Saddam Hussein's regime. During both of these conflicts, the destructive power of state-of-the-art warfare and the social chaos that ensued immediately thereafter was enormous.

Despite the advice given to the US military by historians, archaeologists, and heritage protection experts regarding probable threats to Iraq's cultural patrimony, coalition forces overlooked the need for any protection against looting. They did not seem to anticipate the period of complete lawlessness that followed their April 2003 arrival in Baghdad. Within two days, Iraqi looters stole an estimated fifteen thousand items from the National Museum of Iraq and the Iraq National Library and Archives. Tragically, the call to provide reasonable wartime protection to the cultural patrimony of one of the world's oldest civilizations went unheeded.[58]

To date, the loss of heritage in Iraq has included historic buildings such as the al-Askari Mosque (also known as the Golden Mosque) in Samarra and the minaret at 'Anah—both casualties of factional fighting—and the archaeological remains at Babylon, which suffered greatly from hosting a military base at its perimeter.

As of this writing, the political situations in Afghanistan and Iraq were not yet conducive to the commencement of reconstruction work, but in New York City, an international competition yielded a new plan for the site of the World Trade Center just two years after its destruction. The proposal was greeted with calls to restore, rehabilitate, and judiciously replace other buildings in Lower Manhattan, some of which date to the eighteenth and nineteenth centuries.

The combined official cost estimates for the reconstruction of Lower Manhattan and the rebuilding of Iraq will certainly total hundreds of billions of dollars, excluding the related costs to local inhabitants and businesses. If nothing else, the costly experiences of the post-9/11 conflicts have brought the world closer to an understanding of our commonalties and differences, so much that some argue another new world order has been instigated at the outset of the twenty-first century. Such destruction is not just the concern of people who want to preserve buildings; the endangerment of historic, sacred, and symbolic sites reflects the peril faced by humanity, both on the broader historical scale and in deeply personal ways.

---

maintain similar block sizes and layouts, but no attempt was made at genuine reconstruction. Still others were rebuilt with modern buildings along the lines of their precedent forms, as can be seen in the greater part of Aachen, Emden, and Mannheim.

Post–World War II reconstruction across Europe and beyond ranged from the faithful reconstruction of Warsaw and Gdansk to the complete replacement of Le Havre, France, and Rotterdam, the Netherlands, with bold new architectural forms; new standards were set in urban rebuilding as well as architectural, planning, and architectural conservation theory. In many ways, those experiences in reconstruction, restoration, and urban planning form the basis for the architectural, planning, and architectural conservation practiced today.

Figure 7-17 The namesake of the International Committee of the Blue Shield preventative conservation program is its blue shield insignia, used to identify heritage that should be protected by all parties during civil conflict.

RISK PREPAREDNESS AND RESPONSE

The ICOMOS' 1999 Heritage @ Risk (H@R) initiative collects examples of inadequate cultural heritage protection from many countries and draws conclusions about threats to historic buildings and sites. This information forms the basis for recommendations that become the field's **preventative conservation practice**. The nominators of endangered sites to the biennially renewed World Monuments Fund's Watch™ List of 100 Most Endangered Sites, established in 1995, also systematically gather information about types and patterns of threats to historic buildings and sites.

The risks to cultural heritage and the roles that building-conservation science can play underline the importance of preventative conservation, a facet of architectural conservation that has long been neglected but is now attracting attention. The concept behind preventative conservation, also called risk preparedness and disaster mitigation, is that it requires both architectural and objects conservators to operate proactively, not just reactively.

To the principal categories of risks posed by humans and nature, one must factor in both the degrees of risk and the rate of deterioration. It is by understanding the causes of risks and what happens when several risk factors are combined—which is usually the case—that risks to cultural heritage can be effectively mitigated. After damage or a loss occurs, the first step is usually identifying and prioritizing conservation problems. In formulating national approaches to heritage conservation, ICOMOS' Heritage @ Risk program recommends that strategic plans for safekeeping architectural heritage include a preliminary inventory of all architectural heritage sites. It should highlight the physical conditions and legal protection afforded to each site and create a *risk map* that enumerates the various issues, priorities, guidelines, and recommendations, and provides an operational plan.[59]

Preventative protection for the world's cultural heritage has also been promoted by the International Committee of the Blue Shield (ICBS), formed in 1996 by ICOMOS in association with the International Council on Archives (ICA), the International Council of Museums (ICOM), and the International Federation of Landscape Architects (IFLA). According to its mission statement, the Blue Shield is the cultural equivalent of the Red Cross, organizing emergency responses for heritage threatened by nature or humanity.[60] This organization disseminates information and raises awareness about potential threats and best practices for preparing for them; it also provides professional expertise and coordinates the distribution of previously identified resources in the event of natural disaster or conflict.

ENDNOTES

1. Bonnie Burnham, "Architectural Heritage: The Paradox of Its Current State of Risk," *International Journal of Cultural Property* 7, no. 1 (1998): 159.

2. This phenomenon, which remains a major peril to built heritage, can especially be seen in the placement of early Christian and Byzantine structures on earlier pagan sites in the eastern Mediterranean.

3. Simultaneous threats pose considerably greater conservation challenges than any of them would alone. In recent years, Venice has suffered from frequent flooding, air pollution, acid rain, and uncontrolled tourism. Considering that Venice contains thousands of buildings, works of art, bridges, outdoor sculptures, and public spaces—each with its own characteristics, history, and special maintenance needs—the task to conserve and present this wealth of historic fabric is vast. Similarly large and complex conservation efforts are underway at other World Heritage Sites, such as St. Petersburg, Russia, and Angkor, Cambodia.

4. It is from the point when either de facto or de jure legislation protecting architectural heritage is in place (when statutory laws become obligatory) that a country's or a town's commitment to heritage protection can be effectively quantified.

5. In Malaysia, Turkey, and other countries in western Asia and North Africa, local *waqf* (in Arabic) and *vakif* (in Turkish) foundations, have purview over most Islamic heritage sites. The Vatican controls Rome's Catholic sites, and the Episcopal Diocese of New York oversees properties owned by the Episcopal Church in New York City.

6. Until now, only a limited number of international organizations such as the United Nations Educational, Scientific and Cultural Organization (UNESCO), the International Council on Monuments and Sites (ICOMOS), the International Centre for the Study of the Preservation and Restoration of Cultural Property (ICCROM), the World Monuments Fund (WMF), Patrimoine sans frontières (PSF), the Getty Conservation Institute (GCI), and various intergovernmental assistance arrangements have been involved in architectural conservation projects in most countries.

7. In recent years, revenues from oil discovery and transshipment have offered new financial prospects in both of these examples.

8. Some scientists have argued that recent, subtle global climate changes may be responsible for increasing the number of tropical storms, typhoons, and hurricanes in warmer regions of the world.

9. In December 1999, a violent hurricane crossed France, destroying millions of trees and causing massive destruction. The park of the Palace of Versailles sustained significant damage. A massive flood in 2002 seriously damaged Prague's Old Town, and in 2004 a tsunami claimed well over one hundred thousand lives and laid waste to parts of Galle, one of Sri Lanka's most beautiful historic cities and a UNESCO World Heritage List site. High winds and storms caused severe flooding. (See endnote 12.)

10. Italy, the Balkans, the Caucasus region, Central Asia, and Latin America have regularly been affected. Turkey's 1999 and 2000 earthquakes caused much damage to both new and historic buildings.

11. Among the most famous volcanic disasters affecting historic cultural heritage are those that destroyed Akrotiri on the island of Thira (Santorini), Greece, and Italy's Pompeii and Herculaneum.

12. One of the most well-known floods of modern times was the November 1966 inundation of Florence, which caused enormous damage to its artistic treasures. A concurrent and equally damaging record flood in Venice saw its lagoon waters submerge the Piazza San Marco under nearly 4.25 feet (130 centimeters) of water. The former was attributable to human error; the latter, to natural phenomena. In 1993, large areas of the upper Mississippi River basin in the United States were flooded. Widespread property damage was sustained by several historic enclaves along its bank, including the sixteenth-century French colonial site of Ste. Genevieve, Missouri. In 2005, Hurricane Katrina caused major damage to the historic American city of New Orleans, when many of its levees were destroyed and large parts of the city's low-lying areas were inundated.

13. Fires periodically devastate forests and contiguous areas of the western United States, often with disastrous results. In July 2002, simultaneous forest fires in the states of Colorado and Arizona destroyed some 7.1 million acres of forest and residential areas. Fires due to arson devastated hundreds of square miles of south-central Greece in the summer of 2007.

14. Ironically, an alarming number of accidental fires occurs during the restoration process. The more stringent fire-prevention and related life-safety measures used recently in the design of buildings, both for new buildings and for rehabilitations, have done much to prevent loss of both life and property.

15. Feilden, *Conservation of Historic Buildings*, 91–111.

16. The crystallization of salts on or behind brick and soft-stone masonry surfaces creates spalling, which can exacerbate deterioration. The freezing of moisture in exposed building materials, especially masonry, can also create spalling.

17. ICOMOS Climate Change Committee findings on how to manage static change in a dynamic landscape. ICOMOS Scientific Council, "Recommendations from the Scientific Council Symposium *Cultural Heritage and Global Climate Change (GCC)*," held in Pretoria, South Africa, October 7, 2007 (final draft, March 21, 2008), http://www.international.icomos.org/climatechange/pdf/Recommendations_GCC_Symposium_EN.pdf.

18. In addition to Feilden's writings, other valuable reference sources, especially these serving the field of architectural conservation science, include technical journals such as the *Journal of Architectural Conservation* (Donhead Publishing, Shaftesbury, UK) and the *APT Bulletin: The Journal of Preservation Technology* (Association for Preservation Technology International, Springfield, IL). Other authors who specifically delve into these subjects include Martin E. Weaver, Samuel Y. Harris, and Giorgio Croci. (See also Appendix D.)

19. Feilden, *Conservation of Historic Buildings*, 2–3.

20. Examples of government-sponsored development schemes include the former Soviet Union's agricultural collectivization programs of the 1930s; China's aim to boost agricultural production by the government's Great Leap Forward initiative, which lasted from 1958 until 1961; and hydroelectric dam projects in these and dozens of other countries.

21. Tung, *Preserving the World's Great Cities*, 17.

22. Pierre-Yves Ligen, *Dangers and Perils: Analysis of Factors which Constitute a Danger to Groups and Areas of Buildings of Historical or Artistic Interest* (Strasbourg, France: Council for Cultural Co-operation, 1968), 10.

23. Ibid., 21. In an effort to reverse this trend, areas of the Plaka in Athens were the subject of neighborhood improvement schemes in the 1980s that merited an award from Europa Nostra.

24. Tung, *Preserving the World's Great Cities*, 248–249.

25. Ligen, *Dangers and Perils*, 10. Solutions for cleaning and restoring the stone exteriors of French architecture have ranged from light water washing to resurfacing. This latter option has been viewed since the nineteenth century as being philosophically dubious, with most agreeing today that it should be undertaken only as a last resort, if at all.

26. Also affected are the limestone exteriors of innumerable Venetian palaces. "Stone disease" decomposes healthy stone surfaces below the dark sulfide-rich crust that has been deposited by airborne pollutants.

27. Similar reports that specifically address historic resources are often referred to as historic structure reports, conservation plans, or conservation resource management plans.

28. Ligen, *Dangers and Perils*, 9.

29. Concurrently, the change in many regional landscapes was accelerated by a dramatic explosion of large-scale, high-intensity corporate farming. Small family farms became encircled by disharmonious power lines, reservoirs, and service facilities and by the remotely located infrastructure necessary to sustain nearby urban centers.

30. Venice's popularity may prove to be its demise. Despite numerous restoration efforts, Venice's town fathers have allowed it to be subjected to some extraordinary pressures—such as the 1989 Pink Floyd rock concert in Piazza San Marco (St. Mark's Square). This spectacularly insensitive example of historic-site programming permitted considerable unnecessary wear, demand on resources, and vandalism to occur in parts of the historic city and effectively shut down the heart of Venice for several days. In January 2008, the local transport situation was so bad for locals that the government instituted a program of boat travel service exclusively dedicated for residents.

31. Examples include the Greco-Roman town of Bosra, Syria; Biban el-Harim (Valley of the Queens) in Luxor, Egypt; and Pagan, Myanmar, where residents living among the ruins of these sites were displaced for tourism purposes.

32. Tim Winter, *Post-Conflict Heritage, Postcolonial Tourism: Culture, Politics and Development at Angkor* (Abingdon, Oxon, UK: Routledge, 2007); is a model of the careful study of the role of tourism and its many special considerations in the Kingdom of Cambodia, past, present, and future.

33. The challenge of providing improved access to Machu Picchu took on other dimensions when a government-backed commercial operation planned the use of cable cars to improve access and double the number of visitors. Local opposition to this idea was joined by UNESCO and ICOMOS, and the idea was shelved. At this stage in the well-established cultural tourism industry, the essential key elements of access, reception, orientation, site touring options, the actual site visit, and local sales and services are such well-known practices that there are a wealth of better examples to examine throughout the world.

34. Stephen Gordon, "Historical Significance in an Entertainment Oriented Society," in Tomlan, *Preservation of What, for Whom?* 58.

35. In part through its regular contributions to the Jewish Heritage Program of the World Monuments Fund, the Ronald S. Lauder Foundation, in particular, has made preserving historic religious sites a goal.

36. Such actions were particularly prevalent in France, Germany, and Belgium and frequently meant the destruction of historic accoutrements such as stalls, altar rails, rood screens, and the like.

37. Ligen, *Dangers and Perils*, 13.

38. A vacant and neglected house will naturally deteriorate to the point that the condition of its materials and structural systems are beyond practical retrieval. When a house is occupied and internal temperatures are maintained within the range of human comfort, thus preventing exposure of historic architectural components and furnishings to extreme temperatures, the fabric of that building is relatively stable and, with periodic maintenance, will last indefinitely.

39. As of 2008, many of the upper floors of Block 96W at the South Street Seaport Museum in New York City had been without commercial office renters since the renovation of these nineteenth-century commercial buildings in 1981.

40. New architecture that is incompatible in design and function set within the context of existing historic buildings is common. I. M. Pei's insertion of the glass pyramid entrance to the Louvre Museum, or Rogers and Piano's radically new kind of architecture, the Pompidou Center, at the edge of Paris's Marais district, are considered by most to be two successful examples. While the "artistic" juxtaposition of new and old structures in this fashion has often appealed to planners and architects, experience has shown that functionally and aesthetically incompatible designs have often been unsuccessful neighbors.

41. The proliferation of tower blocks within sight of historic monuments in Italian cities is one example of the consequences. The Cavalieri Hilton in the Monte Mario district offers excellent views of old Rome, though it is termed an eyesore for many who view it from the city's historic center.

42. Ligen, *Dangers and Perils*, 12.

43. Byzantine sites were also relegated to second-class status by Greece's nationalist archaeologists. Many were destroyed in the search for remnants of the preferred ancient Greek civilization. This attitude has changed over the past few decades, and Greek authorities now recognize sites of Byzantine origin and other types of heritage, such as the Venetian colonial and Jewish religious properties, as important elements of the nation's cultural past. The restoration of the Etz Hayyim Synagogue in Khaniá on the island of Crete in the 1990s is one example.

44. David Lowenthal, *Possessed by the Past: The Heritage Crusade and the Spoils of History* (London: Viking, 1997).

45. New construction has placed so much pressure on archaeological heritage that the field of archaeology developed a salvage archaeology subspecialty concerned with excavating and documenting sites under time constraints. Salvage archaeologists are brought in to work under tight deadlines—when a site is going to be destroyed because of a building project, for example.

46. Wayne Curtis, "A Cautionary Tale," *Preservation: The Magazine of the National Trust for Historic Preservation*, January–February (2008): 23. All existing building fabric contains within it the energy that was originally spent to create it, from the felling of trees, the forming and firing of bricks, the mining of ore, the smelting of iron, the burning of lime, and the hauling of these materials to the building site. Additional energy was expended in site preparation and in the tens of thousands of actions required to erect and finish the structure.

47. Fitch, *Historic Preservation*, 31.

48. Ibid., 32–34. In 1979, the US Advisory Council on Historic Preservation published a book entitled *Assessing the Energy Conservation Benefits of Historic Preservation: Methods and Examples* (Washington, DC: Advisory Council on Historic Preservation, 1979), which included two examples of embodied energy. Equivalency was calculated for a federally funded, low-cost housing project, the Lockefield Gardens apartments in Indianapolis. These represented over 550 billion Btus of energy, or the equivalent of 4.5 million gallons of gasoline. A second analysis was completed on the shell of a Washington, DC, carriage house, the A. Everett Austin House. Referred to as the Austin House, this structure represented over one billion Btus of energy, or about 8,000 gallons of gasoline (US Advisory Council on Historic Preservation, *Assessing the Energy Conservation Benefits*, 52).

49. One source quotes the difference in cost between rehabilitation and new construction as 75 versus 50 percent. National Trust for Historic Preservation, *Economic Benefits of Preserving Old*

Buildings (1976; repr., Washington, DC: Preservation Press, National Trust for Historic Preservation, 1982).

50. See also Fitch, "The Economic Sense of Recycling," chap. 3, in *Historic Preservation*.

51. A 1991 study of New York City office buildings found that on average, buildings erected after 1940 consumed 25 percent more energy than those constructed earlier. Some buildings consumed more than twice as much. Michael L. Ainslie, preface to *New Energy from Old Buildings*, ed. Diane Maddex (Washington, DC: Preservation Press, National Trust for Historic Preservation, 1982, 1978), 3.

52. Diane Maddex, ed., *New Energy from Old Buildings*, 9.

53. While this scale of historic preservation activity reflects the popularity of the field in many countries today, these actions sometimes have unfortunate results. Wholesale improvements to neighborhoods can result in gentrification, which displaces less affluent residents. It has also occasionally invited unsustainable levels of tourism, such as in the Georgetown section of Washington, DC, or London's Covent Garden district.

54. John C. Sawhill, "Preserving History and Saving Energy: Two Sides of the Same Coin," in Maddex, *New Energy from Old Buildings* (Washington, DC: Preservation Press, National Trust for Historic Preservation, 1982, 1978), 17.

55. Ligen, *Dangers and Perils*, 11.

56. Museum of World Religions conference report, September 2002, Taipei, Taiwan.

57. Although Tung, *Preserving the World's Great Cities*, 17, notes that "far more architectural history was destroyed in the urban redevelopment which followed the fighting than by the tens of millions of bombs themselves…much of the loss incurred in the rush to remodel was avoidable, unnecessary, largely irreversible, and therefore tragic."

58. Widely publicized accounts of the looting of Iraq's museums and cultural institutions during this period of conflict will forever taint the military operations associated with this war. Given ancient Mesopotamia's role in world history, the recent loss of its remains in Iraq was a loss to all humankind.

59. Heritage @ Risk program, ICOMOS, Paris, 1999.

60. The blue shield from which this organization takes its name is the symbol specified in the 1954 Hague Convention for marking cultural sites to protect them from attack in the event of armed conflict. International Committee of the Blue Shield, "Working for the Protection of the World's Cultural Heritage," http://www.ifla.org/VI/4/admin/protect.htm.

Trajans's Market (110 CE), one of many areas of Ancient Rome where several
types of conservation intervention are found.

CHAPTER 8

Options for Involvement

Each architectural conservation problem can be viewed in terms of its typology and relative physical magnitude, and each possible solution in terms of its level of impact, or *degree of intervention*. Decisions about these conceptual parameters define the physical scale of any conservation project and set the philosophical basis for the proposed work. Because conservation is largely the art of controlling change and deciding when and how to repair are crucial decisions.

After a potential architectural conservation project has been identified and the owner's permission to proceed has been obtained, the next step is to determine the scope of the project and viable scenarios for planning and implementing the work. Key to this is determining the physical and philosophical parameters of the task. Rigorous research into both the history and the current condition of the building or site are essential. Who created it and why? What were the original designer's and builder's intentions? How and why were any modifications made? Such questions must be asked and answered early on. At the same time, it is necessary to develop an understanding of the pathologies that are affecting the structure in order to design effective conservation solutions. The rate of deterioration, and whether the deterioration process is currently being controlled, are vital questions in planning for conservation.

Accurate answers are important because a building, or a remnant of a building, is much more than its walls, framing, and finishes: As British conservation architect John Warren states, "It is a statement by and about those who created it, about the time of its making and about the subsequent vicissitudes that have laid upon it the patina of age, the scars of events, and it speaks of the social evolution which its adaptation and changes describe."[1]

With the restoration process comes the prospect of alteration or even destruction. An architectural conservation professional therefore has the duty to develop a thorough understanding of the building in question—its significance, origins, how and why it endured through time, and how it will function in the future—before committing to actions that will affect the significance and integrity of its structure and surroundings. When dealing with listed historic buildings especially, conservation professionals entrusted with this task should give their utmost attention to the structure and painstakingly record its building materials and volumetric qualities, along with the rationale behind their judgments. Because attitudes toward the significance of details that make up a historic building may change over time, it is necessary to document thoroughly and objectively as many of a historic buildings' details as possible and to constantly sharpen one's perception of each project.[2]

Conservation architect Bernard Feilden summarizes the task best: "A complexity of ideas and of cultures may be said to encircle a historic building and be reflected in it.... The object of the conservator must be the retention of the fabric and its consolidation for future use in the context of a sympathetic understanding of its past."[3] This is the essence of what historic building and site conservation is all about.

"Buildings are mortal," another prominent British conservation architect, Donald Insall, once stated. "Building conservation, like medicine, demands preventative care which if overlooked can be costly. The earliest signs of problems arising are often slight, and it is necessary to differentiate between important symptoms and those which can be disregarded.... Examples of this are changes in groundwater conditions, or cracks in walls and foundations [that] reflect a change in load pattern and a loss of structural integrity."[4]

Most architectural conservation experts argue for as little intervention as possible and for accomplishing only what is structurally necessary to arrest the most aggressive sources of decay in order to slow the rate of erosion. Most also agree that the less visible the intervention, the more successful the end result.

Sympathetic repairs must be ensured through the use of appropriate materials and techniques. Usually, policies concerning conservation bow to the urgency of the situation, the nature of defects, what threats apply, and the proposed reuse of the building. But when assessing these factors, certain immutable principles must be followed. The most important of these entail a commitment to *minimal intervention* and the *reversibility* of those interventions wherever possible. The time-tested principle of intervening as little as possible while at the same time making sure these actions are capable of being rescinded without compromising the original fabric allows for a wider range of options in the future should other interventions be warranted. The minimal intervention principle also ensures the retention of original or earlier building fabric, which is crucial to the important concept of conserving authenticity.

Of course, some principles are bound to conflict with one another, as will other issues of the "fit" of new functions, compliance with modern building standards, expense, and so on, are accommodated. In such cases, good judgment based upon experience comes into play.[5] John Warren further states the need for architectural conservation professionals to approach their work in an ethical and transparent manner: "It should be undertaken with the utmost *integrity*, which means the conservator must use the materials appropriate to the original purpose. They must have *sympathy* for the old, so that the newer work is appropriate. In addition, *datability* ensures the authenticity of the age and nature of intervention, and *honesty* is integral to defining the work as what is was originally conceived. Finally, *location* as a principle underscores an important relationship of a specific structure to its geographical site, of which it is irrevocably a part."[6]

Neutrality is another facet of conservation that demonstrates respect for the historical context of the original fabric; it is an extension of the concept of authenticity and a guiding principle in the field. A neutral or modestly respectful intervention extends the life of a structure without compromising the building's original architectural character.

The documentation of interventions is an essential part of the conservator's work. Buildings with a long history are, by definition, bastions of time that have outlasted those who were originally involved with their construction and upkeep. Therefore, any records detailing repair and conservation work done over the years become important tools for those charged with their future maintenance. Such records should cite their sources for materials, and the types and extent of work carried out, as well as its sequence and nature. Armed with this information, future architectural conservators will be able to assess the success of past techniques and use this assessment to plan their own work.

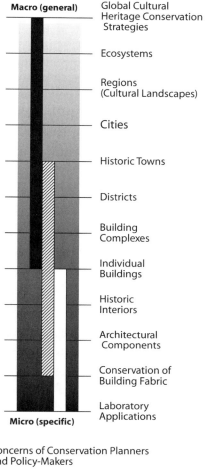

Architectural Conservation: Levels of Participation

Macro (general)

— Global Cultural Heritage Conservation Strategies

— Ecosystems

— Regions (Cultural Landscapes)

— Cities

— Historic Towns

— Districts

— Building Complexes

— Individual Buildings

— Historic Interiors

— Architectural Components

— Conservation of Building Fabric

— Laboratory Applications

Micro (specific)

 Concerns of Conservation Planners and Policy-Makers

 Concerns of most Architectural Conservationists

▢ Concerns of Building Materials Conservation Scientists (e.g., applied science; diagnoses of pathologies and prescription of solutions with an historical perspective

Considerations:

1. The scale is vast (ranging from a global perspective to the microscopic).

2. Conservation professionals usually work at different points on the scale and can often be working on several at the same time.

3. The task of preserving and presenting the built world is both synoptic and cross-disciplinary

4. The methodology for addressing each scale of problem is essentially the same (e.g., rational, deductive reasoning).

Chart 8-1 Architectural Conservation: Levels of Participation

LEVELS OF PARTICIPATION

The problem of conserving buildings and sites should be approached holistically and should consider all related cultural, spatial, structural, and environmental characteristics. After holistic planning—documenting and developing an understanding of the various values and the overall significance of the resource and considering several alternatives—specific planning for conservation can begin. Hard decisions about compromises may be faced that may entail, as Bernard Feilden says, finding the "least bad" solution. An understanding of the available choices depends on an appreciation of the spectrum of possible physical and conceptual parameters of the challenges at hand.

In recent decades the field of architectural conservation has expanded to include a wide range of potential physical involvements and degrees or profundities of intervention.[7] James Marston Fitch was the first to realize that systematizing the parameters of physical intervention in conserving the built world could be useful. As he said, "[D]espite the size and complexity of the field, it is yet susceptible to rational quantification, description, and analysis."[8]

In the early years of the architectural conservation movement, typical concerns rarely extended beyond an individual building and its site. With time, broader scales of interest have developed; for example, planning and architectural heritage protection agencies often preserve entire neighborhoods. In time, this view has enlarged further to include whole districts and even small towns. More recently, the scale of possible physical involvement has widened further to include entire cities and cultural landscapes. Some of today's national and international laws and conventions address the broadest conceptual scales of physical involvement, including whole ecosystems. In 1994, the United Nations Educational, Scientific and Cultural Organization's (UNESCO's) World Heritage Centre adopted its Global Strategy for a Balanced, Representative and Credible World Heritage List, which aimed not only to increase the number of sites in underrepresented countries and regions but also to expand the types of sites on the list to include natural and traditional cultural landscapes.[9]

A conceptual scale of physical involvement outlines the range of possible physical magnitudes within which architectural conservationists may operate (Chart 8-1). Architectural conservation specialists and colleagues in allied fields can work at scales ranging from entire ecosystems to specific building components—all the way down to the microscopic level. In between these extremities are cities, historic districts, and individual buildings.

Inside this range, specialists in the field tend to operate within certain limits. For instance, conservation planners, policy makers, and those involved with international conservation practice are concerned with conservation issues that are usually macro in scale, significance, and influence. The historic resources they address might range from a specific iconic building or site or something even larger—like an entire historic town—to very particular, site-specific conservation issues, the solutions for which, it is hoped, will become contributions to the field. Practitioners such as architects and engineers usually work with physical challenges ranging in scale from restoring and conserving entire historic towns or whole districts all the way down to specific buildings and their essential components. Building materials conservation specialists (or architectural conservators) work on issues pertaining to historic building fabric, which may be represented in the form of a whole building or its miniscule constituent parts, even at the molecular level.

Within this generalized schema, certain patterns point to some useful and reassuring conclusions:

1. The scale's **range** is vast and spans from micro level (e.g., examining marble's molecular composition) to the broadest imaginable (e.g., cultural landscapes on UNESCO's World Heritage List, even regions crossing international boundaries).

2. In actual **practice**, one project inevitably falls at different points on the scale of physical intervention simultaneously, as when a conservation architect is restoring a house museum within a historic village that is also being conserved.

3. Conserving and presenting historic buildings and sites are both **synoptic** and **cross-disciplinary** activities. Conservation project goals and objectives are site specific, and specialization within the field allows for—even demands—a cross-disciplinary approach. For example, it takes a team of specialists to restore *and* interpret a historic building, and additional specialists are needed to conserve its historic environmental context.

4. The **methodology** for addressing each type and scale of physical challenge in conservation practice is usually the same. Each relies on the scientific method: Identify the problem through either deductive or inductive reasoning; establish and test a hypothesis; prescribe and implement a solution; document the entire process; and monitor the results.

5. The **types** of cultural heritage resources being conserved are forever growing in number and variety. The traditional view of only conserving the best representative examples of their type in order to glorify certain aspects of the past has given way to a newer, wider interest in conserving the vernacular, the folkloric, the industrial, and even the controversial—evidence of a broader view of history. Additionally, as more contemporary designers become involved with rehabilitating and recycling old buildings, bold new examples of modernizing and enhancing the built environment are being seen.

6. Examples of different types of cultural heritage and awareness of their significance are broadening as cultural heritage conservation continues to develop as a global concern, for example, government-designated masters of skills in performing or applied arts recognized on an individual or collective basis (Japanese "Law for the Protection of Cultural Properties," 1984). As the breadth of additional forms of tangible and *intangible cultural heritage* expands, so does the number of specialized interests and areas of inquiry within it. Fields range widely, from research on site-specific human activities during prehistoric times (e.g., the Banpo culture in Xi'an, China) to addressing time and change through modern art (for example, American artist Donald Judd's Rooms—places for contemplation of time and space—which are on view at the Chinati Foundation museum in Marfa, Texas). Both the Xi'an and Judd site museums have professional architectural conservators in residence.

DEGREES OF INTERVENTION

In addition to the scale of physical possibilities, various levels or *degrees of intervention* are available to the architectural conservationist (Chart 8-2). Each level on this scale carries with it attendant philosophical implications that are increasingly complex: The greater the intervention, the greater the risk to authenticity and the likelihood of irreversibility. And conserving and presenting artistic and architectural heritage is often complicated when several types of intervention are required during the same project. Such circumstances again underscore the importance of documenting the "as-found" conditions, the determination of a clear rationale for planned interventions based on the character and significance of the building or site in question, a respectful design that considers both practical and aesthetic issues, and carefully executed work.

Whichever level of intervention is chosen, long-term conservation is best served by the continued use of a site in a way that respects its structural integrity and surviving historic architectural fabric. For all interventions, the primary aims should include retaining as much of the existing structure and other building fabric as possible, special care in the replacement of missing elements, and the design of alterations to serve the role of the building within its context.[10]

As noted both in Section I and in the glossary, the field of architectural conservation has appropriated its nomenclature from a variety of sources and languages. The previously defined interventions termed *restoration, rehabilitation, conservation,* and *adaptive use* are among the most common interventions that architectural conservationists rely on. These and several other options reveal a range of choices that spans from the least to the most intrusive to a building's or site's historic integrity. Different options and levels for intervention at historic architectural and archaeological sites include:

- *Laissez-faire:* This approach involves leaving a site alone. There are instances where no action at all is either necessary or justified—when conditions are not right for intervention.[11]

- *Preservation* or *conservation:* A dictionary definition for *preserve* is "to keep safe from harm, to maintain, keep up, and guard against decay"; for *conserve*, "to preserve, retain, keep entire." **Architectural conservation**'s aim is to preserve or conserve as much historic building fabric as possible. This approach is considered "conservative" from a theoretical standpoint.

- *Preventative conservation:* Preventative or defensive conservation has been employed more frequently in the context of objects conservation; it is increasingly being used, however, for conserving historic buildings and building complexes. It has been defined as "all actions taken to retard deterioration and prevent damage to cultural property though the provision of optimal conditions of storage, use and handling."[12] One example of defensive conservation is the prevention of a road from being constructed next to an important building or site.

- *Maintenance:* Every historic structure requires the attention of experienced maintenance personnel, though most buildings also have their own specific requirements. Effective regular maintenance is termed *cyclical maintenance* and comprises a rigid program of periodic inspections. The regularity of maintenance inspections and actions depends on the historic building in question and can range from inspections by outside consultants every one to three years to daily inspections by a variety of experts who may work at the property. Unfortunately, the importance of periodic inspection and routine maintenance is rarely recognized.

- *Consolidation* or *stabilization:* The aim of stabilizing a material, a component, or an entire building is to arrest the decay process. Options for consolidation or stabilization range from minimal to radical—and from visible to invisible. The choices depend on the materials involved, their pathologies, and the physical scale of the problem.[13] A ruined structure can essentially be "frozen in time" by stabilization measures that protect it from further erosion, either through interventions that directly protect the fabric of the ruins, enclosing the site in another structure, or some combination of the two.[14]

- **Restoration:** Restoration returns a building, site, or work of art to an appearance it had at an earlier time. It can involve major interventions to part or all of it. If special circumstances such as subsequently discovered compelling evidence justifies restoration to an original appearance or condition, this may involve the alteration or removal of subsequent changes. This can only be successfully achieved, however, if the decision emerges from a sound, objective, and comprehensively conceived conservation policy.

- **Rehabilitation** or **renovation:** Rehabilitation makes efficient, contemporary use of a property possible once again. The repairs and alterations, however, preserve those portions or features of the property that are significant to its historical, architectural, and cultural values. Rehabilitation entails the extensive renewal or modifications of the elements of a building required to adapt it to a new purpose, as when modern services are introduced. Sensitive rehabilitations include the reuse of original materials where possible.

- **Reconstruction:** The reassembly of a partially or completely collapsed structure on its original site (in situ) using most, if not all, of its original materials. Also called **anastylosis**, it is considered to be a major level of intervention. It is most easily justified in cases of extreme recent damage from catastrophes, such as collapse by earthquake, flood, or bombing.[15]

- **Relocation:** Occasionally, there is no way to save an old building other than to move it. The building, or a significant part thereof, is then disassembled and reassembled—or sometimes moved as a complete entity—to a new site. Such a radical intervention is considered to be a last resort in most instances.[16]

- **Replication:** The replication of a vanished or extant building entails making a copy or **facsimile** at a different site. Justifications for replication are similar to those for reconstruction. Replication can involve the creation of another version of a building or landscape by its original creator, or it can be achieved in a later era. The term **replication** is related to the term **reproduction**, which describes when exact copies of extant examples of missing building elements (or **lacunae**) are used on a project.[17]

An extensive restoration, a reconstruction, or a replica of a damaged or destroyed building will never carry the same value and meaning as the original. Nevertheless, the replication of a lost building or part thereof may be an important consideration in the presentation of the integrity of the whole and therefore has its place in architectural conservation practice. The task might be as simple as replacing a lost component within a known design, or it might be more speculative, based on careful research and related philosophical and aesthetic concerns.

Yet despite all the rhetoric in the field of heritage conservation today—or possibly because of it—many historic buildings and sites are still being treated in heavy-handed ways when more respectful interventions could just as easily have been performed. This is largely due to a lack of awareness of best practices in the field or ambivalence on the part of those responsible for cultural resources. One reason for such ambivalence is a problem with perceptions of ownership—that is, for taking responsibility for the past. (See Chapter 5.) Another has to do with specialized interests that can result in a lack of balance in conservation programs.[18]

Given the built environment's accelerating rate of change, decisions must frequently be made hastily, and decision makers are often pressured to act before receiving adequate technical information and financial support. Taking the time to consider completely all aspects of a decision, including the possibility of deferring any action until greater consensus and coordination can be reached and adequate support obtained, is usually the best approach.[19]

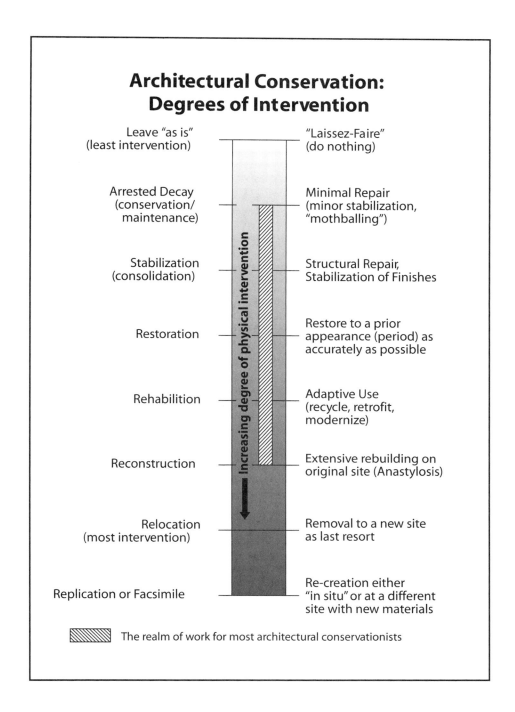

Architectural Conservation: Degrees of Intervention

Leave "as is" (least intervention) — "Laissez-Faire" (do nothing)

Arrested Decay (conservation/ maintenance) — Minimal Repair (minor stabilization, "mothballing")

Stabilization (consolidation) — Structural Repair, Stabilization of Finishes

Restoration — Restore to a prior appearance (period) as accurately as possible

Rehabilition — Adaptive Use (recycle, retrofit, modernize)

Reconstruction — Extensive rebuilding on original site (Anastylosis)

Relocation (most intervention) — Removal to a new site as last resort

Replication or Facsimile — Re-creation either "in situ" or at a different site with new materials

Increasing degree of physical intervention

⬚ The realm of work for most architectural conservationists

Considerations:

1. Conservative vs. Radical Approach

   Conservative—more easily reversed, conserves more authenticity, and often costs less

   Radical—Less easily reversed, affects the authentic quality of the site, and is usually more expensive

2. Objective: Finding the "right" degree of intervention; the conservative approach is usually safer and better

Chart 8-2 Architectural Conservation: Degrees of Intervention

ENDNOTES

1. John Warren, introduction to *Earthen Architecture: The Conservation of Brick and Earth Structures; A Handbook* (Sri Lanka: International Council on Monuments and Sites [ICOMOS], 1993). See also Warren, "Principles and Problems: Ethics and Aesthetics" in (ed.)Stephen Marks *Concerning Buildings*, (Oxford: Butterworth Heinmann), 1996, 34–54.

2. Ibid., xi.

3. Bernard Feilden, "An Introduction to Conservation of Cultural Property" papers at ICCROM, UNESCO, (Paris: 1979).

4. Warren, *Earthen Architecture*, xxi.

5. To this end, architect Lee H. Nelson, former head of the US National Park Service's Technical Preservation Services division, suggested creating a decision-making tree that allowed for the listing of the pros and cons of various conservation interventions under consideration.

6. Warren, *Earthen Architecture*, xxii.

7. Based on the concept of the scale of intervention first articulated in Fitch, *Historic Preservation*, 44. This concept was heavily relied upon in the formation of the 1983 Appleton Charter for the Enhancement of the Built Environment prepared by ICOMOS Canada.

8. Fitch, *Historic Preservation*, 47.

9. As articulated in the Budapest Conference of 1992, the "4 Cs" of its stated objective are *credibility, conservation, capacity-building*, and *communication*. UNESCO, "Global Strategy," http://whc.unesco.org/en/globalstrategy/.

10. Warren, *Earthen Architecture*, 188–89.

11. There may be a mitigating extrinsic circumstance, such as the presence of a recalcitrant owner whose departure may facilitate a future intervention. When a subterranean structure is discovered by remote sensing and can be analyzed by endoscopic photography and otherwise left undisturbed, taking no action can also be optimal.

12. IIC-CG Code of Ethics and Guidance for Conservation Practice, definitions.

13. Flaking paint or a detached plaster surface can be stabilized in situ by material conservation measures. A structurally damaged building can be stabilized relatively simply by measures ranging from temporary shoring to discrete structural interventions.

14. Museums primarily use the "frozen-in-time" approach for their collections of objects because they have the advantage of working in controlled environments. Conservers of architecture in outdoor settings may have the same ambitions for a building or site, but they must inevitably embrace the approach of managed change. The reburial of an archaeological site is an example of this kind of preservation, although this action has occasionally produced unwanted results, such as when changes in drainage or vegetation negatively affect the archaeological resources in question.

15. Reconstruction can be justified in historic terms—a rebuilding on original foundations using as much original fabric as possible, for example. It can also be justified when a destroyed building or landscape was a vital part of an urban scene and its reconstruction is preferred in order to preserve the established historic context. Where the contents of an interior have been saved and can be accurately reassembled, reconstruction may be the best option available.

16. There are long traditions of moving buildings in most parts of the world, with the act in some instances being historically significant in and of itself. For example, new Japanese and Chinese rulers often relocated and recycled decommissioned palatial or temple forms used by their predecessors and integrated them into their new buildings. Such actions also were routine in ancient Rome and Greece.

17. An example is the replica of Michelangelo's famous statue of David in the Piazza della Signoria in Florence; the original is more safely on view in the nearby Accademia di Belle Arti. Replicas can represent an extreme approach from a philosophical point of view, because viewers of the reproduction are not seeing the original.

18. David Baker, *Living with the Past*, 10.

19. One such reaction that has arisen in the art conservation field, and that is taking on currency in the field of architectural conservation, is the laissez-faire policy advocated by James Beck of Columbia University in New York. His proposed "A Bill of Rights for Works of Art" in *Remove Not the Ancient Landmark*, Donald M. Reynolds and Rudolf Wittkower (London: Routledge 1996), 65–72, questions the necessity of restoring several important works of art at all. Until

his death in 2007, Beck argued vehemently against restorations of Michelangelo's ceiling frescoes in the Sistine Chapel; Leonardo da Vinci's *The Last Supper* in Santa Maria delle Grazie, Milan; and the tomb of Ilaria del Carretto in the Cathedral of Saint Marin in Lucca, citing views on the original artists' intentions, the historic and aesthetic value of accumulated patinas, and truths about the reversibility of certain kinds of interventions. Thus far, Beck's views on conservation have centered on movable artworks and art that is integral to buildings and not on complete works of architecture. Nevertheless, buildings conservators would do well to take heed.

THE ILLUSTRATED
BURRA CHARTER

Good Practice for Heritage Places

Meredith Walker & Peter Marquis-Kyle

AUSTRALIA ICOMOS
International Council on Monuments and Sites

CHAPTER 9

Principles, Charters, and Ethics

Accumulated experience in the fields of art and architectural conservation over the centuries has generated a generally recognized body of philosophical, aesthetic, and technical parameters that serve as the operational basis of architectural conservation practice today. These have been forged by, and reflect, many of humankind's major challenges and endeavors: physical needs, psychological needs, social change, economic forces, and technological developments. All along, the cause-and-effect nature of architectural conservation practice has generated seminal questions: Why are we doing this? Why *this* particular building? Why apply *this* philosophy and method and not another? What does *original* mean in this instance? Does authenticity really matter?[1]

The answers to these questions vary depending on the circumstances. While some aspects of conservation theory may seem universal, others have more context-specific applications. Conservation policy developed for the treatment of historic architectural resources, in fact, frequently combines more than one philosophical approach. For example, an urban conservation project may entail carefully restoring building façades while taking more liberties with their interior spaces.

Those participating in the architectural conservation process are expected to ensure that actions that physically affect listed or eligible architectural heritage sites be in compliance with the intent of their relevant legal protection measures. A knowledge of precedents for the application of recognized principles and procedures, and how to get things accomplished in the relevant locale, can make the difference between a conservation project running smoothly and successfully or not.

PHILOSOPHICAL APPROACHES

In the broadest sense, the philosophy of cultural heritage conservation is that the world's cultural resources are common resources for the common good. However, this universalist view, which is held by the United Nations Educational, Scientific and Cultural Organization (UNESCO), its supporting institutions, and most others involved in international architectural conservation practice, offers no practical suggestions for conserving historic buildings, sites, or objects. The ability to judge how best to plan for the conservation of historic buildings and sites comes by examining the history and evolution of philosophies in the field of architectural conservation and cultivating a historical perspective on how attitudes toward protecting historic patrimony evolved.

Despite frequent debates on the applicability of philosophies and the ever-increasing numbers of new charters and guidelines that promote best practices, the overall aims of architectural conservation remain largely the same and will continue to do so for the foreseeable future.[2] The internationality of the heritage conservation field today provides cultural heritage conservationists with an abundance of information on practices in other places, an advantage that encourages discussion.

Within the subject of historiography—in particular, its facets dealing with the history of architectural history, the history of art history, and the history of architectural conservation—attitudes change toward building styles, periods, and their influences, as well as why and how certain historic architectural resources have been conserved. (See also "Cultural Bias" in Chapter 7 and Part III.) Today, experts in cultural heritage conservation and the general public tend to favor conserving evidence of history that predates their own lifetimes.[3] Throughout history, too, such preferences have favored the preservation of certain architecture (and many other things) over others; the result has been the loss of much cultural heritage to the whims of changing interests and taste. In the European Renaissance, for example, the architecture of the Middle Ages was ignored in favor of a renewed interest in Greek and Roman antiquity.[4] The baroque was once despised by some during its time and long after for not having followed the rules of canonical classicism; the neo-Gothic grew in reaction to neoclassicism; and all of architectural history—and most art from all previous periods—was seen as déclassé by many mid-twentieth-century modernists. One conclusion in observing such biases is that more objective determinations of the values imbued in historic objects, buildings, and sites are necessary. At the present time this is certainly occurring, but the record is not perfect, and it probably never will be, since it is human nature to question and to hold opinions.

Since the 1960s, the architectural conservation field has vastly expanded. It now serves a global interest, as public demands have increased for the conservation, interpretation, and enjoyment of history through firsthand experiences. To meet these demands, heritage protection legislation has become increasingly sophisticated, and the number of agencies and administrators having purview over architectural conservation has grown commensurately. In response, conservation professionals have been required to justify their actions in legal, technical, economic, and philosophical terms. Therefore, whether a person has only a lay interest in the subject, is just entering the profession, or is a well-established professional, he or she must always be prepared to make well-considered arguments in favor of, or against, all types of interventions. An informed knowledge of the key conservation philosophies is crucial for modern heritage conservation professionals.

There are millions of conserved buildings throughout the world serving as inspiring and instructive exemplars, and each survived its own ever-changing circumstances. Because each building is unique and because there are often varying interpretations of the significance of such resources, there is no single appropriate philosophic approach applicable to architectural conservation.[5] John Earl's *Building Conservation Philosophy* outlines the range of philosophical positions from three possible key points of view: that of the purist, the pragmatist, and the cynic:

The **purist** considers that the existence of alternative philosophical approaches toward the preservation of buildings is incorrect. Correctness cannot be watered down. A job should either be done properly or not at all.

The **pragmatist** believes that a sound philosophy points in the direction of truthfulness. Its precise application must depend on the building and its circumstances. If someone is in command of all the facts, then the building will tell *him* what to do.

The **cynic** feels that preservation is a completely artificial procedure, one that interferes with the natural processes of decay and obsolescence. Preservation philosophies are therefore necessarily artificial; they are generally used to justify an approach that has already been decided upon.[6]

Certain aspects of architectural conservation philosophy will always be challenging. For example, how is authenticity measured in a structure's material and form? Does it carry the same importance for all structures? In *Earthen Architecture*, John Warren asks, "How does authenticity apply to…a cathedral whose stone had been cut back in the nineteenth century, and an earthen built west African mosque which has all new surfaces due to the demands of earthen architecture where the original form has been preserved?"[7] Warren suggests that an expert would argue an original earthen architectural form that has been faithfully renewed is more authentic than cut-back stone buildings because the construction remains that of the first design. Perpetual maintenance, even if it means extensive use of new, "in-kind" materials, is allowable if the earlier design is retained, because authenticity lies equally in the materials and in the design.

In this example, Warren addresses a philosophical dilemma that architectural conservationists frequently encounter. While the heritage conservation movement is attuned to the essential criterion of authenticity—as is evidenced in the dozens of charters that have been produced over the past century—nonprofessionals may understandably be confused about this issue. Given the number of surrogate historic experiences found in the history-based entertainment attractions developed and operated by the Walt Disney Company and a growing number of other commercial operations with similar aims, especially in East and Southeast Asia,[8] discussions about authenticity in heritage conservation will be with us for many years to come. (A recent example of this tendency was the announcement in January 2008 that the chairman of Emirates Investment & Development intended to build a replica of the historic center of Lyon, France, in Dubai on the Arabian Peninsula.)[9]

Those involved in real architectural conservation practice should observe the most basic philosophical principles and ethical standards. Bernard Feilden enumerates them succinctly in *Conservation of Historic Buildings*:

1. The condition of the building must be recorded before any intervention.

2. Historic evidence must not be destroyed, falsified, or removed.

3. Any intervention must be the minimum necessary.

4. Any intervention must be governed by unswerving respect for the aesthetic, historical, and physical integrity of cultural property.

5. All methods and materials used during treatment must be fully documented.[10]

These basic principles in architectural conservation are fundamental and are, in fact, the same ones used in the allied field of art conservation.[11]

LEGISLATION

Laws and customs for protecting buildings precede even the ancient Greek and Roman civilizations. As detailed in a section in Chapter 12 titled "Prehistoric through Hellenistic Times" (page 157), the earliest documented restoration and preservation actions can be found in Mesopotamia during the second millennium BCE.[12] Beginning with orders from

Emperor Julius in the fourth century CE, Roman law called for the protection and maintenance of older monumental structures. During the late Middle Ages and the Renaissance, papal decrees tried, with limited success, to protect monuments from desecration by those wanting to remove and reuse their building materials. In April 1462, Pope Pius II issued *Cum almam nostram urbem*, the first papal bull to specifically mention the preservation of ancient remains.[13]

From that point forward, formal protection of built heritage accelerated. A 1666 Swedish royal proclamation demanded the protection of all historic monuments, and in 1818, the Grand Duke of Hesse issued a decree concerning surviving historic structures in his territory, now a part of Germany. Throughout the remainder of the nineteenth century, national protection of architectural heritage was legally enshrined in Greece (1834), France (1841), Spain (1860), Italy (1872), Hungary and Egypt (1881), the United Kingdom (1882), Finland (1883), Bulgaria (1889), Romania (1892), and Norway (1897).

The French national legislation in 1841 marked the first efforts to articulate a specific code of conservation principles and guidelines. It established a framework of controls, gave grants to major cathedrals and other significant structures, and guarded recognized buildings against demolition or radical change—but little else. It is at this point that state offices became more broadly involved in conservation issues, compiling heritage resource inventories, documentation standards, and allowable interventions. When France issued its monuments protection legislation, it became a model of heritage protection administration. In the nineteenth century, the French form of cultural heritage administration expanded overseas to its colonies, a relationship that was retained through the interwar years of the twentieth century.

Clearer, more stringent, more rational conservation rules and guidelines were needed, however; all manner of protection and restoration approaches had previously been attempted at various national architectural monuments. It fell to the French administrators who had been appointed to inventory, restore, and maintain these historic buildings to design this integrated approach and to further the legal protection and administration of these buildings. The chief originator of this system was France's first monuments inspector general, the architect Prosper Mérimée, who guided the Service des Monuments Historiques from 1834 to 1853.[14]

From the early twentieth century until the present, a plethora of cultural heritage protection legislation for use at all levels of government has been produced, generating the legal framework within which heritage conservation activities occur in all countries.[15] The practice of architectural conservation began to take on a new dimension in the 1960s with the advent of widely recognized legislation that protected entire enclaves of historic buildings through combinations of incentives and disincentives.[16]

Today, architectural conservation legislation typically calls for the listing of historic buildings and sites, their documentation and monitoring, as well as the establishment of a heritage conservation agency to oversee and coordinate these planning activities. Workable architectural conservation laws require certain basic provisions, including:

- A definition of what is to be preserved, usually in the form of a list of criteria for determining value and significance

- A method by which the authorities will be alerted to possible danger (commonly, laws require a notice or an application to be made before a protected building can be demolished or altered)

- A way of permitting harmless or desirable works to proceed after notifying the controlling authority and its experts (whose approval is often outlined in a certificate of consent that outlines conditions for action)

- Effective, tangible sanctions against offenders (e.g., fines, imprisonment, enforcement, direct action to repair, expropriation)[17]

CODIFICATION OF PRINCIPLES AND DOCTRINE

Theorizing about and questioning the appropriateness of various principles and procedures for conserving buildings began in the eighteenth century. In England in the 1790s, debates on architectural conservation philosophy originated surrounding James Wyatt's restorations at Windsor Castle and Lichfield Cathedral in Staffordshire. These early debates were informed by artistic and aesthetic interests in the picturesque and the *sublime* qualities of historic buildings and landscapes, which had begun earlier with the writings and building achievements of Horace Walpole, Uvedale Price, William Beckford, Humphrey Repton, and others.

Deliberation about conservation issues was initially more so in the public realm in England because there, more so than on the European continent, conservation theory and the legislation that later supported it were developed by antiquarians, advocates, and concerned citizens, rather than by bureaucratic institutions or royal fiat.[18] In the mid-nineteenth century, the debate on how to treat ancient buildings reached a feverish pitch when John Ruskin and William Morris argued for more measured approaches to maintenance and respect for historic building fabric, opposing purely pragmatic architects such as Sir George Gilbert Scott. Scott proposed more liberal avenues, defending the radical restorations that he and others were conducting at the time.

These two competing schools of thought became known as scrape and anti-scrape (a heavy-handed versus a highly restrained approach).[19] An important outgrowth of this polemic was the 1877 Manifesto of the Society for the Preservation of Ancient Buildings, founded by William Morris. It has served as a precedent for the plethora of conservation charters and doctrines that followed it.

The first attempt at an international code of architectural conservation practice, *The Preservation and Restoration of Architectural Monuments*, was drafted in 1904 at the Sixth International Council of Architects in Madrid. It was not until 1931 that another international effort was made to address the core issues of architectural conservation and related ethics, this time at a conference in Athens. Another year passed before the Assembly of the League of Nations formally agreed to communicate to its member states the proceedings of the congress of specialists embodied in the Athens Charter.[20] Since then, many new doctrines, both national and international, have raised standards for architectural conservation intervention and have created efficient mechanisms for transmitting information about solutions and best practices in heritage conservation all over the world. (See also Chapter 16 and Appendix C.)

Following World War II, the United Nations continued the League of Nations' role and has been prominent in cultural heritage protection. Since the 1950s, its affiliate, UNESCO, has passed a number of conventions to safeguard select globally significant heritage sites. These include the concept of World Heritage sites, a legal framework established by its convention of 1972 that seeks to recognize and protect exemplary cultural and natural heritage sites.[21]

As functional regional conservation bodies matured during the mid-twentieth century, the international scope of cultural heritage oversight expanded. Scores of new charters, decrees, and declarations clarified and enhanced existing legislation and administrative procedures. The most influential of these was the Venice Charter of 1964,[22] which along with many others was produced under the aegis of the International Council on Monuments and Sites (ICOMOS). Not only did these charters serve contemporary needs, they also helped stimulate cultural heritage protection in particular, and architectural conservation in general.

The leaders in international heritage conservation advocacy and practice have been supported by organizations such as the International Council on Museums (ICOM), the International Union for the Conservation of Nature (IUCN), and a number of smaller specialized international nongovernmental and private organizations. All serve in increasingly sophisticated ways as useful complements and counterpoints to national legislation. (See Appendix B.)

Regional organizations have also played an important role in the detailing and implementation of international conservation principles. One of the first multinational regional agreements was executed in 1946, when the Cultural Treaty of the Arab League outlined methods of cooperation for various issues, including the safeguarding of intellectual and artistic legacy. The Council of Europe has been one of the foremost producers of conservation guidelines for international application since its organization in 1949. While the charters developed by UNESCO and ICOMOS primarily address architectural conservation principles and issue-specific guidelines, those developed by the Council of Europe have dealt with the social issues of cultural heritage conservation. In cultural heritage and in other matters, the Council of Europe's voice was strengthened by the creation of the European Union in 1993. Today, the council's work in heritage protection occasionally reaches beyond the borders of Europe, in the spirit of international friendship.

Many international conventions, or parts thereof, have also been adopted by conservation practitioners in individual countries. (See Appendix C.) Two examples are Australia's Burra Charter (originally adopted in 1979 and subsequently revised several times) and Mexico's 1993 Declaration of Oaxaca, which addresses the rights of Latin America's indigenous peoples, respect for their special relationship with nature, and the need for industrialized nations to preserve the biosphere. Australian heritage conservationists found that many Venice Charter tenets were not applicable to their needs because one of their greatest challenges was to conserve aboriginal heritage sites so that they could be appreciated by all while still being used by their aboriginal custodians. The resulting Burra Charter's strength lies in its assessment of cultural values as a critical basis for conserving both tangible and intangible heritage. Created under the aegis of Australia ICOMOS and Heritage Australia, the Burra Charter recommends that wherever possible, all established cultural values of a heritage place should be conserved in an integrated way.[23] At Uluru (Ayers Rock), Australia's popular tourist destination, aboriginal peoples were part of the heritage planning process; their special considerations have been integrated into aspects of the site's presentation.

FIVE INFLUENTIAL ARCHITECTURAL CONSERVATION CHARTERS AND DOCUMENTS

Some charters pertaining to architectural conservation have been superseded and abandoned, and others may require updating. Nevertheless, their creation and utilization have been immeasurably beneficial in forging agreements on diverse cultural heritage protection issues over the years. They have also helped others who continue to develop appropriate heritage conservation guidelines and related administrative frameworks.

The Society for the Protection of Ancient Buildings Manifesto

William Morris's 1877 manifesto of the Society for the Protection of Ancient Buildings (SPAB) was the first attempt to set down basic ideals in architectural conservation. While later charters tend to take the case for saving old buildings for granted, the SPAB Manifesto openly argues that preserving buildings is a sound proposition better than most alternatives. It invokes a true sense of heritage by arguing that sites are inherited by the contemporary generation and should be maintained for the future. Morris notes:

It has been said most truly that these old buildings do not belong to us only; that they belonged to our forefathers and they will belong to our descendants unless we play them false. They are not in any sense our property, to do as we like with them. We are only trustees for those who come after us.[24]

The SPAB Manifesto has survived far beyond its historical origins and remains an important guide. Its underlying ideas, as British architect John Earl has noted, "have been adopted and substantially amended as the basis of international creeds such as the Venice Charter of 1964, which was an outgrowth of the Athens Charter of 1931, and which was supplemented by Recommendations of the UNESCO Paris Conferences of 1968 and 1972."[25]

Though the manifesto did not include the word *authenticity*, it laid the foundation for this guiding principle of architectural conservation by suggesting that overly restored and reconstructed buildings and building fragments were forgeries and that only buildings with their original materials on their original sites were truly worthy of protection. It also warned against the conjecture and destruction involved in restoration by arguing: "Those who make the changes wrought in our day under the name of Restoration, while professing to bring back a building to the best time of its history, have no guide but each his own individual whim to point out to them what is admirable and what is contemptible; while the very nature of their task compels them to destroy something, and to supply the gap by imagining what the earlier builders should or might have done."[26]

Unlike subsequent documents, the SPAB Manifesto does not lay down specific principles or procedures. Even today, the society stresses that it is not a blueprint but rather a lens through which a building and its problems can be viewed. It asked conservators only "to stave off decay by daily care," arguing the extreme position that architectural heritage was something contemporary interventions could not "meddle with without destroying."[27] The SPAB Manifesto also expanded the range of architectural styles and building types considered valuable.

The Venice Charter

The Venice Charter is the common name for the International Charter for the Conservation and Restoration of Monuments and Sites, which was drafted in Venice in 1964 and adopted by ICOMOS in 1966. It has been periodically amended since that time. It has had a significant, positive effect on the general field of heritage conservation and is recognized as a standard in legislation around the world. The Venice Charter articulates proper procedures for the restoration and conservation of historic buildings and sites through definitions and stated principles. It encourages precise documentation, scientific investigation, and rational interventions, all in the interest of authenticity.

The Venice Charter comprises sixteen tenets, many of which are concepts developed in the nineteenth century. It supersedes the Athens Charter of 1931 and was an outgrowth of what may have been the largest congress of restorers and architectural conservationists to date: The Second International Congress of Architects and Technicians of Historic Monuments, which convened in Venice, represented the most advanced thinking in the field at the time. The newly formed ICOMOS adopted the Venice Charter the year after its drafting.

An idea of the scope and the spirit of its principles can be gained from a few excerpted articles:

Article 1. The concept of a historic monument embraces not only the single architectural work but also the urban or rural setting in which is found the evidence of a particular civilization, a significant development or an historic event. This applies not only to great works of art but also to more modest works of the past which have acquired cultural significance with the passing of time.

Article 2. The conservation and restoration of monuments must have recourse to all sciences and techniques which can contribute to the study and safeguarding of the architectural heritage.

Article 9. The process of restoration is a highly specialized operation. Its aim is to preserve and reveal the aesthetic and historic value of the monument and is based on respect for original material and authentic documents. It must stop at the point where conjecture begins, and in this case moreover any extra work which is indispensable must be distinct from the architectural composition and must bear a contemporary stamp. The restoration in any case must be preceded and followed by an archaeological and historical study of the monument.

Article 12. Replacement of missing parts must integrate harmoniously with the whole, but at the same time must be distinguishable from the original so that restoration does not falsify the artistic or historic evidence.

Article 13. Additions cannot be allowed except in so far as they do not detract from the interesting parts of the building, its traditional setting, the balance of its composition and its relation with its surroundings.

In the decades since its drafting, some criticisms of the Venice Charter have emerged. It has been argued that it does not necessarily reflect a global perspective on architectural conservation. Since its inception, experts in the United States have argued that it deals largely with the conservation of stone structures—which are primarily European phenomena—and that it does not adequately address the conservation of buildings made of wood and other materials typical elsewhere.[28] Similarly, the Western heritage conservation movement relies on the retention of original material remains, while other places, such as East Asia, attribute greater importance to the retention of the spirit of the place.[29] (See also "European Conservation Principles Abroad" in Chapter 15.)

Indeed, applications of the Venice Charter in most non-European countries have been uneven. The charter did not adequately address nonmonumental and vernacular architecture (such as earthen constructions) and overlooked the importance of certain living traditions for renewing architecture that had evolved over the millennia. There are probably more twentieth-century buildings than all the historic buildings in the world combined—yet aspects of them defy the easy application of the Venice Charter's tenets. In addition, its usefulness to allied professions such as archaeology and the treatment of historic gardens and landscapes has proven to be limited.

Despite its shortcomings—and despite how rarely its provisions are strictly adhered to—the Venice Charter serves remarkably well as a reference point in discussion and practice throughout the world. While there has been talk about updating it, this seems unlikely. Other charters and legislation on standards for conservation have superseded the Venice Charter in many parts of the world.

US Secretary of the Interior's Standards and Guidelines

The passage of the US Tax Reform Act of 1976 marked a new phase in American historic preservation; federal tax incentives were made available to those who rehabilitated qualified income-producing historic buildings, especially in underutilized inner-city areas.[30]

One of the most important aspects of the 1976 act was the institution of a system to ensure that the quality of the restoration projects seeking tax relief were of the highest caliber. Projects are only eligible if they meet *The Secretary of the Interior's Standards and Guidelines for Rehabilitation*, which were developed based on the tenets of earlier international charters and guidelines, including the Venice Charter. It differed from its predecessors in that it provided specific guidance on most every type of conservation intervention. For instance, it recommended how masonry should be cleaned and repaired, how historic wooden windows should be repaired or replaced in-kind, and pointed out the importance of installing new building systems without compromising architectural character. The list of ten basic standards is supplemented by the guidelines portion of the document, which offers a detailed description of what is acceptable and what to avoid during the rehabilitation process. The guidelines are further supplemented by illustrated preservation briefs that describe specific conservation issues and possible solutions in detail.

Architectural conservation theory and practice in the United States reached new levels of sophistication beginning in the late 1970s, when the benefits of historic preservation were widely recognized and appreciated. The construction industry responded with the advent of compatible new construction materials and increased training in restoration craft specialties. As a result of federal tax incentives, several types of new players who had typically shied away from preserving historic buildings entered the field, including more and more commercial property owners and real estate developers. The entrepreneurial opportunities contained in the 1976 Tax Reform Act also encouraged a new business-oriented approach to preservation. The economic benefits of historic preservation proved to be massive, with investors pouring almost $4.4 billion into over 34,800 rehabilitation projects by 2007.[31] In addition, the radically improved technical and administrative apparatus created to handle government-supported historic preservation at the local, state, and federal levels assisted many other large-scale projects, including the restorations of Ellis Island and Grand Central Station in New York City.[32]

The Burra Charter

The popular name of the Australian ICOMOS Charter for Places of Cultural Significance is, like the Venice Charter, taken from the town in which it was created. Originally drafted in 1979, the Burra Charter has been revised several times, most recently in 2004. It clearly and thoroughly details the principles, processes, practices, and guidelines for dealing with architectural and artistic heritage of all types. It also specifically addresses many Venice Charter omissions by emphasizing the conservation of historic places rather than single historic buildings.

Figure 9-1 The cover of *The Illustrated Burra Charter* (Australia ICOMOS, 2004). The Burra Charter was produced in reaction to inadequacies within the Venice Charter of 1964 and addresses Australia's less "monumental," indigenous types of cultural heritage. *(Image courtesy of M. Walker and P. Marquis-Kyle)*

The importance the Burra Charter places on the cultural significance of sites over aesthetic and material values reflects the fundamental difference in sensibilities between it and the Venice Charter. It firmly addresses the importance of establishing, at the outset of a conservation project, the cultural significance of a place. The Burra Charter sensitively approaches the conservation needs of indigenous peoples whose cultural heritage and artistic traditions may be different from other inhabitants of their country. It stresses traditional methods and approaches to both conserving and interpreting sites. The specific recommendations of this extensive document cover such broad topics as how to collect historical information, how to formulate conservation policy and plans, and how to establish reporting procedures.[33] Since the Burra Charter's drafting, other organizations worldwide have borrowed from and augmented it with a number of other charters and declarations addressing specific issues in architectural conservation, such as urban ensembles, archaeological sites, postwar reconstruction, cultural landscapes, conserving authenticity, and cultural tourism and training. (See also Chapter 15.)

BS 7913:1998

In 1998 the British Standards Institute issued architectural conservation guidelines called *The British Standard: A Guide to the Principles of the Conservation of Historic Buildings*, which is more commonly known as BS 7913:1998. It was developed by a committee that represented building conservation organizations in the United Kingdom.

This valuable document is less widely known and less accessible than are the Venice and Burra charters.[34] One of its most important distinctions is that it addresses *why* time-tested principles and guidelines for conservation are recommended. In its aims to promote good architectural heritage conservation practice, it also illustrates current philosophies in the field. BS 7913:1998 directly confronts issues pertaining to standards and legislation, such as when rules, codes, and standards are in conflict with one another.[35] This a useful because architectural conservationists are often faced with dilemmas of this nature.

In addition to the usual notes on the importance of reversibility and documentation, BS 7913:1998 deals with the economic advantages of architectural conservation and matters pertaining to energy conservation. It advocates a cautious and minimalist yet flexible approach and argues in favor of maintenance over restoration. It goes beyond comparable documents in addressing cause and effect, warning, for instance, of the pitfalls of matching materials in restorations: "[D]ifferent materials chosen to match at the outset will… match less well as they age."[36]

Together with the various national heritage protection laws drafted by the governments of individual countries, such national and international standards and procedures make up the canon of theory and practice in the field of architectural conservation today. The dynamic evolution of theory in the field is reflected in these documents and supports one clear lesson: There will always be the need for the existence and testing of such doctrine in the future.

ETHICS AND PROFESSIONALISM

When determining the whys, whats, and hows for the conservation of a historic building or site, architectural conservation professionals are expected to recognize time-tested principles and to apply techniques that are in the building's or site's best interests. Heritage conservation professionals often find themselves entrusted with the heavy responsibility of looking after and representing—even defending—an object, a building, or a site. The field's growing sophistication means that most in positions of responsibility can take comfort in the fact that important conservation decisions are rarely made by one person alone. Nevertheless, shared responsibility does not negate

Concepts Essential to Successful Architectural Conservation

- Accurate appraisals of cultural and architectural (artistic) significance

- Experience and competence on the part of the conservator

- Documentation of "as found" conditions, the history of the resource, and the conservation process being utilized

- Retention of authenticity

- Minimal intervention and minimal loss of fabric

- Avoidance of conjecture

- Discrete indication of interventions

- Conservation of the resource's structural, spatial, aesthetic, and contextual integrity

- Retention and indication of changes over time

- Conservation of patina

- Respect for any related "living heritage"

- Reversibility

- Sustainability

- Cyclical maintenance

Chart 9-1 Concepts Essential to Successful Architectural Conservation

the need for having a clear understanding of, and belief in, professional ethics.

Cultural heritage conservation ethics is first a matter of appreciating values and significance and then of safeguarding them in the most careful, responsible, and respectful way. The decision to conserve rather than restore extensively or replace something is a matter of ethics because it has a bearing on future conservation and presentation options. The concept of reversibility similarly reflects an ethical concern in conservation. A conservative approach and intervention in ways that are well documented are also considered ethical approaches to conserving objects, buildings, and sites.

Despite all the legislation and charters, the architectural conservation field has no specific overarching doctrine that outlines a comprehensive, universally applicable professional code of ethics.[37] Such a dicta may never exist because ethics in architectural conservation are recognized from the cumulative experiences of best practices in the field to date, and are thus constantly, if subtly, evolving.

Although there will probably never be a single universal code of principles, operation, and ethics for all to follow, certain tenets are recognized by those with proper training or experience in the field (Chart 9-1).

ENDNOTES

1. Earl, *Building Conservation Philosophy*, 5.
2. Warren, *Earthen Architecture*, xxiii.
3. With the increase in the conservation of exemplary works of modern architecture beginning in the middle third of the twentieth century, the age criteria in defining eligibility has begun shifting.
4. Mainly due to problems of accessibility, the role of Greece in the story of Roman architecture was not fully appreciated until the mid-eighteenth century.
5. Earl, *Building Conservation Philosophy*, vi.
6. Ibid., endnote 50.
7. Warren, *Earthen Architecture*, 188.
8. The production of surrogate historic experiences is on the rise, with impressive *de novo* history-based attractions found in many countries. In Singapore, after scores of blocks of traditional shop houses were demolished in the 1980s, they were soon missed and "new-old" versions of the same have become popular again. In Beijing, it has been a common practice for years to re-create the ambience of its traditional streets of courtyard dwellings, especially as new eating and shopping venues. In Thailand, the Muang Boran heritage park outside Bangkok, and reenactments of the World War II Allied bombing of the Bridge over the River Kwai at the Thai end of the Burma Railway, are other examples. (See also "Special Challenges Faced in East and Southeast Asia" in Chapter 17.)
9. Elaine Sciolino, "Smitten by Lyon, a Visitor Tries to Recreate the Magic," *New York Times*, January 28, 2008.
10. Feilden, *Conservation of Historic Buildings*, 6.
11. In all branches of the heritage conservation field, such principles are supplemented by various guidelines that more specifically address the types of resources and interventions that would likely be encountered. The various charters and codes of ethics are worded in ways that leave options open for exceptional circumstances. For Feilden, "[E]xperimentation may have its place in the process, keeping in mind that conserving buildings is different in many ways from conservation of objects in controlled conditions; there being differences in both scale and complexity." Ibid, "Introduction," UNESCO/ICCROM papers, 1979.
12. These are actions documented through contemporaneous writing, archaeology, or both. However, evidence of humankind's more ad hoc experiences with memorial-

izing and perpetuating the existence of memories, customs, and objects—certainly including repaired and reused objects and shelters—vastly predates Mesopotamia in the second millennium BCE. (See also Chapter 12.)

13. Jokilehto, *History of Architectural Conservation*, 29.

14. The regulations under Mérimée and later, Eugène-Emmanuel Viollet-le-Duc, were used mostly in dealing with the Gothic buildings of France. In Italy, architects Camillo Boito and Renato Bonelli from the 1880s produced similar doctrines aimed at conserving ancient Roman monuments. In Austria and Germany, specific conservation guidelines for restoring and conserving various churches, castles, and other monuments were articulated and advocated by several noted architects, some in the role of *konservator der kunstdenkmäler*, from Alexander Ferdinand von Quast (appointed in 1843) to Georg Dehio to a number of others from 1891 on. Adding to the effort from 1810 was the highly influential Karl Friedrich Schinkel, and from 1903, the Austrian art historian Alois Riegl, who produced the first systematic analysis of heritage values and of a theory of restoration. See also Jokilehto, "International Standards, Principles and Charters for Conservation" (56), in Marks, *Concerning Buildings*, for a description of an 1864 initiative led by Czar Alexander II of Russia to protect works of art in the case of conflict.

15. The most thorough record of international legal protection of cultural heritage is found in Lyndel V. Prott and P. J. O'Keefe, *Law and the Cultural Heritage* (Abingdon, Oxon, UK: Professional Books, 1984).

16. Entire ensembles of buildings had been given legal protection (i.e., historic district zoning) earlier, by the Vieux Carré legislation of 1936 in New Orleans and in Charleston, South Carolina, as early as 1931. Evidently the effect was felt only in the United States.

17. Earl, *Building Conservation Philosophy*, 31.

18. Polemics over the retention and treatment of historic buildings on the Continent predate this English example (e.g., the outcry over the destruction of old St. Peter's Basilica in Rome in the late fifteenth century); however, such instances were isolated by comparison with the political stances and schools of concern that took root and developed first in England in the late eighteenth century, then in France and Italy.

19. "Scrape"—as in scraping off deteriorating stone surface and carving anew. Such renewing of buildings in the process of restoration is warned against in John Ruskin, "The Lamp of Memory," in *The Seven Lamps of Architecture* (London: Smith, Elder, 1849), and in William Morris, *Manifesto of the Society for the Protection of Ancient Buildings*, http://www.spab.org.uk/html/what-is-spab/the-manifesto/.

20. The 1931 Athens Charter for the Restoration of Historic Monuments, adopted at the First International Congress of Architects and Technicians of Historic Monuments under the auspices of the League of Nations, pertaining to heritage protection, should not be confused with the Athens Charter of the Fourth International Congress of Modern Architecture (Congrès International d'Architecture Moderne [CIAM]), held in 1933, whose decisions were later edited by Le Corbusier.

21. Bell, *Historic Scotland Guide*, 4.

22. International Charter for the Conservation and Restoration of Monuments and Sites (the Venice Charter), was produced by the Second International Congress of Architects and Technicians of Historic Monuments in Venice in 1964 and adopted by ICOMOS in 1965.

23. In 2000, the Burra Charter's wider concerns for cultural heritage protection—and hence, its wider applicability—was proven when it was chosen as the basis for Principles for the Conservation of Heritage Sites in China (the China Principles), a project that began with a Getty Conservation Institute initiative in association with China's State Administration of Cultural Heritage (SACH) and ICOMOS China. In addition, ICOMOS New Zealand's Charter for the Conservation of Places of Cultural Heritage Value reflects that country's unique indigenous heritage protection needs. It includes Maori views of significance and value, particularly the Maori belief that places imbued with the spirits of their ancestors should be allowed to decay.

24. Morris, *Manifesto*.

25. Earl, *Building Conservation Philosophy*, 42–43.

26. Morris, *Manifesto*.

27. Ibid.

28. It is for this reason that Great Britain—as represented by Harold J. Plenderleith—and the United States—as represented by Charles Peterson—chose not be signatories to the Venice Charter.

29. Chen Wei and Andreas Aass, "Heritage Conservation: East and West," *ICOMOS Information*, no. 3 (July–September 1989).

30. The provisions of the legislation initially offered a five-year amortization of rehabilitation costs, which attracted many owners and developers to the benefits of America's historic buildings.

31. Statistics provided by the National Park Service in a telephone conversation with the author on May 9, 2008. Across the United States, thousands of sizable architectural preservation projects benefited from the stimulus of the tax incentives, including Pioneer Square in Seattle, Larimer Square in Denver, and Ybor City in Tampa, Florida.

32. Although somewhat diluted in 1986 by the Treasury Department, tax credits for historic preservation in the United States are still considered to be one of the country's most effective instruments for architectural conservation. Another tax-based incentive scheme was passed by the U.S. Congress in 1981, an investment tax credit for rehabilitation; its mix of credits and favorable accounting treatment of expenses made historic rehabilitation projects even more economically competitive through the high-profit potential of new commercial high-rise building.

33. The Burra Charter can be viewed online at www.icomos.org/australia/burra.html. Its applications are explained in extensive detail in a related publication by Michael Pearson and Sharon Sullivan, *Looking After Heritage Places: The Basics of Heritage Planning for Managers, Landowners and Administrators* (Carlton, Victoria, Australia: Melbourne University Press, 1995).

34. Extracts of British Standards Institute (BSI), *Guide to the Principles of the Conservation of Historic Buildings*, BS 7913:1998 (London: BSI, 1998), can only be reproduced by special permission; complete editions of these standards can be obtained by mail from British Standards Customer Services, 389 Chiswick High Road, London W4 4AL, United Kingdom, or from British Standards Online at http://www.bsi-global.com/en/Shop/Publication-Detail/?pid=000000000001331102.

35. An example is found in BSI, *BS 7913:1998*, sec. 5.2, pertaining to calculations and related matters required in structural codes that when applied to a historic building may on occasion be overridden by the professional judgment of qualified engineers and architects.

36. BSI, *BS 7913:1998*, sec. 7.3.4.4.

37. Probably the best effort to date at defining a formal code of ethics for the architectural conservation professional is found in Article 9: Code of Professional Commitment and Practice within the Indian National Trust for Art and Cultural Heritage (INTACH), *Charter for the Conservation of Unprotected Architectural Heritage and Sites in India*, Part IV, Article 9, adopted November 4, 2004. Codes of ethics in the allied museums field exist, and guidelines were adopted at the Conference on Training in Architectural Conservation (COTAC) that address the issue, though indirectly, (http://www.COTAC.org.uk). See also: John Warren, "Principles and Problems: Ethics and Aesthetics," in Marks, *Concerning Buildings*, 34–55.

Façade conservation in Amsterdam involving modernization.

CHAPTER 10

The Conservation Process

T he threats to physical cultural heritage—and the processes of their decay—are widely understood among cultural heritage conservation professionals today; so are the basic steps for physically conserving architecture, designed landscapes, and their constituent elements.

It is a physical fact that everything built by humans tends toward equilibrium with its natural environment. As a result, architectural conservationists are in a perpetual struggle against time to slow the inevitable process of decay. Given what is often at stake, and the subsequent need to act expeditiously, the process of translating ideas for conserving historic buildings and sites into reality is a crucial part of architectural conservation. To this end most practitioners, whether architects, engineers, materials conservation scientists, landscape architects, or preservation planners, take on the tasks of architectural conservation project development in four main phases:

1. **Project identification:** *Determining the project's physical and conceptual parameters.* The tasks of the first stage include documenting the project's status as a historic site— its precise location, its ownership, its physical characteristics, its legal protection, and its financial sustainability; obtaining historical information of all kinds, especially data pertaining to the site's architectural history and its existing condition; and, very importantly, evaluations of the resource's cultural significance.

2. **Planning:** Creating a viable plan of action for the proposed conservation project. Tasks include:
   - Analyzing and testing materials and structural systems
   - Completing research on all necessary technical investigations
   - Developing detailed designs and specifications for restoration and conservation
   - Determining project phasing and any special procedures
   - Project cost estimating
   - Preparing proposed plans for owner and conservation agency approval and for project tendering

- Procuring project approval
- Selecting the project implementation team, including contractors, project managers, craftspeople

3. **Implementation:** *Execution of the planned project.* Tasks include:
   - Securing the necessary permits and insurance
   - Resolving related legal matters
   - Site preparation and protection measures
   - Project implementation according to agreed-upon procedures
   - Creating detailed documentation of the implementation process
   - Job completion
   - Production of the project completion report, which will likely be publicly filed
   - Obtaining final approvals
   - Placement of the completed conservation project into service

4. **Maintenance and protection:** *Design and implementation of a cyclical maintenance and site-protection program.* Tasks of this final, ongoing phase include production of both short- and long-term operation and maintenance plans that consider the physical characteristics of the historic resource, its intended uses, and its vulnerabilities; the implementation of the maintenance plan using trained personnel who appreciate the importance of the task; and finally, periodic reviews and revisions of the maintenance and protection program.

Since the different stages of the architectural conservation process often require people with different talents, it is advisable to use an ***integrated***, team-based approach at each stage of development and to involve the principal parties and appropriate specialists throughout the process. The staged development of heritage conservation projects also serves the equally important role of allowing other participants in the project—from site owners and project funders to heritage management officials and the general public—to provide input in the most efficient and timely manner. Throughout the process it is important to maintain an awareness of the socioeconomic and regional planning contexts of the project.[1]

Because most architectural conservation projects represent significant investments of time, effort, and financial resources, the management of even small projects requires skill and experience. The ability to articulate a project's objectives and the relationships of its various phases is essential, as is having a clearly defined rationale for what is being done and why. For instigators of architectural conservation projects, a major requirement for success is being able to explain the process and to lead the effort as necessary—even if the owner, architect, manager, or special interests groups are actually in charge. In the words of English architect James Strike:

> We need to be able to recognize, and to justify, our position.... [T]o put these thoughts succinctly across to others requires a clear understanding of the criteria...we have to recognize not only the criteria of criticism, but also that conservation is not a static, deterministic commodity. We need to see our point of view as part of a maturing process...[that will]...assist in the way we react to other people's points of view, and also to help us cope with their adjustments to change.[2]

While this outline of the conservation process has in general proven to be a successful method in most countries today, its application will always pose challenges. In his *Architectural Restoration in Western Europe: Contradiction and Continuity*, Dutch conservation theorist Wim Denslagen offers a view of the architectural conservation process that represents the likely reality of taking a project through at least the first stages of the conservation process:

The way monuments are dealt with in our society is all too familiar. All the parties involved have their own interests: the owner of the monument defends his corner, the architect defends the interests of his profession, the civil servant weighs interests in the name of public administration, the judge passes judgment in the event of an appeal on the lawfulness of the decisions taken. Could it be done in any other way? No. Should it be done differently? Again the answer is no, for society as a whole represents a greater interest than that of an institution or individual.... If there is no way of avoiding all of these positions and interests, does it make sense to devise theories about a subject from art history without taking social and ideological aspects into account? And does the person who does so realize that he too is imprisoned or at least influenced by the position he occupies in society?[3]

Denslagen's provocative observations about the conservation process point once again to the importance of having a clear rationale and action plan for the intended project and a commitment to quality from the initial concept through completion.

ENDNOTES

1. Or as Bernard Feilden puts it in *Conservation of Historic Buildings*, "There is one methodology which unites all practitioners of conservation. Conservation is a synthesis of art and science, which in this context includes the natural sciences, archaeology, art history, and architecture."

2. James Strike, *Architecture in Conservation: Managing Development at Historic Sites* (New York: Routledge, 1994), 6.

3. Denslagen, Wim. *Architectural Restoration in Western Europe: Controversy and Continuity* (Amsterdam: Architectura and Natura, 1994), 11–12.

The community practice of earthen roof surface repair, Lhasa, Tibet.

CHAPTER 11

Participants in Architectural Conservation

All facets of cultural heritage conservation—from historical research projects to museum work and heritage education to the protection of historic buildings and sites—are in some way accessible to all who may care to participate in them. And this is as it should be: Cultural heritage conservation is by, for, and about living people. The everyday users of the built environment are, after all, as important to its future as are professional curators, conservators, and managers. Indeed, heritage protection is a shared responsibility.

Participants in architectural conservation include:

- **Individuals:** Owners, users, and caretakers, local management—and perhaps a property owners' association—who, in their daily routine, protect and maintain a property
- **The local public:** Concerned citizens, advocates, and protection agencies who maintain local landmarks or ready them for regional or national listing
- **The wider general public:** People who express concern for a historic resource on a local, regional, or national basis; advocate for national listing
- **The world community:** Those who recognize and express concern for a historic building deemed to be of universal importance and interest—for example, World Heritage listing or a site benefiting from support from international funding organizations

While there continues to be a paucity of trained personnel in heritage conservation professions in most countries, progress has been made in heritage conservation education and capacity building in recent decades through the efforts of national and international groups like International Centre for the Study of the Preservation and Restoration of Cultural Property (ICCROM), the United Nations Educational, Scientific and Cultural Organization (UNESCO), the International Council on Monuments and Sites (ICOMOS), the International Union of Architects (UIA, the French acronym), and various international funding and technical assistance organizations. With tens of thousands of trained heritage conservation professionals now serving the field internationally, experts in many areas of specialization are now available to address most, but not all, problems no matter where they are found.[1]

Chart 11-1 outlines the main relationships of private and organizational entities in relation to conserving recognized historic architecture. The significance of a specific heritage site—which can range from being only of local interest to being recognized internationally—also affects how attention to it is channeled through collaborative efforts. These may include local heritage commissions working in partnership with international heritage protection organizations such as the World Heritage Centre at UNESCO.

Established international heritage conservation organizations operating at all levels must relate to, and when necessary incorporate, a variety of allied support groups. These may include local or national historical, archaeological, and other professional organizations; worldwide membership and professional organizations as well as subsidized private-interest groups; not-for-profit private organizations or foundations, nongovernmental organizations (NGOs), and quasi-governmental organizations (QUANGOs); and international state mem-

Participants in Architectural Conservation

DIRECT INFLUENCES

Owners
Private–individual, partnership, corporate
Public–national, state, local
QUANGO–national, regional, or local trusts
NGO–building trust, foundation, or not-for-profit

Users/occupants
Residents–24 hour inhabitants
Daily workers–office workers
Occasional users–visitors, sightseeing public

Operators/managers
Property manager (custodian) & staff
Chief curator & staff (collections caretakers & presenters)
House architect or engineer
Security personnel–(for users, public, collections, & site)
Maintenance personnel

LESS DIRECT INFLUENCES

Official bodies having purview
Building code regulators—Local, state, national
National, state, and/or local conservation agencies

Support groups
Advocates, NGOs, friends groups
Tenant associations
Local donors
Interested public
Interested international constituencies

Others
Lenders
Financial Institutions
Insurers

OCCASIONAL INFLUENCES/INTERVENERS

Technical Assistance (as required)
Conservation architect
Engineer
Specialty consultants
(conservators, exhibition designers, etc.)
Cyclical maintenance services

Chart 11-1 Participants in Architectural Conservation

bership schemes such as UNESCO and ICOMOS. All of these structures are increasingly being joined by additional local stakeholders—concerned individuals who serve as advocates, volunteers, and supporters—and by special-interest organizations, the most effective usually being those that provide funding to conservation projects in need. Arriving relatively recently in this latter category are the international banking and development organizations such as the World Bank and its subsidiary regional banks and comparable other financial institutions. Preferring to work usually on large-scale urban conservation projects, these international lending or grant-making entities are among the most powerful of the potential players in international architectural and urban conservation practice.

Most architectural heritage sites can inspire a sense of interest or "ownership"—even if only at a symbolic or intellectual level—and can therefore attract their own support group of concerned individuals. The remarkably consistent purposes and procedures of today's architectural conservation field ensure that at practically every level, all who are involved have much in common. Cultural heritage connects people, and the cause to protect it does so even more.

STRUCTURE OF THE FIELD

In recent years, the field of architectural conservation has developed a wide range of specialists and resources to meet the growing demands on it. There are scores of subspecialties within the architectural conservation field that are described in various training manuals, such as those maintained by the various ICOMOS Training Committees and the UK-based Conference on Training in Architectural Conservation (COTAC) proceedings. The growing list includes: architects, engineers, art and architectural historians, landscape architects, building materials conservation scientists, hydrologists and experts on moisture in historic structures, experts in documentation and related analysis, museum professionals, educators, archaeologists, estimators, surveyors, urban planners, specialists in heritage conservation law, cultural heritage resource managers, experts in heritage tourism, builders and contractors, the full range of specialist craftspeople, administrators of historic resources, owners, fund-raisers, administrators, and public advocates.

Age-old professions such as architecture, engineering, and the building trades have adapted themselves to meet the sophistication with which some architectural conservation projects are organized and implemented. They are being joined by an ever-expanding list of specialties and subspecialties that have developed as offshoots of recent technological developments. These include photogrammetry, database development for heritage documentation purposes, and numerous building conservation science applications. Within each of these areas and more are experts who may have been trained formally or informally in specific or combined applications. (The general composition of the professions and specialties that make up the architectural heritage conservation field is tiered, but nearly all are interdependent.)

The growth in stature of the architectural conservation field reflects its many important accomplishments as well as its worldwide influence. Given the dynamic, globally diverse, and potentially chaotic nature of its scope, its participants operate with a remarkably consistent sense of purpose. While the multidisciplinary and synoptic nature of the field are among its most distinguishing characteristics, the common basis for all who participate in architectural conservation is the delight and satisfaction of conserving useful and significant historic buildings and sites. As far as the structure of the profession is concerned, its key players remain:

Cultural Resource Managers

This professional segment includes project instigators and packagers, cultural resource management (CRM) planners, participating owners, leading project participants, others with CRM specialties, municipal- and state-appointed authorities, legal counsel, marketing analysts, and project funders (project managers at funding agencies, among others).

Architects, Engineers, and Planners

Architects, engineers, and planners trained and experienced in architectural conservation practice; quantity surveyors; cost estimators; producers of legal contract documentation; and overseers of the bidding process. The important planning and legal responsibilities of these professions ensure that qualified architects, engineers, and planners hold key roles in decision making and coordination for most architectural conservation projects.

Building Conservation Scientists and Specialty Consultants

The term *building conservation specialist*, which includes, more prominently, *building conservation scientist and specialty consultant*, covers specialty documentation producers, materials analysts, scientists in testing labs, diagnosticians, and prescribers of special solutions; archaeologists, geologists, petrologists, hydrologists, and so forth; and experts in the allied fields of restoration and conservation of historic landscapes, museology, education (at various levels), interpretive programming, cultural tourism, and public relations.

Project Implementers

These include construction project managers, owners' representatives and quality assurance guarantors, accounting and payment specialists, contractors and subcontractors, procurers of materials and logistics specialists, specialty craftspeople, skilled and unskilled workers, and maintenance and site-protection personnel.

Cyclical Maintenance Operations

These include periodic inspection and maintenance personnel, regular site-protection personnel, and those who coordinate insurance and preventative conservation measures.

THE ARCHITECTURAL CONSERVATION PROFESSIONAL DEFINED

While some may disagree, according to historian Roger Kennedy, former director of the US National Park Service, "A professional is simply somebody who stays with something long enough to get good at it.... Advanced degrees are not a definition of professionalism."[2] Kennedy considers the role of the heritage conservation professional, and presumably the historian in particular, as "not one of pontificating history, or of dictating history, but one of facilitating a better understanding and relevance of history."[3] A more precise definition of an architectural conservation professional is "a person who can contribute artistically, intellectually or practically to the process of conservation, so [it] includes craftsworkers, contractors and builders."[4]

An even fuller definition of today's well-rounded architectural conservationists is found in a description of their ideal training offered by James Marston Fitch, the founder of the first graduate-level training program in historic preservation in the United States.[5] In Fitch's view, architectural conservationists must first be generalists with special interests and abilities. They "must see their own special area of expertise as being only one strand in a larger fabric, the warp and woof of which there are many other coequal and coexistent specialties.... The task of retrieving, recycling, and curating the built world is by its very nature... multidisciplinary...," with experts working together effectively in recognition of "common concepts, shared methods and technologies for dealing with it, and a common language for describing it."[6] To the benefit of his many students and followers, Fitch also believed architectural conservation professionals must be literate in the design fields: architecture,

ICOMOS-Recommended Qualifications for Competency in Architectural Conservation Practice[7]

Conservation works should only be entrusted to persons competent in these specialist activities. Education and training for conservation should produce from a range of professionals conservationists who are able to:

- read a monument, ensemble, or site and identify its emotional, cultural, and use significance;

- understand the history and technology of monuments, ensembles, or sites to define their identity, plan for their conservation, and interpret the results of this research;

- understand the setting of a monument, ensemble, or site, their contents and surroundings, in relation to other buildings, gardens, or landscapes;

- find and absorb all available sources of information relevant to the monument, ensemble, or site being studied;

- understand and analyze the behavior of monuments, ensembles, and sites as complex systems;

- diagnose intrinsic and extrinsic causes of decay as a basis for appropriate action;

- inspect and make reports intelligible to nonspecialist readers of monuments, ensembles, or sites, illustrated by graphic means such as sketches and photographs;

- know, understand, and apply UNESCO conventions and recommendations, and ICOMOS and other recognized Charters, regulations, and guidelines;

- make balanced judgments based on shared ethical principles and accept responsibility for the long-term welfare of cultural heritage;

- recognize when advice must be sought and define the areas of need of study by different specialists, e.g., wall paintings, sculpture, and objects of artistic and historical value, and/or studies of materials and systems;

- give expert advice on maintenance strategies, management policies, and the policy framework for environmental protection and preservation of monuments and their contents and sites;

- document works executed and make some accessible;

- work in multi-disciplinary groups using sound methods and;

- be able to work with inhabitants, administrators, and planners to resolve conflicts and to develop conservation strategies appropriate to local needs, abilities, and resources.

landscape architecture, and the decorative arts. They must understand the basic methods of research and documentation of historic artifacts and the means of recording, drafting, and delineating, as well as the general methodology of scientific artifactual conservation, if only to know to whom to turn for collaboration in such matters. And increasingly, they must understand current economic, legal, and legislative forces acting upon historic district planning, since this is the context in which most projects must be analyzed.

Fitch's British counterpart and colleague Bernard Feilden adds to this definition, saying: "Contrary to what the name implies architectural conservationists tend to be forward looking, constructive and imaginative. Accused at times of being unrealistic and impractical, the root concerns of most conservationists are resourcefulness, aesthetic interests, and associations in terms of meaning in art and architecture. One of the field's great advantages is that it addresses site-specific issues and rarely with matters which are arcane and esoteric."[8] The accomplishments of architectural conservationists are seen by its beneficiaries as being useful, positive, and fundamentally constructive.

RELATED READINGS

Alpin, Graeme. *Heritage: Identification, Conservation, and Management.* South Melbourne, Australia: Oxford University Press, 2002.

Baker, David. *Living with the Past: The Historic Environment.* Bletsoe, Bedford, UK: D. Baker, 1983.

Bell, D. *The Historic Scotland Guide to International Conservation Charters*. Edinburgh: Historic Scotland, 1997.

British Standards Institute. *Guide to the Principles of Conservation of Historic Buildings*. BS 7913:1998. London: British Standards Institute, 1998.

Cantacuzino, Sherban ed. *Architectural Conservation in Europe*. London: Architectural Press, 1975.

Earl, John. *Building Conservation Philosophy*. Preface by Bernard Feilden. 3rd ed. Shaftesbury, UK: Donhead and College of Estate Management, 2003. First published in 1996 by College of Estate Management.

Erder, Cevat. *Our Architectural Heritage: From Consciousness to Conservation*. Museums and Monuments series. Paris: UNESCO, 1986.

Feilden, Bernard M. *Conservation of Historic Buildings*. Technical Studies in the Arts, Archaeology and Architecture. 3rd ed. Oxford: Architectural Press, 2003. First published in 1982 by Butterworth Scientific.

Feilden, Bernard M., and Jukka Jokiletho. *Management Guidelines for World Cultural Heritage Sites*. Rome: ICCROM, 1993.

Fitch, James Marston. *Historic Preservation: Curatorial Management of the Built World*. 5ᵗʰ ed. Charlottesville, VA: University Press of Virginia, 2001.

Hunter, Michael, ed. *Preserving the Past: The Rise of Heritage in Modern Britain*. Stroud, Gloucestershire, UK: Alan Sutton, 1996.

Insall, Donald. *The Care of Old Buildings Today: A Practical Guide*. London: Architectural Press, 1972.

Jacobs, Jane. *The Death and Life of Great American Cities*. New York: Random House, 1961.

Layton, Robert, Peter G. Stone, and Julian Thomas, eds. *Destruction and Conservation of Cultural Property*. Andover, Hampshire, UK: Routledge, 2001.

Marks, Stephen, ed. *Concerning Buildings: Studies in Honor of Sir Bernard Feilden*. Oxford: Butterworth-Heinemann, 1996.

Serageldin, Ismail, Ephim Shluger, and Joan Martin-Brown, eds. *Historic Cities and Sacred Sites: Cultural Roots for Urban Futures*. Washington, DC: World Bank, 2001.

Stanley-Price, Nicholas, M. Kirby Talley, Jr., and Allesandra Melucco Vaccaro, eds. *Readings in Conservation: Historical and Philosophical Issues in the Conservation of Cultural Heritage*. Los Angeles: Getty Conservation Institute, 1996.

ENDNOTES

1. In addition, an increasing number of concerned organizations are participating in heritage conservation efforts; often, they focus on specific heritage types of one kind or another. The effectiveness of their roles depends on the degree of their commitment to the task and their organizational and financial capacity.

2. Kennedy, "Crampons, Pitons and Curators," in Tomlan, *Preservation of What, for Whom?* 23.

3. Ibid., 55. For additional material on the ethics of restoration, see Wim Denslagen and Niels Gutschow, eds., *Architectural Imitations: Reproductions and Pastiches in East and West* (Maastricht, Neth.: Shaker Publishing, 2005).

4. Bernard Feilden, "Architectural Conservation," *Journal of Architectural Conservation*, no. 3, (November 1999): 9.

5. Within the Graduate School of Architecture, later named the Graduate School of Architecture, Planning and Preservation at Columbia University in New York City.

6. Fitch, *Historic Preservation*, introduction and chap. 1, ix–12.

7. ICOMOS, "Guidelines on Education and Training in the Conservation of Monuments, Ensembles and Sites," paragraph 5, adopted by ICOMOS General Assembly meeting at Colombo, Sri Lanka, July 30–August 7, 1993. See also: Derek Lindstrum, "The Education of a Conservation Architect: Past, Present and Future" in Marks, *Concerning Buildings*: 96–119.

8. Feilden, *Conservation of Historic Buildings*.

PART III

Conservation of Built Heritage: An Enduring Concern

CHAPTER 12

Prehistory Through the Fourteenth Century

AN INSTINCT TO PRESERVE?

Since the dawn of modern humanity, which physical anthropologists have determined to be about 150,000 years ago, *Homo sapiens* have been opportunistic in providing themselves with shelter and the necessities of life.[1] From at least this point forward their ability to create tools must have been followed not long after by an interest in personalizing things as a way to mark them as their own.[2] Customs and beliefs—faith in the supernatural, the development of ritual, and a sense of a past and a future—also distinguished early humans.

The transfer of remembered customs and beliefs across generations has always been profoundly important because it has allowed knowledge to accumulate.[3] As our *Homo sapien* ancestors came to understand their place in time and history, they began to leave intentional marks and signs of their existence. Through these they sought to preserve, in a most primitive way, their place in the history of their culture or social group. Such an "urge to monumentality"[4] provided a sense of permanence or immortality that was lacking in their often short and brutal lives and expressed a physical desire to be remembered. Revisiting and protecting these expressions of memorialization may be considered an almost instinctive interest of humanity—and thus would be its earliest acts of preservation consciousness.

Apart from their possible inherent meaning, early humans must have realized the practical advantage of reusing things, be they utilitarian objects or habitats. Modern archaeology is constantly reinforcing this likelihood. For about sixty thousand years, cave dwellings near Cussac in France's Dordogne valley were used by successive generations, according to the findings of archaeologist Jean-Philippe Rigaud, director of France's National Center for Prehistory.[5] Studies have found that the site was first inhabited by generations of Neanderthals and then by distinctly different *Homo sapiens*. In the case of the latter, generations left their individual marks on the caves. Caves such as the recently discovered Chauvet Cave (ca. 30,000 BCE) and the famous Caves of Lascaux (ca. 15,000 BCE) both display a maturation of artistic expression as well as confirming a continuous intergenerational use of what must have been considered a significant place.

Archaeology has also verified that burying human remains with consideration of an afterlife is an ancient custom that dates to at least Neanderthal times (100,000–28,000 BCE). Although archaeologists and paleontologists can only speculate about Neanderthal beliefs, there is ample evidence that they customized burial sites with some degree of intention and thought.[6] The custom of memorializing burials and sacred sites with stone markers may be just as ancient. Durable tomb markers represent a desire for the continuation of memory, often beyond the lives of those who created them. At La Ferrassie in France's Dordogne valley, the skull of one of the dead was buried a short distance away in a hole covered by a stone that had several cuplike depressions on its surface.[7] This simple stone placement, some seventy thousand years old, is one of the earliest known grave markers and may be humanity's first intentional monument.[8]

The primitive social fabric of *Homo sapiens* in the Upper Paleolithic era (around forty-two thousand years ago) matured over the next fifteen thousand years into the early Neolithic cultures, during a time that is widely considered to be the eve of civilization.[9] Neolithic tribes domesticated animals, developed agriculture, and transformed themselves from nomadic hunter-gatherers into sedentary agrarian populations. Established settlements required the construction of shelters that were meant to last.

At the sites of the earliest known constructed human settlements in Anatolia, Mesopotamia, and the Chinese Yellow River basin (from the sixth, fifth, and fourth millennia BCE, respectively), archaeologists have found evidence not only of long-term planning but also of structural renovations and recycled building materials. Certain Neolithic building materials required perpetual maintenance, such as the mud brick found in the Tigris and Euphrates region and the thatched roofs of Banpo, China, and Langweiler, Germany. If it safe to assume that people quickly realized that periodic building repair was easier than total structural replacement, the practice of regular upkeep or simple maintenance—the essential ingredients of conserving existing buildings—may also date to the time of the earliest human settlements.

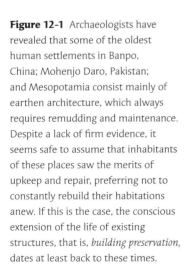

Figure 12-1 Archaeologists have revealed that some of the oldest human settlements in Banpo, China; Mohenjo Daro, Pakistan; and Mesopotamia consist mainly of earthen architecture, which always requires remudding and maintenance. Despite a lack of firm evidence, it seems safe to assume that inhabitants of these places saw the merits of upkeep and repair, preferring not to constantly rebuild their habitations anew. If this is the case, the conscious extension of the life of existing structures, that is, *building preservation*, dates at least back to these times.

Such preservation-minded actions across the millennia can be considered the genesis of today's architectural conservation ethos for two reasons:

1. The continuous use of old buildings forced the concept of extended use, adaptive use, and maintenance, thus making preservation for many structures inevitable.

2. Such maintenance and preservation actions supported the survival of an increasing number of historic buildings and sites.

The simple material value of existing buildings, especially those constructed with some care and expense, could not be ignored. It would be many centuries before more monumental structures and those associated with the ruling elite would be given special consideration, as is evidenced by numerous surviving building inscriptions and historical references. Spiritual reverence and the memorialization of places with historical associations also provided additional reasons for preservation rather than replacement.

Throughout this period, humans became increasingly cognizant of the importance of retaining and preserving objects, including buildings, for reasons beyond their practical value. For Alain Schnapp, professor of Greek archaeology at the University of Paris, the collection and preservation of items for no purpose other than their significance as "carriers of messages from a more or less remote past" has been characteristic of human beings since their cultural and biological debut.[10] From the Caves of Chauvet and Lascaux to the banks of the Tigris and Euphrates rivers, early humans and their embryonic civilizations have consistently shown this to be true.

PREHISTORIC THROUGH HELLENISTIC TIMES

Civilization dawned in southern Mesopotamia's fertile river valleys in what is now Iraq. Although the Neolithic settlements of Jericho (Jordan), Çatalhöyük (Turkey), and Banpo (China) exhibited some of the earliest forms of urbanization and even monumental architecture (such as the legendary Tower of Jericho), they were still isolated examples of developing civilization in an overwhelmingly nomadic age. The consolidation of small Mesopotamian villages into towns represented a far more significant trend because it was regional. As these embryonic conglomerations matured, the Sumerian civilization, with its cult centers serving different communities, emerged.[11]

The Sumerian religion provided another motivation for the continuous habitation of cult centers and provided the impetus for creating impressive and enduring architecture. No other force up to that point in history had been able to harness the energies of humankind in the pursuit of such creative endeavor. At Eridu, 200 miles southeast of Baghdad, the first mud-brick temple incorporating a niche for a cult object arose. This was the first known instance where humans built not just for shelter but also to express a consciousness of something greater than themselves: a reflection of a civilization with an advanced system of beliefs.

Their development of sun-baked and fired mud-brick technology allowed the Sumerians—and later the Babylonians and Assyrians—to build their greatest architectural achievements, the ziggurats. These stepped pyramidal structures of mud-brick masonry were sealed with bitumen. Unlike later Egyptian pyramids, ziggurats had exterior staircases leading to the upper portions of the building and to a temple at their summit. Originally isolated places of worship that were believed to connect heaven and earth, the ziggurats eventually became surrounded by settlements, which in turn interconnected to form cities. Thus, the ziggurat became the religious and administrative focal point for an urban center. Their massive form and purpose made ziggurats monuments in the truest sense of the word.

Urban development itself became more controlled as Mesopotamian civilization developed. While earlier settlements and villages grew slowly and more or less randomly,

Figure 12-2 The original temple at Eridu, Iraq (ca. 5000 BCE) is considered by archaeologists to be the first structure reflecting religious beliefs and group worship to be erected. *(Photo: State Antiquities and Heritage Organization, Baghdad)*

in the eighteenth century BCE, King Hammurabi of Babylon introduced building codes and planning laws. Builders were required to erect strong, sturdy buildings that would adequately protect their users. If a building collapsed and killed its owner, the builder paid with his life; if it killed the owner's son, the builder's son shared that fate.[12] Such legal codes not only reveal a sense of the importance of high-quality buildings and concerns for public safety but serve as precursors—however indirect—of the modern zoning and regulatory codes that would later be expanded to assist in the preservation of buildings and historic city centers.

Mesopotamian rulers also concerned themselves with preserving the sacred mud-brick ziggurats, which deteriorated quickly and required regular maintenance. Over time, ziggurats were either regularly restored, or larger ones were built atop existing structures. While rebuilding a temple over old foundations may have had structural benefits, restoration and reconstruction in situ was also a religious obligation, because Sumerian deities required their temples' continuation on sites that they believed had been used since the beginnings of time.[13] This maintained the covenant between the god and the community, which the ziggurat embodied.[14]

During the five successive Mesopotamian empires—Sumerian, Akkadian, Babylonian, Assyrian, and Chaldean—the monumental ziggurats remained important not only as symbols of religious veneration but also as connections to the past. At the twilight of the Mesopotamian civilization, Chaldean kings sought to create associations with the glories of former rulers by ordering the restoration and rebuilding of earlier structures. This represented a shift in the way Mesopotamians viewed the past, from one that stressed an "eternal continuity after initial creation" in the distant past to one recognizing linear progress.[15] The independence of Babylon following the collapse of the Assyrian Empire in 612 BCE was celebrated by a brief but vibrant revival of Babylonian arts and culture that included these restoration projects as well as monumental new constructions.

In the early sixth century BCE, King Nebuchadnezzar II was intrigued by ancient remains and saw the clear political benefit of reviving Great Babylon, which he rebuilt. He also built the magnificent temple of Marduk, whose famous seven-story ziggurat, Etemenanki, is often referred to as the Tower of Babel. He restored the temple of the Sun God at Sippar[16] and sought out forgotten ancient sites such as the temple of Burnaburiash to give the Babylonian people a tangible sign of their glorious past. This restored temple from the fourteenth century BCE was reinstituted as a sacred place, sending a powerful message to the populace: This living symbol had been resurrected through the greatness of their king, who through it restored the covenants with the gods.[17]

Nabonidus, the last king of Babylon, continued to restore temples with even greater zeal than his predecessor, Nebuchadnezzar II. Notably, he spent a great deal of time and energy excavating and rebuilding the temple of Egipar and the temple of Shamash and Aya, originally built by Nebuchadnezzar I.

These passages represent the oldest known written description of the careful investigation of a long-lost architectural ruin and its extensive restoration and reconstruction:[18]

> At that time Egipar, the holy precinct…was an abandoned place, and had become a heap of ruins…. I cut down the trees, removed the rubble of ruins…. I made Egipar [too] anew as in the olden days, I built its daises and plans anew as in the olden days…[19]

Although in antiquity such projects would likely have meant extensive conjectural reconfiguring and the reuse of old elements where convenient, they served the ultimate purpose of reviving the past—and therefore remain concrete, early examples of architectural conservation in its most general sense.

As civilization began to coalesce in Mesopotamia's Fertile Crescent, the same process occurred in Egypt. Beside the long course of the Nile, a civilization developed for which the past was paramount; it represented a divine and unchangeable legacy that had to be preserved in order to secure favor in the afterlife and stability in the future. This belief profoundly affected the course of Egyptian culture, including the design, construction,

Figure 12-3 The relatively well-preserved ziggurat at Ur-Nammu at Ur (ca. 2100 BCE), seen here before modern partial reconstruction, is typical of several of its predecessors. (*Prof. P. V. Glob*)

Figure 12-4 The stepped pyramid of King Djoser dating from 2650 BCE, considered the first monumental tomb in Egypt, was designed to hold the great ruler's prepared remains and his necessities for the afterlife. The concepts of monumentality, memory, preservation, and longevity were all embodied in Egyptian funerary architecture throughout ancient Egyptian civilization.

Figure 12-5 One of oldest known examples of sophisticated restoration intervention to a monument is evidenced in the repair of a break at the back of this seated figure of Rameses II at the entrance to Luxor Temple. The pair of butterfly-shaped carvings across the stone fracture received iron or bronze cramps (now missing) to keep both sides of the massive fracture together and to prevent slippage.

rebuilding, and preservation of its architectural monuments, which over three millennia continually reused forms and artistic motifs.

The Kingdom of Egypt was united in about 3200 BCE when the king of Upper Egypt conquered the north and created a vast state extending nearly 500 miles (800 kilometers) along the Nile River. It was not until 2650 BCE, however, that the Egyptians engineered their first monumental architectural achievement, the step pyramid of the third dynasty King Djoser. Built by Imhotep, the first master architect whose name is recorded in Egyptian history, this pyramid resembles Mesopotamia's tiered ziggurats. Unlike the ziggurats, Egyptian pyramids were used as monumental tombs rather than temples. Early on, the pyramids evolved and lost their ziggurat-like tiers and eventually assumed the well-known shape best exemplified by the Great Pyramid of Giza, which was built for the Pharaoh Khufu around 2560 BCE.

The apparent investments of time and effort made by the ancient Egyptians clearly reveal that preparation for the afterlife was a major, if not *the* major, concern among the living.[20] Egypt's elaborate burial customs began to be visibly expressed: Monumental buildings were inscribed with the names and deeds of the deceased sovereigns, and pyramids connected the pharaohs with the eternal past and the gods.[21] The monumentality of the pyramids indicated that they were meant to survive for all time and be symbols connecting all Egyptians to their historical roots.[22]

The Egyptians are considered forerunners among the Western civilizations that followed in the protection of monuments and saw to it that their monuments were looked after and maintained.[23] Like the Mesopotamians, they believed that temples and tombs were sacred sites and that the preservation of religious and funerary monuments was an obligation fulfilled to sustain the favor of the gods.

Some of the oldest the evidence of the careful repair or restoration of a monumental architectural form is found on a seated colossal stone figure at the outer entrance pylon of Luxor Temple in Upper Egypt. The bottom third of the 45-foot (14-meter) granite monolith was broken somewhere between its extraction from the quarry and its erection (ca. 1200–1300 BCE). Given the sizable diagonal break at the base of this statue, its builders must have asked the question, Repair or replace? When archeologists discovered it in the 1950s, they noted its repair in antiquity: Two butterfly-shaped cuts had been made across the break to receive either stone or metal inserts (which are now lost) to prevent slippage.

Political considerations also influenced temple reconstruction and restoration, as can best be seen at the temple of Karnak. For more than two thousand years, the temple and its various outbuildings were built, altered, restored, or demolished by pharaohs who wished to create a lasting monument like the pyramids, one that would remain a landmark in time as a symbol of the glorious past they so worshipped. At Karnak, the characteristic ancient Egyptian concern for immortality plays out in the way successive kings attempted to outdo their predecessors. The complex developed in stages over time as new pylons, colonnades, and courtyards were added in front of older ones. The reuse of materials was commonplace during its various periods of construction. Amenhotep III constructed the outermost third pylon in part by using rubble from a previous structure.[24] Rameses II attempted to surpass his predecessor's achievements by constructing the second pylon and completing the temple of Abydos. In a feat of royal narcissism, he had at least one face of the colossus of Amenhotep III recarved to resemble himself.

In both Egypt and Mesopotamia, the symbolism of the past was always strong. The desire of Egypt's rulers to achieve immortality and thereby assume their place in the ever-receding past as well as the mystical future manifested itself in their construction of

Figure 12-6 Construction of the outermost pylon of the temple at Karnak involved the use of recycled building materials, seen here in the turned stones from a previous building. Throughout antiquity, architectural legacies were more likely to be destroyed—not carefully memorialized—so their useful materials could be recycled.

Figure 12-7 The *tel* of Erbil in northern Iraq dates to at least 2300 BCE; it is considered one of the world's oldest settlements. *(Photo: ©Georg Gerster/Panos Photo, London)*

monumental architecture on a scale previously unseen. The continued preservation of its monuments by later rulers—including the Hellenic, Ptolemaic, and Roman administrations—helped Egypt's culture endure long after its political vigor had expired.

Mesopotamia and Egypt were not the only ancient civilizations to actively reuse historic sites and structures. As civilization crept westward across the Mediterranean, new cultures arose. From the second millennium BCE on, examples of reconstruction and building repair are found with some frequency all along the eastern and northern shores of the Mediterranean. The motives for such actions were nearly always practical or religious.

Throughout the region—but especially in the Fertile Crescent—rebuilding towns in antiquity was commonplace. This is evidenced from the *tels*, hills formed by successive settlements. Archaeologists have encountered as many as twenty-two levels of occupation at *tel* sites in Israel. At Knossos on Crete, early twentieth-century British archaeologist Sir Arthur Evans discovered ten distinct layers dating back more than two thousand years at the Palace of Minos. At such sites, salvageable earlier building materials, foundations, street patterns, and fortifications were often reused.

In Turkey—especially along its south and west coasts—historical, archaeological, and visual evidence reveals numerous examples of recycled building materials, renovations, and the long-term preservation of specific buildings. Hittite settlements in the south were conquered and expanded by others that in turn were taken over successively by the Greeks and the Romans. Many of the same sites were continuously occupied through the Byzantine period, with a few remaining in use through the Ottoman period to our time. Natural seaports such as modern-day Bodrum, Antalya, and Izmir, were settled in antiquity and have been used without interruption since then.

The Greeks, like the Egyptians, learned about their past—including details of their predecessors, the Mycenaeans and the Minoans—through mythical stories and surviving monuments.[25] But unlike the Egyptians, they did not possess earlier monumental pyramids or temples. What they did encounter were buried artifacts, large Mycenaean tombs, and ruined cities. To a Greek from the eighth century BCE, the discovery of these tombs inspired awe; respect for them was displayed through offerings that were left on-site.[26] From these first acts came the creation of localized tomb and hero cults,[27] among the Greeks' earliest attempts to establish a link with their past. For some the practice eventually took on the form of ancestor worship; for others—the inhabitants of Messenia, for example—the tombs became landmarks that guided decisions about where to build houses and other tombs.[28] In Mycenae, however, ruins and tombs were not granted such respect. And on Páros, ruins were incorporated into the foundations of new houses and defenses, while tombs were put to use as kilns, mills, trash pits, and even dwellings.[29] Such activities continued the tradition of reuse for purely practical purposes and were reminiscent of the continual habitation and use of sites and structures in Crete, Asia Minor, and the Near East.

Such was the case on the Acropolis in Athens, a site that has been in continuous use since Neolithic times. Damaged building material and statuary on the Acropolis resulting from the Persian Wars were used by Themistocles in the fifth century BCE to rebuild its fortifications.[30] Archaeologists believe that the finely carved and polychromed religious images from the earlier debris were probably buried with ceremony, a preservation-minded action of a different sort.

Continuity of use at the Acropolis, an important religious and symbolic site, is remarkable but not unusual. Throughout antiquity, new buildings often replaced predecessor religious structures for a variety of reasons, from their loss due to fire (a not infrequent occurrence at offering sites) to the need for structural improvements. Especially during the early classical period, earlier temple buildings were reconstructed in more developed forms with more durable materials. Interestingly, for over five centuries, the design of replacement temples and shrines varied little, except for some refinements in construction techniques and in the application of the three canons of

Figure 12-8 In the second century CE, the Roman writer Pausanius described the purposeful retention of old buildings in Greece, mentioning acts of preservation at the Heraion of Olympia. The Erechtheion (pictured here) on the Acropolis was restored twice, once ca. 250 BCE and again in Augustinian times (first century BCE).

Greek architecture: the Doric, Ionic or Corinthian orders. The conservative attitude at that time toward innovation in religious architecture reflects a respect for tradition and the past.

In the second century CE, the Greek travel writer Pausanias noted in his *Description of Greece* that one original oak column at the important Temple of Hera at Olympia (seventh century BCE) had been retained in the building's relatively protected rear chamber, while the forty-three other principal columns of the building were built of marble.[31] Not only does this suggest how the materials for Greek temples likely evolved but also that an original element was purposefully retained as a relic. That Pausanias wrote about the Heraion of Olympia eight centuries after its construction is testament in itself to a sustained consciousness of the importance of the preservation of architectural marvels in ancient Greece.

Another of the earliest travelers to leave a written account of sites he had seen was Herodotus (ca. 484–ca.425 BCE), who described the monumental structures along the Nile and gave a lengthy discussion of Giza's pyramids in his *History*.[32] Other ancient travelers such as Pausanias and Strabo also wrote about the impressive architecture that they observed in foreign places and referred specifically to their "antiquity."[33] Their writings can be considered documentary and preservation-minded views and proved useful in disseminating knowledge of the existence and significance of specific historic sites.

As Greek cities grew, increased attention was paid to the construction of monumental architecture, especially sanctuaries and temples. Starting in the eighth century BCE, Greek cities vied with one another to produce such monuments, which were an important part of urban life.[34] With the construction of such public monuments came provisions for their care. City administrations such as that of Miletus employed architects responsible for inspecting public buildings and streets. Athens went even further, and required that an architect perform maintenance work and be able to repair the buildings quickly if necessary.[35]

The preservation of historic structures and public spaces continued into Greece's Hellenistic period, which lasted from the late third to the first century BCE. Frequently, public spaces in Greek cities integrated new and old structures, and the spatial relationship between the two was carefully considered to form a harmonious ensemble.[36] In this period, historic buildings were usually respected as significant parts of the landscape that required special consideration, not viewed as hindrances to new construction.

From the Near East's Neolithic settlements to urban classical Greece, the preservation of structures and human-made environments has been an integral, if occasional, part of Western civilization's development. By reusing, restoring, or worshipping the glorious monuments and settlements of their forebears, humankind's expanding societies sought to preserve and reinforce their connection to the past. In doing so, these early communities established their legitimacy, which bolstered their collective confidence and enabled them to more forward.

REUSE AND PRESERVATION IN ANCIENT ROME

These excellent buildings are my delight, the noble image of the Empire's power and the witnesses of its grandeur and its glory. It is my wish that you shall preserve in its original splendor all that is ancient and that whatever you may add will conform to it in style.... To leave to future generations, to humanity, monuments that will fill them with admiration is a service full of honor and worthy of every man's strongest desire.

— Theodoric the Great (455–526 CE)[37]

Figure 12-9 Ancient texts and archaeology reveal the Regia ("king's house") and Temple of the Vestals adjacent to the Roman Forum were restored and reconstructed several times in their present location over an eight-hundred year period due to their symbolic significance to the ancient Romans. Seen here are the remains of the Regia's triangular entrance courtyard from the via Sacra, as it appeared in 1956. *(Photo: courtesy Phototeca, American Academy in Rome)*

Roman civilization had flourished for more than six hundred years before one of its leaders spoke these words in defense of the empire's built heritage. Ironically, it was a barbarian Ostrogoth king who spoke them. Theodoric presided over the ruined capital of an empire that was passing into history before his eyes. Like other kings before him, he sought to legitimize his rule by connecting it to the glories of the ancient past, a past when a powerful Rome produced the monuments he sought in vain to preserve.

Rome's origins lie hidden in the mists of historical and mythical time. Scholars today believe that the hills of Rome contained many small settlements of Latin tribes as early as 1000 BCE. Latinium (as Rome was then called) was subsequently occupied by the Etruscans, who filtered into the area between 650 and 600 BCE. Rome's historical founding is most likely to have taken place during this time.[38] Archaeology verifies that settlements have existed on Palatine Hill since the eighth century BCE, when a pattern of reuse began that continued throughout the city's history.

Excavations at the Regia ("king's house") at the nearby Roman Forum have proven that site's long-term continual use as well. Attributed to King Numa (715–654 BCE), one of the earliest Etruscan sovereigns, the Regia was repeatedly reconstructed over a seven-hundred-year period, with each building following the same design and reusing a significant degree of earlier construction material.[39] The prime motive for perpetuating the existence of the Regia in ancient Rome was its historical association with the Etruscan founders of the city.

Although patterns of reuse of specific sacred and urban sites were evident during Rome's early years, there was little official or public appreciation of art or architecture. During the republic's early imperial years of expansion, Roman leaders focused themselves and their construction practices on practical and military considerations. The decor of the religious buildings—the most elaborate civic architecture—was spare compared with the grandeur that developed later in imperial times.

The Romans' architectural preservation tradition almost certainly began with their exposure to Hellenistic culture and their adoption of Greek architectural forms.[40] The change in their perspective became most apparent during the Augustan period (27 BCE–13 CE), which ushered in a new era of peace and security after years of civil war and imperial expansion and included a building program for Rome. As the Roman architect Marcus Vitruvius Pollio wrote in the first century BCE in his famous work *De Architectura*, a manuscript written for the Emperor Augustus, "The majesty of the empire was expressed through the eminent dignity of its public buildings."[41]

Vitruvius's views about protecting the "old" were clear: Because there was continuity in life, there was no conflict between supporting new ideas while preserving what was old.[42] An architect, he insisted, must be multidisciplined, concerned with history and with the accomplishments of the architects who preceded him.[43] Soon, the majesty of the empire was not only expressed in its new construction but through the conscious protection of its historic buildings and sites as well.

Rome's historic structures benefited from Augustus's munificence, an approach that was imitated by many of his successors. As new buildings and imperial schemes were planned and realized in the Forum, the protection of older buildings was taken into account.[44] Specific rehabilitations were also undertaken in an effort to beautify the capital. During the first century, the stylistically outmoded Etruscan Temple of Portunus at the Forum Boarium was updated with a new cladding of travertine marble as part of Emperor Augustus's attempt to transform Rome's appearance.[45]

The nearby round Temple of Hercules, which was built in the second century BCE, remains one of ancient Rome's most intact ancient buildings. It sustained serious damage in the first century CE when a Tiber River flood washed away half of its twenty Corinthian columns. Ten matching replacements were erected during Emperor Tiberius's restoration. The temple was extensively modified in the twelfth century when it was converted into the Church of San Stefano delle Carrozze, later renamed Santa Maria del Sole. In the early nineteenth century the Temple of Hercules was restored to its ancient appearance, except for its roof. Recently, both it and the nearby Temple of Portunus were restored in a manner that respected the changes that had been made to these iconic Roman temple forms over time.[46]

The historic heart of the city of Pompeii, the Forum Triangulare, was built on Greek ruins. The Doric temple of its original sanctuary had largely vanished by the time of Augustus. However, Pompeii's most ancient forum had always maintained a public use. When Marcus Claudius Marcellus became the city's patron during the reign of Augustus, he restored its setting and converted the temple remains into an ornamental ruin, thus preserving the historic site for the pleasure of the Pompeiian citizenry.[47]

In Athens, Augustus himself hoped to impress his Greek subjects by systematically dismantling the 463 BCE Temple of Ares, putting Roman markings next to Greek stonemasons' signs on each stone as references, and transferring it from its location north of Athens to the Athenian agora, where it was reconstructed.[48] Placement in the city's urban center, where it would be looked after more effectively, ensured the temple's preservation.

By the first century CE, Roman attitudes toward the protection of art and architecture had expanded to include a concern for urban environments. Throughout the empire, laws were introduced to regulate everything from construction techniques to building heights. By 44 CE, Herculaneum had laws against the speculative demolition of build-

▶ **Figure 12-10** Views of the Temples of Portunus (top) and Hercules (bottom) in the Forum Boarium, Rome. Both of these archetypal temple forms were restored or improved in antiquity, modified for Christian worship in the Middle Ages, and restored more to their earlier forms during several efforts over the past three centuries.

Figure 12-11 The restoration of wall murals at Il Cenacolo (a dependency of the House of the Silver Wedding Anniversary), located in ancient Pompeii's Insula V2, after the earthquake of 62 CE used recycled building materials.

ings. In ancient Rome, deteriorating buildings and vacant lots were regarded with distaste. Looked upon as disturbances to the urban environment, they were seen as opportunities for improvement through rebuilding. At one site on the central square of Hadrianapolis, Emperor Hadrian ordered the owner of a dilapidated house either to restore and maintain his property or sell it.[49]

Roman emperors also concerned themselves with reconstruction following major disasters; both Hadrian and Vespasian encouraged the rebuilding of housing and public buildings after fires and earthquakes. The city of Pompeii successfully looked to Rome for assistance after its disastrous earthquake of 62 CE and was in the midst of restoration and reconstruction when it was devastated by Mount Vesuvius's volcanic eruption seventeen years later. During that brief interval, the Temple of Isis, which was completely leveled during the earthquake, was rebuilt. Because it commanded rich and influential worshippers, it was completely restored to look exactly as it had before the earthquake—thanks to the patronage of six-year-old N. Popidius Celsinus. This gesture, obviously backed by his wealthy freedman father, was rewarded by the city aldermen, who gave the boy a seat on the municipal council[50]—an early example of how the restoration of a significant public building could be used as a tool for social advancement.

In ancient Rome, rebuilding exact copies of predecessor buildings was the exception rather than the rule. The Pantheon is a case in point. It was constructed as a new and more elaborate version of previous structures on the same site, which were twice lost due to fires. When a new building was completed in the second century CE, the Emperor Hadrian carefully added an inscription honoring Marcus Agrippa, the original patron of the earlier building.[51] In antiquity, such remodeling and redesigning was tempered and influenced by historical idioms,[52] and the general approach to reworking older buildings, especially public religious structures, tended to be conservative.

Critical interpretation of historic sites—which included mostly ruins—emerged during the second century CE. Pausanias, a Greek who visited Asia Minor, Syria, Palestine, Egypt, Macedonia, and Epirus during the height of Roman rule, recorded his impressions of several ancient monuments in his *Description of Greece*. He found Mycenae too small and uninspiring for the capital of what had been a major power, but wisely added that it was difficult to judge entire cultures by their ruins and that further consideration was needed. To illustrate this point, Pausanias offered this comparison to his readers:

Suppose for example, that the city of Sparta were to become deserted and that only the temples and foundations of buildings remained. I think that future generations would, as time passed, find it very difficult to believe that the place had really been as powerful as it was represented to be. Yet the Spartans occupy two-fifths of the Peloponnesos and stand at the head not only of the whole Peloponnesos itself but also of numerous allies beyond its frontiers. Since, however, the city is not regularly planned and contains no temples or monuments of great magnificence, but is simply a collection of villages, in the ancient Hellenic way, its appearance would not come up to expectation. If, on the other hand, the same thing were to happen to Athens, one would conjecture from what met the eye that the city had been twice as powerful as in fact it is.[53]

Pausanias's insights highlight what became an increasing concern for citizens and builders of countless buildings, towns, and civilizations right up until our own time—planned urban monumentality for its own sake and as a sign of strength and power for posterity.

By the third century CE, the Roman Empire stretched from the rolling hills of Great Britain to the Syrian desert. Its powerful military had united disparate nations and kept them together through commerce, citizenship, and military might, but faults were beginning to show. Rome was forced to construct walls to protect it from outside forces, and Christianity had become a force from within that disrupted the empire's social fabric. Physically, the capital began to decline as well. Over the course of a few centuries, Rome was repeatedly attacked and looted, and countless art and architectural treasures were destroyed by invaders.[54]

With the twilight of the Roman Empire came the dawn of the Christian world. Besieged, divided, and dying, the empire lingered on. Acceptance of Christianity in 380 CE led to the destruction of pagan temples. After Theodosius II closed them in 437 CE, many temples—with their shrines vacant—were slowly dismantled.[55] The early Christian intention was often not to destroy Roman temples, however, but rather to claim them for use by the new dominant religion, and thus they were often preserved and adapted to meet Christian liturgical requirements. In the sixth century, Pope Gregory the Great reaffirmed such conversions by commanding, "Do not destroy the pagan temples, only the idols which are found in them. As for the monument, sprinkle it with holy water, erect altars and place relics there."[56]

The closure of the state marble quarries initiated a millennium of building cannibalization that saw Rome's architectural glories dismantled to provide raw material for new buildings. The Arch of Constantine, the first Christian emperor, was constructed using statuary and polished marble removed from the Arch of Marcus Aurelius and the Forum of Trajan.[57] Later emperors such as Leo and Majorian, however, passed laws levying heavy penalties against the destroyers of public buildings.[58] Few fought as hard for these regulations as did Theodoric, the ruler of Ravenna in the early sixth century. He considered himself a "restorer of cities," reestablished the ancient Roman office of *curator statuarum*

Figure 12-12 The Arch of Constantine in Rome, which dates from 312 CE, includes a number of both recycled and replicated sculptures from some four centuries prior.

to protect its statues, and instructed his architect to respect and protect the ancient sites and to make sure new construction related fittingly to them.

Theodoric's aim to preserve the architectural status quo in Rome proved untimely. Rome's glory in the West had passed to the East. When the Roman Empire and the Church split in the third century, Emperor Constantine established a magnificent city at the easternmost tip of Europe on the foundations of the ancient Greek city of Byzantium. Envisioned as the second, or new, Rome, Constantine's city was lavishly embellished with found and acquired Roman stone building fragments, or *spolia*. Soon known as Constantinople, this quickly expanding city was adorned with columns, sculptures, tiles, and marble removed from ancient buildings throughout the Eastern empire.

THE MIDDLE AGES IN EUROPE

The Roman Empire's collapse in the fifth century preceded a chaotic period in history, when the peoples of Europe reorganized and moved into the period we now call the Middle Ages. Although this era has also been called the Dark Ages, from an architectural point of view, it was a fertile period. Although many important historic buildings were lost, urban growth exploded and impressive new works were created, including the sixth-century Hagia Sophia, or the Church of the Holy Wisdom, in Constantinople, whose design was Roman in spirit and incorporated significant quantities of pagan-era building materials.[59]

(Since its construction, the Hagia Sophia has required dozens of conservation interventions and structural enhancement measures, including a twice-rebuilt dome and new buttresses to guard against damage from the region's frequent earthquakes.[60] A focused analysis on the numerous attempts to stabilize, repair, and restore this one building since medieval

Figure 12-13 The east courtyard portal of the church of S. Clemente (first constructed in ca.380 CE, with its present form dating from 1099) in Rome's Subura quarter is one of scores of examples of the reuse of ancient building materials during the Middle Ages. (© ICCROM)

Figure 12-14 The Hagia Sophia in Istanbul is one of several Byzantine churches adorned with fine marbles taken as *spoils* from earlier Roman and Hellenic temples.

times would elucidate the many philosophical concerns that relate to the Hagia Sophia's conservation and interpretation today.)

Meanwhile, throughout the former western half of the Roman Empire, people struggled to establish new societies amid the remains of an increasingly decrepit Roman legacy. The poor condition of ancient sites must have seemed stifling, if not overwhelming, to succeeding generations, because these structures had lost their purposes and meanings. The decline of classical education and the continued official affirmation of Christian belief and culture made the omnipresent remains of Roman grandeur seem irrelevant to contemporary life, or even obstructions to daily existence.

Gradually, communities devised ways to deal with their inherited architectural past, often continuing the reuse and modification of those historic structures that had begun in the later centuries of the Roman Empire. A dramatic example is the city of Split on the coast of what is today Croatia. It was established in the early seventh century CE by refugees seeking safety within the massive walls of the abandoned retirement palace of Emperor Diocletian. The palace's many buildings and spaces, which had been built only a few centuries earlier, were converted by the new arrivals into a fully functional medieval town. Throughout the lands that were formerly part of imperial Rome, materials and forms were recycled for new uses for centuries after the empire's collapse to facilitate the adaptive use of ancient buildings. For example, the Roman basilica, or public meeting hall, a form that had been borrowed from Greece, served as the prototype for the nave and aisle of Christian churches for the next two millennia.

Intriguing examples of how building materials from antiquity were recycled during medieval times are found throughout western Europe. Charlemagne's coronation in 800 by Pope Leo II aligned the Church in Rome with the Carolingian Court, and he reinforced this connection by adorning his palace at Aachen with architectural fragments and elements acquired from ancient Roman structures in Ravenna and Rome.[61] At St.-Gilles-du-Gard Church near Arles, France, ancient marble colonnettes were placed on the new building's façade to give the composition a distinctly ancient flavor.[62] St.-Gilles's twelfth-century portal and niche façade sculptures are remarkably similar to ancient Roman sculptures, complete with figures draped in togalike garments standing *contrapposto*.

St.-Gilles and other churches now called Romanesque were not technically a revival of ancient Roman styles, but classical forms and construction techniques did serve as their inspiration. At the very least, intrinsically valuable objects such as exotic marble columns and richly carved architectural fragments were incorporated into the new buildings. Likewise, certain objects from antiquity, such as cameos, jewelry, and finely carved sarcophagi, were occasionally appreciated through the Middle Ages for their material as well as aesthetic values and were therefore collected and preserved, their pagan associations ignored. Many of antiquity's literary treasures, thought to have disappeared, were rediscovered, transcribed, and circulated within European monasteries and in the madrassas of the Islamic world.

The great Roman capital and its spirit refused to die in the hearts of descendent Romans, although during the Middle Ages the city became a mere shadow of its former glorious self, having been particularly humbled and broken following the Norman sack of 1084. Crowded, with long-neglected ancient sites, several of its hills had become overgrown or converted into refuse heaps. Rome slowly reawakened, but as its population grew, so did the pressures on its surviving buildings. Rome's aristocrats also began to reclaim the great shells of ancient structures: Noble families began to build their palaces adjacent to, or on top of, important ancient buildings; others were converted into tenements and workshops.

Figure 12-15 The church St.-Gilles-du-Garde near Arles, France, incorporates recycled ancient marble and contemporary classicizing details on its façade.

Figure 12-16 Antonio Tempesta's map of Rome, dating from 1593, shows the relationship of its vast numbers of ruins to the living city.

This new construction required building materials, which were seen as readily available in the ruins of the city's unused and unprotected ancient buildings. Marble veneers, columns, and statues were broken up and burned by limekiln owners, who established themselves in places where the mining of marble from ancient buildings was most convenient.[63] The destruction of ancient buildings became alarmingly commonplace as the Catholic Church, the paramount power in the city, reused their materials in the construction of new churches. While there is evidence that in the later Middle Ages the more precious carvings and artistic work were increasingly preserved for their intrinsic value or as objects of curiosity, a vast amount of ancient building material had already been lost.

In the twelfth century, concerned Romans—disturbed by the transformation of their beloved city into an open quarry—set up a senate to gain control of Rome and preserve it from the Church. Their success was brief.[64] The senate attempted to stop the wholesale destruction of the city's ancient sites, and in 1162 passed a decree stating that Trajan's column should be protected "as long as the world shall last" and that anyone attempting to damage it would pay with his life.[65] Despite the senate's best intentions, the destruction of ancient buildings proceeded as the popes continued to cede buildings to the Church or to private individuals for the purposes of demolition.[66]

At the same time, however, the Church's efforts in other fields were also contributing to the maintenance and importance of ancient buildings in Rome. As the center of the Catholic Church, Rome was a major pilgrimage destination for those seeking to visit the relics of many saints, including St. Peter. The *Einsiedeln Itinerary* and the *Mirabilia Urbis Romae* (The Marvels of the City of Rome)[67] were some of the earliest guides to the wonders of the city; they provided tourists and pilgrims with routes for seeing Rome's Christian sites—as well as its ancient pagan ones. This influx of visitors indirectly benefited the protection of historic sites: in 1119, the column of Marcus Aurelius and an adjoining building were rented to an operator who allowed pilgrims to climb it to view the city from its great height—for a fee, of course.[68]

Occasional opposition to the continued destruction of Rome's architectural heritage continued. The English theologian Magister Gregory openly criticized the wanton destruction being carried out at the command of the popes in one edition of the *Mirabilia*. In the early fourteenth century, Cola di Rienzo, later tribune of the people of Rome, was also an avid admirer of the city's ancient monuments. He railed against those he believed to be responsible for the city's decline, exclaiming, "Sublime Rome lies in the dust, she cannot see her own fall since the emperor and the pope have torn her two eyes out!"[69] One of di Rienzo's contemporaries, Giovanni Dondi, was one of the first since antiquity to record accurate dimensions of the monuments he encountered on his journeys. Under

Figure 12-17 Marmashen Church in northwestern Armenia was restored to appear as new after an earthquake in the twelfth century. Details about the restoration, including mention of its donors, are spelled out in its rededication inscription on the façade of the church's west transept.

Figure 12-18 Marmashen. Detail of the dedication inscription from the transept.

his direction the Colosseum, the Pantheon, Trajan's Column, the Vatican Obelisk, and the basilicas of St. Peter and St. Paul were all surveyed.[70]

The most important historic buildings of many other cities—in Europe and beyond—were also documented in the written accounts of visitors during the Middle Ages as well as in later centuries. Chinese scholars and travelers such as Fa-Hsien in the fifth century and Huien Tsang in the seventh century left behind descriptions of various Buddhist sites and cities in India—including Nalanda's monastery, library, and university complex, which was destroyed by the Turks in 1205. Today their writings are the best remaining evidence of this architectural heritage. One of the most famous travel writers in history, the Ottoman official Evliya Çelebi, published accounts of his decades of travels in a ten-volume book called *Seyahatname* (Book of Travels) in the mid-seventeenth century. After ten years spent documenting his native Istanbul, Çelebi set off to observe and describe Anatolia, the Balkans, Persia, the Middle East, North Africa, and what is now Austria and Hungary. His descriptions of hundreds of Ottoman-era buildings in Greece, Hungary, and Serbia are all that remains of many of these sites.

All of these men, in their various ways—whether by denouncing authority or recording evidence for posterity—can be considered some of the earliest architectural conservationists. There are, however, few medieval examples of the restoration of buildings in Europe, as we understand the term today.[71] Historic buildings were frequently modified and reused. In-kind repairs after disasters such as earthquakes occasionally occurred. But restoration to capture a previous or original design, or solely for the sake of restoration, had yet to be attempted.

ENDNOTES

1. Whether considered the genetic predecessors of *Homo sapiens* or—as most physical anthropologists and paleontologists believe—of a different species, the Neanderthal and a host of other proto-*Homo sapian* species having much earlier tool-making abilities date back as far as 2.5 million years. It is in this vast period of time that the human capacity for processing symbolic thought originated.

2. Blow-painted, silhouetted images of hundreds of hand prints in the Caves of Pech-Merle in France made twenty thousand years ago attest to the interest of early *Homo sapiens* leaving their mark. Rock art (petroglyphs) that is more difficult to date is found in sub-Saharan Africa and the Burrup Peninsula of Australia.

3. Given evidence recently uncovered at the Blombos Cave in South Africa, physical anthropologists now believe that cognizant modern man existed nearly seventy thousand years ago. The discovery of finely polished weapon points demonstrates a skill that represents, as John Noble Wilford has said, "a form of consciousness that extends beyond the here and now to a contemplation of the past and future and a perception of the world within and beyond the individual." ("When Humans Became Human," *New York Times*, February 26, 2002).

4. Donald Martin Reynolds, ed., *Remove Not the Ancient Landmark: Public Monuments and Moral Values; Discourses and Comments in Tribute to Rudolf Wittkower* (Amsterdam: Gordon and Breach, 1996), 4. Monumentality is referred to here with a stress on memory and its synonym *monere* or *monumentum*, Latin for "remind" or "warn." John Warren's "Principles and Problems: Ethics and Aesthetics," in Marks, *Concerning Buildings*, 34–35, expands on the idea of memory and presentation in early prehistoric times.

5. Rick Gore, "People Like Us," *National Geographic*, July 2000, 106.

6. In northern Iraq's Shanidar Cave, one of the best-preserved examples of a Neanderthal ritualistic burial, a body was placed in the fetal position on a woven mat and was surrounded by deliberately arranged wildflowers. Richard E. Leakey and Roger Lewin, *Origins: What New Discoveries Reveal About the Emergence of Our Species and Its Possible Future* (New York: E. P. Dutton, 1977), 125.

   Evidence suggestive of a belief in an afterlife has also been found in a mass Neanderthal gravesite in La Ferrassie, France, where flint tools and the presence of animal bones seem to signify that these objects would be useful to the dead, perhaps in the next world. Source: Kharlena Maria Ramanan, "Burial, Ritual, Religion, and Cannibalism," in *Neandertals: A Cyber Perspective*, http://sapphire.indstate.edu/~ramanan/ritual.html. (February 5, 2002).

7. Erik Trinkaus and Pat Shipman, *The Neandertals: Changing the Image of Mankind* (New York: Knopf, 1993), 255.

8. Evidence of human-made habitats dates from a much earlier time. The earliest known human-made structure—a two-million-year-old construction of stacked rocks that held branches in position—was found in Tanzania's Olduvai Gorge. Wally Kowalski, *Stone Age Habitats*, http://www.personal.psu.edu/users/w/x/wxk116/habitat/ (February 5, 2002). Further prehistoric dwellings of between 400,000 and 500,000 years old are found along coastal southern France. Near Nice, the Cave of Lazaret was occupied between 186,000 and 127,000 years ago. Its structures mainly consisted of wooden branches held in place by stone and covered with animal skins or grass. More recent structures—such as the Upper Paleolithic hut from Dolní Vestonice (ca. 21,000 BCE) in the southern Czech Republic and the Mezhirich huts in northern Ukraine (ca. 13,000 BCE)—incorporated other materials, such as the earliest examples of fired earthen building materials and interlocking mammoth bones. The building of Mezhrich was an enormous feat, making use of the mandibles of over one hundred mammoths for the foundations of four huts. Gore, "People Like Us," 112. The newcomer *Homo sapiens* from the beginning of the Upper Paleolithic period (around 42,000 years ago) had technological and artistic capabilities superior to Neanderthals and were better able to adapt. Animal paintings in the Chauvet Caves of 32,400 years ago and contemporaneous ivory figurines found in the Caves of Hohlenstein-Stadel in Germany—including the famous fetish figurine *Löwenmensch* ("man-beast")—are believed to be attempts by the Cro-Magnon community to find meaning in their world. They signify the gradual development of a social fabric. Cro-Magnon man is better known as Aurignacian man, after the town of Aurignac in southwestern France where several Cro-Magnon sites are found.

9. J. M. Roberts, *Prehistory and the First Civilizations*, vol. 2, *The Illustrated History of the World* (New York: Oxford University Press, 1999), 51.

10. Alain Schnapp, *The Discovery of the Past*, trans. Ian Kinnes and Gillian Varndell (London: British Museum Press, 1993), 12.

11. Religion also served to solidify the order of Sumerian new towns, which increasingly took on the role of cult centers and places of pilgrimage. The earliest of these Sumerian cult centers was Eridu, founded ca. 5000 BCE. As populations increased, small, disparate groups worked in tandem to reclaim marshlands, irrigate fields, and fend off others who tried to claim their lands — efforts that required a higher level of human organization than had ever occurred before. Eventually, as groups joined together for more efficient food production and self-protection, the first towns were created. Roberts, *Prehistory*, 77–78.

12. Cevat Erder, *Our Architectural Heritage: From Consciousness to Conservation*, trans. Ayfer Bakkalcioglu (Paris: UNESCO, 1986), 23.

13. Cornelius Holtorf, "The Past in Ancient Mesopotamia," chapter in "Monumental Past: The Life Histories of Megalithic Monuments in Mecklenburg-Vorpommern (Germany)" (PhD diss., University of Wales, 1998).

14. Ibid.

15. Ibid.

16. Erder, *Our Architectural Heritage*, 25.

17. Schnapp, *Discovery of the Past*, 18.

18. The persistence and energy with which Nabonidus restored major monuments foreshadowed the imminent demise of his empire at the hand of the Persian king Darius I. It was as if by restoring the temples and leaving his mark that Nabonidus sought to delay Babylon's fall. Perhaps, in a way, he achieved immortality: Babylon fell, but Nabonidus's name, as well as that of Nebuchadnezzar, lives on.

19. Holtorf, "The Past in Ancient Mesopotamia"; Erica Reiner, *Your Thwarts in Pieces, Your Mooring Rope Cut: Poetry from Babylonia and Assyria* (Ann Arbor, MI: University of Michigan, 1985), 2–5.

20. From around 2800 BCE, bodies of the elite were elaborately mummified, placed in carved sarcophagi, and interred with a variety of grave goods, often including mummified animals. Mummified creatures — ranging in species from tiny shrews to crocodiles, and even a lion — were meant to accompany the deceased human being to the next world. Tomb chamber walls were usually finished with fine polychrome bas-reliefs.

21. Holtorf, "The Past in Ancient Egypt." note 13.

22. Grahame Clark, *Space, Time and Man: A Prehistorian's View* (Cambridge: Cambridge University Press, 1992), 89.

23. Erder, *Our Architectural Heritage*, 23. Ancient Egypt's history is also marked by numerous examples of the purposeful destruction and defacement of buildings, the most infamous example being the attempted excision from the historical record of all images of and references to Queen Hatshepsut by her successor, Thutmose III.

24. Many of Amenhotep III's architectural creations, including his own modifications at Karnak, were dismantled by his successors. The pieces were recycled.

25. Holtorf, "The Past in Ancient Greece."

26. J. N. Coldstream, "Hero-cults in the Age of Homer," *Journal of Hellenic Studies* 96 (1976), 14.

27. *Tomb cults* refer to popular worship and veneration of Mycenaean tomb sites between 770 and 700 BCE. There is some debate about the actual reasoning behind tomb cults; arguments point to the tombs being used as surrogate links to the unknown or imaginary past and also to reinforce the community's link to the land.

28. Holtorf, "The Past in Ancient Greece."

29. Ibid.

30. Piero Gazzola, "Restoring Monuments: Historical Background," in UNESCO, *Preserving and Restoring Monuments and Historic Buildings* (Paris: UNESCO, 1972), 22.

31. Pausanias, *Description of Greece*, vol.2, trans. W. H. S. Jones (Cambridge, MA: Harvard University Press, 1961), chap. 16:54.

32. Alberto Siliotti, *Egypt Lost and Found: Explorers and Travelers on the Nile* (London: Thames and Hudson 1999), 17.

33. Not much is known about the life of Pausanias (mid-second century CE), a Greek traveler and geographer. His *Description of Greece* runs to ten volumes and was meant to be a kind of tourist guide to Greece and its historical and religious artifacts. *Geography* by Strabo (64 BCE to 23 CE), a Greek historian and geographer, runs to seventeen books and is a wealth of information on the historical geography of the area. Both authors have written vivid descriptions of historic architecture that no longer exists today, such as the statue of Zeus at the Temple of Zeus at ancient Olympia. These descriptions, along with other discoveries by archaeologists (in the case of the statue of Zeus, excavations of terra-cotta molds), help in the visual reconstruction of these various sites.

34. Schnapp, *Discovery of the Past*, 57.

35. Erder, *Our Architectural Heritage*, 29.

36. Ibid., 33. When Attalus II, King of Pergamum, built a two-story stoa on the Athenian agora during the second century BCE, its positioning further defined the boundaries of the agora while also commanding a view of the panathenaic processional route.

37. T. C. Bannister quotes from Cassiodorus' *Variae* in his "Comment" in National Trust for Historic Preservation and Colonial Williamsburg, *Historic Preservation Today: Essays Presented to the Seminar on Preservation and Restoration, Williamsburg, Virginia, September 8–11, 1963* (Charlottesville, VA: University Press of Virginia, 1966), 33–34.

38. Human settlements existed on the hills of Rome during the Bronze Age in the middle of the second millennium BCE.

39. L. Richardson, Jr., *A New Topographical Dictionary of Ancient Rome* (Baltimore, MD: The Johns Hopkins University Press, 1992), Regia, 328-29.

40. Erder, *Our Architectural Heritage*, 40.

41. Chester G. Starr, *The Roman Empire, 27 B.C.–A.D. 476: A Study in Survival* (New York: Oxford University Press, 1982), 25.

42. Erder, *Our Architectural Heritage*, 42.

43. Ibid.

44. Jokilehto, *History of Architectural Conservation*, 2–3.

45. A twentieth-century restoration of the Temple of Portunus, known earlier as the temple of Fortuna Virilis, shows the various changes made to it over time. This includes the now scant evidence of its improvements in Augustus's time, which were removed in the nineteenth century by restorers interested in showing this temple more as a rare example of architecture from the Republican period.

46. Both temples had accretions removed during restorations beginning in the early nineteenth century with their most recent restorations occurring during the past decade in a partnership between Rome's Soprintendza di Monumenti and the World Monuments Fund.

47. L. Richardson, Jr., *Pompeii: An Architectural History* (Baltimore, MD: Johns Hopkins University Press, 1988), 73.

48. W. B. Dinsmoor, "The Temple of Ares at Athens and the Roman Agora," *Hesperia* 9 (1940): 383–384.

49. Erder, *Our Architectural Heritage*, 46–47.

50. Robert Etienne, *Pompeii: The Day a City Died*, trans. Caroline Palmer (New York: Harry N. Abrams, 1992), 118.

51. Jokilehto, *History of Architectural Conservation*, 4–5. The English translation of the Pantheon frieze reads: "Marcus Agrippa, the son of Lucius, three times consul, built this."

52. Gazzola, "Restoring and Preserving Monuments and Historic Buildings," 22.

53. Schnapp, *Discovery of the Past*, 48–49.

54. With the exception of the "enlightened barbarian" Theodoric the Great (455–526 CE). Jokilehto, *History of Architectural Conservation*, 5.

55. Erder, *Our Architectural Heritage*, 56.

56. Jokilehto, "History of Architectural Conservation," (DPhil thesis, University of York, 1986).

57. While the marble quarries east of Rome were likely still operating at the time, the recycling of building elements, especially those with fine carving, was commonplace throughout the Middle Ages.

58. Tung, *Preserving the World's Great Cities*, 36. One of the earliest preservation statutes, brutal but ultimately ineffective, dates from 458 CE. Punishment for those who dismembered imperial monuments was two-tiered: a heavy fine for the magistrate who approved the destruction and a beating and the loss of both hands for the workmen who carried out the order. While it proved to be only a minimal deterrent in Rome, a significant pattern of protection was established elsewhere on the peninsula henceforth.

59. Visitors to today's Istanbul can see several sites where impressive reuse of earlier building materials occurred, including not only the Hagia Sophia but also Kariye Camii, Kalenderhane Çamii, and Yerebatan Saray (Cistern Basilica), where construction involved reusing 336 antique stone columns to support its enormous vaulted roof.

60. Erder, *Our Architectural Heritage*, 23. As the great building's remarkably brief five-year construction project neared completion in 537 CE, its huge central dome partially collapsed. It was immediately rebuilt, but in a slightly modified form. Architectural conservation historian Cevat Erder has asked provocatively whether this should be considered repair or restoration or whether it was just a second attempt at construction. Because the design was altered during repairs before the building was placed into service, the work should properly be considered a rebuilding. Four hundred years later, when another section of the dome fell in the earthquake of 989, the extensively damaged vaulting was replaced by the famed Armenian architect Trdat. This third building of the Hagia Sophia's dome entailed no design alteration and is considered a restoration.

61. Erder, *Our Architectural Heritage*, 70.

62. The façade's composition consists of three portals raised on a stylobate; the enriched entablature, divided by bays, is also an amalgam of ancient Roman forms and materials and medieval French church culture.

63. Proven locations were between the Capitoline Hill and the Tiber along the Via delle Botteghe Oscure, in the Forum, and next to the Colosseum.

64. Erder, *Our Architectural Heritage*, 71. The pillaging of ancient building materials for reuse and the relocation or collection of more valuable chance discoveries encountered during excavations continued, despite the efforts of the senate.

65. Schnapp, *Discovery of the Past*, 94.

66. Erder, *Our Architectural Heritage*, 71.

67. Claude Moatti, *The Search for Ancient Rome* (New York: Harry N. Abrams, 1993), 22.

68. Erder, *Our Architectural Heritage*, 71.

69. Moatti, *Search for Ancient Rome*, 25.

70. Schnapp, *Discovery of the Past*, 108. The Vatican Obelisk was placed in its present position in 1586.

71. Existing histories of architectural conservation appear to have overlooked numerous examples of accurate and extensive restorations and reconstructions of medieval buildings—especially churches—in the earthquake-prone Caucasus nations of Armenia and Georgia, where it is common to encounter ancient repairs and restorations to stone buildings that are remarkably modern in their approach.

CHAPTER *13*

The Fifteenth Through the Eighteenth Centuries

THE RENAISSANCE, 1300 TO 1600

Hasten to prevent such damage! It will be an honor for you to have saved these ruins, because they testify to what once was the glory of unviolated Rome.[1]

—Petrarch to Paolo Annibaldi

As Petrarch, the fourteenth-century Florentine poet and scholar, wrote those words, a new age—the Renaissance—was dawning. It was first heralded throughout the cities of Italy and then slowly encompassed the European continent. Petrarch was not alone in his admiration of antiquity, though he is credited as being among the first to spur a revival of interest in all the arts of the classical world. He was also one of the earliest to attempt a periodization of history by suggesting antiquity was followed by dark ages that ended with the awakening of his own time.[2]

Petrarch's successors further shaped the Renaissance that transformed Europe's medieval world. Their impact on architectural conservation was to broaden interest in surviving antiquities from their curiosity and use values to their historic values. According to French historian of architectural theory Françoise Choay, Petrarch saw ancient Roman monuments as legitimizing "literary memory."[3] They individually and collectively bear witness to an ancient Rome mentioned in texts and reflect another, separate time. Petrarch also found that the legend-filled interpretation of local guides was inadequate for helping visitors understand the significance of ancient Rome's remains and believed that the city could only be experienced properly using the ancient authors as a reference.[4] For him, ancient Roman buildings had to be interpreted in the context of their different time and had to be treated as historical objects.

Upon his first visit to Rome, Petrarch was appalled by the sight of the lime works next to the Colosseum and upbraided the Romans for their profound lack of respect for their monuments.[5] Though an edict from 1363 made vandalizing monuments punishable by a fine, such activities continued with abandon.[6] During the fifteenth century, Rome was still

Figure 13-1 View of the Roman Forum, ca. 1535. *(Engraving by Maerten van Heemskerck)*

a city in ruins. Its streets were clogged not only by rubble mixed with building elements, pieces of statuary, and the detritus of everyday life but also by a new wave of pilgrims and visitors who came in search of antiquity, whether for inspiration, to collect, or simply to satisfy their curiosity. Interest in ancient monuments—and more generally, in the cultural heritage of foreign places—had increased as travel had become easier.

With the growth of collections came the need to share this knowledge and the desire to acquire more, a phenomenon that was played out on a broad stage. In the fifteenth century, the Vatican played a major role in amassing artifacts of the past. Toward the end of that century, wealthy individuals interested in the remnants of ancient Rome not only organized private collections but also underwrote its further study and encouraged its revival.

The revival of the classical idiom in art and architecture was expressed in sculpture, painting, literature, and music but most visibly in architecture. Humanism, a fundamentally new world view, had grown slowly but surely during the three previous centuries, thanks to gradual changes in social conditions like the development of banking, the possibility of travel, of universities, the expansion of religious attitudes—and in response to the larger world as gleaned from the Crusades and more distant trade. For the first time, Europeans perceived a distance between the present and the more distant past. This "taste for the antique" reflected a complete reappraisal of history. Two centuries later, it culminated in the radically changed worldviews of the Enlightenment.

While writers penned travel descriptions and poetry espousing a new "cult of ruins," Florentine architects such as Filippo Brunelleschi repeatedly returned to study the construction technologies and principles used in Rome's ancient architecture, then they applied them in their own work. Brunelleschi and his contemporary artists and architects also appreciated surviving ancient buildings for new reasons—their aesthetic and educational values. A consummate scholar, Brunelleschi was also an artist, mathematician, designer, and engineer; as such, he perfectly fit Vitruvius's earlier profile of an architect.

Brunelleschi was enamored with Rome; he participated in excavations and made sketches, measured drawings, and reconstructions on paper. He returned to Florence with a multitude of ideas for buildings. It is believed that the Pantheon inspired his solution for the then incomplete dome of the Basilica of Santa Maria del Fiore in Florence.[7] Elsewhere in that city, he used Roman design principles and details for his work at the Ospedale degli Innocenti and the Church of Santo Spirito.

In 1414, the humanist antiquarian Gian Francesco Poggio Bracciolini discovered Vitruvius's first-century architectural treatise *De Architectura* in the library of the monastery of St. Gall, Switzerland. The find proved to be a welcome revelation for an artistic community hungry for the technological wisdom and radical reasoning of the classical world. Until that time, builders had tried to understand the distant past through observation and scant references to the building arts found in surviving ancient texts. Leon Battista Alberti learned about ancient building practices mainly by translating Vitruvius's treatise on architecture. His approach was that of a scholar, historian, and architect. The newly invented printing press allowed Alberti's translation—and other books on architecture that followed—to gain increasingly wide audiences.

The 1485 publication of *De Re Aedificatoria*, Alberti's updated version of Vitruvius's *De Architectura*, accurately reflected the attitudes of Renaissance architects and their followers, who were inspired by, but often modified, the examples of the ancients. In his treatise, Alberti encouraged architects to respect and adhere to the original intent of the designer when continuing work on unfinished projects or historic buildings. He also advocated the preservation of ancient buildings, not only for their historical value but for their beauty as well, and railed against the negligence and avarice that allowed them to be pulled apart or left open to the elements.

▼ **Figure 13-2** Though never completed, the rehabilitation of the Gothic Church of San Francesco in Rimini, Italy (1450), is an extensive rehabilitation designed by Leon Battista Alberti using rules of proportion learned through his translations of Vitruvius and design details deriving from his firsthand study of ancient Roman buildings.

Alberti's architecture reflected his understanding of ancient Roman design principles as described by Vitruvius, his keen eye from observing Rome's ruins, and his talents as an artist and designer. The same would be said of countless others for centuries to follow. His modifications to the Tempio Malatestiano (1450–1461) to become the Church of San Francesco in Rimini and Santa Maria Novella in Florence were renovations of earlier buildings using a variety of classicizing details. The Tempio Malatestiano was reclad in stone with motifs borrowed from antiquity. At Santa Maria Novella, the primary elevation was remade in a manner that reflected Alberti's mastery of the classical canon regarding proportion. He sympathetically blended Florentine Romanesque with multicolored marble patterning in a mathematically reasoned geometric façade design and based its portal on that of the Pantheon.

Alberti—and Brunelleschi before him—created new architecture based on long-forgotten ancient Roman precedents. No prior attempt at reviving the antique had been so effective. It is impossible to understand Renaissance architecture and its reliance on ancient prototypes without understanding Brunelleschi's and Alberti's views. They heralded a new generation of artists, architects, and builders who learned about ancient architecture by measuring and drawing ancient monuments and ruins and sharing the resulting information with each other. As is usually the case, ambitious patrons who demanded distinctive architecture played a key role as well.

As the Renaissance progressed, scholarship on various aspects of antiquity advanced quickly and sympathy for preserving ancient buildings began to evolve, especially after the 1480s, as printing presses, made more efficient by movable type, accelerated the dissemination of new ideas and sensibilities. Through architectural treatises by Giacomo da Vignola and Sebastiano Serlio and travel accounts by the humanist Cyriacus of Ancona, the histories and descriptions of buildings and cities became more widely known. In the second quarter of the sixteenth century, when books were generously illustrated, the understanding and appreciation of the past developed at an even more accelerated pace.

However, as Françoise Choay has noted, the recognition of the dual historical and artistic values of the monuments of antiquity in the 1400s did not lead to their effective and systematic conservation.[8] Despite a general ambivalence, there were, however, isolated incidents that demonstrated interest in architectural conservation. During the latter half of the fifteenth century, Florentine sculptor and architect Il Filarete (Antonio Averlino) used Roman monuments to explain how poor maintenance can reduce even the best built structures to ruins. Another artist and architect, Francesco di Giorgio Martini, was referred to as a "restorer of ancient ruins" based on his restoration drawings of surviving parts of ancient buildings. He further emphasized the instructional value of ancient buildings as sources of inspiration for the creation of new architecture.

The most visible physical expression of the Renaissance was the redesign of much of medieval Florence and Rome, which was accomplished by applying ancient Roman building principles, especially the five Roman column orders, to new construction. The works of this period were never mere copies of ancient prototypes. Instead, Renaissance architects and artists applied ancient principles to meet contemporary needs. By this time noble Roman families had also appropriated ruins for their own use.[9] The Arch of Trajan became part of the defense wall for a residence on the Forum side of the Palatine Hill. The architect Baldassare Peruzzi built a palace for the Pierleoni family atop the ruins of the ancient Theater of Marcellus, which once held fifteen thousand spectators. The project represents the attitude of the time: Adapt ancient buildings for practical use by utilizing recycled building components wherever possible. Peruzzi leveled the original top story of the semicircular theater and replaced it with palatial quarters—a grand example of adaptive use. Because Renaissance Rome lacked any efficient city administration, there was little to stop its significant historic buildings from being appropriated, either by squatters or nobles.

Antiquarianism, the serious inquiry into the past, rapidly on the rise during the fifteenth century, soon became an official interest of the Vatican as well. The Catholic Church was Rome's most viable institution as well as the center of the city's political and cultural power. Its interest in the city's ancient past was enhanced by the discovery of the Golden House of Nero (the Domus Aurea), which had revealed an abundance of classical treasures.

The early fifteenth-century popes Martin V and Eugenius IV, concerned by the squalid state of Rome—the seat of the Catholic Church—were the first to attempt a form of urban renewal through the removal of debris and demolition of dilapidated buildings. Pope Nicholas V, helped by such notable architects as Alberti and Bernardo Rossellino, embarked on a series of civic improvements to restore the city to its rightful place as a great capital. Still, little effort was made to restore or officially protect ancient monuments, and many historic buildings were lost or damaged during this period.

The first pope to link the monuments of ancient Rome to the history of Christianity (and decide they were therefore worthy of preservation) was Pope Pius II, whose bull *Cum almam nostram urbem* of 1462 was Rome's first piece of protective legislation.[10] Repair and maintenance work on ancient buildings during this period focused mainly on those structures still in use, such as bridges, aqueducts, and fortifications. Minor repairs to the Arch of Titus in 1466 and later the Arch of Septimius Severus were also carried out.[11]

Regardless of the edicts they passed, the Renaissance popes were often contradictory in applying conservation measures. Pope Eugenius IV ordered the protection of the Colosseum from vandals but then allowed his architects to pilfer its marble for his own use.[12] Pope Paul II, an accomplished art collector before his ascension to the papal throne, encouraged the Church's study and acquisition of ancient art. Although his enthusiasm for antiquity expanded Vatican collections, the frenzy of excavations it inspired greatly damaged or destroyed many historic structures. Pope Sixtus IV supported monument protection in his own bull, *Quam provida* of 1474, though he allowed his architects to dig wherever they wished.

While Rome's early intermittent repair and maintenance works cannot be considered restoration in a modern sense, a fifteenth-century intervention to save Rimini's basilica better fits today's definition of architectural conservation. According to the eminent Italian restoration architect, historian, and theorist Piero Gazzola, the basilica, which was famous for its Byzantine mosaics, was raised 6½ feet (nearly 2 meters) to prevent its burial by the silt deposits that accumulated in the river Po over the centuries. The city's remarkable feat of engineering was not documented but is evident from archaeological remains and an observation of the building's construction details. This bold operation was inspired by a concern for saving the historic structure's artistic and architectural integrity; its effective use of various construction, repair, and restoration measures made it comparable to modern restoration.[13]

In the sixteenth century, wealth poured into Rome from the New World and provided the necessary resources to continue its transformation. Major building projects, such as St. Peter's Basilica and many noble palaces, devoured enormous amounts of marble, which was still being pilfered from ancient buildings in the city and throughout the region.

In 1508, at the invitation of Donato Bramante, Raffaello Santi came to Rome to help with the construction of St. Peter's Basilica. Santi (better known today as Raphael) joined a group of humanist scholars connected to the papal court who were growing increasingly concerned about the rate of destruction of Rome's monuments. He joined his colleagues in writing a letter to Pope Leo X, one of the first official protests framed not just as an attack but also as a plea for the preservation of Rome's ancient buildings. It bemoaned the loss of heritage but also offered the ancient capital the opportunity for greatness once again:

> *How many popes…have permitted the ruin and destruction of antique temples, of*
> *statues, of arches and of other structures that were the glory of their founders?…*
> *[T]his new Rome we now see, however great she may be, however beautiful, however*
> *ornamented with palaces, churches, and other buildings, is nevertheless built of lime*
> *produced from antique marbles…. It should therefore, Holy Father, not be one of*
> *the last thoughts of Your Holiness to take care of what little remains of the ancient*
> *mother of Italy's glory and reputation;… they should not be taken away and altogether*
> *destroyed by the malicious and the ignorant.*[14]

As a result of Raphael's impassioned letter, the pope appointed him commissioner of antiquities in 1515 and issued a proclamation that proscribed the destruction of statues and inscriptions and imposed fines on violators.[15] Even Raphael faced conflicts of interest, however. Since Bramante's death the previous year, he had also become the architect of St. Peter's Basilica, a position whose responsibilities included the selection of suitable building materials from excavations sites and quarries.

In 1521, Giacomo Mazzocchi published the *Epigrammata Antiquae Urbis* (1521), the results of his multiyear study of antique inscriptions found in Rome. This epigraphic survey essentially provided the first comprehensive list of surviving ancient Roman buildings, infrastructure, monuments, and fragments, as well as their locations in the city.[16] Soon thereafter Raphael began to work on a map of ancient Roman sites. He so admired the remains of ancient Rome that he proposed rebuilding the ancient capital based on archaeological evidence.

The sack of Rome in 1527 by the French dealt another blow to the protection of the city's built environment. In an eight-day orgy of violence, destruction, and desecration, the population was forced to choose between fleeing the city or being massacred by the rampaging army; churches, shrines, and ancient monuments were looted, burned, or destroyed.

Rome recovered slowly after this attack. Pope Paul III established the Vitruvian Academy to list and evaluate Rome's ancient sites and appointed Latino Giovenale Manetti as commissioner of antiquities to protect monuments, including "arches, temples, trophies, amphitheaters, circuses, aqueducts, statues and marbles."[17] Because the construction of St. Peter's Basilica was exempt from these protections, however, marble taken from excavations—especially from the Forum—was used on that project.[18]

One particularly important undertaking during the second half of the sixteenth century was Michelangelo's conversion of the massive Baths of Diocletian into the Church of Santa Maria degli Angeli. Most of the lavishly decorated early fourth-century structure was still standing, even its great vaults. Michelangelo's design, which was altered by Luigi Vanvitelli in the eighteenth century, incorporated adaptive reuse with minimal intervention. Later alterations superimposed a baroque façade on the church and changed the interior, but the presence of the ruin remained dominant. Tragically, a full third of the original structure was demolished shortly thereafter by Pope Sixtus V.[19]

Pope Sixtus V, the last of the Renaissance popes, inaugurated another period of major construction that, like many before, compromised the protection of Rome's ancient urban fabric. His plan sought to link the past with the present—imperial and Christian Rome—in a glorious tapestry that sometimes required him to "tear down the ugly old and repair the worthwhile."[20] The wide boulevards of this grand new urban plan,[21] carried out by architect Domenico Fontana, necessitated the destruction of hundreds of buildings—including numerous important historic structures. In addition to a large part of the Baths of Diocletian, Pope Sixtus V's schemes also destroyed portions of the Claudian Aqueduct, the Septizonium of Septimus Severus, and a number of early Christian and medieval sites such as the Lateran Palace and the Oratory of Santa Croce.[22]

Figure 13-3 Rome's ancient building materials were frequently recycled or destroyed, and its finer surviving pieces of statuary were sought after by collectors. This eighteenth-century engraving by the artist and engraver Pietro Santi Bartoli illustrates the search for the valuable antiquties that continued with little interruption from the Renaissance through the eighteenth century.

At the same time, Pope Sixtus V's urban renewal plans integrated historic buildings and sites throughout Rome and even highlighted them via a more rational street system. He ordered the clearing of buildings around the Columns of Trajan and Marcus Aurelius, capped them with gold statues of St. Peter and St. Paul, and moved several obelisks to new, prominent locations. A herculean effort was made to erect the massive obelisk taken from the Circus of Nero in front of St. Peter's Basilica.

This massive sixteenth-century urban renewal scheme did not always go smoothly. The citizenry of Rome, through their city council, frequently voiced their opposition to the destruction of what they felt was their patrimony. In 1541, the council opposed the use of stones from the Forum for the construction of St. Peter's Basilica and prohibited the use of stones from the Colosseum for the repair of bridges.[23] Thanks to successful public intervention, the circular tomb of Cecilia Matella was also spared from destruction.[24] The citizens who opposed Rome's modernization rejoiced upon the death of Pope Sixtus V,

DVM·RECTAS·AD·TEMPLA·VIAS·SANCTISSIMA·PANDIT
IPSE·SIBI·SIXTVS·PANDIT·AD·ASTRA·VIAM

▲ **Figure 13-4** The revised plan of Rome ordered by Pope Sixtus V, with its new main thoroughfares connecting key religious sites and the vistas that resulted.

▶ **Figure 13-5** There was interest in France from the early sixteenth century in preserving ancient Roman remains in the vicinity of Nîmes. By the time of the Charles-Louis Clérisseau's engraving *Maison Carrée at Nîmes* in 1778, the building had been partially restored for more than a century.

but his plan had already been implemented. By the end of the sixteenth century, the city had been transformed from a medieval urban maze to a proud capital with wide streets and major thoroughfares complete with new buildings designed in the classical idiom and new presentations of surviving antiquities.

No cogent philosophy of conservation or remarkable conservation techniques emerged during the Renaissance, but the process of critically evaluating the past arose—as did the debate about the importance of protecting historic buildings and sites and preserving a physical link with the distant past.

During the Renaissance, several other countries joined the Italian peninsula and were inspired to initiate their own expansion of the arts and sciences and to address their cultural heritage issues.[25] For many years, the Roman ruins that were scattered across Europe were especially vulnerable because the local populations' connection to them was not as strong as it was on the Italian peninsula, where they were regarded as part of the country's indigenous heritage. As a result, there was less protection afforded them, and many Roman structures in its former Europe provinces were demolished, buried, or radically altered. Only in a few instances were active measures taken to preserve these sites. In what is now France, the governor of Languedoc passed a decree in 1548 that protected ancient buildings in the city of Nîmes from demolition, declaring that these antique structures "from which the connoisseurs draw pleasure and profit in the art of architecture" were "ornament[s] of the country of Languedoc and pride of this kingdom."[26]

In the sixteenth century, dramatic social and political changes altered the way societies viewed their built heritage, and more recent medieval architecture joined the ancient past in being both threatened and protected. In 1517, Martin Luther's condemnation of the excesses of the Catholic Church launched a series of religious conflicts in Europe that remained violent and destructive until the middle of the following century.

In Denmark, Sweden, England, the Swiss Confederation, and other northern European countries, monastery reform laws executed during the 1520s and 1530s transferred control of Church property to the state. These were followed by the destruction of some Catholic churches and the confiscation of art treasures and reusable building materials from others.[27] Some sites were converted for new secular uses—for example, the Dutch city of Utrecht appropriated former Catholic monasteries for use as orphanages, barracks, and government buildings; St. Paul's Abbey became the provincial law courts.[28]

In countries where the Roman Catholic Church remained strong, a counterreformation was launched to reestablish Church supremacy and stamp out what was considered to be Protestant heresy. Throughout Europe, a modern form of *damnatio memoriae* ("the eradication of memory") was practiced by Catholics and Protestants alike. In the hope that the destruction of buildings and objects of another religion would destroy the religion itself, both sides targeted religious properties. In France, the Huguenots melted down gilded sculptures and ornaments from Catholic churches; in turn, the authorities destroyed Huguenot meeting spaces. The Calvinist approach was especially violent. In 1566, their radical opposition to what they considered idolatrous religious imagery led to the destruction of stained glass, sculpture, relief panels, and paintings across northern Europe. Little medieval religious art survived in Holland. England's Queen Elizabeth I issued a proclamation in 1560 against defacing churches or public buildings in a futile attempt to end this unfortunate practice.[29]

Over the next half century, Catholic churches were slowly reconstructed and repaired. Some were converted into Protestant churches; others, located in Catholic-controlled or tolerant countries, were rebuilt more gloriously than before. In Antwerp, the interior of the fourteenth-century Cathedral of our Lady, the largest Gothic church in the Low Countries, was lavishly restored. The work, executed after the Spanish reconquest of Flanders in 1585, revived Catholicism in that city and reflected the Church's return to power. Paintings by Peter Paul Rubens and new stained-glass windows were completed there in the following decades.

According to the eminent art historian Ernst Gombrich, "The more the Protestants preached against outward show in the churches, the more eager did the Roman Church become to enlist the power of the artist. Thus the Reformation…also had an indirect effect on the development of Baroque."[30] These polemics were clearly expressed in architecture, existing work that needed restoration and upgrading, and in new work that expanded further lessons of the antique.

THE BAROQUE PERIOD THROUGH THE ENLIGHTENMENT, 1600 TO 1780

By the seventeenth century, the major cities of western Europe, including Rome, were flourishing, and the Ottoman Empire had replaced Byzantium as the dominant cultural force in Asia Minor. European powers established colonies across the globe and trade routes connected the continents, facilitating the transfer of goods and information as never before. The religious turmoil of the previous century had reached equilibrium in most places, and a more secular world was emerging. Critical and more objective views were increasingly expressed about other times and places as well as about a variety of contemporary phenomena. While this approach—in what we now call the Age of Reason—helped conserve the artistic heritage of classical times through a heightened appreciation of such matters, less attention was given to the medieval world, which was still deemed to be the recent past, above which the Age of Reason, or the Enlightenment, had risen.

In Europe, baroque was the style of the era. Many of the Continent's major capitals— Vienna, Budapest, Prague, and Rome among them—were enhanced with a new architecture based on the principles of classicism that was stylized to a new level of adornment. The baroque also exemplified the triumph of the Roman Church, which was experiencing numerous successes throughout the world. Early Christian and medieval church structures were viewed as inferior aberrations and were given baroque facelifts, which sometimes involved the destruction of works by such artists as Giotto, Fra Angelico, and Pisanello.[31]

In Rome, urban improvements accommodated the city's population among the Eternal City's monuments that survived from ancient times. Through this active building period, the struggle by antiquarians and others to preserve both ancient and more recent historic buildings continued in the face of persistent contradictory moves by the seventeenth-century papacy.

Pope Alexander VII, who reigned for much of the seventeenth century, was responsible for the conservation of two important ancient sites but for two very different reasons.[32] In 1663, he restored the Pyramid of Caius Cestius for its instructive value, arguing that "the ruin of it would have diminished the fame of the magnanimousness of the ancient, and learning from their example [would be] made difficult for the virtuous foreigners."[33]

In contrast, he ordered the restoration of the Pantheon's exterior and the conversion of the interior into a family mausoleum in 1662. He had previously begun to disfigure this ancient monument by asking Gianlorenzo Bernini to perch two bell towers on the structure—additions ridiculed as "ass ears," yet which represented a popular, baroque-era attitude that ancient classical architecture was too severe in its simplicity and was therefore incomplete.[34] The Pantheon's portico was restored with marble taken from an imperial Roman arch that had stood in the piazza in front of it. Improvements to its urban setting also entailed the destruction of the Arch of Marcus Aurelius. On its façade, replacement column capitals matched the originals, except that the coat of arms of Pope Alexander VII's family was integrated into their designs. Mercifully, little of his conversion plans for the Pantheon's nearly completely intact interior was carried out.

The future of the Colosseum, where Christian saints were martyred and numerous religious ceremonies celebrated, was also strongly debated during the seventeenth century.

Figure 13-6 By the mid-eighteenth century, foreigners were on an insatiable quest for classical antiquities in Italy in order to form collections from abroad. This engraving (after Clérisseau, 1763) by Domenico Cunego romantically depicts the search for "the antique."

Time and again, despite its legal protection, papal administrations quarried its stones for building materials. In 1671, plans were drawn up to reuse the Colosseum as a Temple of Martyrs. Nothing of the surviving ancient structure was to be touched; only a small chapel constructed at its center would alter the monument.[35] The plan was revolutionary in terms of minimal intervention, but only its consecration in 1675 was ever carried out.[36]

As with this relatively sensitive proposed treatment of the Colosseum, some baroque architects, such as Francesco Borromini, were remarkably adept at integrating historic fabric into new designs. He successfully incorporated Rome's existing Basilica of St. John Lateran into a new baroque design.[37] The elliptical plan of Piazza Navona, the old Roman Hippodrome, was respected in his design of the Church of Sant'Agnese, located along the piazza's west side.

During the seventeenth century, the selling and buying of antiquities increased. This pastime had the positive effect of spreading interest in classical art and architecture abroad, which brought a regular flow of foreign collectors, artists, and architects to Rome. But it also led to an alarming increase in excavations, which damaged and destroyed many historic structures and archaeological sites.

The popes—motivated by a mix of patriotism and a desire to share in the excavated riches—attempted to regulate the process through a series of decrees. In 1624, exports of antiquities were temporarily halted, and in 1634 a commission was formed to protect Roman antiquities.[38] Collectors' passions for statues, artifacts, and architectural elements, however, overpowered these actions. A 1685 decree reinforced the export ban and represented a legal principle in heritage conservation that gained wider currency in the centuries to follow.[39] More edicts were published in 1701, 1704, and 1707, during the reign of Pope Clement XI, but they did little to dampen the growing interests of both local and foreign collectors. The discovery of well-preserved wall paintings and architectural details in the Palace of Domitian excavation site on the Palatine Hill by the Dukes of Parma in 1720 caused a sensation.[40] Once opened, the palace revealed a suite of rooms elaborately decorated and filled with marble veneer and statuary. The site was destroyed in the ensuing rush to loot the rooms for anything of value. As this occurred on private property, there was little public outcry.

Alongside such wanton destruction, measures were taken to preserve some of Rome's more familiar monuments. The Colosseum was stabilized following an earthquake in 1703. An order by Pope Benedict XIII prohibited the reworking of inscribed or decorated marble to remove their pagan quotations and symbols.[41] Any connection between Rome's historic buildings and Christianity served as a reason for their preservation. In 1731 Pope Clement XII restored the Arch of Constantine, which had been built by the first Christian emperor, and commemorated its restoration with a plaque and a publication.[42] Two years later he also passed an edict concerning the preservation of ancient buildings. In 1744 his successor, Pope Benedict XIV, ordered the protection of the Colosseum and made the removal of its stones tantamount to desecration because the site had been consecrated as a shrine to the martyrs.

During the eighteenth century, wealthy grand tour participants—foreigners who visited Italy in order to view its historic marvels—elevated Rome to the status of the "studio of Europe."[43] Inspired by Rome's ancient buildings and sites, some created great works of literature, art, and architecture. Others rivaled the passion of the Renaissance popes in their mania for collecting antiquities. Private collectors were attracted by the material and aesthetic value of these objects as well as the irresistible social cachet their display conferred back home in England, France, and elsewhere.[44]

Many of these travelers stayed in Rome, expanding its ever-present colony of foreigners. In time, this community became more vocal about the care and maintenance of

Rome's (and later, Italy's) classical monuments. Foreign cultural institutions such as the Académie de France à Rome, which was established in 1666, were joined by other institutions founded to study classical art and architecture. Some, such as the Society of Antiquaries of London, remained abroad but included among their tenets "the encouragement, advancement and furtherance of the study and knowledge of the antiquities and history of this and other countries," including those in Rome.[45]

Far from Italy—but due to contact and familiarity with developments in Rome—a mature conservation ethos and practice developed in early seventeenth-century Scandinavia. Sweden's interest in its past paralleled its political development and entry onto the European stage as a political power. King Gustavus Adolphus sponsored studies and inventories of Sweden's heritage that included objects from all previous time periods and of all types, from coins and runes to churches and earthworks. In the 1630s a list of state antiquities was compiled, and in 1666 the regent for King Karl XI signed an antiquities ordinance to protect the country's cultural heritage.[46] The ordinance "provided protection for antiquities and monuments, however insignificant, if they contributed to the memory of a historic event, person, place or family of the country, and especially of kings and other nobles."[47] At the same time, ordinances were passed that required collectors of antiquities, including the Catholic Church, to inventory and register their holdings with the state. Two years later, an institute for antiquarian studies was established; it later incorporated an archive and museum.

Today, modern historians know little about the effectiveness of Sweden's seventeenth-century preservation edict, which is likely the first public proclamation of its kind.[48] The Swedish edict differed notably from the seventeenth- and eighteenth-century papal bulls. Although the bulls forbade the removal of fragments from excavations and ancient sites for building or collection purposes, their primary mission was to protect and extend the proprietary property rights of the papacy. The Swedish legislation represented a more modern sensibility toward heritage protection. It reflected an interest in preserving sites as part of the kingdom's heritage, not specifically as property of the king or pope. It was inclusive of prehistoric and medieval as well as ancient objects and sites, and it implied an appreciation of conservation as a national priority to be taken most seriously. One of its provisions demanded that anyone who caused damage to a building restore it to its former appearance.

In the late seventeenth and early eighteenth centuries, the idea of what we now call national monuments and antiquities developed further both in England and in France, as a specific interest in historic architecture from before and after Roman colonization emerged. The debates and research of the Society of Antiquaries of London were principally focused on British heritage, and English antiquarians began publishing studies of their country's non-Roman heritage. Two notable works are John Aubrey's 1670 book *Monumenta Britannica* and William Dugdale's *Monasticum Anglicanum* (1655–1673), which focused on English monasteries.[49] The Benedictine monk Bernard de Montfaucon began to devote attention to medieval cathedrals and sculpture in France, initially in *L'Antiquité Expliquée et Représentée en Figures* (Antiquity Explained and Represented in Sculptures) in 1719 and more explicitly a decade later in *Monuments de la Monarchie Françoise* (Monuments of the French Monarchy).[50]

At the same time, French philosophers such as René Descartes, Blaise Pascal, Jean-Jacques Rousseau, and Voltaire introduced ways of thinking that emphasized reason, progress, and personal freedom. Those eighteenth-century ideas were anathema to the absolutist and religiously hierarchical world of the previous centuries and marked a shift in European thought and culture. The Age of Enlightenment profoundly affected the way Europeans viewed cultural heritage and laid the foundation of the conservation ethos and movement we know today.

Figure 13-8 The Parthenon, 1753. James Stuart and Nicholas Revett's *Antiquities of Athens* (1762) illustrated key ancient Greek buildings in their as-found state as introductions to suites of engravings of carefully measured buildings, which also were graphically "restored." Such books were meant for a clientele of patrons, architects, and builders.

This shift in thinking was in part due to the study of the classical democratic societies of the ancient Greeks and the Roman republic. During the mid-eighteenth century, classical Greek culture came back into vogue with the modern European discovery of the Doric temples in Paestum and Sicily and renewed interest in Athens and the Hellenic remains in the eastern Mediterranean. The grand tour also began to attain a new social significance and became a must for the wellborn and the educated, attracting not only scholars and artists but also social luminaries of the day, such as Sir William Hamilton and Lord Elgin. Grand tourists increasingly drawn from the middle class returned home with souvenirs and their sketchbooks filled. European governments began to subsidize trips for scholars, and the Society of the Dilettanti was formed in London in 1733 as a club for travelers to meet, plan, and discuss trips to the sites of classical antiquity.[51] The Society of the Dilettanti's impressions of Athens joined others that addressed similar aspects of architectural history and generated public interest in ancient Greek architecture.[52] As a result, Greek revival became the dominant architectural style both in Europe and in much of colonial North America. The work also increased awareness that historic cities were totalities of their diverse parts—including road systems, fortifications, the full range of necessary building types, and even their hinterlands.

In retrospect, the general collection of antiques from ancient Mediterranean civilizations and their acquisition grew to unseemly proportions at about this time. In 1802, Lord Elgin received permission from Turkish authorities to remove a number of sculptures from the temples of the Acropolis, notably the Parthenon and the Erechtheion. They were transported to London, where they were later bought by the newly formed British Museum.[53]

Figure 13–9 Frontispiece from *Description de l'Égypte.*

Exploration—scientific, geographic, or both—increasingly influenced public interest and taste among the nations involved in such enterprises. The scientists, historians, and artists who accompanied Napoleon to Egypt in 1798 returned to France laden with both archaeological treasures and documentation of numerous aspects of Egypt's past and present culture. The resulting publication, *Description de l'Égypte*, which documented all aspects of this expedition, created an awareness in Europe and beyond about Egypt's vast artistic heritage. Popular interest in Egyptian culture became so profound that it even sparked an Egyptian revival in architecture and the decorative arts.

During the eighteenth century, this fervor for all things ancient inspired numerous books devoted to art and architectural history. Johann Bernard Fischer von Erlach, considered by some to be the father of architectural history, produced the first comprehensive illustrated history of world architecture, *Entwurf einer historischen Architektur* (Draft of Historical Architecture), in 1721.[54] Giovanni Battista Piranesi, in *Vedute di Roma* (Views of Rome) and *Le Antichità Romane* (Roman Antiquities), brought the mostly ruined monuments of ancient Rome to life in haunting images that became some of the most sought-after travel mementos of their day. James Stuart and Nicholas Revett, in their *Antiquities of Athens*, presented measured drawings and details of classical Greek architecture in a book that, along with the Society of the Dilettanti's report, became a primary source for the Greek revival movement in architecture. Other significant publications included David Le Roy's *Les Ruines des Plus Beaux Monuments de la Grèce* (Ruins of the Most Beautiful Monuments of Greece [1758]) and the Comte de Choiseul-Gouffier's *Le Voyage Pittoresque de la Grèce* (Picturesque Travels in Greece [1782]).

The discoveries of the ancient lost cities of Herculaneum and Pompeii were the greatest archaeological achievements of the eighteenth century and drew the attention of all Europe to Naples.[55] Many came to observe the finds as they were pulled from the earth and visited the king's residence at Portici, where they were displayed. What fascinated scholars and visitors alike was that unlike Rome—a capital city judged by its greatest monuments—Herculaneum and Pompeii were two entire Roman cities frozen in time that, through systematic excavation, could be studied and recorded to reveal the daily lives of their inhabitants.

Compared with excavation efforts at lava- and mud-covered Herculaneum, Pompeii yielded its treasures with less effort because the ash that covered it was easier to dig. When Pompeii's more sensational finds were removed, ordinary artifacts and architectural finishes that were judged to be unimportant were often destroyed. In the early years of its rediscovery, the notion of preserving and presenting ancient buildings and their contents in situ had not yet been considered. Important buildings such as the Temple of Isis in 1764 were soon stripped of all of their gold, statues, and frescoes. Sir William Hamilton lamented, "I could have wished, that before they were removed, an exact drawing of the Temple had been taken and the position of the paintings expressed therein, as they all related to the cult of Isis, and would have been more interesting published together than at random, which I fear will be their fate."[56] Hamilton was not the first to voice discontent with the state of the Pompeii excavations: A decades-long battle had been waged between the excavation director Roque Joachim de Alcubierre and his assistant, Karl Weber. Weber's repeated attempts to document excavated discoveries were carefully thwarted by Alcubierre, who believed his job was to hunt for treasure, not record what was found.

Johann Joachim Winckelmann, the eminent German classicist and curator of antiquities under Pope Clement XIII, visited Naples twice. In 1758 the jealous nature of the Neapolitan curators and the court limited his access to the museum and excavations,[57] but he gained better access a few years later. His famous open letter to Count Heinrich von Brühl railed against the crude techniques being employed at the sites and criticized Alcubierre: "This man, who has absolutely no experience working with antiques, is to blame for the many disasters and the loss of many beautiful things."[58] His letter became a catalyst for a shift from treasure hunting to scientific practice that embraced concerns for archaeological conservation.

Winckelmann, a truly enlightened scholar, changed the way Europeans viewed classical works of art and architecture. He was the first to construct a stylistic chronology[59] for dating art and architecture. His *History of Ancient Art among the Greeks* (1764) is an ordered account that places selected annotated works in a historical account.[60] Winckelmann's work elevated the study of classical art, history, and archaeology to the level of a science.[61] As the "father of classical archaeology" and the "father of art history," Winckelmann did much to inaugurate the neoclassical movement. Over the next century, this mode, which emphasized Greek culture and beauty, gained momentum throughout Europe and beyond.

ENDNOTES

1. A. Levanti, *Viaggi di Francesco Petrarca in Franci*, in Germania ed in Italia (Milan: Societa Tipographica, 1820), 1:268, cited in Jokilehto, *History of Architectural Conservation*, 21.
2. Françoise Choay, *The Invention of the Historic Monument* (Cambridge: Cambridge University Press, 2001), 33. The notion of and the term *media tempestas* ("Middle Ages") took currency at this time.
3. Ibid., 28.
4. Schnapp, *Discovery of the Past*, 106.
5. Erder, *Our Architectural Heritage*, 72.
6. Ibid.
7. The structural system of the Pantheon is, however, completely different.
8. Choay, *Invention of the Historic Monument*, 34.
9. The medieval population of Rome lived amid the ruins of the ancient capital. Many of its great public buildings had been taken over for mundane purposes—butchers had moved into the Forum of Nerva and the lower vaults of the Theater of Marcellus; a fish market had been installed in the Porticus Ottaviae; leather workers plied their trade in the Stadium of Domitian; and limekilns and cord makers were set up in the Circus Flaminius. The great baths of Agrippa were inhabited by glassmakers and bottle makers.
10. Eugène Müntz, *Les Arts à la Cour des Papes*, vol. 1 (Paris: E. Thorin, 1878), app. 4:352–53, quoted in Erder, *Our Architectural Heritage*, 76.
11. Jokilehto, *History of Architectural Conservation*, 29.
12. Ibid.
13. Piero Gazzola, "Preserving Monuments," 23–24.
14. Raphael, "Lettera a Leone X," in Renato Bonelli, ed. *Scritti Rinascimentali* (Milan: Editzioni il Polifilo, 1978), 469.
15. Rodolfo Lanciani, *The Golden Days of the Renaissance in Rome* (New York: Houghton, Mifflin, 1906), 246.
16. Jokilehto, *History of Architectural Conservation*, 32.
17. Herbert Thurston, "Pope Clement VII," in *The Catholic Encyclopedia*, vol. 4 (New York: Robert Appleton, 1908). The essay is available online at http://www.newadvent.org/cathen/04024a.htm.
18. Moatti, *Search for Ancient Rome*, 49.
19. More than 107,638 square yards (90,000 square meters) of material were removed from the site for use in construction of roads and for the pope's residence, Villa Montalto. See Jokilehto, *History of Architectural Conservation*, 36.
20. Erder, *Our Architectural Heritage*, 81.
21. This approach had been originally attempted on a smaller scale by Pope Nicholas V and Alberti.
22. Moatti, *Search for Ancient Rome*, 50.
23. Erder, *Our Architectural Heritage*, 82.
24. Ibid., 84.

25. Plans by architect Hernán Ruiz to modify the Great Mosque of Córdoba in Spain in 1523 by installing a Christian capella major in the middle of the monument, along with a new high altar and sanctuary, generated one of the earliest recorded cases of an architectural conservation controversy. After the plan was carried out, King Charles V expressed his regrets, saying, "Had I known what you desired to do, you would not have done it, for what you are doing here can be found everywhere and what you possessed previously exists nowhere." M. Schveitzer, *Hachette World Guides: Spain* (Paris: Hachette, 1961), 720, as cited in Norman Williams, Jr., Edmund H. Kellogg, and Frank B. Gilbert, eds., *Readings in Historic Preservation: Why? What? How?* (New Brunswick, NJ: Center for Urban Policy Research, Rutgers University, 1983), 9.

26. Ibid., 119.

27. Jokilehto, *History of Architectural Conservation*, 41.

28. Renger De Bruin, Tarquinius Hoekstra, and Arend Pietersma, *The City of Utrecht through Twenty Centuries: A Brief History* (Utrecht, Netherlands: SPOU and Utrechts Archief, 1999), 48.

29. Jokilehto, *History of Architectural Conservation*, 41.

30. Ernst H. Gombrich, *The Story of Art*, 16th ed. (London: Phaidon, 1995), 388.

31. Gazzola, "Restoring Monuments," 24.

32. Before Pope Alexander VII, the Baths of Constantine and the Temple of Minerva had been largely destroyed during the papacy of the cultured Borghese Pope Paul V. His successor, Urban VIII, showed little improvement as a preserver of Rome's past: He demolished early Christian churches and lesser Roman monuments, allowed stones from the Colosseum to be used for his nephew's residence, and stripped ancient bronze from the Pantheon. This latter act earned him the epithet, "Quodnon non fecerunt Barbari fecerunt Barberini" (What the barbarians failed to do, the Barberini did). Erder, *Our Architectural Heritage*, 85.

33. Ibid.

34. These towers were removed during an 1883 restoration of the Pantheon. Gazzola, "Restoring Monuments: Historical Background," 25.

35. Jokilehto, *History of Architectural Conservation*, 38.

36. Ibid.

37. Erder, *Our Architectural Heritage*, 85.

38. Ibid.

39. Louis Hautecoeur, *Rome et la Renaissance de l'Antiquité à la Fin du XVIIIe Siècle* (Paris: Fontemoing, 1912), cited in Erder, *Our Architectural Heritage*, 85. By the eighteenth century, Rome became enthralled by the treasure hunt, which was fueled by a never-ending stream of foreign tourists, including wealthy aristocrats ready to pay exorbitant amounts for antiquities to take home.

40. Moatti, *Search for Ancient Rome*, 71–72.

41. Erder, *Our Architectural Heritage*, 88.

42. Jokilehto, *History of Architectural Conservation*, 39–40.

43. Erder, *Our Architectural Heritage*, 84.

44. One result of the formation of antiquities collections was the need for buildings that could appropriately house them. A notable early example is the London residence of master neoclassical architect Sir John Soane, one of that city's earliest museums and an example par excellence of an historic house museum. For the most part, Soane acquired copies of antiquities to create a study collection for his own atelier of apprentices.

45. The Society of Antiquaries of London was founded in 1707 and received a royal charter in 1751. It emerged from the College of Antiquaries, which was established in 1586. Society of Antiquaries of London, "Home" and "History," *Society of Antiquaries of London*, http://www.sal.org.uk.

46. H. Schück, *Vitterhets Historie och Antikvitets Akademien* (Stockholm: 1932), 268, cited in Jokilehto, *History of Architectural Conservation*, 366.

47. Ibid.

48. The interest of Xuanhe, Emperor of the Northern Song dynasty, who made an imperial project of collecting, cataloging, and thus, preserving the artistic and literary heritage of earlier dynasties, could be said to be an analogous imperial dictate from five centuries prior. Emperor Song Huizong, who reigned from 1100 to 1126, collected ancient Shang and Zhou dynasty bronzes. His minister Wang Fu compiled images and texts about each bronze into a book known as

Xuanhe Bogu Tulu (Illustrated Description of Antiquities in the Imperial Collection in the Xuanhe Period). The same emperor also had made a book of artists' biographies and important paintings known as the *Xuanhe Huapu* (The Xuanhe Painting Manual).

49. Choay, *Invention of the Historic Monument*, 50.

50. Ibid., 46–47.

51. Schnapp, *Discovery of the Past*, 261.

52. James Stuart and Nicholas Revett were in charge of this monumental work; it took over a decade to produce just the first three (of five) volumes of engravings of precisely measured buildings, complete with explanatory text.

53. Hellenic Ministry of Culture, "The Restitution of the Parthenon Marbles: The Review of the Seizure," *Odysseus, the WWW server of the Hellenic Ministry of Culture*, http://odysseus.culture.gr/a/1/12/ea125.html (accessed August 7, 2008). As of the date of this publication, a spirited and longstanding debate continues between the British and Greek governments concerning the repatriation of what are popularly known as the Elgin Marbles at the British Museum. A specially designed modern museum in Athens awaits their return.

54. Based mostly on historical evidence, including travelers' accounts and images of architecture found on ancient coins, Fischer von Erlach attempted to explain the history of architecture across time in a rational manner in this richly illustrated, trilingual folio.

55. While sinking a well in 1709, a farmer pulled up several pieces of polished marble and discovered the upper tiers of a Roman theater. Twenty-nine years later, in 1738, excavations under the command of Roque Joachim de Alcubierre, an agent of King Charles III of Naples, positively identified the town as Herculaneum. Ten years later, excavations began at a site later acknowledged as the ancient city of Pompeii.

56. Colin Amery and Brian Curren, Jr., *The Lost World of Pompeii* (London: Frances Lincoln, 2002), 37.

57. Christopher Charles Parslow, *Rediscovering Antiquity: Karl Weber and the Excavation of Herculaneum, Pompeii, and Stabiae* (Cambridge: Cambridge University Press, 1995), 216.

58. Ernesto De Carolis, "A City and Its Rediscovery," in *Pompeii: Life in a Roman Town*, ed. Annamaria Ciarallo and Ernesto De Carolis (Milan: Electa, 1999), 23.

59. Schnapp, *Discovery of the Past*, 258.

60. Ibid., 262.

61. Moatti, *Search for Ancient Rome*, 82–83.

The Arch of Trajan, Rome, Italy, extensively restored in 1818.

CHAPTER *14*

The Forging of a Discipline: The Late Eighteenth to Early Twentieth Centuries

In Europe and the Americas, the nineteenth century was a time of reaction and romanticism, industrialization and revolution, nationalism and unification. The French Revolution and the Napoleonic wars had destroyed whole segments of the European built environment: Churches were vandalized, fortresses were razed, and cities were looted and burned. Out of this destruction came the first voices of international protest toward the wanton destruction of historically significant structures.[1] In midcentury, Enlightenment ideals of the past century were put to the test by an era of political revolutions against absolutism. Europe's ancien régimes played out their final act as they set the stage for the cataclysmic changes of the twentieth century.

Throughout this period of political, economic, and social turmoil and modernization, architectural conservation in Europe developed from being a lay interest of wealthy travelers and the prerogative of mostly self-serving royal and papal authorities to a nascent popular and professional discipline. Art history, archaeology, and architectural history had emerged as scholarly pursuits in their own rights by the beginning of the nineteenth century and played a role in shaping international heritage conservation concerns and the specialty disciplines that addressed it. All share common purposes and methodologies; all offer didactic and tangible displays of the past.

Travel also affected the development of heritage conservation concerns. Western European followers of Renaissance humanist traditions appreciated history and its lessons. Great names in literature and the arts—from William Shakespeare and Edmund Spenser in the seventeenth century to France's Voltaire, Jean-Jacques Rousseau, and Victor Hugo; Germany's Johan Wolfgang von Goethe and Johann Joachim Winckelmann; and England's

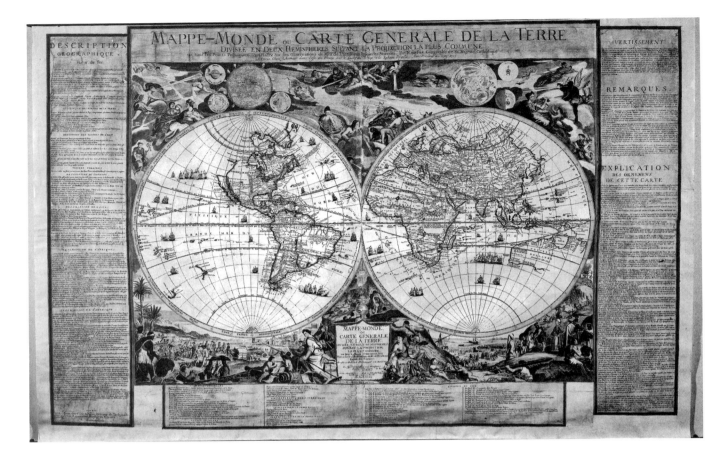

Figure 14–1 Maps of the world ca. 1800 begin to reflect an accurate and advanced understanding of the true lay of the world's continents.

Horace Walpole and Alexander Pope in the eighteenth—presented views on, and uses for, the manifestations of history as found in the ruins of Rome, Athens, and beyond.

Since the late eighteenth century, there have been numerous accounts by travelers about the delights of historic buildings and sites in foreign places, their state of preservation, and concern for their future. The message of Percy Bysshe Shelley's sonnet "Ozymandias," which is about the futility of attempting immortality, is but one notable example:

> 'My name is Ozymandias, king of kings:
> Look on my works, ye mighty, and despair!'
> Nothing beside remains. Round the decay
> of that colossal wreck, bound and bare,
> the lone and level sands stretch far away.[2]

When debris and vegetation were cleared from the pillaged and partially collapsed Colosseum, as it was being prepared for archaeological excavation and display, foreigners who were moved by the renewal work left dramatic accounts about it. The French writer Stendhal wryly commented on restorations in Rome that were beginning to appear at the time. In 1817 he wrote that the Arch of Titus was "the most ancient arch in Rome, and was also the most beautiful until when it was restored by Mr. Valadier. This wretch who, notwithstanding his French name, is Roman by birth, instead of reinforcing the arch… thought it was well to build it from scratch."[3]

Such observations and participation in foreign heritage conservation activities exemplified an interest that would grow to be the international heritage conservation movement that we know today. From the early nineteenth century onward, the interests of the nationals of one country in the artistic patrimony of another increasingly began to influence architectural conservation and urban improvement schemes that benefited both local residents and foreigners alike. This interest was coupled with improved transportation systems and a concomitant realization of the financial benefits of tourism. Thus, the relationship of tourism to the protection and presentation of historic architecture is direct and in most cases even predates the emergence of heritage protection as a distinct discipline, which occurred during the late nineteenth and early twentieth centuries. In the decades that followed the 1815 Congress of Vienna, the dawning of a romantic age coincided with a period of active respect for architectural heritage and nascent nationalism. A broadened consciousness about the merits of protecting historic buildings emerged that heretofore had only applied to monuments surviving from classical antiquity.[4] Particularly in France and Germany, Europe's elite and growing middle classes gained a newfound appreciation of their built heritage in the wake of war and in response to their burgeoning national identities. In England, religious movements provided the impetus for the reexamination and restoration of medieval churches. In the newly independent kingdom of Greece, ancient classical buildings became symbols of a time before the revolution and occupation, reinforced national pride, and harkened back to periods of stability.

These sentiments also influenced the way certain historic buildings were restored. *Historicism* (the utilization of earlier architectural styles) and later *stylistic restoration* (restoration to a perceived earlier style) prescribed the study and analysis of the architecture, design, and history of a building in order to restore it. In practice, however, this translated into enforcing *stylistic unity* on the structure, which often involved the removal of subsequent additions and the re-creation and addition of elements needed to achieve an ideal form that may—or may not—have ever existed. Through his writings and restoration work, French restoration architect and historian Eugène-Emmanuel Viollet-le-Duc became the personification of this approach and influenced architects throughout Europe.

By midcentury, the Industrial Revolution had caused millions to migrate from the countryside to factory jobs in Europe's urban centers. Harsh working conditions fomented political dissent and revolution, and factories became breeding grounds of this dissent; workers were provoked by an intellectual elite and chafed against the repression of authoritarian regimes. Following the French uprisings of 1848, the administrators of Europe's major cities began unprecedented programs of urban renewal in order to control their cities more effectively, improve public health, and display the new wealth of the age. These modernization schemes, which created many magnificent squares and avenues, also exacted a significant toll on the existing urban fabric. Countless historically significant buildings and sites were destroyed in the name of modernity.

Out of this period of upheaval came a reaction to romanticism and its often frivolous treatment of surviving architectural heritage. The scientific and rational study of historic buildings and the use of minimal intervention in order to conserve them more closely to their unaltered states was urged in lieu of returning them to an earlier appearance through **restoration**. In the latter part of the nineteenth century the British art critic, author, and firebrand John Ruskin led the charge against stylistic restoration and other such major interventions and forced a move toward a more conservative and sensitive conservation practice.

Ruskin's disciple, the designer, writer, and social advocate William Morris created England's first architectural conservation group, the Society for the Protection of Ancient Buildings, in 1877. Other prominent art historians and philosophers such Alois Riegl and architect Georg Dehio represented the Austrian and German schools, respectively, and investigated contemporary values associated with significant historic buildings while exploring their justification of preservation for artistic and cultural purposes. Although stylistic restoration still dominated the broader field of architectural conservation in the late nineteenth century, the debate between the views of Ruskin and those of Viollet-le-Duc continued and did much to inform the rationale and philosophies of the growing conservation movement and practice well into the twentieth century. Along the way, an informed respect for the past prevailed. The imposition of often conjectural and heavy-handed period restoration approaches were disdained in favor of authenticity and careful maintenance.

While during the nineteenth century western European architectural conservation practice developed according to national cultural and political environments, architectural conservation in other parts of the world was increasingly influenced by the exchange of views and methodologies between practitioners in different nations. This helped to establish an international architectural conservation movement that became increasingly unified during the twentieth century, especially in the aftermath of World War II.

The modern field of architectural conservation, complete with a growing body of theory and special methodologies, developed mainly in Italy, France, England, and Germany, beginning in the second decade of the nineteenth century. Earlier experiences in adapting and restoring historic buildings, especially in Rome, served as the basis for this increasingly distinct aspect of the larger field of architectural practice. Among the principal concerns of European urban administrators and architects who wished to implement various modernization programs was the question of what to do with the vast number of old buildings in their ancient cities. Their concerns would be mirrored throughout the world.

Figure 14-2 Structural stabilization of the Colosseum after the 1806 earthquake.

ITALY

In 1798 Napoleon's army sacked and occupied Rome and annexed the Papal States. Artworks were scattered and monuments defaced. The destruction generated a harsh reaction from the Italian clergy and the public. Their vociferous outcry was joined by French artists, who signed a petition of protest.[5] The French interest in classical works of art and architecture did result in a series of conservation efforts during this short-lived period of occupation and directly afterward. The excavation of the Roman Forum from 1801 to 1817 was perhaps the first large-scale section of a city to be set aside for historical and archaeological research purposes.[6] In 1803 Pope Pius VII, wishing to improve the settings of monuments such as the Arch of Constantine, ordered the surrounding buildings torn down and the original Roman pavement exposed in order to create a new urban space anchored by the monument.[7] In 1815 he also sent the sculptor Antonio Canova, his commissioner of antiquities, to Paris to negotiate the return of antiquities taken during the French invasion.[8] Further strides in architectural conservation were made when Cardinal Bartolomeo Pacca, Pope Pius VII's secretary of state—who had been personally financing the excavations and exhibits at Ostia[9]—published a legal framework that attempted to catalog significant historic buildings and establish standards for their restoration in 1820.

By the early nineteenth century, treatment of individual historic buildings began to improve as well. Giuseppe Camporesi and Raffaele Stern's conservation work on the Colosseum continued following the 1806 earthquake. Their great buttress, sensitively integrated to stabilize much of the Colosseum's perimeter, was the first big conservation project of the nineteenth century.[10] Architect Giuseppe Valadier's efforts to stabilize and restore other monuments, such as the Temple of Hercules in 1809–1810 and the Arch of Titus in 1821, were remarkably sophisticated interventions. Both were based on careful documentation, a dedication

◀**Figure 14–3** The Arch of Titus as it appeared ca. 1760 (*Engraving from* Verdute di Roma *by Giovani Battista Piranesi*).

◣◣**Figure 14–4** Guiseppi Valadier's restoration of the Arch of Titus in 1818.

▼ **Figure 14–5** Detail of Valadier's restoration of the Arch of Titus. Travertine, not the white marble that was used to construct the original building, was used to replicate the missing elements (*lacunae*) and purposefully different stone finishes were used to distinguish old from new in the restoration.

to retaining as much original architectural fabric as possible, the successful blending of old and new fabric, and a frank contrast between new materials used for repairs and preserved original materials. His example set a standard for all that was to follow.

Because Rome remained prominent as a grand tour destination, its efforts to preserve and maintain its most important historic buildings were widely noticed and served to inspire others. Nevertheless, architectural conservation theory did not become the established principle in Italy until much later in the nineteenth century.

As many European countries initiated massive urban renewal programs, architects began to search for standards applicable to architectural conservation projects and posed questions about how best to restore, preserve, and present both individual historic buildings and enclaves of structures. By the 1850s, spirited debates in France and England compared Viollet-le-Duc's and Ruskin's diametrically opposed approaches: the major intervention versus only (minor) required repairs and maintenance. Both theories profoundly affected the progress of the architectural conservation movement abroad, especially in Italy following unification in 1870.

By midcentury Viollet-le-Duc's theories dominated Italian restoration practice, and his ideas generated a broad spectrum of reactions from Italian professionals such as architects Alfonso Rubbiani, Alfredo d' Andrade, and Luca Beltrami. Rubbiani's re-creations of a mythical, picturesque Bologna, d' Andrade's studied yet creative enhancement of medieval Italian buildings, and Beltrami's restoration of the Sforza Castle in Milan all display variants of stylistic restoration. Beltrami, who has been called Italy's first modern restoration architect,[11] is credited with defining the approach that he called *historical restoration*—in essence, that the restoration of historic buildings should be based on scholarship and the conviction that each monument is a distinct and separate entity. He argued that the artist/re-creator who had identified with the original architect be replaced with the historian/archivist, who should base his activity on established evidence from archives, paintings, and contemporary literature. This and other such published writings were the beginnings of doctrine in the field, which others would either follow or refute.

Political unification of the Italian peninsula became the impetus for the reorganization of the country's cultural property management system but also posed an enormous threat to the country's built heritage. Historic buildings and districts impeded modernization schemes, including the widening of boulevards, the removal of city walls, and the building and enlargement of public squares. Opposition to such endeavors had begun a decade earlier, when the federalist philosopher Carlo Cattaneo fought against the construction of Milan's Cathedral Square in the 1860s.

Cattaneo's writings are early evidence of Ruskin's international influence on conservation movements and approaches. In the 1870s, when he was called in to assess the restoration of St. Mark's Square, Ruskin was dismayed at the poor conservation techniques being employed. Count Alvise Piero Zorzi took up Ruskin's cause and urged minimal intervention. In 1877, Zorzi expanded on his thoughts in his *Osservazioni Intorno ai Restauri Interni ed Esterni della Basilica di San Marco* (Observations on the Restoration of the Interior and Exterior of St. Mark's Basilica), to which Ruskin contributed the introduction.[12]

The late nineteenth century marked a change toward more critical and scientific conservation practice. Roman architect Camillo Boito best personified and articulated this shift in principles and practice. Trained in the tradition of stylistic restoration, his main restoration works in the 1860s and 1870s clearly showed the architect's creative hand. In 1879, his first written set of principles stressed the study of a building's original fabric, its modifications, and its additions. Still, his work favored returning the historic building to its "normal" state, without its historic accretions—and potentially with the addition of re-created missing elements.

Shortly thereafter, Boito reconsidered his approach. In his paper to the Third Congress of Engineers and Architects in Rome in 1883, he stated the fundamental principles of architectural conservation in an even more modern sense. He began: "Monuments have a

Figure 14–6 The Cathedral of Santa Maria Assunta on Torcello Island in Venice is one of Camillo Boito's earlier restorations, which subscribed more to the *unity of style* school of restoration thinking than his later work.

value not only for architectural study, but as evidence of the history of peoples and nations, and therefore must be respected, since any alteration is deceptive and leads to mistaken deductions."[13] Boito stated in a second principle: "Monuments should be strengthened rather than repaired, repaired rather than restored, and additions and renovations should be avoided." A third principle argued, "If additions are unavoidable, they should be sympathetic in character and distinguishable in detail and material." He stated a further key principle: that "additions to a monument should be respected as changes over time."[14]

In 1893, Boito refined and expanded these four principles into eight points. He included more detailed directions, including the importance of the conspicuousness between old and new work in style as well as materials used, the visible inscription and documentation of all new restoration work carried out, and the exhibition of the removed original elements near the restored building.[15] Boito's points became the basis for the first Italian restoration charter, which provided the foundation for the Italian practice of "philological restoration" based on comparable examples informed as much as possible by historical facts.

Boito did not end the battle of conservation ideologies in Italy: He believed both that the period restoration approach and that which preserves changes over time had merit, depending on the case. Echoing Petrarch, Boito divided Italy's more than two millennia of built heritage into three periods: antique, medieval, and modern (which for him included the Renaissance). Each type required a different conservation approach, which allowed various levels of intervention. Classical-era monuments were the most conservatively handled, while conservation treatment of medieval buildings allowed for the replacement of certain elements with re-created ones. For modern structures, Boito favored allowing a studied and restrained stylistic restoration.

Figure 14–7 Extensive urban improvements in and around Rome in the 1920s and 1930s did much to spur archaeology and architectural conservation practice due to the demands it placed on these relatively new disciplines. The Via dei Fori Imperiale (illustrated), for example, was designed to feature the magnificence of ancient Rome, such as the remains of Trajan's Forum and the Basilica of Maxentius; it terminates at the Colosseum.

Boito's writings on theory in art and architectural conservation significantly affected the direction of conservation practice in Italy and beyond. They also laid the early groundwork for the first international charters dealing with architectural conservation. His most immediate effect was the passage of the 1902 Italian law (expanded in 1904) that established a commission to be aided by a central commission of historians and archaeologists responsible for the protection of historic buildings. The expanded law regulated the treatment of historic buildings in private ownership and also set higher standards for restoration work.

Gustavo Giovannoni was heir to Boito's teachings during his tenure as the director of the Royal School of Architecture in Rome and afterward, when he taught restoration techniques. He is recognized for modernizing Boito's philosophy, condensing his principles, and emphasizing scientific methods of conservation. He also called for expanding the application of the *restauro scientifico* approach, Boito's strictest method, to all historic buildings, not just classical monuments. Giovannoni's special interest and one of his most significant contributions, however, was the protection of historic urban centers and towns, including what he termed "minor architecture"[16] or domestic architecture that contributed to the historic environment. He believed that historic centers were significant environments worthy of consideration and protection in the application of urban planning and restoration projects.

In order to encourage good practice, Giovannoni championed a purist approach to conservation, preferring to preserve the authenticity of a historic building, including its later additions. He presented his reinterpretation of Boito's revised principles, including such issues as the preservation of the historic environment and the use of historic buildings, to the first international congress of architects and technicians of historic monuments in Athens in 1931, which was organized by the International Museums Office under the aegis of the League of Nations. Its work led to the creation of the Athens Charter. (See also Chapter 9.)

By the 1930s, Italy's architectural conservation movement had gained sufficient momentum to ensure that its theories and methodologies were constantly the subject of public debate and legislation. In 1938, the Ministry of Education published its first set of standards regulating the restoration of ancient buildings. The following year, the Italian Parliament actively debated wider conservation issues, including historic urban centers, gardens, and environments. These debates and the resulting legislation became the basis of the laws used in Italy today.

FRANCE

Since the late eighteenth century, the French tradition of restoring and conserving historic buildings has slowly evolved to become one of the world's leading forces in architectural conservation. As in Italy, the volume and depth of French architectural history demanded the attention of restorers and conservators early on.

Because ancient Gaul was a distant provincial territory for the Romans, France's monumental architecture was usually simpler and more utilitarian than that of other centers of Roman power. French citizens, therefore, view their heritage from ancient classical times differently than do Italians and see them not as symbols that reflect great national power but more as expressions of local history.[17] Throughout the Middle Ages and the Renaissance, classical monuments in France were treated as they were throughout the lands of the ancient Roman empire—they were dismantled and reused as components for new domestic, religious, and civic structures, especially in fortifications.[18] Continual invasions by marauding armies and actions taken during France's numerous internal conflicts also contributed to the destruction of Roman structures.[19] Under King Louis XIII, who reigned from 1610 to 1643, political stability returned. During this period of relative calm the modern, centralized French state emerged; this, in turn, greatly affected how organized heritage protection developed in France.

By the late seventeenth century, interest in Italian classical themes, which began in earnest with Philibert de l'Orme and his circle in the early 1600s, dominated French architectural style. This trend lasted well beyond the Enlightenment. Many projects glorified the use of classical architectural styles, including the construction of the new royal Palace of Versailles and additions to the Louvre.[20] The era's scientific advances as well as improvements made in research and analytic methodologies and documentation later proved useful for the fields of history, archaeology, and architectural conservation. In the nineteenth century, the Industrial Revolution—and, ironically, the destructive effects of the Napoleonic Wars—also spurred concerns for conserving the historic built environment in their own ways.

The years between the beginning of the French Revolution in 1789 and the establishment of Napoleon's empire in 1804 were an especially uncertain period for historic buildings and towns throughout western Europe because the aftereffects of these powerful conflicts necessitated extensive repair and reconstruction of the built environment. In France, religious buildings and those associated with royalty and the nobility were often specifically targeted during the revolution, but civic buildings suffered as well.[21] The Cathedral of Notre Dame de Paris was looted and defaced and the sculptures of the saints on the west front were mutilated or sold for rubble, but the building itself remained whole. In contrast, near to the cathedral stands the sixteenth-century Tour St.-Jacques, the sole remnant of a formerly important church almost totally destroyed by revolutionaries in 1797.

The revolutionaries' harsh treatment of the architectural symbols of church and state did not go uncriticized and soon transformed directly and indirectly into conservation measures. Through an antiquarian project aimed at documenting and representing France's heritage, Aubin-Louis Millin's six-volume *Antiquités Nationales ou Recueil de Monuments* (National Antiquities or Collection of Monuments) introduced the idea of the national

Figure 14–8 The demolition by revolutionaries of two façades in the Place Bellecour, in Lyon, France, on October 26, 1793. (*Lafosse*)

monument in the early 1790s. Others simultaneously turned their attention to conserving these historic architectural achievements.[22]

The revolutionary administration began to research, document, and consider whether to apply protective measures to select structures as early as 1790, when the Commission des Monuments was established to classify and inventory nationalized property formerly held by the Catholic Church, the crown, and the nobility.[23] The nation's new assets required organization, if only to assess their economic value and to determine their fate. Movable objects were to be displayed in warehouses throughout France for the education of the populace; this plan, however, was never implemented, and the majority of significant movable objects were collected in the Louvre palace and museum.[24] Buildings were more challenging, but the revolutionary government found new uses for many of them, as had been done in Protestant countries during the Reformation. Churches, including Notre Dame, became storehouses; convents became barracks; the Fontevrault Abbey became a prison; and the Church of Ste.-Geneviève in Paris became a pantheon to commemorate French heroes.[25]

Despite the 1791 law that prohibited the destruction of significant historic buildings (which were considered state property) and the formation of a Comité d'Instruction Publique to protect them, it was not until the advent of Napoleon's dictatorship in 1804 that the destruction was halted. One member of the committee, and one of the most vocal opponents of the vandalism, was the Abbé Henri Grégoire, who in 1794 prepared a series of reports that publicly recorded the ongoing destruction of France's historic buildings.[26] When Napoleon came to power, the revolutionaries had weakened, exhausted from more than a decade of conflict, and France's architectural heritage was in disrepair. Napoleon's reign gave the country time to rebuild and grow before its descent into another international conflict.

The impact of archaeological and scientific discoveries and their documentation of them during Napoleon's Egyptian campaign in the late eighteenth century was far-reaching.[27] Global scholarship in Egyptology and archaeology was advanced by the establishment of an Institut Français d'Archéologie Orientale du Caire (French Institute of Oriental Archaeology in Cairo) and the creation of the lavish *Description de l'Égypte* (Description of Egypt), an unprecedented research and publishing enterprise that documented all known aspects of Egypt's history, ways of life, and physical characteristics. In France, Egyptian motifs became hallmarks of the Empire style employed by Charles Percier and Pierre-François-Léonard Fontaine, Napoleon's court architects. Egyptian cultural heritage also benefited: A new national museum and an administrative system to help conserve the country's vast wealth of ancient buildings and antiquities were established by the French.

Napoleon's fall in 1815 and the ensuing Bourbon restoration triggered France's industrial development, to the detriment of many historic buildings. During the early years of its industrial revolution, France's architectural heritage was demolished at an alarming rate. The famous novelist Victor Hugo, in his 1825 article "Guerre aux Démolisseurs" (War on the Demolishers) appealed to French nationals to save their endangered architecture. His objections to the loss of French cultural patrimony through neglect, insensitivity, and overenthusiastic restoration generated considerable interest in the subject from both the public and the intellectual elite.

The situation in France improved in 1830 when the liberal monarch King Louis-Philippe ascended the throne. His reign ushered in a period of prosperity and recognition of the importance of heritage. One of his earliest actions was to establish a new position, that of *inspecteur general des monuments historiques de la France*, who was charged with compiling a new list of significant historic buildings that deserved government consideration and monitoring restoration work. The post was initially filled by Ludovic Vitet, who traveled extensively throughout France to prepare the first national report on the state of historic structures.

After 1834, his successor, the architect Prosper Mérimée, continued to document historic buildings. Mérimée, one of the nineteenth century's best-known conservationists, relied heavily on the Commission des Monuments Historiques, which was established in 1837 by the Ministry of the Interior, to assist him in reporting on endangered historically significant buildings. The commission offered a new approach to building conservation: A seven-person committee determined survey procedures and decided what was to be preserved and how. It also built upon the existing state-sanctioned monuments protection system.

▼ **Figure 14–9** The survey of France's historic monuments under the direction of Prosper Mérimée was aided by the early use of photography. (calotype: Gustave LeGray, Cathedral cloister at Le Puy en Vélay, 1851). *(Avery Architectural and Fine Arts Library, Columbia University)*

The establishment of this commission was in part a response to public pressure, which demanded care for historic sites, notably the restoration of numerous dilapidated and neglected Gothic buildings. Government allocation of public funds for restoration began at this time, and attention focused on the historic buildings inventory system, which employed the principle of listing buildings as a way of protecting them. By 1849, about three thousand significant historic buildings had been documented—mostly religious structures and Gallo-Roman ruins.[28]

Mérimée's conservative approach to restoration was succinctly expressed by his colleague, Adolphe-Napoléon Didron: "Regarding ancient monuments, it is better to consolidate than to repair, better to repair than to restore, better to restore than to rebuild, better to rebuild than to embellish; in no case must anything be added and, above all, nothing should be removed."[29]

Mérimée was aware that one of the greatest problems facing architectural conservation in mid-nineteenth-century France was that its architects received no training about medieval buildings. The situation became especially obvious after several poorly executed restorations, such as those at the Cathedral of St.-Denis, the Church of St.-Germain l'Auxerrois, and the Cathedral of Notre Dame.

Although French attitudes toward restoration were officially conservative during the 1840s, in practice, methodology was moving in another direction. Religious and nationalistic pressures influenced the growing debate between architects and conservation advocates who wanted to preserve existing structures and those who argued for the "restoration" of buildings to appearances they may have never had. This approach, which came to be known as the *stylistic unity* theory of ancient building repair, argued for stylistic consistency or purity.

Stylistic unity called for the removal of later additions to buildings.[30] Later design—and in some cases even original design work that might have been considered inferior—was replaced with restorations that the original builders would have, or should have, built. Later termed period restorations, these interventions were based on analogies to other examples of Gothic architecture in the name of stylistic consistency. Especially vulnerable were France's venerable Gothic buildings, many of which consisted of differing styles within that idiom and all of which were by then over five hundred years old. Some had never been completed in the first place. In most instances, the possibility of conserving historic buildings of national significance in a minimalist fashion—with simple maintenance and judicious repairs—was not considered a viable option.

The most influential proponent of stylistic unity was the architect and historian Eugène-Emmanuel Viollet-le-Duc (1814–1879), whose approach was characterized by an unprecedented scholarship on the history of Gothic architecture and a preoccupation with archaeologically accurate restoration. His own definition of restoration epitomized the stylistic unity theory: For Viollet-le-Duc, "The term restoration and the thing itself are both modern. To restore a building is not to preserve it, to repair or rebuild it; it is to reinstate it in a condition of completeness that could never have existed in any given time."[31] The implication for historic buildings was that they could be restored and "completed" to an idealized possible former appearance.

The results of Viollet-le-Duc's approach can be seen today in scores of French cathedrals, châteaus, and historic centers that were restored between 1840 and 1870. One example is Notre Dame de Paris. When Viollet-le-Duc undertook the commission to restore the seven-hundred-year-old cathedral with his friend and colleague Jean-Baptiste Lassus, it was in perilous structural condition and had suffered greatly during the revolution, when the statues of the saints along the west side above the three monumental entrances had all been decapitated, and the cathedral had been badly defaced and vandalized.

Viollet-le-Duc first examined and documented the existing structure carefully to provide a basis for his restoration designs. All construction details and repairs that postdated the twelfth and thirteenth centuries were to be removed, based on archival evidence,

▶ **Figure 14–10** Master architect, restorer, and architectural theorist, Eugène-Emanuelle Viollet-le-Duc.

▼ **Figure 14–11** Pierrefonds, a medieval fortified castle, before (top) and after Viollet-le-Duc's restoration work in 1855. *(Bibliotheque de Paris)*

observations of the surviving building fabric, and Viollet-le-Duc's extensive knowledge of French Gothic architecture, which is unmatched probably even today. (Figures 14-12 a, b, c)

Despite the physical and technical challenges that Viollet-le-Duc mastered while restoring Notre Dame and scores of other historic buildings and enclaves throughout France, his stylistic unity approach drew increasing criticism from other practitioners—and the public. In particular, his rigid rule of removing nonoriginal additions was considered to be too harsh—and even arrogant—by a growing number of detractors. Debates over his approach drew in the local population, and in time took on an international dimension when opposing principles espoused in England by John Ruskin were taken up by such French writers and critics as Anatole France and, later, Marcel Proust.

During the middle third of the nineteenth century, there was another international debate underway among architectural historians, over where Gothic architecture had been invented—France, England, or Germany. In France, this subject became a matter of state-sanctioned interest. It was ultimately resolved to be a French invention, something Viollet-le-Duc, a fervent medievalist, had believed all along.[32] Thus, the whole debate on both the origins of Gothic style and its appropriate restoration was a matter of national pride.

Viollet-le-Duc's theories of architectural history and restoration were founded on his extensive understanding of the history of architecture, as demonstrated in his ten-volume *Dictionnaire Raisonné de l'Architecture Française du XIe au XVIe Siècle* (Analytical Dictionary of French Architecture from the Eleventh through the Sixteenth Centuries [1854–1869]) and ten-volume *Dictionnaire du Mobilier Français de l'Époque Carlovingienne à la Renaissance* (Dictionary of French Furniture from the Carolingian Era to the Renaissance [1855]). He possessed a rare understanding of historic European buildings, their appointments, and their builders, and as chief architect for the Historic Monuments Commission, was widely influential. While his stylistic unity theory was subsequently judged to be unyielding and extreme, it is often considered as at least a theoretical option when contemplating the restoration of historic buildings. In special circumstances, his commitment to presenting buildings as the sum total of their best stylistic form may even have its place in contemporary preservation theory, if only to represent an extreme possibility. Viollet-le-Duc, however, thought that his was the *only* sensible course to pursue.[33]

Though his philosophy of restoration is, in fact, rarely ever used today, Viollet-le-Duc has been called "the father of architectural restoration" because his rigorous enthusiasm for saving and restoring historic buildings remained constant during the period when the specialty was evolving into a discrete discipline and then into a recognized profession. He was deeply interested in applying archaeological methods and understood the value of such new scientific developments, utilizing them in ways that might be considered significant contributions to the field. He was also among the first to use photography as a research aid; in fact, by 1851, photography was widely used by the Commission des Monuments Historiques. Photogrammetry, invented in France by Aimé Laussedat in 1849, was used in restoration practice to measure historic buildings such as Gothic cathedrals, which posed special challenges to surveyors due to their height and design complexities.[34]

As Viollet-le-Duc was transforming some of France's most important historic buildings and towns, Georges-Eugène Haussmann was transforming France's most important urban center: Paris. Encouraged and supported by Emperor Napoleon III, Baron Haussmann, as he called himself, remade the French capital. What was once a maze of medieval neighborhoods became a newly ordered center of imperial grandeur. Hausmann's Paris was characterized by wide boulevards built over the ruins of anything that stood in his way—including inconveniently placed historic civic and religious buildings. His desire to create an environment conducive to political stability and physical health resulted in the clearance of areas that had been the centers of resistance during the uprisings of 1830 and 1848. Haussmann provided many new open spaces, such as parks and squares, and enhanced prominent historic buildings by clearing areas around them. Although criticized for his heavy-handedness and for isolating a number of important historic buildings from their context, Haussmann made an irrevocable mark on Paris.

In 1870, a series of political events convulsed France. Its defeat in the Franco-Prussian War was humiliating; the monarchy collapsed again; and civil war resulted in the establishment of a ruling populist commune in Paris. During this turbulent time, several prominent historic buildings and building complexes—among them the Tuileries Palace, the Palais Royal, the Palais de St.-Cloud, the Hôtel de Ville, and the Ministries of Finance and State—were reduced to shells. It became the task of the Third Republic to restore order and to choose which buildings merited retention and which were to be demolished.

The public's desire to preserve historic buildings and sites remained strong as national reconstruction followed this latest war and the ensuing revolution. A popular outlet for interest in historic conservation was evidenced in the creation of amenity societies such as the Société des Amis des Monuments Parisiens (Society of Friends of Parisian Monuments) in 1884. The 1879 reorganization of the Commission des Monuments Historiques helped lay the groundwork for the first effective legislation for the protection of historic buildings and sites in 1887. This law, coupled with added regulations established dur-

▼ **Figures 14–12a & b** The construction of the flèche addition, completed in 1860, during the restoration of the Cathedral of Notre Dame de Paris.

Figure 14–13 The destruction of the town of Cambrai in northern France during World War I. *(akg-images, Ltd.)*

ing the following years, reduced the commission to a consultative role; the Service des Monuments Historiques now oversaw all restoration projects, giving it the authority to regulate even privately owned historic buildings.[35]

During this post–Viollet-le-Duc era, Ruskinian philosophy slowly infiltrated France. After Ruskin's *Seven Lamps of Architecture* was translated into French in 1899, the more conservative approaches to conservation as espoused by Ruskin and Morris began to gain ground. This was true not only among French intellectuals (who admired their insistence on authenticity) but also among conservation professionals. The Service des Monuments Historiques was eager to set standards and centralize restoration practice but also needed to cut costs as more historic buildings came under government protection. This was especially the case after the 1905 separation of church and state, after which a flood of church buildings becoming the responsibility of the government. Funding shortfalls required the service to emphasize maintenance and emergency work rather than full-scale restoration campaigns.

The government's position as protector of the nation's architectural heritage was strengthened in 1913 when France's architectural conservation legislation was amended. Religious and private properties that were not formerly considered of national significance could now be listed. Construction and demolition of buildings in the vicinity of a historic building were regulated, a move that recognized the importance of the historic context. A year later, as government policy shifted its focus from restoration to conservation, the Caisse Nationale des Monuments Historiques (National Treasury of Historic Monuments) was established.[36] Among its responsibilities were supervising the allocation of funds used to purchase and repair historic structures and making national heritage sites accessible to visitors.

From 1914 until 1918, World War I inflicted catastrophic damage on scores of European historic buildings, notably in northeastern and eastern France, where combat was most intense. Throughout the war, the Caisse Nationale des Monuments Historiques worked with the army to protect historic structures as best it could, even removing the most significant elements and furnishings to western France for safekeeping.

Following the 1918 armistice, repair efforts began with a major documentation and survey to assess the damage. Some buildings that were deemed beyond repair were de-listed or preserved as ruins. The Service des Monuments Historiques was centralized for efficiency and reorganized under the authority of one architect.[37] It took nearly four years for the first phase of emergency consolidation to be completed, but within one decade after the war most of the buildings had been restored with public funding.

During the 1920s there were further governmental efforts to conserve historic buildings and sites. In 1924 cities were required to carry out more comprehensive master plans, which forced municipalities to assess their historic nature and create proposals for conservation regulations. By 1930, the majority of significant historic buildings had received some sort of governmental financial assistance thanks to a growing belief that the government's regulatory position was strengthened through ownership of, or financial interest in, the nation's architectural patrimony. At times, restoration funding was sourced from overseas.[38]

By the end of the 1930s, France's comprehensive system of architectural heritage protection had made it a world leader in the field. This system, along with France's traditional legal framework, was exported to its colonies and protectorates throughout the world. Many countries still retain French-style legislation and administrative networks for heritage protection despite having become independent. The cumulative experience of architectural conservation before World War II served as a basis for the unimaginable demand for postwar restoration and reconstruction, which resulted in many of the architectural conservation systems that exist today.

GREAT BRITAIN

During the nineteenth century, architectural conservation developed differently in Great Britain than it did in Italy and France, where traditions grew out of a largely governmental or religious institutional reaction to threatened heritage. A far more democratic process occurred within Britain's public, professional, religious, and intellectual spheres before the government was compelled to take action. The broad network of governmental and nongovernmental organizations in Britain today, however, far outpaces other countries in architectural heritage protection.

While there are numerous examples of interest in historic buildings and sites by British antiquarians from the Renaissance through the seventeenth century, a coherent philosophical approach to the subject did not develop until the late eighteenth century. By that time, European travel had been an integral part of a gentleman's education for generations. The effects on British art and architecture from ideas imported by such grand tour participants are legion. In 1615, Inigo Jones, England's first professional architect, returned to London from Italy with a treasure trove of drawings, writings, and design ideas from Andrea Palladio. Jones's interest in classical antiquity and architecture extended beyond mere curiosity; his self-taught expertise in its principles was later skillfully applied to his own architecture and design work. (See also Figure 6-4.)

Eventually, a group of connoisseurs emerged from Great Britain's traveling classes, cognoscenti whose ranks included serious scholars, painters, writers, architects, designers, collectors, and tastemakers. Their growing interest in the study of the classical world and the dissemination of its culture led to the founding of the Society of Antiquaries of London (1717) and the Society of the Dilettanti (1734), which were ostensibly established to assist travelers but which also channeled a concern for the care of ancient buildings abroad.[39] Paradoxically, the British curiosity for the antique stemmed from the growing general knowledge of classical antiquity as seen in Rome and increasingly in Greece, Magna Graecia, and the Near East. Such familiarity deepened along with increased travel among the British upper classes. But most of Great Britain's own ancient pre-Roman structures

Figure 14–14 Antiquarian Sir William Hamilton, Britain's ambassador to Naples, viewing the excavations at Pompeii. (An engraving after a drawing by Pietro Fabris, published in 1776, that is exemplary of several illustrated books describing Hamilton's collections of vases and his interest in vulcanology.)

(rings, circles, and dolmens) and Roman ruins (walls, fortresses, and a few villas)—largely simple and utilitarian buildings—were viewed merely as objects in the landscape and sometimes dismantled for building material.

This elitist fascination with ancient Greek and Roman ruins, fueled by nostalgia and curiosity about all things ancient, spread and soon encompassed Great Britain's wealth of ancient and medieval ruins. Thus began a national examination of the country's architectural heritage.[40] Great Britain's architectural conservation movement started in the 1750s and 1760s when antiquarians such as Edmund Burke and Robert Walpole became increasingly interested in historic British architecture, particularly Gothic structures.

The developing popular appreciation of the more sublime qualities of historic buildings was expressed both in literature and in the newly created picturesque landscape designs in fashion at the time. Ruined buildings held a special fascination, and ruins became regular features in English landscape designs. Where none existed, "sham ruins" were created. Such elements, characteristic of the English picturesque, grew in response to Italian and French landscape design traditions and reflected antiquarianism as vividly as any other artistic expression in late eighteenth-century Great Britain.

While real and re-created ruins and new versions of ancient buildings evoked the picturesque, contemporaneous magazines pondered the state of Great Britain's authentic monastic and medieval ruins.[41] This interest in ruins both coincided with, and was driven by, the rise of the Gothic revival movement. New "Gothic" buildings promoted the study of the true Gothic found in the churches, cathedrals, and ruined monasteries. These had gone out of fashion in Great Britain in the sixteenth century when Gothic had become an anachronistic symbol of Catholicism.

In one of the earliest expressions of Gothic revival, Horace Walpole embraced the nearly forgotten style when he redecorated his country house, Strawberry Hill, beginning in 1750. Walpole's exuberant interpretation of medieval motifs sparked a wave of Gothic revival constructions, as architects became conversant in designing in a variety of styles. By the beginning of the nineteenth century, historicism became commonplace in architecture. The more versatile architects, such as William Chambers, George Dance, John Soane, and John Nash, were building in Gothic revival style—or perhaps even in an Egyp-

Figure 14–15 Strawberry Hill at Twickenham outside London, the Gothic revival house of Horace Walpole.

tian or Chinese style—as successfully as they could in the classical revival style. Each had a thorough knowledge of the history of architecture as it was then understood and served it up to a clientele that had a growing interest in the exotic as well as the historic.

During this same period, new work was initiated on many masterpieces of medieval architecture, and a movement to re-Gothicize cathedrals began. James Wyatt (1746–1813) was perhaps the foremost architect working with historic cathedrals at the close of the eighteenth century. Wyatt, a purveyor of Gothic revival in his commissioned work at Strawberry Hill and Fonthill Abbey, approached projects such as Lichfield, Salisbury, Hereford, and Durham cathedrals with an eye toward stylistic unity and the improvement of interiors, including removing elements or parts of the buildings to make them more functional. Wyatt was not alone in his approach; other architects and builders followed similar philosophies in their treatment of historic structures and were encouraged to do so by the Church and its supporters, who faced the problems of how to repair and improve surviving medieval buildings.

At Salisbury, Wyatt masterminded a series of interventions that so lacked restraint that the cathedral was essentially transformed.[42] The work caused unprecedented comment. Even before Ruskin's polemics, Wyatt's reputation as a restoration architect came under fire for damaging the great cathedral. His terse response to the moniker "the destroyer" was: "Improvement was a long-established tradition."[43]

Richard Gough, president of the Society of Antiquaries, and John Carter, author of *Ancient Architecture in England*, were outspoken critics of Wyatt's work. Gough championed the establishment of a committee for "preserving from mutilation, sacrilege, or even rapid dilapidation, the remains of ancient edifices" in 1788.[44] Carter decried the unskilled hands of restoration workers and argued for greater understanding of medieval detailing.[45] John Milner took the debate further. In his 1798 *Dissertation on the Modern Style of Altering Ancient Cathedrals as Exemplified in the Cathedral of Salisbury*, he not only refuted the justification of changes made to the cathedral but also attacked the Bishop of Salisbury for allowing them.[46]

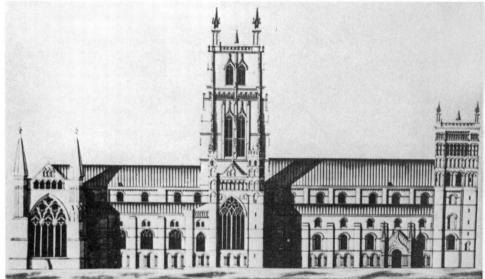

Figures 14–16 and 14–17 Durham Cathedral before (top) and after James Wyatt's restoration to an appearance he considered more Gothic (1780–1800). *(Source: Jane Fawcett, editor, Future of the Past)*

Unfortunately, this early debate on Wyatt's work did not halt the popularity for his style of restoration. Edward Blore at Ripon Cathedral, George Austin at Canterbury Cathedral, Sir Jeffry Wyattville at Windsor Castle, and more famously Sir Robert Smirke at York Minster, continued Wyatt's tradition of restoration combined with improvements. There were, however, a growing number of architects urging a more studied and conservative approach to restoration. William Atkinson was among those who protested the work at Durham, suggesting less intrusive repairs and even recommending that existing portions of buildings be left intact—including any moss growing on them![47] He and others also advocated more scholarly and scientific methods of restoration.

The prosperity that followed Napoleon's defeat in 1815 inaugurated a new industrial age in Great Britain, which increased public demand for new housing and drew popular attention to the medieval quarters of cities. Few churches were built in Great Britain during the first twenty years of the nineteenth century, however, despite the rapid growth of cities and towns. Then in 1818, parliament passed the Church Building Act, which provided £1 million for new church construction. The act stimulated a rush of building activity and focused fresh attention on the stylistic principles of Gothic architecture, further demonstrating the new preference for medieval over classical styles.[48] Over the next fifteen

Figure 14–18 The frontispiece of A. W. N. Pugin's *Contrasts*, an emblem of the battle of the styles that helped bring the topic of architecture to the fore in the public arena. A decade later a similar battle started between the *scrape* and *anti-scrape* schools of restoration.

years, 214 new churches were built, of which more than 80 percent were constructed in the Gothic revival style.[49] At the same time, restoration proceeded on a grand scale: In a sweeping gesture to modernize the Anglican church and boost its role in society, 7,144 existing medieval churches, approximately half of the country's inventory, were restored between 1840 and 1873.[50]

The most enthusiastic Gothic revival architect and advocate was Augustus Welby Northmore Pugin, who assisted Sir Charles Barry in designing the Houses of Parliament in 1840s and 1850s. This was the pinnacle of both the idiom and his career. A. W. N. Pugin incited the "battle of the styles" through his publications and passionately endeavored to replace neoclassicism with neo-Gothic, arguing it was the only appropriate style for religious buildings. In his view, the ultimate function of architecture was to serve the church by inspiring humanity to a higher moral purpose, which he believed only the Gothic style, as the true Christian style, could achieve.[51]

While researching his books *Contrasts* (1836), *The True Principles of Pointed or Christian Architecture* (1841), and *An Apology for the Revival of Christian Architecture* (1843), Pugin traveled extensively and was exposed to many examples of building restoration. He was critical of the treatment of historic buildings, especially church restoration projects. Pugin's objections to, and condemnation of, the work of Wyatt and other Protestant alterations to medieval churches were not without a hint of prejudice: Pugin was Catholic. In principle, Pugin was not against restoration; his main issues were the rearrangement and radical alteration of the churches and the uneducated approach to the imitation of Gothic detailing.

The Gothic revival movement and the romantic age jointly encouraged the revival of Catholic ceremony and traditions, for which the medieval cathedrals were well suited. One of the best-known promoters of church restoration was the Cambridge Camden Society (1839), which was forced underground after questioning Great Britain's religious establishment. As the renamed Ecclesiological Society, it refocused its efforts on restoring churches to their original and purest state.[52] Such "Catholic restoration" marked the birth of stylistic restoration in England. This transition did not occur in a vacuum; by the 1840s, many supporters of this approach and of the Gothic revival were in active contact with their counterparts in Germany and France.

In Great Britain, an initial interest in the study and restoration of medieval architecture led to the creation of professional standards based on restoration principles. E. A. Freeman was most likely the first to attempt to define them. In *The Preservation and Restoration of Ancient Monuments* (1852), which followed his *Principles of Church Restoration* (1846), Freeman described three different approaches to restoration. The "destructive approach" disregarded styles of the past and made repairs or additions in the style of the present time; the "conservative approach" precisely reproduced the details of an ancient building to create a new "facsimile" of the original structure; and the compromise "eclectic approach" carefully evaluated the building's history and remarkable features to arrive at the most desirable restoration procedure. The eclectic approach called for restoration to perfect a building's architecture by removing all later additions and improvements that detracted from the original design.[53] In practice, this philosophy was very similar to that of Viollet-le-Duc and was most certainly influenced by him through various articles as well as by correspondence with members of the Cambridge Camden Society. Overall, Freeman's ideas were conservative in tone.[54]

Sir George Gilbert Scott is perhaps the best-known and most prolific of the English school of stylistic restoration architects. He worked on more than eight hundred buildings, including high-profile projects such as the cathedrals of Ely, Hereford, Lichfield, Peterborough, Durham, Chester, and Salisbury, as well as Westminster Abbey. Although he viewed himself as being at the more conservative end of his profession, in reality he was not.

Many of his clients adhered to Freeman's "eclectic" theory. Freeman's approach troubled Scott, however, because he respected and admired both the historic structures and the needs and desires of his clients. By 1850, Scott was one of the chief targets of a growing movement that supported Ruskin's principle of minimal intervention. Scott set himself on the side of the restorers and nobly defended his profession despite his own apprehensions. His defense against a growing tide of protest was embodied in *A Plea for the Faithful Restoration of Our Ancient Churches* (1850), which argued for pragmatism. Scott divided significant historic buildings into two categories: those understood as evidence of vanished civilizations that had lost their original function, and ancient churches that continued in use and served a higher purpose—and which therefore had to be restored to give them the best possible presentation.[55]

The movement against restoration—stylistic, eclectic, or otherwise—was rooted in Great Britain's rapid industrialization, which transformed ways of life and society itself in the space of a generation. For many, the change was threatening. Some considered the destruction of old buildings as progress, while others saw it as continued erosion of heritage and tradition. In 1845, British architectural conservationists capitalized on this societal anxiety by trying to force a debate on the protection of historic buildings. Property owners and the Church—the custodians of many historic buildings—fiercely opposed any measure to impose control over their possessions. In York, community support saved its medieval walls from demolition by city planners. This important success evidenced the beginning of a growing movement among early heritage conservationists and communi-

Figure 14–19 A portrait of John Ruskin.

ties to counteract widespread societal changes and the loss of historic buildings, either through demolition or through restoration.

The writer, critic, and theorist John Ruskin became the principle spokesperson for this reaction against the destructive treatment of historic structures. He argued passionately against the uncontrolled radical changes to Great Britain's built environment and insensitive renovations of historic buildings. In particular, heavy-handed church restorations in which exterior stonework was refinished and recarved upset him greatly. In both print and public speeches, Ruskin railed against these interventions, proclaiming that they violated both the historic and artistic integrity of old buildings.

Ruskin's thoughtful and poetic writings on nearly every aspect of historic buildings are found in *The Seven Lamps of Architecture* (1849) and *The Stones of Venice* (1853), which reveal his almost irrational passion for the "time worn" qualities of historic buildings. His notion of romantic restoration opposed the purely practical concerns of those who wished to make old buildings look new. He argued against re-creating the old and revered the irreproducible characteristics of age:

> *Neither by the public, nor by those who have the care of public monuments, is the true meaning of the word restoration understood. It means the most total destruction which a building can suffer: a destruction out of which no remnants can be gathered: a destruction accompanied with false description of the thing destroyed…. It is impossible, as impossible as to raise the dead, to restore anything that has ever been great or beautiful in architecture.*[56]

In 1880, in the third edition of *The Seven Lamps of Architecture*, Ruskin added: "Do not let us talk then of restoration. The thing is a Lie from

Ruskin's writings and lectures incited heated debates ⟨…⟩ rve historic buildings properly. He argued that intervention wa⟨…⟩at a significant historic building must remain as it is, and th⟨…⟩ to prevent its falling down. He argued against nearly all inter⟨…⟩or timber props, saying, "Better a crutch than a lost limb."[58] ⟨…⟩erable: "Take proper care of your monuments, and you will ⟨…⟩ew sheets of lead put in time upon a roof, a few dead leaves a⟨…⟩f a water-course, will save both roof and walls from ruin."[59]

Ruskin was a particularly vociferous critic of the work ⟨…⟩his version of stylistic restoration, but he also lashed out at rest⟨…⟩n-derous techniques.[60] Moved by Ruskin's cause, Scott respon⟨…⟩of his philosophies and presented his updated ideas in a paper ⟨…⟩sh Architects in 1862. This paper was revised in 1865 into a ⟨…⟩h-niques called "The Conservation of Ancient Monuments a⟨…⟩id not fully embrace Ruskin's philosophy, it was the first docu⟨…⟩ay of his principles to published by a major professional orga⟨…⟩:d Ruskin's growing influence on British architectural conserv⟨…⟩

Ruskin's sensitivity to the more subtle aspects of historic⟨…⟩or their proper conservation continues to affect his ideologica⟨…⟩l-ist approach to building conservation—which might even ⟨…⟩s sometimes referred to as the "English approach." The En⟨…⟩o embody an almost religious respect for historic buildings. It⟨…⟩ in which they were found as much as possible, a school of ⟨…⟩ widely than Viollet-le-Duc's interventionist approach. Both o⟨…⟩ives, though, are extremes, within which are found a range of more practicable conservation options.

Like Ruskin, William Morris also believed primarily in maintaining historic buildings carefully rather than restoring them extensively. Morris began his career as a writer and

Figure 14–20 A portrait of William Morris. *(Courtesy of the Society for the Protection of Ancient Buildings)*

poet, and he found his way to architecture through the study of Flemish painting and Gothic churches. He was an avid fan of Ruskin's writings and staunchly supported his arguments against scraping off deteriorated or unoriginal parts of old buildings in favor of restoration to their likely original appearance. Morris advocated an appreciation of the crafts traditions that had created England's historic buildings, going as far as to continue them in his own famous designs in the decorative and book arts. He was also concerned about the impact of industrialization on Britain, particularly about its negative effects on the environment and on local traditions of all kinds.

In 1877, Morris established the Society for the Protection of Ancient Buildings (SPAB) "to keep a watch on old monuments, to protest against any restoration that means more than keeping out wind and weather, and to awaken a feeling that our ancient buildings are not mere ecclesiastical toys, but sacred monuments of the nation's growth and hope."[61] This is a prime early example of a cause-related campaign in defense of historic buildings. The organization operated as a social activist society; Morris's SPAB Manifesto of 1877 combined an argument against industrialization's rapid progress with Ruskin's respect for the authenticity of unrestored historic buildings and the merits of simple maintenance. (See also Chapter 9).

Morris brought to SPAB a powerful combination of theoretical and practical knowledge, exceptional organizational ability, and a strong sense of responsibility toward the past. He believed passionately that communication and persuasion were essential tools in any effective application of his ideas. SPAB's message was straightforward: Protection and conservative repair were to be undertaken rather than restoration. Indeed, the organization's creation sounded the death knell of the primacy of stylistic restoration and offered a logic that made state protection of historic buildings and sites more appealing and viable.

In 1882, the Ancient Monuments Protection Act gave the British government regulatory authority over eighty-six ancient buildings, the majority of which were prehistoric sites such as Stonehenge.[62] Local governments responded enthusiastically after being given the power to purchase historic buildings in 1889. The Historic Building Section of the County of Greater London was created during these formative years of British government support for architectural conservation. The Protection Act was expanded in 1900 and again in 1910 to include a wider range of historic buildings, those "of public interest by reason of the historic, traditional, or artistic interest attaining thereto" as well as to protect unoccupied historic structures.[63] In 1913, the first advisory board was set up to assist owners of historic buildings as well as government agencies such as the Ministry of Works, which was responsible for protected buildings. It also helped compile the first list of historic buildings with classifications, which was published in 1921. The Ancient Monuments Protection Act was again amended in 1931—this time to allow a review of intended repairs and prohibit demolition of listed buildings.

Though the government had entered the field, private efforts continued to play a significant role in the early twentieth century. The National Trust, a national not-for-profit organization, was founded in 1895 by Robert Hunter, Octavia Hill, and Hardwicke Rawnsley as an alliance between architectural and land conservationists in order to stem the growing tide of industrialization. It was built upon an awareness of the importance of preserving historic buildings and pristine landscapes as Morris, Ruskin, and others had advocated. Since its inception, the Trust's conservative approach has been carried out by hired professionals and expert consultants such as those from SPAB. By 1914 the Trust had become one of the major landholders in the country[64] and was powerful enough to oppose even the railroads in matters concerning land use and preservation.[65]

During the past century, the National Trust has saved over 250 historic properties and natural sites. Its numerous innovative programs concerning site acquisition, interpretation, and education in Great Britain have served as a model for similar organizations such as the National Trust for Historic Preservation in the United States (1949) and India's National Trust for Art and Cultural Heritage (1984).[66] Today's National Trust accepts donations or bequests of areas of land of significant historic interest or natural beauty and purchases land as well. Over time, the Trust has sharpened its focus, handling only projects and properties that can be conserved and that are financially self-sustaining.

By the outset of World War II, the philosophical foundations of Great Britain's much admired system of historic buildings and sites protection had been well laid, but stronger government action was still required. Restoration work on churches remained out of bounds for government regulators and within the purview of the Anglican Church. Little progress had been made on protecting other features of urban historic environments, especially in the built context around listed buildings, such as historic paving surfaces, parks, and landscapes.

The social and economic changes in Great Britain resulting from both wars posed numerous challenges to the protection of much of Britain's architectural heritage. Often against great odds, heritage conservationists who successfully responded to these challenges set numerous examples in conservation methods, technology, and administration, resulting in today's unmatched heritage protection system in Great Britain.

THE GERMAN STATES AND AUSTRIA

Compared with Italy, France, and Great Britain, the impetus to conserve architectural and cultural heritage in modern Germany started slowly, hampered by fractious principalities and continuous political reorganization. Chiefly driven by romanticism and the yearning for German nationhood, architectural efforts focused largely on completing cathedrals, the re-Gothicization of churches, and the stylistic restoration of historic buildings that were associated with German pride. It was not until the mid-nineteenth century that the first serious debates and critiques of contemporary restoration practices took place. Conservation for historical and age value rather than just for nationalistic reasons became a concern only in the twentieth century.

In the early nineteenth century and especially during the Napoleonic invasions, the German states of central Europe found themselves too ill equipped and disorganized to defend themselves. At that time, what is now Germany was a patchwork of kingdoms, principalities, electorates, and ecclesiastical states that were loosely held together under the declining auspices of the millennium-old Holy Roman Empire, which was dominated by the Austrian Empire. Countless historic buildings were damaged by the occupying French and coalition armies. The defeat gave Germans a yearning for a unified country.

Although fractured geographically and politically, the German states were united by their common language, history, and cultural traditions. This unity was emphasized by the romantic movement, whose nostalgia for the past was expressed through art, literature, and architecture. Patriotic feelings following Napoleon's final defeat in 1815 manifested in an efflorescence of these arts. An interest in medieval buildings and ruins arose out of this romanticism and revival of German customs and traditions, a focus that underpinned the German states' first steps toward the restoration and preservation of its most significant architectural heritage. Traditional German architecture, including the great castles and cathedrals of the medieval period, were reexamined. The Gothic cathedral itself became the enduring symbol of German culture, with influential figures such as Johann Wolfgang von Goethe encouraging its appreciation for aesthetic and patriotic reasons and arguing that Gothic was truly German, untarnished by foreign influences and expressive of the German character.[67]

By 1820 there were voluntary groups in several states, including Saxony and Thüringen, that were studying and conserving historic German buildings. Even composer Franz Liszt contributed by organizing concerts to fund efforts to preserve ruined structures. The first German legislation requiring the protection of historic buildings was enacted in the state

Figure 14–21 Karl Frederick Schinkel's Ober-Bau-Deputation surveyed the historic monuments of the German states. He was involved in several restorations, including the cathedrals of Cologne (illustrated here) and Magdeburg and Marienburg Castle.

of Baden in 1749, with more soon following, including edicts in Bayreuth in 1771 and in Hessen in 1779.

One of the greatest contributors to Germany's early conservation movement was the Prussian architect Karl Friedrich Schinkel, who was renowned for his severe neoclassical buildings but who was also proficient in the Gothic revival style.[68] Because of its perceived symbolism and associations, Schinkel often chose the Gothic style for church or national monument projects.[69] In 1810 Schinkel was appointed a member of the Ober-Bau-Deputation (General Directorate), the state architectural administration of the Kingdom of Prussia. He later became its director.

Almost immediately upon entering the service of the Ober-Bau-Deputation, Schinkel became involved in the restoration and protection of Prussian historic buildings. Restoration practice in the German states was still in its infancy, but already nationalistic and sentimental pressures were shaping its development. Schinkel was sent to survey the conditions of the publicly held buildings in the newly acquired Rheinland in 1815. He returned home disturbed by the war-damaged and dilapidated condition of a number of important historic buildings and works of civic art. His report, entitled "The Basic Principles for the Conservation of Ancient Monuments and Antiquities in Our Country" (Die Grudnsätze zur Erhaltung alter Denkmäler und Alterümer in unserem Lande), proposed the establishment of a state organization to protect important historic buildings. Among its duties would be taking an inventory and creating a conservation plan for each kind of building—religious, civic, military, and so forth—in each region of Prussia.[70]

Schinkel's report expanded the powers of the Ober-Bau-Deputation, which then also became responsible for regulating changes to state-owned buildings. Between 1819 and 1835, the Deputation's powers were augmented another five times as its jurisdiction grew to include abandoned castles, convents, fortifications, significant changes made to historic buildings, and conservation works carried out on buildings of historic, scientific, or technical significance.[71]

Schinkel himself was involved in three of the best-known restorations of this time: the cathedrals of Cologne and Magdeburg and Marienburg Castle. These projects, begun in the 1830s, reveal the issues and contradictions at work in Germany's early nineteenth-century restoration practice. Each structure was either incomplete or heavily damaged; Schinkel's approach was to restore each to an ideal state in order to reflect a connection between the country's glorious medieval past and the future of the powerful Prussian state.[72]

In 1833 Schinkel prepared plans for the completion of Cologne Cathedral, although in 1816 he had been awed by its majesty and had suggested a minimalist approach that would have left the cathedral unfinished. In the survey report he prepared on that earlier occasion, he had declared: "In this situation, man's worthiest determination seems to be to conserve with all care and respect what the efforts of the past generations have left to us."[73] At Magdeburg, Schinkel initially assumed a similarly conservative approach, but eventually he succumbed to pressure to ensure stylistic continuity and modified his design.

At Marienberg Castle, Schinkel was called in to assist with a nationally driven effort to restore this former seat of the Order of the Teutonic Knights, a highly evocative and significant site which had been protected by royal decree since 1804. This restoration was particularly challenging. There was no documentation; there were no examples of comparable details or architectural elements. As an architect, Schinkel admitted to being tempted to indulge in creative fantasy to fill in the gaps where no evidence existed.[74] This was not entirely out of character, for he stated in an 1815 report to the Ober-Bau-Deputation that he believed that the state should be responsible for restoring historic buildings to a form in which they could be appreciated by the public, even at the risk of inauthenticity.[75]

In the 1830s Germany also saw the rise of *purifizierung*, or restoration to a particular earlier style, similar to the stylistic restoration that was popular in England and France.[76] This trend, another consequence of the resurgence of German pride, resulted in the restoration of hundreds of churches to a "pure" medieval state. They were stripped of all baroque accretions that had embellished them during the seventeenth and eighteenth centuries, as these were thought to be associated with France. The cathedrals of Magdeburg (restored 1826–1834), Bamberg (1828–1837), and Regensburg (1827–1839) had all of their high-baroque altars, side chapels, screens, pews, and funerary monuments removed and replaced with neo-Gothic furnishings.[77] Plaster was scraped off the walls down to the stone, regardless of any evidence of medieval paintings. The outcome was austere, imposing, and difficult liturgically, as restorers took little heed of the churches' use or history.[78]

The first glimmers of a systematic restoration approach in Germany came via Greece. Architect Leo von Klenze (1784–1864) had been sent to Greece in 1835 by King Ludwig I of Bavaria to oversee the planning and construction of Athens as the capital worthy of his son Otto, the appointed king of the Hellenes. Von Klenze, an avid classicist, traveled ex-

Figure 14–22 The Parthenon reproduced as Valhalla near Regensburg, Germany, by Leo von Klenze.

tensively through Greece and advocated the protection of all major buildings and twelve primary archaeological sites of outstanding significance. His greatest contribution was the preparation of restoration guidelines for the Acropolis, which introduced the methods of **anastylosis** (the reassembly of fallen building elements) and **reconstruction** to conservation practice in Greece. He also made conspicuous use of new material so as not to confuse it with the original fabric.[79] Von Klenze's guidelines also called for the collection of sculptural elements and fragments, some of which were housed nearby, while others were left in situ to maintain the site's picturesque qualities. Von Klenze did, however, permit the demolition of nonancient buildings on the Acropolis.

The restoration and conservation methods used by the Germans in Greece were brought into domestic practice when Alexander Ferdinand von Quast was appointed *konservator der kunstdenkmäler* ("conservator of monuments of art") for Prussia in 1843. Von Quast was given the task of making the case—and establishing principles—for conservation, and for raising public awareness about the cultural value of historic structures.[80] His duties also included the compilation of a national inventory of historic buildings and a review of all plans for restorations of historic structures, tasks that he accepted with relish. Even before his appointment, von Quast—an admirer of English conservation efforts—had set out to establish his own positions on matters pertaining to both theory and technique.[81]

Soon after von Quast's appointment as conservator, an official document released by the Ober-Bau-Deputation clearly outlined restoration and conservation principles. It warned against restoration practices that erased the patina of age and encouraged a minimalist approach focusing on the repair of damage.[82] It also discouraged *purifizierung* and called for baroque and rococo monuments to remain untouched out of respect for the dead, the community, and the church's sense of history.[83] This set the stage for von Quast's support for the retention of all additions to historic buildings, and he advocated the use of critical judgment in cases where later changes obscured intact older building fabric.[84] But

Figure 14-23 The restoration of the Frauenkirche in Munich was done utilizing the *purifizierung* (unity of style) approach.

von Quast strayed from his own dicta many times. At the Abbey Church of Gernrode in 1858, for example, he designed new decorative wall paintings and stained-glass windows to replace the Ottonian ones that had been lost.[85] Yet regardless of his foibles, von Quast significantly influenced the German architectural conservation movement. His post was eliminated in the 1850s when regional conservators were appointed; however, several of these new appointees filled the position he had held with great skill in Bavaria.

German stylistic restorations actually increased in number during the latter half of the nineteenth century. Several factors were responsible. The Eisenacher Regulativ of 1861 helped fuel restoration by outlining Protestant liturgical requirements, including how churches were to be arranged. At the same time, the emergence of historicism in architectural design, in response to growing nationalistic feelings, searched for the "true" German style and appropriate styles for different building types.[86] The resulting *historismus*, or historicizing of architecture, including modifications to recognized existing historic buildings, led to restorations that made hundreds of churches more Gothic because it was thought to be the most appropriate style for Protestant churches.[87] Stylistic restoration as practiced in France and Great Britain also flourished in Germany.

During the latter half of the nineteenth century, several well-publicized restorations and completions of unfinished buildings took place. Cologne Cathedral and its two massive new towers were finished in 1880, a project that served as the training ground for several restoration architects. Laborious restorations and re-creations at Marienburg and Albrechtsburg castles gave each ornate neo-Gothic interiors. Meissen Cathedral also received two new towers, and the Ulm Cathedral was given an extensive restoration in the tradition of Viollet-le-Duc between 1844 and 1890 that included a massive new neo-Gothic tower.

From the mid- to late nineteenth century, there was growing opposition to the restoration fever that had gripped the German states. The restoration of Munich's Frauenkirche, which was completed in 1861, caused a scandal when details leaked to the press indicating that works of art stripped from the church were being sold or destroyed. Critics such as Wilhelm Lübke condemned the restoration and declared that the church had been nearly destroyed[88] through the work of restorers willing to put political motivations before history.[89] The protest over the Frauenkirche was the first public German debate about restoration and its effects on the integrity of an historic building.

Further political upheavals in 1848, the wars of the 1860s, and political unification in 1871 fuelled the connections between German nationalism and restoration practice throughout the rest of the nineteenth century. In 1900, architect and author Hermann Muthesius's translations of Ruskin's work helped turn the tide away from restoration and toward conservation. Muthesius's own writings emphasized the documentary value of historic buildings,[90] recognized the historical, artistic, and archaeological value embodied in each, and preached the Ruskinian doctrine of maintenance over restoration. Another German admirer of Ruskin was Paul Clemens, *konservator* of the Rheinland. He was influenced by Ruskin but also appreciated Viollet-le-Duc's point of view. Clemens cautiously

Figure 14–24 Debate over the restoration of Heidelberg Castle (illustrated) marked a turning point in German restoration theory; unity of style restoration yielded gradually to the conservation approach.

approached conservation, preferring a slow renewal and noting that preservation is for the next century, not the next decade.[91]

Open debate between the supporters of stylistic restoration and those who now aggressively advocated for conservation began in earnest in Germany in the first years of the twentieth century, and the outcome of these discussions greatly influenced the fate of Germany's architectural heritage. Some, such as architect Baurath Paul Tornow-Metz, attempted to take a centrist position not unlike that of George Gilbert Scott in England, aiming to preserve the historic character of a building while respecting its original intent.[92] Others backed those breaking new ground in the theory behind judicious repair and maintenance and opposed extensively restoring historic architecture.

In Germany, this debate came to a head over the proposed restoration of Heidelberg Castle, which in the seventeenth century had been reduced to ruins by the French. Discussion of possible treatments of the castle began in 1869 and continued for more than thirty years. Those in favor of reconstruction appealed for support as a matter of honor: They wanted to regain a symbol of the newly united Germany and to obliterate the memory of defeat. Finally, in 1891, a portion of the castle, the Friedrichsbau, was restored. Plans for the restoration of the adjacent Otto-Heinrichsbau were drawn up in 1901, when new arguments suggested that the restoration of the entire structure was necessary to conserve its Renaissance façade.

Georg Dehio, considered to be the founder of modern German architectural conservation, joined in the discussion. He held to the dictum "Conserve, only conserve," and argued the proposed restoration would be performed at the cost of the structure's authenticity. In 1906, at the sixth annual *Denkmalpflegetag* (Symposium on Conservation), more than two hundred scholars debated the fate of the castle, with arguments that became very technical and heated. The outcome was surprising: There was no decision. Time passed and created a de facto victory for those advocating a measured conservation approach. For the first time in an official German arena, scientific and technical conservation arguments won out over those that were based on romantic, nationalistic, and political sentiment.[93] Both sides in the Heidelberg conservation debate based their arguments on the needs of the building; arguments for restoration for the sake of style and historical value were abandoned.

At the same time, in nearby Austria, Alois Riegl, an art historian, professor, and architectural theorist, was exploring the reasoning behind conservation. As the general conservator for the *Zentral-Kommission zur Erforschung und Erhaltung der Baudenkmale* (The Central Commission for Research and Conservation of Historical Monuments) in Austria, his theories influenced conservation policy throughout the Hapsburg Empire. Through his extensive writings, he also had a significant impact on developments in Germany. In 1903, Riegl produced what would have been the most sophisticated charter for architectural conservation to date in the form of legislation submitted for approval to the Austrian government. But it was not formally adopted, probably due to his untimely death in 1905.

The Central Commission had been established by the Austrian emperor half a century earlier, in 1850, and functioned mainly as a voluntary organization that coordinated the efforts of local communities, professionals, and private financiers to preserve the empire's cultural heritage.[94] Its tasks included "inventory, documentation, legal protection and approval of restoration projects of historic buildings."[95] In the nineteenth century, most conservation in the Austrian Empire—as in the German states—was influenced by romanticism and historicism, and tended toward stylistic restoration. The work of Friedrich von Schmidt was prolific and influential. After working on the Cologne Cathedral project and also on projects in Milan and Vicenza, Italy, von Schmidt became one of the empire's most important and prolific restoration architects, supervising work throughout the empire, including projects at St. Stephen's Cathedral in Vienna and at churches in Zagreb and Prague.[96]

At the turn of the twentieth century, Riegl rationalized and systematized the types and values of historic buildings, classified monuments as intentional or unintentional, and gave reasons for their conservation: because they fulfilled either memorial or present-day uses.[97] The conservation debate in Austria and Germany at the turn of the century, in Riegl's terms, was one between those who would hold historic value to be most important (the restorers) and those who would hold age value as sacred (the conservators).

Riegl's own categories of restoration also reflected his various "monument values" (see the sidebar "Riegl and the Meaning of Monuments" in Chapter 3). His types of interventions were divided into "radical," "art-historical," and "conservative," and they ranged from minimal intervention for structures primarily with age value, to protection or maintenance for artifacts important as historic documents, to complete reconstruction for structures with aesthetic value or use concerns.[98]

Throughout the early twentieth century, advances in the architectural conservation movement continued. Art historian Max Dvořák developed the first comprehensive inventory of Austrian art and architecture, which was later used as the basis for the enactment of legal protections for cultural heritage. His great work, *Katechismus der Denkmalpflege* (Catechism of Monument Conservation), was revolutionary because it represented the first real handbook for architectural conservationists while also being tailored to the public rather than to other academics. Dvořák believed that conservation was not founded on arcane knowledge but on a very human respect for the past and an appreciation of one's culture. He stood firmly behind the belief that the stylistic restoration of a building represented a loss of artistic and historic significance and destroyed value that should pass to later generations. For Schinkel, von Quast, Riegl, and Dehio, the sight of post–World War II German and Austrian cities would likely have been too much to bear. German rebuilding required the reconstruction of the German architectural conservation movement because the old rules no longer applied in a new landscape where significant historic buildings had additional meanings and required new solutions. In the face of such challenges, the German architectural conservation movement began to restore itself.

AUTHOR'S NOTE: The above explanations of the formative years of restoration and conservation practice in Italy, France, Great Britain, Germany and Austria were chosen over those of several other countries with similar stories because these were among the first in the world to develop well-reasoned conservation approaches that later proved to be especially influential internationally. Other countries also have their own stories of the discovery, adoption, and institutionalization of heritage protection measures, some of which are introduced in subsequent and separate parts of this publication.

RELATED READINGS

Cantacuzino. Sherban. *Re/Architecture: Old Buildings/New Uses*, London: Thames and Hudson, 1989.

Choay, Françoise. *The Invention of the Historic Monument*. Cambridge: Cambridge University Press, 2001. Choay, Françoise, ed. *La Conférence d'Athènes sur la conservation artistique et historique des monuments*, Paris: Editions de l'Imprimeur, 2002.

Crouch, Dora P., and June G. Johnson. *Traditions in Architecture: Africa, America, Asia, and Oceania*. Oxford: Oxford University Press, 2001.

Denslagen, Wim. "Restoration Theories, East and West". *Transactions/Association for Studies in the Conservation of Historic Buildings* 18 (1993): 3–7.

Erder, Cevat. *Our Architectural Heritage: From Consciousness to Conservation*. Museums and Monuments series. Paris: UNESCO, 1986.

Fitch, James Marston. *American Building*. Vol. 2: *The Environmental Forces That Shape It*. New York: Houghton Mifflin, 1972.

Harvey, John. "The Origin of Listed Buildings." *Transactions of the Ancient Monuments Society*, vol. 37, 1–20. London: Ancient Monuments Society, 1993.

Jokilehto, Jukka. A *History of Architectural Conservation*. Oxford: Butterworth-Heinemann, 1999.

Kain, R. J. P. "Conservation and Planning in France: Policy and Practice in the Marais, Paris." In *Planning for Conservation: An International Perspective*. Ed. R. J. P. Kain. London: Mansell, 1981.

Miele, Chris, ed. *From William Morris: Building Conservation and the Arts and Crafts Cult of Authenticity, 1877–1939*. New Haven: Yale University Press, 2005.

Pickard, R. ed. *Policy and Law in Heritage Conservation*. London: Spon, 2001.

Schnapp, Alain. *Discovery of the Past*. Translated by Ian Kinnes and Gillian Varndell. London: British Museum Press, 1993.

Tung, Anthony M. *Preserving the World's Great Cities; The Destruction and Renewal of the Historic Metropolis*. New York: Clarkson Potter, 2001.

UNESCO. *Operational Guidelines for the Implementation of the World Heritage Convention*. Paris: UNESCO, 2005. First published in 1977.

Waterson, Merlin, and Samantha Wyndham. *The National Trust: The First Hundred Years*. London: National Trust and BBC Books, 1994.

Watkin, David. *The Rise of Architectural History*. London: Architectural Press, 1980.

Wines, James. *Green Architecture*. New York: Taschen, 2000.

ENDNOTES

1. Erder, *Our Architectural Heritage*, 91–92.
2. *The Complete Poems of Percy Bysshe Shelley* (New York: Modern Library, 2000), 589.
3. Azienda di Promozione Turistica di Roma [Rome Tourist Board], "The Arches of Ancient Rome," *RomaTurismo*, http://www.romaturismo.it/v2/allascopertadiroma/en/itinerari09.html.
4. Erder, *Our Architectural Heritage*, 126.
5. Ibid., 91.
6. Ibid., 93.
7. Ibid., 92.
8. Ibid. The British helped the Vatican secure the return of their plundered treasures and even offered a ship for their transport to Rome in 1822. Ironically, this was only a short time after the British Museum acquired the Parthenon frieze in one of history's most famous unresolved cases of restitution.
9. Ibid.
10. Jokilehto, *History of Architectural Conservation*, 78–79.
11. Ibid., 205.
12. Alvise Zorzi, *Osservazioni Intorno ai Restauri Interni ed Esterni della Basilica di San Marco*, 1877.
13. *Risoluzione del III Congresso degli Ingegneri ed Architetti* (Rome: 1883). Boito's principles are paraphrased here in English. The original in Italian is found in Camillo Boito, *Questioni Practiche de belle Arti, Restauri, Concorsi, Legislazione, Professione, Insegnamento* (Rome: 1893), 28.
14. Liliana Grassi, *Camillo Boito* (Milan: Il Balcone, 1959), 41–48.
15. Erder, *Our Architectural Heritage*, 101.
16. Jokilehto, *History of Architectural Conservation*, 220.
17. Erder, *Our Architectural Heritage*, 117.
18. St.-Gilles du Garde near Nîmes, contructed in its present form during the twelfth century CE, has a variety of ancient sculptures on its façade, along with well-integrated new work. During the construction of the Basilique St.-Denis near Paris, begun in 1144, Abbé Suger specifically requested that recycled marble columns from the dismantled temple of a Corinthian order be used in the ambulatory of the great church.
19. As the memory of Rome faded during the medieval period, French architects created some of France's greatest buildings—its magnificent Gothic cathedrals. These cathedrals and many

smaller churches suffered damage during the religious conflicts of the Reformation, as French Huguenots vandalized and destroyed many religious structures in retaliation for their own losses at the hands of Catholics. Such conflicts affected buildings from all time periods.

20. During this period, churches were altered or demolished as new, classically styled structures were constructed throughout the country. The Gothic style was derided, and French medieval architecture was deemphasized or mocked as ignoble. One of the sole opponents of the Italian-ization of French architecture was architect Charles Perrault, whose translation of Vitruvius left him well-versed in the classical language of architecture. He decried the importation of foreign architecture as unsuited to the French climate and against the tradition and requirements of French construction.

21. After the monarchy was abolished in 1793, the first ruling body of the new French Republic ordered all royal tombs and mausoleums to be destroyed. Losses included the destruction of fifty-one monuments and the near destruction of the royal tombs at the Basilique St.-Denis. André Thoman, et al., *Chronicle of the French Revolution, 1788–1799* (London: Chronicle Publications, 1989), 357.

22. Choay, *Invention of the Historic Monument*, 64; Jokilehto, *History of Architectural Conservation*, 70.

23. Choay, *Invention of the Historic Monument*, 65–66.

24. Ibid., 67.

25. Ibid., 69; and Jokilehto, *History of Architectural Conservation*, 70.

26. Grégoire coined the word *vandalism*. Choay, *Invention of the Historic Monument*, 63.

27. Napoleon's troops traveled with one hundred scholars and specialists ("*savants*"), including his-torians, engineers, architects, geologists, botanists, and zoologists, who documented everything they encountered in this strategically important and famously exotic land. Bringing scientists on a military expedition and setting up a scientific institute before victory was declared proved to be a landmark in the history of both art and science. The resulting folios and text comprising the *Description de l'Égypte* made history in the literature of the arts and sciences as well in the field of book publishing. See also Figure 13-9.

28. Choay, *Invention of the Historic Monument*, 97.

29. Jokilehto, *History of Architectural Conservation*, 138. Adolphe-Napoléon Didron's early articu-lation of sound principles of restoration and conservation practice curiously remain under-cele-brated in the story of French heritage conservation, possibly because of the towering reputations of Prosper Mérimée and Eugène-Emmanuel Viollet-le-Duc, who respectively preceded and succeeded him.

30. Although, in practice, Viollet-le-Duc did occasionally retain subsequent modifications to his-toric buildings for practical reasons.

31. Viollet-le-Duc, "On Restoration," from *Dictionnaire Raisonné de l'Architecture Française du XIe au XVIe Siècle*, vol. 8, as cited in M. F. Hearn, ed., *The Architectural Theory of Viollet-le-Duc: Readings and Commentary* (Cambridge, MA: MIT Press, 1992), 269.

32. The Basilique St.-Denis near Paris, begun by Abbé Suger in 1136, is the oldest-documented expression of Gothic architecture. The English and the Germans, however, maintained that certain characteristics are uniquely theirs and part of their individual national heritages.

33. Viollet-le-Duc's position is the antithesis of the later written theories of Camillo Boito, in par-ticular his *restauro filologico*, which emphasized that historic value is very important in a resto-ration project. Boito maintained that additions made to a building in all periods of use must be respected, as should its patina. He opposed bringing back the building to a supposed original state, and he maintained that consolidation should be preferred to repairs, and repairs preferred to restorations.

34. Architectural photogrammetry was further perfected and made efficient by Albrecht Mey-denbauer, an Austrian who coined the term *photogrammetry* and used his critical invention of a wide-angle lens in producing a photogrammetric survey of St. Mary's Cathedral in Frey-burg, Germany. From 1959 through 1981, Professor Hans Foramitti, a Swiss working at the Austrian *bundesdenkmalamt* (Austria's federal administration for the conservation of cultural property), developed a practical system of photogrammetric survey techniques for historic buildings, information that was disseminated through his teachings and publications on the subject.

35. Choay, *Invention of the Historic Monument*, 98.

36. In 2000, the name of La Caisse was changed to Centre des Monuments Nationaux.

37. Erder, *Our Architectural Heritage*, 144.

38. By 1930, American philanthropist John D. Rockefeller's donations for projects at the palaces of Versailles and Fontainebleau and at Notre-Dame de Reims totaled more than $2.85 million. This encouraged further government investment in these important and highly visible land-marks of French history. Martin Perschler "John D. Rockefeller, Jr.'s 'Gift to France' and the Restoration of Monuments, 1924–1936," *Research Reports from the Rockefeller Archive Center*, Spring (1997): 13.

39. Schnapp, *Discovery of the Past*, 260–261.

40. While neoclassicism in western Europe is widely considered an eighteenth-century phenom-enon, its roots can be traced to French and English Renaissance architecture, after which it is seen even more clearly by the introduction of Palladianism in the early seventeenth century.

41. Examples are Fountains Abbey, and the ruins of Newstead Abbey that were incorporated as an extension of the poet Byron's country home.

42. His alterations involved a catalog of extensive changes: demolition of two late-Gothic chantry chapels next to the Lady Chapel; repositioning the altar; removing the seventeenth-century reredos; installing new, iron communion rails and screens across the aisles and at the organ loft; repositioning the thirteenth-century rood screen; repaving the Lady Chapel using recut old bluestone grave markers; refinishing the walls from the east end to the transept; moving the larger tombs from behind the altar to the nave; and scraping off the thirteenth-century vault paintings that one critic described as "doing honour to the Italian school." Denslagen, *Architectural Restoration in Western Europe*, 37.

43. Ibid., 34.

44. Ibid., 36.

45. Jokilehto, *History of Architectural Conservation*, 108.

46. Denslagen, *Architectural Restoration in Western Europe*, 49.

47. Jokilehto, *History of Architectural Conservation*, 109.

48. From the seventeenth century on, Protestant England had wholeheartedly embraced Classi-cism's cool simplicity and grandeur. Medieval and Renaissance crafts were laid aside as ar-chitects and builders were taught the new canon of antiquity, encouraged by the ideas of the eighteenth-century Enlightenment. The classical churches constructed during the Restoration and Georgian eras were deemed better suited to Protestant liturgical requirements than the medieval Gothic churches. England's great cathedrals, long symbols of banished popery, were abandoned or altered by Anglican clergy to better support a Protestant liturgy. Jokilehto, *History of Architectural Conservation*, 111.

49. William H. Pierson, Jr., *American Buildings and Their Architects*, vol. 2, *Technology and the Pic-turesque: The Corporate and the Early Gothic Styles* (Garden City, NY: Doubleday, 1978), 151.

50. Hugh Thackeray Turner, "Society for the Protection of Ancient Buildings: A Chapter of Its Early History," *Society for the Protection of Ancient Buildings, 2nd Annual Report* (London: Society for the Protection of Ancient Buildings,1899), 7–37.

51. See also A. W. N. Pugin's *Contrasts* (1836). plate shows the Gothic restoration of St. Mary Overy's southern façade, including a sign indicating "Old material for sale."

52. From 1841 to 1843, the society directed the restoration of the twelfth-century Church of the Holy Sepulchre in Cambridge, essentially as a reconstruction. The western entrance was re-built in the Romanesque style, a fifteenth-century pinnacle was destroyed, the original windows were replaced with Romanesque ones, and vaults were built over the circular central space. The changes also included construction of a new bell tower on the north side of the church and removal of all Protestant pews in order to "purify" the interior. Denslagen, *Architectural Restoration in Western Europe*, 61.

53. Ibid., 62.

54. Ibid., 159.

55. Jokilehto, *History of Architectural Conservation*, 161–62.

56. John Ruskin, *The Works of John Ruskin*, library ed., ed. E. T. Cook and A. Wedderburn (Lon-don: G. Allen, 1903–12), vol. 3:242.

57. John Ruskin, "The Lamp of Memory," *Seven Lamps of Architecture*, Chapter 6.

58. Ibid.

59. Ibid.

60. For the average architect and builder at the time, the solution for restoring a crumbling stone exterior involved cutting down or scraping a building's stone exterior surfaces—deteriorated and otherwise—and refinishing it, complete with new surface treatments and freshly carved stone sculpture.

61. William Morris, "Tewkesbury Minster," letter to *Athenaeum*, March 10, 1877, Marxists Internet Archive, http://www.marxists.org/archive/morris/works/1877/tewkesby.htm. Other founding members of SPAB included John Ruskin, architect Philip Webb, and the artist Edward Burne-Jones.

62. Erder, *Our Architectural Heritage*, 180.

63. Derek Linstrum, *"Conservation of Historic Towns and Monuments."*

64. With ownership of 612,000 acres, the Trust is the second largest property owner in Britain today, after the Crown.

65. Jokilehto, *History of Architectural Conservation*, 112.

66. Today, the membership of the International National Trusts Organization consists of 150 members from 53 countries. The INTO holds biennial meetings in different countries of the world. Vibha Sharma, "INTO Launch Today: Conserving Cultural and Natural Heritage," *The Tribune* (Chandigarh, India), December 2, 2007, http://www.tribuneindia.com/2007/20071203/nation.htm#2.

67. Jokilehto, *History of Architectural Conservation*, 112, 127; and Johann Wolfgang von Goethe, "On German Architecture" (1772) and "On Gothic Architecture" (1823), in John Geary, ed., *Goethe: The Collected Works*, vol. 3, *Essays on Art and Literature* (Princeton, NJ: Princeton University Press, 1986), 8, 10.

68. Barry Bergdoll, *Karl Friedrich Schinkel: An Architecture for Prussia* (New York: Rizzoli, 1994), 40–42.

69. Among Schinkel's Gothic revival designs were a mausoleum for Queen Louise (1810–1812); the war monument on the Kreuzberg in Berlin (1818–1821); and his figurative paintings of fictional cathedrals set above Germanic towns and landscapes.

70. Jokilehto, *History of Architectural Conservation*, 114.

71. Denslagen, *Architectural Restoration in Western Europe*, 169.

72. Jokilehto, *History of Architectural Conservation*, 117.

73. Ibid.

74. Ibid., 120.

75. Denslagen, *Architectural Restoration in Western Europe*, 155.

76. Ibid., 155.

77. Ibid., 154.

78. Jokilehto, *History of Architectural Conservation*, 108.

79. Ibid., 93. Valadier preceded Von Klenze with this type of work in Italy.

80. Denslagen, *Architectural Restoration in Western Europe*, 157.

81. In his 1837 paper "Pro Memoria," Von Quast stated that restoration fueled by too much funding was destructive and counterproductive to conservation, which sought to conform to what already exists rather than create something new. Denslagen, *Architectural Restoration in Western Europe*, 157.

82. Ibid., 158.

83. Ibid.

84. Jokilehto, *History of Architectural Conservation*, 125–27.

85. Ibid., 164.

86. Ibid., 192.

87. Ibid., 193.

88. Denslagen, *Architectural Restoration in Western Europe*, 163.

89. Jokilehto, *History of Architectural Conservation*, 193–94.

90. Ibid., 194.

91. Ibid., 195.

92. Ibid., 196.

93. Ibid., 142.

94. Sigrid Sangl, *Biedermeier to Bauhaus* (London: Frances Lincoln, 2000), 112.

95. Jokilehto, *History of Architectural Conservation*, 164.

96. Ibid.

97. See sidebar "Riegl and the Meaning of Monuments" in Chapter 3, 38.

98. Jokilehto, *History of Architectural Conservation*, 218.

PART IV

Contemporary
Architectural
Conservation
Practice

The Conserved historic center of Florence.

The unprecedented relocation of an entire rock-cut Egyptian temple—Abu Simbel at Aswan—to higher ground in order to save it.

15

International Activities and Cooperation

The years since World War II have been by far the most productive period for the architectural conservation field. The interregnum in world affairs and the destruction caused by this most devastating of all wars provided an important turning point in the history of the field.[1]

The immediate postwar years were characterized by extensive reconstruction in the areas that were most affected by physical conflict and by growing global economic prosperity. The economic upturn was first enjoyed by the United States and later spread to other countries. Especially in Western Europe, the widespread postwar modernization of urban areas and transportation systems challenged the nascent architectural conservation interests that had surfaced during the previous two centuries. These gradually developed into broad-ranging national and international trends.

The field's responses to the pressures of global change over the past half century are reflected in a variety of ways: from the development of architectural conservation charters and the passage of laws to the establishment of specialized government agencies and the creation of a variety of influential heritage conservation organizations. In tandem with these developments has been a growing popular concern for both cultural and natural heritage conservation, an outgrowth of the realization that there are limits to social, economic, and physical development. Heated debates about heritage protection were in some instances met with strong, even violent, resistance. Some of the more notable battles have become milestones that mark the progress of increasingly widespread heritage protection actions around the globe.

The long list of reasons for architectural conservation outlined in Chapter 4 is widely recognized today as outweighing the arguments against it. Added to this is the confluence of concerns about heritage protection from within the allied field of museology, archaeology, and historical studies, and the parallel interests of environmental protection and energy conservation.

Because of the world's interconnectedness, the extent of its development, and its awareness of cause and effect at all levels, concerns for the diverse heritage of various nations and ethnic groups has spread among populations everywhere. Interest in and attempts by individuals, organizations, and governments to help preserve cultural heritage beyond their native lands is now commonplace, although nothing new. As has been noted, international heritage protection efforts have their roots in the history of travel, which for centuries has been the primary means by which cultures learn about one another. Glowing descriptions by travelers of the monumental architecture seen during their journeys fuels interest in the historic sites of foreign places—and subsequently, in their protection The process of discovery, comparison, and learning about other people and places in turn enhances expectations—both local and international—and thus national pride. As a result, a new phenomenon can be clearly observed: conservation for the sake of conservation. The growth of the field of international heritage conservation practice exemplifies this trend.

CONTEMPORARY INTERNATIONAL CONSERVATION PRACTICE—ORIGINS

Since the early nineteenth century, the ideas and approaches of specific restoration projects were shared throughout Europe and influenced the developments of conservation practice elsewhere. For example, Giuseppe Valadier's careful retention and reintegration of original fragments and his efforts to distinguish the old from the new in the restoration of the Arch of Titus in Rome was widely imitated in a restoration that relied on a method later termed *anastylosis*.[2] Eugène-Emanuel Viollet-le-Duc's stylistic unity approach was reflected in several important restorations of civic and religious buildings in all of France's neighboring countries, while John Ruskin's influence dominated the lively debates that preceded the restoration of Venice's Basilica di San Marco in the 1860s.[3] During the early, more experimental years of the field, actions such as these taken in several countries became exemplars and points of reference.

Knowledge of such projects, combined with the increasing quantities of historic buildings under threat in the changing capitals of Europe and the world beyond, underlined the need for more comprehensive philosophies and approaches. Several Italian architects and scholars took up this challenge. The work of Roman architect Camillo Boito offered a middle path between the approaches of Viollet-le-Duc and Ruskin by recommending minimal interventions that did not alter a building's physiognomy.[4] Gustavo Giovannoni, who followed Boito's path in the early twentieth century, created Italy's first national architectural conservation legislation, which in turn laid the groundwork for the Athens Charter, the first effort to address philosophies and techniques for the protection of monuments with an international perspective.[5] (See Chapter 14.)

International Appeals

Over the past century, popular interest in, and concern for, conserving historic architecture and related cultural heritage in foreign places has broadened to include a wide variety of individuals, special interest groups, and nations. Early examples of voluntary private and public participation in international heritage conservation assistance include architects being sent to Demre in southern Anatolia by Czar Alexander II to restore St. Nicholas Church in 1860s, and the joint 1903 purchase of the Keats-Shelley House in Rome by the three national committees (from London, Rome, and New York) of the Keats-Shelley Memorial Association, after years of fund-raising on both sides of the Atlantic.[6]

Post–World War I restoration efforts at the Palace of Versailles, which began as a single soldier's rescue efforts, sparked the interest of American philanthropist John D. Rockefeller Jr., who sponsored much of the restoration in the 1930s. After World War II,

organizations such as the Samuel H. Kress Foundation in New York City supported many restoration works, including projects in France and Italy. These examples of international private aid to monuments are additions to the tremendous local and national efforts at rebuilding and restoring war-damaged monuments and cities in Europe, the Mediterranean region, and East Asia, some of which are still underway.

In the latter half of the twentieth century, these efforts were increasingly joined by many private, nongovernmental, quasi-nongovernmental, and intergovernmental initiatives around the world, both organized and informal, that sought to protect the world's significant architectural and artistic patrimony. (See Appendix B: "Organizations and Resources Relating to International Architectural Conservation.") But it was two specific international appeals during the 1960s to protect sites threatened by both humanity and nature that markedly raised global awareness of the issue.

In 1960, Egyptian and Sudanese plans to construct a second, much higher dam at Aswan on the Nile River threatened to submerge numerous important ancient Nubian and Egyptian monuments and archaeological sites, including Pharaoh Rameses II's famous temple, Abu Simbel. The damming of the river would have allowed its waters to irrigate a greater area of land than did its seasonal floods. The determination of these two countries to modernize at the cost of losing numerous historic buildings and sites along the river's edge raised an international outcry.

▲ **Figure 15-1** Early examples of voluntary private and public participation in international architectural conservation assistance include Czar Alexander II sending architects to Demre, in southern Anatolia, to restore St. Nicholas Church in the 1860s.

▶ **Figure 15-2** The rebuilding of the Santa Trinità Bridge in Florence after its destruction during World War II was sponsored by the Samuel H. Kress Foundation in New York City, which has funded hundreds of European architectural conservation projects since.

In order to save the ancient treasures, Vittorino Veronese, the director general of the United Nations Educational, Scientific and Cultural Organization (UNESCO) at the time, launched the first major concerted international technical assistance effort and financial appeal to assist in the rescue of endangered cultural heritage. His words (page 245) went far toward defining the modern concept of universal heritage.

By most measures, the international campaign to rescue monuments along the Upper Nile was a success. It saved more than twenty structures in Egypt and four in Sudan[7] and launched UNESCO as an organizer of international appeals for highly important cultural heritage sites. But while this impressive feat caught the world's attention, it did not generate sufficient funding to cover the conservation of all deserving sites. Nonetheless, the publicity generated by the Aswan rescue operations opened the way for other similar international participatory actions.

◀ **Figure 15-3** The inundation of scores of ancient Egyptian and Nubian monuments along the Upper Nile by the construction of the Aswan High Dam posed an urgent crisis that had public resonance in the early 1960s. Colossal statues of Rameses II, seen here in the process of being disassembled, were reconstructed at the top of a high plateau overlooking Lake Nasser, shown in the photo's background. *(Photo: AFP)*

▼ **Figure 15-4** The ancient temple of Abu Simbel in the process of reconstruction. As an expression of appreciation to countries that contributed to the Nubian rescue effort, the Egyptian government gave orphaned temple buildings to key donors, including Spain and the United States. *(Photos: AFP/RIA Novosti)*

Figure 15-5 The flooding of Venice on November 4, 1966. *(Photo: AFP)*

Wondrous structures, ranking among the most magnificent on earth, are in danger of disappearing. It is not easy to choose from a heritage of the past and the present for the well-being of a people. It is not easy to choose between temples and crops. These monuments, the loss of which may be tragically near, do not belong solely to the countries, which hold them in trust. The whole world has a right to see them endure. They are the Ajanta frescoes, the walls of Uxmal, and Beethoven's symphonies. Treasures of universal value are entitled to universal protection.[8] *(Vitorino Veranese)*

Only a few years later, on November 4, 1966, Venice was flooded with polluted water as a result of high tides exacerbated by strong northerly winds from the Adriatic Sea. The *acqua alta* ("high-water") level of just over 6 feet (194 centimeters) reached during that flood remains a record. The resulting devastation to Venetian architecture and art, and the damage sustained by Florentine treasures by the coincidental flooding of the Arno River, were so grave they stimulated international relief efforts on an unprecedented scale. Again, UNESCO made an international appeal for help, which resulted in the establishment of an international contribution network to facilitate the channeling of funds to Venice.[9] The International Campaign for the Safeguarding of Venice offered a three-way cooperative scheme between UNESCO, some nineteen national and international private organizations, and the local organs of the Italian Ministry of Culture, known as *soprintendente* ("superintendencies"). The arrangement led to the restoration and conservation of more than one hundred historic buildings and one thousand works of art.

Figures 15-6, 15-7, and 15-8 The restoration of the façade of the fifteenth-century Church of Madonna dell'Orto by the Venice in Peril Fund (Great Britain), with details of the statue of St. Christopher before and after conservation. *(Courtesy Venice in Peril)*

The Venice in Peril Fund was one of several conservation relief efforts initiated shortly after the floods by the former British ambassador to Italy, Sir Ashley Clarke, to help both Venice and Florence; however, it primarily concentrated its efforts on Venetian religious and artistic works.[10] The fund still finances work carried out by specialists in the *soprintendente* of fine arts and monuments, who work under partnership oversight by UNESCO's Venice office and Italy's Ministry of Culture. Its aims and methods were emulated by several other international relief efforts, one of which—the International Fund for Monuments, later named the World Monuments Fund—matured to be a leader in architectural heritage protection on a worldwide basis.[11]

International Agreements and Conferences

Almost a century earlier than the Nubian and Venetian rescue appeals, some European countries were developing cultural heritage protection measures because of concerns for another type of threat—civil conflict. In 1874 in Brussels, Czar Alexander II of Russia convened the first international conference to discuss the wartime treatment of civilians and civilian property, including cultural heritage sites. The declaration issued by the conference argued that culture was the common heritage of humankind and noted the irreplaceability of artistic treasures.[12]

The ideas discussed in Brussels were formalized in two international agreements negotiated in The Hague in 1899 and 1907. Soon thereafter, however, whole regions of Europe's architectural patrimony suffered widespread destruction during World War I, revealing the complete failure of these declarations.[13] Even the deployment of special officers to identify and protect cultural property, which the German army initiated in response to the public outcry caused by the destruction of the library at the Catholic University of Leuven in Belgium and the bombardment of Reims Cathedral in France, was not enough.[14]

Figures 15-9 and 15-10 Acts of *preventative conservation* from World War I aerial bombing are seen in the installation of sandbags within a timber frame used to protect Michelangelo's *David* in Florence and the façade of St. Mark's Basilica in Venice from threat. (*Photographs A. W. Van Buren, 1914*)

Figures 15-11 a and b Extensive damage to hundreds of cities and millions of buildings during World War II forced an assessment of choices: restoration or all-new construction. Gdansk, Poland, chose careful restoration and replication where necessary; Le Havre, France (seen here), chose to build anew, either in the radically modern forms designed by Auguste Perret (bottom) or by constructing replacement buildings that approximated the geometry of those that had been lost (top). The carefully reconstructed façades of the Długi Targ (Long Market) in Gdansk (opposite page) revealed the preferred solution by its citizens and planners for returning the city to its prewar appearance.

In 1931, a multinational symposium on the protection of important historic monuments was held in Athens; it established architectural conservation principles that should be recognized internationally. Rather than simply calling for protection, the Athens Charter focused on the need for closer cooperation among nations and the formation of a forum through which technical information and successful experiences could be shared. Importantly, the charter advised the protection of historic buildings not be just a matter of individual concern: The general public had a right to learn about shared cultural heritage and should take an active role in its protection.

The Athens Charter was drafted in turbulent political and social times. A world economic depression was followed by World War II, which was much more destructive than World War I. Much of Europe was left in ruins: In France alone, nearly 460,000 buildings were destroyed and 15 percent of its listed historic buildings were damaged.[15] Numerous cities in eastern China, Japan, and Southeast Asia were damaged or completely destroyed. In the years immediately following World War II, most countries faced rapid changes because of mechanization and new economic conditions.

While there was serious concern in heritage conservation circles over how war-torn countries would ultimately restore and rebuild their cities, the implementation of postwar rebuilding efforts was often hindered by a lack of funds and focus. Most countries initially allocated the bulk of their limited resources to meeting basic survival and economic recovery needs. Measured against these, the restoration and preservation of historic buildings and sites were usually low priorities. In many countries, the spirit of the time demanded a brighter future based on a need for growth, improved health and education, and an all-around fresh start, rather than on protection of the vestiges of the past. Mass housing and industrial-scale prefabrication were the prevailing modes of postwar construction. Where restorations of historic buildings were undertaken, scientifically based methodologies were among the myriad approaches used, although more expedient rehabilitation measures were usually favored.[16]

▼ **Figure 15-12** Długi Targ (Long Market) Square in Gdansk, Poland, after its complete reconstruction in the 1950s.

In 1954, the turn-of-the-century Hague Conventions were revisited as a result of the extensive destruction of buildings and museum collections during World War II. Based on the earlier precedent, UNESCO organized the drafting of the *Convention for the Protection of Cultural Property in the Event of Armed Conflict*. This immensely influential document, known since as the (revised) Hague Convention, was quickly adopted by 102 states.[17]

The beginning of the present era, when the specialty of architectural conservation practice came into being as a bona fide profession, was marked by an international conference in Venice in 1964. Six hundred representatives from sixty-one countries assembled to discuss issues in architectural conservation and best practices in various parts of the world. As detailed in Chapter 9, one goal of the conference was to produce a charter of conservation principles to supersede those stated in the Athens Charter of 1931.

The International Charter for the Conservation and Restoration of Monuments and Sites, known as the Venice Charter, was drafted by a committee made up of nineteen Europeans, two Latin Americans, one Arab, and one Asian. The Venice Charter assumes that it is "essential that the principles guiding the preservation and restoration of ancient buildings should be agreed and be laid down on an international basis, with each country being responsible for applying the plan within the framework of its own culture and traditions."[18]

Since 1964, the Venice Charter has largely defined the path of architectural conservation throughout the world. Many countries have adopted it, partially or wholly, in various forms. While in the ensuing years there have been numerous additional charters and declarations since its inception—some in reaction against it—the Venice Charter has served as the "datum point."[19] The 1964 Venice Conference marked the birth of the influential International Council on Monuments and Sites (ICOMOS), which among its many duties ever since has been to serve as the principle convener of professionals in architectural conservation and several of its allied professions and disciplines. (See below and Appendix C.)

Over nearly the past half century, most of the charters, declarations, and information dissemination efforts that have enriched the architectural conservation field were produced under the aegis of ICOMOS and its parent organization, UNESCO. The notion of protective inventory, which was first discussed and articulated in the 1965 Palma Recommendation, drafted in Barcelona, developed into a system that has been widely used ever since. That same year in Vienna, conference delegates focused on the reanimation of buildings that had lost their original function.[20] The Bath Conference, held in 1966 in England, looked to define principles and methods of conservation more specifically with the help of members who were specialists in architectural conservation practice. Its discussions mostly addressed British systems of heritage protection, both public and private.

France's 1967 conference in Strasbourg on protecting the county's architectural patrimony is notable for the comprehensive view it took on all architectural conservation issues related to regional and town planning. A highlight of that conference was an analysis of the shortcomings of the protection of Paris's Marais quarter and the presentation of several unprecedented ideas for its conservation and revitalization. A year later, the scope of the Marais district examination was further enlarged at a conference in Avignon entitled "Protection and Reanimation of Sites."

Provisions within the 1954 Hague Convention later led to the development of the UNESCO Convention on the Means of Prohibiting and Preventing the Illicit Import, Export and Transfer of Ownership of Cultural Property in 1970. In 1972, UNESCO's Seventeenth General Conference in Paris followed this with the adoption of the Convention concerning the Protection of the World Cultural and Natural Heritage, which by 2007 has been ratified by over 180 states. This document precisely defines *world cultural and*

International conferences like those held by ICOMOS are the main means of communication among international architectural conservation practitioners. Each conference usually has a main theme. Proposed papers are accepted via a peer-review process; specialty-group meetings are held, and often a declaration is made relation to a particular challenge faced in the field.

Since the 1964 UNESCO conference in Venice—the most influential of all meetings in architectural conservation—scores of additional UNESCO and ICOMOS meetings and other similar gatherings have marked progress in the field. In Barcelona in 1965, the notion of the protective inventory was first discussed and articulated and has since become a widely used tool. That same year, a conference in Vienna focused for the first time on adaptive reuse, which was increasingly becoming a method of saving historic buildings. French conferences in 1967 in Strasbourg and in Avignon in 1968 comprehensively viewed conservation within the context of regional and town planning and encouraged more architectural conservation, neighborhood revitalization, and the reanimation of sites. The Brussels Conference of 1969 launched plans for the European Architectural Heritage Year in 1975, a seminal event in instigating Europe-wide cooperation in the conservation of architectural heritage.

The conferences producing these documents were initially centered on European practice, but they quickly expanded to encompass a wider geographic area and broader conservation concerns. ICOMOS has facilitated a series of declarations addressing different types of heritage with a more global perspective, including the 1981 Florence Charter on historic gardens and landscapes as well as specialized charters for historic towns and urban areas in 1987; for archaeological heritage in 1990; for underwater cultural heritage in 1996; for cultural tourism, historic timber structures, and vernacular heritage in 1999; and for structural restoration and wall paintings in 2003.

In addition, more regionally appropriate charters for non-Western heritage concerns in specific places have been developed in recent years, including ICOMOS Australia's Burra Charter in 1979, ICOMOS New Zealand's 1993 Aotearoa Charter (later termed its Charter for the Conservation of Places of Cultural Heritage Value), and ICOMOS China's Principles for the Conservation of Heritage Sites in China (the China Principles) in 2002, to name a few of the most important. The 1994 Nara Document on Authenticity, developed by ICOMOS professionals at a conference in Nara, Japan, reexamined the World Heritage Convention; it is another important contribution to codifying non-Western approaches to conservation by promoting cultural diversity and focusing on intangible heritage.

natural heritage and stipulates the guiding principles for its implementation. The 1972 World Heritage Convention and its signature program, the World Heritage List, serves as an international standard whose far-reaching influence has been admirably implemented by UNESCO on a global scale. (See Appendix B.)

The Brussels Conference of 1969 set among its goals an important international event—European Architectural Heritage Year in 1975. This precedent-setting program instigated Europe-wide cooperation in conserving architectural heritage, in part because it proffered that the benefits of architectural conservation could outweigh the costs. This topic served as the theme of the 1974 Bologna Conference.

The Amsterdam Declaration, adopted in 1975 as part of the European Architectural Heritage Year, outlined a series of principles concerning the conservation of historic properties and led to the recognition that architectural conservation was an integral part of urban planning and land development. It also established legal and administrative measures for the successful implementation of conservation initiatives. In 1977 ICOMOS adopted the Granada Declaration, which addressed issues pertaining specifically to the protection of rural cultural heritage environments. Since then, scores of additional conferences, usually addressing specialty themes, have been held in various locations throughout the world.[21] (See Appendix C.)

INTERNATIONAL AGENCIES AND FRAMEWORKS

Along with the codification of principles and procedures for architectural conservation via charters, declarations, and agreements, numerous national government agencies and organizations have played increasingly important roles in the conservation of cultural heritage. Since the 1960s many nongovernmental organizations (NGOs) and quasi-governmental organizations (QUANGOs) have emerged to assist in the effort.

UNESCO and Its Affiliates

The United Nations Educational, Scientific and Cultural Organization came into existence as an agency of the United Nations in 1945, in the aftermath of World War II. It was founded by thirty-seven countries "to contribute to peace and security by promoting collaboration among nations through education, science and culture in order to further universal respect for justice, for the rule of law and for the human rights and fundamental freedoms which are affirmed for the peoples of the world, without distinction of race, sex, language or religion, by the Charter of the United Nations."[22]

One of UNESCO's initial tasks was a direct response to the devastation incurred during the recently ended war. It was entrusted with "the conservation and protection of the world's inheritance of books, works of arts and monuments of history and science."[23] This mission was strengthened by its ratification by twenty additional countries the following year. Then in 1946, the International Council of Museums (ICOM) was founded in Paris within the purview of UNESCO. The ICOM's Documentation Centre at UNESCO's Parisian headquarters has since served as a principal resource center for museums all around the world.

Both UNESCO and ICOM began operating at a time when art looted during World War II was being repatriated, much of Asia and Africa was being decolonized, and conscious efforts were being expended to reestablish national and cultural identities. Since much of UNESCO's early work in these areas pertained to movable heritage, cooperation between the two agencies was mutually beneficial.

This support network was further strengthened in 1949 when UNESCO established an International Committee on Monuments, thereby expanding its practical efforts to protect the world's most significant immovable cultural heritage, a responsibility within its broad mandate. UNESCO's missions in architectural conservation began in 1951, when a team of experts from its Monuments Committee traveled to Cuzco, Peru, to assist in postearthquake restoration. Despite UNESCO's preference to advocate for conservation rather than to raise funds for and implement actual projects, the organization's participation triggered a number of important additional rescue operations such as those at Borobodur, Indonesia, and Mohenjo Daro, Pakistan, and more recently at Angkor in Cambodia, Mostar in Bosnia, and various sites in Iraq. The success of UNESCO's first major campaigns was measured by the response that it received from every age group and nationality and tested the organization's effectiveness at mobilizing global attention and resources toward seriously threatened sites. Because it is limited to the power of persuasion, UNESCO's ability to realize its goals is very much dependent on popular support and member state cooperation.[24] Unfortunately, not every international appeal made by UNESCO to save threatened world heritage has succeeded. The most widely publicized recent failure of international organizations to protect a site concerned Bamiyan, Afghanistan's colossal, rock-hewn Buddha sculptures. Despite the mobilization of global interests and UNESCO's sensitive and valiant attempts to influence a different course of action, these irreplaceable artifacts were destroyed by the Taliban regime in March 2001.

Having done so much to illustrate the possibilities of international collaboration early on, UNESCO continues to be the major force among today's various global heritage conservation initiatives. Through its periodic gatherings of international cultural heritage institutions and professionals, the accomplishments of the Word Heritage List, and its assistance in a wide spectrum of training and activities that build awareness about heritage conservation, UNESCO has defined an operational framework and an important point of reference for the cultural heritage conservation field. UNESCO instigated many of the cultural heritage charters discussed previously and together with ICOM and ICOMOS has led the way in establishing principles and procedures in international cultural heritage conservation practice.

At the Ninth UNESCO General Conference in New Delhi in 1956, the need for an international center for the study, preservation, and restoration of cultural properties was discussed. An intergovernmental organization was established in 1959 in Rome to meet this need. It was first known as the Rome Center and later labeled the International Centre for the Study of the Preservation and Restoration of the Conservation of Cultural Property (ICCROM).[25]

ICCROM's primary task is to create an active worldwide network of conservation experts and specialized institutions. It has focused its attention on the multidisciplinary collaboration of archaeologists, architects, planners, curators, materials conservators, educators, and others. From the early 1960s until 2000, it offered short-term courses in the conservation of historic towns and buildings, materials conservation, and other specialized topics. Since then ICCROM has served more as a locus for specialized international meetings on a wide variety of heritage conservation subjects, though in 2006 its renowned architectural conservation overview was reinstituted in the form a shorter program offered biennially. In addition, ICCROM's library continues to be the largest collection of titles on art and architectural conservation in the world.[26] (See also "International Training in Architectural Conservation," page 272.)

The International Council on Monuments and Sites (ICOMOS) was formed in 1965 as a result of the same Congress of Architects and Specialists of Historic Buildings that drafted the Venice Charter. ICOMOS is dedicated to promoting the application of theory, methodology, and scientific techniques to the conservation of *architectural* and *archaeological heritage*.[27]

As a forum for professional dialogue, ICOMOS organizes international conferences to discuss important issues in the field. In November 1994, an ICOMOS meeting was convened in Nara, Japan, to discuss the loss of local cultural identity that accompanies globalization and the concomitant issue of conserving the authenticity of heritage sites. The resulting Nara Document on Authenticity recognized that:

In a world that is increasingly subject to the forces of globalization and homogenization, and in a world in which the search for cultural identity is sometimes pursued through aggressive nationalism and the suppression of the cultures of minorities, the essential contribution made by the consideration of authenticity in conservation practice is to clarify and illuminate the collective memory of humanity.[28]

Since its creation in 1965, ICOMOS has replaced the Committee on Monuments as UNESCO's principal advisor on principles, policies, and techniques that apply to the conservation and protection historic towns, buildings, engineering works, archaeological sites, historic gardens, cultural landscapes, and endangered intangible heritage. It also plays a vital role in identifying and preparing documentation of nominations to UNESCO's World Heritage List. ICOMOS, like UNESCO, is based in Paris but operates through a global network of local offices and national committees.

The World Heritage List

In 1972 UNESCO created its famous institutional charter known as the World Heritage Convention. Among its principal functions is to identify cultural and natural sites of outstanding significance and universal value as candidates for inclusion on UNESCO's World Heritage List. It is the responsibility of individual countries that are party to the

Figure 15-13 UNESCO's Asia-Pacific Heritage Awards for Cultural Heritage Conservation program began in 2000. Through 2007, it has recognized the excellence of 97 projects chosen from 266 entries made by 23 countries. One winner of the 2005 Award of Distinction was the Shaxi historic town conservation project in western Yunnan Province, China, which benefited from a number of local, national, and international technical and financial partnerships. The main building fronting the Sideng Market Square of Shaxi is seen here after its restoration. Contained within is a modest museum that explains the Horse Tea Route that brought Shaxi its wealth in the past. *(Photo courtesy Ralph Feiner)*

convention to nominate sites within their borders for consideration. (For details on the criteria for inclusion on the World Heritage List, see "Types of Value or Significance" in Chapter 3.) In addition to national legal protection measures, sites placed on the World Heritage List are monitored by UNESCO and are thus symbolically placed under the general protection of the international community as humanity's common heritage. The convention also promotes international cooperation and mutual support in the safeguarding of this shared heritage and urges all peoples to assist in the cause through a variety of educational measures, including the Universities and Heritage Program (in collaboration with the International Union of Architects), the Asia-Pacific Heritage Awards for Cultural Heritage Conservation, and UNESCO's subvention of training programs at ICCROM.

The World Heritage List is developed and maintained by the intergovernmental World Heritage Committee, based at UNESCO's World Heritage Centre in Paris. The Committee consists of twenty-one member states elected by those that are party to the World Heritage Convention. It implements a variety of heritage protection advocacy activities throughout the year and holds an annual meeting that aims to:

1. Evaluate properties that have been nominated for World Heritage List consideration and submit to the Representative Assembly of States Parties a select list for their review and acceptance. Following the assembly's decision, an updated World Heritage List is published.

2. Manage the World Heritage Fund, including the examination and approval of states parties' applications for financial and technical assistance.[29]

3. Monitor the state of conservation and management of each cultural and natural property inscribed on the World Heritage List in order to promote improvement of the work.

V ROCE 1992 BYLO HISTORICKÉ JÁDRO MĚSTA TELČE ZAPSÁNO
ORGANIZACÍ SPOJENÝCH NÁRODŮ PRO ŠKOLSTVÍ VĚDU A KULTURU
-UNESCO- DO SEZNAMU SVĚTOVÉHO DĚDICTVÍ. TÍMTO ZÁPISEM
UZNALO MEZINÁRODNÍ SPOLEČENSTVÍ VYJÍMEČNOU KULTURNÍ HODNOTU
TÉTO PAMÁTKY A PROHLÁSILO JI ZA SOUČÁST KULTURNÍHO DĚDICTVÍ
NÁRODŮ SVĚTA V JEJICHŽ ZÁJMU SE TATO PAMÁTKA TĚŠÍ OCHRANĚ
V DUCHU MEZINÁRODNÍ ÚMLUVY O OCHRANĚ SVĚTOVÉHO KULTURNÍHO
DĚDICTVÍ.

EN 1992 LE CENTRE HISTORIQUE DE LA VILLE DE TELČ A ÉTÉ INSCRIT
PAR L'ORGANISATION DES NATIONS UNIES POUR L'ÉDUCATION, LA
SCIENCE ET LA CULTURE -UNESCO- SUR LA LISTE DU PATRIMOINE
MONDIAL. PAR CET ACTE LA COMMUNAUTÉ INTERNATIONALE A RECONNU
L'EXCEPTIONNELLE VALEUR CULTURELLE DE CET ENSEMBLE ET L'A
PROCLAMÉ PARTIE INTÉGRANTE DU PATRIMOINE CULTUREL DES NATIONS
DU MONDE. C'EST DANS LEUR INTÉRÊT QUE CET ENSEMBLE EST PROTÉGÉ
PAR LA CONVENTION INTERNATIONALE CONCERNANT LA PROTECTION DU
PATRIMOINE MONDIAL CULTUREL ET NATUREL.

THE HISTORIC CENTER OF TELČ WAS ADDED BY THE UNITED NATIONS
EDUCATIONAL, SCIENTIFIC AND CULTURAL ORGANIZATION -UNESCO-
TO THE WORLD HERITAGE LIST IN 1992. THE INTERNATIONAL COMMUNITY
THUS RECOGNIZED THE EXCEPTIONAL VALUE OF THIS SITE AND DECLARED
IT A PART OF CULTURAL HERITAGE OF THE NATIONS OF THE WORLD
IN THE INTEREST OF WHICH THIS SITE IS PROTECTED BY VIRTUE
OF THE CONVENTION CONCERNING THE PROTECTION OF THE WORLD
CULTURAL AND NATURAL HERITAGE.

Figure 15-14 The World Heritage List plaque, posted on the town hall of Telč, Czech Republic.

To heighten its capacity to protect, evaluate, monitor, and provide technical assistance at these sites, UNESCO and the World Heritage Committee engage ICCROM, ICOMOS, and the International Union for Conservation of Nature and Natural Resources (IUCN) to act as advisory bodies. ICCROM advises chiefly in areas concerning technical training, research, and documentation pertaining to artistic and cultural heritage; ICOMOS in the field of cultural heritage in particular architecture and its allied fields; and IUCN in the field of natural heritage protection.

As of January 2008 there were 851 sites on the World Heritage List: 660 are cultural, 166 are natural, and 25 are mixed cultural and natural properties (including cultural landscapes).[30] The sites are spread over 141 of the 184 countries that are state parties to the convention. Despite recent efforts to include more sites in underrepresented regions such as Africa, one-third of the sites on the World Heritage List are located in Europe.

The World Heritage Convention divides built cultural heritage into three types based on size and volume: single buildings, groups of buildings, and sites that encompass vast areas of buildings and their environs. According to Article 1 of the convention:

1. Monuments are defined as "architectural works, works of monumental sculpture and painting, elements or structures of an archaeological nature, inscriptions, cave dwellings and combinations of features, which are of outstanding universal value from the point of view of history, art or science."

2. Groups of buildings are defined as "groups of separate or connected buildings that, because of their architecture, their homogeneity, or their place in the landscape, are of outstanding universal value from the point of view of history or science."

3. Sites are defined as "works of man or the combined works of nature and man, and areas including archaeological sites, which are of outstanding universal value from the historical, aesthetic, ethnological, or anthropological points of view."[31]

In addition to the World Heritage List, the World Heritage Committee prepares and publishes the List of World Heritage in Danger, which includes World Heritage sites that are threatened by serious and specific dangers owing to development, armed conflicts, improper management, or natural disasters. A trust fund established under the convention sometimes serves to meet immediate conservation needs of these properties.

The World Heritage List is one of the most effective tools ever devised to protect humanity's and nature's greatest surviving wonders, though the added recognition and valorization given to World Heritage sites by listing and the related publicity has proven to be a double-edged sword in some cases: In a number of instances, World Heritage listing has placed additional stress on heritage sites from increased visitation resulting from their new status. To obviate future problems, a condition was added in 2002 to the nomination process: Each candidate site's application must now be accompanied by a carefully developed conservation plan that addresses such issues.

OTHER REGIONAL AND INTERNATIONAL ORGANIZATIONS

Since its founding in 1949, the Council of Europe has been interested in European reconstruction and revitalization. Over the years, it has become increasingly focused on architectural conservation and on promoting cooperation in heritage policies and technical assistance among its forty-seven member states. In 1963, its Consultative Assembly decided to forego its traditional advisory role and become more proactive in heritage conservation matters, and it has convened numerous conferences on heritage conservation attended by European experts. The resulting conference proceedings represent a wealth of scholarship and thinking on Europe's heritage conservation movement, the challenges it faces, and the solutions that have been proposed. One of the many outcomes of these conferences was the organization of a pan-European administrative apparatus for heritage conservation called the Technical Cooperation and Field Action Unit.

In the 1970s the Council of Europe adopted a number of declarations to formalize its principles and to guide its approaches to cultural heritage protection, including the previously mentioned Amsterdam and Granada Declarations. The council was very active in developing an action plan for Bosnia and Herzegovina following the civil conflicts that laid waste to entire historic towns and countless historic buildings in that country during the early 1990s.

In 1991 the Council of Europe officially launched its highly successful annual program, European Heritage Days, with the support of the European Commission (EC). This initiative became a joint action of the council and the EC in 1999. Throughout Europe, during a weekend in September, European Heritage Days makes numerous historic buildings, sites, and other forms of cultural heritage more accessible to the public with the aim of presenting their shared cultural heritage and encouraging their active involvement in safeguarding it. Annual themes vary in each country and have in the past included such topics as specific forms of heritage (e.g., farmhouses, musical instruments, culinary traditions, garden architecture); specific historic periods (e.g., medieval or baroque heritage); and social approaches to heritage (e.g., heritage and citizenship, heritage and youth). The European Heritage Days initiative has been extremely successful: all forty-nine state parties to the European Cultural Convention actively take part in it. In 2008, the number of annual visitors was estimated to be twenty million at more than thirty thousand participating heritage sites and programs.

The liaison office for European Heritage Days since 2007 has been Europa Nostra, a private sector advocacy group established in 1963. Europa Nostra promotes the protection of Europe's architectural and landscape heritage through annual conferences and helps increase global awareness of conservation excellence by awarding highly sought-after citations for outstanding achievements in restoration and preservation. As with the Council of

Figure 15-15 The award of the Europa Nostra Medal in 1989 to the Landcommanderij Alden Biesen in Bilzen, Belgium, was presented for the restoration and adaptive use of the former "land commandery" as a cultural center. His Majesty King Baudouin of Belgium is unveiling the plaque marking the medal award in the company of Hans de Koster, then President of Europa Nostra. Since 2002, Europa Nostra's excellence in heritage conservation awards have been extended on behalf of the Council of Europe as well. *(Photo courtesy of Europa Nostra)*

Europe, its purview radically expanded after the collapse of the Soviet Union, when newly independent states looked to it for help in overseeing heritage conservation on their territories. Today Europa Nostra brings together more than 220 heritage organizations, 100 regional and local authorities, and 1,300 individual members committed to the protection and enhancement of Europe's built and natural heritage. Its broad scope of activities ranges from focused, in-depth scientific studies on military architecture to the administration of the EC's European Union Prize for Cultural Heritage, which recognizes best practices in European heritage conservation.

Other key players in the international architectural conservation field include a number of nongovernmental organizations such as the Getty Conservation Institute, the World Monuments Fund, the Aga Khan Trust for Culture, and Cultural Heritage without Borders. (See Appendix B for a description of organizations and numerous others active in the field.) Each of these organizations helps to increase international understanding about the importance of cultural heritage protection, and all occasionally collaborate with UNESCO—often with impressive results, such as in the former Yugoslavia and at Angkor since the mid-1990s. In addition, the global attention paid to the World Monuments Fund's biennial Watch™ List of the World's 100 Most Endangered Sites has raised awareness of—and often substantial funding for—many of the threatened sites it has featured. The significance of the World Monuments Watch™ program was realized not long after its inception in 1996 by noted *New York Times* architectural critic Herbert Muschamp, who appraised the first list as being "an extremely important document, much more than a plea to protect history. It is itself history: a record of the growth of consciousness in a shrinking world."[32]

Toward the end of the last millennium, the World Bank led one of the most promising initiatives in the field of cultural heritage conservation. The credo of former chairman James O. Wolfensohn was that since culture was the one thing that all peoples of the world have in common, recognition of its richness and diversity should be a priority as the economies and cultures of the world become increasingly globalized. Wolfensohn's approach, which was adopted by the World Bank, was called the Comprehensive Development Program (CDF). Its significance lay in essentializing culture and identity as elements of a more holistic development approach. In its efforts to aid economic development, the World Bank realized that it needed to perform planning that took into consid-

Figure 15-16 The cover of the first *Watch™ List of the 100 Most Endangered Sites,* a program of the World Monuments Fund launched in 1996.

eration both financial viability and the protection of each site's historic integrity, provide financial and technical support, create partnerships with other organizations, and support physical interventions that were sensitive to the locales that it was supporting. With this focus in mind, the World Bank funded urban conservation projects at Lahore, Pakistan, the medina in Fez, Morocco, the historic district in Tunis, and several other places. (The accomplishments of the World Bank in urban conservation during the period from 1995 to 2000, with explanations of its rationale and the approaches it used, are well presented in *Historic Cities and Sacred Sites: Cultural Roots for Urban Futures* [2001]).

Although the World Bank's initial enthusiasm for Chairman Wolfensohn's ambition to seek out and actively support heritage conservation projects has waned, the bank has retained a sense of heightened awareness of the importance of cultural heritage protection in its various aid programs. Loans from the World Bank have addressed these concerns since the late 1990s, and its emphasis today is on sustainable development that considers cultural heritage protection.

▲ **Figure 15-17** The World Bank's support of infrastructure improvement, selected building conservation projects, and an array of social aid programs in Fez, Morocco, in the late 1990s, represents the tremendous benefits of international funding for large-scale heritage conservation projects. Seen here are delegates to a World Bank–sponsored conference in Beijng, 4 July 2000, that addressed urban conservation challenges and opportunities in the People's Republic of China.

▶ **Figure 15-18** The State Administration for Cultural Heritage (Xi'an) and the World Monuments Fund (New York) have separately provided both financial and technical assistance toward the restoration of the Bogd Khan Summer Palace in Ulaanbaatar, Mongolia. The palace's north gate, said to be constructed with 108 different wood joints, was restored by SACH (Xi'an) in 2007.

Working at a more regional scale are subsidiaries of the World Bank and similar organizations, such as the European Bank for Reconstruction and Development, the Inter-American Development Bank, and the Asian Development Bank. Each has proficiencies for assisting in heritage protection, especially in relation to infrastructure improvements for historic urban areas.

Some wealthier countries participate in international heritage conservation projects through extraordinary financial support via their membership in UNESCO or through direct country-to-country assistance schemes. Spain, Sweden, Germany, France, Italy, Japan, and (more recently) China have generously supported architectural conservation projects in other countries. In some cases, there have been historic ties linking the two countries; in other cases, there have been none.[33]

EUROPEAN HERITAGE CONSERVATION PRINCIPLES ABROAD: ACTION AND REACTION[34]

Europeans have long been involved in architectural conservation in distant parts of the world, bringing the principles they developed to very different contexts and cultures. One positive result has been that methods developed for researching and documenting historic buildings have tended to create similar approaches in international conservation practice, something than can fairly be judged to be helpful since there are so many obstacles to the task. Much of this evolution has occurred in tandem with developments in international affairs over the past two centuries, via the European colonization of relatively undevel-

Figures 15-19 and 15-20 The Taj Mahal, completed in 1653, was in disrepair and had been pillaged for its easily reached semiprecious stone inlay until measures were taken to restore this icon of Mughal art in the early 1900s by the Archaeological Survey of India.

Figure 15-21 The National History Museum in Hanoi, Vietnam, housed in the former archaeological research institute of the École Française d'Extréme Orient, also serves a lasting legacy of international cultural heritage research, documentation, and conservation from the era of French Indochina.

oped places or through the permissions and concessions granted to European researchers and their subsequent assistance efforts. In the majority of cases, those promoting cultural heritage protection and conservation abroad found themselves accommodating the interests and resources of their foreign counterparts, often having little choice other than to include builders and craftspeople who were more knowledgeable about local building traditions—and getting things done in those locales.

In many instances, international assistance helped safeguard historic structures from certain loss and initiate the organization of useful cultural heritage management systems in foreign countries. Two early examples are Great Britain's Archaeological Survey of India (ASI), which was established in 1814, and the École Française de l'Extréme-Orient (French School of Asian Studies) network, which began throughout French Indochina in the 1890s.

The various administrations, resources, and methodologies introduced by Europeans into their colonies were often a positive force in both local and regional heritage protection efforts, having a notable, long-lasting impact in India, Cambodia, Vietnam, and Laos. The Archaeological Survey of India continued to carry on its work even after the British departed in 1947 and is currently responsible for the protection of over five thousand monuments. In turn, these agencies have often directly or indirectly served as models for other countries. For example, the British system of legal protection and of listing and conserving monuments in India influenced efforts in Nepal, Pakistan, Bangladesh, and Sri Lanka. The French system of consolidating responsibility for museums and monuments as separate but equal branches under one ministry of culture is a model used by many countries.

The melding of international and local interests in issues of architectural heritage protection invariably highlights questions of cultural sensitivity, rights, and "ownership of the past." Adding to the complexity of the question of the true benefits of outside assistance in architectural heritage protection is that surviving traditional cultures usually had repair and maintenance techniques for their buildings in place. Thus, the need for outside help is merited in four principal situations:

When traditional building repair and preservation techniques are lost and there is a call for outside help in replacing them

When there is a lack of appreciation of the significance of, and commitment to, the sensitive treatment of historic resources

Where locals may be overwhelmed by an extraordinary technical challenge or the size of the task

Where significant financial assistance that is not available locally may be needed.[35] (See also Chapter 7.)

Local Versus International Cultural Values

Although foreign heritage conservation assistance has proved helpful for many thousands of historic sites throughout the world, such actions do not always meet the needs of local populations. Today's heritage conservation profession is comprised of a broad roster of both seasoned and newly trained professionals from all regions of the world representing a plethora of specialties. Such cultural diversity among experts and other key participants has engendered greater cultural sensitivity at all levels of the field's operation. One outcome of this unprecedented cooperation and quantity of activities has been the growing recognition that conservation principles and procedures that serve one part of the world do not necessarily have a global validity. Over the last half century, noticeable trends toward global cultural homogenization, which began through colonization, were being advanced in other ways by the Athens and Venice charters and their progeny, as well as by a host of supranational organizations such as UNESCO, ICOMOS, ICOM, and ICCROM.

In describing the phenomenal spread of global principles and procedures in architectural conservation, Ken Taylor, a visiting fellow at the Australian National University, has argued that by setting international professional standards—world-recognized best practices—these organizations "impose a common stamp on culture across the world... [as] their policies create a logic of global cultural uniformity [by seeking] to impose standards of 'good behavior.'"[36] In the face of such force and cohesion, it is not surprising that for many years local or traditional values that were not part of a cultural mainstream and remained unknown outside of their own community. Taylor points out that universal and global standards can overwhelm local values and practices.[37]

It is with such concerns that various non-European heritage conservation entities and initiatives confidently and effectively began to challenge Eurocentric precepts of heritage conservation practice toward the end of the twentieth century. New documents re-

Figure 15-22 The cover of *The Principles for the Conservation of Heritage Sites in China. (Image courtesy of ICOMOS China)*

vised and supplemented principles stated within the Venice Charter of 1964. Among the most notable are ICOMOS New Zealand's Charter of Aotearoa, ICOMOS Australia's Burra Charter, ICOMOS China's China Principles, and a number of protocols such as Japan's Nara Document on Authenticity, Vietnam's Hoi An Protocols, and UNESCO's 2003 Draft Convention for the Safeguarding of the Intangible Cultural Heritage. Each of these documents challenged conventional thinking about core philosophical issues and has helped move the field forward toward embracing a more relativistic stance on cultural heritage conservation issues.[38]

New initiatives have superseded the shortcomings of old doctrine and are being addressed through a variety of new or supplemental charters and declarations. The dynamism of this continuing trend reflects both the continuing maturation of international cultural heritage conservation practice and its inherent strengths. Diverse cultural values can produce valid but opposing viewpoints about conservation.

Progress on this subject is constant: More recently, several other national and regional guidance protocols have been proposed and codified, including the 2004 Indian National Trust for Cultural Heritage (INTACH) Charter for the Conservation of Unprotected Achitectural Heritage and Sites in India[39] (see below). These developments reflect that today's modern heritage conservationists recognize that the idea of one "universal," globally applicable conservation philosophy is in most respects both fallacious and impossible; tomorrow's will undoubtedly be endowed with myriad initiatives that will support and validate additional value systems of more of the world's countless examples of cultural heritage.

In the mid-nineteenth century, India's colonial rulers attempted to protect what they perceived to be India's valuable national heritage and designated some five thousand major historic buildings and sites as eligible for state protection. This approach, including the establishment of the Archeological Survey of India (ASI) and the Ancient Monuments Act, was a foreign invention that had the practical and well-intentioned aim of protecting cultural and material assets.

Today, more than a half century after the British Raj period ended, the ASI is joined by other cultural and natural heritage protection organizations with similar aims, most notably the Indian National Trust for Cultural Heritage. To the consternation of many, however, modern India's heritage laws and acts still incorporate British architectural conservation principles and procedures—not those that would better address the needs of modern India's cultural mosaic. The same is true for the former English colonial realms of Sri Lanka (formerly Ceylon) and Pakistan.[40]

As the name implies, the 2004 INTACH Charter for the Conservation of Unprotected Architectural Heritage and Sites in India is meant to supplement, through its offering of even broader considerations and standards, the operating regulations of the long-established Archaeological Survey of India. The main aim of the charter is to address the subcontinent's heritage conservation needs beyond the more than five thousand nationally listed monuments under the purview of the ASI. Its text is extensive. It breaks new ground for national charters through its detailed coverage of the rights and roles of indigenous communities in management, education, public awareness, and the heritage protection equation, as well as in how to treat India's less "monumental" architectural heritage. It additionally (and boldly) offers a detailed code of professional commitment and practice that serves a growing need for clear standards of professional conduct as the heritage protection field expands.

The best minds in heritage conservation practice in India and Sri Lanka, along with some invited international experts, produced the INTACH India Charter in the shadow of a nearly one-hundred-year-old existing system. A brief look at how pre-2004 conservation standards and regulations were imposed on the country illustrates how approaching local needs from a foreign perspective may save sites but can also create incomplete and unsatisfactory results, because what is important to one culture may not necessarily be valued in the same way by the other.[41]

Tangible Versus Intangible Heritage

To continue with the example of India: The details of the ways of life, values, and traditions of the subcontinent's indigenous culture—especially those that relate to heritage conservation—are rarely understood by any outsiders except those who have made a conscious effort to do so, such as cultural anthropologists. A formalized conservation approach is generally unnecessary because heritage conservation is essential to ongoing living traditions. The past may be kept alive through storytelling (oral transmission), songs, and performances, as well as by the traditional building and decoration techniques that are passed down from generation to generation. The subsistence economies of most indigenous communities require them to maintain their shelters in order to avoid costly new construction. In such indigenous cultures, a de facto conservation protocol already exists that is very much a part of everyday life.

Because organized heritage protection agencies in India have mostly overlooked the country's large number of rural populations, a sizable section of the country's cultural heritage has been left behind in the country's heritage conservation process, probably because few had the means, or the interest, to effect such action. The reasons given for why outsiders with broader views have become involved there is twofold: India's caste system, and (the more commonly cited reason) because there is so much else to look after in India's vast inheritance of cultural heritage.

This situation has several important implications for today's Indian architectural conservationists. While Western-oriented heritage conservation professionals continue to focus their attention on the country's surviving monumental structures, Indian conservationists now emphasize the continuity of the traditions that created its monuments.[42] As explained by Indian architect, urban planner, and conservation consultant A. G. Krishna Menon, "In the West their conviction is entirely defensive, while in India there is an emerging perception of the conservation ideology providing an alternate strategy for development...[that is] more concerned with improving the quality of life than preserving authenticity."[43] Additionally, heritage and heritage places have until recently been considered only as isolated artifacts that cater to a material culture rather than to India's profound philosophical and spiritual roots. Perimeter fences both protect ASI-listed sites from vandalism and isolate them from the local populace. Neighboring structures were demolished to create the parks that both encircle some listed buildings and further separate them from daily life.

New Zealand's Charter for the Conservation of Places of Cultural Heritage Value addresses one of the most striking examples of how a dominant culture's approach toward material conservation diametrically opposes the needs and desires of an indigenous minority culture. In traditional Maori culture, everything is seen as having a natural life span.

▼ **Figure 15-23** The Maori of New Zealand believe that everything has a life span and nothing should intervene with the natural process of decay and destruction. This late nineteenth-century painting by a European settler is among the few evidences of what Maori architecture looked like. (Rangihaeta's celebrated house on the island of Mana called "Kaitangata" [eat man] by George French Angas; J.W. Giles [lith] Plate 4 1847) *(Image courtesy of the Alexander Turnbull Library, Wellington, New Zealand)*

When that life span has been spent, the person, object, or natural feature must be allowed to deteriorate and return to dust. Western heritage conservation precepts—especially architectural conservation practice—oppose this spiritual law.

The Maori concept of natural reclamation is shared by a number of other traditional cultures that also believe that "any hand-built dwelling must defer to nature's need for reclamation…[and should be] conceived from the outset as part of a seamless dematerialization back into the environment…."[44] Many rural southern African communities approach the idea of conservation and sustainability in ways very different from those of Europeans and North Americans. Their dwelling constructions are not meant to last indefinitely, nor are they expressions of the wealth or status of the owner. Although their transitory, biodegradable earthen and grass huts may sometimes decompose in less than a decade, their mere existence is tangible evidence of something much more enduring: the oral, intergenerational bequest of traditional building methods. The passage of specific skills and building traditions has a greater life span than does the materiality of the object in question; structures fade, but the memory of heritage remains. Tradition is strengthened by the continual need to replenish the community's building stock. When that need no longer exists—if, for example, modern governments provide buildings constructed of modern materials to replace traditional structures—living traditions are lost as established skills and knowledge fade away. To help counter this problem, in Japan the most revered artisans are honored by being designated as "living national heritage." The creative talent and craftsmanship they expend in creating buildings is in some cases considered more important than the structures themselves.

In the words of James Wines, author of *Green Architecture*, "Architecture is one of the most dependable reflections of a civilization's philosophical foundations."[45] Opposition between humanity and nature is a keystone of Western thought. The Christian Bible itself reinforces a Western belief that humanity has dominion over all living things and that the earth has been provided to it for its pleasure and use.[46] In contrast, non-Western religions and tribal belief systems acknowledge humanity's interdependence with the earth and encourage ecological sensitivity.

Asian religions have no hierarchical ranking, or separation, between humankind and nature. And more than in modern cultures, traditional cultures consider a site's original architectural integrity as secondary to its genius loci—its sense of place. Especially for Asian communities, living traditions are not only kept alive but are enhanced and enlivened by dynamic physical changes at a heritage site. For them, a site's authenticity relies on genius loci, which may not be affected by rehabilitating, enlarging, or rebuilding a structure or place.

Harmony with nature is fundamental in many aspects of traditional life, especially throughout Asia and in most underdeveloped rural communities globally. In architecture, the importance of an appropriate interaction with the natural world is ensured by practitioners of feng shui, a philosophical approach that moved from Asia into pockets of Western culture during the 1990s. Time will tell if this is a first step toward introducing an influential new form of interconnectedness with nature into modern, non-Asian, architecture.

Authenticity and Permanence: Material Versus Traditional

Other Asian religions—Taoism, Buddhism, and Hinduism—agree with the Maoris that a building has a life cycle but disagree on the need for deterioration. As South African sustainable development expert Chrisna Du Plessis has argued:

Figure 15-24 The Ise Shrine in Japan's Mei Prefecture has been ritually reconstructed on an adjacent site every twenty years almost without interruption since 690 CE. The entranceway to the complex is seen here.

It is the idea of the temple and the place on which it is built that is sacred and should be preserved. The temple building is just the vehicle for the sacred and therefore this "body" should be allowed to die and the temple reincarnated into a new "body" in accordance with the cycle of life and death.[47]

In light of this differing attitude, material qualities so privileged in the West are not as critical to the concepts of authenticity and permanence in many Eastern cultures. The approach taken by the Shinto devotees of the Ise Shrine compound in Japan's Mie Prefecture illustrate the practical considerations of this viewpoint. Since the complex was built in 690 CE, the Ise temple's *geku* ("outer") and *naiku* ("inner") shrines have been ritually reconstructed on an adjacent plot of land every twenty years[48] in order to keep spiritual ties with the sun goddess Amaterasu Omikami alive. The effort includes renewed productions of the furniture and decorations for the shrines plus more than one thousand newly produced and installed items of sacred treasures and garments. Although this ancient site holds one of Japan's most revered shrines, the "inauthenticity" of its newly constructed buildings by Western definitions probably makes it ineligible for World Heritage consideration under current regulations.[49]

The provocative recent book *Architectural Imitations: Reproductions and Pastiches in East and West*, edited by Wim Denslagen and Niels Gutschow, includes studies on the tradition of continuous reconstruction and architectural copying in various Asian countries and elsewhere. By juxtaposing East Asian case studies in replication and reconstruction with approaches to the same problems in European and other Western countries, this book does much to explain the differences (and similarities) in viewing the past and attitudes toward its protection among the world's different cultural traditions.[50]

▲ **Figure 15-25** The Mogao Caves, Dunhuang, Gansu Province, China. Hundreds of caves containing Buddhist shrines have evidently been repaired, restored, and reconfigured over the nearly fifteen-hundred-year history of the complex. The conservation philosophy at the site today is to stabilize, conserve, and protect while also showing evidence of changes that have taken place over time.

◀ **Figure 15-26** Painted plaster wall decoration within Mogao Cave IV.

In one of the first comparisons of Eastern and Western architectural conservation approaches, Chen Wei and Andreas Aass illustrated the differences by comparing the conservation histories of two of the world's most important works of architecture: the temple complex of Confucius in Qufu, China, and the Acropolis in Athens.[51] Both were built in the fifth century BCE, both reflect significant architectural modifications over time, and both have played pivotal roles in the cultural sensibilities of their respective locales. Today, each is a recognized UNESCO World Heritage site.

The temple complex in Qufu is the largest Confucian temple in the world. It was built around the house in which the great Chinese philosopher Confucius grew up and has expanded into one of China's largest historic architectural complexes, comparable to Beijing's Forbidden City.[52] The idea of impermanence is central to the belief system of Confucianism and carries over into an approach toward architecture.

The Chinese do not emphasize a static permanence in their buildings as did the builders of most of Europe's historic monuments, and therefore few ancient traditional buildings retain their original forms. Over its lifetime, the Qufu complex has been restored, rebuilt, or enlarged some thirty-seven times—a Western definition of authenticity does not apply. While its architectural details have changed, however, its genius loci—the embedded spirit of Confucianism and Chinese culture—remains unchanged.

In contrast, the cumulative history of the Acropolis, which until relatively recently included religious and defensive buildings from the Byzantine and Ottoman periods, has been sacrificed by restorers who stressed the site's appearance at a particular point in time—the pinnacle of classical Greece's golden age in the fifth century BCE. The "arrested development" of the physical remains at the site has turned it into a museum piece evocative of a selected moment in its distant past, lacking physical evidence of either its prior or subsequent history.

The Group Versus the Individual

Personal individualism is a highly respected trait for Europeans and Americans. This value can be extended to the appreciation of Western architecture, in which visual beauty is often achieved by individuality and autonomy of form. But such individualism often has negative connotations in cultures, in which the right of the collective is considered more important than the rights of one person or community.

The East Asian concept of monumentality carries with it more meanings than does the Western idea of large individual objects. A Chinese palace is not one individual building but is rather an enclave of several buildings. To non-Asian eyes, therefore, "[E]ven the most important and grandest palaces, when looked at in isolation and compared with any famous buildings abroad, will appear small, simple and of inferior appeal," according to Chinese architect and eminent early architectural conservationist Liang Sicheng.[53]

Although Asia has no lack of individually striking structures, beauty there is more often thought to be achieved via harmonious groupings than by a single building. An aesthetic whole takes into consideration building placement within a natural setting and extends over the spaces between buildings and structures. If the onlooker focuses on the beauty of an individual structure rather than on the importance of voids within a complex construct, a large part of what has been achieved by the architect has been missed. "Chinese Taoist architectural thought, which recognizes the important difference between tangible construction and intangible structure, mirrors [Taoism's] basic tenet: that nature is an 'organic whole in which the intangible part is the most vital.'"[54]

For many cultures, building placement is based on religious and astronomical considerations, which themselves may be considered group concerns. Muslim mosques are aligned to the holy city of Mecca; pantheistic sites such as Stonehenge in England and Ireland's Druid circles apparently took solar positioning into account when they were constructed. Asian aesthetics can also reflect the presentation of cosmologically reasoned planning. Three well-known, large-scale examples are the Borobodur temple in western Indonesia, Angkor Wat in northern Cambodia, and the Forbidden City in Beijing. A less widely known example is the Kyeonghoe-ru, a pavilion built in 1492 as a royal banquet hall in Seoul, South Korea.[55]

Such diverse and subtle interests reveal that effective architectural heritage conservation practices throughout the world are being better understood with each passing year, and the appreciation of sometimes divergent viewpoints provides important points of contrast that help cross-fertilize expert opinions. Fortunately, culturally rooted dichotomies

▲ **Figure 15-27** The Buddhist temple of Borobodur in Java, Indonesia, built between the end of the seventh and the beginning of the eighth century CE, is an architectural metaphor for the universe. Its ruins were stabilized on two occasions before its major restoration in 1968 under the aegis of UNESCO. *(© UNESCO - R. Greenough)*

▶ **Figure 15-28** The ancient city of Mohenjo Daro, Pakistan (ca. 2500 BCE), was the seat of the Harappa culture, a key source of Indian civilization. The difficult task of conserving earthen masonry ruins was undertaken here with international expertise organized by UNESCO.

in attitudes toward the built environment and in architectural conservation philosophy do not pose dire problems for the future of the global heritage conservation movement; rather, they emphasize how important and timely the task of cultural heritage protection is. The field of architectural conservation practice, rich as it is now, can only be enhanced by a fuller appreciation of how the so-called East-West philosophical debates on heritage protection translate into the present array of potential solutions for both conserving and interpreting cultural heritage sites.

East Meets West: Two Examples

Although they may not always agree on all core heritage conservation issues, non-Western and Western conservation professionals have joined forces in numerous history-making conservation projects over the past half century. The relatively early Asian architectural conservation projects of Borobodur and Mohenjo Daro illustrate how conservation philosophy and practice can successfully combine the best of both worlds.

Borobodur, a striking example of Buddhist architecture, was rediscovered in 1814 beneath a layer of lava ash and tropical vegetation in central Java, Indonesia. Its terraced pyramid is decorated with Buddhist carvings dating from ca. 842 CE. The site's conservation history has, to a large extent, defined the development of Indonesia's national heritage conservation approach after its independence from the Netherlands in 1945.

Borobodur has been the focus of several documentation and restoration projects since 1907, when Dutch conservators surveyed and cleaned its great pyramidal form to evaluate the extent of its structural instability after years of neglect. With the end of the colonial era, responsibility for the site passed to the new national government, which launched a "save Borobodur" program in 1969. For the next fourteen years, an international team of experts organized by UNESCO, in cooperation with the Indonesian Ministry of Culture, took on the task of restoring and re-presenting Borobodur as a regional primary cultural heritage site. The effort involved hundreds of workers, who dismantled, reassembled, and restored thousands of pieces of stone and brick atop a mostly new stone foundation.

As a developing nation, Indonesia's financial priorities lay elsewhere at the time, so conservation funding had to be raised externally. UNESCO's success in securing $25 million dollars and involving twenty-seven countries in a massive conservation effort was a moving demonstration of the fact that, in the cultural heritage field at least, the international community believes that, as one writer put it, "Each is his brother's keeper."[56] Borobodur became a World Heritage site in 1991; it is today both a symbol of Indonesia and a model both for Indonesian heritage policy and for regional heritage conservation practice.

A similar international rescue effort benefited Mohenjo Daro, a forty-five-hundred-year-old city located in present-day Pakistan that was one of the principal sites of the Indus Valley civilization. Since its rediscovery in 1912 by archaeologist R. D. Banerjee, a substantial number of excavations have been carried out. Unfortunately, most of them had a detrimental effect on the site's surviving architectural fabric. Mohenjo Daro's fragile earthen architectural remains were dissolving due to deleterious actions of rising damp and salt efflorescence caused by an altered natural water table. Archaeologists attributed the problems to the construction of a dam nearby while others claimed that the archaeologists were responsible. In any case, the act of exposing the ruins made them defenseless against the action of water.

In 1964, the then director of ICCROM, Dr. Harold Plenderleith, assessed Mohenjo Daro's site conditions after the Pakistani government appealed to UNESCO for assistance. To eliminate the threat to the site, UNESCO supported the construction of an elaborate drainage system that collected and diverted groundwater and accumulated precipitation.[57] Although this solution only partially mitigated the problem, it has helped.[58] One long-standing recommendation remains unchanged: rebury the entire site in order to preserve it, and then replicate it or represent it abstractly aboveground.[59]

Since the implementation of these two early international assistance strategies, popular interest in and awareness of the importance of architectural conservation has steadily increased in these regions. Other such high-profile international heritage conservation efforts continue to have similar effects, including the ongoing international conservation initiatives at Angkor in Cambodia, Wat Phou in Laos, and a plethora of smaller-scale initiatives being orchestrated by the Asia Pacific office of UNESCO.

INTERNATIONAL TRAINING IN ARCHITECTURAL CONSERVATION

The evolution of professional training in architectural conservation is also a reflection of the growth of the field. The need for organized specialty training in architectural conservation and related subjects was realized in the 1950s, although it took almost another decade for the first higher-education programs to begin to offer instruction in the field. When ICCROM was established in 1959 as part of the mandates of UNESCO, it was a pioneer in the field. Rome was fertile ground for this development, as is evidenced by the contemporaneous start of national Italian instruction in the field via the *Instituto Centrale per il Restauro* (ICR), led for thirty years by the influential Cesare Brandi. Similarly, the University Institutes for Monument Restoration was established in Florence in 1960 by Piero Sanpaolesi. By 1964, these programs were matched in scope and sophistication— albeit from a slightly different perspective—by the graduate programs in architectural conservation offered by the Middle Eastern Technical University in Ankara, Turkey, and at Columbia University in New York.

Today, universities throughout North America, Europe, and the world have added architectural conservation to their curricula, sometimes as an independent program and sometimes as a specialization within more general history, archaeology, or architecture programs.[60] Especially during the last quarter of the twentieth century, a plethora of degree programs and specialty courses have come into existence. In fact, formal training in architectural conservation is offered in numerous countries, which is both a testament to the popularity of the field and the effectiveness of earlier efforts to place heritage conservation on the agenda of most of the world's governments.

Figure 15-29 Since its founding in 1958, the International Centre for the Study of the Conservation and Restoration of Cultural Property (ICCROM) has been based in Rome, the ideal location for an institution with its mission.

In 1993, ICOMOS created its *Guidelines on Education and Training in the Conservation of Monuments, Ensembles and Sites*, which have been adopted by the principal full-time courses on architectural conservation in the United Kingdom and elsewhere in Europe. Its standards are rigorous. The document also provides profiles on the abilities and qualifications that each specialty within the architectural conservation profession should possess. It is used by the Conference on Training in Architectural Conservation (COTAC) as a basis for drafting national vocational qualifications.[61] (See also Chapter 1: "The Architectural Conservation Professional Defined" and Chapter 15: UNESCO and its Affiliates.")

Many of the graduate and postgraduate programs in architectural conservation include an international perspective, and participation though interuniversity collaborations and conservation projects abroad often holds great appeal for students and educators alike. Two of the leading European graduate programs that prepare students for international practice today include the University of York in England (within its Institute for Advanced Architectural Studies) and the Catholic University of Leuven in Belgium. The Center for the Training of Heritage Professionals at l'École de Chaillot in France goes a step further by offering holistic graduate training in heritage management for architects, restoration architects, and urbanists in France, with structured satellite courses in other parts of the world including Damascus; Porto Novo, Benin; and most recently, Siem Reap, Cambodia.[62]

For students, some of the most attractive additional opportunities to gain foreign experience are offered by ICOMOS through its annual international summer internship exchange program. Thus, the field of architectural conservation has an international relations component that is reflected at a macro level by growing support for the sentiment of universal heritage, the thesis upon which the work of UNESCO (and much of the field) is based.

At the same time, many other programs offer instruction in conservation theory and practice that emphasize their countries and locales. For example, since the 1970s the University of Rome and its counterpart universities in Naples, Siena, Florence, Genoa and Milan have offered graduate programs that stress Italian traditions in the field. During the same period England developed a full array of graduate level and specialty training opportunities, ranging from fully developed Masters degree programs (University of York, DeMontfort University, Leicester, and the University of Bath) to part-time and extramural study programs (at the Architectural Association, London, and at the University of Bristol). The robustness of training opportunities in England is exemplified in its specialty training programs including the building and decorative arts craft training program at West Dean and the University of Oxford's part- or full-time course offerings attractive to conservation officers although not specifically for them. [63]

In the USA, Columbia University, the University of Pennsylvania, and Cornell University offer Masters of Science degrees in historic preservation with exposure to, if not specific courses in, international architectural conservation practice.[64]

Other examples of universities that offer high-quality architectural heritage conservation courses with national or region specific emphasis but with offerings appealing to students from other countries in their aims include the University of Rome III and University of Rome La Sapienze in Italy; Academia Istropolitana Nova in Belgrade, Serbia; Deakin University in Melbourne, Australia; the National University of Singapore; Hong Kong University; and Tsinghua University in Beijing.

In addition to ICCROM's aforementioned regional training programs in Africa, the Middle East, Southeast Asia, etc., there are UNESCO Pacific Region office-sponsored Asian Academy in Macau, China, and the newly-established Master's degree in "World Heritage at Work," which is aimed at training World Heritage Site managers at the University of Turin in Italy sponsored by the International Training Centre of the International Labor Organization (http://www.itcilo.org/masters/worldheritage). Due to their evolving natures descriptions of all these programs and educational opportunities (and many others) are best researched on the World Wide Web.

In the first few decades of formal instruction in architectural conservation education, institutions focused on the theoretical and material aspects of the field and related methodologies and stressed aesthetic and historical values; in recent years, however, their graduates—now seasoned professionals—have addressed additional facets of the field, such as conservation planning, archaeological conservation, and the conservation of intangible cultural heritage. These include economic and social values that are equally crucial components of effective heritage conservation practice.[65] Today, these graduates represent a new generation of architectural conservationists who are swelling the field's professional ranks and populating ministries of culture (or their equivalents) and diverse local agencies, architecture and its allied professions, specialty NGOs, and universities around the world. They are carrying out projects as well as training future conservationists, thereby helping to ensure the ongoing formation of the dynamic profession we know today.

ENDNOTES

1. Sequels to this volume will contain more on the history of the formative years of architectural conservation practice during the first half of the twentieth century.

2. Valadier collected displaced elements from around the site and reinstated as many as possible in the arch's restored geometry, carefully distinguishing old from new. It is reported that those pieces that could not be re-reinstated were placed in the attic of the monument. See Appendix A to compare **anastylosis, restoration,** and **reconstruction**.

3. Alvise Zorzi, Osservazion, *Intornoai Restauri Interni ed Esterni Della Basilica di San Marco*.

4. George Christos Skarmeas, "An Analysis of Architectural Preservation Theories: From 1790 to 1975," (PhD diss., University of Pennsylvania, 1983), 83. See also Boito, chap. 16, "Italy."

5. The 1883 Resolution in Italy, the first national charter on restoration authored by Camillo Boito, and the Charter of Madrid of 1904, with their lists of principles, may be seen as a precedent for the Athens Charter.

6. The boarding house in Rome where Keats died in 1821 is now a museum that features memorabilia related to Percy Bysshe Shelley, John Keats, and Lord Byron, the trio of young poets who symbolize the English romantic movement.

7. For many Sudanese, the disproportionate number of monuments saved in Egypt compared with those saved in Sudan is an example of how Nubian cultural heritage is considered less important than that of Egypt.

8. Speech by Vittorino Veronese, director-general of UNESCO, launching a funds appeal for Abu Simbel in 1960. E. R. Chamberlin, *Preserving the Past*. 7.

9. The Florentine relief effort was led by the Italian government—in particular, by its Ministry of Culture.

10. The Venice in Peril Fund's first project was the restoration of the late Gothic church of Madonna dell'Orto. It also helped restore less famous churches in order to bring attention to lesser known monuments and to aid buildings that were otherwise unlikely to receive assistance.

11. See Appendix B for information about the activities of the US-based World Monuments Fund and Save Venice, Inc. Other international assistance to Venice at the time included two initiatives from the Federal Republic of Germany, one from Australia, two additional efforts from the United States, two from France, one other from the United Kingdom, two from Switzerland, and eight from Italy.

12. Jokilehto, *History of Architectural Conservation*, 282.

13. Ibid. In the aftermath of World War I, three reconstruction options were usually considered: Some people wanted to keep ruined buildings and sites with especially poignant wartime associations in their existing state as memorials; some wished to create gardens in place of ruined buildings; and others favored restoring and reconstructing buildings to their prewar appearance.

14. Ibid.

15. Ibid., 285.

16. By 1962, Warsaw had risen from its ashes as a result of a massive campaign of accurate reconstruction and careful restoration. Reconstructed buildings in the new Stare Miasto (Old Town) historic center of Warsaw corresponded to the former ones in outward appearance, but internal changes incorporated modern amenities and occasionally increased the floor area by the insertion of added floor levels.

17. The (revised) Hague Convention was first ratified in 1956. As of 2005, it has been ratified by 114 nations, with the United States and the United Kingdom being the most notable exceptions. That it exists as a standard attests to its strength, though recognition of, adherence to, and enforcement of heritage protection measures has been uneven at best, as was demonstrated during the Balkans conflicts of the 1990s and the Iraq War beginning in 2003.

18. *International Charter for the Conservation and Restoration of Monument and Sites (the Venice Charter)*, http://www.icomos.org/docs/venice_charter.html.

19. Roland Silva, *Problems, Aims and Future Directions to Conserving the Past* [Online] Rev. October 18, 2002. Available: http://www.unescobkk.org/culture/roland.html (Web site since discontinued).

20. Case studies presented outstanding examples of success, such as the Spanish experience in creating its network of *paradores*, and Italy's Ville Venete conservation scheme.

21. As documented by specific conference proceedings and available from the International Council on Monuments and Sites (ICOMOS).

22. *UNESCO 1945–2000: A Fact Sheet*, rev. October 22, 2002. Available: http://www.unesco.org/general/eng/about/history/back.shtml (accessed October 22, 2002.) (Web site discontinued.)

23. UNESCO, Constitution of the United Nations Educational, Scientific and Cultural Organization, adopted in London, November 16, 1945, art. I.2.c, http://portal.unesco.org/en/ev.php-URL_ID=15244&URL_DO=DO_TOPIC&URL_SECTION=201.html.

24. At present, 191 countries subscribe as members of UNESCO, and six are associate members. The long story of cultural heritage protection as a goal within the United Nations Educational, Scientific and Cultural organization is well described in Dr. Henry Cleere's "Protecting the World's Cultural Heritage," Chapter 5, in *Concerning Buildings: Studies in Honor of Sir Bernard Feilden*, ed. Stephen Marks, (Oxford: Butterworth-Heinmann, 1996).

25. ICCROM's history (including the story of the evolution of its present acronym name) and the development of professional training in architectural conservation throughout the world is best documented in Derek Lindstrum's "The Education of Conservation Architect: Past, Present, and Future," Chapter 6 in *Concerning Buildings: Studies in Honour of Sir Bernard Feilden* ed., Stephen Marks. (Oxford: Butterworth_Heinmann, 1996.)

26. At the time of this writing, the libraries of the J. Paul Getty Museum and the Getty Conservation Institute in Los Angeles, California, exceed ICCROM's holdings with respect to the Getty's more general holdings on art history and its numerous indexing projects.

27. ICOMOS, "About ICOMOS," International Council on Monuments and Sites, http://www.international.icomos.org/about.htm.

28. This was the theme of a traveling exhibition entitled Culture and Development at the Millennium: The Challenges and the Response, launched in Washington, DC, in September 1998 by the World Bank. This was followed one year later by an ICOMOS conference in Mexico with the theme Heritage @ Risk.

29. This fund, although not large given its mandate, plays an active role in promoting the protection of important cultural and physical sites in the world, particularly in developing countries and underdeveloped regions.

30. World Heritage Centre, "World Heritage List," UNESCO, http://whc.unesco.org/en/list (accessed January 7, 2008).

31. "UNESCO World Heritage Convention," UNESCO, http://whc.unesco.org/en/convention-text/.

32. Herbert Muschamp, "Monuments in Peril: A Top 100 Countdown," *New York Times*, March 31, 1996.

33. Other countries providing international heritage conservation assistance to specific projects include: Poland, Hungary, India, the United States, Russia, the Czech Republic, Austria, Norway, Finland, Great Britain, Australia, New Zealand, and Canada.

34. For this purpose, the term *European* is defined as countries beyond the geographical borders of present-day Europe so as to include countries that primarily derived from European colonialization and similar direct influences in the New World, in particular North America. As such the terms *West* and *East* are used in this context to describe Euro-American and East Asian cultural and cultural heritage protection sensibilities.

35. There are cases in South and East Asia where perpetual maintenance and even prescribed methods of repair and "restoration" of religious monuments were long-standing traditions. Passages within the fifth-century Sanskrit *Mayamatam: Treatise of Housing, Architecture, and Iconography* (trans. B. Dagens) prescribed repair methods to Hindu religious monuments in southern India and even mention how religious merit can be gained for doing the repairs. Evidence of maintenance and complex repairs and restorations of Buddhist shrines in caves at Mogao in Dunhuang, Gansu Province, China, and temples and shrines at Pagan, Myanmar (formerly Burma), from over five centuries ago, can be seen in visiting these sites today.

36. William Logan, "*Globalising Heritage,*" in Taylor, "Cultural Heritage Management: A Possible Role for Charters and Principles in Asia," *International Journal of Heritage Studies*, 10, No.5, (December 2005): 419.

37. Taylor, "Cultural Heritage Management," 420.

38. Although some have felt the Burra Charter's inclusion of "aesthetic" values somewhat dilutes this point.

39. Professor of Architectural Planning and History Seung-Jin Chung at Hyupsung University in Korea calls for a different approach to conserving East Asian architectural heritage that is distinct from that of the West in an article entitled "East Asian Values in Historic Conservation," *Journal of Architectural Conservation* 11, no. 1 (March 2005): 33–70.

40. Visionaries and heritage enthusiasts Lord George Nathaniel Curzon and John Marshall earnestly applied themselves to Indian architectural heritage protection in their creation and development of the Archaeological Survey of India (ASI). Marshall established specific architectural conservation principles and guidelines, complete with detailed technical recommendations, two decades before the Athens Charter of 1931. The ASI's procedures were updated in the 1980s with the assistance of Bernard Feilden.

41. Heritage protection measures under the British Raj were concerned almost exclusively with India's most important monumental architectural heritage. There was little local input, especially involving rural populations, regarding native Indian preferences toward protecting the country's built heritage.

42. A. G. Krishna Menon, "Conservation in India: A Search for Direction," *Abstracts and Texts, Architexturez.net*, http://www.architexturez.net/+/subject-listing/000058.shtml.

43. Ibid.

44. James Wines, *Green Architecture* (New York: Taschen, 2000), 20.

45. Ibid., 35.

46. Genesis 1:28; "Man's role is to subdue the earth…and to rule over the garden." See also Genesis 2:15. A likely but controversial claim that Western cities have evolved as they have as a direct consequence of biblical sustainability in Chrisna Du Plessis, "Global Perspectives: Learning from the Other Side," *Architectural Design* 71 (July 2001): 16.

47. Ibid.

48. There has been only one breach, during the fifteenth century, of the ritual, which is proscribed in the text from 804 CE, *Record of Rituals for the Imperial Shrine of Ise*. The sixty-first rebuilding, accomplished in 1993, cost $3 million. Dora P. Crouch and June G. Johnson, *Traditions in Architecture: Africa, America, Asia, and Oceania* (Oxford: Oxford University Press, 2001), 364, 367. See also Isao Tokoro, "The Grand Shrine at Ise: Preservation by Removal and Renewal," in Serageldin et al., *Historic Cities and Sacred Sites: Cultural Roots for Urban Futures* (Washington, DC: World Bank, 2001), 22–29.

49. If the Ise shrine was to be nominated to the World Heritage List, its challenge of passing the listing criterion pertaining to "authenticity" could conceivably be countered by citing UNESCO's Convention for the Safeguarding of the Intangible Cultural Heritage, dating from 2003.

50. Denslagen and Gutschow, *Architectural Imitations*, 2005.

51. Chen Wei and Andreas Aass, "Heritage Conservation: East and West," *ICOMOS Information*, n.3 (July/September 1989).

52. Nine courtyards and 466 elegant rooms, added in many dynastic styles, are spread in a symmetrical north-south axis over the twenty-two hectares of Qufu's living religious enclave.

53. Liang Sicheng, "Chinese Architectural Theory," *Architectural Review* July (1947): 19.

54. Amos Ih Tiao Chang, *The Tao of Architecture [originally published as The Existence of Intangible Content in Architectonic Form Based Upon the Practicality of Laotzu's Philosophy]* (Princeton, NJ: Princeton University Press, 1956), quoted in Crouch and Johnson, *Traditions in Architecture*, 332.

55. The original building was burned in the Japanese invasion of 1592; but today's structure, an exact copy built in 1867, provides an excellent example of an aesthetic building treatment that also represents cosmological ideas. Three partitions on the uppermost floor "represent heaven, earth and man; and eight columns...symbolized eight sticks called 'goae' [that represent] the phenomena and shapes of heaven and earth and of all creatures. The middle floor had twelve columns which symbolized the twelve months, and the lowest level had twenty-four columns for twenty-four solar terms." Kim D.-W, "Kyeonghoe-ru, Korean Architecture and the Principle of the I-Ching," *Architectural Culture* October (1983): 47–51.

56. E. R. Chamberlin, *Preserving the Past*, 180.

57. The project's first phase alone cost approximately $7.5 million.

58. Rising damp problems persist, and damage to the foundations and lower levels of the buildings continues.

59. Barraud Dani and Farhat Kenoyer, "Pakistan: Erosion Threatening World's Oldest Planned City," *Radio Australia*, rev. October 22, 2002. Available: http://www.abc.net.au/ra/asiapac/ archive/jul/raap-6jul2001–4.htm (accessed October 22, 2002).

60. In the United States alone, other important graduate programs in architectural conservation are offered at Columbia University, Cornell University, the University of Pennsylvania, and the University of Hawaii. Each program addresses architectural conservation in the broadest sense, though within each curriculum can be found emphases on theory, conservation science, and planning.

61. *Guidelines on Education and Training in the Conservation of Monuments, Ensembles and Sites*, adopted at the Tenth ICOMOS General Assembly in Colombo, Sri Lanka, 1993.

62. L'École de Chaillot is a venerable 120-year-old institution that prepares its graduates for the French civil service and state examinations in restoration architecture, among other things. Its restoration architecture section is guided by Pierre-André Lablaude, *architecte en chef* for Versailles.

63. The best history of formal higher education and its prospects is offered by Derek Lindstrum, founder and long-time head of the architectural conservation program at the University of York. See Lindstrum, "The Education of the Conservation Architect: Past, Present and Future," chapter 6, in *Concerning Buildings*, 96–118.

64. Michael Tomlan, "Historic Preservation Education: Alongside Architecture in Academia", *Journal of Architectural Education* (May 1994): 187–196. Dr. Tomlan is chairman of the (US) National Institute for Preservation Education (NICPE) that tracks all graduate and post-graduate level training opportunities in American historic preservation.

65. The culmination of this interest is reflected in the adoption of the Convention for the Safeguarding of the Intangible Cultural Heritage in 2003. As adopted at the thirty-second session of the UNESCO General Conference in Paris on October 17, 2003, it takes the 1972 World Heritage Convention as its model, but with major modifications, as required by the subject matter.

A street in the Marais district, Paris.

CHAPTER 16

A Multidimensional Field for the Twenty-First Century

As the field of architectural conservation has become an increasingly global phenomenon, it has also become increasingly consistent in its application of its cumulative experiences. The catalysts behind this phenomenon are the universality of its appeal from social, cultural, political, and economic standpoints as well as the modern technologies that have made the world seem smaller. Heritage conservation is what David Pierce has described as "the only architecture-related cause that has ever been truly popular," and its audience has increased in recent years.[1]

Because issues of urbanization, decentralization, and globalization have reshaped the contemporary development landscape, cultural heritage conservation and management require reevaluation. In spite of, and in reaction to, the unprecedented amount of change that has occurred in the past sixty years, architectural conservation in particular has emerged as a viable and useful component of practically every country's agenda. Architectural restoration and preservation has gone from the obscure mission of an embattled elite to a cause universally accepted as worthwhile. In addition to its widespread appeal, local, national, and international tourism has provided a major rationale for the viability of the heritage conservation industry in even the remotest parts of the world.

Forces That Shape International Architectural Conservation Practice

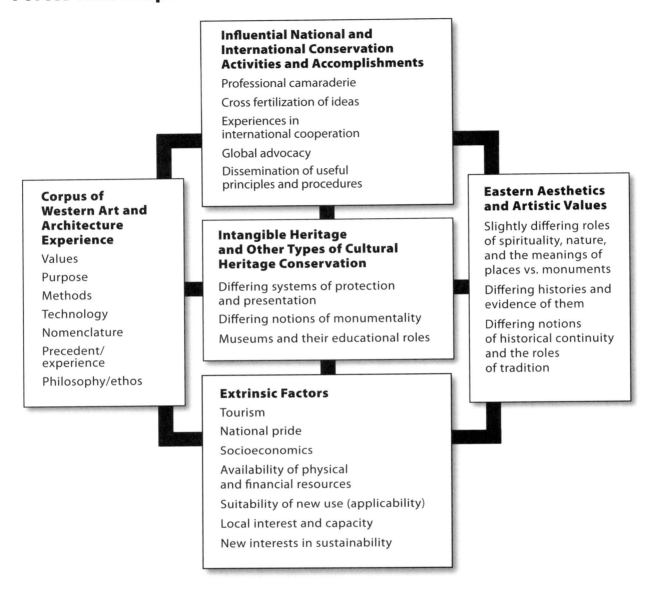

Influential National and International Conservation Activities and Accomplishments

Professional camaraderie

Cross fertilization of ideas

Experiences in international cooperation

Global advocacy

Dissemination of useful principles and procedures

Corpus of Western Art and Architecture Experience

Values

Purpose

Methods

Technology

Nomenclature

Precedent/experience

Philosophy/ethos

Intangible Heritage and Other Types of Cultural Heritage Conservation

Differing systems of protection and presentation

Differing notions of monumentality

Museums and their educational roles

Eastern Aesthetics and Artistic Values

Slightly differing roles of spirituality, nature, and the meanings of places vs. monuments

Differing histories and evidence of them

Differing notions of historical continuity and the roles of tradition

Extrinsic Factors

Tourism

National pride

Socioeconomics

Availability of physical and financial resources

Suitability of new use (applicability)

Local interest and capacity

New interests in sustainability

Chart 16.1 Forces That Shape International Architectural Conservation Practice

Though the problems faced in protecting the world's architectural patrimony are varied, there is considerable consensus among heritage protection professional and interested others about their remedies. The efforts of international organizations, and their determination to address priorities and gaps in the ever-burgeoning field, facilitate the incidental transfer of technology, methodology, principles, and training techniques, which is also aided by the nature of the work itself. Other factors contribute as well. Today, the world is aware of its history on an unprecedented scale as a result of improved education and scholarship and the modern amenities of instantaneous communication and affordable travel.

Twenty Actions That Influenced Today's World Architectural Conservation Practice

1. The outpouring of international interest and support resulting from the extraordinary threats posed by the construction of the Aswan Upper Dam in Egypt in 1964 and the flooding of Venice and Florence in 1966.

2. The observance of the destruction and restoration of famous historic sites, such as Stare Miasto (Old Town) in Warsaw and the Old Bridge in Mostar, Bosnia. The world's visceral reaction to the widely televised destruction of the Bamiyan Buddhas in Afghanistan stands as another example, though they have not yet been rebuilt.

3. The restoration of the large charismatic sites of Borobodur, Indonesia; Angkor Wat, Cambodia; the grand Louvre project in Paris; and the Golden Ring east of Moscow. Earlier examples include the Parthenon (Greece), Colonial Williamsburg (Virginia), Teotihuacan (Mexico), and Tikal (Guatemala).

4. Debate from the mid-nineteenth century of the radical restoration and building-completion philosophy of the French architect Eugène-Emmanuel Viollet-le-Duc in France versus the more conservative approach honoring changes over time promoted by the writer Victor Hugo and archaeologist Adolphe Napoléon Didron in France and artists, historians, and advocates John Ruskin and William Morris in England.

5. Examples set by very large restorations and adaptive uses of seaport areas, transportation facilities, government complexes, and the like in the United States in the mid-1970s and 1980s.

6. The impressive technical achievements of architects, engineers, conservation scientists, and conservators at Abu Simbel and Philae temples at Aswan, Egypt, which were relocated to protect them; at the Cape Hatteras Lighthouse in North Carolina; at the Leaning Tower of Pisa; and at the yet to be completed Moses harbor protection project in Venice. Similar feats in conservation science, including fine art conservation, are the postearthquake restorations in Assisi, Italy, since September 1997, and the cleaning and conservation of Michelangelo's Last Supper in Milan and the Sistine Chapel ceiling at the Vatican.

7. The conservation and display of especially popular historic architectural and archaeological complexes such as the Roman Forum, Pompeii and Herculaneum, the Parthenon and the Acropolis, Macchu Pichu, the Temple of Hatshepsut, and the temples of Angkor.

8. The establishment of restoration crafts training operations and graduate and postgraduate training opportunities in various countries.

9. The more widely publicized illicit trade of antiquities, most notably in Italy, Greece, China, Peru, Cambodia, and Iraq.

10. The realization of the economic development potential of heritage tourism.

11. The development of internationally applicable charters and guidelines, especially the Athens Charter of 1931, the Venice Charter of 1964, the U.S. Secretary of the Interior's Standards and Guidelines for Historic Preservation (1976), the Burra Charter (1979), and the China Principles (2000).

12. The establishment of the United Nations Educational, Scientific and Cultural Organization (UNESCO) and its supporting organizations and programs, including the International Council on Museums (ICOM), the International Centre for the Study of the Preservation and Restoration of Cultural Property (ICCROM), the International Council on Monuments and Sites (ICOMOS), and the World Heritage Centre.

13. The development of key national heritage protection legislation and legal precedents having special influence, such as the Malraux Law in France (1964), for conserving ensembles of buildings.

14. Financial incentives as offered in the United States through federal tax incentives for rehabilitation of qualifying historic buildings (1976), matching grants in aid, and the actions of philanthropic organizations.

(continued)

15. The work of international nongovernmental organizations devoted to the protection of architectural heritage such as the World Monuments Fund (New York), the Getty Conservation Institute (Los Angeles), and the Aga Khan Trust for Culture (Geneva).

16. The example of the British National Trust, founded in 1899.

17. Influential government, corporate, and social leaders and voices in the arts such as André Malraux, John Betjeman, Jacqueline Kennedy Onassis, Lebanon's Rafik Hariri, and the Hadrian Awardees of the World Monuments Fund.

18. Distinguished educators and professional art and architectural historians and architects such as Cesare Brandi and Giovanni Carbonara (Italy),

Bernard Feilden (United Kingdom), James Marston Fitch (United States), Raymond Lemaire (Belgium), Liang Sicheng (China), Paul Philippot (Netherlands/Italy), Alois Riegl (Austria), and all the winners of the ICOMOS Piero Gazzola Award.

19. Particularly influential, reform-minded activists such as John Ruskin and William Morris in England and Jane Jacobs and James Marston Fitch in the United States.

20. Computerized information documentation and retrieval systems and special photographic, laser-measuring, and diagnostic techniques adapted for use in heritage protection that speed and simplify everyday fieldwork.

Exemplars of appropriate methods and technologies used in architectural conservation are found throughout the world and can be observed and learned from at any time, by observing first-hand (at least at a distance), examining published project descriptions, and increasingly, viewing almost simultaneous progress reported in print or posted on the World Wide Web. For experts and scholars, information on either ongoing or completed conservation projects is usually easily accessible via related public presentations and other collegial means, such as professional symposia and specially arranged tours. For wider audiences, some of the more famous restorations can be news in and of themselves that the public may follow with interest: The two-year restoration of the Tower of Belem in Lisbon (Figures 17-14 and 17-15) from 1999 was featured in planned regular coverage in Portugal's prominent national newspaper *Público*; the restorations within the past decade of the Bolshoi theater in Moscow and La Fenice opera house in Venice were closely followed by interested local and international theater and opera enthusiasts; and the simultaneous restorations of the Statue of Liberty and parts of Ellis Island located in New York harbor in the 1980s in connection with the statue's centennial celebration garnered almost constant national attention.[2]

The extraordinarily large and complex effort by international teams currently working at Angkor in Cambodia has been described by American preservation expert and teacher William Chapman as being the "single largest laboratory for observing contemporary heritage conservation practice in the world." On visiting Angkor today, one may readily notice more than a dozen large scale restorations and conservation projects at the ancient Khmer capital's numerous stone temples, where the techniques being used by various international teams are generally similar. (See Figure 17-70.) The particulars of each conservation project, complete with the nuances of occasional differences in approach, are on record at the Angkor International Documentation Center and are frequently published. Each national or international team working at Angkor is obliged to report on their progress at biannual meetings of the International Coordinating Committee of the APSARA Authority, having purview over the archaeological park. At the summer technical meetings in particular, the expert teams working at Angkor present proposed work and project progress reports for peer review and approval by the Cambodian authorities, their advisers, and UNESCO, which serves as Secretariat to the Authority.

One may ask, what do these all these architectural conservation projects and their project development teams have in common? From the standpoint of overall project structure and methodology, they are almost identical. Each begins with a proposal to solve an agreed-upon conservation issue; next is its official approval, followed by different stages of implementation of the required conservation work, and finally documentation of the completed work. On placing the conserved architectural resource in service, it is expected that the sites will be properly maintained, presented, and monitored.

Though it is plain to see that cultural heritage conservation has become a globally collaborative effort, complete with similar methodologies and objectives, some point out that sharing knowledge and working internationally has not been so successful. The former ICOMOS Canada president François Leblanc argues that miscommunication and disparate contexts complicate the integration of the global conservation field:

> *There are tremendous cultural differences across the world including different concepts of culture and heritage which often cannot translate from one language to another. If it is an untranslatable spiritual concept and intrinsic to heritage value then communication becomes very difficult. Likewise, issues differ enormously and the issues in one part of the world are completely irrelevant to another part. For example, in northern Mozambique one issue is what techniques to use to survey a site when the principle issue is that surveyors are eaten by lions at certain times of the year. The issues are very different from those in Paris or Tokyo.*[3]

Indeed, heritage conservationists around the world continue to face a great array of challenges. Leblanc is certainly correct in stating that the issues of cultural misunderstandings and contextual specificities continue to be among the most complicated. Yet more positively, there is great promise in learning from the experiences of others. The keys are continued work in improving communications, the education of more professionals, and the generation of wider public support for cultural heritage protection.

ENDNOTES

1. David Pearce, *Conservation Today* (London: Routledge, 1989), 228.
2. In many of these examples, the public dissemination of information about ongoing restorations helped ancillary efforts in project funding.
3. John Ward, "ICOMOS Canada and Sharing Knowledge," *ICOMOS Canada Bulletin* 6, no. 2 (1997), http://archive.canada.icomos.org/bulletin/vol6_no2.html.

CHAPTER 17

A Summary Global Tour of Contemporary Practice: Challenges and Solutions

The absence of an accurate inventory of global architectural conservation practice has left the field faced with fragmentary evidence of its own history and accomplishments. While many studies of cultural heritage conservation efforts in specific places—even entire countries—exist, this information has not been synthesized to show how accomplishments in architectural conservation in subregions of the world fit together to form a whole. Until the time that a fuller catalogue raisonné of global conservation practice is made, complete with statistical analyses, an impression of patterns of contemporary practice and promising directions in architectural conservation throughout the world is all that can be offered.[1]

The following global tour of architectural conservation practice starts with the places with the longest traditions in organized heritage protection and then moves on to locales where the concern is relatively new and perhaps even still forming. The divisions that follow are mostly geographical, although sometimes also historically informed based on cultural relationships and connections that have shaped conservation experiences. An emphasis is placed on the distinguishing characteristics of architectural conservation practice in each region as well as on their contributions to the overall field. Since there are obvious limitations to the number of examples that can be cited, choices have been made about which challenges, solutions, and promising trends are faced in particular regions. Examples of no more than ten current challenges and promising developments are cited for each region of the world.[2]

EUROPE

Despite its tumultuous history and constant border changes, Europe is home to one of the world's oldest and most distinguished civilizations, with a legacy of cultural heritage that includes the monuments of ancient Greece and Rome, medieval and Renaissance cathedrals and cities, and modern technological and architectural marvels. Though one of the smallest continents, Europe has proven to be the most influential in world history, both during antiquity and especially in the past five centuries. This global hegemony has included the professional field of architectural conservation, which originated as a public concern in Europe as a result of its strong civil society, democratic traditions, and nationalist tendencies.

In the period since the divisive world wars, Europe has followed a path of political integration that culminated with the formation and strengthening of the European Union (EU), which today includes twenty-seven countries, with most of the rest of the continent applying to join and waiting out the process of accession. The past sixty years have also been characterized by growing concern for heritage protection in Europe, originally galvanized by the destruction of World Wars I and II and given renewed purpose and promise by the reorganization of political affinities in Europe in the post–Cold War period. The greatest challenge for heritage conservation in Europe today is the strengthening of cultural diversities while simultaneously integrating and standardizing policies and procedures in a newly united continent.

Following the collapse of the Soviet Union, much of Central and Eastern Europe began the difficult process of transition to democratic governments and market economies, and the region's heritage has been threatened by rapid privatization and the loss of significant state subsidies. Though free from the centralized and ideological policies of the Communist era, most countries in that part of Europe are still struggling to cope with these new challenges over a decade later, as well as with the new pressures of uncontrolled development and increased tourism. At the same time, the resurgence of nationalism in Eastern and southeastern Europe has made heritage an issue of importance to more of the peoples in these regions, and it has allowed a renewed focus on building types and periods neglected by the former regimes—especially those of religious heritage.

The countries of Europe have signed regional cultural agreements and have had governmental and nongovernmental organizations to protect and conserve their shared heritage since the 1950s. The European Cultural Convention was the first to promote reciprocal respect and appreciation for the heritage sites of respective countries and to raise the notion of a common European heritage.[3] It has been supplemented by additional agreements, such as the 1975 European Charter of the Architectural Heritage, which addresses architectural conservation issues more explicitly.[4]

Both the EU and the Council of Europe have increasingly promoted regulations and programs that standardize conservation procedures and practices and integrate professional and technological resources throughout the continent, such as through the European Heritage Network. Since its establishment in the 1960s, Europa Nostra, the pan-European federation for cultural heritage, has been Europe's primary organization in the field, offering another platform for collaboration, serving as a watchdog to protect threatened heritage, and offering coveted awards for successful conservation projects.[5] With the EU's enlargement, more and more countries have been included within this culture of shared experiences, and heritage legislation and policies throughout Eastern and southeastern Europe have been updated. In addition, EU programs have extended beyond the borders of Europe, supporting projects and capacity-building abroad through innovative programs like the Euro-Mediterranean Partnership. In recent years, in the spirit of cultural diplomacy, the EU has been assisting heritage conservation efforts as far afield as South and East Asia, sub-Saharan Africa, and the Caribbean.

In fact, for more than a half century Europe has taken advantage of its position as a global leader to promote and support cultural heritage conservation worldwide, and through participation in international organizations, it has encouraged the application of its principles and the adaptation of its policies practically everywhere. As has been previously described, international collaboration for the conservation of the world's cultural *and* natural heritage was largely initiated in Europe, with organizations such as the United Nations Educational, Scientific and Cultural Organization (UNESCO), the International Council on Monuments and Sites (ICOMOS), the International Council of Museums (ICOM), and the International Union for Conservation of Nature and Natural Resources (IUCN). As such, it is fair to say that the modern field of architectural conservation practice was largely founded and guided by European ideals and experts. It was mostly European professionals who organized the conferences that led to the seminal Athens Charter in 1931 and Venice Charter in 1964. These documents reflect Europe's inherent advantages for sharing knowledge and its cooperative spirit; they are also imbued with specifically Western values and notions of heritage that have begun to be reevaluated by the rest of the world in recent decades.

Today, nearly every western and northern European country has well-established and strictly enforced legislation, high-quality educational programs, administrative oversight bodies, and public interest campaigns all working on behalf of its heritage, and the countries of Eastern and southeastern Europe are quickly catching up. Countries throughout Europe that have been overly dependent on government funding for architectural conservation have seen the growth of not-for-profit organizations and have embraced innovative fund-raising schemes devoted to heritage protection in recent decades. Diligent European heritage conservationists have developed new technologies, methodologies, and creative programs that have benefited practice at home and abroad. Perhaps most importantly, the definition of what constitutes valued cultural heritage has gradually expanded in Europe in recent decades as it has begun to learn from the experiences and traditions of other cultures, balancing its formerly mono-directional influence on the rest of the world.

Special Challenges Faced in Europe

Figure 17-1 *Pressures from tourism.* The overwhelming popularity (and subsequent overuse) of many historic European cities during tourist season—such as Venice and Prague, shown here overrun by visitors—has threatened the character and even the physical integrity of many important sites. The socioeconomic integrity of these urban centers is threatened as their local residents are forced out by rising property values, the growth of shops and restaurants catering only to tourists, and the declining quality of life resulting from the crowds and noise. The population of Venice, for example, has dwindled from 190,000 in 1900 to less than 60,000 today, a large percentage of whom work in tourism-related industries serving the city's more than 100,000 daily visitors.

Figure 17-2 *Uncontrolled development.*
Views of urban development beyond the historic centers of Toledo, Spain, and Athens, Greece (illustrated here) reveal how the historic scale and character of many European towns and cities is threatened by inadequately controlled and insensitive development. The areas on the immediate periphery of conservation areas are a particular problem in this respect. The late nineteenth century witnessed the destruction of old city walls and medieval neighborhoods for the construction of boulevards and embankments, and the entire twentieth century was marked by periods of redevelopment for highway and transit schemes as well as for massive housing complexes and industrial expansion. Much has already been lost, and insensitive new design and development is still being done at the expense of its architectural heritage in many European cities.

Figure 17-3 *Accommodating motorized traffic* has been the single largest motive for modernizing historic cities. In addition to encouraging the destruction of historic buildings and dense medieval street patterns, the automobile also threatens architectural heritage due to air pollution and the use of open space for parking—despite the importance of those spaces and the views that are obstructed. Automobiles remain a major problem for heritage protection in Europe today, even though many cities have addressed this issue in various ways. Rome (illustrated here) requires special resident parking permits, and commercial vehicles must respect timed-access restrictions in the districts within the *centro istorico*. For all the convenience automobiles afford, there are no easy, inexpensive solutions to overcome the rising costs of this mode of transportation. *(Photo courtesy of Europa Nostra)*

Figure 17-4 *Out-migration from small towns and rural areas.* Many of Europe's small towns and rural landscapes are at risk as their populations are drawn toward urban centers in search of better employment opportunities and the relative excitement of city life. In southern Tuscany, the ancient hill town of Pitigliano is one of the country's numerous picturesque rural towns that are suffering from a lack of vital energy usually provided by younger generations that remain to live and work. In some cases, these small towns have been discovered by city dwellers seeking second homes in the countryside or have benefited from resettlement as an artist community or corporate retreat; however, others sit idle, with few inhabitants remaining, and with the prospect of deteriorating to a point beyond which conservation is practical.

Figure 17-5 *Conserving archaeological heritage* is an ongoing concern since urban and rural archaeological sites throughout Europe are under constant pressure from illegal excavation and destruction. High land values in European cities have often marginalized archaeological protection in favor of new development. Even without these pressures and under the best of circumstances, it is difficult to preserve and present in situ archaeological remains due to their fragility and the special problems of conserving and featuring recently exposed fragments of structures. In rural areas such as the Valley of the Roses in north-central Bulgaria, the illicit digging for valuable antiquities was rampant for a period in the mid-1990s. Seen here are the remains of a Thracian tomb after robbers plowed through it with earth-moving equipment.

◄ **Figure 17-6** *Paucity of private-sector support.*
Most European countries today have well-developed
heritage protection systems that include interested
nongovernmental organizations and volunteer
groups. However, due to Europe's long tradition of
almost exclusively governmental support of heritage
conservation, some of its wealthiest countries still
lack widespread public support and interest in
architectural conservation. Improvements have been
seen in some places that failed to attract notice for
decades—in Jewish districts in Eastern Europe, for
example, including Kazimierz in Krakow, Poland, which
has witnessed a slow regeneration in recent years. On
the other hand, public awareness and appreciation
of heritage is low in countries such as Romania and
Georgia, where rural inhabitants especially are often
indifferent about significant architectural sites in need
of protection. Even sizable populations near famous
sites—such as Herculaneum near Naples (illustrated
here)—have grown accustomed to assuming that
the Italian government is solely responsible for their
treatment, when in fact there are many additional
opportunities to integrate these unique windows into
history with their adjacent living communities.

▶ **Figure 17-7** *Lack of resources and quantity of work in
Eastern Europe.* Though the European continent is more united
than ever, its four decades of division during the Cold War have
left a legacy of varying economic and administrative capacities for
architectural conservation between Eastern and Western Europe
today. Former state-supported restoration ateliers and their cadres
of experts have found it difficult to adapt to the free-market
economy since the early 1990s. There remains an imbalance in
the amount of work to be done, as Communist-era policies often
had uneven and destructive policies toward certain architectural
heritage types, such as religious buildings and former manor
houses. This discrepancy remains readily apparent in reunited
Germany, where despite concerted planning and renewal efforts,
much remains to be done in bringing architectural protection
in the former East Germany to the same level as the rest of
the country. The historic center of L'viv, Ukraine, is remarkably
intact. But it was preserved mainly due to its remoteness and
thanks to benign neglect, and it will require much effort to
effectively preserve and present its historic buildings and places.
In Russia, conservation and reconstruction priorities today are
often characterized by either very slow or very quick action. The
Constantine Palace on the outskirts of St. Petersburg on the Bay
of Finland was a ruin in 2002 (a detail is illustrated here); by 2006
the entire palace had been completely restored as a high-level
government-reception facility.

Figure 17-8 *War damage.* War is the oldest and historically the most destructive threat to cultural heritage, and it continues to be a problem in Europe today. In the past two decades, the historic built environments in parts of the Balkans and the Caucasus regions have suffered either directly or indirectly from wars and civil strife. In several instances in the former Yugoslavia, architectural symbols of different cultures have been specifically singled out as targets. Scores of historic towns and sites in the central regions of the former Yugoslavia were wantonly destroyed—including Sarajevo's National Library, the bridge at Mostar, and the Croatian city of Vukovar. Progress in reconstruction has differed greatly, with Dubrovnik recovering essentially in a matter of months. Chechnya in the Caucasus has only begun its process of recovery, and damaged sites in Kosovo remain untouched due to other priorities. Because of its forced abandonment during the Balkans conflict and the new delineation of a new national boarder through its hinterlands, the town of Pocitelj, Bosnia and Herzegovina, and its once distinguished mosque (illustrated here) will likely never again see its earlier vitality.

Figure 17-9 *Ethnic and religious differences.* Long-standing ethnic tensions between several countries and peoples of Europe, such as that between Greece and Turkey and within the former Yugoslavia, have often impeded the conservation of architectural heritage sites in those regions. The Armenian architectural heritage of Gaziantep, Turkey, has yet to be fully restored and reintegrated into one of the most historic towns in the region. The deterioration of neglected Greek Orthodox churches above the Green Line in Cyprus and the destruction of the Sarajevo Library in Bosnia (seen here) are two examples. Though pan-European institutions and values have encouraged cooperation, respect for cultural differences, and the revitalization of these resources, there continues to be a lack of public or private consensus about many of these sites—and of support for their proper restoration and reintegration as useful architectural resources.

Promising Developments in Europe

◀ **Figure 17-10** *International cooperation.* As originator of the modern architectural conservation movement and home to most of the world's intergovernmental heritage protection organizations, including UNESCO, ICOMOS, ICOM, and ICCROM, Europe has led the way in promoting and assisting international cooperation. This support has benefited not only the architectural heritage of different countries but also of Europe in general. Examples of cooperation in reconstruction are found where traumas of civil unrest have occurred, as in former Yugoslavia, or in the aftermath of natural disasters as seen in the high-quality restoration of historic buildings and works of art in Assisi in central Italy after powerful earthquakes in the region in late 1997. The multi-year reconstruction of the Old Bridge in Mostar (illustrated here)—destroyed in 1993 during the war in Bosnia-Hercegovina—is one of the most widely celebrated examples of a high quality heritage conservation project completed thanks to the partnership of several mostly European-based governments, international organizations, and private institutions. Prominent among NGOs that helped restore other buildings in post-war Mostar were the Research Center for Islamic History, Art, and Culture (IRCICA), Istanbul, which sponsored several meetings for preserving post-war Mostar, and a potent technical and financial partnership between the World Monuments Fund and the Aga Khan Trust for Culture that planned and restored several representative buildings on both sides of the Neretva River. In the case of Assisi, the Italian government coordinated the material and financial assistance of several regional, national, and international offers of assistance toward restoration and recovery in the region. *(Photo courtesy Dr. Mounir Bouchenaki)*

▲ **Figure 17-11** *Leadership past and present.* Charismatic political and civic leaders throughout Europe have taken an interest in architectural conservation and contributed significantly to raising awareness of heritage issues and in financing specific projects. The tradition of outspoken individuals arguing on behalf of historic protection begun by Victor Hugo, John Ruskin, William Morris, and others continues today. In the United Kingdom in the 1990s, the Prince of Wales's criticisms of planning legislation and development schemes that compromised historic sites have saved a number of important heritage sites, such as the environs of Paternoster Square in London that would have been compromised by a proposed incongruent commercial development. More often, leadership in heritage conservation occurs at the local level. In Istanbul, for instance, local lawyer and heritage protection advocate Çelik Gülersoy demonstrated the value and potential of the city's historic vernacular wooden architecture by restoring a number of structures as modestly scaled heritage hotels. Seen in the foreground here is Gülersoy's Pension Hagia Sophia.

Figure 17-12 *Protecting historic cities and districts.* Europe has witnessed unprecedented success in the protection of its historic ensembles and historic cities as it moved beyond the concept of conserving isolated monuments to conserving entire historic urban areas. France's Malraux Act of 1962 was one of the most important and influential of the laws to protect whole enclaves of historic buildings. The decaying Marais district of Paris (illustrated here) was one of the first neighborhoods transformed through the restoration of its wealth of seventeenth- through early twentieth-century buildings into a vibrant, sought-after mixed residential and commercial locale. Numerous cities throughout Europe have also conserved whole historic urban areas with the aid of effective legislation, technical support, and sophisticated financing schemes. The historic centers of Florence, Bologna, Genoa, Vicenza, and Lucca are a few examples in Italy alone.

Figure 17-13 *High-quality insertions of modern architecture and amenities.* In recent decades, Europe has witnessed a plethora of respectful new construction, including sympathetic new additions to historic buildings within protected historic areas. The scale of such projects ranges from individual building façade restorations to huge urban improvement schemes. In Amsterdam (illustrated here), there are scores of rehabilitated facades and new buildings that fit well among older neighboring buildings. The pièce de résistance of François Mitterrand's grand improvement program for the Louvre Museum and Tuileries Gardens in Paris in the 1990s was the construction of its famous bold new entrance in the form a glass pyramid designed by American architect I. M. Pei. The project provided much-needed improved access to the complex and added space in extensive excavated areas beneath the principal courtyard of the complex.

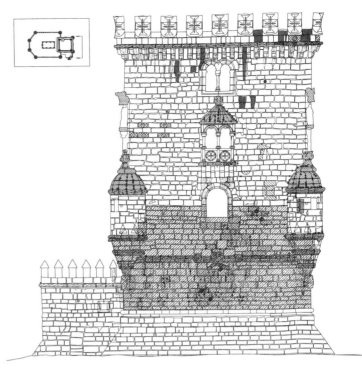

Figures 17-14 and 17-15 *Sophisticated conservation technologies and documentation systems.* Introduced in recent decades, new conservation technologies, methodologies, and creative implementation programs have transformed possibilities in architectural conservation, with several applied research laboratories in both the public and private sectors in Europe playing key roles in these developments. Noninvasive investigative techniques such as ultrasonic masonry analyses, photogrammetry, and endoscopic analyses, as well as advanced documentation methods such as aerial photography and computer-aided geographic information systems (GIS) and global positioning systems (GPS) mapping, are all regularly employed in European architectural conservation practice at the present time. At the Tower of Belém in Lisbon, conservation architects and professors from the Instituto Superior Técnico, Lisbone and Laboratório Nacional de Engenharia Civil (LNEC), Lisbon, together with private consultants, devised computerized quantitative and qualitative surveys of the historic masonry forming this highly important five-hundred-year-old building. The project was accomplished via a financial and technical partnership of the Portuguese Instituto Português do Património Arquitectónico, the World Monuments Fund (New York), and World Monuments Fund Portugal.

Figure 17-16 *Conservation of wooden architecture.* The fragility and impermanence of wooden architecture has made it particularly susceptible to the ravages of time and nature, yet in Europe in recent years pioneering solutions have been found to safeguard and restore this type of heritage. Especially in northern Europe, where wood has historically been the most prevalent building material, solutions ranging from organized wood-restoration crafts training courses to sophisticated chemical or water-mist, fire-suppression systems have been developed for the restoration and conservation of wooden structures. Recent projects include initiatives by the Norwegian government to restore all of its surviving medieval stave churches while installing state-of-the-art fire-protection systems in each. Similarly significant measures have been taken at Old Rauma in western Finland, the largest, best-preserved Nordic wooden town. After more than a decade of discussion and planning, the magnificent eighteenth-century Church of the Transfiguration at Kizhi Island in northern Russia (illustrated here) began a fifteen-year stabilization and restoration program that will entail its suspension from a structural steel scaffolding followed by its partial disassembly, structural repair, and reassembly from its foundations up.

▲▲ **Figure 17-17** *Innovative archaeological displays.* The extensive numbers of prehistoric and ancient ruins found throughout Europe have long been recognized as requiring special preservation and presentation measures. The continent's archaeologists and heritage conservationists have risen to this challenge, making Europe, especially its Mediterranean shores, among the world's best places to view innovative protection and display measures for archaeological sites. England has been a leader in archaeological site conservation and display; the in situ display of the remains of a Roman villa at Fishbourne in Sussex (seen here) is an outstanding early example dating from the 1970s. The retrieval of the Swedish warship *Vasa* from Stockholm harbor and its conservation treatment and display within a new museum enclosure set a certain standard in the display of maritime heritage. Elsewhere in Europe, archaeological remains are displayed as features within existing historic buildings such as at Wawel Castle in Krakow and Santa Maria del Fiore in Florence, where ruins at their foundation levels are featured.

▲ **Figure 17-18** The clear-spanned space achieved with glue-laminated trusses forming a completely naturally lit enclosure at Fishbourne Roman Villa carefully avoids damage to its impressive, surviving mosaic floors.

Figure 17-19 *Parador and pousada systems of Spain and Portugal.* Over the course of the twentieth century, Spain and Portugal have developed an innovative reuse scheme for their numerous historic castles, fortresses, palaces, convents, and monasteries that were unused and deteriorating due to changes in need and a lack of maintenance. Hundreds of these structures have been restored and converted into networks of luxury hotels by a state-owned tourism commission in Spain and a private company in Portugal. In addition to conserving and ensuring the future protection of these important historic resources, these schemes have also promoted tourism in rural and other less commonly visited areas of these two countries. The development of a former palace in Trujillo, Spain, to become a *parador* saved an important historic building, gave the fortified upper town a much-needed amenity, and ensures the vitality of the town's historic center.

Figure 17-20 *A guest room* within the Parador de Trujillo.

Figure 17-21 *Conserved British country houses—models for preserving a particular building type.* In an effort to slow the alarming rate of destruction of British country houses, especially since World War II, the hard work of several conservation advocates began to have an effect. The concerted effort, involving historians, heritage conservation activists, the British National Trust, and the group later known as English Heritage, raised the alarm about the loss of many the country's houses, explicitly pointing out the consequences and the merits of conserving this special national historic resource. By leading the way with examples and using a variety of techniques such as the formation of civic trusts for acquisition, conservation, and accommodation of public access, the effort not only saved numerous houses by making their continued operation more viable, but it also did much to popularize Great Britain's architectural heritage in general. The opening of portions of Belvoir Castle in Leicestershire to the public on a year-round basis while its owners, the family of the Duke of Rutland, remain in residence elsewhere in the large estate, is an example. *(Photo used by kind permission of the Trustees of the Ninth Duke of Rutland's will)*

Figure 17-22 *Adaptive use of industrial heritage.* Europe has also used innovative adaptive-use schemes to conserve a number of its historic industrial buildings that outlived their original purposes. By converting former steel manufacturing plants along the Ruhr Valley in Germany into commercial developments, viable new uses, creative designs for reuse, and sound economic development strategies have been combined for the benefit of townships, developers, and investors. Sometimes such conversions pose complicated reuse challenges, such as the Tour and Taxis Transportation Hub in Brussels, which has recently been partially adapted as a mixed-use commercial center. Factories and wharves from London to Istanbul have been converted into museum and art-gallery complexes and mixed-use new developments, as are seen in large harbor redevelopment projects in Liverpool, England; Genoa and Naples in Italy; Lisbon; Bergen and Hamburg in Germany; Copenhagen (seen here); and other cities.

▲ ▲ **Figure 17-23** *Conserving masterpieces of modern architecture.* As the birthplace of modern architecture, Europe has no shortage of landmarks of twentieth-century design. Though many of these buildings are threatened and much remains to be done, especially in Moscow, with its rare collection of avant-garde architecture by Konstantin Melnikov, Moisey Ginzburg, and other masters, elsewhere landmarks of twentieth-century architectural design have been carefully restored. Impressive examples include Le Corbusier's Villa Savoye near Paris; Josef Hoffman's Stoclet Palace in Brussels; Walter Gropius's Bauhaus School in Dessau, Germany (seen here before restoration); and Erich Mendelsohn's Einstein Tower in Potsdam, Germany. The restoration of Adolf Loos's Villa Müller in Prague in 2000 set a new standard for quality in restoring modernist landmarks that should be matched in years to come in the much-needed restoration of Ludwig Mies van der Rohe's Villa Tugendhat in Brno, Czech Republic. The international organization DOCOMOMO (the International Working Party for *DO*cumentation and *CO*nservation of Building Sites and Neighborhoods of the *MO*dern *MO*vement) has led the way in identifying and researching exemplary twentieth-century architecture and advocates its preservation.

▲ **Figure 17-24** *The Bauhaus in Dessau, Germany,* after its careful restoration in 1999.

Figure 17-25 *Cultural landscapes and greenways.* The scale of physical concern for the human-shaped environment in Europe in the late twentieth century has expanded to include historic cultural landscapes, which often encompass hundreds of square miles. Since 1992, UNESCO has recognized a number of European mixed cultural and natural heritage sites that give unique testimony to historic interactions of nature and humankind. In addition, many of the nearly two hundred UNESCO biospheres in Europe, which ensure the protection of examples of the natural environment and biodiversity, also include cultural heritage sites. One of Europe's more innovative combined cultural and natural conservation programs started in southern Moravia in the Czech Republic in 1992, when the vast areas surrounding the *zameks* ("castles") of Lednice and Valtice were recognized for their international significance. Planning and various demonstration architectural conservation projects orchestrated by the World Monuments Fund in cooperation with the Czech Ministerstvo Kultury helped create a synergy and momentum that soon greatly expanded to the sites being placed on UNESCO's World Heritage List. In connection with these activities, enterprising local nature enthusiasts with international assistance reactivated old trail systems in the area and reestablished historic pathways and thoroughfare connections between towns in the region. The Czech Greenways program presently extends throughout the Czech Republic and into several neighboring countries to the extent that it is now possible to hike or bicycle the entire historic route from Prague to Vienna and from Budapest to Krakow.

At the nexus of Europe, Asia, and Africa, the countries along the southern and eastern edges of the Mediterranean and on the Arab peninsula are home to cultural heritage of vital importance, not only to this region but also to numerous modern civilizations and the history of humankind in general. This truly universal heritage includes some of the oldest evidence of human cultural production in the world, as well as extensive remains of the earliest cities, with layer after layer of history documenting thousands of years of occupation. Today's cultural heritage conservationists in the region are responsible not only for the monuments and archaeological remains of Mesopotamian, Egyptian, and Persian civilizations but also for the medieval Islamic cities and evidence of the Crusaders, colonizers, and modern developments that coexist with the remnants of this ancient past.

The region's long history is rich with examples of the reuse of old structures and the repair and maintenance of important sites; however, conservation for the sake of conservation is a twentieth-century endeavor in North Africa and the Middle East. In many cases, these ideas were imported by Europeans but quickly found their place in newly established ministries of culture throughout the region. In the half century after World War II, the countries of the region developed in different directions, and a diverse range of conservation policies emerged.

Nevertheless, the countries forming North Africa and the Middle East share aspects of their cultural histories and today face many of the same threats to their historic sites. Among the most common of these are looting to feed the profitable trade in illicit archaeological objects, loose enforcement of legislation, political instability, population growth, insensitive infrastructural development, and a harsh desert environment that has in some ways contributed to the deterioration of built heritage.

In recent decades, conflicts in Iraq, Iran, Israel, the Palestinian Territories, and Lebanon have caught valuable architectural sites and urban ensembles in the crossfire. In many cases, ongoing conflicts in the region inhibit local initiatives or international assistance for conservation projects. To draw attention to the detrimental effect of conflict on historic sites, the World Monuments Fund included the cultural heritage of the entire country of Iraq on its 2006 Watch™ List of 100 Most Endangered Sites. While a few countries of the region can claim their weak economies complicate conservation efforts, many Middle Eastern countries, especially the Gulf States, have abundant funds as a result of their extensive deposits of crude oil, though they do not always prioritize heritage concerns.

In North Africa, rich cultural heritage resources are only adequately protected in Egypt, whose powerful Supreme Council of Antiquities has broad powers and a complex bureaucracy. Other countries of the region have done little beyond officially recognizing their cultural heritage sites. These limited efforts have focused almost exclusively on designated World Heritage Sites, leaving hundreds of other important historic structures, towns, and cities without attention or protection. For cultural and political regions, colonial-era heritage has been even more neglected. Cultural heritage tourism has brought income to North Africa, but that is tempered by some of the most attractive sites in the region remaining difficult to access. A comprehensive approach to sustainable tourism is urgently needed even in Tunisia, especially since its successful urban conservation projects are being closely watched by its neighbors for the good examples they may represent.

The heritage of North Africa and the "Holy Land" has been of interest to Europeans for centuries. As explained earlier, the international heritage protection movement matured in part in reaction to the construction of the Aswan Dam in Egypt. Since then, international organizations such as UNESCO, the World Bank, and the Aga Khan Trust for Culture have assisted with conservation at important sites throughout the region. The ICCROM has raised awareness and trained local professionals through its Support Programme for the Cities of North Africa and Near and Middle East Countries (NAMEC).

The unresolved conflicts that have plagued the Arab world in the past half century, especially the chronic tensions that exist between Israel and its neighbors, have made heritage concerns low among the region's priorities. Political solutions and stability are almost a prerequisite for advancing conservation in the region. Moving away from isolated museum sites and toward linking heritage conservation's values and benefits to the wider community is also necessary for the trend to grow and mature in this region. Recognizing local development projects based on cultural heritage conservation will only reinforce recognition, appreciation, and protection of sites in the region. Integrating the educational potential of heritage conservation with stronger governmental support and international aid is key to ensuring the protection of the built heritage of North Africa and the Middle East. In addition, more intraregional collaborative opportunities and knowledge-sharing networks among these countries could greatly benefit sites and improve contemporary conservation practice in the region. With increased promotion of cultural-heritage tourism and international best-practices in field projects, the Middle East and North Africa could quickly become world leaders in architectural conservation practice.

Special Challenges Faced in North Africa and Western Asia

◀ **Figure 17-26** *Reconciling modern development needs and protecting archaeological heritage* is a special challenge in parts of the Middle East, where important archaeological remains are beneath many of the regions prime building locations. Preserving and presenting the ruins of the ancient Phoenician city of Tyre in Lebanon (of which a gateway from the Roman period is seen here) is a case in point: The remains of the ancient seaport dating to 900 BCE have posed obstacles to new coastal roadways and harbor developments. The answer lies in sensible land-use planning based on thorough archaeological investigations of the area, where sensitive landscape, architectural, and engineering designs should reconcile new infrastructure needs with the conservation and presentation of ancient Tyre's scant surviving remains.

▼ **Figure 17-27** *Multilayered histories and choices for their presentation* are special problems in the Middle East since evidence of earlier occupations at numerous sites dates back thousands of years. Beginning in the nineteenth century, when archaeologists and historians began to search for Biblical sources when some histories are favored over others for nationalist purposes, the questions always remain: Whose history is whose, and which of these histories will be favored in reuse and interpretation schemes? No sites in the Middle East better exemplify the problem of conserving and featuring different histories in the same location than the Dome of the Rock (seen here), the Wailing Wall, and the Temple of Solomon in Jerusalem, where two great religions claim essentially the same location as among their most hallowed heritage. Jerusalem is also the seat of the Christian faith, with the Church of the Holy Sepulchre and sites that led to the end of the life of Christ, all being related to the city.

Figure 17-28 *Working through and recognizing priorities of the waqf system* in the Muslim world adds to the complexity of restoring, preserving, and featuring heritage sites in flexible and sustainable ways. Ownership or control of a historic building by a *waqf* (a long-established Islamic religious body having purview over land and buildings) can be problematic, especially when buildings such as *sabils* (charitable water dispensaries) and madrassas (teaching facilities) are allowed to deteriorate and/or be abandoned before new uses for them are found. Muslim architecture owes much to these religious and community trusts that likely built the region's impressive architectural heritage in the first place. Today myriad restoration and adaptive-use opportunities exist in historic cities across the Arab world that are not easy to launch due to the complexities of the *waqf*, which must usually be involved even when a project may be government sponsored. Challenges remain for heritage conservationists and *waqf* authorities to find better ways to negotiate the protection of historic buildings that fall into this category. Until then some of the best architecture in the region is at risk of falling into further disrepair. The *sabil* of Yusuf Bey in Cairo, dating from 1634, illustrated here, is a case in point. *(Photo courtesy of Faisal Ali Rajper)*

Figure 17-29 *Rejection of traditional building techniques in favor of modern architecture* of lesser quality is frequently seen in developing countries of North Africa and the Middle East. The broad acceptance of Western-style steel, concrete, and glass buildings has had its appeal since it represented comfortable modernity, and its cost-efficiency for the usable floor area gained is hard to surpass. However, the thermal comfort afforded by many of these buildings and the cost of air-conditioning and maintaining such buildings in hot climates has been questioned in recent years. Since the mid-twentieth century, the substitution of traditional solid earthen construction with concrete- and masonry-block construction has fallen short of expectations of them as better building methods. The remarkably tall earthen architecture (with hewn natural stones) of Tarim, Sana'a, and Shibam (illustrated here) in Yemen show the potential of age-old earthen construction. Such construction methods were fast disappearing until the preservation of Yemen's earthen architecture was promoted through the efforts of a few international architectural conservationists working with locals who appreciated their uniqueness. While it is hard to envision a widespread return to building in sun-dried mud brick, there are lessons from it with regard to its thermal retention and transmission properties, its cost-efficiency, and the ease and economy of repairing it. The creation of efficient yet imaginative new architectural designs for today's needs was urged throughout the 1970s by Egyptian architect Hassan Fathy, but mostly to no avail.

Figure 17-30a and b *Sound and useful twentieth-century architecture neglected* today is commonplace in North Africa, the Middle East, and elsewhere. Most major cities in the Arab world were designed or redesigned by European architects and planners in the nineteenth and early twentieth centuries. New buildings at the time were usually high-quality and designed with sensitivity for the local environment. The climatically suited buildings of all types predating the independence of the various Middle Eastern and North African countries is often better than their replacements from the standpoint of energy consumption, scale, and aesthetics. The ATBAT housing complex in the Cité des Jeunes in Casablanca, Morocco, was built by Léon Aroutcheff and Robert Jean and was featured in the French magazine *Architecture d'Aujourd'hui* as a success in new housing design. Today the building's distinguishing features, such as its balconies and overall color scheme, have been erased by successive alterations and infill campaigns performed by local residents. Meanwhile, Arts Decoratif monuments such as Hubert Bride's 1917 Immeuble Bessoneau (also known as the Hotel Lincoln) have suffered from neglect. *(Photos courtesy of Meisha Hunter)*

Figure 17-31 *Uneven development of heritage offerings* can negatively affect both a country's tourist economy and its more popular heritage destinations. Having a greater number of options and heritage themes available for interested visitors adds to a country's potential appeal to visitors deciding on their destinations. In addition, having numerous offerings can relieve pressures on the most popular sites. Libya and Tunisia have extraordinary cultural tourism potential, with Libya especially still needing to engage in the final planning and preparation of several of its sites for organized preservation and presentation. (The city of Sabratha, one of dozens of Roman sites in Libya, is seen here.) There are lessons in the ways Morocco and Jordan have handled the same problem, which is to feature their key sites in terms of heritage circuits, where lesser sites along the way are featured as being interesting as well. This approach is both obvious and inevitable; viewing, developing, and presenting national heritage as a system of offerings has proven effective in generating increased tourism revenues, spending by outsiders in locales where it is needed, extended stays, and satisfying promises made in tourism promotion. *(Courtesy Byron Bell)*

Promising Developments in North Africa and Western Asia

Figure 17-32 *Success at preserving and featuring a large-scale heritage area* as seen at Petra in Jordan, where years of efforts at master planning and balanced site management have yielded results. Famous since the nineteenth century as a special destination for travelers, Jordan's Department of Antiquities and other related agencies, in cooperation with the Petra National Trust, has over the past two decades managed this World Heritage site with increasing success. Along the way, hard decisions had to be made, such as disallowing access by horses—a romantic notion but with its practical problems—and the removal of a Bedouin community that sold wares to tourists from the center of the archaeological park. A number of site improvements were made including enhanced site circulation, partial restoration of ancient water drainage systems to prevent flooding, and the installation of wayside markers and other interpretative aids throughout the vast site. While there is more to do at this huge site in the areas of stone conservation and interpretation, significant progress has already been made.

Figure 17-33 *Innovation in adaptive use of buildings for tourism* is seen at several sites in Jordan, such as the rehabilitation of the large caravansary near Amman to be a restaurant featuring traditional cuisines and entertainment. At Petra, where there has been much worry about spoiling the ambience of the greater site with uncontrolled hotel construction, a partnership was created under the leadership of a European entrepreneur to reuse the entire small village Taybet Zaman as overnight accommodations for tourists. The scant remaining population of the village was made shareholders of the enterprise and, after voluntarily relocated to modern housing nearby, they worked at the hotel in roles ranging from management to operating its restaurant to continuing as artisans in traditional industries such as glassblowing, metalwork, and baking.

Figure 17-34 *Successful conservation of historic urban centers* in the medinas of Tunis and Fez in the 1990s can be credited in large part to the efforts of the World Bank. Both places were carefully studied as a basis for the insertion of new infrastructure, including water supply, waste removal, and power supply, after which its difficult installation was carried out without major interruption to the communities being served. World Bank projects and other similar loan programs carry with them the added benefits of specialized socioeconomic analyses often utilizing specially developed economic and planning models. The research involved and feedback gained in these large urban conservation projects has done much to inspire similar projects elsewhere in the world and has generally raised the stakes for such undertakings. These kinds of projects have also brought a number of new and powerful players into the heritage protection arena.

Figure 17-35 *Featuring differing histories in the same location via archaeology* has been accomplished at two prominent sites in the Middle East, one in Jerusalem and one in Aleppo, Syria. An earlier successful urban conservation project is seen in the interpretation of Old Jerusalem, where the Israeli Antiquities Authority conducted excavations in the 1970s and 1980s, finding residential quarters dating to as early as 500 BCE that are effectively interpreted as architectural and archaeological palimpsests for residents and visitors to Old Jerusalem. At the Citadel of Aleppo (seen here), the Aga Khan Trust for Culture, in partnership with the Syrian Ministry of Culture and with the support of the World Monuments Fund, has investigated, stabilized, and conserved a number of structures atop this prominent ancient site that is one of the world's oldest settlements. Being a multilayered *tel*, archaeology has revealed much over the past century, including the recent discovery by archaeologists from the University of Heidelberg of a remarkably intact ancient Hittite temple. The quality of the research and conservation work carried out at the Citadel of Aleppo since the early 1990s has served as an example for the region.

▶ **Figure 17-37** *Post-conflict recovery in Iraq* will be extensive and will take many years. The destabilization of the former firmly controlled national heritage protection program caused by both Gulf Wars has led not only to the rampant spoliation and destruction of hundreds of Iraq's heritage sites from all periods but has put the country's Ministry of Culture and museums systems in disarray. The surviving masonry arch of Ctesiphon dating from the third century CE (illustrated here) was not helped by the nearby placement of military facilities the 1980s. In an effort to help prepare Iraqi heritage protection professionals for the task of recovery when peace returns, a joint effort led by the World Monuments Fund and the Getty Conservation Institute has offered a number of heritage-documentation and training programs to cadres of Iraqi professionals at workshops conducted outside the country since 2004. Other entities are poised to help further when conditions improve, such as an International Coordinating Committee formed by UNESCO and an international conservation initiative sponsored by the government of the Czech Republic that is aimed at helping to conserve the ancient city of Erbil.

Figure 17-36 *Tourism management at world-famous heritage sites* has an impressive record in Egypt, in part because the country's magnificent cultural heritage has lured foreign travelers for so long. While the very large sites of the pyramids and sphinx on the Giza plateau and the huge temples of Karnak and Luxor pose no real problems in interpretation or circulation, certain other "must-see" sites in the Valleys of the Kings and Queens in Luxor do. Overcrowding upon entering the more famous tombs, including the recently discovered multilayered Rameses II tomb has been so serious in recent years that it posed urgent problems related to the management of the number of visitors. In cooperation with the Supreme Council of Antiquities, the Theban Mapping Project under the American University in Cairo, with financial support from the World Monuments Fund and the American Express Corporation, led an effort to better present the Valley of the Kings. One of the ideas was brilliantly simple: Have several identical, durable, and attractively designed sign panels on display in strategic locations for tourists to study while waiting to enter the tombs. This reduced both boredom among visitors and the time spent inside once they've entered.

Figure 17-38 *Various international partnerships for heritage conservation* in North Africa and western Asia have yielded impressive results, especially within the past decade. In cooperation with the host governments of several countries, the Aga Khan Trust for Culture has applied considerable funding and conservation expertise at several important heritage sites in the region. Its most recent achievement has been the creation of the Al-Azhar Park in Old Cairo, where about 74 acres of rubble that had been deposited against the city wall over the centuries were removed to create a richly landscaped urban park, complete with fountains and a number of restored historic buildings. As often happens in such large projects, a certain synergy takes place along the way. In this instance, not only did the Egyptian Supreme Council of Antiquities participate in a number of valuable ways, but other international NGOs—such as the World Monuments Fund and the United States's Ford Foundation—joined in and co-funded several of the historic building conservation projects. *(Photo © Aga Khan Trust for Culture/Aga Khan Cultural Services-Egypt)*

Figure 17-39 Impressive technical achievements in architectural conservation have occurred at some sites in the Middle East, especially in Egypt. In cooperation with the Egyptian Supreme Council of Antiquities, the Getty Conservation Institute addressed the very challenging problems of conserving painted finishes in the Tomb of Nefertari in the Valley of the Queens in Luxor. Other international assistance in conservation has been provided by the German Archaeological Institute, the Polish PKZ conservation atelier that did extensive restoration work at the Temple of Hatshepsut in the 1980s (illustrated here), and the Oriental Institute of the University of Chicago in its long-standing efforts to document and conserve stone carving at Luxor Temple. One of ICCROM's most effective programs, the Support Programme for the Cities of North Africa and Near and Middle East Countries (NAMEC), established in 2001, has accomplished much in the region as well in areas of technical assistance and professional education.

SUB-SAHARAN AFRICA

The overwhelming cultural and architectural diversity of the African continent is united by the shared experience of wholesale exploitation and colonization by outside forces. Though many world regions grapple with the complications of post-colonialism, this problem is especially acute in sub-Saharan Africa, where this legacy pervades all contemporary experiences, including heritage conservation.[6] It is the root of three of the greatest challenges faced by heritage conservation professionals in most sub-Saharan countries today, including ineffective governmental institutions, destitute economies, and conflicted senses of ownership and responsibility. The first two factors have resulted in a lack of funding for heritage conservation, of enforcement of heritage protection policies, and of trained professionals throughout sub-Saharan Africa, but the third factor is in many ways the most difficult to overcome.

Traditional cultural heritage management systems existed in sub-Saharan Africa even before the establishment of European-modeled structures and polices by colonial powers. Ritual use, taboos, and religious restrictions ensured the survival of sacred sites and complexes for centuries throughout the African continent.[7] The most important aspect of these traditional systems was their involvement of the entire community in heritage protection, an aspect lost over the course of the past century when Western-style legislation and agencies and Western-trained conservation specialists took over the care of their historic sites.[8] Though traditional connections to heritage sites have been severed in most of Africa, Botswana's community-trust program offers a positive example of how local groups can maintain a sense of ownership and benefit economically from cultural heritage that could be emulated across the continent.

Of all of the world's continents, Africa is plagued with the most challenging threats to architectural conservation. Though not immune to the development pressures and natural disasters that trouble the rest of the world, heritage in Africa suffers much more from the rightful preoccupation of governments and aid workers with humanitarian concerns, such as the HIV/AIDS epidemic and malnutrition, which drain resources and energies. Most African countries often find themselves trapped between international pressure to better protect their cultural heritage sites and local demands for improved infrastructure and economic development. In addition, political instability and guerilla-style conflict hampers conservation in the central and northern regions of sub-Saharan Africa as it does in the Middle East.

Prospects for heritage look grim in some African countries, such as Zimbabwe, which takes its name and much of its pride and identity from its cultural monuments yet has failed in its efforts to protect and conserve them effectively.

However, other countries reflect encouraging trends, such as South Africa, which has emerged as a regional economic and cultural leader with architectural heritage conservation successes that have allowed it to foster developments in neighboring countries.

Fortunately, international recognition of African architectural heritage and financial support for its conservation has increased in recent years. The ambitious Africa 2009 program recently launched by ICCROM has offered a new source of hope for historic sites in sub-Saharan Africa by working to improve local awareness and appreciation of cultural resources, augment professional capacities, and establish an information exchange network.[9] UNESCO has recognized dozens of cultural heritage sites in sub-Saharan Africa, and when combined with the rich wildlife and scenery, these designations have already contributed to the growth of tourism and economies in East Africa. South Africa is a leader in cultural heritage conservation in the continent today, with a balanced program of conserving all kinds of history that occurred in its lands, ranging from the colonial heritage of Cape Town, Johannesburg, and Pretoria to its recent successful nomination to the World Heritage List of the Mapungubwe Cultural Landscape. This and other listings of Africa's cultural landscapes and intangible heritage sites reflect a positive trend toward accepting the importance of more of Africa's traditional social reference points and routes and its sacred natural elements.

In the past decade, there has been an increasing sensitivity on the part of international experts and government bodies to the interests of local communities and a concerted effort to involve them from the beginning in the planning and management of sites.[10] Many recognized West African sites, such as Timbuktu in Mali and the Royal Palaces of Abomey in Benin, are still active ritual centers and functioning towns, and thus conservationists must carefully balance the needs of their users with maintaining the sites and their integrity.

In sub-Saharan Africa, improving contemporary conservation practice over the long term will require the building and rebuilding of local awareness of heritage protection, the restoration of traditional patterns of ownership and use, the enforcement of existing legislation, and increased intra-African cooperation. The international heritage conservation community must also continue to play an active role to ensure future conservation successes in Africa. It must carefully balance aid and advice with respect for difference, and it should focus on empowering local communities by improving local capacities to carry out and finance projects independently.

Special Challenges Faced in Sub-Saharan Africa

Figure 17-40 ***The "difficult" histories posed by European colonialism*** are omnipresent in sub-Saharan Africa, so much so that it is hardly noticed today. The wealth of their natural resources, their agricultural potential, and their location have made the countries comprising Africa's shorelines especially susceptible to outside influence. While in many respects colonization drew some areas of the continent into the modern world, cultural heritage legacies of Africa are sharply divided between indigenous and colonial, there being great needs today to tend to both. For example, there are still tangible reminders of the slave trade that existed along both the western and eastern shores of the continent – as illustrated by this image of a Gambian slave castle. Helping to ensure the protection of historical documentation of such difficult histories is UNESCO's Slave Trade Archives project, which has begun digitizing documentation of slave transactions via local projects in Gambia, Senegal, Ghana, and Benin. The island of Gorée, about 2.5 miles (4 kilometers) off the coast of Dakar, Senegal, served as a slaving post stronghold for nearly two centuries. Based on a conservation program for the site provided by UNESCO in 1978, the Senegalese government has since presented this infamous site to visitors of the island. Illustrated here is a view from one of the "slave castles" on Gorée. *(Courtesy Byron Bell)*

Figure 17-41 *Breaks in patterns of society and systems of inheritance* in Africa over the past four hundred years have ruptured understandings and roles of the past in the lives of many Africans today. In such situations, senses of place, belonging, and continuity are at risk. One of the best emblems of people migrating and resettling is seen in Johannesburg (illustrated), where immigrants from various African nations have settled in different blocks of the city's former central business district, though they have remained together through their language and ethnic ties. It remains to be seen how largely immigrant populations often living in former commercial buildings can coexist, and what the future holds for them.

Figure 17-42 *Other social priorities*—sickness, famine, and civil conflict in some areas of sub-Saharan Africa—have drawn attention and resources away from organized heritage protection efforts. The overpopulated Soweto district just to the east of Johannesburg (illustrated here) exemplifies "temporary" settlement that continues on indefinitely. Saving lives and rising above dire living circumstances will understandably always be a priority for national and foreign relief agencies. Heritage conservation programs, however, are frequently among the first activities to be on hand when civilized societies develop and begin to prosper. Two of the more prominent of such programs are ICCROM's Africa 2009 program, which helps educate heritage managers in successfully integrating heritage management and conservation practices, and the New Partnership for Africa's Development (NEPAD), which promotes appropriate management of African immovable cultural heritage as a tool toward sustainable development and poverty alleviation. The university-based CRATerre-EAG, the International Centre for Earth Construction in Grenoble, France, which is devoted to conserving earthen architecture, has significantly assisted several of the countries in Africa in actual hands-on architectural work.

Figure 17-43a and b *Rock art (petroglyphs) in peril*—an acute problem throughout Africa from its Mediterranean shores to South Africa. Along with the fossil record of earliest man, the rock art of Africa stands as the most enduring evidence of the continent's claim to being the site of the origins of humankind. Monuments in their own right, the thousands of rock-art sites in Africa have, on the whole, not fared well in the last century especially. Problems range from vandalism and theft to purposeful desecration of rock-art sites to keep visitors away. Systematic examination and documentation of the problems of conserving rock art in Africa is being led by the International Federation for Rock Art (IFORA). A cliff-face shelter at in northwest Zimbabwe and the images it contains are portrayed here. *(Courtesy Werner Schmid—1999)*

Figure 17-44 *Sub-Saharan Africa holds the record for exotic threats* to effective cultural heritage protection. In addition to the region having most of the usual threats to cultural heritage posed by humans and nature, there have been problems with wild animals: elephants toppled walls and stele in Ungwana, Kenya; burrowing aardvarks undermined stone wall foundations at Khami National Park in Zimbabwe (illustrated here); lions have threatened heritage documentation teams in several countries of Central and South Africa. The harsh tropical climate in equatorial Africa also threatens the survivability of all but the most durable constructions, such as the region's historic stone buildings.

Promising Developments in Sub-Saharan Africa

Figure 17-45 *The effective conservation of earthen architecture* in several sub-Saharan locations such as Mali and Ghana has proven to be an example of good heritage conservation practice for the continent and beyond. In Mali, age-old traditions in maintaining earthen architecture are consciously continuing after an interlude involving scientific analyses of ways to conserve finely painted exterior polychromy with technical assistance from the Getty Conservation Institute. Technical assistance from CRATerre-EAG has recently been very effective in restorations such as Larabanga Mosque in Ghana. The mosque in the village of Djenné-Djeno (illustrated here) is an example of both African earthen architecture that continues to serve its community well and whose periodic repairs ensure a continuity of age-old building traditions. *(Photo courtesy of Byron Bell)*

Figure 17-46 *The accomplishment of a number of impressive architectural conservation projects* is seen at places throughout sub-Saharan Africa at sites ranging from stabilized ruins in Kenya to some extraordinary documentation and site presentation work currently underway at the rock-cut churches of Lalibela, Ethiopia. In Cape Town, South Africa, heritage conservationists have undertaken the restoration of a number of buildings using European restoration principles at this oldest European settlement in South Africa. The Italian colonial city of Asmara in northwestern Eritrea represented a utopian vision when it was built in the 1930s as a collection of avant-garde designs (illustrated) produced by some of Italy's leading architects of the time. Asmara has survived mainly due to a lack of change and its relative remoteness. The architecture and story of Asmara has been well covered through recent documentation and publication efforts; its survival is thus more likely. *(Photo courtesy and © Edward Denison, 2003)*

Figure 17-47 *Conserved intangible heritage in sub-Saharan Africa* is exemplified by the separate listings of the Richtersveldt (South Africa) and the Mapungubwe cultural landscapes to the World Heritage List. These large territories with their scant evidence of human usage reflect the antithesis of consciously built "monumental" architecture found elsewhere. Instead, the buildings and material culture of some of the region's indigenous populations subtly reflect thousands of years of African history, which is mainly evidenced by the living practices of many of the indigenous populations of the continent today. The most prominent form of cultural heritage of the nomadic Nama people that inhabit the present Richtersveldt cultural landscape in northwestern South Africa is the oval hut made of short-lived construction materials consisting of bent sticks covered by woven reed mats to form oval huts. Similar buildings are on display as replicas of the reed-covered shelters of the Nam people on exhibit in Pretoria, at the historic village re-creation seen here.

Figure 17-48a and b *Growing interests in the restitution of art removed to other countries is well exemplified by the* Italian government's recent return of the Aksum Obelisk to its original location in Aksum, Ethiopia, in 2006. This 78-foot (24-meter) once-monolithic structure stood as the tallest of several obelisks at the ceremonial center of Aksum from the time of its erection during the fourth century CE until its removal by Italian engineers in 1937 to be the centerpiece of a traffic circle in front of the Ministry for Italian Africa (later the building for the United Nations Food and Agricultural Organization) in Rome. Italy lost Ethiopia as a colony during World War II. Nearly a half century later, as a gesture of friendship, Italy organized the return of this icon of Ethiopia's cultural heritage to its home, where it was joyously celebrated on 4 September 2008. *(Photos courtesy Ethiopian Embassy, London, and © ICCROM)*

CENTRAL AND SOUTH ASIA

The diverse and extensive heritage of Central and South Asia has witnessed both the destructiveness of man and of nature in the recent past, with the March 2001 destruction of the colossal Buddha sculpture in Bamiyan, Afghanistan, by the iconoclastic Taliban regime, and the December 2004 tsunami damage to the old town of Galle and other cultural heritage sites in Sri Lanka. In Central Asia, the conservation and protection of cultural heritage is a nascent trend plagued by weak economies and differing priorities, but South Asia has a stronger tradition for heritage management and systems that have permitted some recent conservation successes.

The five landlocked Central Asian countries have been a crossroads of trade routes and a borderland of empires for most of their long history. The importance of this region to both Western and Eastern civilizations is only now being widely recognized and appreciated, since recent political developments have opened these countries up to international attention. International involvement is a key component of Central Asia's contemporary architectural conservation, since the governments of many of these newly independent countries are preoccupied with modernization, industrialization, and humanitarian problems. Restoration of religious sites in these newly desecularized countries has received the most attention from local sources, and international organizations such as UNESCO and the Aga Khan Trust for Culture have supported additional architectural and other cultural heritage conservation activities in the region.

The legacy of Soviet domination, continued instability in Afghanistan, and heightened religious fundamentalism throughout the region have all undermined efforts to protect cultural heritage in Central Asia, adding to the region's uncertain future. Central Asia also requires more local professionals and training opportunities to maintain and expand the projects initiated by outside organizations. The quality of workmanship in the region is often low, public interest in and support of heritage protection concerns is minimal, and urban conservation is almost completely lacking.

In South Asia, rapid urbanization and population growth threatens heritage as new developments encroach on historic sites and pollution and waste management problems degrade the environment. The cultural complexity of the region also poses a significant challenge for conservators, but at the same time the region's shared concerns offer an opportunity for cooperation, professional exchanges, and knowledge sharing that can promote common ground for overcoming tense political relationships—especially between Pakistan and India.

Modernization and economic development have dominated both government and private agendas in recent decades, and cultural heritage conservation has often been marginalized by these processes. Public awareness of the importance of conserved architectural heritage and of its economic potential has been raised since 1984 by the Indian National Trust for Art and Cultural Heritage (INTACH), a not-for-profit voluntary organization; but, as in many other parts of the world, its message requires constant reinforcement.[11] Though architectural conservation is now a noticeable part of India's agenda, the country finds itself lagging behind in some conservation practices and standards today. Its strong economy and extensive bureaucratic support structure are allowing it to catch up quickly, however.[12] Other South Asian countries are following India's lead with mixed success, a result of lesser resources in the face of overwhelming conservation needs.

South Asian societies have maintained strong links to their traditional heritage and sacred landscapes; even the colonial experience did not sever these connections as it did elsewhere in the world. Unfortunately, however, since independence, government policies in many South Asian countries have not built on these connections but rather have undermined local senses of responsibility for historic sites. Today, however, an understanding of the importance of these relationships is becoming more widespread, and contemporary practice is witnessing the incorporation of more holistic and anthropological approaches to architectural conservation. Innovative new programs are addressing community-based conservation initiatives, such as the revival of architectural woodworking crafts in Nepal, linking Sri Lankan students with nearby temples to ensure the temples' protection, and the integration of cultural heritage with sustainable tourism in Pakistan.[13]

With its burgeoning population, strong community ties to heritage, and increasingly influential economies, South Asia will likely play an ascendant role on the world stage of professional cultural heritage management in the coming decades. Projects such as Nepal's Kathmandu Valley Preservation Trust and Sri Lanka's Cultural Triangle demonstrate that improved understanding of regional cultural realities leads to more effective conservation practice. A significant new contribution to heritage protection in India, to the region, and to the field in general, has been INTACH's Charter for the Conservation of Non-Listed Cultural Heritage Sites in India, adopted in 2004, which has several distinct innovations. (See also Chapter 16.) With India as an economic and organizational leader, the region is well-poised to continue its traditions and innovations in architectural conservation. Truly blessed with more similarities than differences, the countries of South Asia are in a unique position to combine efforts for heritage conservation and overcome residual conflicts in the region with this shared purpose.

316

Special Challenges Faced in Central and South Asia

Figure 17-49 *Overzealous renovation and restoration work* has been a common problem in efforts at heritage protection in Central Asia all the way east to Mongolia, in part due to the region's relatively brief participation in the field and also due the heavy-intervention philosophy of Russian restorers assigned to these regions through much of the twentieth century. With a lack of a robust conservation ethos and so few examples of more subtle, best practices in conservation, it has proven hard to overcome their tradition of extensive restoration. It can be fairly argued that in many instances involving severely deteriorated earthen architecture or masonry architecture clad in glazed tile, measured conservation approaches toward featuring partial ruins are not viable, since unless a structure can be made to adequately withstand threats from water intrusion and seismic tremors, its protection will likely be short-lived. Some decisions about the degree to which buildings are restored have been overtly political, with perhaps the best example still being Saddam Hussein's directive to extensively rebuild the ruins of Babylon in the 1980s to reflect his regime's power, an act that one could argue today has its own historicity. A similar problem of over-restoration involving a different building type occurred at Bahla Fort in Oman, (illustrated here).

Figures 17-50 and 17-51 *War and wanton destruction* can bring instant ruin to cultural heritage sites that often took years to create and that existed for centuries. Vivid images of this were broadcast around the world on television in the weeks after the March 2001 explosion of the Bamiyan Buddhas in Afghanistan, which dated from 632 CE. More an act of religious iconoclasm or simple vandalism than an act of war, the deliberate destruction of these rock-hewn Buddha images carved in the cliff faces 125- and 180-feet (38- and 55-meters) high was over in an instant. Valiant efforts on the part of UNESCO to negotiate with representatives of the Taliban regime in the weeks before this incident did not help, and today the country wishes to have them reconstructed. *(Intact Buddha image [1972] courtesy Byron Bell ; destroyed Buddha image courtesy Giorgios Toubekis)*

▶▶ **Figure 17-52a and b** *Technical problems in architectural conservation such as protecting sculpted caves and structures excavated* from rock escarpments are not uncommon in Central Asia and the Indian Subcontinent. Examples include the former Bamiyan Buddhas in Afghanistan; the Ajanta Caves in Maharashtra, southern India; and the rock-cut features of Sigiriya in Sri Lanka. Most can only be effectively addressed after extensive and complicated geotechnical studies, and the problems of their conservation can be large and expensive. At the Ajanta Caves (illustrated here), difficult structural repairs and efforts to mitigate water intrusion have in the past involved the use of concrete reinforcing and patches, which has in instances proven to be an ineffective long-term solution. *(Courtesy ©ICCROM/Rodolfo Luján Lunsford)*

▲ **Figure 17-53 *Crushing population and development pressures*** in most urban areas of the subcontinent pose problems at sites in urban locations or peripheral areas that once had carefully considered and often generous *curtilages* (enclosed areas surrounding a structure) that may have contained support buildings or landscape features that were integral to the principal building. Housing shortages and uncontrolled settlements characterize many of the subcontinent's cities and towns. Removing these settlements and relocating their inhabitants to more suitable locations is no easy matter but one that has been tackled in the region for well over a century. Examples include the Taj Mahal in Agra, India, and the Humayun's Tomb in New Delhi (illustrated here). Water features and the spatial character of these buildings have been restored, though their original landscaping is only suggested by modern planting schemes.

▶ **Figure 17-54 *Pressures by throngs of pilgrims*** at religious heritage sites throughout Asia have posed problems at times to the protection of sacred sites. Christian sites in Jordan; Muslim sites, especially at Mecca, the prophet Mohammed's birthplace; and huge numbers of worshippers on holy days at the Temple of the Tooth in Kandy, Sri Lanka, are good examples of how highly important religious heritage sites can attract and almost overwhelm a significant heritage site. The number of pilgrims can be quite high, as illustrated here at one of the most revered Sikh sites, the sixteenth-century Sikh temple Sri Hamandir Sahib in Amritsar, eastern India. *(Courtesy © Raghu Rai, Magnum Pictures)*

Promising Developments in Central and South Asia

Figure 17-55 *The silk routes of central and western Asia* are world landmarks for the roles they played in the history of commerce. From antiquity through as late as the mid-nineteenth century, the goods and cultural influences that passed over these numerous routes enriched towns along their way save for the period of the Mongol invasions in the thirteenth and fourteenth centuries. Growing interest in the silk routes, including their documentation and related research, combine to make these famous transportation routes a promising new offering in heritage tourism. International friendship and heritage advocacy schemes led by the famous musician Yo-Yo Ma and the artist Ikuo Hirayama have done much to underscore the importance of trade history and the international cooperation that the silk routes fostered in their day. The site of Ayaz Kala, Uzbekistan (illustrated here) is one of many sites, including Samarkand and Bukhara, Uzbekistan, and Kaifeng, China, on the northern section of the silk route, that should benefit from the increased offerings in cultural tourism in central Asia.

Figure 17-56 *On-site training in architectural conservation* is a hallmark of the work being done at Chogha Zanbil, Iran's 3300-year-old mud-brick citadel. Conservation issues range from uneven settling, erosion, poor water drainage, intrusive modern brick and concrete repairs, and visitor damage. Owing to the site's importance, in the 1990s work at Chogha Zanbil (illustrated here) became the first internationally supported conservation project in Iran since the 1979 Islamic Revolution. The project is being jointly executed by UNESCO; CRATerre-EAG; and the Iranian Cultural Heritage Organization (ICHO), with financial assistance given also by the Japanese government. A key component of the project is a multiyear, on-site training effort that helps Iranian architectural conservationists and other regional participants focus on the variety of issues associated with the conservation of earthen architecture. Regional participation includes young professionals from Iran, Azerbaijan, Kazakhstan, Kyrgyzstan, Tajikistan, and Turkmenistan. The training program has established a permanent on-site conservation staff for Chogha Zanbil and serves as a basis for the Iranian government's decision to construct a number of additional research centers at other key historic sites throughout the country.

Figure 17-57 *Large heritage sites* have been preserved and presented in several places in India and Sri Lanka. The estates and towns of Rajput rulers in northern and western India, the ancient sacred sites in their dramatic landscape settings that comprise the Golden Triangle in north-central Sri Lanka, and the remains of the former Hindu kingdoms of Champaner and Hampi are examples. Many of these sites have benefited from conservation planning during which priorities were determined, circulation patterns considered, and modern amenities were planned and provided, enabling them to become sustainable heritage tourism destinations. The many sites that comprise the UNESCO-listed Golden Triangle in Sri Lanka, of which Vadatage Polom is one (illustrated here), offer an amazing blend of long history, exotic geological and geographical marvels, and impressive architectural and artistic achievements.

Figure 17-58 *The heritage hotel system in Rajasthan, India,* is an exemplar of heritage tourism route development and stands as one of the most special of all possible visitor experiences in India. Established in the early 1970s, this innovative concept consists of welcoming paying guests into adaptively used palaces and their support facilities. Accommodations range in price, proximity to one another, and degrees of luxury. Visitors are generously welcomed and made to feel that they are guests of the Raj's family amidst reminders of life in these former kingdoms. The systemic nature of the former Raj palace network of guest accommodations allows for a variety of touring options and side activities such as palace tours, special dining, nature treks, and the like. The heritage hotel system of Rajasthan has done much to provide revenue needed for the upkeep of these legendary places. The Umaid Bhawan Palace in Jodhpur, with part of it serving as a heritage hotel, is illustrated here.

Figure 17-59 *Progress in urban conservation* is seen in several examples in India, namely at historic districts in Calcutta and Ahmadabad, where initiatives toward urban environmental improvements have yielded impressive results. Indian conservation architect Debashish Nayak has perfected ways to reach locals and engage the women and children in cleaning up and upgrading their neighborhood settings, paying special attention to conserving significant historic buildings. In Ahmadabad, in partnership with the city and an administrator of a Ford Foundation grant for family health improvement, Nayak arranged for micro-loans, heritage education, and walking tours led by youngsters as parts of an innovative scheme they labeled the Health and Heritage Program. (See Figure 1-6.) There are a growing number of other examples, such as the ongoing step-by-step urban improvements in the Dalhousie Square business district in Calcutta dating from British colonial times. (The restored Writer's Building on Dalhousie Square is shown here.) Somewhat similar foreign-assisted key building conservation and site improvement projects are underway at the fortified Rajasthani towns of Jaisalmer and Nagaur. Both are being conducted as partnerships involving the Archaeological Survey of India. Jaisalmer is receiving international technical and financial assistance from the World Monuments Fund, and Nagaur Fort is being addressed in a partnership involving the Getty Conservation Institute and the Maharaja of Jodhpur.

EAST AND SOUTHEAST ASIA

Throughout East and Southeast Asia, the spiritual traditions of Buddhism, Confucianism, and of general respect for ancestors have long fostered an ethic of cultural heritage protection that has extended to historic buildings and sites. While most Eastern cultures have long histories of maintaining and perpetuating memory and traditions associated with historic places, such cultural heritage ranging in scale from the traditional form of Asian cities to decorative details on individual buildings is threatened throughout the region. Despite the wealth of significant artistic patrimony to be preserved, most East and Southeast Asian countries have insufficient management policies and resources for the task and have been unable to relate architectural conservation to their larger development agendas. China and Japan are exceptions in some respects and have been especially receptive to new approaches that work in cultural heritage management and have also begun to make their marks on global heritage conservation. Additionally, some projects throughout Southeast Asia have provided models and opportunities for the development of international conservation practice.

The strong East Asian economies in recent years have enabled the channeling of significant resources toward heritage concerns. In addition, strong grassroots support for conservation has encouraged legislation and institutional development in Japan since the 1960s.[14] Japan has long been known for its tradition of reconstruction, most famously at the Shinto shrines at Ise, as well as for its preference for the new and modern. But Japanese culture also appreciates *sabi*, or patina, in craft objects and architecture. Today, however, the lack of craftsmen versed in traditional construction techniques is one of the greatest challenges in conserving the country's historic structures. A frequent supporter of UNESCO's activities and one of the largest donors to the World Heritage Fund, the Japanese government has enabled the completion of successful conservation projects throughout the world.[15]

South Korea has a firmly established centralized management system that has been successful at mitigating developmental pressures on many of its cities, although its extensive bureaucracy with overlapping responsibilities has frequently left local governments ineffective. Fortunately, nongovernmental organizations have played an important role in monitoring historic cities and sites in South Korea. While North Korea remains resistant to outside influences, UNESCO's efforts to recognize its cultural heritage may help bring this isolationist country into broader conservation trends. Though there has been distrust and enmity between the Koreas and their powerful neighbor Japan, the strong cultural ties between these Far Eastern countries have led to increased partnerships and sharing of expertise and technology in the early twenty-first century.

If ever there was a place with an outstanding and long-term interest in its history and a tradition of referring to and revering its past, it is China. Few countries can claim the centuries of cultural continuity and wealth of surviving heritage that China enjoys. The past has always been a major presence in Chinese life and culture, except for a brief period in the twentieth century, and the maintenance of traditional values, continuous use of sites, and growth of Western-style professionalism have all reinforced its conservation field in recent years.

Among the greatest challenges for architectural conservationists in China today is protecting the historic architecture of its cities that are threatened by development and growth happening on an unprecedented scale and at unprecedented rates. Today's focus on modernization and industrial and economic growth after decades of poor planning and massive urban renewal schemes has left contemporary Chinese cities faced with significant losses and in desperate need of attention. UNESCO, the World Bank, and the Chinese State Administration for Cultural Heritage sponsored an international conference in Beijing in 2000 to study this problem and propose viable solutions.[16]

China's increasing cooperation and integration into today's global economy has opened it up for this kind of international collaboration, benefiting both Chinese cultural heritage and the international professional heritage conservation community, which has modified its own standards and practices in many instances to accommodate China's traditions and approaches. A series of professional exchanges and conferences led to the ratification of the China Principles by ICOMOS China in 2000.[17] (See Chapter 9.) The process and international partnership from which this document emerged has quickly become a model for designing specific heritage conservation guidelines for non-Western countries interested in protecting their cultural heritage according to basic international standards.

Cultural and historic links connect the heritage of China with that of Mongolia and Taiwan, and the management policies and conservation practices in these countries also reflect these interrelationships. Due to political differences, in the late twentieth century, both Mongolia and Taiwan have attempted to distinguish their identities from the People's Republic of China, and their governments and heritage professionals have sought independent relationships and connections with more distant partners and international organizations. However, because of its exclusion from the United Nations, Taiwan has not benefited from UNESCO's assistance or collaborative participation in other international organizations as Mongolia has. China's occupation of Tibet remains a question today, at least in the minds of many

Tibetans, and with the survival of many aspects of Tibetan cultural heritage hanging in the balance. This seems ironic since the two places earlier enjoyed centuries of long and generally peaceful relations.

The more famous monuments of Southeast Asia, including Angkor and Borobudur, have attracted the attention of local and international scholars, travelers, and heritage conservationists since at least the mid-nineteenth century and have formed the basis from which the region's involvement in the architectural conservation field has developed. These sites have drawn professionals from around the world, creating examples, working relationships, and institutions through which new conservation techniques and procedures were developed. The emergence of a pool of talented local heritage conservation professionals holds promise for the transfer of knowledge and experiences gained through the internationally supported projects at the region's well-known historic monuments to thousands of other important buildings and sites.

Various intergovernmental technical assistance and support programs involving France, Japan, Germany, New Zealand, Australia, and lately, the United States and international organizations such as UNESCO, ICOMOS, ICCROM, the World Monuments Fund, and the Getty Conservation Institute have been active in Southeast Asia, but regional organizations have also played an important role in architectural conservation. For example, cultural heritage management is one of the many fields in which the Association of Southeast Asian Nations (ASEAN) promotes regional cooperation and collaboration, and it maintains a special fund to support projects among its ten member countries. In recent decades, cultural heritage tourism has become an increasingly powerful force in Southeast Asia, especially in Thailand, Cambodia, and Indonesia. Other regional governments whose historic sites are less widely known have taken note and have also begun initiating wide-ranging efforts to protect and promote their own heritage with varying degrees of success.

Special Challenges Faced in East and Southeast Asia

Figure 17-60 *Modernization and development pressures* in East Asia and most of the Southeast Asian nations have produced astonishing results in the growth cities of Beijing, Shanghai, Hong Kong, Tokyo, Osaka, Bangkok, Kuala Lumpur, and Singapore. The same can be said for the next tier of cities, of which there are hundreds, including Hanoi, Vietnam; Nara and Kyoto, Japan; Chiang Mai, Thailand; Vientiane, Laos; Yangon, Myanmar (formerly Burma); and Denpasar and Djakarta (illustrated here), Indonesia. In each, heritage protection laws and concerns exist, but reports of success in effective architectural heritage protection are varied. It is in the smaller historic towns where the greatest successes in urban conservation are found; in places like Hoi An, Vietnam; Luang Prabang, Laos; Lijiang, Yunnan Province, China; and Georgetown, Malaysia, UNESCO World Heritage listing, or the prospects for it, has been a decisive factor in the nearly intact survival of these historic towns—proof again of the power of universal heritage interests, both real and perceived.

Figure 17-61 *The exportation of architectural and archaeological heritage* from the countries of East and Southeast Asia in the late nineteenth and twentieth centuries is widely seen throughout the world today because many the most significant of these items have ended up in museums or in notable private collections. This phenomenally active business of buying and selling cultural heritage is well reflected in the offerings of specialty antique dealers and the more-famous auction houses as well as in the steep rise in prices for the better examples of Asian antiquities. Another example of this trend is Asia Week in New York, where in 2007 no fewer than five large specialty antique shows and auctions occurred that featured "Asiana." The tightening regulations on the illicit trade of antiquities are closing the openness of this trade in the United States, which is having an effect on acquisitions practices of museums and prices. When viewed in broader terms, the problem is that the current international concern over this subject is "too little, too late." The easy acquisition of the better examples of architectural sculpture at many of Asia's and the world's historic architectural sites has already occurred. For instance, through the 1970s, publicly displayed religious sculpture, as seen in this Hindu stele in Kathmandu, Nepal, were commonplace. The few remaining such sculptures that survive out of doors today are usually caged in ironwork to prevent their theft.

Figure 17-62 *Inexperience and/or lack of commitment in heritage conservation practice* is not uncommon in Asia, especially in some countries such as Mongolia, North Korea, Bhutan, and Myanmar, where traditions and systems for organized heritage protection are not well established. In Mongolia, there is a paucity of monumental cultural heritage today, hence the lack of an effective system for protection. In North Korea and Myanmar, political agendas do not support recognized international conservation practices very fully (although several NGOs have attempted work in Myanmar, and UNESCO has advised North Korea on a few conservation projects). Specialty consultants and some NGOs have recently begun to help in Bhutan, the challenge there being its physical isolation more than anything else. Concerned heritage conservationists can only hope that when more robust heritage conservation practice does get underway in these countries that the hard-won field lessons that have been gained in other countries will be adopted—with modifications as necessary—rather than having to be relearned.

Figure 17-63 *The paucity of qualified conservation personnel and professional training opportunities* remains an issue in East and Southeast Asia, although much progress has been made in recent years in formal heritage conservation training. Training at various levels can be gained in conservation courses and programs within a number of university architecture and archaeology graduate programs and also in a plethora of on-site training courses offered by the numerous NGOs working in this subject area. The World Monuments Fund has offered on-site learning opportunities to graduates in archaeology and architecture from the Royal University of Fine Arts in Phnom Penh, Cambodia, since 1991. ICCROM has offered several programs in Southeast Asia especially, one of which is its Living Heritage Sites conservation program. The UNESCO Regional office in Southeast Asia and the Pacific Region has been particularly effective in cultural heritage crafts training programs. The shortage of trained architectural conservation professionals in East and Southeast Asia is offset by surviving traditional building skills and a wealth of artistic ability found throughout the region.

Figures 17-64, 17-65, and 17-66 *Examples of overdevelopment for tourism purposes* may be seen in the complete renewal of infrastructure and the re-presentation of the historic town of Lijiang in Yunnan Province in southern China. Some of the terraced streets that follow its small river do remain authentic in appearance. But straightened, repaved streets and plazas have also been provided, and a multitude of shops—many offering identical tourist merchandise for sale—have been added. Together with the dwindling Naxi minority populations, who built and live in Lijiang, it gives the restoration of this classic historic Chinese village an inauthentic quality—especially when compared with the real thing, which can be seen, unrestored, in historic towns throughout the region. Another example of such overdevelopment can be found in distant Cambodia and derives from the 2008 decision to allow *son et lumière* (sound and light) performances each evening at Angkor Wat. The introduction of such nighttime entertainment at this most revered of all the country's national heritage sites—a structure that was designed in consideration of lunar and solar movements in the first place—is viewed by many as being unnecessary and disrespectful of the sanctity of the place.

Figure 17-67 *The marketing of history takes on new dimensions when essentially all-new surrogate* experiences are developed. In some cases, more visitors can only be accommodated with the addition of prosaic architectural elements that are aesthetically incongruous and historically inaccurate. While this raises questions regarding authenticity, this likely enables such places to relieve threats from overvisitation. Two such examples (with differing levels of attention to historical accuracy) are found in Thailand. The more ambitious of the two is Muang Boran (Ancient City) near Bangkok (illustrated here), which preserves a number of relocated historic buildings, though it mainly displays replicas of Thailand's key historic monuments located in positions within a 320-acre park that is a simulacrum of the country today. Great attention was paid to the accuracy and detailing of the components of this open-air museum, with overnight guest quarters in replicated Thai buildings and a range of educational offerings. Another facet of Thailand's history exists at the country's border with Myanmar, where those who died building the Burma Railroad in World War II are commemorated. The touching story is rather incongruously depicted by reenactments of the destruction of the Bridge over the River Kwai (made famous by the movie *The Bridge on the River Kwai*) on a scheduled basis during the tourist season with sound and light special effects and fireworks.

Figure 17-68 *Nongreen architecture and juxtaposed scales* are characteristics of new urban architecture in the rapidly growing cities of East and Southeast Asia and most other parts of the world as well. The radically different scale, materials, and overall design notwithstanding, most of the many new glass-clad skyscrapers of Bangkok, for instance, are not well suited to region's environmental conditions. This view of the old section of Bangkok along its Chao Phraya River shows the historic Catholic Cathedral of the city, which lies next to the historic Oriental Hotel amid a growing number of skyscrapers replacing Bangkok's historic river shoreline.

Promising Developments in East and Southeast Asia

Figure 17-69 *Strong laws and policies, when enforced,* are an asset in East and Southeast Asian cultural heritage conservation practice. Central government-led planning in China ensures a certain control of what cultural heritage is protected (and what is not). The violation of laws relating to the protection of classified cultural heritage is punishable by fines, imprisonment, and even death. The looting and illicit trade of antiquities is slowly being stemmed as a result of international governmental cooperation—but at the same time, much of the lucrative trade has simply been driven underground. The trade of movable heritage such as bronzes and ceramics is beyond the scope of this book. However, when parts of historic buildings are broken away for illicit sale on the international antiques market, the topic does fall under the purview of architectural conservation. Recent laws in some countries (namely the United States) pertaining to the import of antiquities from certain countries, as well as some recent precedent-setting and broadly issued calls to return stolen antiquities, have had an effect at least on museum acquisitions practices. Other measures, such as improved site protection, have deterred looting and illicit sales of antiquities, as seen in increased surveillance among site guards and the actions of the Heritage Police at Angkor in Cambodia, who are under "shoot-to-kill" orders to protect temple sculpture from thieves to stop them when necessary.

◀ **Figure 17-70** *Effective international collaboration for cultural heritage protection* is seen today in the historic city of Angkor in Cambodia. A provisional administrative body called the Authority for Protection and Management of Angkor and the Region of Siem Reap (APSARA) was established to protect the Angkor Archaeological Park. The authority, which has grown to have a staff of hundreds of administrators and specialists, has succeeded remarkably well at safeguarding the vast, protected Angkorian cultural landscape, including its over forty significant temples and other structures, at a time when the country's cultural heritage continues to be vulnerable to serious loss or compromise. At their twice-yearly meetings, the International Coordinating Committee of the APSARA Authority reviews all proposed work, work in progress, and other matters relevant to the safeguarding of this World Heritage site primarily by means of a peer-review process. (A site visit to the temple of Ta Prohm to observe the work of the conservation team in charge is illustrated here.) Under the aegis of UNESCO and the APSARA Authority, over a dozen foreign teams have worked cooperatively to conserve and present Angkor. ICOMOS, ICCROM, the World Bank, and other entities such as the Asia Society and the World Monuments Fund have conducted regional workshops and foreign assistance efforts in both East and Southeast Asia. Organizations operating elsewhere in the region on a more localized basis include the Heritage of Malaysia Trust, which has spearheaded community conservation efforts at the historic town of Georgetown, Malaysia; the US-based Kathmandu Valley Preservation Trust, which has restored numerous buildings in the Kathmandu Valley; and the SEAMO Regional Centre for Archaeology and Fine Arts (SEAMO-SPAFA) in Bangkok, which has conducted a variety of research and conservation efforts in Thailand and neighboring countries.

▲ **Figure 17-71** *Increasingly sophisticated tourism offerings* in the areas of cultural heritage, nature, and leisure tourism—or combinations thereof—are in demand in East Asia and elsewhere in the world. Tourism in most East Asian countries has rapidly increased in the past few years, in step with the region's expanding prosperity and opportunities to travel. In turn, there is an increase in offerings of custom tours: Visits to places and with people considered to be behind the scenes or off the beaten path. While the main beneficiaries of high-end tourism are often foreign tour companies, at a more basic level some remarkably innovative ideas for capturing foreign tourist dollars at heritage sites can be found throughout East Asia. These are first seen in the almost-overwhelming quantity of merchandise for sale in prescribed areas at the entrances to the more popular tourist sites. Canny merchants sometimes devise nearly irresistible tourist enjoyment experiences, like restored historic restaurants offering vintage recipes, "cyclo-tours" of historic districts, boat tours, and the like. The author has jumped at participating in various historic experience reenactments ranging from visiting the war rooms and crawling through underground tunnels at Cu Chi Tunnels on the outskirts of Ho Chi Minh City, Vietnam, to paying 30 *yuan* (approximately $1) to shoot arrows from a longbow from atop the Great Wall of China at Badaling at bales of hay below. Bicycle touring in Southeast Asia is increasingly popular since more can be seen very inexpensively. Illustrated here is a Czech-American bicycler discovering the byways and villages of central Vietnam. (*Courtesy Sean McLaughlin and Lubomir Chmelar*)

◀ **Figures 17-72 and 17-73** *Progress has been made in resolving conflicting philosophies* for preserving authentic historic details and finishes versus restoring and replicating historic buildings to look like new. Diverse international architectural conservation projects and programs that have been conducted in Asia over the past two decades have done much to harmonize traditional differences in architectural conservation philosophy. (See also "European Heritage Conservation Principles Abroad" and the sidebar "East Meets West" in Chapter 15.) The negotiated solution of how to restore and preserve painted finishes dating from the Ming and Qing periods at Xiannongtan (the Temple of Agriculture) at the former south edge of Beijing is a case in point. In a technical and financial partnership between the Beijing Municipal Administration of Cultural Heritage and the World Monuments Fund, after three years of research, tests, pilot projects, and discussions, it was agreed to restore the exteriors of several of the buildings of this important historic complex to their as-built appearance, mainly because they must again perform their role as a protective envelope for what is within. A different and new (at the time) philosophy in Chinese architectural restoration was employed for preserving the interiors of the buildings—their largely intact original painted finishes on ceiling beams and rafters were simply cleaned, stabilized, and presented in their as-found condition.

▲ **Figure 17-74** *Pollution clean up and improved living environments* are certainly top agenda items among government agencies in Asia, though the record of accomplishment in these areas is quite uneven mainly due to limited financial resources in most locales. Clean water and improved sanitation schemes are increasing, sometimes with the aid of international loan programs such as the World Bank and the Asian Development Bank. Others are purely local initiatives, such as a hugely ambitious project to restore one section of the Grand Canal in central China at a time. The great canal system that extended some 1,115 miles until the early nineteenth century has been likened to the Great Wall and once linked Hangzhou with Beijing, connecting the country's great west-to-east river systems. Its construction began in 486 BCE and was completed during the reign of Kublai Khan. Whole sections remain in use. Newly restored sections have been opened recently, and there are plans for reopening others. A move is underway among the State Administration for Cultural Heritage bureaus in each province where the Grand Canal exists in China to nominate it to the World Heritage List.

The Pacific Ocean covers more than a third of the earth's surface and contains over thirty thousand islands. The often vast distances between these islands and their climatic and geographic variations have resulted in numerous diverse indigenous cultures—all with distinctive heritage. This region was colonized by Europeans beginning in the sixteenth and seventeenth centuries, and many sites from those early interactions also survive. Today, the success of cultural heritage management in the countries of the Austro-Pacific Region, also called Oceania, largely rests on negotiating multiple perceptions and forms of heritage and on forging feasible socioeconomic approaches. Australia and New Zealand are especially influential regional partners.[18]

Contemporary heritage conservation practice began in Australia in the 1970s, as public interest in historic sites rose and legislation at all levels of government responded to that interest in order to protect and manage the evidence of the continent's early European settlements, which were threatened by development.[19] At that same time, extensive surveys were made of the country's historic, cultural, and natural resources, including its aboriginal sites, which were not yet valued by the wider Australian community. Today, however, Australia's progressive conservation approach includes and validates its complete range of cultural heritage. In recent years, Australia's indigenous peoples have increased their profile and asserted their rights in relation to their own heritage, leading to additional legislation specifically concerning aboriginal sites.

Australia has emerged as an international leader in the field of conservation and is often looked to for guidance on cultural heritage issues and specific projects, not only in the Pacific but throughout the world. Especially since the establishment of the Burra Charter, first drafted by ICOMOS Australian 1979, Australia has served as a model of culturally inclusive heritage policies, integrated natural and cultural conservation, and the development of effective conservation management and practices.[20] The New Zealand Charter for the Conservation of Places of Cultural Heritage Value (also known as the Aotearoa Charter), adopted by ICOMOS New Zealand in 1992 to guide conservation practice there, explicitly addresses the concerns of aboriginal peoples and non-Western concepts of heritage even more so than the Burra Charter, but its contextual specificity has made it less influential.[21]

An appreciation for the cultural heritage of the Maori, New Zealand's indigenous people and a general understanding of the advantages inherent in safeguarding places of cultural significance have always characterized this country's conservation movement. Organized heritage protection in New Zealand began in the early twentieth century with concern for natural sites and expanded in the 1950s to include historic cultural sites as more and more were threatened with destruction. Many argue that in New Zealand, investment in building conservation still takes a backseat to environmental protection; however, the government has worked to ensure that important artifacts from its history are preserved in private and public collections.[22] New Zealand is home to the first-ever cultural landscape inscribed on the World Heritage List, Tongariro National Park, whose pristine scenery and impressive mountains have religious significance for the Maori people.

Throughout the Pacific islands of Micronesia, Melanesia, and Polynesia, architectural conservation is often not even differentiated from the protection of other forms of heritage: In most of Oceania, natural, built, and intangible wonders and traditions are all highly valued. Local modes of connecting to the past are embedded in the transfer of indigenous knowledge, oral traditions, and performative practices from generation to generation, making the past personally relevant and socially significant to the present. Sometimes this intangible heritage also finds physical embodiments in archaeological sites, monuments and buildings, and in special natural or cultural landscapes. In many of the island countries of Oceania, traditional leaders and their private land tenures are greatly influential in heritage management practice, making cooperation with these communities vital to successful conservation as well as to the interpretation of sites.[23]

Oceania's built heritage also includes evidence of its colonial past, yet some Pacific Islanders see the preservation of Western-style resources as a hindrance to the development of their own heritage forms.[24] Alternatively, continued political ties with former colonizers have greatly benefited heritage protection in many Pacific countries, which often have administrative and legal frameworks based on imported European models and which often rely on foreign financial and technical assistance. The United States and France have been particularly active in assisting cultural heritage conservation efforts in their former colonies and presently held territories in the Pacific.

Challenges for conservationists in Oceania today include not only the frequent lack of financial resources but also a lack of training opportunities and scholarship on the region's heritage and culture, which has led to inconsistent standards and applications. In fact, very little of the cultural heritage of the Pacific has even been documented or received any conservation or basic maintenance: Many of the region's important sites are threatened by constant biodeterioration—in particular, vegetation growth—and rising sea levels.[25] Uncontrolled tourism threatens to exploit and commercialize Oceania's heritage, as it does at sites elsewhere in the world. As tourism increases, it needs to be managed carefully, especially since so many Pacific island sites are located far from accessible urban centers.[26]

Nonetheless, Oceania is building on its past accomplishments and beginning to make valuable contribu- tions to the larger conservation field, especially relative to the protection and perpetuation of multicultural heritage, through the engagement of local communities. As the Pacific islands hone their individual approaches and strengthen regional dialogues and cooperation with the more established cultural heritage conservation traditions of Australia and New Zealand, they will surely gain the recognition from the international heritage protection community that they deserve.

Special Challenges in the Austro-Pacific Region

Figure 17-75 *The great diversity of types of cultural heritage,* its location in often vastly disparate places across thousand of miles of ocean, and the fact that much of the region's heritage is not "monumental" in the traditional sense pose special challenges to heritage protection efforts in the Austro-Pacific region. Figures 17-75 through 17-78 and 17-81 through 17-86 illustrate the remarkable range of cultural heritage resources. Above is a well-conserved and well-presented *moai* at Easter Island (Chile).

Figure 17-76 The site of artist Paul Gauguin's home and studio in French Tahiti, which now has an interpretive center.

Figure 17-77 Wreckage of a Val bomber on the former Japanese airbase of Rabaul in the South Pacific.

Figure 17-78 *Great Kau Ravi* ("men's ceremonial house") in Kaimari, Papua New Guinea. There are *a lack of suitable heritage conservation methodologies* used in the Pacific region, usually because the models that have been applied are based on heritage documentation and protection systems of the colonizers of the places under study. This results in surveys conducted by people without a background or full understanding of the values and concerns of the people and places under consideration. Much of the region's proudest heritage is intangible, and the more monumental buildings and sites can themselves be temporary in nature. Anthropologists and sociologists are usually better prepared to undertake this type of heritage assessment for conservation purposes than are cultural heritage experts trained in the European and American methods of cultural heritage documentation and protection. In addition, there frequently are disconnects between foreign governing bodies having control of other countries and indigenous populations as found in American Samoa, British Fiji, and parts of the Philippines. *(Photo courtesy of the Australian Museum, AMS320; Frank Hurley Photographs, V4852)*

Figure 17-79 *Weather conditions, tidal surges, and sea-level change* are all potential threats to the island nations and cultures of the Pacific. Typhoons, tsunami tidal waves, and the world's new threat—slowly rising sea levels—are all naturally of great concern. Many cultures of the Pacific are situated on low-lying atolls, and all have seaports and some degree of seaside inhabitation. Vulnerability to natural disaster is very real, as is evidenced by reports of typhoons and, occasionally tsunamis, the most deadly one on record having occurred in December 2004 near the western edge of the region off the coast of Sumatra in the Indian Ocean, which affected regions as far west as the African coast. The results of a typhoon on Wake Island in September 2006 are illustrated here. *(Courtesy U.S. Air Force/ Tech. Sgt. Shane A. Cuomo)*

Figures 17-80 and 17-81 *The inadequacy in the protection of petroglyphs (rock art)*, which is frequently the only surviving evidence of distant human occupation, is a problem across the Austro-Pacific region, as it is elsewhere. Specialists have worked to conserve symbolic and artistic expressions carved into volcanic tuff outcroppings at Easter Island, and the petroglyphs (rock art) of the aboriginal peoples of Australia are considered a symbol of the nation. Unexpectedly, however, despite great efforts on behalf of many Australian heritage conservationists, probably the largest and oldest collection of aboriginal rock art in the world is at risk from modern human-induced threats on the Burrup Peninsula in Western Australia. There are an estimated one million examples of aboriginal rock-art engravings near the industrial port of Dampier that are threatened by nearby industrial processes, including the production and shipping of liquefied natural gas and minerals processing. Encroachment on the extensive fields of rock art for development purposes and air pollution resulting from related industrial processes have noticeably affected what most experts consider to be among the earliest expressions of art by humankind (dating to between 20,000 and 30,000 BCE). Even the prestigious and influential Australian heritage conservation community, the aboriginal peoples lobby within national government, and members of the country's high government seem to be at a loss for solutions, since relocating the industrial seaport is not considered a viable solution. *(Photographs by Robert G. Bednarik, with permission)*

Promising Developments in the Austro-Pacific Region

▶ **Figure 17-82** *The development of national heritage conservation charters* that take into account the concerns of a nation's often specialized heritage conservation concerns, as found in Australia's Burra Charter and New Zealand's Aotearoa Charter, are among the most impressive examples of theory applied to practice in heritage conservation anywhere. These charters address some of the most difficult questions in the field, such as the Maori belief that cultural heritage in the form of objects is expected to die a natural death. (See also Chapter 15.) Despite these charters, it remains difficult to protect the more intangible heritage addressed in these charters, since it is difficult to guide those who are not aware of these matters as to its importance. For instance, tourists who arrive to view Uluru (Ayer's Rock) in north-central Australia are forewarned that it is a special aboriginal sacred site, and signs actually dissuade their climbing it. Nonetheless, most make "the climb" anyway. Whether it's the Aotearoa Charter, which was primarily meant to protect Maori heritage, or the Burra Charter, with its even broader purview and potential, these charters are especially instructive for other countries with ethnic minority populations that are not wholly covered in national heritage protection legislation. The topic of heritage charters deriving from Australia and New Zealand is symbolized here by a movable object, a Maori spear.

◀ **Figures 17-83 and 17-84** *Local participation in heritage protection* is growing in the Austro-Pacific region, with there being a number of accomplishments that may serve as exemplars. On Easter Island, after years of resistance, at the urging of the Chilean National Forest Corporation (Corporación Nacional Forestal, or CONAF) and with the aid of international NGO's, Rapa Nuians (locals) are participating in the establishment and management of heritage trails for viewing numerous monuments on the island. There has been success in forging multicultural alliances for heritage protection and conserving cultural diversity in Levuka township in Fiji (illustrated here), where the heritage conservation interests of local residents against the background of the island's British colonial regime were clarified in a series of town meetings. There are several excellent NGOs throughout the Austro-Pacific Region such as the New Zealand Historic Places Trust, Australian Heritage, the National Trust of Fiji, and the Cook Islands Cultural and Historic Places Trust, whose role as conveners and communication channels are invaluable to heritage conservation in the region. It is usually groups like these that organize well-attended periodic conferences during which principles of the Burra, Aotearoa, and Ename charters, the Nara Document on Authenticity, and perhaps other experiences in the world are considered in the light of local heritage conservation interests. (*Courtesy Bhupendra Kumar and photographer Manhar Vithal of Lomaitivi Studio, Levuka, Ovalau, Fiji*)

Figure 17-85 *Looking after "sites of conscience"* is a special facet of heritage conservation practice, with Australia having shown the way in two kinds of examples. The first was by incorporating aboriginal populations in the heritage protection process as exemplified in the creation of the Burra Charter in 1979. A second example is seen in the use of the same heritage values-based approach to documenting and incorporating "difficult" histories, an example being prison and convict heritage at sites such as the prominent penal colony of Port Arthur in Tasmania, Australia (illustrated here). More recently, conservation interest groups on and for the island of New Caledonia have undertaken a similar initiative. Measures to document, preserve, and memorialize World War II heritage sites in the region (in addition to the hundreds of memorials established by the military services that fought there) can also be seen in the same light. (See also Figure 17-77.)

Figure 17-86 *The concept of protecting entire cultural landscapes* was formalized by the nomination and listing by UNESCO of the first-ever cultural landscape inscribed on the World Heritage List, Tongariro National Park in New Zealand, whose pristine scenery and impressive mountains have religious significance for the Maori people. Likewise, in Australia, the Kakadu National Park represents a mixed (natural and cultural) World Heritage site. Other important landscapes—such as the Philippine rice paddies illustrated here—also benefit from such focus and care. UNESCO's World Heritage Centre has been active in supporting heritage conservation in New Zealand and Oceania in the past several years, with actions like its "World Heritage–Pacific 2009" workshop (held in October 2005), which was attended by participants from several nations in Oceania, the French Territories, and Easter Island (Chile). That the workshop was funded by the Nordic World Heritage Foundation and the Italian Fund-in-Trust shows the reach and global interest of other countries wanting to assist with heritage conservation in Oceania. (*Courtesy Byron Bell*)

In North America, the period since World War II has been characterized by the ever-greater expansion of industry, housing, and commercial enterprises as well as by the extension of cities outward through the growth of suburbs. Though demolition of historic buildings in inner cities characterized the first few decades after the war, so did a rising consciousness of the intrinsic and economic value of these resources in both the United States and Canada. The losses of familiar urban environments and of cherished historic buildings galvanized communities in both countries.

Canada's heritage and its heritage protection policies and practices reflect a combination of the cultural and legal traditions of Britain and France, its parent countries, and the populist and economic influences of its strong southern neighbor. Over the course of the twentieth century, Canada has continuously reorganized and consolidated its conservation mechanisms and updated its heritage legislation. There has recently been an important development in this long history: the administrative restructuring of Canada's cultural resources management system in utilizing a management approach focusing on preventative maintenance and continuous care by Parks Canada, the custodian of the country's national parks and historic sites.[27] In 2002, Parks Canada and the Department of Canadian Heritage launched a joint project called the Historic Places Initiative to further improve the culture of heritage conservation in Canada by updating legislation and standards and increasing enforcement and implementation.[28] Canada's decision to decentralize its heritage system along the lines of the system used by the United States has given much responsibility to provincial authorities and has successfully encouraged local participation and innovation.

Despite a century of positive action, experts estimate that 21 percent of Canada's built heritage was lost in the last thirty years and that strong measures are needed to ensure the survival of remaining historic properties, especially federally owned ones.[29] Immediate challenges requiring attention include shoreline erosion, which threatens to erase some of the country's most important archaeological sites, and abandoned churches and historic industrial buildings, for which new and appropriate uses are a struggle to find. In addition, development pressures continue to jeopardize historic environments in Canada's inner cities and, some say, even threaten World Heritage sites such as the Historic District of Old Quebec.

Architectural conservation practice in the United States has always taken a remarkably populist approach and has always relied on local initiatives for its success. This has resulted from minimal government support, a general belief that heritage conservation is the responsibility of "good citi-

zens," and the popular appeal of profit-driven motivations and emphases on pragmatic and practical—rather than theoretical—methods and solutions. As a result of financial incentives, participants in American *historic preservation*—which is the preferred term in the United States—have included commercial property owners, real estate developers, and general investors to a greater extent than elsewhere in the world. In addition, the United States' wealth and generosity has always engendered a tradition of philanthropic support of benevolent causes such as historic preservation. This public financial support includes not only the country's wealthiest families and occasional significant corporate support but is also noticeable in tens of thousands of ordinary citizens who have joined the country's numerous voluntary organizations.

The most important, national-level nongovernmental organization concerned with conserving historic architecture in the United States is the National Trust for Historic Preservation. This private, voluntary organization was founded in 1949 to provide "leadership, education, advocacy, and resources to protect the irreplaceable places that tell America's story."[30] Recent innovative public-private partnerships that it has initiated or participated in have included the Main Street program, focused on America's smaller towns, and the White House Millennium Council, focused on key national monuments.

Though compared with European countries and to Canada, the United States government has contributed less financially and has participated less extensively in architectural conservation projects, it has been significantly involved in the documentation of the country's heritage for nearly a century through the Historic American Building Survey and the Historic American Engineering Record. In addition, the National Park Service (NPS) maintains a sizable number of national historic buildings and sites and an honorary list of important historic sites, called the National Register of Historic Places, in order to promote preservation and encourage collaboration. The NPS and the individual state historic preservation offices have since 1976 overseen the implementation of a system of effective tax incentives to further encourage private participation in the preservation of historic buildings and sites.

Given the United States' successes in historic preservation thus far, the focus of many projects has shifted from restoration and rehabilitation to preventative maintenance, and the entire rehabilitation industry is expected to remain robust for the foreseeable future. In addition, as special interest groups increase their profiles and raise their voices, sites important to Native Americans, native Hawaiians and Alaskans, Hispanics, African Americans, and others having specific sociocultural interests, will likely increasingly be protected and valued as the heritage of all Americans. Experiences in the United States have inspired cultural heritage conservationists elsewhere in the world today to broaden their definition of what is historically important: not only landscape vistas and sizable historic districts but also postwar commercial architecture, suburban housing developments, and sites of scientific importance. Emulated American practices also include its powerful grassroots volunteerism and not-for-profit networks and effective tax incentives designed to spur economic development in ways that include and respect historic buildings.

Special Challenges Faced in North America

Figure 17-87 *Suburbanization and urban sprawl* have been hallmarks of North American life through most of the twentieth century, especially since World War II. Expansion in this form reflects strong beliefs in property rights, desires for home ownership, and at times the pursuit of a better quality of life away from urban centers. Since the 1970s, due in large part to the growing historic preservation movement and good transportation systems, a new appreciation of urban life resulted in a "back-to-the-city" movement that in turn stimulated the creation of increased urban amenities. This trend also reflected a realization among many US citizens and Canadians alike of the limits of growth, even in the abundant lands of North America, and there is now new interest in using presently developed land more efficiently. Detroit, beyond its central business district (illustrated here), was developed with such a profligate use of space and is so suburbanized at this point that it is hard to imagine that any kind of back-to-the-city movement could ever restore the vitality of its historic center without further subdivision of its many oversized land parcels.

Figure 17-88 ***Dependence on the automobile*** is not unique to North America, though the United States is a leader in having developed its lands and cities assuming the widespread use of automobiles and other motorized vehicles. In many of America's cities it is not possible to live without using automobiles since there inevitably will be areas that mass public transportation cannot efficiently serve. Los Angeles (shown here), Houston, and Atlanta are three of scores of major cities in the United States whose growth was made possible mainly by the automobile. Accommodating motorized transportation with their required road systems and support facilities has famously had a major impact on America's historic built environments. It is by now well-known that the creation of the national Interstate highway system in the USA and its counterpart major thoroughfares in Canada, from the late 1950s through the early 1970s especially, did more to stimulate the creation of the historic preservation movement in these countries than did anything else. In a classic case of cause and effect, urban dwellers often quickly became preservationists in reaction to the destruction of historic areas deemed "blighted" as a basis for the insertion of new highways and extensive "urban renewal."

▲ **Figure 17-89 *Underappreciation of the intangible benefits*** of preserved historic buildings, districts, and cultural landscapes is often a problem in the North American economies. Economic viability is always an important criterion when planning architectural conservation projects, but there are other considerations as well. Less tangible dimensions of the historic built environment that are also valuable include: the special sense of place that many communities have, the authentic variety that derives from mixed use, and special landscape features whether natural or human made. The rare surviving sense of place and lifeways of the Amish community living in parts of Lancaster Country, Pennsylvania (shown here), is an example of a culture's persistent belief in tradition in the fast-changing American society. Despite protection measures and wide sympathy for its preservation, the prognosis for Amish country in central Pennsylvania is not very good. Increased real estate development and road-widening projects in the vicinity spell change for this renowned American cultural landscape.

▲ **Figure 17-90 *Local history museums and a number of traditional heritage attractions*** are not addressing the interests of a growing number of Americans. Various studies have shown that not only has visitation fallen at most of the nation's key historic sites but that younger visitors expect more by way of nontraditional—if possible multimedia—presentations that take less time and that are more entertaining. This has meant that educators and museum directors and their staffs need to adapt the ways they tell the stories of America's historic places in order to engage the attention of their visitors while also not trivializing content. The challenges faced today in the presentation and interpretation of historic building museums are not easy to solve, though a start in addressing the problems should include an understanding of the values and significance of a place both in history and at the present time. Colonial Williamsburg, Virginia (illustrated here), noticed this problem early in the 1990s and responded by enhancing the visitor experience to the nation's first capital. Today, visitors may encounter purposefully untidy conditions at Colonial Williamsburg, such as a wooden clapboards in need of paint, the smell and sight of autumn leaves burning, and less-than-pristine streets and pathways.

Promising Developments in North America

Figure 17-91 *US federal tax incentives for rehabilitation* continue to be one of the most powerful tools for encouraging wide participation in the improvement of historic urban areas having underutilized and aging buildings. Through 2007, the expenditure of some $4.35 billion on the certified rehabilitation of some 34,800 income-producing buildings is evidence of this, and administrators of the program do not count the valorizing effect or added value that a rehabilitated property has, nor the "multiplier effect" that an improved historic property may have on its surroundings. There is an interest in some circles in expanding these incentives to include private-property owners, which could have a massively beneficial effect on preserving America's built environment across the nation. Hundreds of cities and towns around the country have benefited from the federal tax incentives for historic preservation. Seen here is a San Francisco mansion that was preserved by its transformation into law offices.

Figure 17-92 *Preservation planning* as a component within urban and rural land use planning practice has made a significant positive difference in improving living environments in the United States and Canada since the 1980s and promises even greater possibilities as limitations on built and natural resources are more widely realized. Restored urban parks and "smart-growth" planning is exemplified in one of the first North American projects of this type, Riverwalk in San Antonio (illustrated here). The vision of one architect backed by a whole community for the possibilities of converting mostly rundown commercial buildings along the San Antonio River was realized; over thirty years later, it is more successful than ever. Several other exemplary adaptive-use schemes, most notably Ghirardelli Square in San Francisco and Faneuil Hall-Quincy Market rehabilitation project in Boston, served as models for numerous similar other projects across North America and even elsewhere in the world.

Figure 17-93 *Since the 1970s, the military services of the United States have taken the task of protecting important US military history* both at home and abroad seriously. Historic surveys have been made at the various historic military bases, and care has been taken to place decommissioned military properties in the hands of preservation-minded organizations. The transfer of the Presidio of San Francisco, a former U.S. Army base with origins dating back to the eighteenth century Spanish settlement of northern California, is an example of a multiyear effort to adaptively use a decommissioned historic military facility. Managed by the Presidio Trust, an independent federal agency, buildings such as the Montgomery Street barracks (illustrated) in the National Historic Landmark District are leased to civilian entities in order to generate revenue that supports operations of the former base as well as conservation and interpretive programs.

Figure 17-94 *Improved physical security at recognized cultural heritage sites* has been a priority within the US Department of Interior since September 11, 2001. Through a series of national workshops and other means of demonstrating examples and solutions, improved security at heritage sites of all kinds throughout the United States has been advocated to good effect. The multifaceted nature of this subject is reflected in the fields of expertise involved, including architects, landscape architects, museum professionals, educators, experts in physical surveillance, law enforcement agencies, preventative conservation specialists, and a host of materials manufacturers. A new direction in cultural heritage protection in America and in several other countries has developed involving landscape architects, engineers, and security specialists, who have the difficult task of enhancing physical protection of significant historic buildings and sites while also maintaining their appeal and easy accessibility. The Washington Monument on the Mall in Washington, DC, was entered by a doorway at its base until after 2002, when the site was made more secure. A new reception and access area was installed so that visitors now approach the site from an initial receiving area approximately 150 feet away, walk up one of two curving paved ramps, and enter the structure via a security screening facility, which was appended to the base of the monument.

Figure 17-95 *"Green architectural design" for both new buildings and rehabilitated existing buildings* is an especially promising trend in North America. Evidence of this interest is seen in an increasing number of energy-efficient buildings that comply with new standards such as the Leadership in Energy and Environmental Design (LEED) rating system for measuring energy efficiency. Just as important is a wider realization of the value of existing buildings and their materials as recyclable resources, whether as historic building components that can be reused in renovations and new construction or for reconstitution as new products within the burgeoning industry of recycled metals, glass, and paper products. An example of an office building in the United States rehabilitated in ways that were specifically designed to conserve energy is the headquarters of the Christman Construction Company in Lansing, Michigan, which received an unprecedented double-platinum LEED certification in 2008 for its renovation of a commercial building built in 1928. Many character-defining features such as historic brass door and stairway hardware and the structure's wood floors, trims, and windows were used, as was more than 90 percent of the existing exterior fabric. Natural daylight and views benefit a large portion of the interior in part via a new atrium, while a computerized environmental systems management system optimizes climate and light needs for its occupants. The final cost of the rehabilitation was no greater than a conventional new building of the same size. *(Courtesy The Christman Company/Gene Meadows, photographer)*

Figure 17-96 *Interest in preserving outstanding examples of modern architecture* is increasing in North America. This is partly because there are many good examples to choose from and partly because this type of architecture has finally "come of age." Modern design fetches high prices in the antiques markets and advocacy for its protection has become ever more vociferous. The main promoters of conserving the better examples of twentieth-century design in architecture in North America (and in some instances elsewhere in the world) are the US National Trust for Historic Preservation, DOCOMOMO-US, and the World Monuments Fund through its World Monuments Watch™ program and, since 2007, WMF's Modernism at Risk initiative. The efforts of these organizations have been spurred by the losses of a number of major landmarks in twentieth-century architectural design. The last-minute salvation of modernist architect Edward Durrell Stone's residence for A. Conger Goodyear in Westbury, Long Island, New York, built in 1931 (illustrated here) is an example of both what is at stake in conserving important examples of modernism and how it is possible to help. The building was saved through the fast action of a partnership between the World Monuments Fund and the Long Island Historical Society. The property was purchased by this impromptu partnership only days before it was to be destroyed, prepared for re-sale, and sold to more appreciative owners.

LATIN AMERICA AND THE CARIBBEAN

Latin America, including Mexico, Central and South America, as well as the Caribbean islands, encompasses a significant geographical area spanning two continents. The region's heritage includes colonial settlements and religious monuments built by Europeans, as well as indigenous cultural landscapes, villages, and monumental vestiges of prehistoric grandeur. Though comprehensive legislation to protect this heritage has existed since at least the mid-twentieth century, it was not until the 1990s that widely effective heritage protection actions were carried out to secure its future. These latest policies in many cases reflect a sophisticated combination of environmental and cultural heritage protection, yet much of the region's heritage remains at risk today nonetheless.

The current threats to Latin America's heritage include pillaging of archaeological sites, unstable political conditions, development pressures, migration to cities from rural areas, and a lack of economic resources and public interest in cultural heritage protection. Regional environmental threats include very damaging earthquakes, such as those that have resulted in the rebuilding of Quito, Ecuador (2007); Mexico City (1985); Puebla, Mexico (1999); Peru (2007); and so on, as well as frequent hurricanes and tropical storms, such as Hurricane Mitch, which battered Central America in 1998, causing extensive damage at several towns and cites in the region including key heritage sites such as the Copán Archaeological Park in Honduras and other national heritage sites in Guatemala.

South America's many distinct regions, including the Andes, Brazil, and the Cono Sur (the southernmost tip of the continent), each have their own histories and contemporary cultures; however, the heritage of the continent shares many characteristics, including the existence of indigenous civilizations predating the 1500s and similarities of the Iberian canonization regimes.

South America's wide range of cultural and natural assets offers an excellent potential opportunity for tourism, but much of what could be developed for tourist revenue is at risk because of the relatively low priority governments assign to heritage conservation and the low public appreciation of and involvement in cultural heritage protection. In addition, effective historic urban conservation presents perhaps the biggest challenge for cultural heritage protection professionals throughout South America today because of the rapid and often uncontrolled growth of its cities.

The outlook for South America's urban and architectural heritage is, however, growing brighter in some respects, since private and local institutions are becoming increasingly involved in its protection. Local entities have also formed partnerships with international organizations and European governments to improve training, educate the public, and complete model conservation projects. The lack of a pan–South American organization focused on conservation and heritage issues isolates the individual accomplishments that have been made and prevents cooperation and information sharing for the benefit of the historic architecture and cities of all the continent's thirteen countries.

Central America, by contrast, is home to a number of important regional organizations working on behalf of its shared heritage, including ICCROM's Conservation of Cultural Heritage in Latin America and the Caribbean Programme (2008–2019) (LATAM)), which was established in 2008 "with an aim to improving and strengthening capacities for conservation, enhancing communication and exchange and increasing awareness in the region."[31] LATAM's activities will center around the five main themes selected as priorities for at least the first phase of the programme (2008–11): education and training for the conservation of cultural heritage; illicit traffic of cultural heritage; definition of economic indicators for conservation activities; risk management for cultural heritage; and cultural heritage conservation publications and their dissemination.[32] Within the region, Mexico has a particularly rich tradition of protecting and conserving its architectural heritage through an extensive network of conserved archeological sites and museums as well as preserved historic town centers, much of which are under centralized control. There is also a greater public value placed on cultural heritage in Mexico than in other places in Latin America, which serves to keep government priorities and policies in check.

The architectural heritage of the Caribbean all suffers from extensive exposure to intense sun, seismic activity, tropical storms, and high precipitation levels. In response to these issues as well as others that cause seasonal and quixotic patterns of tourism, cooperative efforts among the Caribbean islands, such as those organized by the Organization of the Wider Caribbean on Monuments and Sites (CARIMOS), have proven particularly beneficial. Nonetheless, the conservation experiences of these numerous island countries varies significantly as a result of differing amounts of government support, levels of public participation and not-for-profit involvement, and the adverse effects of tourism and development. Collaboration with European countries has also helped in several Caribbean nations, and the successful nominations of the historic centers of Havana and Santo Domingo, Dominican Republic, to the World Heritage List have encouraged further architectural conservation activity in those locales. The insular political nature of Cuba has produced some remarkably creative and successful heritage protection schemes, especially in relation to the restoration and rehabilitation of Havana's rich architectural heritage.

Recent charters and agreements reached through agencies such as the Organization of American States (OAS) reflect the maturation of cultural heritage protection in Latin America and the Caribbean: Once narrowly focused on individual buildings and historic districts, it now encompasses a vision of cultural diversity and intangible expressions of culture. At the same time, stronger legislation, increased government commitment, and public education in the individual countries of the region are essential to protect the richness and diversity of its heritage. Despite the numerous challenges, the collaborations and successful projects of the 1990s have established a solid foundation from which momentum is building in a field that is more and more effective each year.

Special Challenges Faced in Latin America and the Caribbean

Figure 17-97 *Serious natural threats to the historic built environment* in areas of Latin America, such as el niño (periodic extreme weather conditions associated with Pacific Ocean currents), earthquake hazards throughout most of Latin America's central areas and western coasts, and tropical storms in the Caribbean region, in addition to the usual high levels of biodeterioration found in tropical climates, combine to make conserving historic buildings a continuous struggle for architects, engineers, and materials conservators in the region. The major earthquake of August 2007 in Lima, Peru, is one of the more recent natural catastrophes to affect Latin America. Cliffside erosion along the Rio Moche at Huaca del Sol, Peru, caused by the el niño phenomenon in January 1998 is seen here. *(Photo courtesy of Carlos Wester La Torre)*

▶ **Figure 17-98** *Latin America and the Caribbean are lacking in pan-regional collaborative efforts in cultural heritage conservation,* especially architectural conservation. While professional membership and advocacy organizations such as CARIMOS, serving the Caribbean nations, and the programs within the OAS are committed to cultural heritage protection, there is a greater potential for international partnership projects. A conference organized by the World Monuments Fund in São Paolo, Brazil, in May 2002 was viewed by its participants as the first assembly of architectural conservation professionals from all thirteen South American nations (a conference poster is illustrated here). A number of successful urban conservation projects to date in South America, funded by the World Bank and the Inter-American Development Bank, have shown the enormous potential for more subvention of this kind.

▼ **Figure 17-99** *Complicated property inheritance systems and complex ownership conditions* negatively affect the protection of significant historic architecture in several Caribbean nations. Property owners from former ruling countries such as Great Britain, Spain, and France often abandoned estates, including substantial architectural legacies, to their followers, who had less interest and need for properties such as manor houses and sugar mills. Such uncertain ownership and ambiguities over upkeep responsibility are not favorable conditions for historic buildings and sites. For instance, under British law, property in the Bahamas was inherited by a single family member under the primogeniture system. Under Bahamian law today, inherited property is equally divided among all heirs, which is not unusual. However, this radically new system of inheritance and responsibility has often created scores of owners for a single property. The problem is further complicated in cases in which properties were abandoned or taken during regime changes without compensation or a clear legal transfer of title. Add to this apathy or disdain over the heritage of "others" whose histories may be viewed as exploitative. Such is the case with a number of eighteenth-century English colonial houses on the island of Eleuthera in the Bahamas, as shown here.

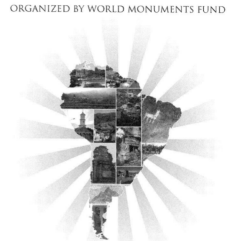

Heritage Conservation in
South America
Challenges and Solutions
ORGANIZED BY WORLD MONUMENTS FUND

Conference Abstracts

São Paulo, Brazil
April 11–14, 2002

Promising Developments in Latin America and the Caribbean

Figure 17-100 *A growing number of thematic heritage conservation initiatives* are proving helpful in Latin America such as the Colonial Church's conservation program in the Mexican Yucatan and the reactivation schemes for the Ruta de Maya trails in the Yucatan and northern Guatemala. Along the way are restored towns, convents, and haciendas where visitors can comfortably learn about lifeways past and present in the region, taking as much time as they wish. The archaeological site and small town of Uxmal (illustrated here) is one of many places that has been preserved through adapting to tourism in the Yucatan. Similar thematic and heritage route initiatives are found in the binational Los Caminos del Rio program, which connects the historic river towns on both the Mexican and US sides of the Rio Grande, and in the efforts to conserve a collection of historic wooden churches on the archipelago of Chiloé in southern Chile.

Figure 17-101 *Experiencing cultural and ecological systems*
and their relations to one another are appealing to outsiders wishing to learn about a new place, especially when accommodations are adequate and interesting and when tour routes do not involve backtracking. The Ministry of Culture in Guatemala has worked to present a variety of Mayan heritage sites as *systems* of tour offerings. The famous site of Tikal (illustrated here) is presented in a forest setting, although its ancient court area and the jungle immediately surrounding it have been judiciously cleared. The Mayan site of Ceibal near the town of Flores has a similar setting, although it is visited almost exclusively for its remarkable surviving Mayan carved stelae. Since 2004 the ministry has worked to feature the large site of El Naranjo, where the plan very purposefully aims to leave the ancient city in its undisturbed jungle setting, which is not easy to get to. Preserving and presenting a variety of similar cultural heritage sites so their commonalities and differences are carefully featured represents a sophistication in national cultural heritage management that serves as an exemplar. *(Courtesy Byron Bell)*

Figure 17-102 *Conferences on shared cultural heritage and its protection,* such as the international historic fortifications conservation seminar in Campeche, Mexico, in March 2004, are occurring with increased frequency in Latin America and the Caribbean. Another example is the international collaborative effort that began in 2002 to better preserve and present the seventeenth- and eighteenth-century system of Guaraní Jesuit Missions that spread across the borders of Paraguay, Argentina, and Brazil. (The San Ignacio Mini in Argentina.) This program, which was funded by UNESCO, the Fundación Antorchas (Argentina), and the American Express Foundation and others via the World Monuments Fund, involved several international technical workshops, a number of conservation projects to preserve the surviving distinctive stone construction of the missions, and the creation of an interpretive center.

Figures 17-103 and 17-104 *Successful architectural conservation accomplished within severe budget restraints* is seen widely in Havana, mainly as the result of the foresight and leadership of one individual, the city historian Eusebio Leal Spengler. Faced with a crisis in the mid-1990s—a wealth of historic buildings that were rapidly deteriorating and very little government or outside funding—the indefatigable Leal tackled the task as if it were an emergency triage situation. The first rehabilitation projects included former hotels to accommodate foreign visitors. With revenues gained from these developments, additional former commercial buildings—such as apothecaries, department stores, and a few former mansions—were tastefully restored to serve Havana's burgeoning tourist market. In effect, Leal developed a soundly managed, not-for-profit urban redevelopment corporation with revolving funds. What is most remarkable here, however, is how the program involved such a wide variety of building types. After restoration, they were used for sensible commercial purposes, the proceeds from which were then reinvested toward taking on even more ambitious projects. To the credit of Leal and his team of young professionals, the level of research, documentation, and restoration work is extremely high. These images depict a once-common scene in Old Havana and a sign of the future: buildings near the point of collapse and a restored streetscape.

Figure 17-105 *Increasing private sector support for architectural conservation* is seen in parts of Latin America, most notably in Mexico. Innovative programs such as Adopte una Obra de Arte (Adopt a Work of Art)—which started as a club of art patrons in Mexico City interested in conserving paintings—now works throughout Mexico on restoring historic buildings as well. The restoration of the rich, gilded interiors of the Cathedral of Salamanca in the State of Guanajuato, Mexico, is one of dozens of art and architectural conservation projects it has undertaken. Some of the larger banks—with the leading example being Banamex—have generously given to architectural conservation projects, as have a few private philanthropists. Several of these projects have involved matching funding from the World Monuments Fund. *(Courtesy Agustin Espinosa / Ricardo Castro Mendoza y Ciencia y Arte en Restauración S.A. de C.)*

Figures 17-106 and 17-107 *Former colonial ruling government assistance* is currently underway in several countries of Latin America through the Spanish International Cooperation Agency for Development (AECID) program based in Madrid. Among its most notable projects is its support of *escuela talleres* (specialized job training programs) for architectural conservation in the countries of Cuba, Mexico, and Peru. In addition, substantial financial support has flowed from the AECID program to restore and conserve specific buildings such as the churches of the Colca Valley cultural landscape (illustrated here); the historic center of Arequipa, Peru; and Jesuit Guaraní Missions in Paraguay. Obligations on the part of host governments and local municipalities include project management in-kind contributions (of at least 25 percent) and occasionally donations of property for heritage conservation purposes.

Figure 17-108 *High-quality restoration and imaginative adaptive-use projects* are found throughout the Caribbean and Latin America, as seen in the Drax Hall historic house restoration in Barbados, Citadelle Henri in Haiti, and the Annaberg Sugar Mill in St. John, Virgin Islands, plus a plethora of well-rehabilitated town architecture in many of the Caribbean nations. Over the past half century, a number of outstanding conservation projects have been accomplished throughout Central and South America as well, including countless examples of town architecture in the continent's more-established historic cities such as Cartagena and Bogota in Colombia; Recife, Ouro Preto, and Rio de Janeiro in Brazil; Santiago, Chile; Cuzco, Peru; and Quito, Ecuador. Mexico has excelled in its abilities to restore both its colonial (most notably its religious architecture) and its pre-Colombian heritage. The adaptive use of La Fundidora, the former power plant for Monterrey, Mexico (illustrated here), for cultural and commercial uses is a particularly good example of the imaginative reuse of an impressive historic industrial structure.

THE POLAR REGIONS

Antarctica and the Arctic Circle present significantly different cultural heritage protection challenges than anywhere else on earth. Concerns for conservation in the polar regions has all along focused more on environmental rather than cultural or historic architectural matters; however, the archaeological sites, buildings, and settlements that do exist are all the more important because of their rarity and fragility. In both of these extremes of the earth's surface are found the legacies of intrepid European and North American explorers, both modern and from more distant times past, who braved the harsh climates to investigate and to claim territory. These remains range in form from sturdy expedition huts, food deposits, and other base-camp buildings, to caches and cairns, to the early fishing industry establishments, to memorials. The cultural heritage of the Arctic is more diverse than that of Antarctica, as it includes indigenous sites as well as evidence of early whaling, mining, and fishing operations.

The unique cultural heritage of the polar regions has recently received international recognition and attention, and important preliminary steps for its protection have been taken. The harsh climate of these regions poses the greatest challenge to conservation. In addition to there being limited amounts of time that conservation work can be carried out in these areas due to weather conditions, there are the threats of wind-driven snow and ice, corrosion, mold, and fungi that all affect building materials. Two architectural conservation experts have posited that rates of deterioration of building materials may be increasing due to increasing ultraviolet light that has resulted from global warming.[33] On the other hand, the permanently frozen environment of most of the polar regions has retained many sites in a state of preservation impossible in other world climates.

While tourism to these remote regions is still relatively rare, there are no official controls on what little there is and it has occasionally threatened the integrity of these fragile sites. The International Association of Antarctica Tour Operators, established in 1991, has created strict guidelines for tourists to the southernmost parts of the world. This helps, though some sites, such as the fragile wooden expedition huts of explorers Carsten Borchgrevink (1898–1900), Ernest Shackleton (first expedition 1907–1909), and Robert Falcon Scott (1901–1904 and 1910–1913) remain vulnerable from occasional "tourist wear," since visitors are invariably shown the place in groups. Some of these sites also suffer from being largely unprotected from diverse wildlife that may take up residence, a situation that is difficult to control.

The lack of a clear political authority in Antarctica to make decisions on behalf of cultural heritage deserving protection has hampered conservation there. Uncoordinated efforts, competing territorial claims, and poorly delineated responsibilities have left management of cultural heritage to the domain of private institutions and international organizations. Efforts at cultural heritage protection in the Arctic, which has been divided among eight separate countries (Canada, Finland, Greenland [a province of Denmark], Iceland, Norway, Russia, Sweden, and the United States), has fared slightly better, but it also suffers from a lack of cooperation and standardized approaches.[34]

Fortunately, a number of cultural and natural heritage conservation organizations have begun working in the polar regions. The not-for-profit Antarctic Heritage Trust, founded in New Zealand in 1987, was the first to concern itself with conserving the legacy of the late nineteenth- and early twentieth-century (1895–1917) explorers of the South Pole. The Trust is recognized as the organization responsible (on behalf of the international community) for the care of four bases from this period and has launched the Ross Sea Heritage Restoration Project to conserve the bases built during these expeditions. All four sites are listed as Antarctic Specially Protected Areas under the Antarctic Treaty System. In 2004 and 2006, Shackleton's hut was listed on the World Monuments Fund Watch™ List of 100 Most Endangered Sites in the world. Scott's hut was listed in 2008.

In 2000 ICOMOS formed an International Polar Heritage Committee (IPHC) to inventory and raise the profile of the key cultural heritage sites of both Antarctica and the Arctic. It has thus far identified seventy-six sites that deserve special protection measures, and it has established markers at these sites.[35] Though not actively engaging in any specific conservation projects, the IPHC has provided a means for experts in polar heritage conservation to exchange information. In the Arctic, many conservation projects, such as those initiated by the US Department of the Interior, have forged partnerships with indigenous groups who have lived in the region for centuries and are keen to preserve their histories.

While heritage conservation practice in the polar regions is only in its formative stages, governments with jurisdiction over the Arctic and international organizations working at both of these extremes of the earth's surface have begun to respond to the unique challenges of conserving the scant but important early evidence of human activity in these vast areas. Though much is yet to be accomplished, the important first steps of realizing and documenting the existence of historic sites in the polar regions are underway, and groups and experts skilled at working in these extreme climates have emerged. These developments have come none too soon, given growing commercial interests in arctic regions and recent scientific conclusions about climate change that will affect them.

Special Challenges Faced in the Polar Regions

▲ **Figure 17-109** *The harsh weather conditions that deteriorate building materials* and other objects in the polar regions are difficult, if not impossible, to control. While the relative stability of below-freezing temperatures is an ideal condition for preserving organic materials, other environmental problems pose risks to buildings and objects, such as the corrosive effects of wind-driven snow and ice on wood and other fragile surfaces, the corrosion of metals, and biological growth. These pathologies pose serious threats to the long-term existence of construction materials and systems that were usually designed to be short-lived in the first place. One prominent example of significant polar heritage at risk is Captain Robert Falcon Scott's base (illustrated here), associated with the British Antarctic Expedition 1910–1913 and the attempt for the South Pole, Cape Evans, Antarctica. *(Photo courtesy © Antarctic Heritage Trust, http://www.nzaht.org/AHT)*

▲ **Figure 17-110** *The lack of control and monitoring of cultural heritage sites in the polar regions,* especially in relation to occasional vandalism and pilfering, can be a problem. The remoteness of the sites makes them vulnerable to salvagers and souvenir hunters. As many as four thousand visitors a year may visit the more popular Antarctic heritage destinations, the various explorers' huts, and base camps. Another (and somewhat amazing) threat to some expedition huts in Antarctica results from their serving as roosting positions for sea birds and penguins, whose guano has caused conservation problems at outbuildings that are important to the interpretation of these sites. The dog kennel and storage building areas at Ernest Shackleton's hut at Cape Royds (illustrated here) exemplify this problem, though the issue is even more acute at the expedition hut of Norwegian explorer Carsten Borchgrevink, who made the first confirmed landing on Antarctica in 1895.

▲ **Figure 17-111** *Sea level changes are affecting certain low-lying settlements* of indigenous populations in the Arctic regions. The site of Herschel Island (illustrated here) that has been used as a whaling station for hundreds of years faces going out of existence due to receding shorelines in the area. There are other changes to traditional lifeways of indigenous inhabitants of the Arctic as well, mostly having to do with mechanization. While it is quite understandable how Aleut and Inuit hunters and communities would quickly adopt snowmobiles, prefabricated building materials, power boats, and modern hunting weapons to replace their traditional dwellings and means for survival, each technological adaptation carries with it changes to living heritage patterns. *(Courtesy M. D. Olynyk, Government of Yukon)*

▶ **Figures 17-112 and 17-113** *Methodical inventories, analyses, and plans to conserve noted polar cultural heritage sites* have for many years been undertaken by nations whose boundaries extend through the two regions. Such activity is organized by experts within each country's own national heritage framework and represents important first steps in polar cultural heritage conservation. ICOMOS' International Polar Heritage Committee (IPHC) was established in November 2000 to create a network of experts and facilitate the transfer of ideas and information about polar conservation techniques and practices. One important IPHC initiative, which as of 2008 is before the Arctic Council, is the creation of a circum-Arctic analysis of internationally significant heritage sites. The IPHC also works with authorities to improve cultural heritage protection for sites of significance, such as base camps, cairns, and memorials located in the international territories of the Arctic or Antarctic. Two such examples, illustrated here, are the remains of an early twentieth-century trapper's hut in Svalbard, an Arctic archipelago that is part of Norway, and Roald Amundsen's ship *Maud* lying in Cambridge Bay, in north Canada. The site of the hut is a national monument for Norway, but it is also part of the history of its present location, where it adds to the tourist potential of the area. *(Courtesy Susan Barr, photographer)*

Promising Developments in the Polar Regions

Figure 17-114 *Interest in conservation of both the natural and cultural heritage* of the polar regions has grown in relation to increased scientific investigations and ever-widening concerns in recent years over the effects of climate change. A few architectural and other cultural heritage conservation projects now underway may serve as examples for others to follow. The New Zealand Antarctic Heritage Trust has taken the lead in polar heritage conservation through its Ross Sea Heritage Restoration Project, which aims to conserve the expedition huts of Shackleton, Scott, and Borchgrevink. With funding assistance from its sister organization, the United Kingdom Antarctic Heritage Trust, and from the international community, Ernest Shackleton's hut at Cape Royds has recently been confirmed as structurally secure and watertight, and conservation work on the 4,500 artifacts completed. Trust representatives are currently working year-round in Antarctica undertaking the work program to save Captain Scott's 1910 base at Cape Evans (shown here). Over the past five years the building has experienced unprecedented climatic conditions, and the building is at real risk of loss due to resultant structural damage (see Figure 17-109). Documentation efforts by the Yukon Historical and Museums Association at the centuries-old whaling station at Herschel Island (see Figure 17-111) in northernmost Canada anticipate no plan to relocate the community as its shoreline recedes but to record it before it disappears. All three of these sites have been placed on the World Monuments Watch™ List of 100 Most Endangered Sites. *(Courtesy © Antarctic Heritage Trust, http://nzaht.org/AHT/)*

ENDNOTES

1. UNESCO or ICOMOS are in the best position to produce such a detailed country-by-country survey of the status of heritage conservation in the world. A step in this direction was begun by US/ICOMOS in the 1970s, through its sponsorship of national reports for France, Poland, and the Netherlands, Turkey, and other countries. Since 1999, members among the leadership of ICOMOS international have admirably attempted a version of this through its Heritage @ Risk program, resulting in biennial status reports on heritage thought to be in danger—with candid mention of the reasons for the threats—on a country-by-country basis. A somewhat similar initiative was completed under the leadership of Arlene Fleming, heritage conservation consultant for the World Bank, who led an effort at compiling a database of useful heritage conservation contacts, legislation, administrative structures, and other information for countries the World Bank serves.

2. The author thanks the World Monuments Fund for its support. As one of its senior staff members since 1990, I have gained a knowledge of international architectural conservation practice without which this book could not have been written. Opinions found within this book are mine and should not necessarily be viewed as those of the World Monuments Fund organization. Five additional volumes were drafted as part of the present *Time Honored: A Global View of Architectural Conservation* project; these are more specific about the roles of, solutions to, and challenges in architectural conservation around the world. Additional information of this kind, though usually from more specialized perspectives, can be found in the publications and Web sites of organizations like the United Nations Educational, Scientific and Cultural Organization (UNESCO), the International Council on Monuments and Sites (ICOMOS), Europa Nostra, the Getty Conservation Institute, the World Monuments Fund, the newly established Global Heritage Fund, and a plethora of national heritage publications. (See also Appendices B and C.)

3. Council of Europe, "European Cultural Convention," Paris, open for signature on December 12, 1954, and entered into force on May 5, 1955, *Council of Europe*, http://conventions.coe.int/Treaty/EN/Treaties/Html/018.htm.

4. Council of Europe, "Convention for the Protection of the Architectural Heritage of Europe," Granada, open for signature on October 3, 1985, and entered into force on December 1, 1987, *Council of Europe*, http://conventions.coe.int/treaty/en/Treaties/Html/121.htm; and Council of Europe, "European Convention on the Protection of the Archaeological Heritage (Revised)," Valletta, Malta, open for signature on January 16, 1992, and entered into force on May 5, 1995, *Council of Europe*, http://conventions.coe.int/Treaty/en/Treaties/Html/143.htm.

5. Europa Nostra, "About Europa Nostra," *Europa Nostra*, http://www.europanostra.org/lang_en/index.html.

6. Colonizing countries also left behind their own contributions to Africa's built heritage, from slave-trading forts on the continent's west coast to plantation estates in the east. Today's African governments must make difficult decisions about these painful physical reminders of past oppression, and limited budgets seldom make room for these sites.

7. Webber Ndoro, "Traditional and Customary Heritage Systems: Nostalgia or Reality? The Implications of Managing Heritage Sites in Africa," in *Linking Universal and Local Values: Managing a Sustainable Future for World Heritage*, ed. Eléonore de Merode, Rieks Smeets, and Carol Westrik, World Heritage Papers no. 13, conference proceedings, Amsterdam, May 22–24, 2003 (Paris: UNESCO World Heritage Centre, 2004), 81.

8. Ibid.

9. ICCROM, "Africa 2009," *ICCROM*, November 21, 2007, http://www.iccrom.org/eng/prog_en/04africa2009_en.shtml.

10. Dawson Munjeri, "Anchoring African Cultural and Natural Heritage: The Significance of Local Community Awareness in the Context of Capacity-Building," in de Merode et al., *Linking Universal and Local Values*, 79.

11. O. P. Jain, "The Practical Experience in Implementing Conservation Objectives" (paper delivered at the WMF Conference "Heritage Conservation: New Alliances for Past, Present and Future," Colombo, Sri Lanka, July 28, 2004).

12. Ibid.

13. Gamini Wijesuriya, "'Livingness' in Asian Contexts and Attitudes Towards the Past: Alliances Within" (paper delivered at the WMF Conference "Heritage Conservation: New Alliances for Past, Present and Future," Colombo, Sri Lanka, July 28, 2004); and "Northern Areas Conservation Strategy: Background Paper on Cultural Heritage and Sustainable Tourism," *IUCN Pakistan*, October 2001, 16.

14. Junko Goto and Arnold R. Alanen, "The Conservation of Historic and Cultural Resources in Rural Japan," *Landscape Journal* 6, no. 1 (1987): 45.

15. Japan has provided technical and management expertise to foreign countries and has demonstrated its role as a leader in conservation theory as well, due in large part to the 1995 Nara Document on Authenticity. This document codified several non-Western conservation approaches by stressing intangible heritage, the roles of craft traditions, and how diversity and respect for conflicting heritage values should be accommodated.

16. UNESCO World Bank, *China-Cultural Heritage Management and Urban Development: Challenge and Opportunity*, conference proceedings, Beijing, July 5–7, 2000, *World Bank*, http://www.worldbank.org.cn/Chinese/content/culture.pdf.

17. "Conservation and Management Principles for Cultural Heritage Sites in China," *Getty Conservation Institute*, http://www.getty.edu/conservation/field_projects/china/.

18. William Chapman, "Asia and the Pacific: A Big Area to Cover!" in "Preservation in the Pacific Basin," special issue, *CRM (Cultural Resource Management)* 19, no. 3 (1996): 4.

19. The struggle by Australia's heritage conservation community has yet to be completely won. Some of the country's greatest heritage of all—the large field of aboriginal rock carvings and paintings at Dampier on the Burrup Peninsula—is threatened by industrial development, including harmful air pollution. (See Figures 17-80 and 17-81.) Further details may be found in Robert G. Bednarik's recent publications, *Australian Apocalypse: The Story of Australia's Greatest Cultural Monument* (Melbourne, Australia: Australian Rock Art Research Association, 2006); and "The Science of Dampier Rock Art—Part 1," *Rock Art Research* 24, no. 2 (November 2007): 209–46.

20. "The Australia ICOMOS Charter for the Conservation of Places of Cultural Significance (the Burra Charter)," adopted at Burra, Australia, August 19, 1979, with many subsequent revisions.

21. ICOMOS New Zealand, "Charter for the Conservation of Places of Cultural Heritage Value," adopted in New Zealand, October 4, 1992; and Dinah Holman, "Local Planning and Conservation Charters," *Planning Quarterly*, no. 100 (1990): 22.

22. Stephen Rainbow, "A National Tragedy," *New Zealand Historic Places*, no. 64 (1997): 9.

23. Dirk H. R. Spennemann and Neal Putt, "Heritage Management and Interpretation in the Pacific," in *Cultural Interpretation of Heritage Sites in the Pacific*, ed. Dirk H. R. Spennemann and Neal Putt (Suva, Fiji: Pacific Islands Museums Association, 2001).

24. Chapman, "Asia and the Pacific," 4.

25. Felicia R. Beardsley, "Jungle Warfare 2000," in "Pacific Preservation," special issue, *CRM (Cultural Resource Management)* 24, no. 1 (2001).

26. Richard Williamson, "The Challenges of Survey and Site Preservation in the Republic of the Marshall Islands," in "Pacific Preservation," special issue, *CRM (Cultural Resource Management)* 24, no. 1 (2001).

27. ICOMOS Canada, "H@R!: Heritage at Risk; National Reports, Canada," *ICOMOS*, http://www.international.icomos.org/risk/canad_2000.htm.

28. Heritage Canada, *Towards a New Act: Protecting Canada's Historic Places* (Ottawa: Minister of Public Works and Government Services, Department of Canadian Heritage, 2002), 2.

29. ICOMOS Canada, "Canada: Heritage at Risk! 2001-2002" (ICOMOS: 2001), (http://www.international.icomos.org/risk/2001/cana2001.htm).

30. National Trust for Historic Preservation, "About the National Trust for Historic Preservation," *National Trust for Historic Preservation*, http://www.nationaltrust.org/about/.

31. "Launch meeting: LATAM—Conservation of Cultural Heritage in Latin America and the Caribbean Programme (2008–2019)."

32. LATAM phase one info, see http://www.iccrom.org/eng/news_en/2008_en/events_en/07_30 meetinglatamCOL_en.shtml.

33. Susan Barr and Paul Chaplin, "H@R 2001–2002: Polar Heritage," *ICOMOS*, http://www.international. icomos.org/risk/2001/polar2001.htm.

34. For example, in Canada, the Yukon government has taken the initiative to preserve the decaying remains of the region's built heritage and to attract tourists. The Department of Tourism and Culture has listed a number of historically significant buildings and archaeological sites that require protection under its Historic Sites program.

35. International Polar Heritage Committee, "Historic Sites and Monuments in Antarctica," *International Polar Heritage Committee*, http://www.polarheritage.com/index.cfm/sitelist01up.

Castello Rivoli, Turin. Adaptive use of the Manica Luonga to be the
Turin Modern Art Museum. (*Andrea Bruno, Architect*)

CHAPTER *18*

The Past in the Future

MEETING THE CHALLENGE AND BEYOND

The long evolution of the field of cultural heritage conservation—in particular architectural conservation—is best characterized as a struggle against great odds, against various acts of humans and nature, and against occasional destructive economic and social trends. For its leaders, it has also been a constant battle to show the way forward by example through endless work on behalf of the essentially defenseless artistic creations of humanity. But the efforts that led to today's systems for conserving the built environment have been imperfect and have met their share of tragic lessons and great frustrations along the way.

The increasing roles that governments and international organizations are playing reflect the fact that architectural conservation is no longer a matter of taste but an expression of basic social responsibility. As such, it seems safe to assume that public interest in the subject—and demands for the proper handling of cultural patrimony—are here to stay. While the attitude that older is better, which was championed by nineteenth-century antiquarians and activists, is not a rationale heard frequently today, the attitude that older is definitely rarer, and thus worthy of attention and protection, has become stronger than ever.[1]

The maturation of the field of architectural conservation, especially in the past two decades, has created a global community of like-minded individuals with remarkably consistent views of the challenges ahead and of the best ways to address them. As people throughout the world seek meaning and stability in their environments and are increasingly interested in protecting it, cultural heritage conservation and all its related concerns have solidified into a growth industry that reaches practically everywhere.

This widespread interest in the past says much about the present. Globalization poses threats to local cultural differences; rapid modernization and growth changes physical surroundings at disquieting speed; and apprehension about an unknown future makes the past comforting. These and other factors have combined to encourage the ascendancy of cultural heritage during the twentieth century, and especially in recent decades. As the dynamics of change increase and the world seems to get smaller with every passing year,

367

the words of David Lowenthal ring ever more true: "The need to return home, to recall the view, to refresh a memory, to retrace a heritage, is universal and essential."[2]

As the interest in organized cultural heritage conservation has spread and developed throughout the world, broad patterns can be discerned. Major campaigns to conserve and re-present examples of authentic national cultural heritage have been given new impetus in countries like Russia and those of Eastern Europe, which are emerging from previously unsupportive political ideologies; countries undergoing rapid physical and social change, such as China; and those recovering from conflict, such as Cambodia, Afghanistan, and the countries that made up the former Yugoslavia. Cultural heritage has been an important mechanism for countries and regions working toward economic unification, such as those within the European Union and the many members of the Association of Southeast Asian Nations (ASEAN). Slow but sure struggles to improve heritage conservation practice in developing countries with less tumultuous recent histories in sub-Saharan Africa and Central Asia still face great challenges. Ongoing conflicts and differing priorities in places like Iraq and the Palestinian Territories prevent conservation action from taking place at all. Yet worldwide awareness of and interest in protecting significant examples of cultural heritage has also been invigorated by heart-wrenching incidents of destruction during recent tensions and conflicts, such as in Bamiyan, Afghanistan; Ayodhya, India; and throughout the former Yugoslavia.

Despite its successes, the conservation of architectural heritage in most countries remains a herculean task complicated by threats from nature as well as from humans and by a general shortage of trained specialists and necessary funds. Historic buildings and sites, whether as individual entities or as parts of ensembles, are lost every day as a result of the inevitable deterioration of most building materials. No place on earth is immune to these threats: In the past few years, historic European cities like Prague and Dresden, Germany, were inundated by floods; earthquakes have reduced historic sites like Bam, Iran, to rubble; a major tsunami destroyed lives and cultural heritage in several countries of South and Southeast Asia; and hurricanes and flooding have ravaged New Orleans, Louisiana.

Even greater menaces than these natural disasters are the pressures that humans place on their physical environment. Though urban and town planning and contemporary architectural practice is today more sensitive to the need to integrate historic buildings into new designs than in the past, the losses are still great. Unfortunately, however, in many parts of the world, rather than wisely planned land development and building, the accumulation of countless separate, unplanned, and often illegal construction projects in cities and rural areas combine to pose significant threats to both the built and the natural environments.

Since the Venice Charter of 1964, few years have passed without a new declaration or charter exploring some aspect of architectural heritage and conservation. Though they often seem similar, most have made important original contributions to the field. Their cumulative effect has promoted dialogue on many issues and ideas. *Charettes* (holistic planning sessions during which experts usually reach consensus and identify specific solutions) and large-scale conferences, such as ICOMOS' fifteenth biennial meeting in Xi'an, China, in 2005, have become increasingly efficient and have had a positive impact on the field.[4] Declarations of principles made as a result of many of these meetings, and the preponderance of recent charters, make keeping track of the dynamic heritage conservation field an unending task but also reflects its importance and multifaceted nature. (See also "International Conferences and Declarations: Milestones of Progress" in Chapter 15, as well as Appendix C.)

Despite these challenges, the field has benefited from some unusual advantages and is currently witnessing some important, promising developments. The widespread appreciation of its practical merits and an even wider sympathy for the cause that it represents are foremost among the factors that have improved the likelihood of having more resources—and examples of architectural conservation—in the future.

That communities in need can turn to international heritage conservation organizations and other experts for help is also of tremendous value. Since the end of the Cold War there have been almost no geopolitical barriers for governmental and nongovernmental organizations (NGOs) concerned with architectural conservation attempting to help anywhere in the world. (Of course, invitations to participate by appropriate government ministries and the legal owners of the various historic properties and protocols concerning work procedures and other responsibilities must be in place before any in-depth planning or implementation can occur.) This unprecedented reach and access, in combination with the cause-related and solutions-oriented nature of the field, has boosted international heritage projects in a variety of ways. It has involved increasingly sophisticated methods of cooperation in the technical and financial partnerships realms, which in turn allows the participating organizations and governments to complement each other's strengths and abilities.

Since the early 1990s, the World Bank and several of its affiliates have done much to shape international thinking about making culture key to efforts at international assistance. The United Nations Educational, Scientific and Cultural Organization (UNESCO) and other international organizations working in heritage conservation definitely took notice and advocate in new ways to use cultural heritage as a tool to promote both economic sustainability and responsible development.

The numbers of bi- and multilateral intergovernmental initiatives for heritage protection are also increasing. Well-established, state-sponsored institutions such as l'École Française d'Extrême Oriente, continue their research and conservation work in Cambodia and India; international cooperation has expanded to include a number of new participants; the Indian government has been active at Angkor in Cambodia; Turkey offered assistance throughout the Balkans in the aftermath of war in the former Yugoslavia; Polish government–sponsored ateliers have helped conserve important historic sites in Egypt and Vietnam; and Saudi Arabia has funded conservation all across the Islamic world. (See also Chapters 15 and 16.)

Examples of philanthropy from the American Express Corporation, the Samuel H. Kress Foundation, and the Getty Conservation Institute in the United States and other private and corporate foundations in England, Portugal, Mexico, India, Japan, Hong Kong, and elsewhere have brought much-needed funding to architectural conservation all over the world. A long list of individuals who are substantial private donors can be added to this list. The thousands of not-for-profit organizations—large and small—working worldwide on aspects of cultural heritage conservation reflect a widespread realization that the gaps between government needs and available local resources need to be filled. Centrally placed in these scenarios are always individuals whose roles are often underappreciated, but who should not be overlooked. It is the community leaders and advocates, the government officials and their staffs, the curators, teachers, architects, engineers, and specialty consultants, as well as the craftspeople and workers at the projects, who are the backbone of the field.

Ever-evolving management policies and procedures for cultural heritage protection and new documentation and conservation technologies have greatly improved practice worldwide in recent years, and more such developments are likely to follow. The accessibility of computerized inventories and databases and their ease of use have permitted information sharing on a scale and at speeds unimaginable even a few decades ago.

Degree programs in architectural conservation, short courses by institutions such as the International Centre for the Study of the Preservation and Restoration of Cultural Property (ICCROM), a host of other university-level educational opportunities, and international internship programs such as those offered by the International Council on Monuments and Sites (ICOMOS), have significantly raised the level of experience, expertise, and professionalism of practitioners. The allied fields of archaeology and architectural history have embraced conservation as an important part of their mandates, with examples of impressive combined excavation, education, research, and conservation work being done at the ancient Greek colonial site of Tauric Chersonesus; at Sevastopol, Ukraine, by the University of Texas; at Genghis Khan's capital of Karakorum in Mongolia by the University of Heidelberg in Germany; and at Pompeii by the University of Bradford in England. In addition, more schools of architecture and urban planning have begun to *require* courses in design for historic contexts, urban rehabilitation, and architectural conservation within their curricula. Likewise, at least remedial instruction in both object and site conservation is part of most all graduate programs in archaeology today.

Important steps have also been taken to address failings in the field, such as the lack of balanced global representation on the World Heritage List. These discrepancies are in large part due to a lack of understanding, reinforcing the idea expressed in the UNESCO constitution that "ignorance of other cultures is a root cause of conflict."[3] Recent expansion of the possible categories by which heritage sites may be listed and protected by UNESCO has helped. Previously, sites could either be listed as cultural or natural; now a "mixed" listing is recognized, since some cultures do not support the distinction. Good progress is being made in UNESCO's and ICOMOS' efforts at balancing the World Heritage List to include more sites from more places by adding new member states and sponsoring more varied specialized conferences and events. At the same time, several of the more prominent NGOs, such as the World Monuments Fund, the Getty Conservation Institute, and the Aga Khan Trust for Culture, have reached high levels of sophistication and effectiveness in recent years. While their methods of operation may vary, the main aim of each is to raise wider awareness of the importance of conserving architectural and related cultural heritage. Reinforcement of the same message from these and the many other voices in the heritage conservation field works well for showing the possibilities and winning public support.

GOING FORWARD

By 2020, an estimated 70 percent of the earth's land surface will be serving human needs in one way or another, with a large amount it supporting the built environment. By 2025, the world's population is projected to reach eight billion. These dramatic statistics suggest that despite all the successes in architectural conservation to date, the pressures of growth and development will only increase. Protecting global cultural heritage is, therefore, an endeavor from which there can be no respite. Constant vigilance and new solutions and initiatives are required to ensure the continued protection of currently recognized cultural heritage sites. To extend this protection to yet more sites will be a major challenge.

In the future, international institutions will continue to play useful roles in promoting cultural heritage conservation policies and in providing information, financing, and access to expertise. However, advances must be made to better coordinate international efforts to prevent redundancies.

Poverty reduction efforts should include support for the conservation of the cultural heritage of poorer and marginalized groups in order to improve their self-esteem and empower those communities to take charge of improving their own circumstances. The poor are particularly at risk from large-scale development projects that result in displacement—often to worse conditions that further undermine their values and dignity. Heritage protection should be built into more development projects, as restored and properly maintained architectural heritage not only builds local confidence and pride but also encourages sustainable cultural tourism and its economic benefits.

New solutions must be developed to mitigate the deleterious effects mass tourism has on the most popular heritage sites. Constructing facsimiles, such as the surrogate Lascaux Cave, is not always possible or desirable; therefore, visitors should be limited and better controlled at sites such as the Acropolis, the tombs of the Valley of the Kings, and sites at

Some Ideas That Would Help[5]

1. Limit new land development until presently developed (built) areas are more efficiently utilized. Recognize more fully the merits of "smart growth," especially as it relates to architectural heritage enhancement and protection.

2. Provide additional tax relief and other government-provided financial incentives in more countries for conserving architectural heritage.

3. Reduce energy consumption through even broader "green design" planning, such as reducing the distances that people must travel for amenities and to their places of employment.

4. Ensure that all who are being trained in architecture, planning, and real estate development and those who are relevant government policy administrators have access to at least introductory courses in architectural heritage conservation.

5. Institute additional cleanup, repair, and urban improvement schemes along the lines of the US National Trust's Main Streets program and the *escuela taller* systems aimed at heritage site enhancement and protection in Spain and Latin America.

6. Foster, document, and celebrate local invention toward sustainable cultural heritage conservation.

7. Reward writers and the media for outstanding journalism on heritage conservation.

8. Teach more well-planned heritage awareness programs at the grade school level.

9. Support the efforts of ICOMOS to create an international observatory for cultural heritage that would document and share knowledge about why and how destruction to cultural heritage occurs, how protection is achieved, and what is the relevance of heritage conservation to world culture is.[6]

10. Ensure new architecture is suitable to the climate for which it is planned and design for later physical adaptability.

11. Develop a broader corpus of literature about the field of cultural heritage protection.

12. Recognize the extent of military spending throughout the world and work to reduce it, and spend significant portions of the savings on enhancements to built environments and cultural heritage conservation.

13. Increase participation of global banking entities and other key financial institutions in historic urban infrastructure improvement schemes and related architectural conservation.

Angkor Wat, where overuse threatens the physical integrity of these historic resources. In addition, special measures are necessary in some instances to prevent historic sites from being operated as hollow caricatures devoid of their local life and character.

Not all worthy conservation projects are economically viable. Many believe that governments must intervene more to preserve their national heritage, though there are differing opinions as to how this should be accomplished and to what extent it should occur. This is all the more clear in a world increasingly dependent on the marketplace for initiative and investment. When the costs of rehabilitation and revitalization are factored in, government subvention of one kind or another is often required. Ensuring that cultural heritage conservation is an element in annual budgets, national environmental action plans, and legal and regulatory mechanisms such as land use planning, building codes, and design guidelines is, therefore, essential. In turn, planners with heritage protection administrations should also ensure that all building types, communities, and historical themes are addressed in the process of conserving the built environment, even when it may involve "difficult" history such as tragedies and failures.

Cultural heritage is a self-reinforcing component of education. Communicating its value through education, beginning with school children and including all levels of society, is perhaps the best investment that communities can make in their future. This may take the form of school-organized site visits, educational materials, heritage-oriented programs in drawing and photography classes, and even offerings via the electronic media such as the Internet. As in the past, many of the most innovative ideas and solutions for cultural heritage protection, including architectural conservation, will come from interested local amateurs, volunteers, and activists. This stands to reason: It was such individuals who likely created the built environments and life ways they seek to preserve in the first place.

As the cultural heritage conservation movement faces the future, its many purposes—especially those of ensuring continuity and retaining key examples as inspirations from the past—should remain viable indefinitely. Considering all that is at stake and the field's progress to date, there is little doubt that future heritage conservationists will strive to embrace the challenge.

RELATED READINGS

Ashworth, G. J. and J. E. Turnbridge, eds. *Building a New Heritage: Tourism, Culture and Identity in the New Europe.* London: Routledge, 1994.

Barnett, Jonathan, ed. *Smart Growth in a Changing World.* Washington, DC: APA Planners Press, 2007.

Bednarik, Robert G, *Australian Apocallypse: The Story of Australia's Greatest Cultural Monument* Occasional AURA Publication 14, Melbourne: Australian Rock Art Research Association, 2006). "The Science of Dampier Rock Art"—Part 1, *Rock Art Research* 24 (2) 2007: 209–246.

Brandon, Peter, and Patrizia Lombardi. *Evaluating Sustainable Development in the Built Environment.* Oxford: Blackwell Publishing, 2005.

Cunningham, Storm. *The Restoration Economy: The Greatest New Growth Frontier.* San Francisco: Berrett-Koehler, 2002.

Cuno, James. *Who Owns Antiquity? Museums and the Battle Over Our Ancient Heritage.* Princeton, NJ: Princeton University Press, 2008.

Feifer, Maxine. *Tourism in History: From Imperial Rome to the Present.* New York: Stein and Day, 1985.

Feilden, Bernard M., and Jukka Jokilehto. *Management Guidelines for World Cultural Heritage Sites.* 2nd ed. Rome: ICCROM, 1998.

Fladmark, J. M., ed. *Cultural Tourism.* Papers presented at the Robert Gordon University Heritage Conference, 1994. Shaftesbury, UK: Donhead, 2000.

Fladmark, Magnus, ed., *Cultural Tourism.* Donhead, St. Mary: Donhead Publishing, 1994.

Fowler, Peter J. "Archaeology, the Public and the Sense of the Past," in *Our Past Before Us: Why Do We Save It?* Edited by David Lowenthal and Marcus Binney. London: Temple Smith, 1981.

Herbert, D. T., ed. *Heritage, Tourism and Society.* London: Mansell, 1995.

Hewison, Robert. *The Heritage Industry: Britain in a Climate of Decline.* London: Methuen, 1987.

Hoffman, Barbara. *Art and Cultural Heritage: Law, Policy, and Practice.* Cambridge: Cambridge University Press, 2005).

ICCROM Conservation Studies 3 (2005). Stovel, H. Stanley-Price, N., Killick, R., eds. *Conserving Religious Heritage,* papers from the ICCROM Forum on "Living religious heritage: conserving the sacred," held in Rome on 20–22 October 2003.

Joffroy, Thierry, ed. *Traditional Conservation Practices in Africa.* ICCROM Conservation Studies 2. Rome: ICCROM, 2005.

Jokilehto, Jukka. "A Century of Architectural Conservation." *Journal of Architectural Conservation,* no. 3 (November 1999): 14–33.

Lowenthal, David. *The Heritage Crusade and the Spoils of History.* Cambridge: Cambridge University Press, 1998.

MacDonald, S, ed. *Preserving Post-War Heritage: The Care and Conservation of Modern Architecture.* Shaftsbury: Donhead, 2001.

Quaedvlieg-Mihailović, Sneška, and Rupert Graf Strachwitz, eds. *Heritage and the Building of Europe.* Berlin: Maecenata, 2004.

Prudon, Theodore H. M. *Preservation of Modern Architecture.* Hoboken NJ: John Wiley & Sons, 2008.

Serageldin, Ismail, and Joan Martin-Brown, eds. *Culture in Sustainable Development: Investing in Cultural and Natural Endowments: Proceedings of the Conference on Culture in Sustainable*

Developments, World Bank, Washington, DC: 28–29, 1998. Washington, DC: World Bank, 1999.

Serageldin, Ismail, Ephim Shluger, and Joan Martin-Brown, eds. *Historic Cities and Sacred Sites: Cultural Roots for Urban Frontiers.* Washington, DC: World Bank, 2001.

Stille, Alexander. *The Future of the Past.* New York: Farrar, Straus and Giroux, 2002.

Teutonico, Jeanne Marie, and Frank Matero, eds. *Managing Change: Sustainable Approaches to the Conservation of the Built Environment.* Los Angeles: Getty Conservation Institute, 2003.

Towse, Ruth, ed. *A Handbook on Cultural Economics.* Northampton, MA: Edward Elgar, 2003.

UNESCO. *Final Act of the Intergovernmental Conference on the Protection of Cultural Property in the Event of Armed Conflict.* Conference held at The Hague in 1954.

UNESCO. http://unesdoc.unesco.org/images/0008/000824/082464mb.pdf. Legislation that serves as the basis for all subsequent discussion on cultural heritage protection prior to and during times of conflict.

World Commission on Environment and Development. *Our Common Future (The Bruntland Report).* Oxford: Oxford University Press, 1987.

ENDNOTES

1. Pierce, *Conservation Today,* 232.

2. Lowenthal and Binney, *Our Past Before Us,* 236.

3. W. Brown Morton, III, "What Do We Preserve and Why?"167.

4. Over one thousand delegates from around the world attended the five-day ICOMOS Fifteenth General Assembly and Scientific Symposium in Xi'an, China, which offered hundreds of scholarly and specialist presentations and numerous specialty optional study tours. The proceedings were immediately published on the World Wide Web, a resolution addressing development around heritage was passed, and a regional outpost for ICOMOS in Asia was launched.

5. See also illustrations of "Promising Developments" in the region by region summary coverage of "Special Challenges" and "Promising Developments" throughout the world. (Chapter 17).

6. A proposal made in 2005 by architect Dinu Bumbaru, vice president of ICOMOS International.

APPENDIX A

Nomenclature Used in International Architectural Conservation Practice

SOME KEY TERMS

Since the eighteenth century, the nomenclature used by practitioners of architectural conservation has evolved as the subject progressed from being a lay interest to a discipline to the multifaceted profession it is today. Many widely used terms have what at first glance seems to be an obvious meaning due to familiar Greek and Latin roots. However, care should be taken to fully understand their meaning (or meanings) as often an accurate definition incorporates nuances.

Translation has added other subtle distinctions to architectural heritage conservation's professional nomenclature. Over the past several decades, as heritage conservation transcended political boundaries to become a matter of global concern, a concurrent and rapid adoption of terms by professionals working in disparate global regions created the remarkably uniform nomenclature used in today's international heritage conservation practice. This vocabulary has also been enriched by terms contributed by different cultures. As a result, practitioners of architectural conservation have at their disposal a broad lexicon that reflects both the field's rich diversity as well as its global applicability.

The various international charters and declarations promulgated by the United Nations Educational, Scientific and Cultural Organization (UNESCO), the International Council on Monuments and Sites (ICOMOS), the International Council of Museums (ICOM), and some of the other key heritage conservation advocacy groups working alongside them have done much to harmonize the field's nomenclature. Therefore, the best sources for locating the representative operative terminology of these organizations can be found in their work. Other fruitful sources are in the more influential and detailed charters such as Australia ICOMOS Burra Charter, ICOMOS New Zealand's Charter for the Conservation of Places of Cultural Heritage Value (the Aotearoa Charter), and the *Secretary of the Interior's Standards and Guidelines for Archaeology and Historic Preservation*, and in online databases such as the Getty Conservation Institute's Art and Architectural Thesaurus.

Below are defined some key terms and their sources, where possible, used in the international practice of architectural conservation. This list is by no means comprehensive; for example, specialized technical terms are outside the scope of this glossary. In many cases, definitions of the same term from different sources are listed in order to show how a single term can incorporate different nuances of meaning.

SOURCES AND ABBREVIATIONS

AKTC: The Aga Khan Trust for Culture.

BC: The Australia ICOMOS Burra Charter, Burra, Australia, 1999 (and subsequent revisions).

BMF: Bernard M. Feilden, *Conservation of Historic Buildings* (London: Butterworth Scientific, 1982).

DM: *Dictionnaire Moderne Français — Anglais* (Paris: Librairie Larousse, 1960).

EP: Eric Partridge, *Origins: A Short Etymological Dictionary of Modern English*, 4th ed. (New York: Macmillan, 1966).

G: Getty Vocabulary Program, Getty Conservation Institute.

HSG: D. Bell, *The Historic Scotland Guide to International Conservation Charters* (Edinburgh: Historic Scotland, 1997).

IIC-CG: International Institute for Conservation—Canadian Group, Code of Ethics and Guidance for Conservation Practice for Those Involved in the Conservation of Cultural Property in Canada (Ottawa, Canada: IIC-CG, 1985).

JJ: Jukka Jokilehto, *A History of Architectural Conservation* (Oxford: Butterworth-Heinemann, 1999).

JMF: James Marston Fitch, *Historic Preservation: Curatorial Management of the Built World* (Charlottesville, VA: University Press of Virginia, 1990).

JS: James Strike, *Architecture in Conservation: Managing Development at Historic Sites* (London: Routledge, 1994).

MW: *Merriam-Webster Online Dictionary*, http://www.merriam-webster.com/

NZ: The New Zealand ICOMOS Charter for the Conservation of Places of Cultural Heritage Value (the Aotearoa Charter), Auckland, 1992.

RHUD: *The Random House Unabridged Dictionary*, 2d ed. (New York: Random House, 1993).

SI: US Secretary of the Interior's Standards and Guidelines for Archaeology and Historic Preservation. USPO, Washington, DC.

VC: Venice Charter of 1964, as adopted by ICOMOS in 1965.

WM: William J. Murtagh, *Keeping Time: The History and Theory of Preservation in America* (New York: John Wiley & Sons, 1997).

WP: Mark Fram, *Well-Preserved: The Ontario Heritage Foundation's Manual of Principles and Practice for Architectural Conservation* (Ontario, Canada: Boston Mills Press, 1988).

adaptation: Modifying a place to suit the existing use or a proposed use (BC).

adaptive use (see also *rehabilitation*): 1. A form or structure modified to fit a changed environment (RH). 2. Converting a building to a use other than that for which it was designed, e.g., a factory into housing, by altering the building (after WM, 213). 3. Modifying a place to suit proposed compatible uses (art. 1.9, 1.10, BC; art. 22, NZ).

anastylosis: (Greek: *ano*, up or above; *stylo*, column; *stylosis*, derivative of *styloun*, to prop up with pillars; EP.) 1. "The restoration of a ruined monument or building by reassembling fallen parts and, when necessary, incorporating new materials" (RH). 2. "The re-establishment or rebuilding of a monument with its own materials and according to its own methods of construction. It allows the discreet and justified use of new materials in replacement of missing stones without which their original elements could not be repositioned" (George Balanos, restorer of the Athenian Acropolis, ca. 1932). 3. "The reassembling of existing but dismembered parts" (VC).

archaeological heritage: "That part of the material heritage whose primary information has been provided by archaeological methods. It comprises all vestiges of human existence and consists of places relating to all manifestations of human activity, abandoned structures, and remains of all kinds (including subterranean and underwater sites) together with all the portable cultural material associated with them." (International Committee for the Management of Archaeological Heritage [ICAHM], Charter for the Protection and Management of the Archaeological Heritage [Lausanne, 1990.])

architectural conservation (see also *conservation, historic preservation, preservation, restoration*): (Latin: *servare*, to keep safe or well, to preserve.) 1. "All the processes of looking after a place so as to retain its cultural significance. It includes maintenance and may according to circumstance include preservation, restoration, reconstruction, and adaptation and will be commonly a combination of one or more of these" (art. 1.4, BC; art. 22, NZ). 2. "All actions aimed at the safeguarding of cultural property for the future. Its purpose is to study, record, retain and restore the culturally significant qualities of the object with the least possible intervention" (IIC-GC). 3. A main aim of cultural heritage conservation is "the maintenance and enhancement of reference patterns needed for the expression and consolidation of citizenship" (1987 Petropolis Charter). 4. "The object of conservation is to prolong the life of cultural heritage and, if possible, to clarify the artistic and historical messages therein without the loss of authenticity and meaning" (HSG, 24).

architectural heritage (see also *cultural heritage, cultural property (general)*): 1. Groups of buildings: homogenous groups of urban or rural buildings conspicuous for their historical, artistic, scientific, social or technical interest that are sufficiently coherent to form topographically definable units. 2. "Architectural heritage shall be considered to comprise the following permanent properties: i. Monuments: all buildings and structures of conspicuous historical, artistic, scientific, social or technical interest, including their fixtures and fittings; ii. Sites: the combined works of man and nature, being areas which are partially built upon and sufficiently distinctive and homogeneous to be topographically definable and are of conspicuous historical, archaeological, artistic, scientific, social or technical interest." (Council of Europe, *Convention for the Protection of the Architectural Heritage of Europe*, Granada, 1987.) 3. "The European architectural heritage consists not only of our most important monuments: it also includes the groups of lesser buildings in our town and characteristic villages in their natural or manmade settings...entire groups of buildings, even if they do not include an example of outstanding merit, may have an atmosphere that gives them the quality of works of art, welding different periods and styles into a harmonious whole. Such groups should also be preserved...." (Council of Europe, European Charter of the Architectural Heritage, Amsterdam, September 26, 1975.)

architectural value: "Factors which comprise a building's perceptible architectural value as expressed in the way the building looks, the irreplaceable craftsmanship of its construction, the skill evident in its component parts and their combination on a distinctive piece of ground, and quality of construction of a specific era, now gone forever" (WP).

associations: "The special connections that exist between people and a place. Significant associations between people and a place should be respected, retained and not obscured. Opportunities for the interpretation, commemoration and celebration of these associations should be investigated and implemented" (BC).

authentic (see also *original, prototype*): (Greek: *authentikos*, original, primary; Latin: *auctor*, an originator, an authority.) 1. Not false or copied; genuine, real; shares the sense of actuality and lack of falsehood or misrepresentation (RH). 2. "'Authentic' means that the object was made contemporaneously with its style, that it is not a copy.... 'This is an authentic copy' means that it is an accurate copy, the historical details of the replica are correct' (JS, 138). 3. "Original as opposed to a copy, real as opposed to pretended, genuine as opposed to counterfeit. Authentic does not mean the same as identical. Authentic refers to original and there can only be one original" (JJ, 298). 4. Being true in substance, as really proceeding from its reputed source or author (*Shorter Oxford English Dictionary*, cited in HSG, 22). "One must be careful not to confuse 'authentic' with 'original': all original fabric is authentic, but not all authentic fabric is original. Often restorations which have removed accretions, and reconstructions, gain a greater aesthetic or 'period' consistency at the cost of the authentic record of the site's existence" (HSG, 28).

branding (see also commodification of culture): "The overall image of a heritage attraction is an amalgam of its name, logo, content, promotional message and location." (Kenneth Robinson et al in "Selling the Heritage Product" in *Manual of Heritage Management*, edited by Richard Harrison [Boston: Butterworth-Heinmann, 1994], 382.) Branding connects all important information (Who? What? Where?) about a historic resource or organization with a promotional message. Branding is used to trigger instant recognition (brand recognition) and with that, familiarity of a product. The more familiar, the likelier it is accepted and eventually appreciated or demanded by users. Depending on the product and the image it is connected with, the ways of its promotion will vary widely.

buildings (historic): "A 'historic building'... has architectural, aesthetic, historic, documentary, archaeological, economic, social, and even political and spiritual or symbolic values; but the first impact is always emotional, for it is a symbol of our cultural identity and continuity; a part of our heritage" (BMF, 1).

built environment: "The aggregate of human-made structures, infrastructural elements and associated spaces and features" (G).

commodification of culture (or history) (see also branding): Takes place when economic value is assigned to something not previously considered in economic terms; the treatment of things as if they were a tradeable commodity. (*Wikepedia*) Examples in the field of cultural heritage include controlled daily access by the use of tiered fee systems to sites such as the Roman Forum or the multi-day passes necessary for access to the temples of Angkor. Such control may include efforts by local authorities to restrict the types of presentations of their histories, an action is in effect *branding*. Industries like tourism are renowned for the commodification of culture in more indirect ways. Hotels, airlines, travel agents, and guidebooks are among those that create (and mobilize) particular representations of place, people, and the past for touristic consumption. Typically, such processes of commodification feature the exotic, the ethnic, the romantic, or the mysterious to secure the tourist dollar.

compatible use: "The functions of a place, as well as the activities and practices that may occur at the place. Compatible use means a use which respects the cultural significance of a place. Such a use involves no, or minimal, impact on cultural significance" (BC).

conservation (see also *architectural conservation, historic preservation, preservation, restoration*): 1. "All the processes of looking after a place so as to retain its cultural significance" (BC). 2. The discipline involving treatment, preventive care, and research directed toward the long-term safekeeping of cultural and natural heritage (G). 3. "Conservation involves maintaining the presence of the past in the present. That involves preserving, restoring and/or adapting old buildings; designing new ones that respect their neighbors and the continuity of history; weaving old and new together in an urban fabric of variety and richness." (Khairul Enam and Kaleda Rashid, "Planning Tools for Conservation," AKTC, 68. 4.) "Conservation is flexible: it can include restoration, creation, or simply respect for the environment and climate. It implies a desire to live in harmony and sympathy with the global scheme....

Conservation has a broader meaning, one which includes an attitude of the creative mind willing to delve into the past." (Mohamed Makiya, "A Practicing Architect Looks at Conservation," AKTC, 100–101.)

conservation area (see also *historic and architectural area*): A designation of towns or zones within which particular precautions must be taken in development, and outside of which there perhaps lies a further protective or buffer zone in which controls of traffic movements, industrial pollution, the heights of new buildings, types of land use, and so forth, are enforced (SU).

conservation (integrated): The interdependence of the different facets of conservation work, including the integration of: 1. various areas of professional expertise, including architecture, technology, archeology, history, sociology, and economics; 2. expertise on the varied components to be conserved within a buil,ding so that the site is considered as a whole not and not as disparate parts; 3. the opinions, wants, and needs of the community into the action plan, and the integration of the site into community activities; and 4. the integration of protection and protectionist aims into the economic and social development of urban and regional planning (HSG).

conservation (preventative): Used more frequently in the context of objects. "All actions taken to retard deterioration and prevent damage to cultural property though the provision of optimal conditions of storage use and handling" (IIC-CG). 2. "Prevention entails protecting cultural property by controlling its environment, thus preventing agents of decay, and damage from becoming active. Neglect also must be prevented by sound maintenance procedures based on periodic inspections" (BMF, 9). 3. Conservation that is aimed at preventing future deterioration of materials or artifacts, including providing suitable environmental conditions (G).

conservator: (Latin: *seruaure /seruus*, guardian; EP.) 1. In the generic sense, any person whose primary occupation is the conservation of cultural property and who has the training, knowledge, ability, and experience to carry out conservation activities (IIC-CG). 2. People responsible for treatment, preventative care, and research directed toward the long-term safekeeping of built and natural heritage (G).

consolidation: (Latin: *solidare*, to establish firmly.) 1. "Solidification; strengthening" (RH). 2. "The physical addition or application of adhesive or supportive materials into the actual fabric of cultural property, in order to ensure its continued durability or structural integrity" (BMF, 9). 3. The stabilization of degraded or weakened areas by introducing or attaching materials capable of holding them together (G).

cultural ecology: The mutual relations between humans and their cultural environment. Cultural ecology must be kept in balance, just as the ecology of nature must be kept in balance. (Ernest Allen Connally, "Historical Preservation as an Ethical Concept and a Social Asset," in *Symposium on Monuments and Society: Leningrad, USSR, 2–8, September 1969* [Paris: ICOMOS, 1969], 36.)

cultural evolution: 1. Evolution: "Any process of formation or growth; biologically, a change in the gene pool of a population from generation to generation by such processes as mutation, natural selection and genetic drift. A gradual, peaceful or progressive change" (RH). 2. "A change in the body of non-genetic information that we humans have, including what is stored in our brains, what is stored in our books, our buildings, our computer disks, our films, and it is changing all the time." (Paul R. Erhlich, *Human Natures: Genes, Cultures, and the Human Prospect* [Washington, DC: Island Press, 2000.])

cultural heritage (see also *architectural heritage, cultural property (general)*): 1. "The entire corpus of material signs—either artistic or symbolic—handed on by the past to each culture and, therefore, to the whole of humankind. As a constituent part of the affirmation and enrichment of cultural identities, as a legacy belonging to all humankind, the cultural heritage gives each particular place its recognizable features and is the storehouse of human experience." (1989 UNESCO draft medium-term plan) 2. "The present manifestation of the human past." (S. Sullivan,

Reader for Cultural Heritage Planning Workshop, Siem Reap Cambodia, World Monuments Fund (NP), March, 2000.) 3. Cultural heritage possesses "historical, archaeological, architectural, technological, aesthetic, scientific, spiritual, social, tradition or other special cultural significance, associated with human activity (NZ). 4. "Evidence of cultural value" at a site comes from "the comparative quality of a mixture of different factors: construction; aesthetics; usage/associations; context, and present condition" (HSG, 36).

cultural landscape: 1. "The totality of built monuments, natural features and social, historic, ethnographic, and cultural practices that give a particular locality its character. Skills, crafts, local history, populations and rural processes are now also recognized as being the essential fabric that defines and supports a cultural landscape." (Bonnie Burnham, "Architectural Heritage: The Paradox of its Current State of Risk," in *International Journal of Cultural Property* 7, no. 1 [January 1998), 159.]): 2. Land and water areas significantly altered or modified by human actions; used in contrast to *natural landscape*, which designates areas where human effects, if present, are not ecologically significant to the region as a whole (G).

cultural property (general) (see also *architectural heritage, cultural heritage*): 1. An object that is judged by society to be of particular historical, artistic, or scientific importance. 2. "That which forms part of the cultural and national heritage" (UNESCO 1972 definition per HSG, 19). 3. "Not only the established and scheduled architectural, archaeological and historic sites and structures, but also the unscheduled or unclassified vestiges of the past as well as artistically or historically important recent sites and structures" (Preamble [1.2] of the 1968 UNESCO recommendation concerning the Preservation of Cultural Property Endangered by Public or Private Works).

cultural property (immovable heritage): 1. Monuments of nature, architecture, art, or history, and archaeological sites and structures of historical or artistic interest (IIC-CG). 2. "A general term now used to encompass all kinds of material objects, structures, architecture, architectural ensembles, and archaeological sites associated with, and created by, man's multifaceted cultural traditions" (BMF, 6). 3. Historic sites and all works of architecture are encompassed under immovable property, including religious, military, civil, and domestic architecture. Immovable property includes industrial and agricultural buildings, workshops, factories, farms, barns, mills, and indigenous rural housing, and the fixtures, fittings, and furnishings belonging to them, as well as the archaeological deposits associated with their development (BMF, 6–7).

cultural property (movable): 1. Works of art, artifacts, books, manuscripts, and other objects of natural, historical, or archaeological origin (IIC-CG). 2. "All works of art, craft and artifacts which are not in some way specifically connected to structures, architecture or sites…[including] paintings and sculpture, ceramics, furniture, archival material, most textiles, domestic objects and archaeological objects…." (BMF, 6).

cultural significance (see also *site of cultural significance*): "A historic, scientific, social or spiritual value for past, present or future generations…embodied in the place itself, its fabric, setting, use, associations, meanings, records, related places and related objects. Places may have a range of values for different individuals or groups…[and] may change as a result of the continuing history of the place. Understanding…cultural significance may change as a result of new information. The term *cultural significance* is synonymous with *heritage significance* and *cultural heritage value*" (BC).

damnatio memoriae: Latin term for the erasure of inscriptions and images of an individual after his or her death in an effort to expunge him or her from history, as attempted with the physical reminders of the Egyptian pharaoh Akhenaton and the Roman Emperor Domitian, and retaliatory actions associated with the Reformation and Counter- Reformation.

degagement: French trans: "open a view" (DM). At historic sites degagement refers to disengaging the site from the vegetation that obscures it and removal of soil overburden and accumulated debris.

densification: An American urban planning term for an increase in population density, either by plan or natural accretion.

documentation: 1. All of the records, written and pictorial, accumulated during the examination and treatment of a cultural property; where applicable, it includes the examination record, treatment proposal, owner consent, the treatment record and summary, and the recommendations for future use or storage (IIC-CG). 2. An activity and strategy within cultural heritage management that identifies and describes an aspect or aspects of cultural heritage and puts it in a tangible form. Documentation includes the development of publications, public events, and educational programs and is considered a basis for decision making for architectural conservation planning. 3. Gathering and recording information, especially to establish or provide evidence of facts or testimony (G).

duplicate (see also *facsimile, mimesis, replica, reproduction*): (Latin: *duplicare*, to make double; EP.) 1. A copy exactly like an original (RH). 2. "In the context of a collection of images or printed matter,…additional copies in the same format and medium" (G).

easement: 1. A partial interest in real property, through donation or purchase, recorded in the deed, protecting the identifying elements of the interior, exterior, or space around the property to be preserved (WM, 214). 2. A right held by one property owner to make use of the land of another for a limited purpose, as right of way (RH). 3. Usually a not-for-profit interest granted by deed or will that is held by a person in land owned by another and that entitles the holder to a special limited use (G).

ensemble (monumental): 1. All the parts of a thing taken together, so that each part is considered only in relation to the whole (RH). 2. "Groups of movable or immovable things presenting natural, scientific, aesthetic, historic or ethnological interest, confined to a topographical area and embracing surroundings which serve as a protective and intermediate zone and which set off the whole to advantage." (Pierre-Yves Ligen, *Dangers and Perils* [Strasbourg, France: Council for Cultural Co-operation, 1968.])

fabric (architectural): "All…physical material…including components, fixtures, contents, and objects…in a place. Fabric includes building interiors and sub-surface remains, as well as excavated material. Fabric may define spaces and…may be important elements of the significance of the place" (BC).

façade, façadism: 1. "The front of a building, especially an imposing or decorative one; any side of a building facing a public way or space, and finished accordingly" (RH). 2. The retention of only the façade of a historic building during the conversion process, in which the remainder of the structure is severely altered or totally destroyed (WM, 215). 3. The practice of retaining the front elevation of a building and constructing a new and usually larger building behind it (G).

facsimile (see also *duplicate, mimesis, replica, reproduction*: (Latin: *simulare*, to represent exactly, to copy, to imitate.) 1. An exact copy, as a book, painting, or manuscript (RH). 2. A precise reproduction, usually in the same dimensions as the original, especially of books, documents, prints, or drawings, today often reproduced photographically, in the past reproduced by engraving or other printmaking process (G).

gentrification: 1. The buying and renovation of houses and stores in deteriorating urban neighborhoods by upper- or middle-income families or individuals, thus improving property values but often displacing low-income families and small businesses (RH). 2. Internal migration such that higher-income populations replace lower-income populations in rehabilitated housing, while the displaced population is compelled to find new accommodations (JMF, 40). 3. Renovation and settlement of decaying urban areas by middle- and high-income people (G).

heritage (general): 1. Something that comes or belongs to one by reason of birth; an inherited lot or portion (RH). 2. The combined creations and products of nature and of man, in their entirety, that make up the environment in which we live in time and space. Heritage is a reality, a possession of the community, and a rich inheritance that may be passed on, which invites our recognition and our participation. (1982 Deschambault Declaration)

heritage resources: "Every element of a historic environment available for use or deserving of protection" (the environmentalist and the planners view) (WP, 8).

historic and architectural area (see also *conservation area*): "Historic and architectural (including vernacular) areas shall be taken to mean any group of buildings, structures and open spaces, including archaeological and paleontological sites, constituting human settlements in an urban or rural environment, the cohesion and value of which, from the archaeological, architectural, prehistoric, historic, aesthetic or socio-cultural point of view, are recognized. Among these areas, which are very varied in nature, it is possible to distinguish the following in particular: prehistoric, sites, historic towns, old urban quarters, villages and hamlets, as well as homogenous monumental groups, it being understood that the latter should as a rule be carefully preserved unchanged." (1976 UNESCO Nairobi Recommendation, 1.1a)

historic conservation district: 1. An urban area of one or more neighborhoods that contains: a. historic properties, b. buildings having similar or related architectural characteristics, c. cultural cohesiveness, and d. any combination of the foregoing. (US National Historic Preservation Act of 1966, section 470) 2. Districts or areas designated by a governing body as being culturally or historically significant, or embodying distinctive characteristics of a period, method of construction, or inhabitants (G).

historic environment: "The historic environment is all the physical evidence of past human activity, and its associations, that people can see, understand and feel in the present world. i. It is the habitat that the human race has created through conflict and cooperation over thousands of years, the product of human interaction with nature, ii. It is all round us a part of everyday experience and life, and it is therefore dynamic and continually subject to change. At one level, it is made up entirely of places such as towns or villages, coast or hills, and things such as buildings, buried sites and deposits, fields and hedges: at another level it is something we inhabit, both physically and imaginatively. It is many-faceted, relying on an engagement with physical remains but also on emotional and aesthetic responses and on the power of memory, history and association." (From "Discussion Document 1" of English Heritage, *Review of Policies Relating to the Historic Environment: Consultation* [London.] English Heritage, 2000]).

historic garden (see also *natural heritage, monument*): 1. Gardens designed to reflect a period in history, either in form or through the use of heirloom plants (SU). 2. "An architectural and horticultural composition of interest to the public from the historical or artistic point of view. As such, it is to be considered as a monument (art. 1). The term 'historic garden' is equally applicable to small gardens and to large parks, whether formal or 'landscape' (art. 6). Whether or not it is associated with a building—in which case it is an inseparable component—the historic garden cannot be isolated from its own particular environment, whether rural, artificial, or natural (art. 7). The historic garden is an architectural composition whose constituents are primarily vegetal and therefore living, which means that they are perishable and renewable. Thus its appearance reflects the perpetual balance between the cycle of the seasons, the growth and decay of nature and the desire of the artist and craftsman to keep it permanently unchanged" (art. 2) (1981 ICOMOS Florence Charter).

historic monument: See *monument*.

historic objects: A categorical term for individual physical historic resources. The term includes works of architecture in Russia and in most countries of the former Union of Soviet Socialist Republics.

historic preservation (see also *architectural conservation, conservation, preservation, restoration*): 1. The North American term for what in western Europe, Australia, and New Zealand is termed *architectural conservation*. It implies the maintenance of an artifact, building, or site in the same condition in which it was received by the preservationist (JMF). 2. "The term 'historic preservation' is functionally obsolete [but] the term 'historic preservation' is so embedded in American practice, so institutionalized in organizational names (e.g., the National Trust for Historic Preservation), legal acts that have been passed, and the educational programs begun, that Americans are going to be called historic preservationists, although the term is no longer adequate." (J. M. Fitch, chapter in *Preservation: Toward an Ethic in the 1980s* [Washington, DC: Preservation Press, National Trust for Historic Preservation, 1980], 140.)

historic site: 1. The position or location of a town, building, etc., especially as to its environment; the area or exact plot of ground on which anything has been, or is to be, located (RH). 2. A specific landscape associated with a memorable act, as, for example, a major historic event; a well-known myth; an epic combat; or the subject of a famous picture (1981 ICOMOS Florence Charter). 3. A defined topographical area constituting a zone worthy of protection by reason of its natural, scientific, aesthetic, historic, or ethnological interest to the public. (Ligen, *Dangers and Perils*.)

iconoclasm: 1. The action or spirit of breaking or destroying images, especially those set up for religious veneration; the attacking of cherished beliefs, trade institutions, etc., as being based on error or superstition (RH). 2. The doctrine, practice, or attitude of one who destroys religious images or opposes their veneration (G).

immovable heritage: See *cultural property*.

intangible cultural heritage: "The practices, representations, expressions, knowledge, skills—as well as the instruments, objects, artifacts and cultural spaces associated therewith—that communities, groups and, in some cases, individuals recognize as part of their cultural heritage." It is manifested in "oral traditions and expressions including language; performing arts; social practices, rituals and festive events; knowledge and practices concerning nature and the universe; traditional craftsmanship." (UNESCO, *Convention for the Safeguarding of the Intangible Cultural Heritage*, Paris, 2003, art. 2.)

integrated conservation: See *conservation (integrated)*.

integrity: (Latin: *integer, integritas*, untouched, whole; EP.) 1. The state of being whole, entire, undiminished; sound, unimproved, or perfect condition (RH). 2. Material wholeness or completeness; an unimpaired or uncorrupted condition. A concept applied in determining the eligibility of historic buildings, ensembles, and heritage landscapes for heritage listing and protection, as in placement on the World Heritage List. (UNESCO, *World Heritage Strategy*. J. Jokilehto, ICCROM Position Paper, 4.2, pps. 52–53), 3. Integrity is a physical as well as a moral quality (HSG, 30).

lacuna: 1. A gap or missing part, as in a manuscript, series, or logical argument (RH). 2. In art and architectural restoration and conservation, a missing element in an artistic or architectural composition. 3. Blank spaces or missing portions of a text or object, such as a painting or manuscript, usually resulting from damage or accidental omission (G).

laissez faire (approach to conservation): to "let alone" or "do nothing" (DM) toward conserving a historic building, site, or work of art. An approach in conservation considered viable when a historic resource is best left as is, as when physical conditions are stable or when the best strategy may be to wait until more favorable conditions to intervene.

living monument: A highly accomplished living figure considered by the society in which he or she is living to be a rare national asset. Both Japan and Korea maintain lists of living treasures, some of whom are associated with the historic building-craft traditions.

living heritage: The continuation indigenous communities' living traditions in the same locale.

living national treasure: See *living monument.*

management planning: The overarching framework by which one establishes a series of appropriate steps to preserve a site, including physical conservation. "In the field of conservation, the terms management and conservation are sometimes used interchangeably to mean all or some of those actions that are taken to ensure that long-term conservation and appropriate use of a cultural site. This may include such steps as documentation policy, significance assessment, physical research and intervention, and visitor management. (Sharon Sullivan in *Conservation of Ancient Sites on the Silk Road*, ed. Neville Agnew [Los Angeles: Getty Conservation Institute, 1997], 30.)

maintenance: 1. The upkeep of property or equipment (MW). 2. The continuous protective care of the fabric and setting of a place…[as]…distinguished from repair. Repair involves restoration or reconstruction (BC).

material culture: 1. "Considered by museum professionals to include artifacts in collections, but often also includes the outside world of buildings and environments" (WP, 8). 2. The aggregate of physical objects produced by a society or culturally cohesive group (G).

mimesis (see also *duplicate, facsimile, replica, reproduction*): (Greek: *mimeisthei*, to imitate.) 1. Imitation or reproduction of the supposed words of another; an aesthetic concept that takes imitation as the primary operative aspect in the creation of a work (G). 2. A consideration in determining outstanding universal value for purposes of a World Heritage Listing. (UNESCO, *World Heritage Strategy*, J. Jokilehto. ICCROM Position Paper, 4.2, 53.)

minimal intervention: A level of intervention in art and architectural conservation where only minimal effective actions are taken to conserve a physical historic resource.

mnemonic: (Greek: *mnaomai*, I remember; *mnestis*, memory.) 1. Assisting or intended to assist the memory (RH). 2. Devices or strategies for aiding the memory, such as verses, rhymes, or imagery (G).

monument (see also *historic garden, natural heritage*): (Latin: *monere*, to remind.) 1. Something erected in memory of a person, event, etc., such as a building, pillar, or statue; any building, megalith, etc., surviving from a past age and regarded as of historical or archaeological importance; an area or site of interest to the public for its historic significance, great natural beauty, etc., preserved and maintained by a government; any enduring evidence or notable example of something (RH). 2. "A tangible, material construction, usually of stone, brick, or metal, that serves to remind passersby of some person, event, or concept" (Wayne R. Dynes, "Monument: The Word," in *Remove Not the Ancient Landmark*, ed. Donald M. Reynolds [Amsterdam: Gordon and Breach, 1996], 27.) 3. The word *monument* in the Venice Charter refers not only to major buildings but to more modest ones that over time go on to acquire a cultural value of their own. ICOMOS recognizes a wide variety of monuments: a. historical monuments to national history, cultural history, folklore, industrial history, history of transport, military history, and archaeology; and b. artistic monuments of town planning and urbanism, architecture, fine and applied art, landscape design, and cultural landscapes. (Ludwig Deiters, "The Differentiation of Monuments: A First Step in Deciding Upon their Social Use and Restoration," in *Symposium on Monuments and Society: Leningrad, USSR, 2–8 September 1969* [Paris: ICOMOS, 1969], 118–19.) 4. The concept of a historic monument embraces not only the single architectural work but also the urban or rural setting in which is found the evidence of a particular civilization, a significant development, or a historic event. This applies not only to great works of art but also to more modest works of the past that have acquired cultural significance with the passage of time (VC).

mothballing: Originally an American term for arresting or significantly reducing the rate of decay of a historic building or parts thereof by measures such as boarding its windows and repairing or revising water-shedding surfaces to be relatively maintenance free and secure from intrusion and vandalism. Mothballing may be an appropriate intervention for surplus properties such as redundant military bases or industrial sites that could serve different uses at a future time.

museialization, museumification: The categorization and interpretation of heritage property using a museum professional's approach.

natural heritage (see also *historic garden, monument*): 1. Natural features consisting of physical and biological formations of outstanding universal value from an aesthetic or scientific point of view. 2. Geological and physiographical formations and precisely delineated areas that constitute the habitat of threatened species of animals or plants of outstanding universal value from the point of view of science or conservation. 3. "Natural sites or precisely delineated natural areas of outstanding universal value from the point of view of science" (UNESCO 1972 Recommendation concerning the Protection, at National Level, of the Cultural and Natural Heritage [2], in HSG, 21.)

original (see *authentic, prototype*): (Latin: *originale*, source [of a spring], origin.) "Belonging or pertaining to the origin or beginning of something, or to a theory at its beginning; new, fresh, innovative; being something of which a copy is made; a primary form or type from which varieties are derived...as opposed to a copy or imitation" (RH).

palimpsest: (Greek: *palim*, again; *psestos*, rubbed smooth.) 1. A parchment or the like from which writing has been partially or completely erased to make room from another text (RH). 2. "A parchment on which two or more texts have been written, each text affected to make room for the next" (JS, 48). 3. Literally, a reused document; in the field of architectural conservation, layers of history as expressed in the fabric of a historic building or site. 4. Writing material, usually parchment, that has been written upon more than once; the previous text may have been imperfectly erased, thus remaining partly legible (G).

past: A collection of memories, both individual and shared (WP, 8).

patina (see also *wabi-sabi*): (Italian, a film or a glaze, perhaps originally from the verdigris that forms on a disused paten, or shallow dish; EP.) 1. An aged appearance caused by environmental factors, acquired naturally or artificially induced; used especially with regard to a surface layer on metal caused by oxidation or corrosion (G). 2. Film or incrustation, usually green, produced by oxidation on the surface of old bronze and esteemed as being of ornamental value; a similar film or coloring on some other substances; a surface calcification on implements, usually indicating great age (RH). 3. Patina forms part of the historic integrity of a resource, and its destruction should be allowed only when essential to the protection of the fabric. Falsification of patina should be avoided (ICOMOS Canada's Appleton Charter for the Protection and Enhancement of the Built Environment, 1983).

picturesque: Of or suggestion of a picture; suitable for a picture. Striking or interesting in an unusual way; irregularly or quaintly attractive (MW). Deriving from the Italian and French words for painter, the term picturesque was applied by eighteenth century English aesthetes to describe either natural or artificially created landscapes usually associated with country houses and parks.

place: "The concept of place should be broadly interpreted...[and can include a] site, area, land, landscape, building or other work, group of buildings or other works, and may include components, contents, spaces and views...memorials, trees, gardens, parks, places of historical events, urban areas, towns, industrial places, archaeological sites and spiritual and religious places.... Places may have a range of values for different individuals or groups" (BC).

planning blight: In urban planning, an economic disease caused by lack of decision or by attempting schemes that are too ambitious (BMF, 12).

preservation (see also *architectural conservation, conservation, historic preservation, restoration*): 1. To keep alive or in existence; make lasting; to keep safe from harm or injury; protect; to keep up, maintain (RH). 2. The identification, evaluation, recordation, documentation, curation, acquisition, protection, management, rehabilitation, restoration, stabilization, maintenance, and reconstruction, or any combination of the foregoing activities. (*National Historic Preservation Act of 1966*, Public Law 89-665, *US Code* 16, 89th Cong., 2nd sess. [October 15, 1966], § 470w.) 3. All actions taken to retard deterioration of or prevent damage to cultural property. Preservation involves controlling the environment and conditions of use and may include treatment in order to maintain a cultural property, as nearly as possible, in an unchanging state (IIC-CG). 4. The act or process of applying measures to sustain the existing form, integrity, and material of a building or structure, and the existing form and vegetative cover of a site. It may include initial stabilization work where necessary, as well as ongoing maintenance of the historic building materials (SI). 5. The action taken to maintain "the fabric of a place in its existing state" and to retard deterioration (art. 1.6, BC; art. 22, NZ). 6. The retention of the existing form, material, and integrity of a site (ICOMOS Canada's Appleton Charter for the Protection and Enhancement of the Built Environment, 1983). 7. Preservation implies the maintenance of an artifact in the same physical condition as when it was received by the curatorial agency (JMF).

preventative conservation practice: See *conservation (preventative)*.

prototype (see also *authentic, original*): (Greek: *prototypon*, original.) The original or model on which something is based or formed; someone or something that serves to illustrate the typical qualities of a class or model; exemplar (RH).

reconstitution (see also *reconstruction, re-creation, replication*): (Latin: *constitutus*, to set up; *constituere*, to stand erect, to establish.) 1. To reconstruct; constitute again (RH). 2. Radical physical intervention to the structure and fabric of a building to ensure its continued structural integrity, during which the building can be saved only by piece-by-piece reassembly, either in situ or on a new site (JMF). 3. An intervention in architectural conservation that is more profound than "heavy restoration" and less profound than complete reconstruction that entails the reuse of original materials, usually in their original configurations serving the same purposes.

reconstruction (see also *reconstitution, re-creation, replication*): (Latin: *reconstruere*, to rebuild.) 1. Construct: to build or form by putting together parts; reconstruct: to rebuild; make over; construct again (RH). 2. Returning a place as nearly as possible to a known earlier state...by the introduction of [old and new] materials into the fabric" (art. 1.8, BC; art. 22, NZ). 3. "Reestablishment of what occurred or what existed in the past, on the basis of documentary or physical evidence" (BS 7913:1998). 4. All actions taken to re-create, in whole or in part, a cultural property based upon historical, literary, graphic, pictorial, archaeological, and scientific evidence. Its aim is to promote an understanding of a cultural property and is based on little or no original material but clear evidence of a former state (IIC-CG). 5. The act or process of reproducing by new construction the exact form and detail of a vanished building, structure, or object (or part thereof) at a specific period of time (SI). 6. Reconstruction is only appropriate when: a site needs to be completed for its survival; it reveals the cultural significance of a site as a whole; it is not conjectural. A reconstruction should not constitute the majority of the work on the site, should be identifiable as new work, and should avoid generalized representations of typical features. Archaeological sites should not, as a rule, be reconstructed (HSG, 49). 7. "Reconstruction...return[s] a place to a known earlier state and is distinguished from restoration by the introduction of new material into the fabric" (BC).

reconstruction (philological): Extensive restoration or reconstruction based on historical and circumstantial information as opposed to physical evidence.

re-creation (see also *reconstitution, reconstruction, replication*): (Latin: *recreare*, to give new life to [hence to revitalize or refresh]; to produce again; EP.) 1. The act of creating anew (RH). 2. The conjectural reconstruction of a place (art. 13, NZ).

rehabilitation (see also *adaptive use*): (Latin: *re-*, again + *habilitas*, to render fit; EP.) 1. To restore to good condition, operation, or management; to restore to former capacity, standing, or rank (RH). 2. The modification of a resource to contemporary functional standards, which may involve adaptation for new use (ICOMOS Canada's Appleton Charter for the Protection and Enhancement of the Built Environment, 1983). 3. The return to good condition deteriorated objects, structures, neighborhoods, or public facilities that may involve repair, renovation, conversion, expansion, remodeling or reconstruction (G). 5. The act or process of returning a property to a state of utility through repair or alteration that makes possible an efficient contemporary use while preserving those portions or features of the property that are significant to its historical, architectural, and cultural values (SI). 6. Rehabilitation is appropriate only when a coherent policy has been evolved for the whole site, a detailed survey and assessment has been made, there is no loss of character, and the inhabitants and public authorities have been made part of the process (HSG, 51).

relocation: To establish in a new place (MW). The moving of an historic structure. Done ideally only as a last resort, relocation entails the removal of a building and its constituent parts from *in situ* (in position) to *ex situ* (away from its original position).

renovation (see also *repair*): (Latin: *renovare*, to make new again; EP.) 1. To restore to good condition, make new or as if new again; repair; reinvigorate; refresh; revive (RH). 2. The questionable modernization of a historic building during which inappropriate alterations are made and important features and details are eliminated (WM, 217). 3. The process of making changes in objects, especially buildings or other structures, with the intention of improving their physical condition and appearance.

repair (see also *renovation*): (Latin *reparare*, to procure again, to procure in exchange, hence to restore or mend.) 1. To restore to a good or sound condition after decay or damage; to mend (RH). 2. To restore to a whole by replacing a part or to put together what is torn or broken, or to otherwise restore to sound condition (G). 3. The primary purpose of repair is to restrain the process of decay without damaging the character of buildings or monuments, altering the features that gave them historic or architectural importance or unnecessarily disturbing or destroying historic fabric. (English Heritage, "Principles of Repair," leaflet, cited in John Earl, *Building Conservation Philosophy* [Reading, UK: College of Estate Management, 1996], 51.)

replica, replicate, replication (see also **duplicate, facsimile, mimesis, reconstitution, reconstruction, reproduction**): (Italian: *replica*, a reproduction, from the Latin *replicare*, to fold back or again—hence to repeat; EP.) 1. *Replica*: A copy or reproduction of a work of art produced by the maker of the original or under his supervision; any close or exact copy or reproduction; *Replicate*: To repeat, duplicate, or reproduce (RH). 2. "To make a copy of an existing place" (art. 13, NZ). 3. Replicas are precise reproductions of valued objects, usually in the same dimensions as the original. The term is used also when more than one similar object is produced by the same artist, craftsman, or studio with little or no variation between them. Replicas are distinct from forgeries and counterfeits, which are produced with an intent to deceive (G). 4. Replication is making precise reproductions of three-dimensional objects in the same dimensions as the original; the process often involves casting from a mold made directly from the original (G). 5. In the art field, replication implies the creation of a mirror image of an extant artifact; in architecture, it implies the construction of an exact copy of a still-standing building on a site removed from the prototype—in other words, the replica coexists with the original (JMF). As both reconstruction and replication attempt to reproduce something that no longer exists, they are often confused. *Reconstruction* always results in new work; *replication* forms as exact a copy as possible and is therefore intrinsically deceptive in intent as well as potentially damaging to a site's authenticity.

reproduction (see also *duplicate, facsimile, mimesis, replica*): 1. Anything made by reproducing an original; copy; a duplicate (RH). 2. Copying an extant artifact, often in order to replace some missing or decayed generally decorative parts in order to maintain its aesthetic harmony (BMF, 11). 3. A copy of an art image, art object, or other valued image or object, with or without an intent to deceive. It implies a more precise and faithful imitation than does the term *copy* (G).

restoration (see also *conservation, historic preservation, preservation, restoration*): (French: *restauration*, Italian: *restauro*.) 1. "The return of something to a former, original, normal, or unimpaired condition; a reconstitution or reproduction of an ancient building…showing it in its original state" (RH). 2. All actions taken to modify the existing materials and structure of a cultural property to represent a known earlier state. Its aim is to preserve and reveal the aesthetic and historic value of physical cultural property and is based on respect for remaining original material and clear evidence of the earlier state (IIC-CG). 3. The act or process of accurately recovering the form and details of a property and its setting as it appeared at a particular period of time by means of the removal of later work or by the replacement of missing work (SI). 4. Returning the existing fabric of a place to a known earlier state by removing accretions or by reassembling existing components without the introduction of new material (art. 1.7, BC; art. 22, NZ). 5. Actions taken specifically to return an object, site, or structure to a state of historical correctness; changes made to an object or structure so that it will closely approximate its state at a specific past time (G). 6. A process of making changes to an object or structure so that it will closely approximate its state at a specific time in history (G). 7. "[Restoration is] based on respect for all the physical, documentary and other evidence and stops at the point where conjecture begins" (art. 14, BC). The term took on negative associations in the latter half of the nineteenth century in England when architectural restorationists were often accused of overrestoring historic buildings.

restorer: (French: *restaurateur*.) The craftspeople and technicians—not the architects or administrators—who carry out specific restoration and conservation interventions. "In mid-nineteenth-century England, restorers were those who valued aesthetic and structural consistency and therefore maintained that every building and every one of its components should be reconstructed, re-created or completed in its predominant style as a creative act. [It was believed that]…the value of the new appearance of their design was well worth the distortion of historical evidence, the loss of aesthetic integrity and the eradication of all the visual and emotional qualities that genuine (or authentic age) brings with it" (HSG, 3).

reversible, reversibility: (Latin: *revertere*, to turn back; EP.) 1. When the original condition can be reestablished after a change by reversing that change (RH). 2. The capability of being changed back to a previous state or condition; the quality of being not irrevocably permanent (G). 3. The use of reversible processes is always to be preferred to allow the widest options for future development of the correction of unforeseen problems, or where the integrity of the resource could be affected (ICOMOS Canada's Appleton Charter for the Protection and Enhancement of the Built Environment, 1983).

safeguard: 1. To guard, protect, secure (RH). 2. "The identification, protection, conservation, restoration, renovation, maintenance and revitalization of historic or traditional areas and their environment" (UNESCO Nairobi Recommendation, 1c).

setting: The area around a place, which may include the visual catchment (BC).

simulacrum: (Latin: *simulare*, to reproduce exactly; to copy; to imitate—hence, to feign [EP].) A slight, unreal, or superficial likeness or semblance (RH).

site of cultural significance (see also *cultural significance*): A site that has "aesthetic, historic, scientific or social value for past, present or future generations" (BC, 1979). Assessing the cultural significance of a site (and, thereby, its "value" to society) requires a delicate balance between local sensibilities and a more impersonal, intellectual global opinion. The 1992 ICOMOS New Zealand Charter notes that indigenous conservation "is conditional on decisions made in the indigenous community and should proceed only in this context" (HSG, 32). A "statement of cultural significance" must be prepared upon the completion of site investigations and surveys. This statement will define the value of the site and outline a philosophy to guide future interventions, and thereby become an integral part of the action plan for that site (HSG, 38).

Skansen: Swedish location of the first open-air architectural museum, which is dedicated to the interpretation of preindustrial Swedish life. The Skansen Principle has since been recognized in numerous other places as an outdoor architectural museum where buildings are displayed in a way analogous to the display of small artifacts in the controlled environment of a museum.

social capital: "By analogy with notions of 'physical capital' and 'human capital'—tools and training that enhance individual productivity—'social capital' refers to features of social organization, such as networks, norms, and trust, that facilitate coordination and cooperation for mutual benefit." (Robert Putnam, Harvard political scientist, quoted by Richard Madsen in paper presented at the Leadership Conference on Conservancy and Development sponsored by the Yunnan Provincial Association for Cultural Exchanges with Foreign Countries and the Center for US-China Arts Exchanges, Lijiang, China, September 25, 1999.)

stabilization (see also *consolidation*): (Latin: *stabilire*, to make firm; EP.) 1. To stabilize: to make or hold stable, firm or steadfast; to maintain at a given or unfluctuating level or quantity (RH). 2. A process that helps keep the fabric intact and in a fixed position (art. 12, BC). 3. A periodic activity to halt deterioration and put the existing form and materials of a site in a state of equilibrium, with minimal change (1987 World Commission on Environment and Development). 4. The act or process of applying measures designed to reestablish a weather-resistant enclosure and structural stability while maintaining the essential form as it exists at present (WM, 217).

sublime: 1. "The surrendering of the senses" (Milton). 2. Grandeur of thought, emotion, and spirit (*Encyclopedia Britannica*, http://www.britannica.com).

sustainable development: 1. Interventional actions (such as a planned revitalization effort) that do not preclude future additional development options (1987 World Commission on Environment and Development). 2. Development designed to ensure that the utilization of resources and the environment today does not damage prospects for their use by future generations (G). 3. Sustainable development "meets the needs of the present without compromising the ability of future generations to meet their own needs" (1987 World Commission on Environment and Development). 4. "A key concept in heritage conservation management, the point being to make sure that current use of the heritage, which is desirable, does not destroy the chances of handing it down to future generations" (1995 Council of Europe Segesta Declaration, 3, in HSG, 33).

universal value: "Universal significance…does not…derive from the notion that all products resemble a particular ideal or model, but from the conception that each is a creative and unique expression…[that] represents the relevant cultural context. For a cultural heritage resource to have universal value does not—in itself—imply that it is 'the best'; rather it means it shares a particular creative quality of being 'true,' original, authentic, as a constituent part of the common, universal heritage of humanity" (JJ, 295–96).

valorization: The act or process of attempting to give an arbitrary price to an object, usually by government intervention often involving subsidization (*Webstern's New International Dictionary*, 2nd ed.) In the cultural heritage field, valorization relates to the advocacy and valuation of both movable and immovable objects. The government purchase or listing of heritage sites implies investment in their restoration; conservation and display therefore valorizes their existence.

vernacular architecture: 1. The expression of the historic and authentic values recognized by a community that respond directly to the needs of the cultural, physical, and economic environment; an architecture of a locality or a region. Its structure, form and constructional materials are determined by the local climate, geology, geography, economy, and culture (1992 ICOMOS Comité International d'Architecture Vernaculaire Thessaloniki Charter, 1). 2. Architecture built of local materials to suit particular local needs, usually of unknown authorship and making little reference to the chief style or theories of architecture (G). 3. "Vernacular architecture and indigenous cultural heritage overlap when the line of cultural development from original to present community is strong and relatively undisturbed" (HSG, 37).

wabi-sabi (see also *patina*): Japanese term for the added aesthetic value acquired by an object resulting from natural aging, patination, or damage.

zeitgeist: (German: the spirit of the time.) 1. The general characteristics of a particular period (RH). 2. The idea that at any period of time there is a common belief was proposed by the early nineteenth-century philosopher Georg Wilhelm Friedrich Hegel, who said that the *geist* ("mind") is manifested in everything at that particular time. The proposition of a "spirit of the times" indicates that this may vary from one time to another. Hegel refers to this development as the "dialectical process," which he attributes to the evolution of individual thought and the inherent conflicts that exist within individual issues (JS, 7). 3. A general intellectual and moral state or the trend of culture and taste characteristic of an era (G).

Organizations and Resources Relating to International Architectural Conservation

Web-Based Resources

I. Bibliographic and Research Databases

Archnet: Islamic Architecture
http://archnet.org/lobby/

This resource focuses on Islamic architecture, urban design and development, and related issues in the Muslim world. It was developed by the Massachusetts Institute of Technology and the University of Texas at Austin Islamic architecture community, with financial support from the Aga Khan Trust for Culture, a private, nondenominational international development agency that works to improve the built environments of societies that have a significant Muslim presence.

Art and Archaeology Technical Abstracts (AATA)
http://aata.getty.edu

AATA Online is a service of the Getty Conservation Institute (GCI) in association with the International Institute for Conservation of Historic and Artistic Works. This database of more than 100,000 peer-reviewed abstracts of international literature related to conservation and heritage management is updated quarterly.

The Bibliographic Database of the Conservation Information Network (BCIN)
http://www.bcin.ca

Since 1987 BCIN, the Web's most complete bibliographic resource for the conservation, preservation, and restoration of cultural property has been supported by a global network of libraries and documentation centers. Its database includes previously unavailable material from private sources as well as books; published and unpublished monographs and serials; conference proceedings; technical reports, journal articles, and theses; audiovisual materials; and software and machine-readable files. Available online since 1987, BCIN is a trusted resource for professionals, museums, and other heritage organizations. It now contains nearly two hundred thousand citations, including the first thirty-four volumes of the Art and Archaeology Technical Abstracts (AATA), published between 1955 and 1997.

United States National Park Service database
http://www.ncptt.nps.gov
Internet resources for heritage conservation and archaeology maintained by the U.S.
National Park Service.

II. International Architectural Conservation Organizations

Aga Khan Trust for Culture
Case Postale 2049
1211 Geneva 2
Switzerland
Telephone: (41) (22) 909-7200
http://www.akdn.org

Since 1988 the Aga Khan Trust for Culture, a private, nondenominational philanthropic
foundation, has looked to improve the built environments of societies with a significant
Muslim presence. It underwrites and develops programs that support excellence in
contemporary architecture and related fields; the conservation and creative reuse of historic
buildings and public spaces to facilitate social, economic, and cultural development;
education for architectural practice, planning, and conservation; and an understanding of
the intimate connection between Islamic culture, history, and the built environment of
contemporary Muslim societies.

Association of Preservation Technology International (APTI)
4513 Lincoln Avenue, Suite 213
Lisle, IL 60532-1290 USA
Telephone: (1) (630) 968-6400
http://www.apti.org

APTI, a multidisciplinary organization formed in 1968, is dedicated to promoting the
best technology for conserving historic structures and their settings. Its cross-disciplinary
membership is international and includes preservationists, architects, engineers,
conservators, consultants, contractors, craftspeople, curators, developers, educators,
historians, landscape architects, students, technicians, and others who are directly
involved in conserving historic structures and sites. Through its publications, conferences,
training courses, awards, student scholarships, and technical committees, APTI provides
anyone involved in the field of historic preservation with a broad range of information
services.

**Authority for the Protection and Management of Angkor and the Region of Siem
Reap (APSARA)**
187 Pasteur Street
Chaktomuk, Phnom Penh
Cambodia
Telephone: (85) (5) 23 720 315
http://www.autoriteapsara.org

Cambodia's government created APSARA to spearhead the research, protection, and
conservation of cultural heritage, as well as urban and tourist development within the greater
Angkor region in north-central Cambodia. As a first step toward full national management of
Angkor Wat's heritage site, APSARA directs the site's management and tourism development.
Since its creation in 1994, the United Nations Educational, Scientific and Cultural
Organization (UNESCO) has served as the secretariat of APSARA.

Cadw Welsh Assembly Government Plas Carew
Unit 5/7 Cefn Coed
Parc Nantgarw
Cardiff CF15 7QQ
Wales
Telephone: (44) (0)1443 33 6000
http://www.cadw.wales.gov.uk

Cadw, the historic environment division of the Welsh National Assembly, promotes the conservation and appreciation of Wales's historic environment, including its historic buildings, ancient monuments, historic parks and gardens, landscapes, and underwater archaeology. It manages historic properties, extends grants for select historic properties, and publishes a range of books about Welsh built heritage.

Council of Europe
Avenue de l'Europe
67075 Strasbourg Cedex
France
Telephone: (33) (0)3.88.41.20.00
http://www.coe.int

Established in 1949, the Council of Europe is headquartered in Strasbourg, France. Cultural heritage for its member states is an important aspect of the council's basic mission of fostering freedom, human rights, and the rule of law. It is also a pillar of the sustainable development model promoted by the council for balanced economic regeneration and environmental conservation in Europe. The council's aim in the field of cultural heritage is to promote cooperation among states adhering to the European cultural convention, elaborate new heritage policies, and provide technical assistance.

Council of Europe: The European Foundation for Heritage Skills
c/o Palais de l'Europe
F-67075 Strasbourg Cedex
France
Telephone: (33) (0) 3.90.21.45.37
www.european-heritage.net

The foundation's training, information exchange, networking, and development opportunities are offered to planning and management professionals (architects, archaeologists, heritage conservation professionals, inventory officials) as well as to technicians, supervisors, and specialist craftspeople. It also helps national bodies develop multinational projects on specific themes.

Cultural Heritage without Borders/Kulturarv utan Gränser (CHwB)
Box 6204
102 34 Stockholm
Telephone: (46) 8 32 20 71
http://www.chwb.org

CHwB was founded in 1995 in reaction to the systematic destruction of cultural heritage during Bosnia-Herzegovina's civil war. It works toward creating public awareness and involvement, and it is focused on specific tasks to restore cultural property in areas ravaged by conflicts or catastrophes or that are otherwise endangered. Recently, CHwB's scope of activity—that includes working to preserve cultural sites, restoration, museum development, archive reconstruction, and the exchange of field experiences—has broadened to include programs in Tibet and Kosovo, Albania.

DOCOMOMO: International Working Party for Documentation and Conservation of Buildings, Sites, and Neighborhoods of the Modern Movement
Institut Français d'Architecture
Palais de la Porte Dorée
293 av. Daumesnil
75012 Paris France
Telephone : +33 (0)1 58 51 52 65
Fax : +33 (0)1 58 51 52 20
http://www.archi.fr/DOCOMOMO/docomomo_fr/index2.htm

DOCOMOMO is a nongovernmental organization that documents and conserves important modernist architecture and heritage sites and also promotes modern urbanism. It was founded in the Netherlands in 1988; its principal objectives are contained in the 1990 Manifesto of Eindhoven. Membership in 2008 exceeded 2,000 persons who are active in 47 organizations on five continents. Its international secretariat is now based in Paris, France.

École d'Avignon
6, rue Grivolas
84000 Avignon
France
Telephone: (33) (0) 4.90.85.59.82
http://www.ecole-avignon.com

Since 1983 l'École d'Avignon has been a leader in imparting technical expertise to architectural heritage conservationists, primarily from the French-speaking world. Its resource center specializes in training and consulting and was created out of a desire to help craftspeople master the skills necessary to restore and conserve France's rich architectural heritage.

English Heritage
Customer Services Department
PO Box 569
Swindon SN2 2YP
England
Telephone: (44) (0) 870 333 1181
http://www.english-heritage.org.uk

English Heritage's mission is to increase the popular understanding of England's past and to conserve the country's historic environments so they may have sustainable future. Its "blue plaque" scheme for London is one of the oldest in the world and has for over 140 years highlighted a significant personage or event at a historic site; it was extended nationally in 1998. The 2002 National Heritage Act has also supported the development of English Heritage's activities by allowing it to assume responsibilities for maritime archaeology in English coastal waters. At present, the agency's functions include securing the preservation of ancient monuments in, on, or under the seabed.

Europa Nostra / International Federation of Associations for the Protection of Europe's Cultural, Architectural, and Natural Heritage
International Secretariat
Lange Voorhout 35
NL-2514 EC The Hague
The Netherlands
Telephone: (31) (70) 302 40 50
http://www.europanostra.org

This non-for-profit pan-European umbrella organization was created in 1965 to protect and enhance European architectural and natural heritage and to promote high architectural and planning standards. Membership includes more than two hundred nongovernmental organizations (NGOs), one hundred local and regional authorities, and about one thousand individual members from thirty-five European countries. Outstanding achievements in European heritage conservation practice are honored through the European Commission's annual European Union Prize for Cultural Heritage–Europa Nostra Awards, a program managed by Europa Nostra.

German World Heritage Foundation / Die Deutsche Stiftung Welterbe
http://www.welterbestiftung.de

Established in 2002 on the occasion of the listing of the historic centers of Stralsund and Wismar to the World Heritage List, the German World Heritage Foundation (GWHF) launched an initiative to actively contribute to the implementation of the World Heritage Convention. Its objectives are: to assist World Heritage sites in regions of the world with fewer resources, to protect and preserve their heritage values, and to assist in preparing nominations of potential World Heritage List sites to further enhance the balance of the World Heritage List. Projects to date are in Mongolia, Ukraine, Latvia, Russia, Serbia, Montenegro, Azerbaijan, and Congo.

Getty Conservation Institute (GCI)
1200 Getty Center Drive, Suite 700
Los Angeles, CA 90049-1684
Telephone: (1) (310) 440-7325
http://www.getty.edu/conservation/institute/

This program of the J. Paul Getty Trust has, since 1985, been dedicated to furthering conservation practice and education about the preservation, understanding, and interpretation of the visual arts, including objects, collections, architecture, and sites. Its activities include scientific research into the nature of decay and treatment of materials; education and training; model field projects; and the dissemination of information through both traditional publications and electronic means.

The GCI's Art and Architectural Thesaurus (AAT), which is found at http://www.getty.edu/research/conducting_research/ is a prime source of information for conservation professionals. AATA Online, its Art and Archaeology Technical Abstracts, is a service provided in association with the International Institute for Conservation of Historic and Artistic Works. This database includes more than 100,000 peer-reviewed abstracts of international literature related to conservation and heritage management and is updated quarterly.

Global Heritage Fund
625 Emerson Street, Suite 200
Palo Alto, CA 94301
Telephone: (1) (650) 325-7520
http://www.globalheritagefund.org

This relatively new not-for-profit international conservancy was established to protect important archaeological and cultural heritage sites in developing countries and to ensure their long-term preservation. It aims to provide timely investment, expertise, monitoring, and advocacy for the conservation of major archaeological sites and ancient townscapes.

Historic Scotland
Telephone: (44) (0)131 668 8716
http://www.historic-scotland.gov.uk

Historic Scotland is an agency that is directly responsible to the Scottish ministers for safeguarding the nation's historic environment and promoting its enjoyment. Through a regional network of five separate teams, it cares for more than three hundred properties. An education unit helps schools create appropriate curricula; through its organization of conferences, short courses, and workshops, Historic Scotland helps improve conservators' skills. Its fellowships, internships, and grants further support conservation and research.

Indian National Trust for Arts and Cultural Heritage (INTACH)

71 Lodi Estate
New Delhi 110 003
India
Telephone: 4631818, 24641304, 24632267, 24632269, 24692774, 24645482
http://www.intach.org

INTACH documents and conserves India's historical, cultural, and natural resources of archaeological, artistic, scientific, and national importance and assists in the protection of a large number of the nation's listed and unlisted monuments and cultural heritage sites. Its mission is to sensitize the public about the value of their cultural legacy through workshops, seminars, and publications and seeks to foster strategic partnerships with educational institutions, cultural organizations, the government, and other national and international agencies. Recently, it initiated a new focus on living heritage, including lifestyles, folkways, and traditional crafts and performances.

International Centre for the Study of the Preservation and Restoration of Cultural Property (ICCROM)

13 Via di San Michele 00153
Rome, Italy
Telephone: (39) (6) 587901
http://www.iccrom.org

ICCROM was founded by UNESCO in 1956 to promote the conservation of world cultural heritage resources by focusing broadly on training (both general and regional), research, and public advocacy. Its mandate as an educator is met via periodic specialized heritage conservation meetings and conducting short courses, as well as by maintaining one of the world's largest reference libraries on cultural heritage conservation.

International Council of Museums (ICOM)

Maison de l'UNESCO
1, rue Miollis
75732 Paris Cedex 15
France
Telephone: (33) (0) 1.47.34.05.00
http://www.icom.org

Since 1946 this not-for-profit organization of museums and museum professionals has developed into an extensive global network focused on the conservation of natural and cultural heritage. Fees paid by its 21,000 members from 140 countries and by governmental and other bodies underwrite educational offerings such as workshops, publications, and training. ICOM's activities are closely aligned with those of UNESCO.

International Council on Monuments and Sites (ICOMOS)

49-51 rue de la Federation
75015 Paris
France
Telephone: 33 (0) 1.45.67.67.70
http://www.icomos.org

ICOMOS, an international nongovernmental organization, is UNESCO's principal advisor on the conservation and protection of monuments and sites and an advisor to the World Heritage Committee on the nomination of sites to the World Heritage List. It was founded in 1965 following the adoption of the Venice Charter in 1964. Via a network of over 7,600 members in over 106 countries, 110 national committees, and 21 scientific committees, ICOMOS seeks to establish international standards for the preservation, restoration, and management of the cultural environment. Many of these standards have been promulgated as charters adopted by the ICOMOS General Assembly.

International Institute for Conservation of Historic and Artistic Works (IIC)

6 Buckingham Street
London WC2N 6BA
England
Telephone: (44) (0) 20 7839 5975
http://www.iiconservation.org

For over fifty years, IIC has promoted the knowledge, methods, and working standards needed to protect and preserve historic and artistic works across the globe via publications, conferences, and national groups. It helps conservation scientists, architects, educators, and students, as well as collection managers, curators, art historians, and other cultural heritage professionals remain aware of technical advances in their fields through its quarterly journal *Studies in Conservation* and the annual *Reviews in Conservation*. Biennially, IIC mounts a major international conference on a topic of current interest.

International Union of Architects–Union Internationale des Architectes (UIA)

51, rue Raynouard
75016 Paris
France
Telephone: (33) (0) 1.45.24.36.88
http://www.uia-architectes.org

The UIA is an international professional organization for architects and students of architecture. It represents professional architects at an international level; formulates official statements for governmental consideration; develops progressive ideas in both architecture and town planning; encourages interaction with other technical disciplines; helps support architectural organizations in developing countries; promotes the development of architectural education; and facilitates the international exchange of architects, researchers, and students.

International Union for Conservation of Nature (IUCN)

Rue Mauverney 28
CH-1196 Gland
Switzerland
Telephone: (41) (22) 999-0000
http://www.iucn.org

The IUCN, founded in 1948 as the first global environmental organization, is the largest environmental knowledge network in the world. Its mission is to assist societies in conserving the integrity and diversity of nature and to ensure that natural resource usage is both equitable and ecologically sustainable. Current membership includes over 10,000 scientists and experts from 181 countries and over 1,000 member organizations including 82 states, 111 government agencies, and more than 800 NGOs. IUCN supports and develops cutting-edge conservation science, implements this research in field projects, and then links both research and results to local, national, regional, and global policy by convening dialogues between governments, civil society, and the private sector. IUCN's databases, assessments, guidelines, and case studies are among the world's most respected and are frequently cited sources of information and reference on the environment.

Japan International Cooperation Agency (JICA)

Sixth–Thirteenth floors, Shinjuku Maynds Tower
2-1-1 Yoyogi, Shibuya-ku
Tokyo 151-8558
Japan
Telephone: (81) (3) 5352-5311/5312/5313/5314
http://www.jica.go.jp

Japan's extension of aid to developing countries began in the 1950s and has increased and expanded yearly. JICA is responsible for the technical-cooperation aspect of Japan's development assistance programs, from emergency disaster relief to extensions of grants for a wide variety of uses, including cultural heritage. JICA's 1,200 staff members work both in Japan and at more than fifty overseas offices.

League of Historical Cities

Secretariat
International Relations Office
City of Kyoto
Teramachi-Oike, Nakagyo-ku
Kyoto City 604-8571
Japan
Telephone: (81) (75) 222-3072
http://www.city.kyoto.jp/somu/kokusai/lhcs

Comprised of sixty-five cities from forty-nine countries, the league was established in 1994 to promote world peace through an understanding of the marvels and accomplishments of historic cities. The strengthening of international affiliations between historical cities is accomplished through its periodic World Conference of Historical Cities.

National Research Institute for Cultural Properties, Tokyo

13-27 Ueno Park, Taito-ku
Tokyo 110
Japan
Telephone: (81) (03) 3823-2241
http://www.tobunken.go.jp

The institute was founded in 1930 by a private philanthropist to investigate and research cultural properties. Today it conducts applied research relative to contemporary issues in heritage conservation in addition to being a locus for research on a wide range of basic studies in art history, the history of performing arts, conservation science, and restoration techniques. Its departments of fine arts and performing arts research Japanese and East Asian fine arts and intangible cultural property like music, dance, folkways, and drama. The department of restoration techniques develops and evaluates restoration materials and techniques in its physics, biology, and chemistry sections. Since 1995, its Japanese Center for International Cooperation in Conservation has conducted various technical training opportunities for international professionals, maintained an information database, and jointly contributed to international symposia with partners such as the Smithsonian Institution in Washington, DC.

The National Trust (England, Wales, Northern Ireland)

PO Box 39
Warrington WA5 7WD
England
Telephone: (44) (0) 870 458 4000
http://www.nationaltrust.org.uk

The National Trust, one of the world's premier heritage conservation organizations, was founded by three philanthropists in 1895 to acquire and safeguard threatened coastline, countryside, and buildings in England, Wales, and Northern Ireland (its Scottish counterpart is the National Trust for Scotland). It now cares for over 612,000 acres of countryside, almost 600 miles of coastline, and more than 200 buildings and gardens, much of which is open to visitors. As a registered charity independent of government, it relies on outside income and membership fees from its over 2.6 million members.

The National Trust for Scotland

Wemyss House
28 Charlotte Square
Edinburgh, Scotland
United Kingdom EH2 4ET
Telephone: (44) (0) 844 493 2100
http://www.nts.org.uk

Established in 1931, the National Trust for Scotland is the guardian of Scotland's architectural, scenic, and historic treasures. With nearly 300,000 members, it operates as an independent charity rather than as an arm of the government.

Patrimoine sans Frontières

61 rue François Truffaut
75012 Paris
France

Founded in 1992 with the support of the French Ministry of Culture and Communication, Patrimoine sans Frontières is an NGO dedicated to preserving endangered or neglected cultural heritage sites worldwide. Its activities include identifying endangered cultural heritage sites and issues, raising public awareness about them, fund-raising, mobilizing a network of partners to support a particular project, providing advice to other heritage conservation bodies, setting up exhibitions, and coediting publications.

SAVE Britain's Heritage

70 Cowcross Street
London EC1M 6EJ
Telephone: (44) (0) 20 7253 3500
http://www.savebritainsheritage.org

SAVE was formed in 1975 by a group of journalists, historians, architects, and planners to help them campaign for endangered historic buildings. Today, it helps to support local conservation efforts by offering advice and issuing press releases. Its Web site includes the United Kingdom's first online register of endangered historic buildings in England and Wales, many of which are listed. SAVE publications cover a wide variety of conservation issues.

Society for the Protection of Ancient Buildings (SPAB)

37 Spital Square
London E1 6DY
England
Telephone: (44) (0) 20 7377 1644
http://www.spab.org.uk

SPAB is the largest, oldest, and most technically expert national pressure group fighting to save old buildings from decay, demolition, and damage. It was founded by William Morris in 1877 to counteract the destructive "restorations" of medieval buildings practiced by many Victorian architects, an issue that remains its principal concern. SPAB membership ranges from conservation professionals to owners of historic buildings to private persons interested in the conservation of built heritage. Its activities include advisory conservation services and education, with a focus on training future generations.

United Nations Educational, Scientific and Cultural Organization (UNESCO)
Physical Property Division and the World Heritage Centre

1 place de Fontenoy
75352 Paris 07SP
France
Telephone: (33) (0) 1.45.68.10.00
http://www.unesco.org

UNESCO, a specialized agency of the United Nations, was established in 1945 to promote international collaboration in the hopes of better safeguarding heritage. Passage of the 1972 World Heritage Convention and maintenance of the World Heritage List (found at http://whc.unesco.org/en/list) placed UNESCO in the vanguard of international efforts to protect global cultural heritage. Its National Commission network extends over 190 countries, and it operates via field offices in nearly 60 countries. UNESCO publishes over 100 titles a year on various topics relative to its mission.

World Bank
1818 H Street NW
Washington, DC 20433
Telephone: (1) (202) 477-1234
http://www.worldbank.org

The World Bank's mission is global poverty reduction and the improvement of living standards. It provides financial resources and technical assistance to developing countries through two development institutions, the International Bank for Reconstruction and Development (IBRD) and the International Development Association (IDA). The IBRD focuses on middle-income and creditworthy poor countries, while the IDA focuses on the poorest countries in the world. Each provides low-interest loans, interest-free credit, and grants to developing countries for education, health, infrastructure, communications, and many other purposes, including cultural heritage conservation.

World Monuments Fund (WMF)
95 Madison Avenue
New York, NY 10016
Telephone: (1) (646) 424-9594
http://www.worldmonuments.org

World Monuments Fund is the foremost private, nonprofit organization dedicated to the preservation of endangered architectural and cultural sites around the world. Since 1965, WMF has worked at more than 500 sites in 91 countries. WMF's work spans a wide range of sites and has program areas that reflect the evolving needs of the field: architectural conservation, capacity building, training and education, advocacy, and disaster recovery. Every two years, WMF issues its World Monuments Watch™ List of 100 Most Endangered Sites, a global call to action on behalf of sites in need of immediate intervention.

International and Regional Conventions, Charters, and Recommendations[1]

by Arlene K. Fleming

CULTURAL HERITAGE

A Selection of Key Charters, Legislation, Declarations, and Guidelines, including related Web Addresses

The US–ICOMOS Web site has a chronological listing of charters, resolutions, declarations, guidelines, and recommendations adopted by international organizations:

http://www.icomos.org/usicomos

See also: Luxen, Jean-Louis. "Reflections on the Use of Heritage Charters and Conventions." *Getty Conservation Institute Newsletter* 19, no. 2 (Summer 2004).

1954: Summary Information on the Convention for the Protection of Cultural Property in the Event of Armed Conflict/UNESCO (1954 First Protocol, 1999 Second Protocol): http://portal.unesco.org/culture/en/ev.php-URL_ID=35744&URL_DO=DO_TOPIC&URL_SECTION=201.html

1964: International Charter for the Conservation and Restoration of Monuments and Sites (The "Venice Charter")/ICOMOS: http://www.icomos.org/docs/venice_charter.html

1968: or Private Works/UNESCO: http://www.icomos.org/unesco/works68.html

1999: The Australia ICOMOS Burra Charter/Australia ICOMOS: http://www.icomos.org/australia/burra.html

ARCHAEOLOGY: Excavations, Sites, and Materials

(See also: "Armed Conflict" and "Transfer and Trade.")

TERRESTRIAL

1956: Recommendation on International Principles Applicable to Archaeological Excavations/UNESCO

1968: Recommendation Concerning the Preservation of Cultural Property Endangered by Public or Private Works/UNESCO

1969: Revised 1992: European Convention on the Protection of the Archaeological Heritage/ Council of Europe

1976: Convention on the Protection of the Archaeological, Historical, and Artistic Heritage of the American Nations/Organization of American States (OAS)

1990: ICOMOS

UNDERWATER

1996: Charter on the Protection and Management of Underwater Cultural Heritage/ICOMOS

2001: Convention on the Protection of the Underwater Cultural Heritage/UNESCO

ARCHITECTURE

1931: The Athens Charter for the Restoration of Historic Monuments/League of Nations, Congress of Architects and Technicians of Historic Monuments

1956: Recommendation concerning International Competitions in Architecture and Town Planning/UNESCO

1964: International Charter for the Conservation and Restoration of Monuments and Sites (The "Venice Charter")/ICOMOS

1968: Recommendation concerning the Preservation of Cultural Property Endangered by Public or Private Works/ UNESCO

1976: Convention on the Protection of the Archaeological, Historical, and Artistic Heritage of the American Nations/OAS

1976: Recommendation concerning the Safeguarding and Contemporary Role of Historic Areas/UNESCO

1985: Convention for the Protection of the Architectural Heritage of Europe/Council of Europe

1987: Charter for the Conservation of Historic Towns and Urban Areas/ICOMOS

1992: Charter for the Conservation of Places of Cultural Heritage Value (the "Aotearoa Charter")/New Zealand ICOMOS

1999: Australia ICOMOS Burra Charter (The "Burra Charter")/Australia ICOMOS

1999: Charter on the Built Vernacular Heritage/ICOMOS

1999: Principles for the Preservation of Historic Timber Structures/ICOMOS

2000: Charter of Kraków/Krakow, Poland

2000: Principles for the Conservation of Heritage Sites in China (the "China Principles")/China ICOMOS

2004: Charter for the Conservation of Unprotected Architectural Heritage and Sites in India/ New Delhi, Indian National Trust for Art and Cultural Heritage (INTACH)

2005: Vienna Memorandum on World Heritage and Contemporary Architecture—Managing the Historic Urban Landscape/UNESCO

2008: ICOMOS Charter for the Interpretation and Preservation of Cultural Heritage Sites (the "Ename Charter")/ICOMOS Quebec, Canada

ARMED CONFLICT

1907: Convention for the Protection of Artistic and Scientific Institutions and Historic Monuments (The Roerich Pact)/Pan American Union

1907: Fourth Hague Convention Respecting the Laws and Customs of War on Land

1954: Convention for the Protection of Cultural Property in the Event of Armed Conflict (The "Hague Convention")/UNESCO

1954: The First Protocol

1977: Geneva Conventions, Additional Protocols I and II (Protocols based on the "Hague Convention" of 1954)/ICRC

1998: International Criminal Court, established by the Rome Statute

1999: The Second Protocol

2003: Declaration concerning the Intentional Destruction of Cultural Heritage/UNESCO

International Conventions addressing the combination of Cultural and Natural Heritage

1954: European Cultural Convention/Council of Europe

1972: Convention concerning the Protection of the World Cultural and Natural Heritage ("World Heritage Convention")/UNESCO

1972: Recommendation concerning the Protection, at National Level, of the Cultural and Natural Heritage/UNESCO

1976: Convention on the Protection of the Archaeological, Historical, and Artistic Heritage of the American Nations/OAS

See also the "Burra" and "Aotearoa" Charters.

INTANGIBLE HERITAGE

2003: Convention for the Safeguarding of the Intangible Cultural Heritage/UNESCO

See also the "Burra" and "Aotearoa" Charters.

LANDSCAPES: URBAN AND RURAL

1962: Recommendation concerning the Safeguarding of the Beauty and Character of Landscapes and Sites/UNESCO

1968: Recommendation concerning the Preservation of Cultural Property Endangered by Public or Private Works/UNESCO

1972: Convention concerning the Protection of the World Cultural and NaturalHeritage (as it evolved to include cultural landscapes)/UNESCO

1972: Recommendation concerning the Protection, at National Level, of the Cultural and Natural Heritage/UNESCO

1976: Recommendation concerning the Safeguarding and Contemporary Role of Historic Areas/UNESCO

1982: Historic Gardens (The "Florence Charter")/ICOMOS

1999: Australia ICOMOS (The "Burra Charter")/Australia ICOMOS

2000: European Landscape Convention/Council of Europe

MUSEUMS AND MOVABLE CULTURAL HERITAGE
(See also "Transfer and Trade", "The "Hague Convention" of 1954, and the First and Second Protocols)

1960: Recommendation concerning the Most Effective Means of Rendering Museums Accessible to Everyone/UNESCO

1976: Recommendation concerning the International Exchange of Cultural Property/UNESCO

1978: Recommendation for the Protection of Movable Cultural Property/UNESCO

1980: Recommendation for the Safeguarding and Preservation of Moving Images/UNESCO

See also the "Aotearoa Charter".

TRANSFER AND TRADE

(See also The "Hague Convention" of 1954 and the First and Second Protocols.)

1964: Recommendation on the Means of Prohibiting and Preventing the Illicit Export, Import, and Transfer of Ownership of Cultural Property/UNESCO

1970: Convention on the Means of Prohibiting and Preventing the Illicit Import, Export, and Transfer of Ownership of Cultural Property/UNESCO

1976: Convention on the Protection of the Archaeological, Historical, and Artistic Heritage of the American Nations/OAS

1976: Recommendation Concerning the International Exchange of Cultural Property/UNESCO

1978: Recommendation for the Protection of Movable Cultural Property/UNESCO

1985: European Convention on Offences Relating to Cultural Property/Council of Europe

1995: Convention on Stolen or Illegally Exported Cultural Objects (The "Unidroit Convention")/Government of the Italian Republic

KEY TO ABBREVIATIONS:

ICOMOS: International Council on Monuments and Sites

ICRC: International Committee of the Red Cross

OAS: Organization of American States

UNESCO: United Nations Educational, Scientific and Cultural Organization

ENDNOTE

1. List prepared in January 2007 by Arlene K. Fleming, Cultural Resource Management Consultant, e-mail: halandarlene@msn.com.

Annotated Bibliography of One Hundred Selected Titles

T he following selection of books about architectural conservation and allied subjects was chosen primarily from the holdings of the Avery Architectural and Fine Arts Library at Columbia University in New York City and the library at the International Centre for the Study of the Preservation and Restoration of Cultural Property (ICCROM) in Rome. It exhibits a preference for books on representative topics and cites relatively few periodicals or individual articles. Selected conference proceedings are included when they are either widely held in key libraries or when they ought to be. The bibliography favors books in the Romance languages and, in particular, those in English.

The literature of architectural conservation can be considered to have two principal aspects: theoretical (e.g., philosophy, history, historiography, archaeology, aspects of culture, concepts of significance, law, ethics, advocacy, pedagogy) and technical (e.g., conservation science, including masonry conservation, conservation of earthen structures, mortars, timber treatments, structural consolidation, project management, technical procedures, and legal regulation). This bibliography primarily addresses the former, acknowledging that it cannot attempt to capture anything approaching the full quantity of available resources on conservation technical matters and case studies, which are better located via the World Wide Web. (See also Appendix B.)

Indeed, there are thousands of publications pertaining to architectural conservation and hundreds of thousands dealing with architecture and culture in general, with new works being published each year. Topics that are also relevant to cultural heritage conservation include aesthetics, environmental psychology, planning, population studies, and the economics of heritage. A selection of titles representing several of these subjects and the more technical aspects of architectural conservation have been included here in order to define the parameters of the general field of cultural heritage conservation and as a means for readers to find their way into more specialized topics via their bibliographies. Numerous additional useful titles are listed in the "Related Reading" lists at the end of some sections in*Time Honored.*

The best general catalogue of publications relating to art and architectural conservation is located at ICCROM, where by 2007 some 90,000 titles in more than forty languages had been cataloged. It also encompasses more specialized ephemeral works and texts printed in limited quantities. Many of these can also be found in the more complete library collections, such as those at the Getty Conservation Institute (Los Angeles), Columbia University Avery Architectural and Fine Arts Library (New York City), and other institutional and university libraries.

A plethora of other resources are available only via the World Wide Web. Four principal Web-based resources are found in Appendix B: Section I, Bibliographic and Research Databases.

Agnew, Neville, ed. *Conservation of Ancient Sites on the Silk Road: Proceedings of an International Conference on the Conservation of Grotto Sites*. Conference proceedings, held at Mogao Grottoes, Dunhuang, China, October 3–8, 1993. Los Angeles: Getty Conservation Institute, 1997. A lucid description of the process of determining the significance of a historic cultural resource as a basis for formulating a conservation plan.

Ahunbay, Zeynep. *Tarihi Çevre Koruma ve Restorasyon*. Istanbul: YEM Yayen, 1996. A textbook in architectural conservation by a prominent Turkish conservation architect.

Alfrey, Judith, and Tim Putnam. *The Industrial Heritage: Managing Resources and Uses*. London: Routledge, 1992. A presentation of the issues faced in conserving industrial heritage sites, including discussions on determining significance, conservation planning, creating constituencies, documentation, and bringing projects to fruition.

Amery, Colin, with Brian Curran. *Vanishing Histories: 100 Endangered Sites from the World Monuments Watch™*. New York: Abrams in association with the World Monuments Fund, 2001. A description of the World Monuments Fund's accomplishments during the first five years of its World Monuments Watch™ List of 100 Most Endangered Sites program. A comprehensive and balanced, though somewhat narrow, view of global conservation activities of this influential, private not-for-profit organization.

Aplin, Graeme. *Heritage: Identification, Conservation, and Management*. South Melbourne, Australia: Oxford University Press, 2002. A rich information source on conserving both natural and cultural heritage from an Australian perspective.

Appleyard, Donald, ed. *The Conservation of European Cities*. Cambridge, MA: MIT Press, 1979. An edited collection of twenty-three case studies and topical essays on conservation programs in European cities, including Venice; Istanbul; Bath, England; Brussels; the Plaka in Athens; Split, Croatia; and inner-city neighborhoods in Amsterdam and London.

————, ed. *Urban Conservation in Europe and America: Planning, Conflict and Participation in the Inner City*. Proceedings of a conference held in Rome, 1975. Rome: European Regional Conference of Fulbright Commissions, 1975. Conference proceedings that address: "Living and Historical Monuments in Athens, Split and Istanbul"; "Physical versus Social Conservation in Venice, Rome and Grenoble"; "Planning, Legislation and Design in Amsterdam, Leuven, Stockholm…."; and "Citizen Participation…."

Ashurst, John, and Nicola Ashurst. *Practical Building Conservation: English Heritage Technical Handbook*, volumes 1–5. London: Gower Technical Press, 1988. A well-organized and richly detailed guide to the specific skills and technologies used in architectural conservation.

Baer, N. S., and F. Snickars, eds. *Rational Decision-Making in the Preservation of Cultural Property*. Berlin: Dahlem University Press, 2001. Addresses the choices faced in materials conservation from the viewpoint of the conservator.

Baker, David. *Living with the Past: The Historic Environment*. Bletsoe, Bedford, UK: D. Baker, 1983. The author makes the case for conserving entire historic environments, widely referred to today as "cultural landscapes."

Bakoš, Ján. "Monuments and Ideologies." *Centropia: A Journal of Central European Architecture and Related Arts* 1, no. 2 (May 2001): 101–7. Previously published by the Slovak Academy of Sciences in its journal *Human Affairs* 1, no. 2 (December 1991). A highly insightful portrayal of the cult of museums and monuments at the end of the twentieth century, informed by and written in the manner of Alois Riegl.

Bell, D. *The Historic Scotland Guide to International Conservation Charters*. Edinburgh: Historic Scotland, 1997. A comprehensive analysis of some seventy national and international statements of conservation principles. It contains useful contextual material on why to conserve, what to conserve, definitions, comparisons of principles, and related matters.

Binney, Marcus. *Our Vanishing Heritage*. London: Arlington Books, 1984. Arranged according to building type, this is a personalized account of the writer—a significant figure in the history of architectural conservation—and of efforts by him and his circle to preserve Britain's vanishing architectural heritage.

Binney, Marcus, Francis Macin, and Ken Powell. *Bright Future: The Re-use of Industrial Buildings*. London: SAVE Britain's Heritage, 1990. A photo-illustrated booklet with evocative images of impressive industrial heritage sites and a case for their reuse and conservation.

Boito, Camillo. *I Restauratori*. Florence: G. Barbèra, 1884. In this work—a landmark in the literature of architectural conservation—Boito articulates his principles for architectural restoration.

Bonelli, Renato. *Scritti sul Restauro e sulla Critica Architettonica*. Introduction by Giovanni Carbonara. Series no. 14, produced by the Studio for the Restoration of Monuments, University of Rome "La Sapienza." Rome: Bonsignori Editore, 1995. The book reprints Renato Bonelli's critical writings, with illustrations by Bonelli and others, on theory, principles, archaeology, garden restoration, etc., relative to architectural conservation.

Boniface, Priscilla, and Peter J. Fowler. *Heritage and Tourism in "the Global Village."* London: Routledge, 1993. Eleven essays on heritage tourism within the overall tourism industry, which refers to the business in line one of the preface as being "the Greatest Show on Earth."

Brandi, Cesare. *Teoria del Restauro*. Rome: Edizioni di Storia e Letteratura, 1963. Translated by Cynthia Rockwell as *Theory of Restoration* (Rome: ICCROM, 2005). Contributions to theory with mention of specific conservation techniques and examples by one of Italy's most accomplished conservators and cultural heritage administrators.

Brown, G. Baldwin. *The Care of Ancient Monuments*. Cambridge: Cambridge University Press, 1905. Unusual for its day, this early work chronicled architectural conservation legislation in various European countries, North African countries, India, and the United States, as a basis for stimulating more effective legislation to protect monuments in Britain. A good source for the history of architectural conservation and a summary of the issues faced at the time.

Campbell, Krystyna. "Time to Leap the Fence." In *Managing Historic Sites and Buildings: Reconciling Presentation and Preservation.* Edited by Gill Chitty and David Baker. Issues in Heritage Management Series. London: Routledge, 1999. An engaging review of the picturesque in English landscape design tradition, followed by a discussion with examples of the choices one faces in preserving and presenting heritage landscape sites.

Carbonara, Giovanni. *Avvicinamento al Restauro: Teoria, Storia, Monumenti.* Naples: Liguori Editore, 1997. At 732 pages, it is surely the most comprehensive and massive architectural restoration textbook ever written. Its seven parts cover theory, history, restoration and science, and urban conservation issues, with nine appendices containing key conservation charters and declarations.

Ceschi, Carlo. *Teoria e Storia del Restauro.* Rome: M. Bulzoni Editore, 1970. Covering the evolution of architectural conservation principles and practices from the Renaissance through the 1960s, the book includes interesting examples of Renaissance treatments of historic buildings by Leon Battista Alberti, Andrea Palladio, and others.

Chitty, Gill, and David Baker, eds. *Managing Historic Sites and Buildings: Reconciling Presentation and Preservation.* Issues in Heritage Management Series. London: Routledge, 1999. A collection primarily of papers presented at a seminar entitled "Presentation and Preservation: Conflict or Collaboration," held in London in October 1997. It addresses in detail a number of issues, ranging from "community archaeology" and conservation issues at country houses and churches to conserving twentieth-century military installations.

Choay, Françoise. *The Invention of the Historic Monument.* Translated by Lauren M. O'Connell. Cambridge: Cambridge University Press, 2001. A deeply insightful presentation on the evolution of modern architectural practice from its roots in France in the late eighteenth century.

Christie, Trevor L. *Antiquities in Peril.* Philadelphia: Lippincott, 1967. Christie makes the case for conserving the great monuments of the world, with descriptions of conservation efforts of fourteen outstanding sites that were "rescued by modern scientific techniques for the enrichment of future generations."

Cleere, Henry, ed. *Archaeological Heritage Management in the Modern World.* London: Unwin Hyman, 1989. Thirty-one essays dealing with key aspects of archaeological heritage management from a global perspective.

Contorni, Gabriella. *Erre come Restauro: Terminologia degli interventi sul costruito,* Firenze Alinea Editrice, 1993. A highly useful reference to nomenclature used in architectural conservation. Written in Italian, it covers only Italian terms, with each translated into English, Spanish, and/or French. Includes an etymology of terms, references, and illustrated commentary.

Crosby, Theo. *The Necessary Monument: Its Future in the Civilized City.* Greenwich, CT: New York Graphic Society, 1970. The author makes the case that architects, planners, and others should obtain a greater appreciation of key monuments in urban contexts. Three representative chapters are "Tower Bridge, London—A Monument in the Balance," "Rebirth of the Paris Opera," and "The Death of Pennsylvania Station, New York."

De Angelis d'Ossat, Guglielmo. *Sul Restauro dei Monumenti Architettonici: Concetti, Operatività, Didattica.* Series no. 13, School for the Restoration of Monuments, University of Rome "La Sapienza." Rome: Bonsignori Editore, 1995. These writings, with supplements, are by a key figure in modern restoration education and practice in Italy. It includes a modest scale of possible levels of intervention, using Italian sites as examples.

Delafons, John. *Politics and Preservation: A Policy History of the Built Heritage, 1882–1996.* London: E. and F. N. Spon, 1997. A clear and fresh view of the political implications of architectural conservation in Britain, which addresses, among other things, the evolution of the field, planning considerations, formulation of policy, policy parameters, priorities, and sustainable conservation.

Denhez, Marc C. *The Heritage Strategy Planning Handbook: An International Primer.* Toronto: Dundurn Press, 1997. A comparison of systems of legal protection for cultural heritage conservation in various countries, followed by a presentation on planning strategies and related issues.

Denslagen, Wim. *Architectural Restoration in Western Europe: Controversy and Continuity.* Amsterdam: Architectura and Natura, 1994. A wide-ranging study of conservative versus radical (anti-scrape versus scrape) approaches to architectural conservation used in northern Europe from the mid-nineteenth through the mid-twentieth centuries, with insightful discussion of their implications.

Denslagen, Wim, and Niels Gutschow, eds. *Architectural Imitations: Reproductions and Pastiches in East and West.* Maastricht, Neth.: Shaker Publishing, 2005. The most comprehensive roundup to date of writings and thoughts on the issue of so-called Western and Eastern approaches to heritage conservation. The editors roundly question recent biases against reconstructions, and the book addresses the topic from both global and historical perspectives.

Domicelj, Jean, and Duncan Marshall. "Diversity, Place and the Ethics of Conservation." Discussion paper prepared for the Australian Heritage Commission on behalf of Australia ICOMOS, 1994. It includes "issues acknowledging the potential for conflict over diverse values associated with heritage places in a pluralist country such as Australia." The work addresses the question of different perspectives of culture, the challenges faced, examples, and a "Draft Code of Ethics of Coexistence in Conserving Significant Places."

Earl, John. *Building Conservation Philosophy.* Preface by Bernard Feilden. Reading, UK: College of Estate Management, 1996. A review of most, if not all, key philosophical issues encountered in Western architectural conservation, with clear explanations and appendices that include the more widely recognized charters.

Enders, Siegfried R. C. T., and Niels Gutschow. *Hozon: Architectural and Urban Conservation in Japan.* Stuttgart, Germany: Edition Axel Menges, 1998. The results of a Japanese-German collaborative effort at analyzing architectural conservation theory and practice in Japan, especially as it relates to the question of authenticity and the ancient Japanese practice of reconstructing and replicating buildings.

Erder, Cevat. *Our Architectural Heritage: From Consciousness to Conservation.* Museums and Monuments series. Paris: UNESCO, 1986. The first detailed and scopic history of architectural conservation in Europe, in which the author, a classical archaeologist, proves it had its roots in early antiquity. Organized both chronologically and geographically, this amply illustrated and very readable narrative traces architectural conservation's "prehistory" through the nascent years of today's profession. Appendices include "On Restoration," by Eugène-Emmanuel Viollet-Le-Duc, and the Madrid, Athens, and Venice conservation charters (1904, 1933, and 1964, respectively).

Fawcett, Jane, ed. *The Future of the Past: Attitudes to Conservation 1174–1974.* London: Thames and Hudson, 1976. Produced in conjunction with an exhibition organized by the Victorian Society from 1970 to 1971, this classic includes eight essays by key figures in the British architectural conservation field including John Betjeman, Mark Girouard, and Sir Nikolaus Pevsner. Pevsner's "Scrape and Anti-Scrape" remains the best overview of the famous nineteenth-century polemic regarding the use of conservative versus radical approaches to preserving historic buildings. Jane Fawcett's "A Restoration Tragedy," which concerns "restorations" of cathedrals in the eighteenth and nineteenth centuries, is a lucid description of treatments of historic buildings that, to a large degree, created the modern field of architectural conservation. The book's first chapter offers an illustrated history of preservation in Britain from the twelfth century on, and the penultimate chapter, "Conservation in America," reveals the breadth of this impressive collection of essays.

Feilden, Bernard M. *Between Two Earthquakes: Cultural Property in Seismic Zones*. Rome: ICCROM; Marina del Rey, CA: Getty Conservation Institute, 1987. A useful handbook on nearly all aspects of protecting historic buildings at risk from earthquakes. Contains thirteen appendices on topics including preventative measures, documentation systems, and proceedings of relevant international conferences.

————. *Conservation of Historic Buildings*. 3rd ed. Oxford: Architectural Press, 2003. First published in 1982 by Butterworth Scientific. This book in its various editions is a landmark in the field of professional architectural conservation science and practice, written by England's most renowned architectural conservation architect. It thoroughly covers sources of decay, problem types, and technical approaches, including specific formulas. *Conservation of Historic Buildings* remains the unmatched bible for the technically oriented, such as architects, conservators, chemists, and specialist builders.

Feilden, Bernard M., and Jukka Jokilehto. *Management Guidelines for World Cultural Heritage Sites*. Rome: ICCROM, 1993. Intended as a management guide for site protection, this book also explains the rationale for World Heritage listing.

Fitch, James Marston. *Historic Preservation: Curatorial Management of the Built World*. Charlottesville, VA: University Press of Virginia, 2001. First published in 1982 by McGraw-Hill. The first worldwide view of architectural conservation practice by the eminent leader in preservation education in the United States. Meant primarily as a textbook, Fitch offers in his inimitable writing style a description of the field in the 1980s and "the forces that shaped it."

Gamboni, Dario. *The Destruction of Art: Iconoclasm and Vandalism since the French Revolution*. London: Reaktion Books, 1997. In the first comprehensive examination of modern iconoclasm, the author reassesses the motives and circumstances behind deliberate attacks carried out on public buildings, religious buildings, sculpture, paintings, and other works of art in the nineteenth and twentieth centuries

Goulty, Sheena Mackellar. *Heritage Gardens: Care, Conservation, and Management*. London: Routledge, 1993. In her concise and clear overview of the subject, the author uses case studies to address the history of garden care, the conservation process, maintenance, and management.

Gratz, Roberta Brandes. *The Living City*. New York: Simon and Schuster, 1989. A call for commonsense appreciation of cities as living entities, which outlines socioeconomic, cultural, and physical assets that need to be taken more seriously by citizens, planning professionals, and municipal decision makers.

Haskell, Tony, ed. *Caring for Our Built Heritage: Conservation in Practice*. London: E. and F. N. Spon, 1993. "A review of conservation schemes carried out by County Councils and National Park Authorities in England and Wales...." A compendium of accomplishments in the form of case studies in archaeology, industrial archaeology, building conservation, town schemes, parks and gardens, and so on, with introductory remarks, citations of laws, and a list of sources.

Herbert, David T., ed. *Heritage, Tourism and Society*. London: Mansell, 1995. Eleven presentations on aspects of heritage tourism, ranging from its educational roles to its economic benefits.

Hunter, Michael, ed. *Preserving the Past: The Rise of Heritage in Modern Britain*. Stroud, Gloucestershire, UK: Alan Sutton, 1996. An excellent collection of writings, including an introduction by Michael Hunter, and chapters on the progress of heritage conservation in Britain from the mid-nineteenth century until the mid-1990s. Its contents address changing attitudes toward preserving the country house ensemble, the vital role of conservation societies, changing attitudes in urban development, and open-air museums and industrial museums. A bibliographical essay on important books pertaining to British heritage conservation and a chronology of key events in the history of architectural conservation in Britain round out this exemplar of British thought and commitment to heritage conservation practice.

ICOMOS. *The Monument for the Man: Records of the Second International Congress of Architects and Technicians of Historical Monuments, Venice, 25–31 May 1964*. Padua, Italy: Marsilio Editore, 1972. Summaries of 168 papers given at the most famous conference in the field of architectural conservation—the occasion of the drafting of the International Charter for the Conservation and Restoration of Monuments and Sites (the Venice Charter, 1964).

Insall, Donald W. *Living Buildings*. London: The Images Publishing Group, 2008. A review of fifty years of experience, rich with practical information from Donald Insall Associates, a top leader in British architectural conservation practice.

Jacobs, Jane. *The Death and Life of Great American Cities*. New York: Random House, 1961. A landmark in architectural conservation literature, its persuasive and influential arguments succeeded in pressuring public officials and developers to respond to popular demands for preservation.

Jokilehto, Jukka. *A History of Architectural Conservation*. Oxford: Butterworth-Heinemann, 1999. A simplified, updated, and better-illustrated version of Jokilehto's doctoral dissertation on the origins and evolution of conservation practice in Western Europe. Other parts of the world are also addressed, and the UNESCO/ICCROM institutional perspective on contemporary architectural conservation issues is well explicated here. Includes an extensive bibliography.

Journal of Architectural Conservation. London. Thrice-yearly publication that has, since 1995, presented up-to-date information addressing the practical and technical aspects of the field, including conference proceedings. Its purview includes historic buildings, monuments, places, and landscapes.

King, Thomas F., Patricia Parker Hickman, and Gary Berg. *Anthropology in Historic Preservation: Caring for Culture's Clutter*. Studies in Archaeology Series. New York: Academic Press, 1977. A useful sourcebook for both anthropologists and cultural heritage conservationists that explains to each how the other's profession works. Included are chapters on anthropology and historic preservation, a history of historic preservation in the United States, law and regulation, defining cultural significance, and survey techniques.

Larsen, Knut Einar. ed. *Nara Conference on Authenticity in Relation to the World Heritage Convention*. Conference proceedings, Nara, Japan, November 1–6, 1994. Trondheim, Norway: Tapir Publishers, 1995. The results of discussions and presentations by forty-five experts from twenty-six countries who specifically addressed the crucial topic of authenticity in heritage conservation.

Latham, Derek. *Creative Re-use of Buildings*. 2 vols. Shaftesbury, UK: Donhead Publishing, 2000. Two volumes, entitled "Principles and Practice" and "Building Types: Selected Examples," address numerous possibilities for the adaptive or extended use of existing buildings.

Lemaire, C. R. *La Restauration des Monuments Anciens*. Antwerp: De Sikkel, 1938. An early history of accomplishments in architectural restoration in Belgium in the wake of World War I.

Leniaud, Jean-Michel. *L'Utopie Française: Essai sur le Patrimoine*. Paris: Editions Mengès, 1992. A comprehensive description of the conservation of the French cultural patrimony, its special characteristics, and the roles that heritage plays in French society.

Ligen, Pierre-Yves. *Dangers and Perils: Analysis of Factors Which Constitute a Danger to Groups and Areas of Buildings of Historical or Artistic Interest*. Strasbourg, France: Council for Cultural Co-operation, 1968. A cogent explanation, rich with examples, of the myriad challenges faced in conserving Europe's historic built environment.

Logan, W. S. ed. *The Disappearing "Asia" City: Protecting Asia's Urban Heritage in a Globalizing World*. Oxford: Oxford University Press, 2002. An important collection of essays by leaders in the field on changes to representative cities in East and Southeast Asia.

Lowenthal, David. *The Past is a Foreign Country*. Cambridge: Cambridge University Press, 1985. A sweeping study, with provocative ideas on how humans have related to their tangible past.

Lowenthal, David, and Marcus Binney, eds. *Our Past Before Us: Why Do We Save It?* London: Temple Smith, 1981. A compilation of studies that evaluate reasons for, and examples of, conservation of historic sites in Great Britain. Issues addressed include changing views, conserving landscapes, workplaces, and historical identities, and the benefits and risks of heritage conservation becoming a widely popular concern.

Lynch, Kevin. *What Time Is This Place?* Cambridge, MA: MIT Press, 1972. A classic on the roles of history and historic preservation in cities, with insightful commentary from a planner's perspective.

MacLean, Margaret, ed. *Cultural Heritage in Asia and the Pacific: Conservation and Policy*. Proceedings of a symposium held in Honolulu, September 8–13, 1991. Marina del Rey, CA: Getty Conservation Institute, 1993. One of the first scopic reviews of the challenges faced in conserving the cultural heritage of East Asia and the Pacific region, with recommendations for conservation policies and various technical methodologies.

Marks, S. ed. *Concerning Buildings: Studies in Honor of Sir Bernard Feilden*. Oxford: Butterworth-Heinmann, 1996. A broad and rich array of ten essays mainly by England's top teachers in the field, which deal with the principles and problems of conserving historic buildings, including international perspectives.

Marquis-Kyle, Peter, and Meredith Walker. *The Illustrated Burra Charter: Making Good Decisions About the Care of Important Places*. Brisbane, Australia: Australia ICOMOS and the Australian Heritage Commission, 1992. New edition published as *The Illustrated Burra Charter: Good Practice for Heritage Places*. Sydney: Australia ICOMOS, 2004. The Burra Charter is a landmark in the history of efforts to articulate cultural heritage standards and practice, and this book is a clearly described, well illustrated and comprehensive companion to it.

Marconi, Paolo. *Arte e Cultura della Manutenzione dei Monumenti*. 2nd ed. Rome: Editori Laterza, 1990. The book contains observations on the performance of various exterior building materials, and it details their roles of providing both protection and ornamentation.

———. *Materia e Significato: La Questione del Restauro Architettonico*. Rome: Editori Laterza, 1999. A direct approach into some of the most difficult aspects of architectural restoration. It includes detailed discussions and illustrations of all manner of design and technical issues, many of which are the distinguished architect-professor's own projects.

McManamon, Francis P., and Alf Hatton, eds. *Cultural Resource Management in Contemporary Society: Perspectives on Managing and Presenting the Past.* London: Routledge, 2000. Proceedings from the third World Archaeological Congress in New Delhi, December 1994. Transcripts of twenty-four scholarly presentations that address a variety of global issues in cultural resource management ranging from the general and more philosophical (e.g., challenges in Africa, Cameroon, Lebanon, and the United States) to the more specific (e.g., rescue archaeology in Japan and "Teaching Archaeology at the Museum San Miguel de Azapa in Northernmost Chile"). A valuable reference for experts.

Nagar, Shanti Lal. *Protection, Conservation, and Preservation of Indian Monuments.* New Delhi: Aryan Books International, 1993. This book offers a valuable and rare historical perspective, with quotes from ancient literature pertaining to architectural and landscape restoration and preservation. Subsequent chapters discuss intervention possibilities, laws, and environmental conservation, followed by sixteen appendices.

Palmer, Marilyn, and Peter Neaverson, eds. *Managing the Industrial Heritage: Its Identification, Recording and Management.* Proceedings of a seminar held at Leicester University in July 1994. Leicester Archaeology Monographs no. 2. Leicester, UK: University of Leicester, 1995. Illustrated conference proceedings with twenty-four essays organized under topics of recording, site context, assessing priorities, and protection measures.

Pearce, David. *Conservation Today*. London: Routledge, 1989. A publication that accompanied an exhibition at the Royal Academy of Arts in London in 1989 in which the author argues that architectural conservation should be a creative process.

Pearson, Michael, and Sharon Sullivan. *Looking after Heritage Places: The Basics of Heritage Planning for Managers, Landowners and Administrators.* Carlton, Victoria, Australia: Melbourne University Press, 1995. A clear, detailed, and well-organized compendium addressing practically all issues relating to the work of managers at heritage places.

Pevsner, Nicolaus. *Ruskin and Viollet-le-Duc: Englishness and Frenchness in the Appreciation of Gothic Architecture.* London: Thames & Hudson, 1969. Views of the chief and most eloquent proponents of Gothic architecture in their day revealing their deep knowledge and passions on the matter and its treatments via either restoration or minimal conservation.

Poulot, Dominique, ed. *Patrimoine et Modernité*. Conference proceedings. Paris: L'Harmattan, 1998. Sixteen essays by leading thinkers in Western Europe on the evolving roles of cultural heritage over the past two centuries. Notions of Western European cultural heritage, its portrayal, government support for its protection, and its role in politics are principle themes.

Reynolds, Donald M. *Remove Not the Ancient Landmark: Public Monuments and Moral Values; Discourses and Comments in Tribute to Rudolf Wittkower.* Documenting the Image 3. Amsterdam: Gordon and Breach, 1996. Twenty-two essays by prominent art historians—including James Ackerman, James Beck, David Rosand, Oleg Grabar, and Stephen Murray—on the purpose, meaning, and the conservation of planned "monuments" throughout history in the Western world. Includes an essay on the etymology of the word *monument*.

Riegl, Alois. "The Modern Cult of Monuments: Its Character and Its Origin." Translated by Kurt W. Forster and Diane Ghirardo. *Oppositions* 25 (1982). The most famous of the writings on architectural restoration by the influential Viennese art historian, advocate, and philosopher. The best English translation of the classic *Der Moderne Denkmalkultus*.

Rodwell, Dennis. *Conservation and Sustainability in Historic Cities.* Oxford: Blackwell Publishing, 2007. A clear, concise, and well-illustrated coverage of conservation, re-use, design, and matters of sustainability pertaining mainly to European cities by the leading architect-planner specialist in the subject. Excellent bibliography.

Ruskin, John. "The Lamp of Memory," in *The Seven Lamps of Architecture* (London: Smith, Elder, 1849). In chapter 6, article 16, Ruskin declares that, after simple maintenance, it is better to pull down a building than to artificially extend its life since "The thing (restoration) is a Lie from beginning to end…"

Schmidt, Hartwig. *Wiederaufbau: Denkmalpflege an Archäologischen Stätten Band 2.* Stuttgart, Germany: Konrad Theiss, 1993. A comprehensive, and technical presentation of the history of archaeological monuments conservation in the Mediterranean region and the state of the art today.

Schuster, J. Mark, John de Monchaux, and Charles A. Riley, II, eds. *Preserving the Built Heritage: Tools for Implementation.* Salzburg Seminar series. Hanover, NH: University Press of New England, 1997. Proceedings of Salzburg Seminar no. 332, held in December 1995, entitled "Preserving the National Heritage: Policies, Partnerships, and Actions." The synthesis of a solutions-oriented symposium that involved mostly planners, senior policy makers, and the representatives of nongovernmental organizations from thirty-one countries. It includes insightful speculations on the optimum roles of government, nonprofit organizations, and the private sector in effectively conserving architectural heritage. An annotated bibliography and a guide to preservation resources online (by Katherine Mangle) are also provided.

Society for the Protection of Ancient Buildings (SPAB). *Repair Not Restoration.* London: SPAB, 1977. Printed for the centenary of SPAB. A reprinting of speeches and writings by John Ruskin, Auguste Rodin, W. R. Lethaby, and William Morris that eloquently argue against destructive, heavy-handed restorations.

Stanley-Price, Nicholas, ed. *Conservation on Archaeological Excavations with Particular Reference to the Mediterranean Area.* Rome: ICCROM, 1995. First published in 1984. Proceedings from a specialist symposium held in Cyprus in 1983 that dealt with aspects of conserving in situ archaeological remains ranging from "first aid" for finds to sheltering systems.

Stanley-Price, Nicholas, M. Kirby Talley, Jr., and Alessandro Melucco Vaccaro, eds. *Historical and Philosophical Issues in the Conservation of Cultural Heritage.* Readings in Conservation. Los Angeles: Getty Conservation Institute, 1996. A valuable compendium of selected writings on theory and principles in art and architectural conservation. In their own words, we hear from John Ruskin, Bernard Berenson, Kenneth Clark, Alois Riegl, and others on art and connoisseurship, the intent of artists, reintegration of loss, patina, and historiography. This book is the best handy reference for the key theories in architectural conservation, with writings by both mainstays through the early twentieth century and more recent figures such as Cesare Brandi, Paul Philippot, and Giovanni Carbonara.

Stipe, Robert ed. *A Richer Heritage: Historic Preservation in the Twenty-first Century*. Chapel Hill, NC: Historic Preservation Foundation of North Carolina and University of North Carolina Press, 2003. The best text and reference to date on historic preservation practice in the United States, consisting of essays by over a dozen leaders in the field.

Stipe, Robert E., and Antoinette J. Lee, eds. *The American Mosaic: Preserving a Nation's Heritage*. Washington, DC: US/ICOMOS, Preservation Press, National Trust for Historic Preservation, 1987. Written initially for the Eighth General Assembly of ICOMOS in Washington, DC, this book is organized into three parts: a description of the American preservation system; what is or should be preserved and why; and an appraisal of the field and recommendations for the future.

Stovel, Herb. *Risk Preparedness: A Management Manual for World Cultural Heritage*. Rome: ICCROM, 1998. A sourcebook for historic property managers and others on ways to mitigate the effects of human-caused and natural damage to cultural heritage through measures that should be taken before the damage occurs.

Strike, James. *Architecture in Conservation: Managing Development at Historic Sites*. London: Routledge, 1994. A detailed and well-illustrated discussion of considerations when planning new architecture for conservation projects.

Tomlan, Michael A., ed. *Preservation of What, for Whom? A Critical Look at Historical Significance*. Conference proceedings, Goucher College, Baltimore, Maryland, March 20–22, 1997. Ithaca, NY: National Council for Preservation Education, 1998. Eighteen papers reflecting various views on defining values and significance at historic cultural resources, and to its audiences.

Tschudi-Madsen, Stephan. *Restoration and Anti-Restoration: A Study in English Restoration Philosophy*. Oslo: Universitetsforlaget, 1976. A succinct, lucid, and well-researched analysis of the intense struggle in Great Britain for acceptable theories and methodologies in architectural conservation in the nineteenth century, with reference to its antecedents and later influences.

Tung, Anthony M. *Preserving the World's Great Cities: The Destruction and Renewal of the Historic Metropolis*. New York: Clarkson Potter, 2001. A comprehensive view, rich with insights, of the roles that architectural conservation and preservation planning have played (or have not played) in eighteen of the world's greatest historic cities.

Von Droste, Bernd, Harald Plachter, and Mechtild Rössler, eds. *Cultural Landscapes of Universal Value: Components of a Global Strategy*. Jena, Germany: Fischer Verlag in cooperation with UNESCO, 1995. A report on progress to date in defining, documenting, and placing cultural landscapes on the World Heritage List. This volume includes several case studies and references that were meant to form a baseline for launching a global strategy for protecting the world's most significant cultural landscapes.

Von Droste, Bernd, Mechtild Rössler, and Sarah Titchen, eds. *Linking Nature and Culture: Report of the Global Strategy, Natural and Cultural Heritage, Expert Meeting*. Held in Amsterdam, March 25–29, 1998. Conference proceedings that address the aims of UNESCO and partners to conserve both natural and cultural landscapes through the mechanism of the World Heritage List.

Warren, J., J. Worthington, and S. Taylor, eds. *Context: New Buildings in Historic Settings.* London: Architectural Press, 1998. Perspectives on new design for historic settings, o.e of the best in the genre on this topic.

Warren, John. *Conservation of Earthen Structures.* Oxford: Butterworth-Heinemann, 1999. A thorough examination of all issues related to conserving earthen structures, and their constituent parts, including construction techniques, pathologies, repair and conservation techniques, guiding principles, and related practical matters, such as protective shelters and cappings.

Watkin, David. *The Rise of Architectural History.* London: Architectural Press, 1980. A clear account of the history of architectural history that properly credits the role of historians in the architectural conservation movement.

Watt, David S. *Building Pathology: Principles and Practice.* Oxford: Blackwell Science, 1999. A well-illustrated, interdisciplinary approach to the study of building defects and appropriate remedial action.

World Monuments Fund (with US/ICOMOS). *Trails to Tropical Treasures: A Tour of ASEAN's Cultural Heritage.* New York: World Monuments Fund, 1992. An introduction to key historic buildings and sites in the Association of Southeast Asian Nations (ASEAN) and conservation practice in the region based on contributions by local authorities and experts. Its companion volume, *Trails to South American Treasures* (1997), remains the best overview of architectural conservation practice and the challenges that remain in the thirteen countries that comprise South America.

Photo Credits

The author wishes to thank the institutions and individuals who have kindly provided photographic materials for use in *Time Honored*. In all cases, every effort has been made to contact copyright holders but should there be any errors or omissions, the publisher would be pleased to insert the appropriate acknowledgement in reprints of this book.

Particular appreciation is given to the trustees and staff of the World Monuments Fund, who have generously allowed access to its image library. Gratitude is also expressed to ICCROM's director general for allowing access to its image archives and the kind assistance its staff provided to the author.

Frontispiece: Creative Commons Attribution-Share Alike license, v2.5

Chapter 1 opener: Photo Disc, Inc.

1-1: akg-images, Ltd.

1-2: Courtesy World Monuments Fund

1-3: GNU Free Documentation license, v1.2, http://www.gnu.org/copyleft/fdl.html

1-4: © ICCROM

1-5, 1-6: Courtesy World Monuments Fund

1-7, 1-8: Courtesy World Monuments Fund; Atotonilco, 1-8 by R. Ross for WMF, National Institute for Archaeology and History (INAH) heritage site

1-9: John H. Stubbs

1-10: Courtesy World Monuments Fund

1-11: John H. Stubbs

2-1: Courtesy World Monuments Fund

2-2: Courtesy World Monuments Fund

2-3, 2-4: Courtesy of the Mount Vernon Ladies' Association

2-5: John H. Stubbs

2-6: Creative Commons Attribution-Share Alike license, v2.5

3-8: Creative Commons Attribution-Share Alike license, v2.5

3-1: Creative Commons Attribution-Share Alike license, v2.5

3-2: Courtesy World Monuments Fund

3-3: Creative Commons Attribution-Share Alike license, v2.5

3-5: John H. Stubbs

4-1, 4-2: Courtesy World Monuments Fund

4-3, 4-4: © BlackStar/Mark Simon

4-5: Creative Commons Attribution-Share Alike license, v2.5

4-6: John H. Stubbs

4-7: Courtesy World Monuments Fund

5-1: Creative Commons Attribution-Share Alike license, v2.5

Chapter 6 opener: Hypnerotomachia Polyphili woodcut

6-2: Courtesy of Susanne K. Bennet and the Museum of African Art/Jerry L/ Thompson, photographer

6-7: Courtesy World Monuments Fund

6-8: Image courtesy of JPL/NASA

6-9: Courtesy World Monuments Fund

Part II opener: Courtesy World Monuments Fund

Chapter 7 opener: Corbis Digital stock

7-1, 7-2, 7-3: Courtesy World Monuments Fund

7-4a: John H. Stubbs

7-4b: Agence France Presse/CHOO Youn-Kong 2005

7-4c: Courtesy World Monuments Fund

7-4d: John H. Stubbs

7-5, 7-6: Courtesy World Monuments Fund

7-7: John H. Stubbs

7-8, 7-9, 7-10, 7-11, 7-12, 7-13: Courtesy World Monuments Fund

7-14: John H. Stubbs

7-15: Creative Commons Attribution-Share Alike license, v2.5

7-16, 7-17: Courtesy World Monuments Fund

Chapter 8 opener: Creative Commons Attribution-Share Alike license, v2.5

9-1: Photo courtesy of M. Walker and P. Marquis-Kyle, *The Illustrated Burra Charter: Good Practice for Heritage Places* (Burwood, Victoria: Australia ICOMOS Inc., 2004)

Chapter 10 opener: John H. Stubbs

Chapter 11 opener: John H. Stubbs

Part III opener (and 14-15): Courtesy World Monuments Fund

Chapter 12 divider (and 12-5): John H. Stubbs

12-1: Courtesy World Monuments Fund

12-2: Courtesy of State Antiquities and Heritage Organization, Baghdad

12-3: Prof. P. V. Glob

12-4: Creative Commons Attribution-Share Alike license, v2.5

12-5, 12-6: John H. Stubbs

12-7: © Georg Gerster/Panos Pictures

12-8: Creative Commons Attribution-Share Alike license, v2.5

12-9: Phototeca, the American Academy in Rome

12-10a, 12-10b: Creative Commons Attribution-Share Alike license, v2.5

12-11: Courtesy World Monuments Fund

12-12: John H. Stubbs

12-13: © ICCROM

12-14, 12-15, 12-17, 12-18: Courtesy World Monuments Fund

Chapter 13 divider (and 13-5): engraving, *Maison Carrée at Nîmes* by Clérisseau

13-2: John H. Stubbs

Chapter 14 opener: John H. Stubbs

14-2, 14-4, 14-5: John H. Stubbs

14-7: John H. Stubbs

14-9: Gustave LeGrey, Cathedral cloister at Le Puy en Vélay, 1851. Courtesy Avery Architectural and Fine Arts Library, Columbia University

14-13: akg-images, Ltd.

14-15: Courtesy World Monuments Fund

14-20: Courtesy of the Society for the Protection of Ancient Buildings

14-21: GNU Free Documentation license, v1.2, http://www.gnu.org/copyleft/fdl.html

14-22: Creative Commons Attribution-Share Alike license, v2.5

14-23: Creative Commons Attribution-Share Alike license, v2.5

14-24: Creative Commons Attribution-Share Alike license, v2.5

Part IV opener: Corbis Digital

Chapter 15 opener (and 15-3): Agence France Presse, 1966

15-1, 15-2: John H. Stubbs

15-4: Agence France Presse / RIA Novosti

15-5: Agence France Presse, 1966

15-6, 15-7, 15-8: Photos courtesy of Venice in Peril

15-9, 15-10: A. W. Van Buren, "Some Italian Sculptures in Italy during War Time." *Art and Archaeology* 7, no. 7 (July–August 1918): 225–31

15-11a, b: Courtesy Cristiana Peña, 2008

15-12: Courtesy World Monuments Fund

15-13: Photo courtesy of Ralph Feiner

15-14: Courtesy World Monuments Fund

15-15: Photo courtesy of Europa Nostra

15-16, 15-17, 15-18, 15-19, 15-20, 15-21: Courtesy World Monuments Fund

15-22: Image courtesy of ICOMOS China

15-23: Alexander Turnbull Library, Wellington, New Zealand

15-24: Creative Commons Attribution-Share Alike license, v2.5

15-25: Creative Commons Attribution-Share Alike license, v2.5

15-26: Courtesy World Monuments Fund

15-27: © UNESCO/R. Greenough

15-29: John H. Stubbs

Chapter 16 opener: John H. Stubbs

Chapter 17 opener: top: courtesy World Monuments Fund; courtesy of Byron Bell; middle: Creative Commons Attribution Share Alike license v.2.5; courtesy of and ©Raghu Rai, Magnum Pictures; courtesy World Monuments Fund; bottom: Creative Commons Attribution ShareAlike license v.2.5; courtesy of Susan Barr

17-1: Courtesy World Monuments Fund

17-2: John H. Stubbs

17-3: Courtesy of Europa Nostra

17-4, 17-5, 17-6, 17-7, 17-8: Courtesy World Monuments Fund

17-9: GNU Free Documentation license, v1.2, http://www.gnu.org/copyleft/fdl.html

17-10: Courtesy of Dr. Mounir Bouchenaki

17-11: Courtesy World Monuments Fund

17-12, 17-13: John H. Stubbs

17-14, 17-16: Courtesy World Monuments Fund

17-17, 17-18: John H. Stubbs

17-19, 17-20: Courtesy World Monuments Fund

17-21: By kind permission of the Trustees of the 9th Duke of Rutland's will

17-22: John H. Stubbs

17-74: Creative Commons Attribution-Share Alike license, v2.5

17-75, 17-76: Courtesy World Monuments Fund

17-77: Creative Commons Attribution-Share Alike license, v2.5

17-78: Australian Museum, AMS320 Frank Hurley Photographs; V4852

17-79: Courtesy US Air Force/Tech. Sgt. Shane A. Cuomo

17-80, 17-81: Photograph by Robert G. Bednarik, with permission

17-82: GNU Free Documentation license, v1.2, http://www.gnu.org/copyleft/fdl.html

17-83, 17-84: Courtesy of Bhupendra Kumar and photographer Manhar Vithal of Lomaitivi Studio, Levuka, Ovalau, Fiji

17-85: Creative Commons Attribution-Share Alike license, v2.5

17-86: Courtesy of Byron Bell

17-87, 17-88: Creative Commons Attribution-Share Alike license, v2.5

17-89, 17-90, 17-91: John H. Stubbs

17-92: Creative Commons Attribution-Share Alike license, v2.5

17-93: Courtesy of Presidio Trust, San Francisco

17-94: Creative Commons Attribution-Share Alike license, v2.5

17-95: Courtesy © 2008 The Christman Company/Gene Meadows, photographer

17-96: John H. Stubbs

17-97: Courtesy of Carlos Wester La Torre

17-98: Courtesy World Monuments Fund

17-99: John H. Stubbs

17-100: Creative Commons Attribution-Share Alike license, v2.5. A National Institute for Archaeology and History (INAH) heritage site

17-101: Courtesy of Byron Bell

17-102, 17-103, 17-104: World Monuments Fund

17-105: Courtesy Agustin Espinosa/Ricardo Castro Mendoza y Ciencia y Arte en Restauración S.A. de C. A National Institute for Archaeology and History (INAH) heritage site

17-106, 17-107: Courtesy World Monuments Fund

17-108: Creative Commons Attribution-Share Alike license, v2.5

17-109: Courtesy of © Antarctic Heritage Trust, http://www.nzaht.org/AHT

17-110: Courtesy World Monuments Fund

17-111: Courtesy of © M. D. Olynyk, Government of Yukon

17-112, 17-113: Courtesy of Susan Barr, photographer

17-114: Courtesy of © Antarctic Heritage Trust, http://www.nzaht.org

Chapter 18 opener: Courtesy of Andrea Bruno, Studio Bruno

Charts created by Ken Feisel

Index

423